A HISTORY

OF

AMERICAN LAW

Second Edition

Lawrence M. Friedman

A TOUCHSTONE BOOK
Published by Simon & Schuster
New York London Toronto Sydney

Rockefeller Center
1230 Avenue of the Americas
New York, New York 10020

SIMON AND SCHUSTER, TOUCHSTONE and colophons
are registered trademarks
of Simon & Schuster, Inc.
Designed by Irving Perkins Associates

Manufactured in the United States of America

30 29 28 27 26 25 24 23 22   Pbk.

Library of Congress Cataloging in Publication Data

Friedman, Lawrence Meir, date.
A history of American law.

Bibliography: p.
Includes index.
1. Law—United States—History and criticism.
I. Title.
KF352.F7   1985   349.73'09   85-10781
347.30'09

ISBN 0-671-81591-1
ISBN 0-671-52807-6 Pbk.

To Leah, Jane, Amy, and Sarah

CONTENTS

Introduction • The Skeleton of Colonial Law: The Courts • The Colonial Judicial System in the 18th Century • Civil Procedure • Land Law • Succession at Death • Criminal Law • Government, Law and the Economy • Commerce and Labor • Slavery • The Poor Laws • Statute and Common Law in the Colonial Period • The Legal Profession • The Literature of the Law

Revolutionary Ardor • Constitutions: Federal and State • The Judges • The Organization of Courts • Civil Procedure • The Law of Evidence

The Frontier • The Civil Law Fringe

Laissez-Faire and Its Limits • The Business Corporation

Marriage and Divorce • Family Property • Adoption • Poor Laws and Social Welfare • Slavery and the Blacks

PREFACE

American legal history, for a variety of reasons, has been a rather neglected field. It may come as a surprise to hear that this book, whatever its merits and demerits, is the first attempt to do anything remotely like a general history, a survey of the development of American law, including some treatment of substance, procedure, and legal institutions. The United States has four times the population of England; but it has nothing to compare with Sir William Holdsworth's *History of English Law*, a massive work in fifteen volumes; or with a number of solid one-volume histories of English law, good, bad, and indifferent. To be sure, there is a rich literature about certain American subsystems of law. This book could not have been written without them. There are dozens of articles and books about the Supreme Court, about great judges, great cases, about the legal profession, about this or that aspect of law. There are patches and pieces; but no fabric as a whole.

It is a serious thing, for a branch of history, to lack a general treatment. It means there is no tradition, no received learning, no conventional wisdom. But tradition is needed: to define what is important and what is not, to guide students, researchers, other historians—and the general public. Without tradition, there is no framework, no skeleton, nothing to hang one's ideas on, nothing to attack and revise.

The state of legal history is no mere accident. Part of the problem has been that in the United States, there was no place for legal history to come *from*. The conceptual blindness of legal education was not conducive to creative scholarship, at least not until recently. The dominant ideology of law schools was such that these were not centers of legal research. They taught legal method, legal reasoning, analytical skills, how to take cases apart, and how to put them together again. Legal scholars and lawyers were interested in precedents, but not in history; they twisted and used the past, but rarely treated it with the rigor that history demands. Historians, for their part, were not aware of the richness and importance of legal history; the lawyers, jealous of their area, showed them only a dreary battlefield of concepts; historians were unwelcome there; the landscape was technical and strewn with corpses and mines. Both of these attitudes are mellowing. Legal history is finally coming into its own. The literature is growing, and growing in quality. Lawyers and historians are making joint contributions.

This book is timely, then; and is offered up, not as a solution to the problems of legal history, but as a stage along the way: even, in a sense, as a whipping boy, a primer, something to react to; a shape for the field, even if others find it misshapen. The time is ripe; and the opportunity is here. Not that the obstacles are any the less—the embarrassment of primary sources, and the thinness of the secondary; the confounding factor of fifty separate state jurisdictions; the problems of definition of the field. These obstacles are balanced by opportunities. These include, first, the important work of scholars of first rank, men like Willard Hurst. Second, the development of modern social science, which, for all its deficiencies, gives us a way of looking at the world of law and legal history, a hope of cracking the code, a skeleton key to the horrendous mass of detail.

This key has been eagerly, even passionately grasped. This is a *social* history of American law. I have tried to fight free of jargon, legal and sociological; but I have surrendered myself wholeheartedly to some of the central insights of social science. This book treats American law, then, not as a kingdom unto itself, not as a set of rules and concepts, not as the province of lawyers alone, but as a mirror of society. It takes nothing as historical accident, nothing as autonomous, everything as relative and molded by economy and society. This is the theme of every chapter and verse.

A word or two about the scope and limitations of this book. The main narrative moves chronologically, from the beginnings in the 17th century, when a distinctive American law emerged, through the close of the 19th century. I have not attempted to trace the story past 1900 in any detail. But one final chapter tries to sum up main themes of the 20th century.

Historians of law have, quite understandably, paid more attention to national, federal developments, than to the separate histories of the law of the fifty states. In particular, constitutional law, and the Supreme Court, have inspired a rich literature, overshadowing most of the law. In this book, I try to redress the balance. State law occupies a central role in the narrative. I have deliberately kept to a minimum the story of constitutional law, partly because that story has been told, and told well; partly to try to bring forward the more mundane workings of the system, the pawns, foot soldiers, worker bees of law.

A person who writes a book runs up many debts. A glance at the footnotes shows how parasitic is such an enterprise as this. One major influence, not adequately reflected in citations, should be mentioned: the work, personality, and spirit of Willard Hurst, of the law school at the University of Wisconsin. American legal history stands enormously in his debt; and this work, whatever its merits, would be unthinkable without him. His influence, I think, is on every page.

During the years that I spent at the University of Wisconsin, I learned a great deal from my colleagues. There was an atmosphere of ferment that centered about studies in legal history and in law and the social sciences. A good deal of credit for this atmosphere must be ascribed to two private foundations, the Rockefeller Foundation, which supported legal-economic history at Wisconsin for many years, and the Russell Sage Foundation, which stimulated work in law and the social sciences. For the last few years, I have also benefited greatly from my colleagues at Stanford University.

Many colleagues and friends have also been helpful with substance and style. I thank them all, and particularly, Herbert L. Packer, Robert B. Stevens, Leah Friedman, Charles Rosenberg, Stanley Kutler, and Stanley Katz. The libraries and staffs of three university law schools, St. Louis, Wisconsin, and Stanford, were unfailingly helpful over the years. Generations (it seems) of typists labored over draft after draft of the text. I will not list them all, but I cannot ignore Mrs. Joy St. John, the last and most sorely burdened. Finally, I wish to acknowledge the special, subtle contributions of my family.

LAWRENCE M. FRIEDMAN

Stanford, California
1972

PREFACE TO THE SECOND EDITION

As I write this, more than eleven years have gone by since the first edition of this book saw the light of day. I am glad to have this chance to bring the text up to date, to correct the mistakes that I or other people caught, and to take into account the progress made in the field since 1973.

At that time—the early seventies—the field was an infant, or at best a toddler. I think it is fair to say that it is now on its way to maturity. The literature expands like a balloon, and it gets harder and harder to keep up: impossible, some would say. There are fresh viewpoints, new areas opened up, old fields rediscovered. It is a vigorous, healthy subject. Of course, not all the work is top quality, and nobody could honestly talk about break-throughs; but still, much more has been accomplished than I, or anybody else, would ever have dared to hope.

My main job in this revision has been to take account of the new work, to add fresh references, to retell the story in places where we have learned more precisely what the story was, and to rewrite more or less substantially those passages about fields (criminal justice, for example) which have at last come into their own. A tremendous amount of work is left to be done—of course it can never be finished—but there are, I think, fewer absolute voids.

I have substantially reworked large parts of the text. What I have not changed, however, is the general approach. If anybody took the trouble to compare the editions line by line, they would find shifts in emphasis, some fudging here, some unfudging there; but the main message is essentially unaltered. I have listened carefully, even respectfully, to most of my critics (not all); I have tried to keep an open mind; I throw them a bone here and there; but on the whole, to be perfectly honest, I have tended to stick to my

15

guns. I retain the general bias set out in the preface to the first edition. Nothing since then has shaken my confidence in the underlying assumptions. Work done since the early 1970s, in the main, only confirms me in my stubbornness.

I continue, as before, to be grateful to all of my invisible colleagues—the scholars, young and old, whose digging and writing have so enriched American legal history and given me so much raw material to draw on. I owe a special debt to the library staff of the Stanford Law School, and in particular to Myron Jacobstein and Iris Wildman, and to those others of the staff whose names I do not know, but who (no doubt cursing under their breath) had to run here and there to find or borrow the endless numbers of books and articles I wanted or needed. As before, too, I have to acknowledge the indispensable help of Joy St. John, who prepared the manuscript (over and over again), with her usual accuracy, intelligence, and patience. To my family too: thanks for everything.

LAWRENCE M. FRIEDMAN

Stanford, California
December 1984

PROLOGUE

Modern communications and technology have made the world smaller. They have leveled many variations in world culture. Yet people still speak different languages, wear different clothes, follow different religions, and hold different values dear. They are also subject to very different laws. How different is not easy to sum up. Clearly, legal systems are not so different as different languages. The new world—urban, industrial—implies a certain kind of society; this society depends on and welcomes certain kinds of laws. An income tax, for example, is a common feature in the West. But the exact form that a tax law takes depends on the general legal culture. Americans are naturally used to American laws. Law is an integral part of their culture. They could adjust to *very* alien laws and procedures about as easily as they could adjust to a diet of roast ants or a costume of togas. Judge and jury, the familiar drama of a criminal trial, an elected assembly or council at work making laws, wills and deeds, licenses to get married, to keep dogs, to hunt deer—these are all part of a common experience and culture peculiar to the United States. No other legal culture is quite like it. Presumably, no other culture fits the American system quite so aptly.

People commonly believe that history and tradition are very strong in American law. There is some basis for this belief. Some parts of the law can be traced back very far—the jury system, the mortgage, the trust, some aspects of land law. But other parts of the law are newborn babies. The living law in a broad social sense, including tax law, traffic codes, and social-welfare laws, contains some very recent accessions. While one lawyer is advising his client how to react to a ruling from Washington, issued that very day, another may be telling his client that some plausible course of action is blocked by a statute well known to the lawyers of Henry

17

VIII or by a decision of some older judges whose names, language, and habits would be unfathomable mysteries to both attorney and client. As a spoken language, American English is an incredible mixture. Some of its words, its grammatical postures, sounds, and phrases are new; some are old; others are borrowed from Latin or French; some (the most basic part) are derived from Old English or go back to even older strains. Part of the law is like that, too; layer on layer of geological formations, the new pressing down on the old, displacing, changing, altering, but not necessarily wiping out what has gone before. Law, by and large, evolves; it changes in piecemeal fashion. Revolutions in essential structure are few and far between. That, at least, is the Anglo-American experience. Some of the old is preserved among the mass of the new.

But what is kept of old law is highly selective. Society in change may be slow, but it is ruthless. Neither evolution nor revolution is sentimental. Old rules of law and old legal institutions stay alive when they still have a purpose—or, at least, when they do not interfere with the demands of current life. The trust, the mortgage, the jury, are of ancient stock; but they have the vigor of youth. They have come down from medieval times, but the needs they now serve are 20th-century needs. They have survived because they found a place in the vigorous, pushy society of today—a society that does not hesitate to pour old wine into new bottles and new wine into old bottles, or throw both bottles and wine away. At any rate, the theory of this book is that law moves with its times and is eternally new. From time to time, the theory may not fit the facts. But more light can be shed on legal history if one asks: why does this survive? than if one assumes that law, unlike the rest of social life, is a museum of accidents and the mummified past.

In one sense, law is always up-to-date. The legal system always "works"; it always functions. Every society governs itself and settles disputes. Every society, then, has a working system of law. If the courts, for example, are hidebound and ineffective, that merely means some other agency has taken over what courts might otherwise do. The system works like a blind, insensate machine. It does the bidding of those whose hands are on the controls. The laws of China, the United States, Nazi Germany, France, and the Union of South Africa reflect the goals and policies of those who call the tune in those societies. Often, when we call law "archaic," we mean that the power system of its society is morally out of tune. But change the power system, and the law too will change. The basic premise of this book is that, despite a strong dash of history and idiosyncrasy, the strongest ingredient in American law, at any given time, is the present: current emotions, real economic interests, concrete political groups. It may seem a curious beginning to a book of history to downgrade the historical element of law. But this is not really a paradox. The history of law has meaning only if we assume that at any given time the vital portion is new and changing, form following function, not function following form. History of law is not—or should not be—a search for fossils, but a study of social development, unfolding through time.

American social development and law have a long, elaborate history. Compared to some, the United States is a new country—but Boston and New York are more than three hundred years old, and the Constitution is one of the world's oldest *living* organic laws. In short, enough time has elapsed for American law to be essentially American—the product of American experience.

But American law has, and has had, close affinities to other legal cultures. The immediate ancestor is easy to identify. The basic substratum of American law, as of American speech, is English. Before the Europeans came, the country belonged to the native Americans. Europeans came late, but they came in force. They settled first along the coast. The Spanish settled Florida; the French built New Orleans. Swedes settled briefly on the Delaware; the Dutch pushed them out. Then the Dutch were overwhelmed by the English. The Hudson and Delaware settlements were added to a chain of tiny colonies, all English-speaking, along the Atlantic coast. Their populations grew. More Englishmen came. And English speakers, as Englishmen or Americans, ultimately threw out the native peoples, and the French, and the Spanish, and established an empire, stretching from sea to sea.

Each cultural group had brought in its own law. Of the native law, and of Swedish law, it is fair to say, not a trace remains.[1] Some scholars have claimed to find a speck or two of Dutch legal influence surviving to this day. The office of district attorney may be Dutch in origin. French law gained a more or less lasting

---

[1]The law of the native peoples, of course, still has some relevance to those native communities which are more or less autonomous. The law of these peoples, past and present, is a rich field of study in itself. See, for example, K. N. Llewellyn and E. A. Hoebel, *The Cheyenne Way* (1941); John P. Reid, *A Law of Blood: The Primitive Law of the Cherokee Nation* (1970).

foothold in Louisiana, and there (in translation) it stays. Spanish law sent down wider if not deeper roots; no state can call its law Spanish, but pieces of Spanish or Mexican law (for example, the community-property system), live on in California and in other parts of the West. Everything else, if not strictly native, is English, or comes by way of England, or is built on an English base.

It is not easy to say what part of English law was the immediate forebear of colonial law. For one thing, "colonial law" is an abstraction; there was no "colonial law" any more than there is an "American law," common to all fifty states. There were as many colonial systems as there were colonies. The original union was made up of thirteen states; but this thirteen represents, if anything, only a head count at one arbitrary time. Some colonies—Plymouth and New Haven—were swallowed up by larger colonies. New Jersey was the product of a merger of two separate entities. Each entity once had its own legal system.

Each colony, moreover, was founded at a different time. At least a century separates the beginnings of Massachusetts from the beginnings of Georgia. During this time, English law did not stand still. This meant that the colonies began their careers at different points in the process of legal development. During the colonial period, the colonies were subordinate to England. The law of the mother country was theoretically superior. But the colonial condition was not like the relationship of a ward to a city, or a county to a state. Even as a matter of theory, it was not clear which acts of Parliament and which court decisions were binding on the colonies. Throughout the colonial period, the colonists borrowed as much English law as they wanted to take or were forced to take. Their appetite was determined by requirements of the moment, by ignorance or knowledge of what was happening abroad, and by general obstinacy. Mapping out how far colonial law fit English law is almost a hopeless job. Legal cultures differed in different colonies. New England deviated from standard English law more than the Southern colonies did. The connection between the two sides of the Atlantic was always strong but never harmonious. The colonies quarreled with the mother country over law as well as over politics and taxes. Even after the Revolution, the legal connection was not severed. A complex legal relationship survived after 1776. English law continued to be imported, in some quantity, when and as needed. Even today a thin, thin trickle remains, when and as needed.

The date when a colony was first settled gives some rough

indication of the parts of English law likely to be transported. But
what was English law? Two decades before the Revolution, Sir
William Blackstone reduced to writing what he considered the
essence of the royal common law. His *Commentaries on the Law of
England* prints out to one very thick but manageable book. This
book, in its sluggishly elegant style, became a great bestseller, both
in England and America. Despite errors and failings, Blackstone
did manage to put in brief order the rank weeds of English law.
But even his picture was partial and defective, like a dictionary
that omitted all slang, all dialect, all colloquial and technical words.
And even this imperfect guide was not available to colonials before
the 1750s. They lacked a handy key to English law. Yet a key was
desperately needed. The English common law is one of the world's
great legal systems—but one maddeningly hard to know.

English law stood apart and still stands apart from most European systems of law. It resisted the reception of that modified,
modernized form of Roman law which swept over much of the
Continent. Modern Continental law finds its highest expression
in a code. "The law" in France and Germany is statutory. "Common law," on the other hand, was "unwritten law," as Blackstone
called it. "Unwritten" was not meant literally; English and American law are, if anything, overwritten. But by "unwritten" Blackstone meant that the ultimate, highest source of law was not an
enactment, but "general custom," as reflected in the decisions of
the common-law judges. These judges were "the depositaries of
the laws—the living oracles, who must decide in all cases of doubt,
and who are bound by an oath to decide according to the law of
the land." (1 Bl. Comm. *69). Common law was judge-made law—
molded, refined, examined, and changed in the crucible of actual
decision, and handed down from generation to generation in the
form of reported cases. In theory, the judges drew their decisions
from existing principles of law; ultimately these principles reflected the living values, attitudes, and ethical ideas of the English
people. In practice, the judges relied on their own past actions,
which they modified under the pressure of changing times and
changing patterns of litigation. In other words, common law adhered to precedent as a general rule.

Precedent is commonly considered one of the basic concepts
of the common law. It was never quite a straitjacket, as some
laymen (and lawyers) have tended to think. American judges have
always assumed power to overrule an earlier case, if they considered it egregiously wrong. The power was seldom exercised in

the past. Still, it was there, along with the more important power to "distinguish" an embarrassing precedent. In any event, the common law was and is a system in which judges, whether following or distinguishing precedent, play a vital role in creating and expounding principles of law; in its prime, the decided case was one of the basic building blocks of law. For a long time, the proud judges looked at statutes with great suspicion. Statutes were unwelcome intrusions on the law, and were treated accordingly. In Continental law, all law (in theory) is contained in the codes. In common law many basic rules of law are found nowhere but in the recorded opinions of the judges.

What Parliament can do in a month's intensive work, a court can do only over the years—and never systematically, since the common law does not look kindly on hypothetical or future cases. It confines itself to actual disputes. If no one brings up a matter, it is never decided. It is no answer to say that all important questions will turn into disputes; "disputes" are not litigation, and only litigation—primarily, appellate litigation—makes new law. Nor is it easy for judges to lay down quantitative rules, or rules that need heavy public support (in the form of taxes) to carry out, or rules that would have to be enforced by a new corps of civil servants. Judges are supposed to decide on the basis of pre-existing principle. This could hardly tell them what the speed limit ought to be, or the butterfat content of ice cream. An English (or American) court could not possibly "evolve" a Social Security law. The common law is therefore not only slow; it is impotent to effect certain kinds of significant legal change.

Older English law was often as devious in making changes as it was (sometimes) slow. Obsolete doctrines and institutions were often not formally abolished, but merely superseded and ignored. Trial by battle, a favorite of medieval romance and costume movies, was not done away with in England until 1819. For centuries, it slept in its sarcophagus; but a chance mistake in court, in 1818, reminded the legal profession that battle was still a legal possibility. An embarrassed Parliament quickly buried the corpse (59 Geo. III, c. 46, 1819).

Evolution sometimes took place through the use of shortcuts called *legal fictions*. The rise of the action of ejectment is a famous example. Suppose two men—we will call them Henry Black and Richard Brown—are in dispute over title to a piece of land. Brown is in possession, but Black has a claim to it. Each thinks he is the rightful owner. The medieval common law had a form of trial that could be used to resolve this dispute. As it happened, this form of action was slow and heavy-handed. Ejectment developed as a way around it. In ejectment, the pleadings—papers filed in court—told an odd story. A man named John Doe, it seems, had leased the land from Henry Black. Another man, named William Styles, held a lease from Richard Brown. Styles (it was said) had "ejected" John Doe. In fact, Doe, Styles, and the two leases were pure figments of legal imagination. Black and Brown were the only real people in the case. This mummery (which everybody, the court included, knew to be false) served the purpose of bringing the issue of title before the court; but at the same time, because it was a *lease* case, the ancient land actions (which did not apply to leases) were avoided. In the course of time, ejectment itself came to be considered as too complicated, and a nuisance. But the action was not streamlined in England until past the middle of the 19th century.

The tortuous story of ejectment is not an isolated example of high technicality and fiction. What is the nonlegal mind to make of a social institution which treats corporations as "persons," which at times classified slaves as real estate, and which allowed a plaintiff to state that the city of Paris was located in England, refusing to let the defendant contradict him? One of these, the corporate fiction, is still alive (and useful); the others served their purpose and then died out. But though fictions were functional, they were dreadfully hard to manage.

Enough high technicality survives to make Anglo-American law a difficult system to master. But the common law was involute, overformalized, and fiction-ridden not because it was changeless, but precisely because it was constantly changing. Part of the problem lay in traditional theories, in which the common law lay tightly swaddled. In theory, the common law was not man-made in the ordinary sense; the judges uncovered the law (or "found" it); they did not make it, or tamper with it as it was found. The modern idea of law as essentially man-made, as essentially a tool or an instrument, was foreign to the classic common law. Change then had to be hidden, disguised. Blunt, overt reforms (by judges) were out of the question. Moreover, working doctrines of law, however quaint they may seem, must be acting as the servants of some economic or social interest. In a society with many rough, contentious holders of power, at war with each other, the court can effect power relations only slowly and subtly. Otherwise a delicate balance is upset.

Moreover, foolish traditions are tolerable as long as they are harmless. The abolition of trial by battle illustrates this point. If trial by battle had not been all *but* dead, it could not have survived to the 19th century. Powerful engines of change can and do exist *inside* the legal system but *outside* the courts. Some major changes take place in law by means of opening and shutting institutional valves. Subject matter moved from legal agency to agency. The courts gained work, lost work, then gained new work. Parliament's role got stronger; the king's waxed and waned. In the course of these changes, some ancient, specialized, essentially marginal business stayed with the courts. Because they are colorful and old, these fossils attract more attention than they deserve. They give an impression of the archaic, sometimes a false one.

Then, too, a good deal of the law is not addressed to the public directly. Lawyers stand between the laymen and the lawmaker. It is the business of the lawyer to tolerate and master artifice. After all, technical difficulty is the sole social excuse for the lawyer's monopoly, his stranglehold on court work, on the drafting of documents, on the counseling of clients. The English bar was, by the time our story opens, an important influence on the shape of English law. The evolution of the bar was complicated, full of riddles. But by 1600, English lawyers were plainly professionals—men educated in the law. They were not, however, trained at universities, at Oxford or Cambridge. Lawyers came out of the Inns of Court, in London. The Inns had no connection with the universities, hence no connection with Roman law and the general legal culture of Europe. Young men at the Inns, if they learned anything, learned English law, English pleading, English legal experience. Legal training was primarily practical, not jurisprudential. This peculiar bent in English legal education helped the common law to survive, while Continental law fell under the spell of a rejuvenated Roman law. In England, too, the bench was recruited from the bar. Lawyers and judges made up a single legal community, with a shared background and common experiences, as they do to this day. They were a cohesive group sharply set off from the public.

For a variety of reasons, then, the common law came down through the centuries with some of its past sticking to it, like a skin it never quite succeeded in molting. This skin was strongly colored by the feudal past. Medieval English practice left deep marks on the language and habits of common law. The common law was utterly obsessed by two central topics: formal legal process and the law relating to land. A second's thought tells one, however, that these two topics could not have been *all* of the living law of England, any more than the life of great lords could have been the life of everyone in England. Common law was, essentially, the law of the royal central courts. It was this law, basically, that the great English jurists, up to and including Blackstone, described. But the royal central courts, by and large, handled the legal problems of a tiny group of people. Leaf through the pages of Lord Coke's reports, compiled in the late 16th and early 17th century; here one will find a colorful set of litigants, all drawn from the very top of British society—lords and ladies, landed gentry, high-ranking clergymen, wealthy merchants. Common law was an aristocratic law, for and of the gentry and nobility. The masses were hardly touched by this system and only indirectly under its rule. There was law on the manor—law that controlled the common people and bound them to their betters. This was largely subterranean law and made little impact on the treatises. Lawbooks were written at the seat of power: they dealt with the king's kind of law. Day-to-day law of the lower orders was barely chronicled.

Nor did common law, which was royal law, the law of the realm, in fact cover the whole kingdom. Authority was not so welded and compact. There was no single focus of law, no single legal culture. English law was pluralistic, comparable (at least roughly) to the loose aggregations of the later colonial empire, especially in Africa, where official law, derived from the mother country, ruled in the capital, among expatriates and businessmen, while in the countryside, customary law was left largely to fend for itself. In England, too, in the Middle Ages, many local customs, like local dialects, survived alongside common law. Primogeniture, for example—inheritance of land by the eldest son—was the common-law rule, but not the rule in the county of Kent. In Kent, under the system known as gavelkind tenure (abolished in 1925), land descended to all the sons equally. And local and customary law had an important bearing on the law of early America. Colonial practice derived in part from that law which the settlers knew best: the local laws and local customs of their communities back home.

Even for important affairs of important people, the reign of the common law was not undisputed; it had to contend with rival courts, institutions, and subsystems of law. Many of the rivals were eventually brought to heel. But the common law won only by granting deep concessions. Language once more is a useful analogy. The Anglo-Saxon language held out against onslaughts of Norse and French, and two culture tongues, Latin and Greek. But the surviving language—English—was drenched with foreign words, and heavily overlaid with foreign syntax. Modern common law is full of Roman-law words and ideas, and is also heavily indebted to equity, admiralty, and the law merchant.

Of the formal rivals of the common law, the most astounding was the peculiar system, administered by the chancellors, known as *equity*. Since early medieval times, the chancellor had been an important royal official. The chancellor's office, the chancery, was responsible for issuing writs to the common-law courts. Through a long and complex process, chancery itself became a court. But it was a court with a difference. Chancery did not follow strict common-law rules. Looser principles governed, principles in accord with prevailing ideas of "equity." The chancellor was said to be "keeper of the king's conscience." As such, he had the power to dispense with unjust rules. Actually, the chancellor, a literate clergyman, with a staff of scribes, "commanded the machinery which sooner or later would have to be set in motion to give redress to petitioners."[2] This power gave him a strategic position in the royal system of justice. Over the course of time, the chancellor, as the king's delegate, loosened the rules of the common law in a number of fields of law. The theory of "equity" developed to explain the chancellor's power, and reduce his work to some kind of logical order. The *ad hoc* character of equity rules gradually disappeared. One could speak of rules, principles, and doctrines of equity as well as of "law." Equity became, in short, almost a system of antilaw.

In England, then, two contradictory systems of civil law coexisted—and not always peacefully. Yet in many ways law and equity complemented each other. The common law could proclaim duties and rights; but it could not compel any kind of performance, other than the payment of money. Equity, on the other hand, had a whole battery of other remedies. The injunction was one of these. An injunction is an order commanding a person to do some specific act or to forbear from something he had been or might be doing. It is enforceable because, if a defendant disobeys, the chancellor can declare him in contempt and put him in jail. Equity had power over persons, not over things. It could

---

[2]Theodore F. T. Plucknett, *A Concise History of the Common Law* (5th ed., 1956), p. 180.

not render judgments that bound the title to land, for example; it could only act on the parties. The chancellor could order B to give A's land back to him. If B refused, the chancellor could send him to jail; but he could not give A the land. Procedurally, the two systems were very different. Continental and ecclesiastical law heavily influenced the ideas and processes of equity. This meant an infusion of Roman-law culture. The jury was a common-law institution; no jury sat in chancery. On the other hand, many familiar doctrines, and some whole branches of law, such as the law of trusts, grew out of equity.

What was curious, perhaps unique, was the mutual isolation, within one legal system and one country, of law and equity. It was possible for a man to have a claim which equity would enforce but common law would not, and vice versa. For example, the common law tended to treat a deed of land as valid, if it was executed in proper form. In equity, however, the deed was good only if it was free from undue influence, fraud, or deceit. A claim based on a deed might win or lose, depending on which courtroom door the plaintiff went in. Courts of common law ignored doctrines of equity, and equity courts would dismiss a case if the plaintiff had an "adequate remedy at law."

Relations between the two systems were different, of course, at different times. In Tudor-Stuart days, open bitter conflict broke out between equity and law. The common lawyers did not succeed in crushing their rival, though they would have liked to. After a time, the two systems came to a rough and ready coexistence. In the 19th century, equity and law finally "merged." This meant, basically, that a single court administered both systems. Where rules of law and equity collided, equity usually prevailed. In the United States, the distinction between law and equity lingered on for a surprisingly long time. Some states—Massachusetts for one— never had a system of equity; New Jersey not only had separate courts, but did not abolish them until 1947. In Delaware, there is a separate chancery court to this very day. The historical distinction between equity and law still makes a difference in lawsuits. It may decide whether one has the right to a jury or not.

Chancery was not the only court which did not follow strict norms of common law. The court of star chamber was an efficient, somewhat arbitrary arm of royal power. It was at the height of its career in the days of the Tudor and Stuart kings. Star chamber stood for swiftness and power; it was not a competitor of the common law so much as a limitation on it—a reminder that high state policy could not safely be entrusted to a system so chancy as English law. The special commercial courts—also outside the common law—lasted longer than star chamber. The royal central courts, absorbed in the tangle of land titles, paid little attention to the Lombard merchants, and to the bankers and tradesmen, foreign and native, who came after them. The mercantile courts, however, were sensitive to the habits and customs of businessmen.

In these mercantile courts a body of law called the *law merchant* governed, rather than the ordinary law of England. The law merchant was international; its rules were derived from the general customs and law-sense of European traders. There were many types of merchant courts, including the colorful courts of pie-powder, a court of the fairs where merchants gathered. Sir Edward Coke spoke of it as a court of "speedy justice... for advancement of trade, and traffic," as fast "as the dust can fall from the foot."[3]

Through fair courts and merchant courts English law and practice at last gave recognition to the merchant's basic ways of doing business and dealing in money. From these sources, English law learned to handle the documents from which modern checks, notes, bills of exchange, and bills of lading are descended. The special merchant courts decayed when the common law woke up to the interests of business; the law merchant was gradually absorbed into the bloodstream of the common law. By the 17th century the process was well advanced. The final major figure in this development, by common consent, was the Scotsman Lord Mansfield, who died in 1793. Mansfield, deeply versed in Roman and Continental law, had a sure touch for commercial cases. His decisions were sensitive and responsive to the merchant's needs and ways.

Admiralty, the law of the high seas and maritime commerce, was another "rival." Admiralty had a long, involved international tradition, quite separate from the common law. As early as the 16th century, the English court of admiralty came into conflict with the common-law courts. The struggle for control over sea law was not finally resolved for many years. It was not the romance of the sea that was at stake, but power over naval policy and international transport.

Family law—marriage and divorce—was also largely outside

---

[3] 4 Co. Inst. 272. The name "piepowder" is said to be a corruption of two French words meaning "dusty foot."

the pale of common law. Marriage was a sacrament; church courts, even after the Reformation, maintained jurisdiction. The law of succession to property (in modern law, wills and estates) was curiously divided; the common law governed the descent of land; church courts governed distribution of personal property. The two kinds of court used quite different rules. If a man died intestate (without a will), his eldest son inherited his land. But his personal property (money and goods) was equally divided among his children. The ecclesiastical courts, like the courts of equity, did not use common-law procedures; a jury, therefore, had no role in its decisions.

This prologue has laid heavy stress on courts. But the reader must not assume that *all* English law was judge-made. A great deal of law came, directly or indirectly, from King and Parliament. In Renaissance England, there was nothing like the steady stream of statutes one is familiar with today. But the state did not leave so important a matter as law to the sole care of judges. Some statutes fundamentally altered the structure and substance of law. Some were carried over into the colonies.

English law was never static. The law of Charles II was not the law of Edward I; it was light years from the law of King Alfred. Mostly, what has been described is the end product of evolution and enactment, roughly at the time of the settlements. England, in 1600, stood on the brink of a period of the most profound changes, a period which has not yet ended. From the legal standpoint, the single most important aspect of this modern period is a revolutionary shift in the attitude of society toward law. In traditional cultures, law was a divine or time-honored body of rules which defined people's place in the order of society. In modern times, law is an instrument; the people in power use it to push or pull toward some definite goal. The idea of law as a rational tool underlies all modern systems, whether capitalist, socialist, fascist, whether democratic or authoritarian. Law was a prime social mover in England, and then in America. By and large, the period covered by this book is a period of ceaseless and insatiable change.

PART I

The Beginnings: American Law
in the Colonial Period

INTRODUCTION

The colonial period is, for most lawyers and laymen, the dark ages of American law. The two sources of law an American lawyer first considers when he faces a legal problem are statutes and reports of high-court cases. The American lawyer has probably never seen, dealt with, or even heard of colonial cases and statutes. Reports of American cases did not become handy and accessible until well after Independence. Even now, only scattered collections of colonial cases have been published. Many colonial statutes survive only in ancient or rare editions; some have been altogether lost. The *Laws and Liberties of Massachusetts* (1648), one of the most important colonial codes, had utterly vanished, until a copy turned up in the 20th century.

That so much of the native tradition disappeared is not really surprising. Law constantly changes; and old law is basically useless, except to scholars. Only collectors and historians care much about the laws of Massachusetts of 1830. The laws of 1648 are even deader; they were already quaint and outdated when John Adams was alive. Conditions between the time of settlement and Independence were worlds apart; the legal needs of a small settlement, run by clergymen, clinging precariously to the coast of an unknown continent, were fundamentally different from the needs of a bustling commercial state. Gross trends in the growth of the law followed gross trends in the larger society. In the 18th century, for example, colonial law seemed to swing back toward English models. Even after the Revolution, American law appeared to become, in some ways, a bit more English. This was not really a paradox. "English" is a misleading term. Economic growth and social division of labor called for tools of law the Puritan oligarchs of 1650 had no need of and no use for. The new tools were not to be found in the colonial past; but some could be imported from

33

abroad. Only England had a supply of law that American lawyers could use without translation; and England was itself in the process of social change.

As a result, the native tradition was neglected. Colonial law was not widely studied or read. It had no strong written record. It slipped easily out of memory. It also bore the stamp of local law, that is, inferior law, lacking dignity and general authority, stigmatized as a jargon, a dialect. Later colonial systems of law, from Australia to Zanzibar, suffered the same fate of indignity and obscurity. American jurists tended to accept the legal standards of England. The colonial tradition was buried in the rubble of indifference and myth. How much remained alive is difficult to say.

Only in the last thirty years or so have scholars begun to reverse the pattern of neglect. But colonial law has been so slowly and so randomly excavated that scholars have tended to see, like the blind man first meeting an elephant, only a trunk, a tail, a leg, rarely the whole. The whole is very hard to describe. One hundred and sixty-nine years went by between Jamestown and the Declaration of Independence. The same length of time separates 1776 and the end of the Second World War. No one would consider this last span of time a single "period." The comparison may be misleading, since social (and hence legal) change does not necessarily move at an even pace. Even so, colonial times were hardly a single, uniform period.

Some early points of view toward colonial law can by now be safely discarded. George L. Haskins, in a fine study of Massachusetts Bay, summed up a number of older misconceptions. One was "that the law of the colonies was essentially the common law of England, brought over to the extent applicable to colonial conditions." This theory denied "any native legal achievements in the colonial period"; it was demonstrably false. A corollary assumption, that "because the law of the colonies was essentially that of England, colonial law was basically the same everywhere," was equally incorrect. Some scholars, too, treated colonial law as far more innovative than the facts really warranted. They observed that colonial law (especially in early years) was very different from English law. They took English common law as somehow the norm; colonial differences, then, were examples of some sort of rude primitivity. The law of Massachusetts Bay, to these scholars, was a strange, radical departure from a known standard. Massachusetts law was not common law at all; it was a new-fangled system of law, based on the Bible. These theories, too, if not downright wrong, were wildly overstated.[1]

Professor Haskins proposed his own generalization: "The conditions of settlement and of development within each colony meant that each evolved its own individual legal system, just as each evolved its individual social and political system. Geographical isolation, the date and character of the several settlements, the degree of absence of outside supervision or control—all had their effect in ultimately developing thirteen separate legal systems."[2] At any particular time, then, each colony had a legal system built up out of various and diverse materials. These were of three general types: First, there was what might be called remembered folk-law—those aspects of living English law which the settlers brought with them. Second, there were those norms and practices which developed indigenously, to cope with new, special problems of life in the settlements. England, for example, had no need to consider, in its law, the problem of hostile native tribes. Third, there were norms and practices that the colonists adopted because of who they were—the ideological element. Puritans in power made law which was certainly different from English law, and which was not dictated by climate, conditions, or crisis, but by their own tight set of beliefs.

These three elements made up the legal system, in varying degrees, in the different colonies. No wonder, then, that the law looked strange, from the standpoint of English law. What enhanced the (apparent) strangeness was the fact that the colonists did not bring over standard English law—the law of the royal central courts. They brought with them the law they knew: and this was primarily local law, local customs. But local law often deviated greatly from the London standard.[3] And the colonists, as they arrived from England, represented different local traditions. Though they "essentially reproduced ... the ordering of life as they knew it before their emigration," the result was often to "recreate" the "diversity of local England in the New England countryside."[4]

[1]George L. Haskins, *Law and Authority in Early Massachusetts* (1960), pp. 4 ff.
[2]Haskins, *op. cit.*, p. 6.
[3]On these points, see the classic article by Julius Goebel, Jr., "King's Law and Local Custom in Seventeenth-Century New England," 31 Columbia L. Rev. 416 (1931).
[4]David Grayson Allen, *In English Ways: The Movement of Societies and the Transferal of English Local Law and Custom to Massachusetts Bay in the Seventeenth Century* (1981), p. 20.

Colonial law, throughout its history, was made up of the three elements just mentioned. In the 18th century, an English element became, perhaps, stronger and more standardized. After the Revolution, the element of (current) English law became thinner and thinner as time went on. Diversity *within* England became a less and less important formative element. Diversity within the colonies and states was, however, always significant. Both colonial law and the law of the United States were subject to centrifugal and centripetal forces: forces that pulled jurisdictions apart; forces that pushed them together. The mother country, its agents, its superior legal culture—these acted centripetally, before Independence. Geographical isolation, local politics, and the sovereignty (in law or fact) of colonies and states were centrifugal forces. One of the great, and constant, themes of American law is the pushing and pulling of these forces: uniformity and diversity, in constant tension over time.

Professor Haskins mentioned thirteen separate legal systems. This number cannot be taken too literally. Throughout the colonial period, big colonies swallowed up littler ones. Moreover, if one stopped the clock at any particular moment in colonial times, one would find colonies in vastly different stages of economic and social growth. Each colony suffered through a first, precarious period, before the social order solidified. In a way, it is more enlightening to compare early Georgia to early Massachusetts, than to compare a bustling, mature Massachusetts, in the 1700s, to the infant colony of Georgia. Within each colony, too, old and new were mixed together—established population centers and frontier toeholds. Early Massachusetts, middle Virginia, late New York: each showed a specific adaptation of English law to local problems, experience, and habits. Each colony had its commercial center and its hinterland. The year 1776 did not witness a sharp break in legal (or social) life. A similar point can be made about America in the 19th century. At any cross section of time, there was wilderness and civilization; there were isolated farms, boom towns, ports and railroad centers; capitals and outposts, seacoast and hinterland. Each type of community implied different modalities of living law.

In this chapter, we can touch on only a few main themes of colonial law. Colonial legal experience was richly diverse from the outset, because conditions were so varied in the colonies. Some variations were natural—they stemmed from climate or the lay of the land; others were structural, depending upon whether the colony was a crown colony, a chartered colony, or a proprietorship. Others were ideological: Puritanism in New England, William Penn's "Holy Experiment" in Pennsylvania, the proprietary adventure in Maryland. Initial differences in land or structure led to still further differentiation. A rich soil and a mild climate, to take one instance, favor certain crops—tobacco, cotton, rice. It takes a certain climate and soil to develop a plantation economy; but this kind of economy in turn molds social conditions in its community. This was, at least, the American experience.

Part of this chapter will show how differences in condition led to legal mutations. The theme of unity is also strong. There were underlying similarities in the colonial experience: the texture of social and economic life was open; there was abundant land; the home government exerted weak but growing control. English tradition gave way to something uniquely American, different in the various colonies but generally moving in parallel directions.

THE SKELETON OF COLONIAL LAW: THE COURTS

Generally speaking, court organization in the colonies followed one fundamental social law. The colonies began with simple, undifferentiated structures, and developed more complex ones, with more division of labor. England boasted an amazing, cumbersome collection of courts, at the same time highly specialized and wildly overlapping. Sir Edward Coke spent a whole volume, the fourth part of his *Institutes,* describing them. He listed about one hundred courts, ranging from the royal courts, with general jurisdiction, to such special local bodies as the courts of the stanneries, which dealt with tin mines and tin workers, in Cornwall and Devon. That a hundred settlers huddled on an island near what is now the city of Newport, or freezing in the Plymouth winter, should have reproduced this system exactly, would have been both miraculous and insane. And indeed no such thing happened.

Life in the colonies was precarious. The factors that made the judicial system of England possible were completely absent. Necessity was the supreme lawmaker; the niceties came later. The "laws" laid down in early settlements, such as Virginia, were something like military orders. In the beginning, judicial business in the colonies was not separated from public business in general. The same people made laws, enforced them, decided cases, and ran the colony. A special court system grew, and divided into parts, only when there were enough people, problems, and territory to make this sensible.

The government and law of Massachusetts Bay went through many convolutions between 1630 and 1639, when a more permanent scheme of courts was established. The charter of Massachusetts Bay (1629) was typical of charters modeled after those of trading companies. It granted a tract of land, and recognized that the land had to be governed. But in other respects it was much like the charter of a business corporation. The "Governour and Companye, and their Successors," were to have "forever one comon Seale, to be used in all Causes and Occasions of the said Companye." The general court, equivalent to the meeting of stockholders of a corporation, was made up of the officers and all the freemen. The court of assistants (governor, deputy governor, and a number of assistants) constituted a smaller in-group, comparable perhaps to a board of directors. On the other hand, David Konig argues that the company had been reorganized before ever arriving at the Bay and that the true analogy is with another form of corporation: the English borough. The system of government was basically modeled after the government of an English town.[5]

In any event, the ruling bodies of the company had rule-making power: they could make "Lawes and Ordinances for the Good and Welfare of the saide Companye, and for the Government and orderings of the saide Landes and Plantation, and the People inhabiting and to inhabite the same." These laws and ordinances, however, were not to be "contrarie or repugnant to the Lawes and Statutes of this our Realme of England." No one knew or knows exactly what "contrarie or repugnant" was intended to mean. But it was a significant phrase; it appeared in other charters, too, including proprietary ones. The Maryland charter of 1632, granted by the king to "his well beloved and right trusty Subject Caecilius Calvert, Baron of Baltimore," used similar language; Calvert's laws had to be "consonant to Reason, and ... not repugnant or contrary, but (so far as conveniently may be) agreeable to the Laws, Statutes, Customs, and Rights of this Our Kingdom of England."

One thing is clear: there was no clear-cut theory that the set-

[5]David T. Konig, *Law and Society in Puritan Massachusetts: Essex County, 1629–1692* (1979), p. 23.

tlements automatically transplanted common law into their midst. The king and his ministers had no idea what problems would arise in the new plantations; they hardly even knew what shape the new ventures would take. The Virginia colony was managed, initially at least, from a London home office; the charter of Massachusetts Bay envisioned management at the seat of the colony, probably from the very start; the proprietary colonies looked toward still another kind of formal structure.

The original charter of Massachusetts Bay gave power to two bodies, a general court and a court of assistants. Neither was primarily a court in the modern sense. They handled all the affairs of the infant enterprise. Thus a "Court holden at Boston June 14th, 1631," in Massachusetts Bay, ordered "that noe man within the limits of this Jurisdiction shall hire any person for a servant for lesse time than a yeare, unles hee be a setled housekeeper." The court also noted that "Mr. John Maisters hath undertaken to make a passage from Charles Ryver to the newe Towne 12 foote broad and 7 foote deepe for which the Court promiseth him satisfaction according as the charges thereof shall amount unto." William Almy was fined "for takeing away Mr. Glovers cannoe without leve"; Mr. Pelham was ordered to pay over to another settler a sum of money "which the Court hath awarded him to pay to make good a covenant betwixte them." At a court held "att Boston," on July 26, Lucy Smith was "bound as an apprentice" to Roger Ludlow for seven years; it was ordered "that there shal be a watch of sixe and an officer kept every night att Boston"; and Francis Perry was ordered "whipped for his ill speeches and misbehavior towards his maister."[6]

As the colony grew, it had to break through the bounds of this simple, undifferentiated structure. The general court was a body of all "freemen"; and though the ruling magistrates defined "freeman" to include only men of the right religious sort, membership in the general court increased. The court very quickly demanded the right to govern, as the charter had promised. Later, the court became a representative body—a body of the elect, rather than of those with a share in the enterprise.

In 1639, Massachusetts Bay had a full system of courts, organized in a way that would not strike a modern lawyer as unduly exotic. The general court, acting both as legislature and as the

<hr />

[6]*Records of the Court of Assistants of the Colony of the Massachusetts Bay, 1630–1692*, vol. II (1904), pp. 15–16, 17–18.

highest court, stood at the crown of the system. As a court, it confined itself mostly to appeals, though its exact jurisdiction was a bit vague.[7] The court of assistants, made up of governor, deputy governor, and magistrates, heard appeals from lower courts, and took original jurisdiction in certain cases—for example, cases of divorce. Below it were the county courts.[8] They had the same power in civil and criminal causes as the courts of assistants, but "tryalls for life, lims or banishment" were "wholly reserved unto the courts of Assistants."[9]

The county courts were a vital part of the system of social control. They were never merely courts. Rather, they acted as general instruments of government. From time to time, laws gave them important administrative functions. They dealt with "probate and administration, apportionment of charges for the repair of bridges, provision for the maintenance of the ministry, punishment of interference with church elections, punishment of heretics, ordering highways laid out, licensing of ordinaries, violations of town orders regulating wages, settlement of the poor, settlement of houses of correction, licensing of new meeting houses, and punishment of vendors charging excessive prices."[10] The county court, in brief, was "the critical institution for dealing with important matters of local community concern,"[11] and this was true, whether or not an observer today would consider these matters "judicial."

The county courts in Massachusetts also had a kind of appellate function. They were not the absolute base of the system. There were other courts (some *ad hoc*) underneath them, handling small cases or special matters. Single magistrates had judicial and administrative power, something on the order of English justices of the peace. By an order of 1638, magistrates could hear and decide cases where the amount at issue was less than 20 shillings. Later laws gave them more powers: they could deal, for example, with people who broke laws against drunkenness. Single magistrates also had power to give oaths to inspectors of pipe-staves, to perform marriages, to impress laborers for repair of bridges and

[7]Joseph H. Smith, *Colonial Justice in Western Massachusetts, 1639–1702; The Pynchon Court Record* (1961), p. 66.

[8]These were originally called particular courts or inferior quarterly courts. The first counties were established in 1642.

[9]*The Laws and Liberties of Massachusetts, 1648* (1929 ed.), p. 15.

[10]Smith, *op. cit.*, p. 69.

[11]Konig, *op. cit.*, p. 36.

highways, to deal with vagabonds and drunken Indians, and to whip wandering Quakers.[12] In 1677, the general court formalized the status of the magistrates; each one was to have a commission from the court, under the seal of the colony. In 1692, upon the fall of the Andros regime, the role of the magistrate devolved on a new official, who was in fact called "justice of the peace." Local government had become thoroughly secularized; and, from then on, took on a rather more English look.[13]

One habit—creating special courts outside the regular pyramid of courts, to handle particular sorts of business—had appeared early in Massachusetts. A law in 1639 established strangers' courts, for the "more speedy dispatch of all causes which shall govern Strangers, who cannot stay to attend the original Court of Justice." These courts had the same jurisdiction as the county courts, but their sessions were not confined to regular terms of court.[14] Rather than tinker with the ordinary county courts, the colony chose to set up a separate agency. This kind of choice had been frequently made in England.

The Massachusetts pattern has been described in detail, because it illustrates some basic characteristics of colonial courts. As in England, separation of powers was notably absent. Jobs were handed over to this or that institution, without worrying whether court functions ought to be separate from legislative or executive ones. All but the lowest and highest levels of courts had mixed jurisdiction; they tried cases and also heard appeals. New Hampshire, Connecticut, and Rhode Island had, roughly, the same plan of organization.

In Virginia, one finds different names, but a more or less parallel development. Dale's code—the "Lawes Divine, Morall and Martiall" of 1611—set up a stern, undifferentiated system of authority; a single ruling group held tight control of the colony; there was little division of labor in government. The "Martiall" part of the code dealt with the duties of soldiers. The "Divine" and "Morall" parts consisted of rules about crime and punishment, and special regulations for the colony. The code was neither lawyer's law nor English law in the usual sense. But neither was it entirely foreign. David Konig has pointed out the relationship

[12]Smith, *op. cit.*, pp. 72–74.

[13]John M. Murrin, *Anglicizing an American Colony: The Transformation of Provincial Massachusetts* (Ph.D. thesis, Yale University, 1966), pp. 156–58.

[14]*Laws and Liberties of Massachusetts*, p. 15. The governor or deputy governor, "with any two other Magistrates," was empowered to form a strangers' court.

between the regime this code established and English rule in other restless, outlying areas—Ireland, for example—and its relationship to Tudor modes of maintaining order among unruly populations.[15] To be sure, the code also reflected the crudities of life in Virginia: the Indians, the "starving time," real or imagined problems of discipline. On paper, the code seemed quite severe; it threatened death for trivial crimes. But the harsh "penalties for embezzlement of public stores or the stealing of boats, speak not so loudly of severity as they do of the importance of the stores and of the boat."[16]

Once the colony was on firmer footing, Dale's code was no longer needed. It was gone by 1620. The colony needed men; and only a certain degree of mildness, and a promise of self-government, could attract them to a new world. In the 1620s, the forerunner of the Virginia legislative assembly was already in operation. By the late 1630s, Virginians were making laws for themselves through an organization in which local people had a share of the power. But the savagery of Dale's code did not vanish completely, or overnight; and at least one scholar feels that "the old tradition of swift and discretionary justice unbound by common law" continued to "thrive" in Virginia; that its "logical continuation" was, ultimately, felt in the governance of slaves.[17]

As in Massachusetts, the highest court in Virginia was more than a court. The governor and council (and the house of burgesses) decided cases and also made rules. Governor and council functioned as a "Quarter Court"; in 1658, sittings were reduced to three a year, in 1661, to two; the body was then called a "General Court." The general court handled the trial of serious crimes. It also reviewed cases initially decided in the county courts. The county courts began as "Monthly Courts" in 1623; the name was changed in 1642; by then, county government had become fully established. The county courts were manned at first by "commissioners"; after 1661, these men were called justices of the peace. The county courts, as in Massachusetts, were also more than courts; they handled a wide range of what would now be considered administrative matters—tax collecting, road building, regulation

[15]David T. Konig, "'Dale's Laws' and the Non-Common Law Origins of Criminal Justice in Virginia," 26 Am. J. Legal Hist. 354 (1982).
[16]Wesley Frank Craven, *The Southern Colonies in the Seventeenth Century, 1607–1689* (1949), p. 106; see also W. F. Prince, "The First Criminal Code of Virginia," *Ann. Rpt. Am. Hist. Ass'n.*, vol. I (1899), p. 311.
[17]Konig, *op. cit.*, at 375.

of taverns and ferries. They also handled probate affairs. This feature of county courts was quite typical in colonial America. It was replicated in other colonies too.[18]

The county courts were at the heart of colonial government. As more and more of their records are published, a vivid picture of colonial justice unfolds. For example, one can now look in on the county court of Prince Georges County, Maryland, meeting "att Charles Towne the twenty fourth day of November in the Eight yeare of the Reigne of our Sovereigne Lord William the third" (1696). Five commissioners were present. The weather was hard, however, so the court "did Immediately Adjourne to Mr. David Smalls Store house by reason the new house Intended for a Church is Soe open that they Cannot Sitt." At Small's, the court discharged its business—judicial, administrative, quasi-legislative. James Paine, a seven-year-old boy, was bound over as an apprentice "by his Fathers Consent." James was to serve Samuel Westley "untill he arrives to twenty one years of Age." Benjamin Berry and Robert Gordon had been drunk at an inn, "profanely Cursing and Swareing"; they were ordered to be put in the stocks. A number of citizens recorded marks for their animals; William Bailey recorded "an over halve and an under bitt on the Right Eare and a Swallow forke on the Left Eare." George Hutcheson humbly petitioned that "by Gods providence" he had "been Grievously Afflicted with an ulcerated Legg for these many years" without a cure, and "being thus...disenabled from getting my Livelyhood by any hard Labour I gett a poore maintenance in teching of Childred to reade but being growne in years and my Ability or Capasity being but Small I only gett my Accomedations and a few old Cloaths to Cover my nakedness"; he begged to be "Excused...from paying his Leavye"; this the court allowed. Estate matters were handled, constables chosen. A grand jury met and made presentments: "Elizabeth Pole Servant woman...for haveing a bastard."[19] At another session, the court licensed Jonathan Wilson to "keepe Ordinary [an inn] in the Saide towne Called Charles Towne dureing pleasure," complying with "the Act of Assembly Conserning Ordinary keepers." At another, it was

---

[18]On Virginia, see George B. Curtis, "The Colonial County Court: Social Forum and Legislative Precedent, Accomack County, Virginia, 1633–1639," 85 Va. Mag. Hist. & Biog. 274 (1977); see also Paul M. McCain, *The County Court in North Carolina before 1750* (1954).

[19]Joseph H. Smith and Philip A. Crowl, eds., *Court Records of Prince Georges County, Maryland, 1696–1699* (1964), pp. 59 ff.

ordered "that the Sherife receive of every Taxable person Ninety three pounds of Tobacco." At another, they appointed overseers of highways, and heard a complaint that a bridge was "so much out of repair that wee cannot goe over there without the Danger of horse and man."[20]

Some 17th-century colonies organized their systems in ways somewhat different from the patterns in Virginia and Massachusetts. But the over-all structures tended to be the same—less divergent in practice than the names of the courts suggest. The grand council of South Carolina, in the 17th century, was the basic, undifferentiated court of that colony; it sat now as a court of probate, now as chancery, now as admiralty, now as a common law court.[21] It dealt with the defense and safety of the colony, allocated lands, and laid down rules and regulations. In the province of East New Jersey, a court of common right was established in 1683 "to hear, try and determine all matters, causes and cases, capital, criminal or civil, causes of equity, and causes tryable at common law." The court had a unique name; but its broad jurisdiction was otherwise not unusual in the English-speaking colonies. The grand council had an interesting fate. It became labeled as a tool of the proprietors' interests. This made it unpopular with leaders of the colony who opposed the proprietors. The court was, in short, associated with one class, one party, one economic interest. To defeat that interest meant to overthrow the court. When proprietary government collapsed, the court, "devoid of any litigants save the Proprietors themselves, inconspicuously, perhaps unknowingly, adjourned for ever."[22] This was in 1702.

In New York, legal institutions began work, quite literally, in a different language. Its *schouts* and *schepens* were Dutch. When the colony passed into English hands, in the middle of the 17th century, cultural domination took longer to perfect than political domination. In New York City, the old court of burgomasters and schepens changed its name to the "Mayor's Court," in 1665. English procedure was supposedly introduced at this time. But Dutch speech, personnel, and procedures lingered on. As late as 1675, when a plaintiff "declared in action of the Case," the defendant "read his answer and Soe replickt and duplickt, upon which, a

[20]Smith and Crowl, *op. cit.*, pp. 168, 375–76, 615.

[21]Anne K. Gregorie, ed., *Records of the Court of Chancery of South Carolina, 1671–1779* (1950), pp. 22–25.

[22]Preston W. Edsall, ed., *Journal of the Courts of Common Right and Chancery of East New Jersey, 1683–1702* (1937), p. 34.

Jury was empanneled," a "curious melange," in the words of Professor Morris, "of Dutch terminology and English remedy and procedure." By the early 1680s, however, "English verbiage culled from the standard folios on writs and entries published in the mother country supplanted the informal language of the previous [Dutch] record."[23] This was the first American success of common-law imperialism; the process would be later repeated, with varying results, in Louisiana, Florida, Illinois, Texas, and California.

There were exceptional courts in some of the colonies. In Pennsylvania, William Penn had a Quaker's distaste for formal law and litigation. Penn's laws (1682) called for appointment of three persons in each precinct as "common peacemakers." The "arbitrations" of these peacemakers were declared to be as "valid as the judgments of the Courts of Justice."[24] These peacemakers were an early but not unique example of a certain Utopian strain in American law, or at least in popular legal culture. There were similar experiments elsewhere: in Dedham, Massachusetts, for example, from 1636 on, where disputes were mediated by "three understanding men," or by "two judicious men," chosen by the disputants or by the community. There were also attempts at replacing trials with arbitration proceedings in South Carolina, Connecticut, and New Jersey.[25]

The tendency manifested itself, from time to time, in the noble experiment of prohibiting lawyers—there was a feeble attempt in this direction in early Virginia—or in attempts to reduce or abolish formal law. The dream of doing without lawyers has been a persistent one; and the cognate dream of a simple, clear, natural

[23]Richard B. Morris, ed., *Select Cases of the Mayor's Court of New York City, 1674–1784* (1935), p. 43. In Westchester County, however, which was settled by English-speaking people, common-law terminology was used from the beginning. In court records of March 22, 1659, there is a plaintive remark of the clerk that "the coppi of the sentence of the high corte being ritten in Duch we could not understand it." Dixon R. Fox, ed., *Minutes of the Court of Session, Westchester County, 1657–1696* (1924), pp. 12–13. On the transition to common law in New York, see also Herbert A. Johnson, *Essays on New York Colonial Legal History* (1981), pp. 37–54.

[24]Edwin B. Bronner, *William Penn's "Holy Experiment"* (1962), p. 36; on the use of peace bonds, see Paul Lermack, "Peace Bonds and Criminal Justice in Colonial Philadelphia," 100 Pa. Mag. Hist. & Biog. 173 (1976).

[25]Jerold S. Auerbach, *Justice without Law? Non-legal Dispute Settlement in American History* (1983), pp. 25–30. But arbitration itself underwent a process of "legalization" in the 18th century, according to the research of Bruce H. Mann, centering on Connecticut; Mann connects this process with the decline of communalism. Bruce H. Mann, "The Formalization of Informal Law: Arbitration before the American Revolution," 59 N.Y.U. L. Rev. 443 (1984).

form of justice, a book of law that everyone might read for himself, also never died. Indeed, the codification movement of the 19th century drew strength from this source, among others.

Early court organization in Maryland was unrealistic, but not Utopian; and in rather a different direction from arbitration as it existed in Quaker Pennsylvania. On paper, the proprietors established a whole battery of courts after English models: hundred courts and manorial courts, courts of hustings and piepowder in St. Mary's and Annapolis, county courts, courts of oyer and terminer, a chancery court, a court of vice-admiralty, and a prerogative court, among others. Some of these apparently never came to life at all. Records of one manorial court survive; it actually sat between 1659 and 1672. But this transplant was on the whole as hopeless and transient as the introduction of ostriches and camels in the American West.

In short, despite diversity and experimentation, colonial conditions shaped court organization, and moved it in all, or almost all, the colonies along similar lines in the 17th century. Court structures evolved from simple to complex. English models, English terms, and English customs were more or less influential everywhere. Nowhere were executive, legislative, and judicial powers clearly fenced off from each other. But as time went on, there was more marked differentiation. Legislatures still heard appeals; but they conducted few trials or none.

For all their isolation, the colonies owed some sort of allegiance to the crown. They were, in one sense, lost, distant islands, floating alone and unsupervised. But their charters expressed an explicit duty: colonial law must conform to the law of England. The far-off king held at least some nominal authority, particularly in chartered colonies. The settlements of the trading-company type were also beholden, at least in theory, to a distant authority: the company's home office, usually located in London. In proprietary colonies, the proprietor held some sort of appellate power.

Some colonies actively resisted English authority. The Child Remonstrance, in Massachusetts Bay (1646), is a well-known incident. Dr. Child attacked the ruling circles of the colony, in writing. He called for a return to the "Fundamentall and wholesome Lawes" of England. He pointed to the large gap between the laws of England and the laws of Massachusetts Bay. Implicitly, he appealed to the English to close the gap in some way. The colony tried to keep Child's writings from reaching England. John Cotton supposedly warned a shipmaster not to "carry any Writings" that were "complaints against the people of God"; it would be "as *Jonas* in the ship," he said. If "storms did arise," the master should "search if they had not in any chest or trunk any such Jonas aboard"; any such writings should be thrown to the boiling sea.[26]

The colony did not rely on the storm gods alone; it also argued, in England, that its charter precluded appeals from the colony to London. By this time, it was already clear that the relationship between the center in London and the periphery—the outlying colonies—was a problem that would have to be resolved. It was also clear that the colonies would resist encroachments from London. England did not really found an empire; it stumbled into one. It worked out an imperial policy slowly and haltingly; meanwhile, the tiny settlements along the coast grabbed almost total autonomy. The colonies were small, of marginal importance, and a long way from London: all of this insulated them from king and council. If colonial and English law, in substance and procedure, converged at all in the 17th century, it was not imperial policy so much as convenience and free will. And English law *was* convenient. Massachusetts Bay was the most independent of the colonies. But when the colonists compiled their code of 1648, they sent to England for six legal texts, including *Coke on Littleton*.[27]

Especially in proprietary and crown colonies, there were absentee landlords and overlords. They assumed, naturally enough, that the law of England was in force in their properties. Also, fresh boatloads of Englishmen constantly landed in America; doctrines, documents, and devices came with them. There was constant tension between the colonial legal dialects, and the mother tongue. A controversy in East New Jersey, in 1695, illustrates this point. In 1676, Governor Carteret had granted, by patent, to Simon Rouse, certain land, including "58 acres of arable land & six acres of meadow" situated "upon Raway River in the County of Essex." The grant read: "to Have and to Hold to him the said Simon Rouse his Heires or assigns for ever." Rouse left the land by will to Frances Moore. Litigation arose over whether Moore had a valid title to the land. One side referred to the doctrine in "My Lord Cooks Institutes," that to make a grant in fee simple (that is, full ownership), the grantor had to use the words "to A and his heirs and assigns." The word *and* was essential; if the grantor used *or* what resulted was "only an Estate for life," so that

[26]Robert Child, *New England's Jonas Cast Up at London* (1869), p. 26.
[27]Haskins, *op. cit.*, p. 135.

Rouse had no power to leave the land by will; his title ended at his death. This mumbo-jumbo was indeed the law of England, according to the gospel of Sir Edward Coke; and a jury verdict so decided. The verbal misstep had been made, it seems, "through the ignorance of those infant times."

But the decision was a crucial one; it cast in doubt the rights of many landholders, who claimed through Moore. The province was thrown into uproar. Remedial legislation was proposed, but the governor blocked it, hoping to exact payment of unpaid quit-rents as the price of quieting the disputed titles. Ultimately, the proprietary party conceded the point, and an act was passed declaring that all of Governor Carteret's "grants, charters, or patents" bearing the "particle or ... in the habendum" should be "taken, deemed and esteemed as effectual in law" as if the word and had appeared in place of the or. The complexity of law was perilous, in a land with too few technicians; but landowners inevitably invoked English sources of law in disputes where English interests, using English legal documents and techniques, clashed with colonial habits and desires.[28] Little of this was imposed by the London government. In the 17th century, the strings that bound colonial law to English law were less political than social and cultural. Colonial law was more a child of English law than its subordinate.

THE COLONIAL JUDICIAL SYSTEM IN THE 18TH CENTURY

The colonial courts in the 18th century looked noticeably more English—partly by choice, partly because England was more serious about governing. At the end of the 17th century

> a new policy of constructive imperialism was introduced which proposed the supplanting of chartered colonies by royal governments, the combination of smaller self-governing or proprietary units into large units of administration, and the strengthening of the executive power at the expense of representative assemblies.[29]

[28]Preston W. Edsall, ed., *Journal of the Courts of Common Right and Chancery of East New Jersey, 1683–1702* (1937), pp. 105–8, 273.

[29]Richard B. Morris, *Studies in the History of American Law* (2nd ed., 1959), p. 62.

These policies failed in the long run. But the British government at least managed to make colonies pay more attention to London's demands. It was "necessary," said the Massachusetts charter of 1691, "that all our Subjects should have liberty to Appeale to us our heires and Successors in Cases that may deserve the same." In cases where "the matter in difference" was worth more than three hundred pounds sterling, there was a right to appeal to London. As for legislation, copies of all "Orders Laws Statutes and Ordinances" were to be sent to England "by the first opportunity," for "approbation or Disallowance." Any laws disallowed in London, within three years after passage, "shall thenceforth cease and determine and become utterly void and of none effect."

It might have been possible to give the royal courts, in London, appellate jurisdiction over colonial courts. The royal courts, then, could have forced a certain amount of conformity on the colonial courts. But this was not the system chosen. Appeals ran, not to the law courts, but to a special committee of the Privy Council. The committee cared little for the purity of common law as such. It cared about politics and policy.

The council was never an efficient overseer of the routine legal work of the courts. The volume of "appeals" was always small. Distance, expense, and political recalcitrance discouraged appeals. Rhode Island was the most appeal-prone colony; yet it sent, on the average, less than a case a year—76 between 1696 and 1783.[30] The council's working habits also limited its influence. Few council orders

> were embodied in the printed reports; few attained currency in manuscript form—most probable was verbal circulation in garbled form. For this reason the jurisdiction of the Privy Council was largely exercised in *ad hoc* fashion, from appeal to appeal with little lasting effect.[31]

A few Privy Council decisions were great cases, that is, they touched on issues of major significance. One such case was *Winthrop* v. *Lechmere* (1727–28), a rare, controversial example of judicial review.[32] This case threw out, as void, Connecticut's intestacy

---

[30] These figures are from Joseph H. Smith, *Appeals to the Privy Council from the American Plantations* (1950), p. 668. Smith's study is the source for much of the text on the work of the Privy Council.

[31] Smith, *ibid.*, p. 660.

[32] On this famous case, see Smith, *ibid.*, pp. 537–60.

laws. In general, the Privy Council was rather permissive and incompetent. Legislation, too, was reviewed in a haphazard way. Delays were frequent. The council found it hard to decide on a method of review. Practically all colonial statutes were in some way repugnant to the laws of England. In theory, the council could have thrown them all out. In fact, most deviations were tolerated.

It is hard to assess the results of the council's work. Quantitatively, it was not unimportant. According to one authority, 469 colonial laws were disallowed by orders in council—about 5.5 per cent of 8,563 laws submitted for approval.[33] The council struck down some laws because they crossed the invisible, shifting boundary between acceptable and unacceptable repugnance. The council voided some laws as too carelessly written, or so garbled as to be absurd. Still other laws fell because they contradicted English policy or English interests, as the council conceived them. When South Carolina placed a ten per cent duty on goods imported from England, an Order in Council of 1718 declared the law "null and void."[34]

Council orders were not always obeyed. Review sometimes took years, and meanwhile the laws continued in force in the colonies. Still, in ways difficult to measure, the council may have had an effect on legal behavior. Assemblies debating a proposal, or litigants pursuing lawsuits, were perhaps aware of this distant shadow; they may have modified their action in real but unknowable ways.

Judicial organization as such did not change fundamentally in the 18th century. Each colony had its pyramid of courts. The court at the top was almost always more than a court—the governor and council, either as such, or sitting as a special high court. Below the high court were various basic intermediate courts, and at the base a single judge, justice of the peace, or the equivalent. In most colonies, the county courts functioned as a general trial court, and also retried cases decided by justices of the peace or single magistrates. As in England, jurisdictional lines were fuzzy, and courts overlapped; "appeal" often meant to do the whole case over, rather than sending a few difficult issues upstairs on review.

As in the 17th century, the county courts, or their equivalent, were very versatile, very influential in the life of their districts. These courts handled a huge volume of workaday administrative tasks. In Connecticut in the 18th century, the towns chose a group

[33]Morris, *Studies*, p. 63.
[34]Smith, *Appeals*, p. 535.

of men, called the *grand jury,* to help the county court in its work.
As of 1747, these jurors

> were required to oversee workmen in clearing the commons,
> to present idle persons...to take care that the Sabbath be
> observed, to present persons for selling drink [and]...for
> not attending public worship...to inform against killing deer,
> to meet with selectmen and constables in nominating tavern
> keepers, to present servants for being out unseasonable hours,
> to see that Indian children learned to read, to present persons
> for setting up lotteries, to inspect taverns, and to pull down
> secular notifications posted on the Sabbath or a Day of Fast.[35]

This was a unique system; but the general idea was standard.
The county lower court was a *governing* court; it did not merely
settle disputes. And local rule was rule by the local powers. In
a colony like Virginia, the county court represented planters
and their interests. Everywhere, the judges were mostly laymen.
But lay judges were not ignorant men by any means. They knew
a good deal of the relevant law. In England, too, country gentlemen knew the working law of the community. Law was the raw
material of government, and they were the governors. This was
equally true in the new world. The Virginia judges were the
local elites: rich planters, men of reputation, powers in their
own community. Lay judges in America too knew enough to
run their little worlds. In Virginia, the "gentlemen justices" took
"peculiar pride in their literate, if homely, legal ability. As one
planter observed, 'It is a shame for a gentlemen to be ignorant
of the laws of his country.'"[36]

These were courts that settled disputes; and through them
authority penetrated into every local settlement, no matter how
small. It is extraordinary how *pervasive* they were. This was true
both in the 17th and the 18th centuries. In Accomack County,
Virginia, in the 1630s, during a seven-year period, 695 different
people were "involved in litigation before the court either as plaintiffs, defendants, witnesses to the suits, or applicants for registration of land patents." This was in a community whose adult

---

[35]John T. Farrell, ed., *The Superior Court Diary of William Samuel Johnson, 1772–
73* (1942), xlii. See also Hendrik Hartog, "The Public Law of a County Court:
Judicial Government in Eighteenth-Century Massachusetts," 20 Am. J. Legal Hist.
282 (1976).

[36]A. G. Roeber, *Faithful Magistrates and Republican Lawyers: Creators of Virginia
Legal Culture, 1680–1810* (1981), p. 77.

population was estimated at 800.[37] Of course, all this activity was more than litigation. And other institutions too—the churches, for example—worked at dispute-resolution, as rivals of courts, or as partners in rule. As the years went by, the towns grew in size, new people flocked in, and the tight communalism of the early years became attenuated; now the courts became even more useful—in resolving disputes between people who were not in face-to-face contact; who were members of different churches; or residents of different towns.[38] Justice became less patriarchal, more lawyerly and professional.[39] This meant that courts were at once both more and less useful: less useful, as places where simple, natural justice was dispensed, or as the point where the rulers most obviously ruled; more useful, as forums for resolution of disputes among strangers, or as vehicles for solving problems that could not be solved on the basis of traditional norms and traditional patterns of authority.

There was more functional specialization of courts in the 18th century than there had been before. Two court systems, vice-admiralty and chancery, call for special comment. Courts of admiralty handled violations of trade and navigation laws, and traditional admiralty questions of prize law, seamen's wages, salvage, and maritime commerce. These courts did not exist as such in the 17th century. In crown colonies, the governor was *ex officio* vice-admiral; beginning in 1696, he had the power to "erect one or more Court or Courts Admirall" in his jurisdiction. By 1763 nine separate vice-admiralty courts had been set up in the American colonies.[40] They were mostly staffed by native judges. The courts followed traditional English admiralty procedure, which meant, among other things, that cases were tried without juries.

[37]George B. Curtis, "The Colonial County Court, Social Forum and Legislative Precedent, Accomack County, Virginia, 1633–1639," 85 Va. Mag. Hist. & Biog. 274, 284 (1977). In a study of seventeenth-century New Haven, M. P. Baumgartner found that "high-status" people were more likely to *initiate* action; "low-status" people were more often found as defendants. M. P. Baumgartner, "Law and Social Status in Colonial New Haven, 1639–1665," *Research in Law and Sociology*, vol. 1 (1978), p. 153.

[38]See David T. Konig, *Law and Society in Puritan Massachusetts: Essex County, 1629–1692* (1979); William E. Nelson, *Dispute and Conflict Resolution in Plymouth County, Massachusetts, 1725–1825* (1981); Bruce Mann, "Rationality, Legal Change, and Community in Connecticut," 14 Law & Society Rev. 187 (1980).

[39]Roeber, *op. cit.*

[40]See, in general, Carl Ubbelohde, *The Vice-Admiralty Courts and the American Revolution* (1960); Henry J. Bourguignon, *The First Federal Court: The Federal Appellate Prize Court of the American Revolution, 1775–1787* (1977), pp. 21–36.

In a sense, the colonies needed these courts; overseas trade was the lifeblood of commerce. But the vice-admiralty courts were unpopular. The crown had a mighty interest in these courts; they were a natural forum for enforcement of English trade policy. And, from the English standpoint, the lack of a jury was icing on the cake. Jurors were partial to American (colonial) interests. As resistance to British policy grew, it spilled over naturally into resentment of vice-admiralty courts.

To make doubly sure of subservience, England established an overall, all-colonial court in 1763, and gave it concurrent jurisdiction with the existing courts. The court sat, rather inconveniently, at Halifax, Nova Scotia. Its judge was William Spry, an Englishman trained in civil law. Unfortunately, no one came to use this court; Spry sat in his cold little town, waiting vainly for cases. Later, London assigned to Spry, and the other vice-admiralty courts, jurisdiction to decide cases under the Stamp Act. The Stamp Act had nothing to do with the sea. But in England the Exchequer court specialized in matters of crown revenue; there was no such court in the colonies; only the vice-admiralty courts were loyal enough to be trusted with such matters.

Spry's court was abolished in 1768. The British next tried a network of four regional courts, sitting in Halifax, Boston, Philadelphia, and Charleston. These regional courts were to share jurisdiction with the older vice-admiralty courts. But in practice the regional courts merely replaced courts in the towns where they sat.[41] Then came the Revolution. Curiously, the courts did not vanish from the scene. Militants had objected to these courts on two grounds: first, their modes of procedure were abominable, and, second, they enforced abominable laws. Since regular courts also heard some maritime matters, the real issues were policy and power: who controlled the courts? When war broke out, the new state governments found it useful to create their own vice-admiralty courts—for cases of prize law, for example. Massachusetts, among other states, created a system of these courts in 1775—though, true to ideology, issues of fact were to be decided by "twelve good and lawful men."[42] But soon the jury was abandoned, ostensibly because sea law was too intricate for the "good and lawful men." The "wisdom of all civilized nations" decreed that in admiralty there should be "one judge to try, facts as well as

[41]Ubbelohde, *op. cit.*, p. 158.
[42]Ubbelohde, *op. cit.*, p. 196; Bourguignon, *op. cit.*, p. 59.

law."[43] Dispute over procedure in admiralty, then, was only a screen for conflict over interests. A centralized network of admiralty courts was a dismal failure in colonial America. Yet in 1787 the Constitution put admiralty law in the federal, central courts; and there it stays.

The history of chancery in the 18th century has a certain resemblance to the history of admiralty. The immediate background was complicated. Some colonies—Massachusetts and (except for one brief episode) Pennsylvania—lacked separate courts of equity. In these colonies other courts handled, piecemeal, some essentials of the law of equity. Another group of colonies—the Carolinas, Maryland, New York, New Jersey, and Delaware—had actual courts for matters of chancery. Even in these colonies, equity was not always totally separated, institutionally speaking. In Delaware, for example, the court of common pleas, a common-law court, simply sat four times a year as an equity court.[44] In some colonies, the governor bore the title of chancellor. In 17th-century New Hampshire, the governor and council made up the "high Courte of Chancery"; and the governor had the right to "depute, nominate and appointe in his Stead a Chancellor" and staff. In 1699, when the Earl of Bellomont was acting as governor, a new judiciary act eliminated the court of chancery. Instead, the act gave courts of general jurisdiction the power to "moderate the Rigor of the Law" in certain cases.[45] The Southern colonies quite generally had separate courts of chancery. In New York, a supplement to the Duke's laws in 1665 provided that when the original complaint was a "matter of equity" the action should proceed "by way of Bill and delivering in Answers upon Oath and by the Examination of witnesses, in like manner as is used in the Court of Chancery in England." By 1684 a master of the rolls, a register, and clerks of chancery had been appointed. A separate court of chancery survived New York's many court convolutions, and was embodied in the Judiciary Act of 1691.[46]

Hostility to chancery was widespread in the 18th century. Governor William Burnet of New York (1720–28) used the chancery court as a court of exchequer, to collect unpaid quitrents. This

[43]Ubbelohde, *op. cit.*, p. 200.
[44]Roscoe Pound, *Organization of Courts* (1940), p. 76.
[45]*Laws of New Hampshire: Province Period, 1679–1702* (1904), p. 665; Elwin L. Page, *Judicial Beginnings in New Hampshire, 1640–1700* (1959), p. 42.
[46]Paul M. Hamlin and Charles E. Baker, *Supreme Court of Judicature of the Province of New York, 1691–1704*, vol. 1 (1959), pp. 17, 53.

added nothing to the court's popularity.[47] Chancery was closely associated with executive power, in turn with the English over-lords. Equity also worked without a jury; thus there were no barriers against the use of these courts as tools of imperial policy. Besides, equity courts sat, as a rule, only in the capital; unlike the common law, equity was not brought to everyman's doorstep. Litigants complained, too, that procedures were clumsy, inefficient, interminable. An essay in a New York newspaper, written in 1752, reported ru nors of equity suits "at Issue these Thirty Years Past." Chancery was a "Gulf, that will in the End swallow up the Estates of its Suitors."[48] This was a century before Dickens' *Bleak House*. In South Carolina, when the proprietary government was overthrown in 1720, the short-lived revolutionary party stripped the governor and council of chancery powers. Instead, they were to appoint a chancellor, removable only by the king.[49] Yet, despite all the uproars and complaints in the 18th century, the Revolution did not mean the end of courts of chancery. Equity merely passed to new masters. Procedural abuses, once wrenched from political context, lost their power to stir revolt.

In England, ecclesiastical courts handled questions of probate. These courts had no counterpart in the colonies. Massachusetts, by acts of 1685 and 1686, simply made probate courts out of its county courts, with "full power and authority as the ordinary in England." (The *ordinary* was an ecclesiastical official.) In Maryland, up to 1673, the provincial court managed probate matters, or appointed a justice specially to do so; in 1673, "the English organization, with a prerogative court and a commissary general, was reproduced."[50] In New York, the Duke's laws gave probate matters to the courts of sessions. A constable and two "overseers" took inventory and reported to the court. All wills were registered in New York City, where the probate process was gradually centralized. Ultimately, the governor delegated his probate powers to a subordinate, who presided over a "prerogative court."[51]

Some colonies borrowed from the English the idea of roving

[47]Beverley W. Bond, Jr., *The Quit-Rent System in the American Colonies* (1919), pp. 268–69.

[48]Milton M. Klein, ed., *The Independent Reflector* (1963), p. 253.

[49]Gregorie, *op. cit.*, p. 7. In 1721, the old structure was restored.

[50]Carroll T. Bond, ed., *Proceedings of the Maryland Court of Appeals, 1695–1729* (1933), xvii.

[51]On this court, see Herbert A. Johnson, "The Prerogative Court of New York, 1686–1776," 17 Am. J. Legal Hist. 95 (1973).

courts—courts of oyer and terminer and general gaol delivery. These courts "heard and determined" criminal cases, held over in the local community to await the coming of the court. New York established such courts in 1683; they were staffed by local justices of the peace, joined by an itinerant judge, who represented the central authorities, and who rode on circuit from county to county. Some cities, too, had borough courts. Georgia instituted a latter-day version of the old Bay Colony strangers' court. And the Southern colonies set up special courts, with summary procedures, to deal with the offenses of slaves.

CIVIL PROCEDURE

Common-law pleading and procedure were exceptionally intricate. Colonial process never attained the heights, or depths, of the English common law. There were wide differences between colonies—between the loose, informal justice of early Massachusetts and the more conservative, more formal process in the Middle Atlantic and Southern colonies. But everywhere, the general, long-run trend was the same: from simplicity and innovation to more complexity, and ever greater doses of secondhand English form.

Certainly, as compared to what happened in the 18th century, or to the royal English courts, 17th-century procedure was exceptionally lax. But it is easy to exaggerate this trait. When judges are laymen, and not fussy about the separation of powers, a court is bound to be run informally. County court government was government at the point where rules were applied to ordinary life. Justice of that sort has a loose, unstructured look; but if one compares colonial process, not with England's high courts but with English local courts, the differences are not quite so striking.

Direct and pragmatic though it was, 17th-century procedure did not—and could not—ignore the English background. The fundamentals—jury, grand jury, writ, summons, written pleadings, and oral testimony—were in use in the colonies, as they were in England, though never exactly the same. In detail, colonial procedure was a curious mixture. In 1656, in the "Court of trials of the Colony of Providence Plantations," in an "action...of detenew for detaining certaine...horsis and mares," the court "fownd in the Plaintifs declaration a Verball oversight"; the word plaintiff "should have beine writ defendant." No matter: the court ordered "that it may be Rectified according to the Answer put in by the defendant whoe clearly understood & Answers according to the scope of it." In one breath, the court brushed aside technicality; almost in the next breath it used an ancient English form of action ("detinue"). The same court, in a criminal matter, fussed over the "want of A Tittle" in one word in an indictment.[52]

We have already mentioned the use of conciliation and arbitration in colonial law. Such methods of course avoid technical courtroom procedure. The courts themselves sometimes referred matters out for arbitration. In Kent County, Delaware, in 1680, Peter Groendyk and William Winsmore, by "Joynt Consent," referred their differences to the court for resolution. It was a matter of "account of debt and Credit." The court "thought fi[t to] appoint" two arbitrators to decide the case; these two would, in case of a "non agreement...chuse a third person as an Umpire [to] make a final End thereof."[53]

Professor Haskins carefully examined civil process in Massachusetts Bay, and found little that was truly haphazard. The Puritan "zeal to reform every aspect of human activity" led to many legal innovations, including reforms of civil procedure. Procedure "was simplified so as to render justice inexpensive and easily accessible, and yet formal enough to provide adequate safeguards for litigants."[54] Process was speedy and cheap, compared to English process; costs were measured in pennies, not pounds; judgment was generally given on the day of the trial. The Massachusetts summons, unlike the English writ, was stripped of jargon, translated from Latin to English, and greatly streamlined in form. Forms of action were reduced to a few simple headings. The worst excesses of English law stayed out of Massachusetts, though there was a certain amount of backsliding in the 18th century. This trend toward English standards shows plainly in the surviving records—even those of the lowest courts. In New Hampshire, where pleadings had always been simple, clear, and direct, the lawyers introduced more sophistication and complexity during

[52]*Records of the Court of Trials of the Colony of Providence Plantations, 1647–1662* (1920), vol. I, pp. 19, 32.

[53]Leon de Valinger, Jr., ed., *Court Records of Kent County, Delaware, 1680–1705* (1959), pp. 4–5.

[54]George L. Haskins, "The First American Reform of Civil Procedure," in Roscoe Pound, ed., *Perspectives of Law: Essays for Austin Wakeman Scott* (1964), pp. 173, 178.

the years 1692 to 1700; the action of ejectment, the writs of *scire facias* and *supersedeas,* the action of *trespass de bonis asportatis,* entered New Hampshire as immigrants at this time.[55] Students of Massachusetts law on the eve of the Revolution have declared it to be quite conservative, at least by earlier standards. English law was held up as a model. In civil procedure, common-law writs were used "in full vigor." Courts were sticky about the niceties of pleading. Both civil and criminal actions could be, and sometimes were, turned out of court for failure to state a party's name in full, flawless form; if the name was misspelled; if defendant's occupation was wrongly described.[56]

But this convergence was always a matter of more or less. Early colonial government had been oligarchic, paternal. In the 18th century, merchants and landowners gained greater influence in government. The merchant's idea of a good legal system was one that was rational and efficient, conforming to his values and expectations—traits that neither lay justice nor the baroque extravagances of English procedure supplied. Eighteenth-century civil process, on the whole, was an uneasy mixture of several strands: lawyer's law, the needs of the merchants, the will of the sovereigns, and local tradition.

LAND LAW

In theory, the principle of tenure governed both the land law of the colonies and the land law of England. No one could own land absolutely. One could speak accurately, not of ownership of land, but of rights *to* land or *in* land. These rights might be arranged in layers of space and time; three, six, ten or more persons could have different sorts of interest in one tract of land—a right to receive rent, or a right to the land when and if someone else died childless; and still other people might actually live on the land

---

[55]Page, *op. cit.,* p. 96.

[56]See William E. Nelson, *Americanization of the Common Law: The Impact of Legal Change on Massachusetts Society, 1760–1830* (1975), pp. 72 ff. See also John Adams's Pleadings Book, in L. Kinvin Wroth and Hiller B. Zobel, *Legal Papers of John Adams* vol. I (1965), pp. 26 ff. For a glimpse of New York process during this period, see Herbert A. Johnson, "Civil Procedure in John Jay's New York," 11 Am. J. Legal Hist. 69 (1967). On Virginia procedure, see Warren M. Billings, "Pleading, Procedure, and Practice: The Meaning of Due Process of Law in Seventeenth Century Virginia," 47 J. Southern Hist. 569 (1981).

and grow crops. Imagine an apartment building, rented out to tenants, with a mortgage held by the bank, and administered on behalf of a widow who enjoys the rents until she dies, when her children (if they live so long) will take over her interest. The bank collects the rents, and pays itself a fee. The state collects property taxes. Who "owns" the building? There are many "estates" or interests in the building, but no single, individual owner. All these interests or estates have names; all have had a solid wall of law built up around them.

In England, land was the basis of wealth and social standing, and land law was the heart of the royal common law. Land was a scarce commodity in England. It was parceled out in the Middle Ages in tiers of estates, with the king at the apex, and various vassals and subvassals underneath. The feudal apparatus was mostly gone by 1650. But a complex law of estates remained; and social and economic power still paralleled the distribution of rights to land. The colonies, on the other hand, were short of people, cattle, and hard money, but had land to burn. The social system did not follow lines of estates in land, as it did in England. Many elements—tradition, state policy, the market, colonial conditions—jostled for influence on American land law. Traditional elements of course survived. Land law was essentially English, though simplified, varied, and adapted. Parts of it, too, derived from vulgar English law, rather than from classic common law. The early New England towns had common fields, and common herding of cattle; they scattered land in allotments of a few acres each, rather than in compact grants, thus reconstructing "the community life ... known in England insofar as consonant with local conditions and with the objectives of [the settlers'] migration."[57] Land tenure customs were not uniform in England; there was considerable local variation, and this variation showed up in details of tenure and practice in the New England towns.[58]

The ultimate overlord of all colonial land was, in theory, the king. He had granted the land to others: to proprietors, like Lord Baltimore, or by way of charter to settlers, as in Massachusetts. These grants were not, theoretically, absolute; the crown retained some interest. Throughout the colonial period, most of the land, outside of New England, was liable in law to pay an annual rent

[57]George L. Haskins, *Law and Authority in Early Massachusetts* (1960), pp. 69–70.

[58]David G. Allen, *In English Ways* (1981).

to the overlord. These rents, called quitrents, were payable in some cases in money, and sometimes in commodities, like wheat. They were due, in some colonies, to the proprietor, in others to the crown.

In England, the quitrent system was the end-stage in a long process which liberalized the position of a tenant of land. To pay a small perpetual rent was much to be preferred to older, more onerous feudal obligations. But in America quitrents did not seem modern or liberal. They were out of place in a land-rich country. Crown and proprietors were drawn to the quitrents by their desire for cold cash. But attempts to collect the rents led to endless bickering and strife. They probably yielded less in revenue than they cost in disaffection. At the outbreak of the American Revolution, they vanished forever.[59]

The quitrent system never took root in New England. Here there was no attempt to use land rights to squeeze money from holders of land. But the magistrates and leaders in New England were as unprepared as crown and proprietors for the realities of life in a country with plenty of land. They never intended a society of freeholders freely trading in land. New England villages used land tenure and land allocation as a means of social control. How this was done has been carefully documented in Sumner Powell's study of Sudbury. In Sudbury, Massachusetts, a person's station in life determined the size of his allotment. Strangers were not lightly given land in this community. In the 1640s, if a man left town without permission, he apparently forfeited his land.[60] But in New England, too, a swelling population, and the abundance of land, doomed this form of tenure and social control.

In Plymouth, the first plan called for land to be owned in common. Settlers would work seven years for the general good; at the end of that period, they would divide profits and improved land among themselves. More than a century later, the new colony of Georgia adopted a strange land system of indivisible grants in *tail male*. If a grantee died without sons, his land reverted to the trustees of Georgia. Leases were forbidden, and there were restrictions on the maximum size of holdings.[61] Land communism

[59]See, in general, Beverley W. Bond, Jr., *The Quit-Rent System in the American Colonies* (1919).

[60]Sumner C. Powell, *Puritan Village: The Formation of a New England Town* (1965), p. 122.

[61]Milton S. Heath, *Constructive Liberalism: The Role of the State in Economic Development in Georgia to 1860* (1954), p. 35.

was moribund in Plymouth by 1623; by 1738, the Georgia plan had to be modified. Plymouth had been planned as a business venture. Other colonial schemes were abortive Utopias. A grandiose plan for the Carolinas was drawn up, perhaps by John Locke. Carolina was to have an elaborately stratified society, with a nobility of landgraves and "caciques," hereditary, indivisible domains, baronies, manors, and seignories. None of the Utopias, or planned economies—or any other *a priori* social system—really ever took hold.

Elsewhere, conditions proved just as hostile to the opposite urge: the attempt to reproduce too closely English land law and tenure. "Lords of the Manor" actually held brief court in Maryland. There are records of manor-court proceedings for St. Clements Manor in St. Mary's County, between 1659 and 1672. In 1660, jurors presented Luke Gardiner "for not doeing his Fealty to the Lord of the Mannor," and fined him 1,000 pounds of tobacco.[62] The Maryland manors apparently died off quickly.

One other remnant of feudalism apparently had longer-range consequences. In the Dutch patroonships on the Hudson, settlers owed perpetual fealty to the patroon, and, more importantly, perpetual rent. When New York passed into English hands, the new overlords accepted the claims of the patroons. Even more significantly, Governor Thomas Dongan, in the 1680s, continued the policy of making large land grants, with manorial privileges. In 1685, the patroonship of Van Rensselaer became an English manor, with some 850,000 acres. Other baronial grants, overlapping and vague, were made to English aristocrats in upstate New York. Livingston manor had 160,000 acres. Within these vast domains, great families like the Livingstons and the Philipses held land in an almost feudal form of tenure. They were granted, originally, the right to make rules, and to run their own manorial courts, in the style of the old English manors. There is little evidence, however, that such courts really functioned; disputes within the manors were handled by regular courts, and after a while the leases made no mention of courts manor at all. But even without feudal privileges, these were great estates, and the working farmers were tenants, not owners. The landlords actively encouraged settlement; but on condition that a nagging rent be paid to the grantor forever. Some lords of the manor required a fee each time a piece of land changed hands. Some leases were perpetual; other tenants held land on lease for life; they owed rent and had no formal

---

[62]*Archives of Maryland*, vol. 53 (1936), p. 629.

guaranty that their heirs would have the right to renew. This archaic land-tenure system was an anomaly, and it bore bitter fruit; unrest plagued the New York lands in the 18th century. The causes of the unrest were complex: some tenants were genuinely dissatisfied; in some areas, squatters lay behind the conflict; there is even evidence of outside agitation (from Massachusetts). In any event, the manors lasted until the middle of the 19th century, when the antirent movement finally broke the power of the landlords.[63]

All in all, it was easier to use land as a cheap, convenient subsidy than as a means to fetter a restless population. Hence, in general, land policy tended to shake off many aspects of its past, and to grow quite prodigal. The king gave empires to his friends. In early New England, simple servants, after serving out their term, gained acres of land. William Penn's "Concessions" of 1681 offered fifty acres for each servant that a master brought over, and fifty acres to the servant when his term expired. In Virginia, too, anyone who brought over one body, to add to the population stock, earned a "head right" of fifty acres.

By and large, it was a country without skilled conveyancers, particularly in the 17th century. Simplified land forms were thus a necessity, the more so because of the high turnover of land. Colonial deed forms were bastard but effective documents. They were roughly based on the English deed form called bargain and sale. Land was not always transferred by written document. Sometimes *livery of seisin*, an old English form of symbolic delivery, was used, particularly in the 17th century. The grantor gave the land symbolically to his grantee, investing him through "turf and twig." The custom was most common, it seems, in the conservative South. But there are references elsewhere as well. In Maine (then part of Massachusetts), according to a deposition of 1685, Thomas Withers used a "turf and twig" to transfer half of an island to his daughter Elizabeth.[64]

This archaic survival is striking; but there was striking innovation in land transfer too. In some colonies, land passed from person to person in a free and easy way. Conveyancing habits developed that were unheard of in old England. These new, in-

---

[63]This paragraph draws heavily on Sung Bok Kim's elaborate study of the manorial system, *Landlord and Tenant in Colonial New York: Manorial Society, 1664–1775* (1978).

[64]*Province and Court Records of Maine,* vol. 4 (1958), p. 127.

formal modes of conveyance flourished alongside of classic forms. In early Maryland, conveyances of land were often made by written assignment on the back of the original patent, like the endorsement on a check. The patent thus "passed from hand to hand," until some purchaser, to be on the safe side, recorded ownership by enrollment in court.[65] Land transactions shifted from status to contract; land rights were no longer matters of family, birth, and tradition; rather, land was a commodity, traded on the open market. This was a slow but inexorable process. It was not complete until the 19th century, and in a sense not even then. But one of the first American innovations, legally speaking, was a system for registering and recording titles to land.[66] Recording acts, and the recording system, were invented in New England, in the early days of 17th-century settlement, though there was perhaps some basis in the experience of English towns. The essence of the system was that the record itself guaranteed title to the land. An unrecorded deed could not stand up against a recorded deed, even though the recorded deed was *issued* later than the unrecorded deed. The recording system began as a tool of state policy; it made it easier to govern and control the settlements. But in time it became a tool of the market. Americans felt the need for a way to prove title to land, in a volatile, broadly based market, earlier than the English did.

The complicated, protean system of equitable estates, from which the modern trust is descended, also crossed the Atlantic. In 1664, Dr. Luke Barber, a Maryland physician, who faced a heavy suit for damages, transferred all of his property to two men "in trust to the only use and behoofe" of his "most deare...Wife Elizabeth...and her heyres for ever."[67] But it was not the form of this branch of English law so much as substance and function that first found their way into colonial life. In 1641, in western Massachusetts, the "widow Horton" made an arrangement with Robert Ashly, her intended husband, in the presence of a magistrate. The widow

> doth assigne and set over her house and house lott...and all her hogges litle and greate...into the hands of Robert Ashly

[65]*Archives of Maryland,* vol. 53 (1936), xxxvi.
[66]See George L. Haskins, "The Beginnings of the Recording System in Massachusetts," 21 Boston U. L. Rev. 281 (1941); David T. Konig, *Law and Society in Puritan Massachusetts,* pp. 40–43.
[67]*Archives of Maryland,* vol. 49 (1932), p. 120.

> for the use and behafe of her two sonns one sucking and the
> other about Three years ould caled Jermy to be paid to them
> . . . when they shall come to the age of Twenty and one yeares:
> and the said Robert is to have the use and profits of the said
> land and hogges for the educatinge of her said Two sonns:
> and when they shall come to the age of 13 or 14 yeares . . . to
> put them out as apprentises to some usefull trade.[68]

This was, in essence, a trust; it provided protection for the sons
at a time when the widow, still unmarried, had full power to
control her property. It also sheds some light on the much vexed
question of the legal status of women in the colonies. The document would be meaningless *if* a married woman controlled her
property; on the other hand, it does show a practical way to avoid
the strict bite of the law.

In classic English law, land law was entangled in a maze of
actions and writs, some of amazing technicality. In the colonies,
land was hardly of less importance than in England. But ownership was spread out among many more people. Even servants
could become landlords on a modest scale. Land actions and writs,
like the rest of the law, became more "English" as population grew.
But even in the mid-18th century, American land actions were
simpler, freer, and more innovative than those of England. As in
England, the legal system had to have some device to test title,
that is, some method whereby Mr. A, who claimed to own a piece
of land, could challenge Mr. B, who claimed the same land, in
court. The old ways, the so-called *real actions,* had died out by the
time of Queen Elizabeth I. The action of ejectment replaced them;
but ejectment itself was cumbersome and riddled with legal fictions. (In ejectment, as was mentioned in the Prologue, plaintiff
had to assert an imaginary lease, with shadow men, often with
names like John Doe or Richard Roe, in the picture.) In the Southern colonies (except, apparently, 17th-century Virginia), in New
York and in East New Jersey, ejectment was the principal method
of trying title to land. In 17th-century New Jersey, the pleadings
did not usually name fictional people, though at least one instance—Robert Sumer against James Winter—was recorded in

---

[68]Joseph H. Smith, ed., *Colonial Justice in Western Massachusetts, 1639–1702*
(1961), p. 210, On the subject of women's rights, see also Joan R. Gunderson and
Gwen V. Gampel, "Married Women's Legal Status in Eighteenth-Century New
York and Virginia," 39 William and Mary Q. (3rd ser.) 114 (1982); Marylynn
Salmon, "Women and Property in South Carolina: The Evidence from Marriage
Settlements, 1730 to 1830," *ibid.,* 655 (1982).

1695.[69] New England was more innovative. There is not a single mention of ejectment in the Pynchon court record (Massachusetts, 1639–1702).[70] The New England colonies used simpler forms of testing title—for example, an action of trespass to land. In 18th-century Connecticut, the favorite device was an action "for Surrendry of Seizin and Possession," which was something like ejectment, with a new name, and stripped bare of fictions.[71] In Massachusetts, in the 17th century, litigants used the action of "case," a residual action, not used for this purpose at all in England.[72] In the 18th century, all the old actions disappeared, and a single, all-embracing form replaced them, called a plea of ejectment, or a plea of entry, or, most simply, a plea of land. This plea avoided all the old technicalities and led to an ordinary civil suit.[73]

SUCCESSION AT DEATH

When a person died in England, the property left behind was under the regime of two quite different sets of rules. Common-law rules and courts governed the land; church law and courts the personal property. If the deceased left no will, the common law gave the land to the eldest son; the church courts divided money and goods in equal shares among the children. The colonies either had no church courts or fused, as in early Massachusetts, the laws of Caesar and God. Probate power was given to regular courts or to special (but secular) branches of these courts. The courts also handled closely related matters—guardianship of minors, for example.[74] In general, the probate process, including the filing of inventories, was carried over into the colonies. But there was considerable innovation in the *substance* of succession.

The colonies greatly modified the law of descent of lands. In standard English law, primogeniture was the rule; lands de-

---

[69]Preston W. Edsall, ed., *Journal of the Courts of Common Right and Chancery of East New Jersey, 1683–1702* (1937), pp. 84–85.

[70]Smith, ed., *op. cit.*, p. 160.

[71]John T. Farrell, ed., *The Superior Court Diary of William Samuel Johnson, 1772–1773* (1942), xxxiii–xxxv.

[72]David T. Konig, *Law and Society in Puritan Massachusetts*, pp. 60–62.

[73]William E. Nelson, *Americanization of the Common Law*, p. 74.

[74]See Lois Green Carr, "The Development of the Maryland Orphans' Court," in Aubrey C. Land, Lois Green Carr, and Edward C. Papenfuse, eds., *Law, Society, and Politics in Early Maryland* (1977), p. 41.

scended to the eldest son. Primogeniture fulfilled a definite function in the days of military tenure. Even in England, primogeniture was not universal; local customs superseded it in some parts of the kingdom. In Kent, there was so-called gavelkind tenure; land descended to all sons in equal shares. The New England colonies, remote from upper-class English law and upper-class English society, had little use for primogeniture. Except for Rhode Island, all of New England rejected the rule. The 17th-century Massachusetts codes gave the eldest son "a double portion" of the "whole estate reall, and personall."[75] This special birthright was apparently a gesture to the Bible, not to English law. The double portion was also a feature of the law of Pennsylvania. In New York, the Duke's laws provided that property, after the widow's share, was to be divided "amongst the Children, provided the oldest Sonne shall have a double portion, and where their are no Sonnes the daughters shall inherit as Copartners."[76] But primogeniture was a feature of the law in the Southern colonies—Maryland, Virginia, and the Carolinas—until Revolutionary times.[77]

Scholars do not agree on where New England's system of partible descent (that is, division of land among children) came from. Some suspect direct borrowing from local English custom. Many colonial charters granted lands to be held of the king "as of his manor of East Greenwich." East Greenwich was located in Kent. Was it the purpose or effect of these charters to bring in gavelkind tenure? The evidence is confusing, inconclusive, and probably irrelevant. Partible descent was the practice in New England, from a very early date—probably long before anyone thought of arguments based on the charters. Primogeniture and the fee tail survived in the South, partly because of their system of land use. Southern planters used slave labor, and grew sugar, rice, and tobacco on large estates. English land tenure, and the English way of life among landed gentry, fit this social order more than was true in the North.

Primogeniture and its substitutes were rules about *intestacy;* a property-owner could make some other disposition, if he went to the trouble to make out a *will*. This basic document for gifts at

[75]*Laws and Liberties of Massachusetts, 1648* (1929 ed.), p. 53.

[76]See David E. Narrett, "Preparation for Death and Provision for the Living: Notes on New York Wills (1665–1760)", 57 N.Y. Hist. 417, 420 (1976).

[77]On the subject of colonial land law, especially primogeniture and fee tail, see Richard B. Morris, *Studies in the History of American Law* (2nd ed., 1959), pp. 69–125.

death—the last will and testament—came over as part of the colonists' cultural heritage. The English middle class used wills widely. Form was regulated by such laws as the Statute of Wills (1540). But the statutes presupposed, and modified, customs already in existence. And the content of wills tended to follow, in a rough and ready way, what was in the intestacy laws. A study of Virginia wills (17th century) showed that property owners were anxious to keep their property within the bloodline. Few men left more than a life interest to their wives; and sons were much preferred over daughters, since land left to daughters would fall out of the bloodline when the daughter married.[78]

The traditional (English) form of the will appeared early in the colonies. The formal written will, signed by the decedent and attested by witnesses, was part of the general legal culture. So was the oral (nuncupative) will. The Provincial Court of Maryland, for example, heard oral testimony of two witnesses that John Smithson, in 1638, "lying then very sick," had promised, "in case God should call him," to leave his estate to his wife; upon "these depositions...the Judge did approve the said last will and testament."[79]

The essential patterns of the will were part of English folk-law. These patterns recurred in the colonies, preserved in the memories of men and women far from home. Wills from Maine to Georgia strikingly resembled English wills and each other, particularly in their use of singsong, almost balladlike phrases. Shakespeare's will begins with the words: "In the name of God Amen ...I commend my soul into the hands of God my Creator...and my body to the earth whereof it is made."[80] The will of Henry Simpson, written in Maine in 1648, begins as follows: "In the name of God Amen, I, Henry Simpson...Doe make this my last will and testament.... First commending my soule to God that gave it...And my body to Christian buriall."[81]

Thousands of colonial wills have survived. They shed a great deal of light on colonial society. Some were drawn up by important people and disposed of substantial estates. Slaves, servants, and

---

[78]James W. Deen, Jr., "Patterns of Testation: Four Tidewater Counties in Colonial Virginia," 16 Am. J. Legal Hist. 154, 160–61 (1972).

[79]*Archives of Maryland*, vol. IV (1887), pp. 45–46. For another vivid example of a nuncupative will, see Narrett, "Preparation for Death," p. 429.

[80]Quoted in Virgil M. Harris, *Ancient, Curious and Famous Wills* (1911), pp. 305–306.

[81]*Province and Court Records of Maine*, vol. I (1928), p. 126.

the very poor stood outside the property system and left no wills to speak of. Many ordinary people probably left so little behind that nothing went through probate. Others died intestate, that is, without wills. But between 1690 and 1760, New York City recorded 1,600 estates with wills, and only 535 estates without.[82] Wills were by no means only for the rich, at least in the early years of the colonies, when the local law and the local courts were at the fingertips of every man and woman. Many wills in this period disposed of nothing but a few household goods and other odds and ends. Bethia Cartwright of Salem, Massachusetts, who died in 1640, disposed by will of her bedding and bed, pewter platters, a "double saltseller... half a dozen spoones and a porrenger," and a "box of linning, with a payre of shetes."[83]

In the early days, probate administration was quite loose by English or later American standards. In classic English law, the widow's share of her husband's estate—called dower—was a life interest in one third of her husband's lands. Colonial law, particularly in New England, was apparently less rigid. In Massachusetts, magistrates had discretion to modify the wife's share, according to her needs and local social and ethical standards. Rules were not hard and fast: even the eldest son's double portion was not an absolute right; the general court "upon just cause alledged" could "judge otherwise." The rules got stiffer and more absolute over time. The small face-to-face communities grew larger and became societies of strangers. At this point, the demands of economic rationality and the need for predictability and certainty asserted their claims. This meant more formality; and more hard-and-fast rules. But the gulf between rules about land and rules about goods was never so great as in England. And some colonial innovations—particularly partible inheritance—survived every attack.

CRIMINAL LAW

The earliest criminal codes mirrored the nasty, precarious life of pioneer settlements. Dale's laws in Virginia (1611) were severe, almost martial—draconian rules for a small, imperiled commu-

---

[82]David Narrett, "Preparation for Death," p. 430.
[83]*Records and Files of the Quarterly Courts of Essex County, Massachusetts, 1636–1656*, vol. I (1911), p. 18.

nity. In an important sense, they were only a phase. Once the colony became more secure, Virginia's criminal procedure shed most of the harshest aspects of Dale's laws. They came to resemble more the general tradition of criminal justice; but colonial criminal justice, in Virginia and elsewhere, was "on the whole less formal and more direct" than English law; here too, as time went on, there was a certain amount of "conformity to the English practice."[84]

In Massachusetts, early political struggles weakened the power of the oligarchy; and the colony embarked on an extraordinary course of drafting codes. Behind this creative urge was a simple penal philosophy: no one should be punished for crimes not clearly and openly labeled. To accomplish this end, the criminal law had to be plainly written down. *The Laws and Liberties of Massachusetts* (1648) was an early product of this movement. It contained many rules of criminal law. Most of the standard crimes—murder, arson, theft—were included, as well as more exotic ones. The aim of the code was to correct and teach the weak and to cut off from the community, as a last resort, those people who were incorrigibly harmful.

Thus, there was heavy use of open punishments, like public whipping or the pillory and stocks. These were small, inbred, gossipy communities. Public opinion and shame were important instruments of punishment. Under the code, if a man forged legal documents, so as to "pervert equities and justice," he was to "stand in the *Pillory* three several lecture days and render double damages to the party wronged." But Anabaptists were liable to be "sentenced to Banishment"; they were presumably incurable (and perhaps infectious). Burglars, for the first offense, were to be "branded on the forehead with the letter (B)," for the second offense, whipped, for the third, "put to death, as being incorrigible." A burglar who committed his crime on the "Lords day" lost an ear as additional penalty. If he did it again, he lost his other ear. The crime of "fornication with any single woman" was

---

[84]Arthur P. Scott, *Criminal Law in Colonial Virginia* (1930), p. 136; on Dale's laws, see David T. Konig, "'Dale's Laws' and the Non-Common Law Origins of Criminal Justice in Virginia," 26 Am. J. Legal Hist. 354 (1982).

The literature on colonial criminal justice has been growing steadily. In addition to the books and articles cited in the notes to this section, see Douglas Greenberg, "Crime, Law Enforcement, and Social Control in Colonial America," 26 Am. J. Legal Hist. 293 (1982); Kathryn Preyer, "Penal Measures in the American Colonies: An Overview," *ibid.*, at 326; Donna J. Spindel, "The Administration of Criminal Justice in North Carolina, 1720–1740," 25 Am. J. Legal Hist. 141 (1981).

punishable by fine, by corporal punishment, or "by enjoyning to marriage." "Inhumane, barbarous or cruel" punishments were forbidden; and though the *Body of Liberties* (1641) and later codes had accepted torture as a legitimate device, its use was, on paper at least, severely limited:

> No man shall be forced by Torture to confesse any Crime against himselfe nor any other unlesse it be in some Capitall case where he is first fullie convicted by cleare and suffitient evidence to be guilty. After which if the cause be of that nature, That it is very apparent there be other conspiratours, or confederates with him, Then he may be tortured, yet not with such Tortures as be Barbarous and inhumane.[85]

Particularly interesting was a small subcode of "Capital Lawes," imbedded in the early Massachusetts lawbooks, and copied by other New England and Middle Atlantic colonies. Some scholars used this subcode as prime evidence that the basic stuff of Bay law was biblical, not English common law. The capital laws did have a strong Mosaic flavor; in print, each of them was buttressed by a biblical citation: "If any man or woman be a WITCH, that is, hath or consulteth with a familiar spirit, they shall be put to death. *Exod.* 22.18 *Levit.* 20.27 *Deut.* 18.10.11." But not all biblical crimes were Massachusetts crimes, or vice versa. The Puritan mind filtered out of the Bible what was usable and appropriate for their wishes and their days. For many of these crimes, English law could have been cited as easily as Exodus or Leviticus. And the capital laws were only a small part of the criminal law, which was itself a small part of the law as a whole.

Neither in theory nor in practice was colonial law very blood-thirsty. There were fewer capital crimes on the books than in England. In England, death was a possible punishment for any thief; in Massachusetts, only for repeaters. The Quaker laws of West New Jersey substituted restitution of property or hard labor for hanging. The death penalty was not carried out very fre- quently in the colonies. In Massachusetts Bay, for example, it was a capital crime to "curse" or "smite" one's father or mother; but nobody was put to death for such offenses. One study found a total of forty executions in the colonies, before 1660. The figure is perhaps a bit understated; but it does not suggest wholesale carnage. There were fifteen executions in Massachusetts in this

---

[85]*Colonial Laws of Massachusetts, 1660–1672* (1889), pp. 43, 187. *General Laws and Liberties of Massachusetts, 1672,* p. 129.

period: four for murder, two for infanticide, two for adultery, two for witchcraft, one for "buggery"; four Quakers were also put to death.[86]

Some of the Southern colonies recognized the so-called benefit of clergy, which mitigated the surface severity of the penal code. Benefit of clergy was a privilege originally (as the name suggests) for clergymen only. Later it came to cover anybody who knew how to read. A person condemned to death, who claimed the privilege, would be presented with a Bible. The book was opened to the so-called "neck" verse, a line from Psalm 51: "Have mercy upon me, O God, according to thy loving kindness; according unto the multitude of thy tender mercies blot out my transgressions." He would read the verse; this averted the death penalty; a lesser penalty (branding with a hot iron) was then carried out. Thus Edward Reddish of Virginia, convicted of manslaughter in 1671, "did read and by the Governor's clemency and mercy was acquitted from burning."[87] In 1732, Virginia passed an "Act for settling some doubts and differences of opinion in relation to the benefit of Clergy; for allowing the same to Women; and taking away of Reading." This law abolished the reading test completely.[88] Despite "clergy," colonies reimposed the death penalty for crimes that seemed particularly heinous. In Maryland, where tobacco was king, a statute of 1737 decreed "Death as a Felon . . . without Benefit of Clergy" for anyone who broke into and robbed a tobacco house.

Famous periods of hysteria, such as the notorious Salem episode, beginning in 1692, have unduly blackened the colonial reputation. In this "terrible assize" nineteen persons were put to death; fifty or so were tortured or terrified into confessions. On September 22, 1692, eight persons were led to the gallows. Bloodletting also followed slave or servant riots and insurrections. County courts in 18th-century Virginia sometimes used castration as a punishment for slaves convicted of rape.[89] In Massachusetts, the

---

[86]Bradley Chapin, *Criminal Justice in Colonial America, 1606–1660* (1983), p. 58.
[87]George W. Dalzell, *Benefit of Clergy in America and Related Matters* (1955), p. 98; see also Bradley Chapin, *Criminal Justice in Colonial America*, pp. 48–50.
[88]Dalzell, *op. cit.*, pp. 103–4.
[89]Hugh F. Rankin, *Criminal Trial Proceedings in the General Court of Colonial Virginia* (1965), p. 221. There is a large literature, of course, on the Salem witch trials. See Kai T. Erikson, *Wayward Puritans* (1966); David T. Konig, *Law and Society in Puritan Massachusetts*, ch. 7; Paul Boyer and Stephen Nissenbaum, *Salem Possessed: The Social Origins of Witchcraft* (1974).

death penalty was imposed on those who particularly outraged the morals of society. In 1673, Benjamin Goad, "being instigated by the Divill," committed the "unnatural & horrid act of Bestiallitie on a mare in the highway or field." This was in the afternoon "the sun being two howers high." The Court of Assistants sentenced him to hang; and the court also ordered "that the mare you abused before your execution in your sight shall be knockt on the head."[90]

The colonial laws punishing gaming, idleness, drunkenness, lying, and disobedient children are famous. A New Hampshire law of 1693—of a common type—punished those who "on the Lords day" were found to "doe any unnecessary Servall Labour, Travell, Sports," or to frequent taverns, or "Idly Stragle abroad."[91] In colonial times, these moral laws were by no means empty words. They were taken quite seriously. Rules about personal conduct, and about sexual morality, according to the evidence of county court records, fell most heavily on the lower social orders—on servants, on the poor, and on slaves. Early colonial law was strongly paternal. Trials were, in Garfinkel's striking phrase, status degradation ceremonies.[92] Punishment was frequently open and corporal; its goal was to reteach and retouch the erring soul, and it used, as means to this end, confession, public humiliation, and infamy. One Pennsylvania law of 1700 (disallowed by the British five years later), was aimed at persons "clamorous with their tongues"; it gave the magistrate discretion to sentence the offender to be "gagged and stand in some public place."[93] Stocks and pillory were in common use. Crime and punishment meant shame, and beyond that, reform. The codes and their enforcers never abandoned this aim.

Indeed, the most commonly punished crimes in 17th-century Massachusetts were fornication and drunkenness. The 18th-century situation is a bit more complicated.[94] William E. Nelson an-

---

[90]*Records of the Court of Assistants of the Colony of the Massachusetts Bay, 1630–1692,* vol. I (1901), pp. 10–11. Punishing or forfeiting the thing or animal that had done wrong was an old English institution, called *deodand.* In Maryland in 1637, a tree that caused the death of one John Bryant was "forfeited to the Lord Proprietor," *Archives of Maryland,* vol. IV (1887), p. 10.

[91]*Laws of New Hampshire, Province Period, 1679–1702* (1904), p. 564.

[92]Harold Garfinkel, "Conditions of Successful Degradation Ceremonies," 61 Am. J. Sociol. 420 (1956).

[93]*Statutes at Large of Pennsylvania, 1682–1801,* vol. II (1896), p. 85.

[94]Edwin Powers, *Crime and Punishment in Early Massachusetts, 1620–1692, A Documentary History* (1966), pp. 404–7.

alyzed all the prosecutions in seven Massachusetts counties between 1760 and 1774. There were 2,784 in all; 1,074 of these—38 percent—were for sexual offenses. Almost all of these were for fornication; and almost all fornication actions were directed against mothers of illegitimate children. Often there was an economic point to the proceedings: who will support the bastard child? Thirteen percent of the cases, 359 in all, were for religious offenses: blasphemy, profanity, nonattendance at church. Even at this late period, Nelson feels, "all crime was looked upon as synonymous with sin...The typical criminal was not...an outcast from society, but only an ordinary member who had sinned."[95]

There is evidence that the point of the fornication actions changed between, say, 1650 and the 1760s. The element of pure punishment for sin declined; the economic point increased.[96] Control of sin was certainly a factor in all of the blue laws of the 17th century. Servant codes and slave law were aimed at sin, too; and also had the job of keeping social lines distinct, maintaining order in the lower ranks. If an indentured servant refused to serve his term, he was punished with extra years of service. This, too, was the usual fate of servant girls who gave birth to bastards. Fines were useless against the poor; imprisonment would have punished the master as well as the servant. Extra service was the most effective sanction; it was freely used. In a typical example, in Kent County, Delaware, in 1704, John Mahon brought a mulatto servant, Charles, to court. Charles had been a runaway for twenty-six days; it cost his master three pounds, three shillings, and sixpence to bring him back. The court ordered the boy to serve "for his Runaway time...One Hundred and thirty days and for the said sume of three Pounds three Shillings and Six pence soe Expended...he shall serve the said John Mahon or his Assigns the time and terme of six Monts," all this to begin *after* his regular term of service had expired.[97]

In cases of fornication, idleness and the like, defendants were

---

[95]Nelson, *Americanization of the Common Law*, p. 39.

[96]See Hendrik Hartog, "The Public Law of a County Court: Judicial Government in Eighteenth-Century Massachusetts," 20 Am. J. Legal Hist. 282, 299–308 (1976); Richard Gaskins, "Changes in the Criminal Law in Eighteenth-Century Connecticut," 25 Am. J. Legal Hist. 309, 317–18 (1981). In New York, "morals issues were *never* very important." Douglas Greenberg, "Crime, Law Enforcement, and Social Control in Colonial America," 26 Am. J. Legal Hist. 293, 307 (1982).

[97]Leon de Valinger, Jr., ed., *Court Records of Kent County, Delaware, 1680–1705* (1959), pp. 283–84.

overwhelmingly servants and the poor. Few clergymen or merchants or substantial landowners were whipped or put in the stocks
for fornication. Yet prominent people *were* punished in Puritan
Massachusetts for religious infractions (heresy, for example); or
for contempt of authority.[98] And the general theory of crime as
sin led to a certain amount of leniency in practice. Sinners, after
all, can become repentant; and a whipped or punished child can
mend its ways. Eli Faber's study of Puritan criminal justice turned
up the fact that, in some towns, offenders punished by the courts
later became prominent citizens, holding elective or appointive
offices. Concord named Abraham Wood a town clerk and select-
man in 1701; he had been found guilty of fornication in 1684.
The policy of the law, after all, was "reabsorption" into the community.[99]

In criminal justice, as in other aspects of colonial legal experience, it is sometimes treacherous to generalize. Place and period
made a significant difference. The picture one gets of early Massachusetts is a picture of a pervasive, intrusive, but *effective* system
of social control. Yet Douglas Greenberg has painted a contrasting
picture for 18th-century New York: erratic, chaotic, and on the
whole ineffective. He finds a general "failure of institutional arrangements to keep pace with social change."[100] No doubt many
features of New York's history and society were special. But his
evidence is consistent with a more general thesis, too. As the colonies grew in size, as economic and social life became more complex, as mobility (of all sorts) increased, the techniques and mental
habits that worked in the early days lost a good deal of their bite
and their magic. Criminal justice was ripe for reform and for
change.

To label behavior as criminal means, among other things, that
authorities punish that behavior at their own initiative and at
government expense. A crime is a wrong whose remedy is charged

[98]Eli Faber, "Puritan Criminals: The Economic, Social, and Intellectual Background to Crime in Seventeenth-Century Massachusetts," in 11 Perspectives in
Am. Hist. 81 (1977–78).

[99]Faber, *op. cit.,* at 138–43. Quite naturally, then, as the colonies grew in size,
and the theories and practices appropriate to the small, tight settlements became
impractical, one would expect a shift away from leniency. This is perhaps why, in
New York, after 1750, whipping as the punishment of choice for convicted thieves
dropped off (from 70% to 25%); the death penalty and branding rose substantially.
Douglas Greenberg, *Crime and Law Enforcement in the Colony of New York, 1691–
1776* (1976), p. 223.

[100]Greenberg, *Crime and Law Enforcement,* p. 213.

to the state. Criminal law, then, in any period, expresses more than current standards of morality. It is a vehicle for economic and social planning and an index to the division of power in the community. Economic crimes are as much part of criminal law as murder, rape, theft, and crimes against morality. Of course, the lines between economic control, control of morality and status, and suppression of dangerous behavior are quite artificial; the laws governing servants and slaves had all of these objectives. The organization of economic life explains many peculiarities of the criminal codes. In Virginia, hogs were more vital than sheep; stealing hogs, then, was a more serious crime than stealing sheep.[101] In 1715, New York made it unlawful "from & after the first day of May, until the first day of September Annually to gather, Rake, take up, or bring to the Market, any Oysters whatsoever, under the penalty of Twenty shillings for every Offence"; or for "any Negro, Indian or Maletto [sic] Slave to Sell any Oysters in the City of New York at any time whatsoever."[102] Criminal laws naturally expressed economic policy in societies with a strong sense of authority and few special agencies of economic control. In Puritan New England, civil obedience and respect for authority were the essence of social order; proprietary and crown colonies had a somewhat different definition of authority, but the same habits of command.

Thus, though the criminal codes were suffused with concepts of sin, they contained a heavy dose of politics and economic policy as well. Civil disobedience was not always deviance or sin. Often, in colonial history, part of the population opposed this or that aspect of the penal code as oppressive. Form was less objectionable, of course, than substance, or, at times, the allocation of power—not how but who governed. Influential colonists objected to laws against smuggling, the Stamp Act, and the Acts of Trade, in the middle of the 18th century. The war of 1776 was a war of independence. But independence did not mean the right to be free from law; it meant, not a ship without a captain, but a ship whose captain could be trusted, a captain of native heart and mind.

[101] Arthur P. Scott, *Criminal Law in Colonial Virginia* (1930), pp. 225–27.
[102] *Colonial Laws of New York*, vol. I (1894), p. 845 (law of May 19, 1715).

GOVERNMENT, LAW AND THE ECONOMY

Colonial regulation of business was primitive by modern standards. Yet in some ways it was fairly pervasive. The colonies regulated those businesses which were what would now be called public utilities and common carriers. The settlements depended on roads, ferries, bridges and gristmills for transport, communication, and the basic food supply. These enterprises were therefore the public's concern, though private enterprise built them and ran them. In a typical grant, East Haven, Connecticut, gave to a certain Heminway in 1681 an old dam, some land, timber, and stone, and exempted him from tax; in exchange, Heminway agreed to erect and maintain a gristmill, to attend to the mill one day a fortnight, to grind all the corn brought that day, and to limit his toll to the legal rate.[103] The miller's rate of toll was regulated throughout the colonial period. In New Hampshire, for example, an act of 1718 set up "the Toll for grinding all Sorts of Grain" at "one Sixteenth part, and no more," except for "Indian Corn, for which the Mill shall take One Twelfth."[104] Government also regulated markets, road building, and the quality of essential commodities. As in England, the inns and taverns along the roads were controlled by colonial authorities.

Inevitably there were taxes to be raised. Money was scarce in the colonies. To build roads, a labor tax was commonly used. Every adult man was liable to pay the tax in money, produce, or sweat, whichever he could best afford. So, a New York law of 1713, "for Mending and keeping in Repair the Post-Road from New York to Kings-Bridge," began by deploring the "ruinous" and "very dangerous" condition of the road. The act then provided for surveyors, to chart out the necessary repairs, and directed the people who lived in the affected wards to "meet and convene with Carts and Carriages, Shovels, Spades, Pick-axes, Mattocks, and other Tools," either to do the work themselves or to provide "sufficient working hands."[105]

---

[103]Henry Farnam, *Chapters in the History of Social Legislation in the United States to 1860* (1938), p. 96.

[104]*Laws of New Hampshire, Province Period, 1702−1745,* vol. 2 (1913), p. 265.

[105]*Colonial Laws of New York,* vol. I (1894), pp. 792−95 (act of Oct. 23, 1713). The act provided that "no person shall be compellable to work above Eight Days in the year, nor at any time in seed-time, Hay or Corn-Harvest."

A century before Adam Smith, the proprietors, squires, and magistrates of America certainly did not believe that that government was best that governed least. But the desire to rule, and rule broadly, was tempered by the modest means, in taxes and staff, that rulers had at their command. Regulation tended to be local, and as cheap in money and men as possible. When a government wished, therefore, to control the output of bread, it made bakers brand their bread. Under a Pennsylvania law of 1700, every baker had to have "a distinct mark to be set on all the bread he shall bake"; the better to facilitate control over size, taste, and price.[106] For many commodities, the laws provided for "viewers," "searchers," and "inspectors." These men were generally paid through users' fees, not out of tax funds. Fees supported public officials in general. The law tried to achieve other social ends by forcing private persons to do public work. To light its dark streets, the town fathers of New York ordered householders to hang lights on a pole, from the upper windows of houses, "in the Darke time of the moon." Philadelphia ordered citizens in 1700 to plant shade trees in front of their doors, "pines, unbearing mulberries, water poplars, lime or other shady and wholesome trees," so that the town might be "well shaded from the violence of the sun in the heat of the summer and thereby be rendered more healthy."[107]

From England, the colonies copied laws about public markets. These laws told where and when important products could be sold. A scattered market is difficult to administer. When all sellers of wood, or hay, or grain meet at one place and time, regulation can be cheap and effective. A South Carolina law, passed in 1739, set up a public market for the sale of meat and "other butchery wares" in Charleston. No meat could be sold except at the market, and during proper hours.[108]

As in England, too, local—county and city—courts held much of the power to run the economy. This worked well enough, except for those important commercial laws imposed by far-off England. The legal structure meant that local gentry, and local magistrates, could make or break imperial rule. Local rule is efficient, from the standpoint of the center, only if local people can be trusted. American squires and American merchants had fallen out with

[106]*Statutes at Large, Pennsylvania*, vol. II (1896), pp. 61–62 (act of Nov. 27, 1700).
[107]Carl Bridenbaugh, *Cities in the Wilderness* (1938), p. 169.
[108]James W. Ely, Jr., "Patterns of Statutory Enactment in South Carolina, 1720–1770," in Herbert A. Johnson, ed., *South Carolina Legal History* (1980), pp. 67, 69.

their English overlords long before 1776—over the Stamp Act, the Acts of Trade, and other aspects of British rule.[109]

Colonial government made a constant effort, not always effective, to keep its staple crops under some kind of quality control. In Virginia and Maryland, tobacco was the major crop. A long series of laws governed the growth and sale of this commodity.[110] Very early, Virginia tried to reduce the dependence of the colony on a single cash crop, and to improve quality and price of tobacco. In 1619, the Virginia House of Burgesses set up a system of tobacco inspection. Any tobacco which might "not proove vendible" was liable to be burned. In 1621, settlers were restricted to one hundred plants per person, and nine leaves to a stalk. The purpose of this act was to draw people away "from excessive plantinge of Tobacco." Maryland enacted its first inspection law in 1640. In 1657, second crops were outlawed, to prevent a glut on the market, and to cut down the flow of substandard tobacco, which depressed prices and ruined the reputation of Maryland tobacco.

Twentieth-century farm schemes were foreshadowed in old Maryland and Virginia: quality control, inspection laws, regulation of the size of containers, subsidies for planting preferred kinds of crop, public warehousing, export controls. In the 1660s, the tobacco colonies were fearful of a radical oversupply. Maryland in 1666 ordered a complete stop to tobacco cultivation, between February 1667 and 1668, if Virginia and Carolina followed suit (they did). (Lord Baltimore voided this act; he felt it was harmful to Great Britain.) Tobacco regulation was, if anything, more pervasive in the 18th century. Maryland, in 1747, enacted its most comprehensive statute, modeled on an equally elaborate Virginia law of 1730. The law required all tobacco to be brought to public warehouses and forbade the export of bulk tobacco. Inspectors at each warehouse would inspect, weigh, and repack the tobacco, branding each cask with the name of the warehouse, the tare, and the net amount of leaf. There were to be some eighty warehouses in all. Unacceptable tobacco was to be burned or repacked by the owners. Inspectors were to give out tobacco notes, transferrable and redeemable, for all tobacco brought to the ware-

[109]See, for example, on the Stamp Act resistance, Edmund S. Morgan and Helen M. Morgan, *The Stamp Act Crisis* (1953).
[110]See, in general, Vertrees J. Wyckoff, *Tobacco Regulation in Colonial Maryland* (1936).

house in payment of debts. These notes were legal tender—a kind of money. A later form of the act, passed in 1773, was in force when the Revolution came.

Virginia and Maryland were not the only colonies that regulated their staple crop. Connecticut grew tobacco too, and passed an inspection law in 1753. A Pennsylvania law of 1724 forbade the export of any flour not submitted to an inspecting officer, "who shall search and try the same in order to judge of its goodness." Merchantable export flour had to be branded with the "provincial brand-mark, ... sufficient and capable to impress in a fair and distinguishable manner the arms of the province of Pennsylvania with the letter P on each side"; for his trouble, the officer was to have from the shipper "one penny per cask and no more."[111] Flour for domestic consumption was also to be inspected and branded, though with less stringent controls. A statute of the same session continued in effect a bounty of a penny a pound for hemp "to the end that the people of this province may be further encouraged in the raising of good and merchantable hemp." Georgia began colonial life as a planned economy, with public sawmills, farms, and herds of livestock. Even after Georgia became a crown colony (1752), lumber inspection laws were passed (1760), followed by laws setting up grades and specifications for beef, pork, pitch, tar, and turpentine. Later, special legislation dealt with leather and tobacco.[112] Massachusetts Bay had had a leather statute for more than a century. Under the *Laws and Liberties* of 1648, towns were empowered to "choose one or two persons of the most honest and skilfull" to act as "Searchers" of leather. Searchers had power to seize all leather made contrary to the dictates of the law, which limited the tanning trade, and gave directions for the proper manufacture of leather:

> Nor shall any person or persons using or occupying the mysterie of tanning, set any their Fats [vats] in tan-hills or other places, where the woozes or leather put to tan in the same shall or may take any unkinde heats; nor shall put any leather into any hot or warm woozes whatsoever on pain of twenty pounds for everie such offence.[113]

---

[111] *Statutes at Large, Pennsylvania, 1682–1801*, vol. IV (1897), p. 5 (act of Mar. 20, 1724/5).

[112] Milton S. Heath, *Constructive Liberalism: The Role of the State in Economic Development in Georgia to 1860* (1954), pp. 55–56.

[113] *Laws and Liberties of Massachusetts, 1648* (1929 ed.), p. 33. "Wooze" is a variant of "ooze," and refers to the liquid in the tanning vats.

COMMERCE AND LABOR

When the colonies were first settled, the *law merchant*—the rules and practices of commercial law—were not fully "received" into common law, that is, the royal courts of England did not yet recognize them. (Special merchants' courts in England filled the gap.) Yet on both sides of the Atlantic merchants followed much the same legal customs and practices. This was only natural. The law merchant was, in theory, international. More to the point, colonial merchants did business with English merchants; their ties with each other became even tighter in the 18th century. Negotiable instruments were known and used in all the colonies. In the 18th century, many colonies experimented with paper currency. In some, chattel notes were common; tobacco notes were ubiquitous in Maryland and Virginia.

By mercantile custom, commercial paper circulated freely, from hand to hand; a holder in due course—one who came into possession in the ordinary way—had full rights to use, sue, and collect on the note or the bill. The common law, however, was quite stiff about honoring the rights of a person to whom intangibles had been transferred. Colonial law ran far ahead of English law. As early as 1647, Massachusetts provided by statute that "any debt, or debts due upon bill, or other specialtie assigned to another; shall be as good a debt & estate to the Assignee as it was to the Assigner at the time of its assignation ... provided the said assignement be made upon the backside of the bill or specialtie." This statute also appeared in Connecticut (1650), Pennsylvania (1676), New York (1684); and in Delaware, New Jersey, and colonies to the South. The colonies depended upon ocean commerce. They were free from—indeed, often ignorant of—the rigid institutions and doctrines that held back the union of common law and commerce law in England. Hard currency was in short supply in America. This meant that merchants were even more dependent on commercial paper, for carrying on trade. In the 18th century, commercial law, like other branches of law, seemed to creep closer to the standards that governed in England. The societies on this side of the Atlantic were commercially more mature; they were tied more closely to the great world of international trade. Still, many of the local variants were useful, and became permanent parts of the living law.[114]

Labor was as essential and problematic a factor of production as money. The colonies drew up codes of labor law, and constantly tinkered with them. These codes were not totally indigenous; they owed a good deal to mercantilist theory, and of course to English law. As always, specific colonial needs and conditions gave these codes their special character. England had no law of slavery; its law of apprenticeship was the nearest thing to the law of indentured service. The colonies, by grim necessity, had to attract and hold a population, organize a work force, and keep it in place. Some fateful choices were made. On the one hand, indentured servitude, for all its abuses and inequities, held open a promise of freedom, and a decent living at the end of the road. Servitude quietly evolved into a system of free labor.[115] The other new branch of labor law, the law of slavery, led downward into lasting oppression and grief.

In the early days of colonial life, it was a common rule, both North and South, that every able-bodied man had a duty to work. Idleness was a punishable offense. No person, said the *Laws and Liberties of Massachusetts* (1648) shall "spend his time idlely or unprofittably under pain of such punishment as the Court of Assistants or County Court shall think meet to inflict." This principle was never formally abandoned. But in time, it became a matter of caste and class. The magistrates of early New England had to work hard with their hands, just as servants did. In the 18th century there was a definite leisure class, the families of rich merchants and planters. Only the poor were impressed into work gangs; only the poor paid their road taxes in personal sweat.

Some colonies tried to control the cost of labor. Scarcity had pushed up the workingman's price. John Winthrop reported that in Massachusetts in 1633 "the scarcity of workmen had caused them to raise their wages to an excessive rate, so as a carpenter would have three shillings the day, a laborer two shillings and

[114]Frederick Beutel, "Colonial Sources of the Negotiable Instruments Law of the United States," 34 Ill. L. Rev. 137, 141–42 (1939). On the increasing sophistication of modes of handling and evidencing debt, see Bruce H. Mann, "Rationality, Legal Change, and Community in Connecticut, 1690–1760," 14 Law & Society Rev. 187 (1980).

[115]On indentured servitude and labor conditions in general, see Richard B. Morris, *Government and Labor in Early America* (1946).

sixpence." As a result, commodity prices were "sometimes double to that they cost in England." The general court took action; they "made an order, that carpenters, masons, etc. should take but two shillings the day, and laborers but eighteen pence, and that no commodity should be sold at above four pence in the shilling more than it cost for ready money in England." Oil, wine, and cheese were excepted, "in regard of the hazard of bringing."[116] Massachusetts Bay later provided that "the freemen of every Town may from time to time as occasion shall require, agree amongst themselves about the prizes and rates of all workmens Labour and servants wages."[117] Particularly vital occupations, like draymen and ferrymen, were most prone to be regulated. Price regulation, in turn, fell on suppliers of vital commodities, such as bakers. Wage-price regulation was virtually abandoned by 1700. It was briefly and ineffectively revived during the Revolutionary War, as an emergency measure. The shortage of labor probably frustrated all attempts to regulate wages and prices.

Throughout the colonial period, colonies were anxious to attract and keep skilled workmen. South Carolina, in 1741, prohibited artisans from keeping taverns, a less essential occupation. Skilled laborers tried, in some instances, to control entry into their trades and keep prices high. These attempts were no more successful than wage controls. New York and other colonial cities at one time restricted crafts to men who enjoyed the "freedom" of the city. By the middle of the 18th century this system too was dead; the "freedom of the city" was available to all, practically for the asking.

Up and down the coast, indentured servants acted as farm and household workers, hewers of wood, drawers of water—the laboring hands and feet of the colonies. Indentured servants were in essence temporary slaves, the personal property of their masters. "Indentures" were written documents, somewhat similar to English articles of apprenticeship, under which many such servants served. In the early 17th century, many servants, with or without indentures, were Indians or blacks. Many white immigrants (probably more than one-half) arrived either as "redemptioners" or became redemptioners on arrival. This meant that they sold their labor, for a definite period of time, to pay for the

[116]John Winthrop, *The History of New England from 1630–1649*, vol. I (1853), p. 116.
[117]*Colonial Laws of Massachusetts, 1660–1672*, vol. I (1889), p. 174.

price of passage. Some signed indentures in England, before sailing. They signed themselves over to the master of the ship; when ship and passenger landed, a New World broker would sell the indenture in the market, to raise the price of passage. Indentured servitude usually lasted from four to seven years. Those who came without indenture, and without money to pay the captain, had to serve "according to the custom of the country." This "custom" depended on the age and condition of the servant. Often, young immigrants and orphans were brought into court for a decision (or guess) about their age. Court records are full of such proceedings. In Kent County, Delaware, in 1699,

> Mr. John Walker brought into Court a Servant boy named Richard Cundon, to be Judged, he cominge in without Indentures, which being Considered, the Court doe deeme him the said Richard Cundon to be about Twelve years of age, and doe order that he shall serve the said John Walker or his Assignes, Untill he shall arrive to one and twenty years of age, and that at the Expiration thereof, the said John Walker or his assignes shall pay him his Corne, Cloaths and Tolls, according to Law.[118]

At the end of his term, the servant went free, and in addition, recovered by right certain "freedom dues." In early Maryland, servants, whether indentured or not, had the right upon severance to an outfit of clothes, a hat, ax, hoe, three barrels of corn, and (until 1663) fifty acres of land.[119] In later times, clothing, food, and a sum of money were more typical dues (the "Corne, Cloaths and Tolls" of the example).

By no means all indentured servants were "free-willers." England dumped a certain number of convicts onto the colonies as indentured servants, to the distaste of the residents, who attempted (futilely) to legislate against "jail birds." Some unlucky people were kidnapped in England and sold into servitude. For others, servitude was their punishment for crime. But most people sentenced to a term of labor were already servants; they had no goods or lands to satisfy debts or pay fines. They paid their debt to society by adding on to their term of service.

Even more than England, colonial society used indentures of

[118]Leon de Valinger, Jr., ed., *Court Records of Kent County, Delaware, 1680–1705* (1959), p. 152.

[119]*Archives of Maryland*, vol. 53 (1936), xxxii.

apprenticeship to handle poor orphans and abandoned children. This shifted a social problem to private masters. Masters and mistresses gained extra hands; in exchange, masters were supposed to teach boys to read and write, and to introduce them to some useful trade. Girls learned to cook and sew and do household work. The indenture system fulfilled a great many functions. It was a method of organizing labor, of financing immigration, a penal sanction, a way of training the young, a kind of welfare institution, and a crude instrument of credit. Court records show surprising uses of this protean device. In 1703, in Delaware, a "poor Aged lame Man," Leviticus John Wassell, "did bind himselfe a Servant to One Edward Starkie...for the time and terme of foure years In Consideration that the said Starkies Wife Would cure the said Leviticus John Wassell his sore leg." And Joseph Groves "bound himselfe to serve Thomas Bedwell" for two years "In consideration Whereof the said Thomas Bedwell being here present in Court did Promise to learn the said Joseph to write and Cypher soe far as the said Joseph should be capable of receaving during the said time."[120]

Some men of wealth or position began their careers as servants or apprentices. Roger Sherman, for example, was apprenticed as a boy to a shoemaker. Daniel Dulany came to Maryland in 1703 as an indentured servant; he had the good fortune to be sold to Colonel George Plater, who needed a clerk in his law office. Ten years later, Dulany was a lawyer and a landowner.[121] These success stories were not rare; but neither were they typical. More commonly, former servants continued to work at their trades, only now as free men. So, Abraham Daphne, a carpenter, advertised in 1753 that he was "now acquitted and discharged" from servitude, and ready "to undertake any work in his business."[122] Many more no doubt never made it very far up the ladder. A study of indentured servants, in late 17th-century Maryland (Charles County), underscores this point. The servants in the county mostly died or disappeared from the records; many apparently simply left the county. Of those that finished out their term, and became free, 58 percent remained laborers or, at best, tenant farmers. About a third became smallholders. About 17 percent ended up

[120]Valinger, op. cit., pp. 274–76.
[121]Louis B. Wright, The Cultural Life of the American Colonies, 1607–1763 (1957), p. 14.
[122]Warren B. Smith, White Servitude in Colonial South Carolina (1961), p. 88.

with more than average holdings (250 to 600 acres); some 5 percent achieved substantial wealth. Servitude was not a dead end,
by any means; but true success stories were by no means the rule.[123]

The lot of the servant, during his term, was not always a bed
of roses. Many Englishmen or Germans, enticed into servitude by
glittering propaganda, found they had chosen a life of hardship
and tyranny. The servant, by law, had the right of redress against
a cruel or incompetent master. Court records are full of complaints by servants, about beatings, bad food, nakedness, cold, and
general misery. No doubt the vast majority of ill-used servants
were too ignorant or frightened to complain. Thousands of servants ran away. And servants were subject to many legal disabilities.
They could not marry without their master's consent. They could
not vote or engage in trade. Masters could buy and sell their labor.
They were, in short, slaves for the time being.[124]

SLAVERY

Indentured servants were a vital part of the labor system in the
North, in Southern towns, and in frontier regions. But in the
tobacco, rice, and sugar colonies, black slavery more and more
replaced white servitude. The first blacks were servants, not slaves;
their status was perhaps hardly different from that of white servants or Indian captives. But blacks were pagans, and a different
race. A special sentiment gradually crystallized about the growing
numbers of blacks. The American style of black-white relations
can be traced far back into the colonial past. For whites, it consisted
of a peculiar mixture of bigotry, dread, sexual envy, and economic
oppression. The exact legal origins of slavery are obscure; but
clearly it was developing custom that guided the lawmaker's hand.
Slavery did not exist in the mother country. Early references to
slaves and slavery have a certain vagueness and ambiguity. Yet
before the end of the 17th century, slavery had become a definite
legal status in both North and South; it was peculiarly associated
with the blacks; it had become a terrible, timeless condition, inherited by children from their mothers. The legal status of the

[123]Lorena S. Walsh, "Servitude and Opportunity in Charles County, Maryland,
1658–1705," in Aubrey C. Land, Lois Green Carr, and Edward C. Papenfuse,
Law, Society, and Politics in Early Maryland (1977), pp. 111, 115–18.

[124]See, in general, Abbott E. Smith, *Colonists in Bondage, White Servitude and
Convict Labor in America, 1607–1776* (1947).

slave, as it took shape in statute books, reflected and ratified social discrimination and the sense of race.[125] In Virginia, insofar as these developments can be dated, evidence points to the period between 1660 and 1680 as the period in which the status was formalized. In 1662, it became law in Virginia that children of slave mothers would themselves be slaves, regardless of the status of the father.[126] Originally, there was a notion that Christians should not be slaves; but as early as a Maryland law of 1671, baptism no longer brought escape from slavery.[127] From that time on, converted slaves had to wait for freedom in another world.

Once the fundamental lines of the law were set, the colonies, particularly in the South, carried the logic of slavery to its grim outer limits. The slave was property, a capital asset of his master. He passed by will, was bought and sold, could be seized for his master's debts, and was taxed like other property. Virginia, in 1705, in fact declared him to be real estate, the same as houses, trees, or land. This strange law had a certain logic: it meant that some rules of law (on inheritance, for example) applied uniformly to all of an "estate"—both the land and the slaves that worked it.[128] Slaves themselves had few legal rights. They could not testify in court against whites. Slaves could not vote, own property, or (legally) marry. The master was bound by law to treat slaves with a certain minimal fairness, to feed them and clothe them, and to punish no more severely than the situation demanded. These rights were occasionally enforced in court. But of course slaves had neither the power nor the support in public opinion to translate these paper rights into living law very often. Sheer rationality was probably more of a restraint on cruel masters than fear of the law. Slaves were valuable assets; an owner would want his property sound, alive, in good health. But the system had no real guarantees against masters who made mistakes or who were cruel,

---

[125]Carl N. Degler, *Out of Our Past: The Forces that Shaped Modern America* (1959), p. 30; Winthrop D. Jordan, *White over Black: American Attitudes Toward the Negro, 1550–1812* (1968), pp. 91–98. On the colonial slave codes, see William M. Wiecek, "The Statutory Law of Slavery and Race in the Thirteen Mainland Colonies of British America," 34 William and Mary Q. (3rd ser.) 258 (1977).

[126]John H. Russell, *The Free Negro in Virginia, 1619–1865* (1913), p. 37.

[127]James M. Wright, *The Free Negro in Maryland, 1634–1860* (1921), p. 22.

[128]In South Carolina, too, after 1690, slaves were considered "freehold property" in most respects. M. Eugene Sirmans, "The Legal Status of the Slave in South Carolina, 1670–1740," in Stanley N. Katz, ed., *Colonial America: Essays in Politics and Social Development* (1971), pp. 404, 408.

drunk, or irrational. Nor was any account taken of the feelings, hopes, and desires of the slaves themselves.

Slaveholders, North and South, had many fantasies about blacks—about their intelligence, strength, and sensibilities. They were capable of believing, and saying, that blacks were best off as black slaves. Yet in a sense most whites never quite convinced themselves that slaves were happy in their slavery. On the contrary, the white population had a desperate fear of slave violence. There is incessant complaint about the "insolence" of slaves, about the need for firm control. Some slaves indeed dared to raise a hand against their masters. According to one account, 266 slaves were convicted of killing whites in Virginia in the period from 1706 to 1864.[129]

More serious was the threat of actual revolt. This too was not sheer paranoia. There were any number of actual disturbances— all futile, all put down with barbarous severity.[130] Even so, fear of uprising verged at times on hysteria. Slave codes grew steadily more repressive. In North Carolina, for example, the Fundamental Constitutions codified the custom that slaveowners had "absolute power and authority over negro slaves."[131] The statutes were revised in 1715, restricting free whites from trading with slaves, and forbidding intermarriage of blacks and whites. A master could be fined for permitting blacks to build a "house under pretence of a meeting house upon account of worship." This was presumably to avoid risks of paganism and conspiracy. Emancipated slaves had to leave the colony within six months. Those who did not could be sold to some person who would undertake to get them out of the state. An act of 1729 prohibited slaves from hunting with dog or gun on any but the master's land. In 1741, the right to carry a gun and hunt, even on the master's land, was limited to slaves who carried a certificate, signed by the master and countersigned by the chairman of the county court. Only slaves who had performed "meritorious services," certified by the local courts, could be set free. A 1753 law set up a system of

[129]Philip J. Schwarz, "Forging the Shackles: The Development of Virginia's Criminal Code for Slaves," in David J. Bodenhamer and James W. Ely, Jr., eds., *Ambivalent Legacy: A Legal History of the South* (1984), pp. 125, 133.

[130]Edward Franklin Frazier, *The Negro in the United States* (1957), pp. 86–87.

[131]For the following discussion, see John Spencer Bassett, *Slavery and Servitude in the Colony of North Carolina* (1896).

"viewers" to deal with slave problems. Courts were authorized to divide their counties into districts and appoint such "viewers," who could search slave quarters and seize any weapons found. A ghastly fog of fear hovered about the plantation world.

The master himself was law, judge, and jury in his household; this was inherent in the system of slavery. But in North Carolina, at least as early as 1715, there were special courts for slaves who disobeyed the law. Whipping was the common mode of punishment. Serious crimes called for the death penalty; but a dead slave injured his owner's pocketbook; hence owners were repaid out of public funds. For serious crimes, castration was an alternative punishment, though this was eliminated in 1764. But in 1773 a black was burned alive for murdering a white man.

Few of the North Carolina provisions were original or unique. They were typical of the law in the southern colonies. Each jurisdiction added or subtracted a detail here or there. A Georgia statute of 1770, fearful that blacks might wish to "plot and confederate together," forbade slaves to "buy, sell, trade, traffic, deal, or barter for any goods or commodities," except under special circumstances. Slaves could not own or keep "any boat, perriagua, or canoe" or breed cattle. To avoid "ill consequences," groups of seven or more slaves were forbidden to go on the highway, unless accompanied by a white man; violators could be whipped. Since "inconveniences" might arise from book learning, anyone who taught a slave to read or write was liable to be fined. Under a Virginia act of 1748, slaves who, "under pretense of practising physic, have prepared and exhibited poisonous medicines" were to suffer "death without benefit of clergy."

New England slave codes were milder than those of the South. Only Massachusetts had a statute against intermarriage; and Northern blacks were allowed to testify in court. But where blacks lived in sizable numbers (in Rhode Island, for example), or during times of panic over possible black unrest, Northern communities were capable of reacting with great severity.[132] Boston, in 1723, in fear of black arson, enacted emergency regulations to punish all blacks caught near a fire. Under an ordinance of South Kings-

---

[132]In 1741, New York prosecuted more than 150 slaves and 20 whites for a supposed conspiracy involving arson, robbery, and perhaps a general uprising. Thirteen blacks were burned at the stake; sixteen more were hung, along with four whites. Seventy blacks and seven whites were banished. See Thomas J. Davis, introduction to Daniel Horsmanden, *The New York Conspiracy* (1971), p. vii.

ton, Rhode Island (1718), if a slave was found in the house of a free black, both slave and host would be whipped. In the 1750s, no black in South Kingston might own a pig or cow or livestock of any kind. No cider could be sold to a slave. Indians and blacks could not hold outdoor gatherings. In New York, after 1705, a slave found traveling alone forty miles from Albany could, on conviction, be put to death.[133]

There were many free blacks in the colonies in the 18th century. Some were emancipated slaves; some were descended from the class of early free blacks. As the racist element in the slave codes increased, the legal position of free blacks deteriorated. A great fear—that blacks as a group might conspire against whites—cost them dearly. Free blacks were discriminated against by law, and hounded from colony to colony. Law and society debased this class and used their low status as an excuse for further debasement. By 1776, the free black was a kind of half slave in many parts of the country.

THE POOR LAWS

In 1647, a Rhode Island statute enjoined the towns to "provide carefully for the reliefe of the poore, to maintayne the impotent ...and [to] appoint an overseer for the same purpose. See 43 Eliz. c.2."[134] The reference was to the Elizabethan poor laws, passed in the 43rd year of the reign of Elizabeth I (1601). These famous laws were thus part of the colonists' legal background. The New England colonies copied the poor laws, at least in their general features. Local rule was one of the main characteristics of the poor-law system. Each town maintained its own poor—those who were "settled" in the town. But the concept of settlement was exceptionally tricky. It grew luxuriantly through litigation. Towns were most eager to dodge the problems and costs of their paupers; thus the records are full of cases in which one town sued another town, trying to palm a pauper off. By the Plymouth laws of 1671, any person who had been "received and entertained" in a town became the responsibility of that town, if he later became destitute.

[133]Lorenzo J. Greene, *The Negro in Colonial New England, 1620–1776* (1942), pp. 142, 161.

[134]Quoted in Margaret Creech, *Three Centuries of Poor Law Administration: A Study of Legislation in Rhode Island* (1936), p. 8.

The town escaped this duty if the new settler was "warned by the Constable, or some one or more of the Select men of that Town, not there to abide without leave first obtained of the Town."[135] Out of this kind of law grew the custom of "warning out." Between 1737 and 1788, 6,764 persons were "warned out" in Worcester County alone.[136] "Warning out" was not a sentence of banishment, but a disclaimer of responsibility; some towns "warned out" practically every new arrival. "Warning out" threw the burden of support back on the former place of settlement. Thus the system discriminated against unfortunate strangers. Kindly impulses were expended on friends and neighbors who fell on evil days. There the sympathy stopped.

The poor laws were only part of the welfare system of the colonies. Orphans became apprentices. Adults who were poor but could work became servants; an indenture was their ticket to relief. Poor laws were used, then, for a helpless residue of society. For all others, poverty and want meant an adjustment of status, not a draft on the public purse.

STATUTE AND COMMON LAW IN THE COLONIAL PERIOD

Colonial law, to a striking extent, was codified law. Yet these were common-law jurisdictions, after all; and common law was essentially uncodified. There was certainly no English precedent for general codification. Why then were there American codes, even in the earliest days and in the earliest colonies?

In one sense, codification is natural in a colony. A new settlement cannot sit back and wait for evolution. England could make do with an unwritten constitution; the United States could not. Any fresh start demands codification. When Japan and other countries decided to adopt a "modern" legal system, they turned to the European codes. The common law seemed too shapeless, too complex. There were too many books. The law was too unknowable. It could never be restated authoritatively. A code may be a behavioral mirage; it may not mean what it says; it may be

---

[135]Josiah H. Benton, *Warning Out in New England* (1911), p. 54; see also Douglas L. Jones, "The Strolling Poor: Transiency in Eighteenth-Century Massachusetts," 8 J. Social Hist. 28 (1975).

[136]Benton, *loc. cit.,* p. 59.

"interpreted" totally out of shape. But at least it has an authoritative text. It can be copied in the letter, if not in the spirit. The first codes of the colonies were fresh-start codes. Later ones were often borrowed from the earlier codes.

Each code had, of course, a unique history of its own. The first Massachusetts codes rose out of political struggle in the colony. The desire for a code was, among other things, a desire to limit autocracy. The power and discretion of the magistrates in Massachusetts Bay was at first virtually unlimited. Out of an urge by some to control this power came the *Body of Liberties,* drafted by Nathaniel Ward and adopted by the Massachusetts General Court in 1641. In 1648, a far more important and comprehensive code was adopted, the *Laws and Liberties of Massachusetts.* This was not a code in the sense of a logical, systematic arrangement of the law. Rather, it was a collection of important legal rules, arranged alphabetically by subject. The code began with a noble paragraph: "no mans life shall be taken away," or his "honour or good name ...stayned, or his person arrested, or his goods taken, except by the vertue or equity of some expresse law of the Country, or in defect of a law in any particular case by the word of God." Then came a provision on "Abilitie" (persons over 21 may make out wills and dispose of property), then "Actions," "Age," and "Ana-Baptists," ending (except for some "Presidents and Forms of things frequently used") with "Wrecks of the Sea." The code dealt with the general framework of government, the court system, and many particular subjects of legal regulation. Once these laws had been printed, the colonists could proudly assert that their laws were "now to be seen by all men, to the end that none may plead ignorance, and that all who intend to transport themselves hither may know that this is no place of licentious liberty."[137]

The code also reflected, as Professor Haskins has put it, the "traditional Puritan belief in the importance of the written word," evidenced by "literal use of the Bible as authority and by Puritan demand for explicit church canons which would leave no doubt as to what the law was."[138] Precise, knowable law is law that a citizen can easily follow—and law that rulers too must follow; if they do not, their defaults can be clearly seen.

[137]Edward Johnson, *Wonder-Working Providence* (Jameson, ed., 1910), p. 244.
[138]George L. Haskins, "Codification of the Law in Colonial Massachusetts: A Study in Comparative Law," 30 Ind. L.J. 1, 7 (1954). On the code-making impulse, see also G. B. Warden, "Law Reform in England and New England, 1620–1660," 35 William and Mary Q. (3rd ser.) 668 (1978).

Case law—court decisions—did not easily pass from colony to colony. There were no printed reports to make transfer easy, though in the 18th century some manuscript materials did circulate among lawyers. These could hardly have been very influential. No doubt custom and case law slowly seeped from colony to colony. Travelers and word of mouth spread knowledge of living law. It is hard to say how much; thus it is hard to tell to what degree there was a common legal culture.

To borrow statutes (even whole codes) was easier to do. Partly for this reason, some colonies had great apparent influence on the others—almost as great as the influence of the mother country. Legal skill was a rare commodity; hence newer settlements found it convenient to borrow laws from older neighbors, who had similar outlooks, goals, experiences, and problems. Virginia, in the South, and Massachusetts Bay, in the North, were major exporters of laws.

The Massachusetts example is the most striking. The *Laws and Liberties of 1648* were widely emulated.[139] Of 78 provisions in Robert Ludlow's Connecticut code of 1650, 22 were copied, almost verbatim, from the Massachusetts code, 36 were adopted with certain deletions or amendments, 6 came from other Massachusetts sources; only 14 (chiefly on local matters) were "original."[140] The New Haven code of 1656 was also much indebted to Massachusetts. Before the code was drafted, the general court charged the governor to "send for one of the new booke of lawes in the Massachusetts colony, and to view over a small booke of lawes newly come from England, which is said to be Mr. Cottons, and to add to what is already done as he shall thinke fitt."[141] New Hampshire drew most of its code of 1680 (the so-called Cutt code) from laws of Massachusetts and Plymouth. The famous Duke's laws of 1664, in force in New York, Pennsylvania, and Delaware, were "Collected out of the Severall Laws now in force in his Majesties American Colonyes and Plantations."[142] Massachusetts Bay was the source of many of these laws; Virginia also made a contribution. The criminal code of East New Jersey (1668—75) bor-

---

[139]Stefan Riesenfeld, "Law-Making and Legislative Precedent in American Legal History," 33 Minn. L. Rev. 103, 132 (1949).

[140]George L. Haskins and Samuel E. Ewing, "The Spread of Massachusetts Law in the Seventeenth Century," 106 U. Pa. L. Rev. 413, 414—15 (1958).

[141]Quoted in Haskins and Ewing, *op. cit.*, p. 416. The Cotton code had never been adopted in the Bay colony.

[142]*Charter to William Penn and Laws of the Province of Pennsylvania* (1879), p. 3.

rowed provisions from the Duke's laws, and also from the laws of the Northern colonies. Like the *Laws and Liberties*, the Duke of York's laws were arranged alphabetically by subject headings; this code contained organic law, matters of procedure, and matters of substance. It was hardly a slavish imitation of Massachusetts; as much was rejected as accepted. In Pennsylvania, too, when it became a freestanding colony, borrowings (from the Duke's laws, and from the New England colonies) were selective, eclectic, and never random or blind.[143]

By the 18th century, the period of wholesale borrowing of codes had largely ended. In developing bodies of statutory law, the colonies worked within three distinct traditions: their own, that of their neighbors, and that of the mother country. Incipient nationalism operated to sustain, deepen, and enhance the local element in all these laws; commercial dependence and English governance pulled law toward the common legal source. Statutes of the 18th century were more skillfully drafted than their predecessors. The Privy Council, as we have seen, reviewed colonial statutes; it had a certain influence on substance and style. There were new codes in New Jersey and Pennsylvania, at once closer to English models, and yet more original, than the Duke's laws. The influence of Massachusetts faded. Trott's laws, compiled by Nicholas Trott and formally adopted by South Carolina in 1712, merely declared which English statutes were in force in the colony. Many laws of England, Trott conceded, were "altogether useless" in South Carolina, "by reason of the different way of agriculture and the differing productions of the earth of this Province from that of England"; others were "impracticable" because of differences in institutions.[144] That left 150 relevant statutes; the code reprinted these and declared them to be law.

[143]George L. Haskins, "Influences of New England Law on the Middle Colonies," 1 Law and Hist. Rev. 238 (1983).

[144]*Statutes at Large of South Carolina*, vol. II (1837), p. 401. Trott's laws were not actually published until 1736. See Beverly Scafidel, "The Bibliography and Significance of Trott's Laws," in Herbert Johnson, ed., *South Carolina Legal History* (1980), p. 53.

THE LEGAL PROFESSION

The early colonial years were not friendly years for lawyers. There were few lawyers among the settlers. In some colonies, lawyers were distinctly unwelcome. In Massachusetts Bay, the *Body of Liberties* (1641) prohibited pleading for hire. The "attorneys" of early Virginia records were not trained lawyers, but attorneys-in-fact, laymen helping out their friends in court. In 1645, Virginia excluded lawyers from the courts; there had been a ban in Connecticut too. The Fundamental Constitutions of the Carolinas (1669) was also hostile; it was considered "a base and vile thing to plead for money or reward." Apparently, no lawyers practiced law in South Carolina until Nicholas Trott arrived in 1699.[145] The Quaker colony at Burlington, West New Jersey, made do with a single lawyer until the end of the seventeenth century.[146] In Pennsylvania, it was said, "They have no lawyers. Everyone is to tell his own case, or some friend for him... 'Tis a happy country."[147]

There is some evidence, then, to back Daniel Boorstin's comment that "ancient English prejudice against lawyers secured new strength in America... [D]istrust of lawyers became an institution."[148] Thomas Morton, who arrived in Plymouth about 1624 or 1625, has been called the first Massachusetts lawyer. He was jailed and expelled for scandalous behavior. Thomas Lechford, who had some legal training, arrived in 1638. He practiced in the colony as a courtroom attorney, and as a draftsman of documents. Lechford had unorthodox religious views, which won him no friends among the magistrates, nor did the fact that he meddled with a jury by "pleading with them out of the Court." It was an uncomfortable, hostile environment; Lechford eventually sailed back to England.[149]

---

[145]Anton-Hermann Chroust, *The Rise of the Legal Profession in America*, vol. I (1965), p. 297.

[146]H. Clay Reed and George J. Miller, eds., *The Burlington Court Book: A Record of Quaker Jurisprudence in West New Jersey: 1680–1709* (1944), xlii.

[147]Quoted in Francis R. Aumann, *The Changing American Legal System: Some Selected Phases* (1940), p. 13.

[148]Daniel J. Boorstin, *The Americans: The Colonial Experience* (1958), p. 197.

[149]In England, he published *Plaine Dealing, or Newes from New England,* and warned, "Take heede my brethren, despise not learning nor the worthy lawyers ... lest you repent too late." (1867 ed.), p. 68.

Distrust of lawyers arose from various sources. The Puritan leaders of Massachusetts Bay had an image of the ideal state. Revolutionary or Utopian regimes tend to be hostile to lawyers, at least at first. Lawyers of the old regime have to be controlled or removed; a new, revolutionary commonwealth must start with new law and new habits. Some colonists, oppressed in England, carried with them a strong dislike for all servants of government. Merchants and planters wished to run their affairs, without intermediaries. The theocratic colonies believed in a certain kind of social order, closely directed from the top. The legal profession, with its special privileges and principles, its private, esoteric language, seemed an obstacle to efficient or godly government. The Quakers of the Middle Atlantic were opposed to the adversary system in principle. They wanted harmony and peace. Their ideal was the "Common Peacemaker," and simple, nontechnical justice. They looked on lawyers as sharp, contentious—and unnecessary—people. For all these reasons, the lawyer was unloved in the 17th century.

In the 18th century, too, there was sentiment against lawyers. The lower classes came to identify lawyers with the upper class. Governors and their royal parties, on the other hand, were not sure of the loyalty of lawyers, and were sometimes afraid of their influence and power. In 1765, Cadwallader Colden, lieutenant governor of New York, told the Board of Trade in England that the "Gentlemen of the Law" had grown overmighty. They ranked just below the large landowners, and just above the merchants in society. Lawyers and judges, said Colden, had such power that "every Man is affraid of offending them"; their "domination" was "carried on by the same wicked artifices that the Domination of Priests formerly was in the times of ignorance."[150] Lay judges, too, may have resented the lawyers' threats to their competence and prestige. And as law became more "rational" and "professional," it became more confusing and remote to merchants and businessmen.

How strong the resentment against lawyers was, how deep it went, is hard to say. The evidence is partly literary; pamphlets and speeches are notoriously unreliable as measures of actual feeling among a diverse population. Some hatred was surely there; there is hard evidence of riots and disorders against lawyers and

[150]*Colden Letter Books, 1765–1775,* vol. II (Collections of the New York Historical Society, 1877), pp. 68, 70, 71.

judges. Lawyers, like shopkeepers, moneylenders, and lower bureaucrats, are social middlemen; they are lightning rods that draw rage during storms in the polity. In 18th-century New Jersey, the "table of the Assembly groaned beneath the weight of petitions ...invoking vengeance on the heads of the attorneys." The "Regulators," in late colonial North Carolina—a kind of vigilante group—rose up to smash corrupt and incompetent government. Lawyers were in the camp of the enemy. They perverted justice; they were "cursed hungry Caterpillars," whose fees "eat out the very Bowels of our Common-wealth."[151] In Monmouth and Essex counties (New Jersey), in 1769 and 1770, mobs rioted against the lawyers.[152]

But the lawyers were, in the end, a necessary evil. In the end, no colony could even try to make do without lawyers. In the very beginning, to be sure, there were makeshift alternatives. Lay judges knew enough English law to run their local courts; and a few practical books of English law circulated in the colonies. In Maryland in 1663, a layman, Dr. Luke Barber, accused of slandering a woman by calling her a whore ("taken...with her coates up," and with a "rogue" with "his Breeches downe") argued his own case and cited, in his own behalf, a recent English lawbook, "Shephard, and his authorities."[153] The magistrates of Massachusetts Bay, who struggled to keep out lawyers, made use of their own legal knowledge in drafting legislation and in governing. John Winthrop was one such magistrate. Nathaniel Ward, who drafted the *Body of Liberties* (1641), had had some legal training in England. Richard Bellingham, former town recorder of Boston, England, was governor of the Bay Colony in 1641; according to a contemporary, this "much honored" man worked to "further civill Government of this wandering people, he being learned in the Lawes of England, and experimentally fitted for the worke."[154]

As soon as a settled society posed problems for which lawyers had an answer or at least a skill, lawyers began to thrive, despite the hostility. Courts were in session; merchants were drawn into

---

[151]H. T. Lefler, ed., *North Carolina History as Told by Contemporaries* (1956), p. 87.

[152]Richard S. Field, *The Provincial Courts of New Jersey, with Sketches of the Bench and Bar* (1849), pp. 171 ff.

[153]*Archives of Maryland*, vol. 49 (1932), p. 116. The reference is to William Sheppard, *The Faithful Councellor, or the Marrow of the Law in English;* a second edition of this book was published in 1653.

[154]Edward Johnson, *Wonder-Working Providence* (Jameson, ed., 1910), p. 97.

litigation; land documents had to be written, and the more skill the better. Men trained in law who came from England found a market for their services; so did laymen with a smattering of law; there were semiprofessionals, too, with experience for sale. In the late 17th century, justices of the peace, sheriffs, and clerks, acted as attorneys in New Jersey.[155] In the literature, there are constant complaints against unauthorized lawyers, pettifoggers, shysters, and lowlifes—unprincipled men stirring up unprincipled litigation. These complaints, like the outcry against ambulance chasers more than a century later, sometimes had a curiously inconsistent quality. Lawyers were criticized both for incompetence and for wrongful competence. And an unauthorized or underground bar has been common in many societies; it crops up when the need for legal services outstrips the supply of legitimate lawyers. At any rate, there was a competent, professional bar, dominated by brilliant and successful lawyers—Daniel Dulany of Maryland, Benjamin Chew of Philadelphia, and many others—in all major communities by 1750, despite all bias and opposition.

No law schools in the colonies trained these men. Particularly in the South, where there were no colleges, some young men went to England for training, and attended the Inns of Court, in London. The Inns were not law schools as such; they had "ceased to perform educational functions of a serious nature," and were little more than living and eating clubs. Theoretically, a man could become a counselor-at-law in England without reading "a single page of any law book."[156] But the Inns were part of English legal culture; Americans could absorb the atmosphere of English law there; they read law on their own, and observed English practice.

The road to the bar, for all lawyers, was through some form of clerkship or apprenticeship. The aspiring lawyer usually entered into a contract with an established lawyer. The student paid a fee; in exchange, the lawyer promised to train him in the law; sometimes, too, the lawyer would provide food and lodging.[157] Apprenticeship was a control device as well as a way of learning the trade. It kept the bar small; and older lawyers were in firm command. How much the apprentice learned depended greatly

[155]Anton-Hermann Chroust, *op. cit.*, p. 198.
[156]Paul M. Hamlin, *Legal Education in Colonial New York* (1939), p. 16.
[157]Charles R. McKirdy, "The Lawyer as Apprentice: Legal Education in Eighteenth Century Massachusetts," 28 J. Legal Educ. 124 (1976); Hoyt P. Canady, "Legal Education in Colonial South Carolina," in Herbert Johnson, ed., *South Carolina Legal History* (1980), p. 101.

on his master. At worst, an apprentice went through a haphazard course of drudgery and copywork, with a few glances, catch-as-catch-can, at the law books. William Livingstone, who was clerking in the office of a New York lawyer, denounced the system in a letter to the *New York Weekly Post-Boy* (Aug. 19, 1745). The system was an "Outrage upon common Honesty...scandalous, horrid, base, and infamous to the last degree!" No one could "attain to a competent Knowlege in the Law...by gazing on a Number of Books, which he has neither Time nor Opportunity to read; or ...be metamorphos'd into an Attorney by virtue of a *Hocus-Pocus.*" A young clerk "trifle[d] away the Bloom of his Age...in a servile Drudgery nothing to the Purpose, and fit only for a Slave."[158] Other young men found clerkship valuable experience. Some senior lawyers were good teachers and good men. Some famous lawyers trained or attracted clerks, who themselves became famous. Thomas Jefferson was a student of George Wythe. James Wilson studied with John Dickinson, paying Dickinson a fee from the sale of a farm.[159] The first law schools, as we shall see, grew out of law offices which became so good at teaching that they gave up practice entirely.

From the 17th century on, the British exported some lawyers to help them govern their colonies. This was another fountain-head of the American bar. Nicholas Trott, an English lawyer, arrived in Charleston in 1699 as attorney general. He came to dominate the judicial life of South Carolina. In 1703, he was chief justice; he was also a member of the court of chancery, judge of the vice-admiralty court, the court of common pleas, and of the king's bench; he compiled the *Laws of the Province of South Carolina.* Contemporaries complained that "the sole Judicial Power [was] lodg'd" in his hands, "a Trust never repos'd in any one Man before in the World."[160] In 1719, when proprietary government was overthrown, he lost his power. Some lawyers emigrated from England, and eventually held office in the colonies. Mathias Nicolls arrived in New York in 1664. He had been a barrister of Lincoln's Inn and Inner Temple; he had fifteen years' practice in London. In 1683, Governor Dongan appointed him a judge of the court of

---

[158]Reprinted in Paul M. Hamlin, *op. cit.*, pp. 167–68.
[159]Charles P. Smith, *James Wilson, Founding Father, 1742–1798* (1956), p. 24.
[160]Anne K. Gregorie, ed., *Records of the Court of Chancery of South Carolina, 1661–1779* (1950), pp. 6, 53. On Trott, see Herbert Johnson, ed., *South Carolina Legal History* (1980), pp. 23–64.

oyer and terminer.[161] In Massachusetts, too, most good lawyers in the generation after 1690 at one time or another held appointive office.[162]

Each colony had its own standards for admission to the bar. New Jersey tried to set up a graded profession, on the English plan. By a rule of 1755, the colony's supreme court established the order of *serjeants-at-law,* a rank higher than ordinary "counselors." Only the court could appoint to the higher rank; and the court later restricted the number of serjeants to twelve. The serjeants had the power and duty to conduct examinations for admission to the bar.[163] In Virginia, a law of 1748 gave its high court control over licensing and admission to the bar. In Massachusetts, in the 18th century, each court admitted its own lawyers. In 1762, the chief justice of the Superior Court, Thomas Hutchison, instituted the rank of barrister; twenty-five lawyers were called to this rank.[164] In Rhode Island, any court could admit; but admission to one was admission to all. In many colonies, the requirements for admission included a long period of apprenticeship, though in some colonies, if a man was a college graduate, the term was a year or two less.

The legal profession was one road to money and success in the 18th century. Wealthy lawyers tried to keep up their prices and prestige and keep down the supply of practitioners. They never quite succeeded. The lower levels of the bar were hard to control. Lawyers, like actors and painters, were often part-timers and amateurs. In 17th-century Maryland, most lawyers were planters, who spent part of their time on the practice. It was only in the 18th century that it was possible to speak of lawyers in Maryland as "professional" at all. Of 207 attorneys in Maryland, between 1660 and 1715, 79 were planters; others were clerks or merchants; only 48 could be described as professional lawyers.[165] Up to the

[161]Paul M. Hamlin and Charles E. Baker, *Supreme Court of Judicature of the Province of New York, 1691–1704,* vol. I (1959), p. 19.

[162]John M. Murrin, "The Legal Transformation: The Bench and Bar of Eighteenth-Century Massachusetts," in Stanley N. Katz, ed., *Colonial America: Essays in Politics and Social Development* (1971), pp. 415, 423.

[163]Anton-Hermann Chroust, *op. cit.,* p. 200.

[164]Gerard W. Gawalt, *The Promise of Power: The Emergence of the Legal Profession in Massachusetts, 1760–1840* (1979), pp. 16–17.

[165]Alan F. Day, "Lawyers in Colonial Maryland, 1660–1715," 17 Am. J. Legal Hist. 145, 164 (1973). For 33 lawyers, there was no information. On the increasing sophistication of the profession in the 18th century, see also Stephen Botein, "The

time of the Revolution, part-time lawyers made up a sizable part of the Connecticut bar. Joseph Adams of New Haven "combined the duties of attorney and innkeeper"; he "did not do very well at either, for his estate proved insolvent when he died in 1782." Another Connecticut lawyer in the 1750s, Peletiah Mills of Windsor, doubled as "principal taverner of his home town." Other Connecticut lawyers were cloth merchants, clergymen, and soldiers.[166]

In the 18th century, the demand for lawyers' skilled services increased; the bar became much more professional; yet in many colonies, the bar was extremely, and artificially, small. There were only 15 lawyers in Massachusetts in 1740—one for every 10,000 inhabitants. Even in 1775 there were only 71.[167] So few trained lawyers were qualified to practice before the New York Supreme Court, that an act of 1695 ordered litigants not to hire more than two "Attorneys at Law" to handle a case "in any of the Courts of Record Within this Province." Apparently, it was possible to "fee" all the attorneys, that is, hire the whole New York bar, leaving one's opponent high and dry.[168] As of 1700, only about a dozen men practiced before the New York high court. Between 1700 and 1720, six attorneys had the lion's share of practice in New York's mayor's court. In 1731, the New York City charter gave seven attorneys (mentioned by name) a monopoly of this practice. Two years before, a group of New York lawyers had formed an "association" to supervise legal education, regulate practice, and control admission to the bar. In 1756 these "gentlemen of the law" agreed to take on no clerks, except their own sons, for the next fourteen years.[169]

There were similar guildlike movements in other colonies. In Rhode Island, eight lawyers signed a "Compact" in 1745 to make sure fees would always be "sufficient for our support and subsistence." No case was to be pleaded at Superior Court for less than a three pound fee; only a "standing client" was "to be trusted

Legal Profession in Colonial North America," in Wilfrid Prest, ed., *Lawyers in Early Modern Europe and America* (1981), p. 129.

[166]John T. Farrell, ed., *The Superior Court Diary of William Samuel Johnson, 1772–1773* (1942), l–li. On part-time and self-trained lawyers in Massachusetts, see Gawalt, *op. cit.*, pp. 24–25.

[167]Gawalt, *op. cit.*, p. 14.

[168]Paul M. Hamlin and Charles E. Baker, *op. cit.*, pp. 99–101.

[169]Richard B. Morris, ed., *Select Cases of the Mayor's Court of New York City, 1674–1784* (1935), pp. 52 ff.

without his note." Attorneys were not to sign "blank writs and disperse them about the colony, which practice ... would make the law cheap." They agreed not to defend any client whose lawyer was suing for his fee unless three or more "brethren" determined that the lawyer's demand was "unreasonable."[170]

The struggle for control of the trade went on incessantly. John Adams complained, in 1759, that the "practice of Law [was] grasped into the hands of deputy sheriffs, pettifoggers and even constables who filled all the writs upon bonds, promissory notes, and accounts, received the fees established for lawyers, and stirred up many unnecessary suits." No doubt he saw it that way. There were upper and lower lawyers, rich and poor, exclusive lawyers and lawyers hungry for clients, just as there are today. Many lawyers had to struggle for bread and paper. The "professionals," on the other hand, were often rich—or got rich. The rich lawyers resented the poor ones, who threatened and disgusted them; and there were also amateurs and quacks, grabbing for a share of the trade. Many aristocrats, of mind and money, were lawyers.

Politically, many lawyers were conservatives. But lawyers, or men who called themselves lawyers, were among the founders of the Republic. John Marshall, John Adams, Thomas Jefferson, James Wilson, John Jay of New York, George Wythe of Virginia, Francis Hopkinson of Pennsylvania—all these were lawyers. Some leading lawyers—Anthony Stokes of Georgia and William Smith of New York—chose the losing side in the Revolution and left the country. Smith later became chief justice of the province of Quebec. Many lawyers, if not most, were loyalists; yet twenty-five of the fifty-six signers of the Declaration of Independence were lawyers, and thirty-one of the fifty-five delegates to the Constitutional Convention were lawyers. What these facts show, according to Professor Boorstin, is "the pervasiveness of legal competence among American men of affairs and the vagueness of the boundary between legal and all other knowledge in a fluid America."[171] Yet these men identified themselves as lawyers, not as doctors,

[170]Quoted in Wilkins Updike, *Memoirs of the Rhode Island Bar* (1842), pp. 294–95. For the situation in Maryland, see Day, *op. cit.*, at 150.

[171]Daniel J. Boorstin, *The Americans: The Colonial Experience* (1958), p. 205. John M. Murrin, commenting on the "signs of creeping respectability" in the 18th-century bar in Massachusetts, remarks that "Before 1730, many gentlemen felt qualified to practice law on the side without bothering to study it. A generation later, gentlemen were beginning to study it with no intention of practicing it." Murrin, *op. cit.*, p. 432.

politicians, or historians. The line between lawyer and laymen was not as indistinct as it had been in earlier years. There was a pride of profession among these men, who thought of themselves as attorneys, and a common fund of experience and training, whether or not they had ever replevied a cow or drawn up a chancery bill.

THE LITERATURE OF THE LAW

In one sense, colonial legal literature is quickly disposed of: there was no such thing worthy of the name before 1776. Law libraries were scarce, small, and scattered. In the 17th century, few people who called themselves lawyers owned many lawbooks at all. Lawbooks were more common in the 18th century. But a lawyer's library was not full of books about *American* law; the books were English law books, with perhaps a few local statutes thrown in. Most popular were English practice manuals.[172] Native lawbooks were few and utterly insignificant. No substantial body of case law was in print until after the Revolution. When Blackstone's *Commentaries* were published (1765–69), Americans were his most avid customers. At last there was an up-to-date shortcut to the basic themes of English law. An American edition was printed in 1771–72, on a subscription basis, for sixteen dollars a set; 840 American subscribers ordered 1,557 sets—an astounding response. Not all subscribers were lawyers and judges, but many were; and Blackstone's text became ubiquitous on the American legal scene.[173]

Literature is a conscious creation; but it is also recorded life. In this sense, the toiling scribes of colonial courts made literature. A few of their records were printed in the 19th century. Slowly, more have been unearthed; some have been edited and published. Most of the material is useful, but dreary, as formal legal prose tends to be. Yet among the reports are flashes of extraordinary vividness and color. These records, like no others, lift the veil that hides the face of daily life. They paint a marvelous picture, distorted to be sure by the fact that social disorders, large and small, make up the major subject of these chronicles. No one reading these records can cling to the view that Puritan life, for example, was uniformly solemn, dour, and high-minded gray. Joseph War-

---

[172]See Herbert A. Johnson, *Imported Eighteenth-Century Law Treatises in American Libraries, 1700–1799* (1978).
[173]Paul M. Hamlin, *op. cit.*, pp. 64–65.

rinar and Peter Swinck swore, in the Pynchon Court Record, for June 20, 1661,

> that in the forenoone last Sabbath in sermone tyme they saw Samuell Harmon thrust and tickle Jonathan Morgan and Pluckt him of [off] his seate .3. tymes and squeased him and made him cry.[174]

The cruelty of life is recorded, along with lust and sin. William Myers, testifying in West New Jersey in 1686, shows us slavery bare and unadorned:

> Hee heard at a Considerable distance many blowes or stripes ...hee thought hee heard a Negro Cry out many tymes... he supposed it to be James Wills beating his Negro woman, and heard still many Lashes more and Crying out, until hee was greevd and went into his owne house and shut the dore, and said to his wife oh! yond cruell man.[175]

The voice of truth sounds, too, in pleadings and formal speech. Legal phrases and popular speech mingled, for example, in the papers of South Carolina's chancery court (1721), where Mrs. Elisabeth Weekley, the "Relict" and "Executrix" of Richard Weekley, "Planter," told how she was induced to intrust her share of the estate to Mrs. Sarah Rhett:

> the said Mrs. Sarah Rhett did advise your Oratrix That it was not safe for your Oratrix being a Widow and an Ancient Woman and living on the Broad Path to keep soe much moneys in here own House least she should be robbed thereof by her Negroes or otherwise and offered to take charge thereof.... Your Oratrix...delivered over to the said Mrs. Sarah Rhett the said four hundred and Eighty pounds in Bills of Credit who took the same out of a paper Wrapper ...and the said Mrs. Sarah Rhett then counted the said Bills into her lap...and cryed Lord Bless me Woman here's five hundred pounds wanting twenty pounds I did not think you had soe much money...then taking your Oratrix by the hand put her other hand upon her own Breast and told your Oratrix that the said moneys should be as safe as if it were in

[174]Joseph Smith, ed., *Colonial Justice in Western Massachusetts, 1639–1702: The Pynchon Court Record* (1961), p. 253.

[175]H. Clay Reed and George J. Miller, eds., *The Burlington Court Book: A Record of Quaker Jurisprudence in West New Jersey 1680–1709* (1944), p. 57.

her...own hands and that as she was a Christian she would never wrong Your Oratrix of a Farthing.[176]

These and similar happenings were carefully preserved in court records. Thus the living law is in some ways more knowable for this forgotten period of American law than for later, more accessible times. An avalanche of papers and forms smothered the minds and the mouths of ordinary litigants in the 19th and 20th centuries. The clear sound of American law, in its lusty youth, speaks from the pages of colonial county courts.

[176]Anne K. Gregorie, ed., *Records of the Court of Chancery of South Carolina, 1661–1779* (1950), p. 272.

PART II

From the Revolution to the
Middle of the 19th Century:
1776–1850

CHAPTER I

THE REPUBLIC OF BEES

REVOLUTIONARY ARDOR

In 1776, the colonies declared themselves independent. The bitter war that followed ended in an American victory. Peace, of course, raised as many questions of government as it answered. A plan of government is a plan for distribution of the power and wealth of a society. The choice of system, then, is no idle exercise in political theory. How to plan the new American government was the major policy issue of the late 18th century. The first grand scheme was embodied in the Articles of Confederation. It proved unsatisfactory to powerful circles in the country. After the failure of the Articles, a federal Constitution was drawn up, and ratified in 1787.

Each colony, too, underwent its own revolution. Colonies became states, and embarked on new courses of action with new problems and new programs. First, they had to fight a war and patch up domestic disruptions. All this called for a major outburst of lawmaking. In Pennsylvania, for example, a constitutional convention, in 1776, declared a general amnesty and established a new form of government. Old officials were replaced by men loyal to the Revolution. The ordinary business of government was to continue, where possible; and the emergencies of war had to be coped with. In October 1777, British troops "penetrated into [the] state, and after much devastation and great cruelty in their progress," seized Philadelphia; the state government then created a "council of safety," with vast and summary powers "to promote and provide for the preservation of the Commonwealth." It had power to seize goods "for the army and for the inhabitants," punish traitors, and "regulate the prices of such articles as they may think necessary." But the "ordinary course of justice" was to continue as far as feasible. In the same year, the legislature passed a bill of attainder against a number of men who had "traitorously and wickedly" gone over to the king. The state redefined and punished treason, declared bills of credit of the Continental Congress and the state to be legal tender;[1] and, inevitably, legislated about the militia, army supplies, taxes, and the policy of war.

When the war ended, debates over law continued. The king of England and his government had been successfully overthrown. Should the king's law be also overthrown? Should ordinary private law be radically altered? The first generation seriously argued the question. The common law was badly tarnished; so was the reputation of the lawyers, many of whom had been Tories. It seemed to some men that new democratic states needed new institutions, from top to bottom, including fresh, democratic law. A pamphleteer, who called himself Honestus, asked, in 1786: "Can the monarchical and aristocratical institutions of England be consistent with...republican principles?" It was "melancholy" to see the "numerous volumes" of English law, "brought into our Courts, arranged in formidable order, as the grand artillery to batter down every plain, rational principle of law."[2] Thomas Paine, an old firebrand, spoke for at least some zealots when he denounced, in 1805, the "chicanery of law and lawyers." He complained that Pennsylvania courts, even at that late date, had "not yet arrived at the dignity of independence." The courts, he said, still "hobble along by the stilts and crutches of English and antiquated precedents," which were often not democratic at all, but "tyrrannical."[3] During Shays's Rebellion, in Massachusetts (1786), mobs stopped the courts from sitting, and forcibly staved off execution of judgments against debtors. It was easy to attribute class bias to the courts, and attribute this class bias in turn to the antiquated, oppressive, inappropriate common law.

There were two apparent alternatives to the stilts and crutches. The common law could be replaced by some rival system. Or all systems could be abandoned in favor of natural principles of justice. The first alternative had some slight basis, in hope if not in fact. There *were* other systems of law. After the French revolution, American liberals were particularly attracted to the French civil law. In the early 19th century, the Napoleonic Code served as a

[1]*Statutes at Large, Pa., 1682–1801*, vol. IX (1903), p. 149 (act of Oct. 13, 1777); p. 201 (act of Mar. 6, 1778); p. 34 (act of Jan. 29, 1777).

[2]The strictures of Honestus were ultimately published in Boston, in 1819, under the title *Observations on the Pernicious Practice of the Law;* and have been reprinted in 13 Am. J. Legal Hist. 244, 257 (1969).

[3]Philip S. Foner, ed., *Complete Writings of Thomas Paine*, vol. II (1945), p. 1003.

symbol and model of clarity and order. Some civil-law jurists were translated into English during this period: *A Treatise on Obligations, Considered in a Moral and Legal View,* "translated from the French of [Robert] Pothier," appeared in New Bern, North Carolina, in 1802. To some small extent, French scholars influenced American legal thought. Compared to civil law, common law seemed, to a number of jurists, to be feudal, barbaric, uncouth.

In hindsight, the common law had little to fear. It was as little threatened as the English language. The courts continued to operate, continued to do business; they used the only law that they knew. Few lawyers had any grasp of French. French lawbooks were rare and inaccessible; English authorities flooded the country. To be sure, there were some American jurists who had the education and skill to handle Continental law—James Kent of New York, for example. Joseph Story, who served on the Supreme Court, was a tower of erudition. These men cited and used bits of foreign law in their writings and opinions. But they were not revolutionaries. They believed in purifying and improving the law, not in overthrowing it. They were willing to snatch doctrines and ideas from Continental Europe; but even English law did that. One of the culture heroes of the American legal elite was England's Lord Mansfield, who died in 1793. Mansfield was Scottish by birth and an ardent admirer of Roman-flavored civil law.

And of course the common law had many defenders. Not everybody saw the common law as old and despotic. It was also the birthright of free men, a precious inheritance, perverted by the British under George III, but still a vital reality. One rhetorical pillar of the men of 1776 was that the common law embodied fundamental norms of natural law. The first Continental Congress, in 1776, adopted a Declaration of Rights; it declared that the colonies were "entitled to the common law of England," in particular the right of trial by jury. Americans were also entitled to the benefit of those English statutes which "existed at the time of colonization; and which they have, by experience, respectively found to be applicable to their several local and other circumstances."[4]

Common-law lawyers were among the heroes of the Republic. John Adams was one; Thomas Jefferson, for all his ambivalence toward common law and its judges, another. Lawyers mostly

[4]Quoted in Elizabeth G. Brown, *British Statutes in American Law, 1776–1836* (1964), p. 21.

drafted the state and federal constitutions. Courts were increasingly manned by lawyers, who listened to the arguments of other lawyers. Lawyers moved west with the line of settlement; they swarmed into state capitals and county seats. Wherever one looked in political life—in town, city, county, state, and national government—the lawyers were there. Unlike some later revolutions, and some earlier colonial Utopias, the new republic did not try to do business without lawyers. Old lawyers continued to function, training new lawyers in their image, who, like their teachers, turned almost instinctively to common law. The common law was also a weapon of integration. The Northwest Ordinance imposed common law on the lands of the American frontier. In the prairies and forests, where French settlers lived and worked in the path of the American onrush, the common law was an agent of American imperialism.

The common law would have to be Americanized, of course. Now that the states had freedom to choose, what parts of English law would remain in force? This was a tortuous question, not easily solved. Many states passed statutes to define the limits of the law in force. A Virginia law of 1776 declared that the "common law of England, all statutes or acts of Parliament made in aid of the common law prior to the fourth year of the reign of King James the first, and which are of a general nature, not local to that kingdom ... shall be considered as in full force."[5] The Delaware constitution of 1776 (art. 25) provided that "The common law of England as well as so much of the statute law as has been heretofore adopted in practice in this State, shall remain in force," except for those parts which were "repugnant to the rights and privileges" expressed in the constitution and in the "declaration of rights."

The New York experience was particularly complex. A law of 1786 declared the common law in force, and such English statutes as were in effect in the colony on April 19, 1775. Later, New York specifically re-enacted some British laws—the Statute of Frauds, for example, a law first passed in 1677, and which had virtually become a part of the common law. In 1788, a New York law, "for the Amendment of the Law, and the better Advancement of Justice," declared that "after the *first* day of *May* next," no British statutes "shall operate or be considered as Laws" in the state.[6] The

[5]William Walter Henning, *Statutes at Large . . . of Virginia*, vol. 9 (1821), p. 127.
[6]On the New York reception laws, see E. G. Brown, *op. cit.*, pp. 69–75.

New York Constitution of 1821 (art. VII, sec. 13) stated that "Such parts of the common law, and of the acts of the legislature of the colony of New York, as together did form the law of the said colony" on April 19, 1775, and the resolutions of the colonial Congress, "and of the convention of the State of New York," in force on April 20, 1777, would continue to be law, unless altered or repealed, and unless they were "repugnant" to the constitution. No mention was made of British statutes; for good measure, an act of 1828 specifically pronounced the British statutes dead.

Yet even this flock of New York laws fell short of solving the problem. A New York court later held that some English statutes had become part of the "common law" of the colony.[7] This meant that an undefinable, unknowable group of old laws somehow maintained a ghostly presence. They lived on, of course, only insofar as they were not "repugnant" to the constitution or unsuitable to conditions. One could never, then, be sure if an old law were dead or alive. New York was not the only state whose judges held that some of the old statutes were valid, and thus sentenced the legal public to a certain amount of uncertainty. To this day, an occasional case still turns on whether some statute or doctrine had been "received" as common law in this or that state. The question of "reception" had troubled the colonials too. Independence merely altered the form of the question. And in a broader sense, the question is an abiding one in all common-law jurisdictions. Judges must constantly re-examine the law, to see which parts still suit society's needs, and which parts must be thrown on the ash heap, once and for all.

The reception statutes dealt with the *older* English law. What about new law? There was, as expected, a strong burst of national pride. To Jesse Root of Connecticut, writing in 1798, it was "unnecessary, and derogatory" for courts of an independent nation to be governed by foreign law. His ideal was "the republic of bees," whose members "resist all foreign influence with their lives," and whose honey, "though extracted from innumerable flowers,"[8] was indisputably their own. In pursuit of the republic of bees, New Jersey passed a law, in 1799, that

> no adjudication, decision, or opinion, made, had, or given,
> in any court of law or equity in Great Britain [after July 4,

[7]*Bogardus* v. *Trinity Church*, 4 Paige 178, 198–99 (1833), discussed in E. G. Brown, *op. cit.*, pp. 72–73.
[8]1 Root's Reports (Connecticut), xlii, xliii (1798).

1776]...nor any printed or written report or statement thereof, nor any compilation, commentary, digest, lecture, treatise, or other explanation or exposition of the common law,...shall be received or read in any court of law or equity in this state, as law or evidence of the law, or elucidation or explanation thereof.[9]

Kentucky prohibited the mere mention of recent British law. Its statute, passed in 1807, declared that "reports and books containing adjudged cases in...Great Britain...since the 4th day of July 1776, shall not be read or considered as authority in...the courts of this Commonwealth."[10] During Spring Term, 1808, Henry Clay, appearing before the court of appeals of Kentucky, "offered to read" a "part of Lord Ellenborough's opinion" in Volume 3 of East's reports; the "chief justice stopped him." Clay's co-counsel argued that the legislature "had no more power to pass" such a law than to "prohibit a judge the use of his spectacles." The court decided, however, that "the book must not be used at all in court."[11]

But Lord Ellenborough was not so easily banished, in New Jersey, or Kentucky, or elsewhere. The New Jersey statute was repealed in 1819. As a practical matter, English law continued to be used by lawyers and courts, throughout the period, throughout the country. England remained the basic source of all law that was not strictly new or strictly American. The habits of a lifetime were not easily thrown over, despite ideology. Indigenous legal literature was weak and derivative. There was no general habit of publishing American decisions; American case reports were not common until a generation or more after Independence. To common-law lawyers, a shortage of cases was crippling. To fill the gap, English materials were used, English reports cited, English judges quoted as authority. In the first generation, more English than American cases were cited in American reports. Ordinary lawyers referred to Blackstone constantly; they used his book as a shortcut to the law; and Blackstone was English to the core. Sometimes curiously old-fashioned bits of law—phrases, old doctrines, old writs—turned up in curious places (for example, the American frontier); the reason was the ubiquity of Blackstone.

American law continued, in short, to borrow. The English over-

---

[9]Quoted in E. G. Brown, *op. cit.*, p. 82.

[10]Quoted in E. G. Brown, *op. cit.*, p. 132.

[11]*Hickman* v. *Boffman*, Hardin 356, 372–73 (Kentucky, 1808). Vol. III of East's Reports contains cases from the court of king's bench for the years 1802 and 1803.

lay was obvious, pervasive—but selective. The English doctrines that were invited to this country were those which were needed and wanted—and only those. Sweeping changes took place in American law in the years between 1776 and the middle of the 19th century. During that time, there developed a true republic of bees, whose flowers were the social and economic institutions that developed in their own way in the country. They, not Lord Ellenborough and Lord Kenyon, were the lawmakers that made American law a distinctive system: a separate language of law within the family founded in England.

The second apparent alternative to the common law was also a mirage. To abolish the tyranny of lawyers and their rules, to reduce law to a common-sense system, at the level of the common man's understanding, a system of simple, "natural" justice: this was an age-old yearning, but it flared up with special vigor after 1776. As one citizen of Kentucky put it, the state needed "a simple and concise code of laws...adopted to the weakest capacity."[12]

In part, the antilaw movement was an outgrowth of radical politics. One current of thought distrusted the common law on the grounds that it was remote from the needs of ordinary people, and was biased toward the rich. Another current of thought distrusted the law because it was archaic, inflexible, irrelevant; it did not suit the needs of merchant or businessman. Both groups could make common cause against lawyers' law, which suited nobody's wants but the lawyers. There was a general interest, then, in a reform of legal institutions, in which rich and poor, radical and conservative could share. In a complex society, however, it was Utopian to imagine that lawyers' law could be overthrown and replaced by natural justice, whatever that might mean. On the contrary, more and more rules, of more and more definite shape, were needed as time went on. The reform urge, as we shall see, did not abate; but it came to mean, not artlessness, but adaptation to the needs of a market economy.

One basic, critical fact of 19th-century law was that the official legal system penetrated, and had to penetrate, deeper and deeper into society. Medieval common law was not the law everywhere in England; nor was it everybody's law. American law was more popular, in a profound sense. It had no archaic or provincial rivals. It had no competitive substratum. Paradoxically, American law,

---

[12] Quoted in Charles M. Cook, *The American Codification Movement: A Study of Antebellum Legal Reform* (1981), p. 16.

divided into as many subsystems as there were states, was less disjointed than the one "common law" of older England.

Of course, millions were beyond the reach of formal law and indifferent to it. But comparatively speaking, American law had an enormous range. It drew its strength from the work and wealth of millions, and it affected the work and wealth of millions more. In 16th- or 18th-century England, few people owned or dealt in land. Only a small percentage were inside the market economy. Only a few were potential customers for family law, the law of torts, the law of corporations. There was surely less oligarchy in the United States than in the old kingdoms of Europe. A law for the millions, for the middle class, had to develop. And this law, to survive, had to be more pliant and accessible than a law for the wealthy few.

In short, law had to suit the needs of its customers; it had to be at least in a form that lawyers, as brokers of legal information, could use. What happened to American law in the 19th century, basically, was that it underwent tremendous changes, to conform to the vast increase in numbers of consumers. It is dangerous to sum up long periods and great movements in a sentence. But if colonial law had been, in the first place, colonial, and in the second place, paternal, emphasizing community, order, and the struggle against sin, then, gradually, a new set of attitudes developed, in which the primary function of law was not suppression and uniformity, but economic growth and service to its users. In this period, people came to see law, more and more, as a utilitarian tool: a way to protect property and the established order, of course, but beyond that, to further the interests of the middle-class *mass*, to foster growth, to release and harness the energy latent in the commonwealth: "Dynamic rather than static property, property in motion or at risk rather than property secure and at rest."[13]

It was not only property to which the word dynamic seemed more and more apt. These two polar words—dynamic and static— aptly describe a fundamental change in the concept of law. The source of the change lay not so much in the Revolution as in revolution: the transformation of economy and society that oc-

[13]J. Willard Hurst, *Law and the Conditions of Freedom in the Nineteenth Century United States* (1956), p. 24; on the general issue of the extent to which the Revolution itself was a great watershed, see Hendrik Hartog, "Distancing Oneself from the Eighteenth Century: A Commentary on Changing Pictures of American Legal History," in Hendrik Hartog, ed., *Law in the American Revolution and the Revolution in the Law* (1981), p. 229.

curred in the machine age and the age of rational thought. A dynamic law is a man-made law. The Constitution talked about natural rights, and meant what it said; but these rights did not define the duties and status of the subject; rather, they served as a framework for the fulfillment of people's needs and desires. Gradually, an instrumental, relativistic theory of law made its mark on the system. It meant a more creative view of precedent. It meant asking for the functions of past law, and measuring these against demands of the present and future. Once, change in law was looked on as rare and treated almost apologetically. But in the 19th century, Americans made law wholesale, without any sense of shame. Basically, this was legislative law, law made by elected representatives, rather than law made by judges. To be sure, the boldness of the judges and the rapidity of social change meant that there was room for both institutions in the house of creative law-making; the judges seized this opportunity, and played a mighty, if secondary, role in making fresh law.

CONSTITUTIONS: FEDERAL AND STATE

The Revolutionary period was, by necessity, an age of innovation in fundamental law. The old ties with England had been snapped. The states and the general government decided to put their basic political decisions in the form of written constitutions. Some states had begun as chartered colonies; they had gotten into the habit of living under these charters, and had even learned to revere them, as guarantees of their liberty. American statesmen tended to look on a written constitution as a kind of social compact—a basic agreement among citizens, and between citizens and state, setting out mutual rights and duties, in permanent form.

The Articles of Confederation (1777) envisioned a loose, low-key grouping of highly sovereign states. It did not provide for a strong executive. It had no provision for a federal judiciary. Congress, however, was given some judicial power; it was "the last resort on appeal in all disputes and differences...between two or more states concerning boundary jurisdiction or any other cause whatever." Congress also had power over matters of admiralty law, with "sole and exclusive right" to establish "rules for deciding, in all cases, what captures on land or water shall be legal," and how prizes might be "divided or appropriated." Congress also had sole right to set up "courts for the trial of piracies and felonies committed on the high seas," and courts "for receiving and determining, finally, appeals in all cases of captures" (art. IX).

The Articles of Confederation, by common consent, were a failure; the Constitution of 1787 was a stronger, more centralizing document. The Northwest Ordinance (1787), which set up a scheme of government for the Western lands, and which was enacted shortly before the Constitution, took it for granted that all future states would have a "permanent constitution." Any new states carved out of the Northwest Territory would have a "republican" constitution, consistent with federal law (Northwest Ordinance, 1787, art. V).

The original states had in theory the option to write or not write constitutions. But most of them quickly chose the way of the new-written word. Within a short time after the war broke out, eleven states had drafted and adopted new constitutions. To some, a constitution was a rallying point, a symbol of unity during war. The New Jersey Constitution (1776) put it this way:

> in the present deplorable situation of these colonies, exposed to the fury of a cruel and relentless enemy, some form of government is absolutely necessary, not only for the preservation of good order, but also the more effectually to unite the people, and enable them to exert their whole force in their own necessary defense.

A few states chose to rest upon their original charters. But these, too, were eventually replaced by new documents, of the constitutional type. Connecticut discarded its charter and adopted a constitution in 1818. Eventually, every state in the union came to have a constitution in the strict sense of the word. All, in short, embarked on careers of making, unmaking, and remaking constitutions.

Constitutionalism answered to a deep-seated need, among members of the articulate public, for formal, outward signs of political legitimacy. This urge had driven tiny, isolated colonies in what is now Rhode Island or Massachusetts to express the structure and principles of government in the form of an agreement—a visible, legible bulwark against the lonely disorder of life outside the reach of the mother country. Much later, but by something of the same instinct, the remote Oregon pioneers, in a no-man's land disputed among nations, drew up a frame of government and called it a constitution. So did the residents of the "lost state of Franklin" in the 1780s, in what is now part of eastern Tennessee. So did the handful of citizens of the "Indian Stream Republic," in disputed territory near the border of New Hampshire and Canada. And so did the Mormons of the "State of Deseret." These "constitutions," to be sure, were mostly copycats; they borrowed provisions from existing constitutions, taking a phrase here, a clause there, and making whatever changes were considered appropriate. They were short-lived and of dubious legality. But they illustrate how strong the *idea* of the written constitution had become in American life.

There have been dozens of state constitutions. Their texts, style, and substance vary considerably. Some of the earliest ones, written before the 1780s, were quite bold and forward-looking for their times. The first Pennsylvania Constitution (1776) represented a sharp victory for the liberals of the state. Virginia pioneered a Declaration of Rights (1776). The idea and content of the Bill of Rights came from sources in the states. The federal Constitution could not have been ratified, without the promise of a bill of rights, which took the form of ten amendments.[14] After 1787, the language and organization of the federal Constitution became in turn a powerful model for state constitutions. One feature, however, was not easily transferred to the states: durability. There has been only one federal Constitution. It has been amended from time to time—but never overthrown. A few states (for example, Wisconsin) have also had only one constitution. Other states have followed a more variegated, or chaotic, constitutional career. Louisiana has had nine constitutions, perhaps ten, depending on how one counts. Georgia has had at least six.

The federal Constitution was marvelously supple, put together with great political skill. The stability of the country—Civil War crisis aside—has been the main source of its amazing survival. But the Constitution itself deserves a share of the credit. It turned out to be neither too tight nor too loose. It was in essence a frame, a skeleton, an outline of the form of government; on specifics, it mostly held its tongue. The earlier state constitutions, before 1787 and for some decades after, also guarded themselves against saying too much. There were, of course, some idiosyncratic features, even before 1787, in state constitutions. New Hampshire (1784),

[14]On state constitutions and their Bills of Rights, see, in general, Robert Allen Rutland, *The Birth of the Bill of Rights, 1776–1791* (1962); Willi Paul Adams, *The First American Constitutions: Republican Ideology and the Making of the State Constitutions in the Revolutionary Era* (1980).

in the spirit of Yankee thrift, solemnly declared that "economy" was a "most essential virtue in all states, especially in a young one; no pension shall be granted, but in consideration of actual services, and...with great caution,...and never for more than one year at a time."[15] But most state constitutions began with a bill of rights, described the general frame of government, and left it at that.

A constitution, if at all different from ordinary law, has two functions. First, it provides a terse exposition of the structure of government—its permanent shape, the nature of its organs or parts, and their boundaries and limits. Second, it may contain a list of essential rights, essential limitations on government, essential rules—all those propositions of high or highest law, which the drafters mean to secure against the winds of temporary change. But this second function has no natural boundary. Opinions differ from generation to generation on what rights and duties are most fundamental. Even the federal Constitution was more than mere framework. Imbedded in it were fragments of a code of law. Trial by jury, for example, was guaranteed (art. III, sec. 2, par. 3). The Constitution defined the crime of treason (art. III, sec. 3), and set out minimum requirements for convicting any man of this crime. The Bill of Rights contained a miniature code of criminal procedure.

What existed in embryo, and in reasonable proportions in the federal Constitution, was carried to much greater lengths in the states. The inflation of constitutions reached its high point (or low point) after the Civil War. But the process began long before that. Even the state bills of rights became bloated. The federal Bill of Rights had ten sections; Kentucky, in 1792, had 28. Some of these were quite vague: "elections shall be free and equal" (art. XII, sec. 5); others seemed hardly to warrant their exalted position—for example, that estates of "such persons as shall destroy their own lives shall descend or vest as in case of natural death."[16]

The Delaware constitution of 1792 was another offender. It included many details of court organization and procedure; for example, "No writ of error shall be brought upon any judgment ...confessed, entered, or rendered, but within five years after the

---

[15] N.H. const., 1784, art. XXXVI.
[16] Art. XII, sec. 21. This was not by any means a unique clause. See Alabama const., 1819, art. I, sec. 21; Mississippi const., 1817, art. I, sec. 21; Tennessee const., 1796, art. XI, sec. 12; Delaware const., 1792, art. I, sec. 15.

confessing, entering or rendering thereof."[17] This constitution also specified minutely how courts should handle accounts of executors, administrators, and guardians. The Alabama constitution of 1819 provided that "A competent number of justices of the peace shall be appointed in and for each county, in such mode and for such term of office, as the general assembly may direct." Their civil jurisdiction, however, "shall be limited to causes in which the amount in controversy shall not exceed fifty dollars."[18] Clearly, the fifty-dollar limit was no immutable right of man. The Tennessee constitution of 1796 set a ceiling on the governor's salary ($750 a year) and forbade any change before 1804.[19] No one could deduce these numbers from natural law.

There was a point to every clause in these inflated constitutions. Each one reflected the wishes of some faction or interest group, which tried to make its policies permanent by freezing them into the charter. Constitutions, like treaties, preserved the terms of compromise between warring groups. These sometimes took the form of a clause that postponed the power of the state to enact a given kind of law. The federal Constitution left the slave trade untouchable until 1808; until that year "the Migration or Importation of such Persons as any of the States now existing shall think proper to admit, shall not be prohibited by the Congress" (art. I, sec. 9, par. 1). Ohio (1802) made Chillicothe the "seat of government" until 1808; the legislature was not to build itself any buildings until 1809.[20] For very delicate issues, the tactics of constitutionalism appeared essential. Otherwise, slight changes in political power could upset the compromise. One legislature can swiftly repeal the work of another; a constitution is harder to change.

Between 1790 and 1847, state constitutions became more diverse and diffuse. Some developments, like some problems, were peculiar to one state, or to one group of states; some were common to the country as a whole. The most general problems were apportionment and suffrage. Any change in the electoral map or in the right to vote meant a reallocation of political power. The suffrage was a bottleneck of law; who voted determined who ruled. Hence, constitutional disputes over suffrage and apportionment were widespread and sometimes bitter. In Rhode Island, the fran-

[17]Delaware const., 1792, art. VI, sec. 13; const., 1831, art. VI, sec. 20.
[18]Alabama const., 1819, art. V, sec. 10.
[19]Tennessee const., 1796, art. I, sec. 20.
[20]Ohio const., 1802, art. VII, sec. 4.

chise was narrow, and the apportionment scheme outdated. Only those men who owned real estate worth $134 were entitled to vote; this excluded perhaps nine out of ten even of white males over 21. Conservatives stubbornly resisted any change. The so-called "rebellion" of Thomas Dorr (1842) was an unsuccessful, mildly violent attempt to force a change. A new constitution, which went into effect in 1843, finally brought about some measure of reform.[21]

In other states, bloodless revolutions overthrew constitutions and reformed the suffrage. The search for permanence was constant, but permanence escaped men's grasp. The Pennsylvania constitution of 1776, a product of advanced 18th-century liberalism, was replaced in 1790 by a much more conservative constitution; and in 1838 by a moderate one. Statute books were supple; new governments changed them as they wished. Constitutions were brittle. They could be patched up at times; but when they were too deeply impregnated with the policies and interests of an old or lost cause, they had to be completely redone. Inflexibility was the vice of constitutions, as well as the virtue.

An observer with nothing in front of him but the texts of these state constitutions could learn a great deal about state politics, state laws, and about social life in America. The Southern constitutions gave more and more attention, over time, to the protection of slavery, and the repression of free blacks. Legislatures were forbidden to emancipate slaves, unless the master agreed and was compensated. In Pennsylvania (1838) any person who fought a duel, or sent a challenge, or aided or abetted in fighting a duel, was "deprived of the right of holding any office of honor or profit in this State."[22] The Connecticut constitution of 1818, though it paid lip service to freedom of worship, froze every resident into his "congregation, church or religious association." A man might withdraw only by leaving a "written notice thereof with the clerk of such [religious] society."[23] Constitutions often dealt with the state militia, a matter of considerable interest to the Revolutionary generation. In Ohio (1802) brigadiers-general were to be "elected by the commissioned officers of their respective

---

[21]Peter J. Coleman, *The Transformation of Rhode Island, 1790–1860* (1963), pp. 254–94. Rich material on suffrage questions is contained in Merrill D. Peterson, ed., *Democracy, Liberty and Property: The State Constitutional Conventions of the 1820s* (1966); Adams, *The First Constitutions*, pp. 197–217.

[22]Pennsylvania const., 1838, art. VI, sec. 10. Many states had similar clauses.

[23]Conn. const., 1818, art. VII sec. 2.

brigades."[24] Some states barred practicing clergymen from public office. The Tennessee constitution of 1796 testily remarked that "ministers of the gospel are, by their professions, dedicated to God and the care of souls, and ought not to be diverted from the great duties of their functions."[25] The draft constitution of "Franklin," in 1784, would have extended this ban to lawyers and "doctors of physic." The Georgia constitution of 1777 declared that "Estates shall not be entailed; and when a person dies intestate, his or her estate shall be divided equally among their children; the widow shall have a child's share, or her dower, at her option."[26] As early as 1776, North Carolina provided that "the person of a debtor, where there is not a strong presumption of fraud, shall not be confined in prison, after delivering up, *bona fide*, all his estate real and personal, for the use of his creditors, in such manner as shall be hereafter regulated by law."[27] Many 19th-century constitutions contained provisions of this general type, on the subject of imprisonment for debt.

State constitutions reflected the theories of the day on separation of powers, and on checks and balances. The earlier the constitution, however, the weaker the executive branch. For example, 18th-century constitutions gave only feeble powers to the chief executive (called a governor, like his colonial antecedent). His term of official life was typically brief. The Maryland constitution of 1776 solemnly asserted that "a long continuance" in "executive departments" was "dangerous to liberty"; "rotation" was "one of the best securities of permanent freedom." This constitution practiced what it preached. The governor—a "person of wisdom, experience, and virtue"—was to be chosen each year, on the second Monday of November, for a one-year term, by joint ballot of the two houses of the legislature. But he could not continue his wisdom in office "longer than three years successively, nor be eligible as Governor, until expiration of four years after he shall have been out of that office."[28]

[24]Ohio const., 1802, art. VIII, sec. 4.
[25]Tenn. const., 1796, art. VIII, sec. 1.
[26]Ga. const., 1777, art. LI.
[27]N. Car. const., 1776, art. XXXIX. This was also a feature of the Pennsylvania constitution of 1776.
[28]Maryland const., 1776, declaration of rights, art. XXXI, const., arts. XXV, XXXI. The governor had to be rich as well as wise. Only residents above twenty-five years of age, "and having in the State real and personal property above the value of five thousand pounds, current money (one thousand pounds whereof, at least, to be freehold estate) shall be eligible as governor" (art. XXX).

The Pennsylvania constitution of 1776 showed a similar bias. It too called for rotation in office. In England, office tended to depend on the crown or the great grandees; public office was essentially a nice warm udder to be milked. American constitutions firmly rejected this notion. According to the Pennsylvania constitution of 1776, "offices of profit" were not to be established; such offices led officeholders to a state of "dependence and servility unbecoming freemen," and created "faction, contention, corruption, and disorder" in the public (sec. 36). But, as the emphasis on rotation shows, these constitutions also rejected the modern notion of politics as a specific career. Rather, it was a duty, a form of public service, open to the virtuous amateur. This notion, alas, did not long survive.

Early constitutions, as was mentioned, slighted the executive; they preferred to give the lion's share of power to the legislature. In the light of American political history, this was only natural. The colonial governor—and the judiciary, to a certain extent— represented foreign domination. The assemblies, on the other hand, were the voice of local influentials. The Pennsylvania constitution of 1776 gave "supreme legislative power" to a single house of representatives. No upper house or governor's veto checked its power.[29] Over the course of the years, however, the states became disillusioned with legislative supremacy. The governor was one beneficiary of this movement. Typically, he gained a longer term of office, and the power to veto bills. In the federal government, the President had this power from the start.

Judicial power, too, increased at the expense of the legislature. Judicial power took the form of judicial review; the judges, in private litigation, passed on acts of other branches of government; and had the right to declare these acts void if, in the judges' opinion, they were unauthorized by the constitution. Ultimately, judicial review fed on constitutional detail; the more clauses a constitution contained, especially clauses that did something more than set out the basic frame of government, the more potential occasions or excuses for review. But wholesale use of the power was, on the whole, an unsuspected sword in this period. True, in the landmark decision of *Marbury v. Madison* (1803), John Marshall and the Supreme Court, for the first time, dared to declare an act of Congress unconstitutional. But the Court made no clear use of this power, against Congress, for over 50 years. The weapon

[29]J. Paul Selsam, *The Pennsylvania Constitution of 1776* (1936), pp. 183–84.

was used more frequently against *state* statutes. State supreme courts, too, began to exercise judicial review. It was an uncommon technique; it was hated by Jeffersonians; some judges resisted it; it made little impact on the ordinary working of government. But when its occasion arose, it was an instrument of unparalleled power.

Legislative supremacy declined because influential citizens were more afraid of too much law than of not enough. In a number of states, scandals tarnished the reputation of the legislatures. Blocs of voters became afraid that landlords, "moneyed corporations," and other wealthy and powerful forces were too strong in the lobbies of these assemblies. A movement arose to limit the power of the legislatures. Rules to control legislation were written into one constitution after another. The process began modestly enough. Georgia's constitution (1798) outlawed the practice of legislative divorce, except if the parties had gone to "fair trial before the superior court," and obtained a verdict upon "legal principles." Even then, it took a "two-thirds vote of each branch of the legislature"[30] to grant a divorce. Indiana, in 1816, forbade the establishment by statute of any "bank or banking company, or monied institution for the purpose of issuing bills of credit, or bills payable to order or bearer."[31]

The Louisiana constitution of 1845 was something of a turning point. More than those that came before, this constitution was a charter of economic rights and obligations, and a code of legislative procedure, as well as a plain frame of government whose economic import was implicit. The constitution sharply restricted the state's power to pledge its credit or to lend its money. The state was not to "become subscriber to the stock of any corporation or joint-stock company." Lotteries, legislative divorces, and special corporate charters were forbidden. Every law was to "embrace but one subject, and that shall be expressed in the title." No new exclusive privileges or monopolies were to be granted for more than twenty years. No banks of any sort were to be chartered.[32] These were not chance notions. They were not, in the eyes of contemporaries, extreme. The state was trying to reach legitimate legislative goals; but what was new (and ominous) was that it was doing it through anti-legislation: by foreclosing whole areas of law to statutory change. Other states enthusiastically followed

[30]Ga. const., 1798, art. III, sec. 9.
[31]Indiana const., 1816, art. X, sec. 1. But a state bank was allowed.
[32]Louisiana const., 1845, arts. 113, 114, 116, 117, 118, 121, 122, 123, 124, 125.

Louisiana's lead. But when times changed, and conditions changed, these overblown constitutions became all too often embarrassments. They were therefore evaded, or amended, or done over completely.

No two state constitutions were ever exactly alike. But no constitution was pure innovation. Among the states, there was a great deal of copying, of constitutional *stare decisis*.[33] A clause or provision tended to spread far and wide, when it met some felt need, or caught the fancy of lawmakers and constituents. New states embarked on statehood with constitutions that borrowed heaps of clauses and sections from constitutions in older states. Some new states favored the latest, most recent model; others looked to their neighboring states; others to the home state of their settlers. The New York constitution of 1846 left a deep mark on Michigan, and later on Wisconsin. The first constitution of California was heavily indebted to Iowa; Oregon was indebted to Indiana.

Borrowing and influence are not, of course, the same. The states shared a common political culture. Michigan was not a legal satellite of New York; the people in the two states were Americans of the period, and, for the most part, thought alike on political and legal issues. The New York constitution was a recent model; thus people in Michigan used it. When convenient patterns were readily at hand, it was inefficient to start drafting from scratch. Borrowing was always selective. No constitution was swallowed whole. On matters of great importance, conscious choice was never absent. No state was *bound* to adopt the constitution of another state, or any part of it. They adopted out of expedience and fashion.

THE JUDGES

In a common-law system, judges make at least some of the law, even though legal theory has often been coy about admitting this fact. American statesmen were not naive; they knew it mattered what judges believed and who they were. How judges were to be chosen and how they were to act was a political issue in the Revolutionary generation, at a pitch of intensity rarely reached before

[33]J. Willard Hurst, *The Growth of American Law: The Law Makers* (1950), p. 224.

or since. State after state—and the federal government—fought political battles over issues of selection and control of the judges.

The bench was not homogeneous. Judges varied in quality and qualification, from place to place, and according to their position in the judicial pyramid. Local justices of the peace were judges; so were the justices of the United States Supreme Court. English and colonial tradition had allowed for lay judges, as well as for judges learned in law. There were lay judges both at the top and the bottom of the pyramid. In the colonies, the governor frequently served, *ex officio*, as chancellor. New Jersey continued this system, in its constitution of 1776. This constitution also made the governor and council "the court of appeals in the last resort in all causes of law as heretofore."[34] Since governor and council were or might be laymen, this meant that nonlawyers had final control over the conduct of trials and the administration of justice. In the New York system, too, laymen shared power at the apex of the hierarchy of courts. The constitution of 1777 set up a court "for the trial of impeachments, and the correction of errors," consisting of senators as well as judges.[35] This system lasted well into the 19th century.

The lay judges were not necessarily politicians, though this was ordinarily the case. But they were invariably prominent local men. William E. Nelson has studied the background and careers of the eleven men who served as justices of the superior court of Massachusetts between 1760 and 1774, on the eve, that is, of the Revolution. Nine had never practiced law; six had never even studied law. All, however, of these lay judges had "either been born into prominent families or become men of substance." Stephen Sewall, chief justice in 1760, was the nephew of a former chief justice; he had served thirteen years as a tutor at Harvard College.[36]

The base of the pyramid was even more dominated by laymen. Lay justice did not necessarily mean popular or unlettered justice at the trial court level. The English squires were laymen, but hardly men of the people. Lay justice in America had something of the character of rule by the squires. Nor was lay justice nec-

[34]New Jersey const., 1776, art. IX.

[35]New York const., 1777, art. XXXII. In England, too, the highest court, the House of Lords, included laymen as well as judges.

[36]William E. Nelson, *Americanization of the Common Law: The Impact of Legal Change on Massachusetts Society, 1760–1830* (1975), pp. 32–33.

essarily informal. Laymen, after years on the bench, often soaked up the lawyer's jargon and tone. After all, the difference between lawyers and nonlawyers was not that sharp; frequently, a man came to the bar after the briefest of clerkships and with little more than a smattering of Blackstone. The way lay judges absorbed their law was not much different from the way men in general learned to be "lawyers."

There are many anecdotes in print about the coarseness and stupidity of lay judges. Old lawyers, writing years later, and historians of bench and bar, have tended to drag the reputation of these judges through the mud. For sentimental and other reasons, these lawyers and lawyer-historians wanted to exaggerate the rawness and vulgarity of pioneer judges, and to make the point that laymen who wore the clothing of judges must be incompetent. The actual facts are harder to unearth. Popular feelings against the courts, in the late 18th century, had nothing to do with whether judges were laymen or not. The complaint was not that justice was crude, but that it was biased in favor of creditors, in favor of the rich.

In any event, the lay judge was in slow retreat throughout the period. Eventually, he disappeared entirely from upper courts. The first lawyer on Vermont's supreme court was Nathaniel Chipman (1752–1843). He took office, in 1787, as an assistant judge of the court. Not one of the other four judges was an attorney.[37] On such a court, a lawyer found it easy to take the lead. Chipman later became chief justice, and edited law reports for Vermont. In other states, professionalization came even earlier. All five of the judges of the Virginia Court of Appeals, established in 1788, were lawyers; Edmund Pendleton headed the court.[38]

Historically, judges were appointed from above. But American democracy put strong emphasis on controls from below. This implied some more popular way to choose the judges. The Vermont constitution of 1777 gave to the "freemen in each county" the "liberty of choosing the judges of inferior court of common pleas, sheriff, justices of the peace, and judges of probates."[39] Under the Ohio constitution of 1802, "judges of the supreme court, the

[37]Daniel Chipman, *The Life of the Hon. Nathaniel Chipman, Ll. D.* (1846), p. 69.
[38]See S. S. P. Patteson, "The Supreme Court of Appeals of Virginia," 5 Green Bag 310, 313–18 ff. (1893).
[39]Vermont const., 1777, ch. II, sec. 27. See, in general, Evan Haynes, *The Selection and Tenure of Judges* (1944).

presidents and the associate judges of the courts of common pleas" were to be "appointed by a joint ballot of both houses of the general assembly, and shall hold their offices for the term of seven years, if so long they behave well."[40] This gave the electorate at least an indirect voice in judicial selection. Georgia in 1812, and Indiana in 1816, provided for popular election of some judges;[41] Mississippi in 1832 adopted popular election for all. New York followed in 1846, and the rush was on.

The movement, according to Willard Hurst, was "one phase of the general swing toward broadened suffrage and broader popular control of public office which Jacksonian Democracy built on the foundations laid by Jefferson." It was a movement, however, "based on emotion rather than on a deliberate evaluation of experience under the appointive system."[42] The hard facts about judicial behavior were never easy to come by. There is no simple way to compare elected and appointed judges. Still, if judges were not elected, how could they be forced to respond to the will of the people?

There was plenty of evidence from which a jaundiced mind could conclude that judges were political men, and had to be kept in check. Thomas Jefferson, and his party-members, in particular, were quite convinced of this. Federal judges were appointed for life. Before Jefferson came to power, they were naturally Federalists. Their behavior was quite controversial. To Jefferson's men, the judges seemed "partial, vindictive, and cruel," men who "obeyed the President rather than the law, and made their reason subservient to their passion."[43] As John Adams was leaving office,

[40]Ohio const., 1802, art. III, sec. 8.

[41]In Georgia, the "justices of the Inferior Courts" were to be elected for four-year terms, Georgia const., 1798, art. III, sec. 4 (amendment, ratified 1812); in Indiana, the supreme court was appointed by the governor, the president of the circuit court by "joint ballot of both branches of the General Assembly"; associate judges of the circuit courts were to be "elected by the qualified electors in the respective counties." Indiana const., 1816, art. V, sec. 7.

[42]J. Willard Hurst, *The Growth of American Law: The Law Makers* (1950), p. 140. Jacksonian democracy did not mean, necessarily, that every man could or should be a judge. Jackson himself, for example, did not appoint the common man to the bench. His appointments were men of high status, by background or achievement, just as Adams's were. But the Jacksonian *attitude* differed from the earlier one; this may have led to change in the long run. See Sidney H. Aronson, *Status and Kinship in the Higher Civil Service* (1964), p. 170.

[43]Quoted in Charles Warren, *The Supreme Court in United States History*, vol. I (1923), p. 191.

in 1801, Congress passed a Judiciary Act.[44] The act created a flock of new judgeships, among other things. Adams nominated judges to fill these new posts; they were confirmed by the Senate in the last moments of the Adams regime. Jefferson's party raged at these "midnight judges." It was a final attempt, Jefferson thought, to stock the bench forever with his political enemies.

The law that created the "midnight judges" was repealed; the judges lost their jobs; but the other Federalist judges stayed on serenely in office. These holdover judges threatened Jefferson's program, he felt; there was no easy way to be rid of them: "Few die and none resign." He wanted to limit their power; he wanted to make them more responsive to national policy—as embodied, of course, in Jefferson and in his party. John Marshall, the Chief Justice of the United States, was particularly obnoxious to Jefferson. He was a man of enormous talents, and (as luck would have it) enjoyed good health and long life. He outlived a score of would-be heirs to the office, including Spencer Roane of Virginia, and cheated a whole line of Presidents of the pleasure of replacing him. Equally annoying to Jefferson and his successors was the fact that later justices, who were not Federalists, seemed to fall under Marshall's spell, once they were safely on the bench. Madison appointed Joseph Story, who was at least a lukewarm Democrat. On the bench, he became a rabid fan of the Chief Justice. Roger Brooke Taney, who finally replaced John Marshall, had been a favorite of Andrew Jackson, and a member of his cabinet. But Taney, too, became living proof of the perils of lifetime tenure. He outlived his popularity with dominant opinion, at least in the North. The author of the *Dred Scott* decision tottered on in office until 1864, when the Civil War was almost over.

The prestige of federal courts stands high today, particularly with liberals and intellectuals. An independent court system is (at least potentially) a tower of strength for the poor, for the downtrodden, for the average person facing big institutions or big government. Hence Jefferson's famous fight against the Federalist judges is one policy of his party that has not done well in the court of history. Yet, undeniably, some federal judges behaved in ways that would be considered disgraceful today. Federal judges did

[44] 2 Stats. 89 (act of Feb. 13, 1801); repealed, 2 Stats. 132 (act of March 8, 1802). See Erwin C. Surrency, "The Judiciary Act of 1801," 2 Am. J. Legal Hist. 53 (1958).

not run for re-election; but they played a more active political role than is standard for judges today. Some Federalists made what were in effect election speeches from the bench. They harangued grand juries in a most partisan way. This gave some point to Jefferson's attacks. Other judges were more discreet, but (in Jefferson's view) equally partisan. One of the sources of Marshall's strength was his tremendous solemnity. His opinions, mellifluous, grandly styled, even pompous, purported to be timeless and non-political. They appealed to principle, to the sacred words of the Constitution. Their tone implied that their true author was the law itself in all its majesty; the judge was a detached, impartial vessel. This attitude annoyed Jefferson inordinately, who saw in it nothing but a subtle, maddening hypocrisy. Either way, it was an effective piece of political theater.

Jefferson's attacks on the judges did not totally fail. Like Roosevelt's plan to pack the court in 1937, Jefferson and his successors may have lost the battle but won the war. In both cases, an extreme tactic—the threat of impeachment, a court-packing plan—ended in failure. But perhaps, in both cases, the real impact of the tactic was to scare the opposition; it served its chief role as a bogeyman, and not without impact.

The Constitution gave federal judges tenure for life. It left only one way open to get rid of judges: the terrible sword of impeachment. Federal judges could be impeached for "Treason, Bribery, or other high Crimes and Misdemeanors" (art. II, sec. 4). The South Carolina constitution of 1790 permitted impeachment for "misdemeanor in office" (art. V, sec. 3). Literally interpreted, then, the law permitted impeachment only in rare and extreme situations.[45] But there were a few notable cases, in the early 19th century, in which impeachment was used to drive enemies of party and state out of office. In 1803, Alexander Addison, presiding judge of the fifth judicial district in Pennsylvania, was impeached and removed from his office. He was a bitter-end Federalist; as a lower-court judge, he harangued grand juries on political subjects. On one occasion, he refused to let an associate judge speak to the grand jury in rebuttal; impeachment was grounded on this incident. A straight party vote removed Addison

[45]In some states, the wording of the constitution was much less emphatic. So, in New Hampshire, under the constitution of 1792, the governor, with the consent of the council, might "remove" judges "upon the address of both houses of the legislature" (part II, sec. 73).

from the bench. Eighteen Republicans in the Pennsylvania senate voted him guilty; four Federalists voted for acquittal.[46]

On the federal level, the purge drew first blood in 1804. It was a rather shabby victory. John Pickering, a Federalist judge, was impeached and removed from office. He had committed no "high crimes and misdemeanors"; but he was an old man, a drunk, and seriously deranged. It was understandable to want him off the bench; but it was far from clear that the words of the Constitution applied to this kind of case. Pickering's removal was, in fact, a stroke of politics, a dress rehearsal for a far more important assault, the impeachment of Samuel Chase.[47]

This celebrated affair took place soon after Pickering's trial. Chase was a Justice of the United States Supreme Court. He had a long and distinguished career, but he was an uncompromising partisan, and a man with a terrible temper. He too was notorious for grand-jury charges that were savage attacks on the party in power. President Jefferson stayed in the background; but his close associates moved articles of impeachment against Chase. The articles of impeachment made a number of specific charges of misconduct against Chase; among them, that at a circuit court, in Baltimore, in May 1803, he did "pervert his official right and duty to address the grand jury" by delivering "an intemperate and inflammatory political harangue," behavior which was "highly indecent, extra-judicial and tending to prostitute the high judicial character with which he was invested to the low purpose of an electioneering partisan."[48]

But the anti-Chase faction overplayed its hand. In a frank private conversation, Senator Giles of Virginia admitted what was really at stake:

> a removal by impeachment [is] nothing more than a declaration by Congress to this effect: You hold dangerous opinions, and if you are suffered to carry them into effect you will work the destruction of the nation. *We want your offices,*

[46]S. W. Higginbotham, *The Keystone in the Democratic Arch: Pennsylvania Politics, 1800–1816* (1952), pp. 53–55.

[47]Lynn W. Turner, "The Impeachment of John Pickering," 54 Am. Hist. Rev. 485 (1949). It is not certain that the constitutional provision on impeachment was as restricted in meaning as has been commonly supposed. For background, see Raoul Berger, "Impeachment of Judges and 'Good Behavior' Tenure," 79 Yale L.J. 1475 (1970).

[48]*Report of the Trial of the Hon. Samuel Chase* (1805); Appendix, pp. 5–6; see also Richard B. Lillich, "The Chase Impeachment," 4 Am. J. Legal Hist. 49 (1960).

for the purpose of giving them to men who will fill them better.[49]

The trial was long, bitter, sensational. Republicans defected in enough numbers so that Chase was acquitted, by the slimmest of margins. John Marshall and his court were thenceforward "secure." It was the end of what Albert Beveridge claimed was "one of the few really great crises in American history."[50] In January 1805, an attempt was made to impeach all but one of the judges on Pennsylvania's highest court; it failed by a narrow vote.[51] Impeachment was not a serious threat after these years.

Another radical plan to get rid of bad judges was to abolish their offices. Of course, Jefferson could not do away with the Supreme Court, even had he wanted to; that would have meant major Constitutional change, which was clearly impossible. But his administration repealed the Judiciary Act of 1801; that at least put the midnight judges out of business. An ingenious method for removing unpopular judges was tried out in Kentucky. In 1823, the Kentucky court of appeals struck down certain laws for relief of debtors; this act aroused a storm of protest. Under Kentucky law, the legislature could remove judges by a two-thirds vote; the "relief party" could not muster that percentage. Instead, the legislature abolished the court of appeals and created a new court of four judges, to be appointed by the governor. The old court did not quietly give up its power. For a time, two courts of appeal tried to function in the state, and state politics was dominated by the dispute between "old court" and "new court" factions. Most lower courts obeyed the old court; a few followed the new court; a few tried to recognize both. Ultimately, the "old court" party won control of the legislature, and abolished the new court (over the governor's veto). The old court was awarded back pay; the new court was treated as if it had never existed at all.[52]

[49]Quoted in J. Willard Hurst, *The Growth of American Law*, p. 136.
[50]Albert Beveridge, *The Life of John Marshall*, vol. III (1919), p. 220.
[51]S. W. Higginbotham, *The Keystone in the Democratic Arch*, p. 79.
[52]On this controversy, see George DuRelle, "John Boyle," in *Great American Lawyers*, vol. II (1907), pp. 221–59. There were cleaner ways than impeachment or abolition of courts to get rid of old and inconvenient judges. Under the New York constitution of 1821 (art. V, sec. 3), the chancellor and justices of the supreme court had to retire at the age of sixty. (A similar provision, art. 24, had been part of the New York Constitution of 1777.) The clause ended the judicial career of James Kent, who left office in 1823 and took a kind of revenge by writing his famous *Commentaries*.

As these crises died down, it seemed as if the forces of light had triumphed over darkness—that this country was to have a free, independent judiciary rather than a servile mouthpiece of state. The Chase impeachment failed (it is said) because in the end both parties believed in a strong, independent judiciary; both believed in the separation of powers. Many politicians did in fact have qualms about impeachment; it smacked of overkill. Some of Jefferson's men shared these qualms. They did not feel that a sitting judge should be replaced on political grounds. But the failure of impeachment was not a clear-cut victory for either side. It was rather a kind of social compromise. The judges won independence, but at a price. Their openly political role was reduced; and ultimately most states turned to the elective principle. There would be no more impeachments, but also no more Chases. What carried the day, in a sense, was the John Marshall solution. The judges would take refuge in professional decorum. It would always be part of their job to make and interpret policy; but policy would be divorced from overt, partisan politics. Principles and policy would flow, at least ostensibly, from the logic of law; they would not follow the naked give and take of the courthouse square. Justice would be blind; and it would wear a poker face. This picture of the behavior of judges had enough truth, and enough hypnotic force, to influence the role-playing of judges, and to bring some peace and consensus to issues of tenure, selection, behavior, and removal of judges.

This did not mean that judges could, or would, avoid the minefields of politics and policy. High courts faced sensitive issues every term. Some of these issues were so charged with emotion that the veil of objectivity fell or was torn from the judges' faces. *Dred Scott*, in 1857, was an example of the court overreaching itself—a blatant political act, and more significantly, a wrong-headed one.[53] There were many minor *Dred Scotts* at lower levels of decision. Prejudice and arrogance in court did not die out in 1810, or 1820, or ever, but it became less overt; in any event, it became harder to document. Long after Chase, there were political trials in the United States, and judges who persecuted unpopular or dissenting men. In 1845, Circuit Judge Amasa J. Parker presided at the trial of the antirent rioters of upstate New York; his behavior was as partisan and prejudiced as any Federalist judge of the early

---

[53]The definitive treatment of the case is Don E. Fehrenbacher's book, *The Dred Scott Case: Its Significance in American Law and Politics* (1978).

1800s.[54] But more and more, the judges assumed the outward posture of propriety.

Meanwhile, the actual power of judges, as makers of doctrine and framers of rules, may have actually grown somewhat after 1800. The courts had to hammer out legal propositions to run the business of the country, to sift what was viable from what was not in the common-law tradition, to handle disputes and problems thrown up in the course of political, social, and technological change. Once case reports began to be published, judges had rich opportunities to mold law, as logic and social sense directed, and as the docket, responsive to outside pressure and the demands of the litigants, required. They did not let the opportunity slide. The legal generation of 1776 had been a generation of political thinkers and statesmen. The Constitution of the United States is their greatest legal monument. In the next generation, the great state papers, in a sense, were such judicial opinions as *Marbury* v. *Madison*, or the *Dartmouth College Case*. The best of the early 19th-century judges had a subtle, accurate political sense, and firm economic and social beliefs. In particular, the judges turned their attention to law in one of its prosaic meanings: the workaday rules of American life. They built and molded doctrine—scaffolding (as they saw it) to support the architecture of human affairs.

Perhaps the greatest of the judges was John Marshall, Chief Justice of the United States. He, more than anyone else, gave federal judgeship its meaning. It was, of course, conceded that the judiciary made up a co-ordinate branch of government. They were separate, but were they equal? In *Marbury* v. *Madison* (1803), John Marshall invented or affirmed the power of judicial review over acts of Congress. But the *Marbury* decision was only a single dramatic instance of Marshall's work. His doctrines *made* constitutional law. He personally transformed the function and meaning of the Supreme Court. When he came on the bench, in 1801, the Supreme Court was a frail and fledgling institution. In 1789, Robert Hanson Harrison turned down a position on the court to become chancellor of Maryland. John Jay resigned in 1795 to run for governor of New York.[55] In the first years, the court heard very few cases; it made little impact on the nation. By the time

[54]Described in Henry Christman, *Tin Horns and Calico* (1945), pp. 220–41.

[55]The election for governor of New York was held in April, 1795, and Jay's opponent happened to be Abraham Yates, chief justice of the New York supreme court; in short, no matter who won, it was inevitable that a judge would desert the bench for a governorship.

Marshall died, the court was fateful and great.

Marshall had a sure touch for institutional solidity. Before he became Chief Justice, the judges delivered *seriatim* (separate) opinions, one after another, in the English style. Marshall, however, put an end to this practice. The habit of "caucusing opinions," and delivering up one unanimous opinion only, as the "opinion of *the Court*" had been tried by Lord Mansfield in England. It was abandoned there; but Marshall revived the practice. Unanimity was the rule on the Court; for a while, until William Johnson (1777–1834) was appointed by Jefferson, in 1804, the unanimity was absolute, with not a single dissenting opinion. Johnson broke this surface consensus.[56] Yet neither Johnson nor any later justices could or would undo Marshall's work. Doctrines changed; personalities and blocs clashed on the court; power contended with power; but these struggles all took place within the fortress that Marshall had built. The court remained strong and surprisingly independent. Jefferson hoped that Johnson would enter the lists against Marshall. Yet Johnson more than once sided with Marshall, in opposition to Jefferson, his leader and friend. The nature and environment of the court—life tenure, the influence of colleagues—loosened his other allegiances. It was to be a story often told. Joseph Story betrayed Madison; Oliver Wendell Holmes bitterly disappointed Theodore Roosevelt; the Warren Burger court slapped Richard Nixon in the face.

There were strong leaders and builders in the state courts, too. James Kent dominated his court in New York, in the early 19th century. As he remembered it, "The first practice was for each judge to give his portion of opinions, when we all agreed, but that gradually fell off, and, for the last two or three years before I left the Bench, I gave the most of them. I remember that in eighth Johnson[57] all the opinions for one term are '*per curiam.*' The fact is I wrote them all...."[58] Kent's pride in his work was justified. But the opportunity for creative work was there. The judges were

[56]Donald G. Morgan, *Justice William Johnson: The First Dissenter* (1954), pp. 168–89; the phrase about "caucusing opinions" is from a letter written by Jefferson. See also Karl M. ZoBell, "Division of Opinion in the Supreme Court: A History of Judicial Disintegration," 44 Cornell L.Q. 186 (1959).

[57]That is, the eighth volume of Johnson's *Reports* of New York cases. Kent is referring to the October term, 1811, of the New York Supreme Court. 8 Johns. 361–492. *Per curiam* means "by the court," that is, the opinion is not signed by any particular or specific judge.

[58]Quoted in William Kent, *Memoirs and Letters of James Kent* (1898), p. 118.

independent in two senses: free from England, but also free, for the moment, from stifling partisan control. Also, they were published. The colonial judges, who left no monuments behind, are forgotten men. From 1800 on, strong-minded American judges, whose work was recorded, influenced their courts and the law. In New York there was, as we mentioned, Chancellor Kent (1776– 1847); in Massachusetts, Theophilus Parsons (1750–1813) and Lemuel Shaw (1781–1861); in Pennsylvania, John B. Gibson (1780–1853); in North Carolina, Thomas Ruffin (1787–1870); in Ohio, Peter Hitchcock (1781–1853); in Louisiana, Francis Xavier Martin (1762–1846).

The spheres of these state judges were less floodlit, of course, than the Supreme Court in its greater moments. Their work had less national significance. But in their states, and in the world of the common law, they made a definite impact. Some were excellent stylists; all wrote in what Karl Llewellyn has called the Grand Style:[59] their opinions were often little treatises, moving from elegant premise to elaborate conclusion, ranging far and wide over subject matter boldly defined. They were, at their best, far-sighted men, impatient with narrow legal logic. Marshall, Gibson, and Shaw could write for pages without citing a shred of "authority." They did not choose to base their decisions on precedent alone; law had to be chiseled out of basic principle; the traditions of the past were merely evidence of principle, and rebuttable. Their grasp of the spirit of the law was tempered by what they understood to be the needs of a living society. Some were conservative men, passionately attached to tradition; but they honored tradition, not for its own sake, but for the values that inhered in it. And they became famous not because they stuck to the past, but because they worked on and with the living law. Most of the great judges were scholarly men; a few were very erudite, like Joseph Story, who could stud his opinions with acres of citation—a thing Marshall tended to avoid. The great judges were creative, self-aware, and willing to make changes. James Kent described his work as chancellor as follows:

> I took the court as if it had been a new institution, and never before known in the United States. I had nothing to guide me, and was left at liberty to assume all such English Chancery

[59]Karl N. Llewellyn, "Remarks on the Theory of Appellate Decision and the Rules or Canons about How Statutes Are to Be Construed," 3 Vanderbilt L. Rev. 395, 396 (1950). See below, part III, ch. XI, p. 622.

powers and jurisdiction as I thought applicable.... This gave me grand scope, and I was checked only by the revision of the Senate, or Court of Errors....

> My practice was, first, to make myself perfectly and accurately... master of the facts.... I saw where justice lay, and the moral sense decided the court half the time; and I then sat down to search the authorities until I had examined my books. I might once in a while be embarrassed by a technical rule, but I most always found principles suited to my views of the case....[60]

Kent noticed that no one ever cited the work of his predecessors. Their opinions, unpublished, were gone with the wind. He made sure he would not share that fate. He worked closely with William Johnson (1769–1848), who reported his cases. Other judges did this job themselves. F. X. Martin compiled Louisiana decisions from 1811 to 1830; during much of this time, he was himself one of the judges. Many judges were active in collecting, revising, or digesting the statutes of their states, and in writing or rewriting treatises. Joseph Story wrote a series of definitive treatises on various branches of law. James Kent, after retiring from the bench, wrote his monumental *Commentaries.* John F. Grimke (1753–1819) published the laws of South Carolina, wrote a treatise on the "Duty of Executors and Administrators," and the inevitable "South Carolina Justice of the Peace" (1788). Harry Toulmin (1766–1823) edited the statutes of Kentucky; then, as judge of Mississippi Territory, he edited the territorial statutes. Still later, in Alabama Territory, he edited the statutes there too.

Many appellate judges were versatile and highly educated. George Wythe of Virginia (1726–1806), chancellor of the state from 1788 to 1801, was perhaps the foremost classical scholar in the state; as "professor of law and policy" at William and Mary (1779–1790), he occupied the first chair of law in an American college. Augustus B. Woodward (1774–1827), judge of Michigan Territory from 1805, prepared a plan for the city of Detroit, wrote on political subjects, and published a book called *A System of Universal Science.*[61] Some judges were classicists, had gifts for science or language, or, like Story, wrote bad poetry. Theophilus Parsons

---

[60]Quoted in William Kent, *Memoirs and Letters of James Kent* (1898), pp. 158–59.

[61]On Woodward, see Frank B. Woodford, *Mr. Jefferson's Disciple: A Life of Justice Woodward* (1953).

of Massachusetts published a paper on astronomy, and dabbled in mathematics. His "Formula for Extracting the Roots of Adjected Equations" appears as an appendix to the memoir of his life, which his son published in 1859. Parsons was also a Greek scholar and wrote a Greek grammar, which was never published. John Gibson of Pennsylvania was a devotee of French and Italian literature, a student of Shakespeare and an excellent violinist. He was probably the only major judge who designed his own false teeth. William Johnson, while a Supreme Court justice, wrote and published a life of Nathanael Greene, in two volumes, nearly 1,000 pages long.[62] He was also an active member of the Charleston, South Carolina, horticultural society, and wrote a "Memoire on the Strawberry" in 1832.[63] John Marshall himself wrote a life of George Washington.

Most frequently, judges had political careers before they reached the bench. Although most of them willingly "put aside ambition" when they "donned the ermine," their prior lives probably included elective or appointive office. On the frontier, judging was only one aspect of a politician's busy life. Harry Toulmin, in the Old Southwest, was "also postmaster, preached and officiated at funerals and marriages, made Fourth of July orations, practiced medicine gratuitously and in general was the head of the settlements."[64] Before his arrival in the territory, he had been secretary of state in Kentucky. John Boyle (1774–1835), chief justice of Kentucky, was a member of Congress before he became a judge. Joseph Story was speaker of the Massachusetts House when he was appointed to the court. For some judges—John Jay, for example—judgeship was an interlude between other political posts.

Judgeship, then, was not a lifetime career for all judges. It was a stepping-stone, or a refuge from politics, or a political reward. It was not a distinctive career, with its own distinctive pattern of training and background, as in many Continental countries. Judgeship was a matter of luck and opportunity, not special skill, background, or aspiration. It was and is an offshoot of the bar— of that part of the bar active in political affairs. Kermit Hall studied the men appointed to the federal bench between 1829 and 1861.

[62]Donald G. Morgan, *Justice William Johnson: The First Dissenter* (1954), pp. 148–49.

[63]Irwin F. Greenberg, "Justice William Johnson: South Carolina Unionist, 1823–1830," 36 Pa. Hist. 307, 331n (1969).

[64]Dunbar Rowland, *Courts, Judges and Lawyers of Mississippi, 1798–1935*, vol. I (1935), p. 21.

An astonishing 78 percent of the judges had held prior elective public office. This was the Jacksonian era; but it was also true (though to a slightly lesser degree) of the pre-Jacksonians—65 percent of those federal judges had served in elective office.[65]

A prominent lawyer usually took a cut in income when he became a judge. The salaries of judges, as of public officials in general, were not generous. Judges continually complained that they were pinched for money. By statute in 1827, New Jersey fixed the salary of the justices of the state supreme court at $1,100. The chief justice earned $1,200. The governor earned $2,000.[66] Lemuel Shaw became chief justice of Massachusetts in 1830, at a salary of $3,000. The low salary, in fact, was the only source of reluctance for Shaw. For trial judges, the fee system was common. A New York law of 1786 awarded fees to the "judge of the court of probates ... to wit; For filing every petition, one shilling; for making and entering every order, six shillings; for every citation, under seal, to witnesses, or for any other purposes, six shillings ... for copies of all records and proceedings, when required, for each sheet consisting of one hundred and twenty-eight words, one shilling and six-pence."[67] Under the fee system, some lower-court judges got rich. Still, a seat on a state Supreme Court paid off in the coin of high status.

THE ORGANIZATION OF COURTS

The Constitution of 1787 created a new system of federal courts. Like the privy council before 1776, the federal courts had power to review the work of state courts. The extent of that power was and still is a matter of constant redefinition. It was limited severely in scope by the Constitution; yet, in its sphere, it was more potent than colonial review by the British government. Federal courts were close at hand; no ocean intervened; they were familiar with local problems and how to handle them. The Constitution gave the federal courts jurisdiction in admiralty; and, on matters of federal law, litigants could appeal from state to federal courts. In nonfederal matters, however, the states and their courts were

[65]Kermit L. Hall, *The Politics of Justice: Lower Federal Judicial Selection and the Second Party System, 1829–61* (1979), p. 166–67.
[66]Acts N.J. 1827, p. 9.
[67]Laws N.Y. 1778–92, vol. I (1792), p. 240.

supreme. Of course, the judicial clauses of the Constitution merely set an evolution in process and marked off some of its obvious limits. No one even dreamt of the vast powers that would grow from these 18th-century seeds. In the late 18th century, and in the first half of the 19th, the federal courts clearly played second fiddle to the state courts. Where they were supreme, they were supreme; but the realm was a narrow one. Little is known about the way the lower federal courts functioned. A pioneer study, by Mary K. Tachau, examined the records of the federal court in Kentucky, between 1789 and 1816. She found a surprisingly active, useful, and competent court, handling a large volume of casework, in a place that was at the very rim of American civilization.[68]

The federal Constitution was a document of its time, bearing the mark of contemporary theory. In particular, it embodied concepts of separation of powers, and the idea of checks and balances in government. These theories also influenced judicial organization in the states. But the states did not immediately move to seal off judicial power from the rest of the government. It was a deep-seated tradition to mix branches of government at the highest level. In Connecticut, the governor, lieutenant governor, and council constituted a "Supreme Court of Errors." Formerly the legislature itself had acted as the court of last resort.[69] In New Jersey, under the constitution of 1776, the governor held the office of chancellor; and together with his council, constituted "the court of appeals in the last resort." In New York, the court for the "trial of impeachments and the correction of errors"—the highest court, under the constitutions of 1777 and 1821—consisted of the president of the senate, the senators, the chancellor, and the justices of the supreme court.[70]

One by one, however, states began to give their highest court final judicial authority. In New Jersey, the constitution of 1844, in New York, the constitution of 1846, put the seal on this change. Rhode Island was the last state to join the movement. As late as the 1850s, the legislature passed an act which in effect granted a new trial in a pending case. The Rhode Island court, in 1856, interposed itself, labeled the practice intolerable, and appealed to

[68]Mary K. Bonsteel Tachau, *Federal Courts in the Early Republic: Kentucky, 1789–1816* (1978).

[69]Roscoe Pound, *Organization of Courts* (1940), p. 95.

[70]New Jersey const., 1776, art. IX; New York const., 1777, art. XXXII; New York const., 1821, art. V, sec. 1.

the concept of separation of powers.[71] By that time, political opinion, almost universally, rejected this kind of legislative pretension.
On the other hand, throughout the period legislatures passed
private acts that filled functions now thought of as purely judicial
or executive. They granted charters for beginning corporations,
and divorces for ending marriages. They quieted title to property,
declared heirships, and legalized changes of name.

As in colonial days, in most states there was no clear-cut division
between trial and appellate courts. High-court judges often doubled as trial or circuit judges. Appellate terms of court were held
in the capital at fixed times of the year. In between, judges spent
part of the year on coach or horseback, traveling circuit. Circuit
duty was a considerable hardship. The country was large and
sparsely settled, the interior a wilderness. Roads were made tortuous by mud or dust, depending on the season. Often, the judges
rode circuit in their home districts, which somewhat lightened the
burden. Still, many judges complained ceaselessly of their gypsy
life. The system did have some virtues. It brought justice close to
home; it conserved judicial manpower. Circuit duty gave the appellate judge actual trial experience. This gave him exposure to
real litigants, and this (some felt) was good for his soul.

Trial work also cemented relations between bench and bar.
Around 1800, in York County, in what later became the state of
Maine, judges and lawyers traveled together, argued together,
joked together, drank and lived together; this traveling "collection
of lawyers, jurors, suitors, and witnesses filled up the small villages
in which the courts were held." Often there was literally no room
at the inn. "It was quite a privilege, enjoyed by few, to obtain a
separate bed." The members of the bar "were no ascetics. The
gravity and dignity of the bar...were very apt to be left in the
courtroom—they were seldom seen in the bar room."[72] On the
frontier, the circuit system bred a rugged type of judge. In Missouri, around 1840, Charles H. Allen, appointed to one of the
Missouri circuits, traveled "on horseback from Palmyra," his home,
about two hundred miles; then "around the circuit, about eight
hundred more. This he did three times a year, spending nearly
his whole time in the saddle. He was, however, a strong, robust
man, and capable of the greatest endurance. He always traveled

---

[71]*Taylor & Co.* v. *Place,* 4 R.I. 324 (1856).
[72]William Willis, *A History of the Law, the Courts, and the Lawyers of Maine* (1863),
p. 278.

with a holster of large pistols in front of his saddle, and a knife with a blade at least a foot long. But for his dress, a stranger might have readily taken him for a cavalry officer."[73]

As the states grew in wealth and population, they tended to sharpen the distinction between trial courts and courts of appeal. Some states established tiers of intermediate courts, called circuit courts, superior courts, or courts of common pleas. These middle courts were typically trial courts of quite general jurisdiction. They also heard appeals, or retried matters begun in the lowest courts. The supreme court tended to become more and more an appeal court, even if the judges, on occasion, still rode circuit.

Only the highest courts, chiefly the Supreme Court of the United States, have been the subject of any sizeable amount of historical research. The judges of the Supreme Court wore robes, stood heir to a great tradition, and heard cases of far-reaching importance. The further down one goes in the pyramid of courts, state or federal, the thinner the trickle of research. Yet it is certain that the everyday courts, churning out thousands of decisions on questions of debt, crime, family affairs, and title to land, were of vital importance to society. Who were the trial court judges? And what sorts of people served as justices of the peace? What was their background and influence? The justice of the peace was "arch symbol of our emphasis on local autonomy in the organization of courts," reflecting the "practical need, in a time of poor and costly communications, to bring justice close to each man's door."[74] But what was the quality of that justice? How much of the justice's work was social control of the English type—autocratic guidance through democratic forms? The role and function of lower-court judges probably changed greatly between 1790 and 1840; and there were probably great differences between East, West, and South. But little about form, function, and staff is definitely known.

State courts tended more toward specialization than the federal courts. Some states, for example, used separate courts for wills and probate matters. Others, as is the practice today, gave these problems over to courts of general jurisdiction. In New Jersey, the "ordinary" probated wills, and granted letters of administration and guardianship in his "prerogative court." Other estate matters were handled in New Jersey by the oddly named orphans'

---

[73]W. V. N. Bay, *Reminiscences of the Bench and Bar of Missouri* (1878), p. 211.

[74]J. Willard Hurst, *The Growth of American Law: The Law Makers* (1950), p. 148. For a rare study of the lower courts in a state, see Robert M. Ireland, *The County Courts in Antebellum Kentucky* (1972).

court.[75] This tribunal was composed of judges who also served on the court of common pleas in the New Jersey counties.[76] Some states kept separate courts for equity. Georgia's constitution of 1789 (art. III, sec. 3) declared that "Courts-merchant shall be held as heretofore"; but the constitution of 1798 deleted the clause. In Delaware, there were courts of oyer and terminer, and courts of general sessions and jail delivery. Memphis, Cairo, and Chattanooga had their own municipal courts, New York its mayor's court; Richmond's hustings court preserved an ancient, honorable name. The St. Louis Land Court (1855) was an unusual example of specialization.

Unlike the state constitutions, which often discussed the structure of courts in some detail, the federal Constitution was quite laconic on the subject. Judicial power was to be vested in a "Supreme Court" and such "inferior courts" as "the Congress may from time to time ordain and establish." For a few types of cases, the Supreme Court was to have "original" jurisdiction, meaning that these cases came to the Court right off the bat, and not by way of appeal. This was true for cases involving ambassadors, and those to which a state was party. Congress had power to decide how much appellate jurisdiction, and of what sort, the Supreme Court would enjoy. The President had power to appoint justices, subject to Senate confirmation. The Senate proved to be no rubber stamp. George Washington appointed John Rutledge of South Carolina to succeed Chief Justice Jay. A bloc of Federalists, annoyed that Rutledge had opposed Jay's treaty, punished him by refusing confirmation, though Rutledge had already served a few months on an interim basis, and had even written a few opinions.[77]

Under the Constitution, Congress could have dispensed with any lower federal courts. State courts would then have had original jurisdiction over all but a few federal issues. The famous Judiciary Act of 1789 provided otherwise.[78] It divided the country into districts, each district generally coextensive with a state, each with a Federal District Court, and a District Judge. The districts, in turn, were grouped into three circuits. In each circuit, a circuit court, made up of two Supreme Court justices and one district

[75]Pennsylvania, too, had a court with this name. An "ordinary," in England, had been an official in the church courts.

[76]Stats. N.J. 1847, p. 205.

[77]Charles Warren, *The Supreme Court in United States History*, vol. I (rev. ed., 1935), pp. 128–39.

[78]For the early history of federal jurisdiction, see Felix Frankfurter and James

judge, sat twice a year. In general, the circuit courts handled cases of diversity of citizenship—cases in which citizens of different states were on opposite sides of the case. The district courts heard admiralty matters. In certain limited situations, the circuit courts heard appeals.

One defect of the system was that it forced the justices to climb into carriages and travel to their circuits. At first, the justices were on circuit twice a year. Later, the burden was lightened to once a year. Additional judges were added to the court, and new circuits were created as the country grew. But these changes helped only a little. In 1838, Justice McKinley traveled 10,000 miles in and to his circuit (Alabama, Louisiana, Mississippi, Arkansas). Five other justices traveled between 2,000 and 3,500 miles each.[79] As with state courts, there were those who argued that circuit duty was beneficial. It brought the judges closer to the people; it retaught them the legal problems of trial work. But as Gouverneur Morris pointed out, no one could argue that

> riding rapidly from one end of this country to another is the best way to study law.... Knowledge may be more conveniently acquired in the closet than in the high road.[80]

Reform proved politically impossible. In Congress, a strong states-rights bloc was hostile to the federal courts. This bloc saw no reason to cater to the judges' convenience. The Judiciary Act of 1801 abolished circuit riding for Supreme Court justices. Unhappily, this was the famous act of the midnight judges. It was an admirable law in the technical sense, but doomed by its political implications. The Jefferson administration promptly repealed it. Again and again, reform proposals became entangled in sectional battles or battles between Congress and the President, and went down to defeat. As was so often true, notions of technical efficiency were sacrificed to more powerful values and interests.

Landis, *The Business of the Supreme Court* (1928), pp. 4–52.

[79]Frankfurter and Landis, *op. cit.*, pp. 49–50.

[80]Quoted, *ibid.*, p. 17.

CIVIL PROCEDURE

Left to themselves, the colonies might have developed modes of procedure more rational and streamlined than anything in England. The process was retarded in the 18th century by the trend toward Anglicization. Many lawyers and judges were English-trained; English legal texts were in use. Imperial rule, English prestige, and the growth of a professional bar led to a reaction against the "crudities" of colonial procedure. The colonial systems became compromises between English law and native experiment. By the time of the Revolution, colonial procedure was bewilderingly diverse.

There was no chance that classical English pleading would be established after Independence. For one thing, the American bar was simply not equipped to handle this dismal lore. Nor was it in anybody's interest to introduce into law the complexities of English pleading, least of all in the interests of merchants. It was one thing to evolve such a system, as the English had; to bring it in from outside was quite another. But since English lawbooks were easily available, English procedure did have a certain degree of influence. This was particularly true of the first generation after 1776, and for the upper reaches of the profession. Some pleading and practice manuals were written in America, stressing local forms and procedures. When Joseph Story published *A Selection of Pleadings in Civil Actions* (1805), he took some of his forms from Massachusetts lawyers; and he justified his book on the basis of differences in "customs, statutes, and common law" between England and Massachusetts. But basically the book was English, some of it culled from fairly ancient sources. It was merely adapted for Americans, in a process that had the merit of avoiding "the high price of foreign books." James Gould's *Treatise on the Principles of Pleading in Civil Actions,* published in Boston in 1832, made the rather grandiose claim of setting out principles of pleading as a "science." It paid scant attention to American law as such:

> As the *English* system of pleading is, in general, the basis of that of our country; the former has, in the following treatise, been followed exclusively, without regard to any peculiarities

in the latter; excepting a very few references to those, which
exist in the law of my native State.[81]

In fact, the more popular English manuals were in actual use
in the United States. In addition, special American editions of
English treatises were prepared. Joseph Chitty's treatise on pleading was so well received that an eighth American edition was
published in 1840. Chapter 9 of this dreary book bore the following title: "Of Rejoinders and the Subsequent Pleadings; of
Issues, Repleaders, Judgments non Obstante Veredicto, and Pleas
Puis Darrein Continuance, or now Pending Action; and of De-
murrers and Joinders in Demurrer." In this book, the American
lawyer could drink in such strictures as the following:

> A traverse may be *too extensive*, and therefore defective, by
> being taken in the *conjunctive* instead of the *disjunctive*, where
> proof of the allegation in the conjunctive is not essential.
> Thus, in an action on a policy on ship and tackle, the de-
> fendant should not deny that the ship and tackle were lost,
> but that *neither* was lost.[82]

Clearly, English common-law pleading was no model to follow
slavishly. Pleading was an elaborate contest of lawyerly arts, and
winning a case did not always depend on substantive merits. There
were too many rules, and they were too tricky and inconsistent.
The idea behind English pleading was not itself absurd. Pleading
was supposed to distill, out of the amorphousness of fact and
fancy, one precious, narrow issue on which trial could be joined.
Principles of pleading were, in theory, principles of economy and
order. Pleading demanded great technical skill. Those who had
the skill—highly trained lawyers and judges—saw no reason to
abandon the system. But the country was not run by lawyers.
Merchants, bankers, and landowners were more important in
American life. To these, the "science of pleading" could not appear otherwise than obfuscation, a lawyer's plot to kill justice, or
to frustrate the expectations of ordinary people of affairs. It is a
question, what Chitty's ship-merchant would have thought of dis-
junctive and conjunctive traverses.

English procedure, then, was too medieval for the modern
world. (One wonders why it was not too medieval for the Middle

[81]Preface, ix.
[82]Joseph Chitty, *Treatise on Pleading*, p. 645.

Ages.) Reform of civil procedure, at any rate, found fertile soil in the United States. Pleading reform was one of the changes made necessary by the explosion in legal consumers. Legal skill was a resource; and it was scarce. It had to be husbanded. Shrewdness in pleading was not cheap enough and universal enough to pay its way in American society. Popular democracy, the colonial tradition, business demands for rationality and predictability: these too were allies in opposition to the strict "science of pleading." Against them were arrayed a few troops of bench and bar. But this was a raggle-taggle army, halfhearted in defense of its position. Francophile judges had contempt for the common law. Rank-and-file lawyers were too untrained for Chitty. English procedure had become like a drafty old house. Those born to it and raised in it loved it; but no outsider could tolerate its secret panels, broken windows, and on-again, off-again plumbing.

Reform did not come in one great burst. The actual practice of courts, particularly trial courts, was freer and easier than one might assume from reading manuals of procedure. As more research is done, more variance between book learning and reality comes to light. Alexander Hamilton prepared a manuscript manual of practice in 1782, probably for his own use in cramming for the bar. In it, he noted a decline in "nice Learning" about pleas of abatement. These pleas, he said,

> are seldom used; and are always discountenanced by the Court, which having lately acquired a more liberal Cast begin to have some faint Idea that the end of Suits at Law is to Investigate the Merits of the Cause, and not to entangle in the Nets of technical Terms.[83]

New York was, relatively speaking, quite conservative in legal affairs. Hamilton's manual of New York pleading, if it can be trusted, shows deep dependence on English formalities and forms. Yet even here many cracks in the armor appear, many defections in favor of "the Merits of the Cause." Other jurisdictions departed much further from English propriety. Georgia, in the 18th century, passed a series of laws that went a long way toward rationalizing civil procedure. The climax was the Judiciary Act of 1799. Under Georgia's laws, a plaintiff might begin civil actions simply by filing a *petition*, setting out the case "plainly, fully and substantially"; the defendant would file his *answer*, stating whatever was

---

[83]Quoted in Julius Goebel, Jr., ed., *The Law Practice of Alexander Hamilton, 1757–1804*, vol. 1, *Documents and Commentary* (1964), p. 81.

necessary to constitute "the cause of his defense."[84] Georgia's law was, among other things, a courageous attempt to unite equity and common-law pleading. It also got rid of the forms of action, those ancient pigeonholes (or straitjackets) of procedure into which pleaders were forced to fit their pleas, or else. Conservative Georgia courts, outraged by the reforms, supposedly undermined the Georgia scheme and led to its downfall. But the evidence for this charge rests on nothing more than scraps of talk from appellate courts. Quite possibly, the reform had lasting effects on trial court behavior in Georgia.

By the 1830s, reform of procedure was in the air. In England itself, native lair of the common law, reform was a definite force. Jeremy Bentham cast a long shadow. Lord Brougham, in Parliament in 1828, fairly begged for reform. These men and their supporters set off a process with enormous significance for the common-law systems of law. After all, England too was a modernizing society, years ahead of America in industrial development, if not in class structure. During the 19th century the two nations were mutually influential—their experiences meshed neatly, in parallel currents of change. But most of the key developments happened toward the middle of the century, or later.[85]

In the Middle Ages, equity courts had been a source of law reform. Equity boasted a flexible collection of remedies; hence it had often prodded and pushed the more lethargic common law toward rationality. But equity had itself become hidebound; by 1800, it needed procedural reform as desperately as the common law; it was equity, not law, that was the subject of Dickens's *Bleak House*. The very existence of equity was an anomaly—a separate and contradictory jurisprudence, living uneasily beside the "law." In the United States, many states simply handed over equity jurisdiction to the general courts of common law; the same judges decided both kinds of case, merely alternating roles. North Carolina, for example, in an act of 1782, empowered "each superior court of law" to "be and act as a court of equity for the same district."[86] In a few states (Mississippi, Delaware, New Jersey), the courts were distinct, with different judges for law and equity. This was true of New York until the 1820s, when the circuit judges

---

[84]Robert W. Millar, *Civil Procedure of the Trial Court in Historical Perspective* (1952), p. 40.
[85]See below, part III, ch. III.
[86]Laws N. Car. 1782, ch. 11.

were made "vice-chancellors," and given full equity powers within their circuits. But a loser could not appeal from these "vice-chancellors" to ordinary appellate courts; instead, he had to appeal to the chancellor.[87] Finally, some states had no developed system of equity at all (as distinct from "law"). Louisiana was one of these, because of its civil-law heritage. Massachusetts and Pennsylvania were outstanding common-law examples. Before 1848, however, only Georgia (and Texas, whose history was deviant) had actually *abolished* the distinction.

States that lacked "equity" had developed a rough union of their own. Statutes made equitable defenses available in cases at "law." In Massachusetts, the supreme judicial court had "power to hear and determine in equity all cases... when the parties have not a plain, adequate and complete remedy at the common law." The statute listed what these "cases" were, for example, "All suits for the specific performance of any written contract."[88] In Pennsylvania, "Common law actions were used to enforce purely equitable claims; purely equitable defenses were permitted in common law actions; and, at rare times, purely equitable reliefs were obtained by means of actions at law."[89] Throughout the period, Pennsylvania legislatures, by private laws, gave permission to individuals to do acts which, in other states, were within the scope of equity power. For example, they sometimes permitted executors to sell parcels of land to pay the debts of a deceased.[90] In 1836, on the advice of a law-revision commission, Pennsylvania gave broad equity powers to some state courts. Thus Pennsylvania (and Massachusetts), by a piecemeal process, attained a "curious anticipation of future general reforms."[91] In essence, "law" was bent to suit "equity"; but not all the change was in one direction. Equity was addicted to documents and written evidence, and classically tolerated nothing else; the common law favored the spoken word. But the Judiciary Act of 1789 provided for oral testimony in federal equity cases. Georgia allowed trial by jury in some causes

[87]Rev. Stats. N.Y. 1829, vol. II, part III, ch. 1, title II, sections 2, 59.

[88]Rev. Stats. Mass. 1836, ch. 81, sec. 8.

[89]Spencer R. Liverant and Walter H. Hitchler, "A History of Equity in Pennsylvania," 37 Dickinson L. Rev. 156, 166 (1933).

[90]Thomas A. Cowan, "Legislative Equity in Pennsylvania," 4 U. Pitt. L. Rev. 1, 12 (1937).

[91]Millar, *op. cit.*, p. 40. The Pennsylvania law of 1836, incidentally, did not put an end to private acts of "legislative equity"; these lasted for almost forty more years.

which by tradition belonged to the equity side of the bench. North Carolina, in a statute of 1782, did the same. And a North Carolina law of 1801 provided a simple way to continue equity actions after the death of a party on either side. This replaced the "bill of revivor," one of the prime procedural culprits, a device so slow and technical that it gave rise to the suspicion that a chancery bill, once begun, would never come to an end.[92]

In English law there were countless kinds of "appeal," calling for different pleadings and forms, full of dark mysteries, tripping and trapping the unwary. The word *appeal,* strictly speaking, applied only to review by higher equity courts. The states, continuing a trend that began in the colonial period, fixed on and emphasized two kinds of review by higher courts: the equity *appeal* and, for common-law actions, proceedings by writ of *error* or the equivalent. Local variations were frequent. In North Carolina, instead of writs of error, writs of certiorari were used—a form of review which in England was confined to review of noncommon-law courts.[93] In Connecticut the writ of error reviewed decisions in equity, usurping the place of the appeal.

The basic problem of review or appeal is how to avoid doing everything over again—which would be a tremendous waste— but at the same time make sure that lower-court mistakes are corrected. In essence, writs of error corrected only some kinds of errors, those that appeared on the face of the formal record. These were pleading errors mostly, except insofar as a party, in a bill of exceptions, preserved the right to complain about other kinds of "error"—if the judge, for example, had let in improper evidence. These "errors" rarely went to the heart of the matter. The appeal system suffered from what Roscoe Pound has called "record worship"—"an excessive regard for the formal record at the expense of the case, a strict scrutiny of that record for 'errors of law' at the expense of scrutiny of the case to insure the consonance of the result to the demands of the substantive law."[94]

This system was not completely irrational; it could be defended as a reasonable way to divide powers and functions between high and low courts. High courts expounded the law, low courts decided cases. By correcting errors of record, high courts were able to adjust any kinks in formal doctrine. But at the same time, they

[92]Laws N. Car. 1782, ch. 11; 1801, ch. 10.
[93]Roscoe Pound, *Appellate Procedure in Civil Cases* (1941), p. 288.
[94]Roscoe Pound, *Criminal Justice in America* (1930), p. 161.

left the day-to-day work of the trial courts alone. Still, record worship meant that a lot of mistakes and injustices could never be reviewed by a higher court; at the same time, high courts sometimes reversed perfectly proper decisions on highly technical grounds. But the actual control of lower courts by upper courts— and the actual impact of record worship on the life cycle of a typical trial—is exceedingly hard to measure.

Record worship was a disease that probably did not randomly infect every type of case. Courts are stickier, for example, about small errors in cases where life or liberty is at stake. It would be no surprise, then, to find that the law of criminal procedure outdid civil procedure in record worship and technical artifice. This branch of law had a special place in American jurisprudence. The Bill of Rights contained what amounted to a miniature code of criminal procedure. Warrants were not to be issued "but upon probable cause, supported by Oath or affirmation, and particularly describing the place to be searched, and the persons or things to be seized" (art. IV). No person "shall be held to answer for a capital, or otherwise infamous crime" without presentment or indictment by grand jury (art. V). No one "shall be compelled in any Criminal Case to be a witness against himself" or be "deprived of life, liberty, or property, without due process of law" (art. V). The accused "shall enjoy" the right to a "speedy and public trial," by an "impartial" jury of the vicinage; he must be told the nature of his crime; must be able to confront the witnesses; must "have compulsory process for obtaining witnesses in his favor" and the "Assistance of Counsel for his defense" (art. VI). "Excessive bail" was not to be required (art. VIII).

Many states adopted their own bills of rights even before the federal government did. Other states copied or modified the federal version. Criminal procedure was a major part of all of these bills of rights. The basic rights of man turned out, in large part, to be rights to fair criminal trial. These rights were supposed to guard against the tyranny of autocrats and kings. Abuse of power by Federalist judges only strengthened the ideas that underlay the Bill of Rights. Criminal procedure, on paper, gave a whole battery of protections to persons accused of crime. The defendant had the right to appeal a conviction; the state had no right to appeal an acquittal.[95] In a number of cases, it seemed as if the

[95] *State* v. *Jones,* 5 N. Car. 257 (1809).

high court searched the record with a fine-tooth comb, looking
for faulty instructions, improper evidence, error in formal pleadings, or prejudicial actions by the judge. Sometimes the upper
court quashed an indictment for a tiny slip of the pen or set aside
a verdict for some microscopic error at the trial. In *State* v. *Owen*,
a North Carolina case of 1810, the grand jurors of Wake County
had presented John Owen, a cabinetmaker, for murder. According to the indictment, Owen, in Raleigh, on April 21, 1809,

> not having the fear of God before his eyes, but being moved
> and seduced by the instigations of the Devil ... with force and
> arms, at the city of Raleigh ... in and upon one Patrick Con-
> way ... feloniously, wilfully, and of his malice aforethought,
> did make an assault ... with a certain stick, of no value, which
> he the said John Owen in both his hands then and there had
> and held ... in and upon the head and face of him the said
> Patrick Conway ... did strike and beat ... giving to the said
> Patrick Conway, *then and there* with the pine stick aforesaid,
> in and upon the head and face of him the said Patrick Conway,
> several *mortal wounds*, of which said mortal wounds, the said
> Patrick Conway then and there instantly died.

Owen was found guilty and appealed. His attorney argued
that the indictment was defective, in that it did not "set forth
the *length and depth* of the mortal wounds." A majority of the
supreme court of North Carolina regretfully agreed: "It appears
from the books, that wounds capable of description must be
described, that the Court may judge whether it be probable,
that death might have been produced by them." Since the indictment did not allege that the wounds were two inches long
and four inches deep, or the like, the case had to be overturned,
and Owen won a new trial.[96]

Roscoe Pound has called this kind of case the "hypertrophy of
procedure."[97] This hypertrophy, he felt, was an example of 19th-
century individualism run riot. The criminal law tolerated "hypertrophy" because it served the needs of the dominant American
male—the self-reliant man, who lived in a small town or on the
frontier. Such a man was supremely confident of his own judgment, but tended to be jealous of the power of the state. Better

[96]*State* v. *Owen*, 5 N. Car. 452 (1810). The North Carolina legislature promptly
passed an act (1811) to remedy such excesses. See also the provisions of the New
York revised statutes of 1828 dealing with indictments.

[97]Pound, *Criminal Justice in America* (1930), p. 161.

to let the guilty free on a technicality than allow courts and prosecutors real power or discretion.

There is a serious question how far Pound's description fits the
working law and how much *State* v. *Owen* describes a real phenomenon rather than an occasional mutation. Pound's picture of
criminal procedure best describes a tiny group of instances, preserved in appellate records like flies in amber. Recorded appellate
cases have always been a small minority of litigated cases. Who
was it that took advantage of procedural rights and the record
worship of appellate courts? Certainly not the slaves, the dependent poor, the urban masses. It is hard to tell how fair the *average*
trial was. American law had its dark underside—vigilantism,
lynching, mob rule. These show that in some communities, for
some cases, public opinion did not tolerate the niceties of fair trial.
Some *formal* rights, recognized today, were not recognized in the
19th century. Thousands were arrested, tried, and sentenced without lawyers. Yet only a good lawyer could make effective use of
the full guarantees of the Bill of Rights, let alone take advantage
of record worship and "hypertrophy." Probably the average criminal trial fell far short of the ideal of procedural due process. The
average trial, no doubt, was simple and short. And there were
even some major trials—trials with political overtones—that were
by any standards unfair.

THE LAW OF EVIDENCE

There is good reason to believe that the law of evidence tightened
considerably between 1776 and the 1830s. Judging from surviving
transcripts of criminal trials, courts had rather loose attitudes
toward evidence around 1800. In the trial of the so-called Man-
hattan Well Mystery—the transcript was found among Alexander
Hamilton's papers—hearsay was freely admitted; and "some of
the most important testimony was not elicited by questions" from
the attorney, but rather "by allowing the witnesses to give a con-
secutive and uninterrupted account."[98] Opposing counsel did not
meekly wait their turn to cross-examine. Rather, they broke in
with questions whenever they wished.

---

[98]Julius Goebel, Jr., ed., *The Law Practice of Alexander Hamilton: Documents and
Commentary*, vol. 1 (1964), p. 701.

When a field of law becomes cancerously intricate, some fundamental conflict of interest, some fundamental tension between opposing values, must lie at the root of the problem. The American political public has always resisted strong, central authority. Power tends rather to be fragmented, balkanized, dispersed. This attitude, which found expression in the theory of checks and balances, affected the law of evidence too. The modern European law of evidence is fairly simple and rational; the law lets most everything in, and trusts the judge to separate good evidence from bad. But American law distrusts the judge; it gives the jury full fact-finding power and, in criminal cases, the final word on innocence or guilt. Yet the law distrusts the jury as much as it distrusts the judge, and the rules of evidence grew up as some sort of countervailing force. The jury only hears part of the story, that part which the law of evidence allows. The judge's hands are also tied. If he lets in improper testimony, he runs the risk that the case will be reversed on appeal. Hence the rules of evidence bind and control both jury and judge.

It was during this period that many rules of evidence received classic formulation. The rules were heavily influenced by the jury system and the attitude of the law toward the jury. In medieval times, the jury had been a panel of neighbors—knowing busybodies, who perhaps had personal knowledge of the case. When the function of the jury changed to that of an impartial panel of listeners, the law of evidence underwent explosive growth. Rules were devised whose point was to exclude all shaky, secondhand, or improper evidence from the eyes and ears of the jury. Only the most tested, predigested matter was fit for the jury's consumption. Consequently, in the 19th century, the so-called *hearsay rule* became one of the dominant rules of the law of evidence. This was a bizarre kind of rule—one simple, if Utopian, idea, along with a puzzle box of exceptions. The general rule was that juries should not hear secondhand evidence: they should hear Smith's story out of his own mouth, and not Jones's account of what Smith had to say. But in many situations, the rule was deemed too strict, and there were recognized exceptions. These ranged from involuntary utterances ("ouch!"), to shopbooks, to the dying words of a murder victim, naming his killer.

Hearsay rules grew luxuriantly, on both sides of the Atlantic. Most of the doctrines appeared first in England; but not all. The business-entry rule admits records made in the ordinary course of business, even though these are, strictly speaking, hearsay. The rule seems to have started in America around 1820.[99] In general, the American law of evidence outstripped English law in complexity, perhaps because of a deeper American fear of concentration of power.

The rules relating to witnesses were as complicated as rules about the kind of evidence that could be heard, and for similar reasons. In 1800, husbands and wives could testify neither for nor against each other. No person could testify as a witness if he had a financial stake in the outcome of the case. This meant that neither the plaintiff nor the defendant, in most cases, was competent to testify on his own behalf; their mouths were shut in their very own lawsuits. During the period, some fresh restrictions were added. The doctor-patient privilege, for example, prevents a doctor from giving medical testimony without his patient's consent. It seems to have first appeared in a New York law of 1828. Missouri passed a similar law in 1835.[100]

In theory, the rules of evidence were supposed to be rational rules of legal proof. Trials were to be orderly, businesslike, and fair. Each rule had its reason. But the rules as a whole, in their sheer complexity, tended to defeat the rationale. They seem bewildering and irrational, as liable to cheat justice as to fulfill it. Exclusionary rules, said Jeremy Bentham, had the perverse effect of shutting the door against the truth; the rules gave "license to oppression by all imaginable wrongs." Quakers would not take an oath on religious grounds; the rule excluding their testimony,

> in a case of rape...includes a license to the whole army to storm every quakers' meeting-house, and violate the persons of all the female part of the congregation, in the presence of fathers, husbands, and brothers.[101]

It is unlikely that this particular gang rape ever took place. But there was plenty of real and possible abuse, in the law of evidence, to feed the appetite for reform. Indeed, the law of evidence began to be purged of excesses at the very time that courts were putting

[99]*Two Centuries' Growth of American Law 1701–1901* (1901), pp. 324–25.

[100]John H. Wigmore, *A Treatise on the System of Evidence in Trials at Common Law,* vol. IV (1905), sec. 2380, pp. 3347–48.

[101]Jeremy Bentham, *Rationale of Judicial Evidence,* vol. IV (1827), pp. 491–92. This particular horrible example could not occur in the United States. Quakers were, in general, competent witnesses in the United States. They were allowed to make "affirmations" instead of taking oaths.

the final building blocks in place. But major changes were achieved only later in the century.

At the close of a trial, the judge instructs the jury—tells them about the applicable law. In the 20th century, the lawyers write these instructions themselves, or copy them from form-books. The instructions tend to be stereotyped, antiseptic statements of abstract rules. In many cases, it is hard to see how juries can make heads or tails out of them. They seem to matter mostly to lawyers, who argue about the wording and base appeals on "errors" in instructions. In 1776 or 1800, judges tended to talk more freely to the jury. They summarized and commented on the trial; they explained the law in simple, nontechnical language. Instructions were clear, informative summaries of the state of the law. Chief Justice Richard Bassett, of Delaware, explaining adverse possession to a jury, in 1794, remarked: "If you are in possession of a corner of my land for twenty years by adverse possession, you may snap your fingers at me."[102] All this changed in the 19th century; there was to be no more finger snapping, no more vivid language, no more clarity, no metaphors. As early as 1796, a statute in North Carolina made it unlawful, "in delivering a charge to the petit-jury, to give an opinion whether a fact is fully or sufficiently proved," since that was "the true office and province of the jury."[103] In the 19th century, a number of state statutes took away the judge's right to comment on evidence. This made the jury less liable to domination by the judge. The stereotyped instructions may have confused the jury, but they helped maintain its autonomy. The judge was more rulebound than before—hamstrung, one might even say.

In the early years of the 19th century, the roles of judge and jury were subtly altered and redefined. Up to that point, both judge and jury had been relatively free to act, each within its sphere. According to William Nelson, the jury "ceased to be an adjunct of local communities which articulated into positive law the ethical standards of those communities." It was rather an "adjunct" of the court, whose main job was to handle "facts," not "law." Nelson traces to the first decade of the 19th century, in Massachusetts, the articulation and definition of what became a

[102]Daniel J. Boorstin, ed., *Delaware Cases, 1792–1830,* vol. I (1943), p. 39.
[103]Laws N. Car. 1796, ch. 4. See the comments on this statute by Ruffin, in *State* v. *Moses,* 13 N. Car. 452 (1830).

classic definition of powers and roles: that the judge was master
of "law," the jury of "fact."[104] The result, in theory at least, was a
better balance of power. Ultimately, it made possible a more rational, predictable system of justice, especially in commercial cases.
At least that much seemed plausible. And within the little world
of the courtroom, the two major powers, judge and jury, were
locked into tighter, better definitions. Checks and balances were
more than constitutional concepts; they pervaded the whole of
the law.

[104]William E. Nelson, *Americanization of the Common Law: The Impact of Legal
Change on Massachusetts Society, 1760–1830* (1975), pp. 170–71; Note, "The Changing Role of the Jury in the Nineteenth Century," 74 Yale L.J. 170 (1964). Very
little is known, however, about the actual behavior of jurors. See David J. Bodenhamer, "The Democratic Impulse and Legal Change in the Age of Jackson:
The Example of Criminal Juries in Antebellum Indiana," 45 The Historian 206
(1982).

CHAPTER II

OUTPOSTS OF THE LAW:
THE FRONTIER AND THE CIVIL LAW FRINGE

THE FRONTIER

Colonial America was a coastal country. But even before Independence, the line of settlement had crept far inland. The colonies claimed vast tracts of inner wilderness. The Louisiana Purchase added another immense and largely unsettled area. Throughout the period, population flowed into the West and Southwest. These lands of forest and plain, great gushing rivers, fertile soil, and sweeping distances captured and held the American imagination. In 1800, the American frontier represented an empire of the future. By 1900, the frontier was an empire of the past, whose death was widely mourned in scholarship and myth. In literature, the frontier was a land of heroes. Life on the edge was lawless but vital; here the democratic spirit flourished, without the defects and troubles of the older East. The withering eye of modern scholarship has reduced the myth of the frontier to a more human, and reasonable, scale. The law of the frontier, too, has been gradually stripped of its husk of legend.

At Independence, the states faced the problem of what to do with the western lands. The new republic, a collection of former colonies, itself became a kind of colonial power—once the decision was made to treat the western lands as common property of the nation. The Ordinance of 1787—the so-called Northwest Ordinance—prescribed basic law for that huge area of forest and plain which later became Ohio, Indiana, Illinois, Michigan and Wisconsin. The Ordinance of 1798 extended the influence of the 1787 ordinance into the Southwestern territories—to Alabama and Mississippi.

The Ordinance of 1787 is one of the most important documents in American legal history. It adopted a bold policy of decolonization. Everyone expected that the territories would gradually fill with settlers. When enough people had arrived and taken root, the territories would take their place in the Union as full, free, sovereign states. First, however, came a period of tutelage. Until such time as "five thousand free male inhabitants, of full age," lived in the territory, the lawmaking power was vested in a governor and three judges. The three judges had to reside in the district; any two could "form a court." They were to exercise "a common-law jurisdiction."[1] They had to be men of means, each of whom owned in the district "a freehold estate, in five hundred acres of land, while in the exercise of their offices." The governor and a majority of the judges had power to "adopt and publish in the district such laws of the original States, criminal and civil, as may be necessary, and best suited to the circumstances of the district."[2] Congress had veto power over these laws. This power formed a striking—and by no means accidental—parallel to the British power of review over the colonial statutes.

The phrase "adopt and publish" was troublesome, and confusing, from the start. It seemed to mean that the territories had no right to make law on their own. They had only the power to pick and choose, for their use, among the various laws already on the statute books in older states. The provision could not be literally carried out. At the very least, dates and place names had to be changed in borrowed statutes. In practice, the "adopt and publish" rule was avoided and evaded. Some territories adopted laws from states like Kentucky, which was not an "original" state. Some statutes were patched together from more than one statute in the older states. One critic charged that

> They parade the laws of the original states before them, on the table, and cull letters from the laws of Maryland, syllables from the laws of Virginia, words from the laws of New York, sentences from the laws of Pennsylvania, verses from the laws of Kentucky, and chapters from the laws of Connecticut— jumble the whole into such form as they conceive the most suitable to facilitate their schemes . . . and then call it a law.[3]

---

[1] The term "common law" was ambiguous. Probably—but by no means certainly—the term was meant to exclude equity jurisdiction.

[2] This provision was not applicable to Louisiana and Arkansas territories. On territorial government in general, see Jack E. Eblen, *The First and Second United States Empires: Governors and Territorial Government, 1784–1912* (1968).

[3] Quoted in William W. Blume, ed., *Transactions of the Supreme Court of the Territory of Michigan,* vol. I (1935), p. xxiii.

This was, of course, a gross exaggeration; still, many territorial statutes were in fact a product of scissors and paste.

However odd the "adopt and publish" rule may seem today, in a small sense it merely expressed, in extreme form, and as a norm, a procedure that new states in the West followed in making up their laws, even *without* compulsion. They took texts from older states, adding a patch of novelty here and there. Policy choices were made by choosing among old models, not by drafting fresh law. As might be expected, settlers tended to borrow most from states whose laws they knew best—the states they came from. From 1795 on, the governor and judges of Northwest Territory listed the source of each law they adopted for the territory. From 1795 to 1798, twenty-seven out of forty-nine laws came from Pennsylvania, the home state of the governor, Arthur St. Clair. Michigan Territory, between 1814 and 1823, adopted 168 laws from thirteen states; 134 of these were from Ohio, while Tennessee supplied only one.[4] In 1795, Michigan adopted from Virginia its general statute receiving the common law. In theory at least, this brought the entire body of the common law, and an unascertained number of statutes of Parliament, into force in the forests of Michigan.

Under the Ordinance of 1787, a territory reached a second stage of organization when it had a population of "five thousand free male inhabitants, of full age." Government at this stage, too, had a certain family resemblance to British colonial practice. The governor and judges were to share lawmaking power with an elected body. Property owners were to choose one representative "for every five hundred free male inhabitants," up to twenty-five; beyond this "the number and proportion of representatives shall be regulated by the legislature." The elected assembly was to nominate ten persons to serve on the governor's council. Every nominee had to be a resident; and each had to be "possessed of a freehold in five hundred acres of land." Congress was to select five councilmen from these ten nominees. The governor, council, and house had authority "to make laws," so long as the laws were "not repugnant" to the ordinance. The third stage, statehood, became possible when sixty thousand free inhabitants lived in the territory.

The pattern set by the Ordinance was both durable and work-

[4]William W. Blume, "Legislation on the American Frontier," 60 Mich. L. Rev. 317, 334 (1962).

able. It guided the territories of the old Northwest and Southwest smoothly along the road that led to statehood.[5] Colonial unrest was avoided. The Wisconsin territorial act of 1836 was the next major model. It eliminated the first stage of territorial life. Property qualifications were discarded; the population elected its legislature directly. The new model also paid more attention to details of court organization. Wisconsin's law, for example, specified "a supreme court, district courts, probate courts, and...justices of the peace."[6] But even in this, and later territorial laws, there were strong echoes of the Northwest Ordinance. Residents of Wisconsin Territory were guaranteed "all the similar rights, privileges, and advantages granted and secured to the people of the territory of the United States northwest of the river Ohio, by the articles of the compact contained in the ordinance for the government of the said territory, passed on the thirteenth day of July, one thousand seven hundred and eighty-seven."

The working law of the frontier cannot, of course, be deduced from its outer skin. Patient research[7] has dispelled some mists and legends about frontier law, and added to the stock of new knowledge. Civilization advanced in undulating waves, generally along river valleys. Law followed the ax. The land was not empty before the Americans came. There were native tribes scattered throughout the area. In the Mississippi Valley, a cluster of Frenchmen lived by a half remembered form of the law of France. The Americans, by sheer force of numbers, overwhelmed this alien system.

Only in the very earliest days was frontier law as crude as its reputation. At the outset, rough men of the forest administered justice. What they did passed for government, until the settlers and the opportunists arrived. If the tales of the pioneers are true, a drunken, corrupt form of personalized justice governed in the earliest courts. At Green Bay, in 1816, two decades before Wisconsin Territory was established, an "old Frenchman" named Charles Reaume, who "could read and write a little," acted as justice of the peace. In his court, it was said, "a bottle of spirits was the best witness that could be introduced." Once, when the losing party scraped up some whiskey for the judge, Reaume ordered a new trial and reversed his prior decision, on the strength of this "witness." Reaume's "court" was a long, difficult journey

[5]Louisiana and Florida territories were differently handled.
[6]Act Establishing the Terr. Govt. of Wisconsin (1836), sec. 9.
[7]Notably by Francis Philbrick and William Wirt Blume.

from the county seat. His word, in effect, was final. He took care not to decide cases against those traders who were "able to bear the expense of an appeal"; hence his incompetence was not exposed to a wider public. At Prairie du Chien, at the same period, Nicholas Boilvin, a French-Canadian, was "clothed with the dignified office...of Justice of the Peace." Boilvin was as uneducated as Reaume. He owned a library of exactly three lawbooks: the statutes of Northwest, Missouri, and Illinois territories. But in deciding a case, "he paid no attention to the statute"; he merely "decided according to his own idea of right and wrong."[8]

Polish and legal skill were in short supply, too, in the Illinois country. A small group of amateur lawyers, merchants, and political adventurers ran the government. Litigation on land claims and grants was the staple business of the courts. The judges were speculators themselves, and judged their own claims. A federal board of land commissioners was appointed in 1804 to investigate land claims in the Illinois country. The board uncovered "incredible forgeries, fraud, subornation and perjuries," the "very mire and filth of corruption."[9] A certain Robert Reynolds had rushed to file claims with the commissioners, which was an act of great "effrontery," since Reynolds "forged the names of witnesses, deponents and grantors...gave depositions under an assumed name, and appeared before a magistrate with deponents who deposed under false names for his benefit. He forged a grant to himself from a slave woman."[10] Yet Reynolds had once been a judge. He had been appointed a county court judge in 1801 and "attended very regularly to his duties."

Reynolds was not the only forging judge. He was, however, the only one ever indicted for fraud; and his indictment, it was said, was due more to his political enemies than to public outrage. Even after Illinois became a state, "a great rascal" named William P. Foster served on the state supreme court. According to Governor Thomas Ford, Foster was "no lawyer, never having either studied or practised law; but...a man of winning, polished manners, and ...withal a very gentlemanly swindler." Foster was assigned to hold courts "in the circuit on the Wabash; but being fearful of exposing his utter incompetency, he never went near any of them."

[8]James H. Lockwood, "Early Times and Events in Wisconsin," *Second Annual Report and Collections of the State Historical Society of Wisconsin*, vol. II (1856), pp. 98, 105, 106, 126.
[9]Francis S. Philbrick, ed., *The Laws of Indiana Territory, 1801–9* (1930), lxxxvii.
[10]*Ibid.*, lxxxix–xc.

After a year he resigned, pocketed his salary, and left the state to become a "noted swindler, moving from city to city, and living by swindling strangers, and prostituting his daughters, who were very beautiful."[11]

Life was undeniably violent and crude in parts of the frontier. Henry Marie Brackenridge visited Missouri in 1810–11. He saw lawyers and judges who went about armed with pistols and knives. Duels were an everyday affair.[12] Governor Ford of Illinois has given us a graphic description of a trial court at work in Illinois, around 1818:

> The judges...held their courts mostly in log-houses, or in the barrooms of taverns, fitted up with a temporary bench for the judge, and chairs or benches for the lawyers and jurors. At the first circuit court in Washington county, held by Judge John Reynolds, the sheriff, on opening the court, went out into the court-yard and said to the people: "Boys, come in, our John is going to hold court." This was the proclamation for opening the court. In general, the judges were averse to deciding questions of law if they could possibly avoid doing so. They did not like the responsibility of offending one or the other of the parties, and preferred to submit everything they could to be decided by the jury. They never gave instructions to a jury unless expressly called for; and then only upon the points of law raised by counsel in asking for them. They never commented upon the evidence, or undertook to show the jury what inferences and presumptions might be drawn from it; for which reason they delivered their instructions hypothetically, stating them thus: "If the jury believe from the evidence that such a matter is proved, then the law is so and so." This was a clear departure from the practice of the judges in England and most of the United States; but the new practice suited the circumstances of the country. It undoubtedly requires the highest order of talent in a judge to "sum up" the evidence rightly to a jury, so as

[11]Governor Thomas Ford, *A History of Illinois from Its Commencement as a State in 1818 to 1847* (1854), p. 29.

[12]William F. Keller, *The Nation's Advocate: Henry Marie Brackenridge and Young America* (1956), pp. 101, 104. It may be worth mentioning, however, that the most famous duel among lawyers was the duel in which Aaron Burr killed Alexander Hamilton, who was (among other things) a successful commercial lawyer at New York. The duel took place, not on the frontier, but in Weehawken, New Jersey. Dueling was also common in the South, frontier or not, as an aspect of the Southern code of honor. See Edward L. Ayers, *Vengeance and Justice: Crime and Punishment in the Nineteenth-Century American South* (1984), ch. 1.

to do justice to the case, and injustice to neither party. Such talent did not exist to be put on the bench in these early times; or at least the judges must have modestly believed that they did not possess it.[13]

Still, Ford felt that the judges were "gentlemen of considerable learning and much good sense." The power of the judge to comment on evidence was declining in Eastern trial courts as well as on the frontier, for reasons already explored. The modesty of the judges, then, like a lot of other behavior lovingly labeled as the product of the frontier life and mind, was actually part of the mainstream of American legal life. The laxity and informality of Reynolds's court had parallels in other times and places, including some 20th-century traffic courts.

There was, to be sure, trained legal talent on the frontier, along with the fraud and the animal cunning. The level of legal sophistication in a community depended on its size, on its economic base, and on whether it was close to the centers of government. Men like Reaume and Foster were perhaps distortions or exceptions. After territorial government was organized, the "primitive" stage of frontier justice usually ended for good. Samuel Holden Parsons and James Mitchell Varnum, solid lawyers with good reputations, were among the first judges of Northwest Territory. In Michigan Territory, Augustus Brevoort Woodward, a versatile, cultured lawyer with a college education, compiled the Woodward Code, a collection of thirty-four laws adopted in 1805. The governor of Michigan was also a lawyer, and another Michigan judge had studied law, though he had never practiced.[14]

In time a mobile, vigorous bar flourished in the West: a bar made up of quick-witted, adventurous young operators. Law practice required their full cunning. Joseph G. Baldwin (1815–1864) described them, with frontier hyperbole, as they were during the "flush times" of Alabama and Mississippi. In those days

> many land titles were defective; property was brought from other States clogged with trusts, limitations, and uses ... universal indebtedness ... made it impossible for many men to pay, and desirable for all to escape paying ... a general looseness, ignorance and carelessness in the public officers ... new statutes to be construed ... an elegant assortment of frauds

[13]Ford, *op. cit.*, pp. 82–83.
[14]William W. Blume, "Legislation on the American Frontier," 60 Mich. L. Rev. 317 (1962).

constructive and actual...in short, all the flood-gates of litigation were opened, and the pent-up tide let loose upon the
country. And such a criminal docket! What country could
boast more largely of its crimes? What more splendid role of
felonies! What more terrific murders! What more gorgeous
bank robberies! What more magnificent operations in the
land offices!...Such superb forays on the treasuries, State
and National!...And in INDIAN affairs!...the romance of
a wild and weird larceny!...Swindling Indians by the nation!
...Stealing their land by the township!...Many members of
the bar, of standing and character, from the other States,
flocked in to put their sickles into this abundant harvest.[15]

There were fortunes to be made. The new states and territories
were ripe for the plucking, ripe with careers for ambitious young
men. The economic base was land: town land and country land.
Who, if not a lawyer, had the skill to decipher titles to land? Who
could master the maze of rules on land grants, or on the sale and
transfer of land? Government jobs were another rich plum. The
territories at first were net importers of the taxpayer's money.
Judgeships and clerkships were patronage jobs, to be given out
in Washington. Local jobs became available by the thousands—
in courts, in legislatures, and in the executive branch, and in
territory, state, county, and town. The lawyer, again, was peculiarly
suited for these jobs. He scrambled for public office. He also
collected debts for Eastern creditors; he dabbled in land speculation and townsite booming. He scrounged around for any niche
that required the skill of a jack-of-all-trades. He did whatever his
nose sniffed out as promising and lucrative. In the process, many
young lawyers failed, and moved on to other jobs or places. Others
stayed with it; and some became rich.

The lawyers of the West were a mixed lot. If we can believe
Baldwin, at the bar of the old Southwest there were "no seniors:
the bar is all Young America. If the old fogies come in, they must
stand in the class with the rest."[16] Some of these young lawyers
had gone West after college and clerkship. Others learned their
law as they went along. In any case, frontier law was not book law
in the usual sense. There were no libraries, and books were expensive. The practice put no premium on erudition. The best trial

---

[15]Joseph G. Baldwin, *The Flush Times of Alabama and Mississippi: A Series of Sketches*
(1957), pp. 173–74. See also Elizabeth G. Brown, "The Bar on a Frontier: Wayne
County, 1796–1836," 14 Am. J. Legal Hist. 136 (1970).
[16]Baldwin, *op. cit.*, p. 171.

lawyers used and enjoyed good tricks, jokes, a neat technicality or two. The poverty of source materials left a vacuum, filled in by Blackstone, local statutes, and native wit. Few lawyers could know how to distinguish the fossils in Blackstone from the living law back East. For this reason, court law was, simultaneously, free-wheeling and curiously archaic. The papers of Thomas Rodney, judge in the Old Southwest (1803–1811), preserve such museum pieces as the writ of account and *de homine replegiando*.[17] Rodney wrote that "Special Pleading is adhered to in our Courts with as much Strictness Elegance and propriety as in any of the States, so that Even the young Lawyers are obliged to read their books and be very attentive to their business or want bread."[18] In one equity proceeding, when a litigant objected that "the practice in G.[reat] B.[ritain] does not apply here," the judges replied:

> We Shall be guided by The practice in England So far as it is admissible here because there is no Other Safe and Regular guide, for there it has been brought to perfection by long Experience and the practice of the ablest Judges, and being Contained in their books of practice They can always be re-sorted to—without which the practice here would be always irregular and Uncertain.[19]

Professor William W. Blume studied the work of the court of common pleas of Wayne County, Michigan (1796–1805). He saw

> almost no evidence of the informality often supposed to be a characteristic of frontier justice. Instead, we find a strict compliance with applicable statutes, and, where the procedure was not governed by statute, with the English common law.[20]

Though most territorial statutes had been passed or adopted to solve real problems of legal behavior or the organization of the legal system, a few of these, too, had the musty air of museum pieces. The laws of Michigan mentioned essoins and wager of law,

[17]The writ, literally "for replevying a man," was a means of procuring the release of a prisoner—an earlier equivalent of the writ of *habeas corpus*.

[18]William Baskerville Hamilton, *Anglo-American Law of the Frontier: Thomas Rodney and His Territorial Cases* (1953), pp. 137–38.

[19]Hamilton, *op. cit.*, p. 197.

[20]William W. Blume, "Civil Procedure on the American Frontier," 56 Mich. L. Rev. 161, 209 (1957); to the same effect, Cornelia Anne Clark, "Justice on the Tennessee Frontier: The Williamson County Circuit Court, 1810–1820," 32 Vanderbilt L. Rev. 413 (1979).

no doubt needlessly; most lawyers would have been just as bewildered by these medieval rags and tatters as the layman. The first Illinois legislature "imported [laws]...for the inspection of hemp and tobacco, when there was neither hemp nor tobacco raised in the country."[21]

Blume and Elizabeth Brown found in frontier law "two general attitudes and resultant influences attributable to frontier life." The first was a "strong desire to have all statute law published locally so that reliance on laws not available on the frontier would be unnecessary—codes were welcome." The second was a "lack of 'superstitious respect' for old laws and legal institutions; in other words, a readiness to make changes to suit new conditions."[22] These attributes of frontier law—archaism and hypertechnicality on the one hand, crudity, rough-hewn justice, and frontier impatience with form on the other—were not as inconsistent as they might seem. They flowed from the need to make law work in a transplanted setting. The Western communities swallowed batches of old law whole. This was not because of some sentimental attachment to tradition, but because this course of action was, under the circumstances, the most efficient way to get on with the job. There was neither time nor skill to make it all up anew; to use borrowed law was like buying clothes off the rack, or renting a whole suite of furniture at once.

Once a territory became a state, of course, it had complete power over its own law, and could do exactly as it wished. But in fact there was a great deal of continuity, just as there was continuity of law in the thirteen original states after they broke away from England. Governor Ford thought that Western legislatures passed too many laws, that they overturned too much too soon: "A session of the legislature was like a great fire in the boundless prairies of the State; it consumed everything. And again, it was like the genial breath of spring, making all things new."[23] But this is surely an exaggeration. The statute books of the Northwest states were, by modern standards, skimpy and undernourished. New states and territories were thankful for legacies of law. Ohio kept the statutes of Northwest Territory, even after statehood. The territorial laws were handed on to Indiana Territory (1800); Indiana passed them

[21]Ford, op. cit., p. 34.
[22]William W. Blume and Elizabeth G. Brown, "Territorial Courts and Law: Unifying Factors in the Development of American Legal Institutions," Part II, 61 Mich. L. Rev. 467, 535 (1963).
[23]Ford, op. cit., p. 32.

to Michigan and Illinois territories (1809); Michigan Territory was the source of the earliest laws of Wisconsin Territory (1836), which in turn gave them to Iowa (1838) and Minnesota (1849). In the Southwest the line went from Louisiana to Missouri Territory (1812), from there to Arkansas (1819), and from Mississippi to Alabama (1817).

In most cases the basic process was simple: the old territory divided, like an amoeba, into two pieces; and the laws of the original territory now governed in both parts.[24] Without particular thought or debate, a bundle of well-worn statutes was handed on to new jurisdictions. The statute of frauds and the statute of limitations traveled cross-country without major change. In 1799, Northwest Territory enacted a statute "making Promissory Notes and Inland Bills of Exchange negotiable"—another standard American law. These statutes became part of the basic legal framework. Town laws, election laws, laws about the militia, tax laws, laws on court process: all were freely borrowed and passed along from jurisdiction to jurisdiction.

In time, some of the new states repaid their legal debt. They trained new legal and political leaders. Henry Clay (born and educated in Virginia), Thomas Hart Benton, and Abraham Lincoln were all Western lawyers. The West was mobile, fluid; like the colonies in comparison to Britain, it was freer from the dead hand of the past, freer from the friction and inertia of tradition. Out of the West, then, came legal innovations that became enduring features of the law. The homestead exemption began in Texas; from there, it spread to the North and the East. The first Married Women's Property Act was passed in Mississippi. A number of important legal institutions began life in experimental milieus, on the outskirts of American society.

THE CIVIL LAW FRINGE

In the first generation of independence, the civil-law domain, vast but sparsely settled, encircled the domain of the common law. Civil law—French and Spanish—governed along the Mississippi and the river bottoms of its tributaries; in Kaskaskia, St. Louis, New Madrid, and St. Charles; in the bustling port of New Orleans;

[24]William W. Blume and Elizabeth G. Brown, "Territorial Courts and the Law," Part II, 61 Mich. L. Rev. 467, 474–75 (1963).

in the Floridas, and in Texas. When this empire became American property, it fell subject to American government and law.

A massive invasion of settlers doomed the civil law everywhere, except in Louisiana. The new judges and lawyers were trained in the common-law tradition. They supplanted judges of French and Spanish background. The United States did not disturb rights of property that had vested under civil law. American courts wrestled for years with civil-law problems of land law, family law, laws of descent and inheritance. Among Thomas Rodney's papers, from the Natchez district, are case records in which points at issue were resolved by reference to Spanish law or jurisprudence, translated for the benefit of jury and court.[25] The Northwest Ordinance, after prescribing its own rules about wills and inheritance, promised to preserve, for "the French and Canadian inhabitants, and other settlers of the Kaskaskies, Saint Vincents, and the neighboring villages," the benefit of "their laws and customs now in force among them, relative to the descent and conveyance of property."

But American policy insisted, for the long haul, that the law must be thoroughly Americanized. Around the old river town of St. Louis, Spanish law was technically in force, supplemented by French customs. From the very first, however, American officials aimed "to assimilate by insensible means, the habits and customs of the American and French inhabitants; by interweaving some of the regulations of the latter into our Laws, we procure a ready obedience, without violence or complaint."[26] As the American population increased, more direct action was used in addition to these gentle and "insensible means." A statute of 1807, applicable to what later became Missouri Territory, repealed the civil law on wills and inheritance, and introduced American intestacy laws and laws about wills. American lawyers lobbied successfully for a law which made the common law of England the basis of law in Missouri Territory (1815–16). When it entered the Union, Missouri had little left of its civil-law past, except some tangled land titles, and a passion for procedural simplicity.

The French in Illinois were similarly doomed. The guarantee of the Ordinance applied only to laws of succession. The French were immediately subjected to an elaborate county and township

---

[25]E.g., Hamilton, *op. cit.*, p. 176.
[26]Judge John Coburn to Secretary of State James Madison, 1807, quoted in William F. English, *The Pioneer Lawyer and Jurist in Missouri* (1947), p. 56.

organization, on the model developed in the British colonies, despite the fact that they had "retained in their isolation...the political and economic traditions of the France of Louis XIV, of common fields and manorial organization."[27] American officials had no particular sympathy for the culture of French settlers. Judge John C. Symmes, who came to Vincennes in 1790, reacted to the French with chauvinistic disgust. They "will not relish a free government," he wrote. "They say our laws are too complex, not to be understood, and tedious in their operation—the command or order of the Military commandant is better law and speedier justice for them and what they prefer to all the legal systems found in Littleton and Blackstone. It is a language which they say they can understand, it is cheap and expeditious and they wish for no other."[28] It was natural for these settlers to resent the coming of Americans. The French lost their influence, and with it, their law. Traces of French *coutumes* lingered on briefly in family law. Gradually, French law and language disappeared.

An indigenous law, without prestige, and in a minority status, can hardly survive. The sheer mass of American settlers easily conquered Spanish law in Florida, where the original population was sparse. In 1821 Andrew Jackson imposed, by proclamation, common-law procedure in criminal cases, including the right to trial by jury. But Spanish law had gained only a temporary reprieve for civil cases. In 1829, a statute established the common law, and English statutes passed before 1776, as norms of decision in the territory. The Spanish period left behind, in the end, only a few archeological traces in Florida's law.

Spanish-Mexican law left a much greater imprint on Texas. Partly this was because Texas was rather fully formed, as a polity, before it passed into American hands. Here, too, however, trial by jury was an early import. The constitution of Coahuila and Texas (1827), during the Mexican period, exhorted the legislature, as one of its "principal subjects," to enact legislation "to establish, in criminal cases, the trial by jury, extending it gradually, and even adopting it in civil cases, in proportion as the advantages of this precious institution may be practically developed."[29] American settlers probably pressed for this enactment. The Texas government later enacted a form of trial by jury, but not exactly in

[27]Francis S. Philbrick, *The Laws of Indiana Territory, 1801–1809* (1930), ccxviii.
[28]Quoted in Philbrick, *op. cit.*, ccxvi–ccxvii.
[29]Coahuila and Texas const., 1827, sec. 192.

the American mold.[30] The constitution of the republic of Texas (1836), in its declaration of rights, affirmed the right of an accused "to a speedy and public trial, by an impartial jury.... And the right of trial by jury shall remain inviolate."

The Texas Constitution also contemplated wholesale adoption of the common law. "Congress," it said, "shall, as early as practicable, introduce, by statute, the common law of England, with such modifications as our circumstances, in their judgment, may require" (art. IV, sec. 13). But Texas never really "received" English law, in any literal or classical sense. Rather, the republic adopted a Texas subdialect of the American dialect of law. There was thoroughgoing acceptance of trial by jury, "that ever-to-be prized system of jurisprudence," as the supreme court of Texas called it in 1840.[31] But from the very start, law and equity were merged in court organization and procedure. The constitution of 1845 specifically gave to the district courts jurisdiction "of all suits... without regard to any distinction between law and equity."[32] In 1840, the civil law was formally abolished; but even then Texas did not introduce the full rigors of common-law pleading. Rather, it preferred to retain "as heretofore" the civil-law system of "petition and answer." Procedure, then, conformed neither to common-law nor civil-law norms. It was a hybrid system. Judges and lawyers, in the early years, seemed genuinely ambivalent about the two rival systems. On the one hand, civil law was alien, and few lawmen could cope with it. The law of 1840, by keeping some parts of civil-law pleading, forced courts (as one judge said) to look for "principles and criteria in a language generally unknown to us." As a result, "Constant perplexities... annoy and delay us at each step."[33] But in a later case, another Texas judge condemned some aspects of common-law pleading as "Bold, crafty, and unscrupulous."[34] Still a third judge took a middle view:

> The object of our statutes on the subject of pleading is to simplify as much as possible that branch of the proceedings

[30]Edward L. Markham, Jr., "The Reception of the Common Law of England in Texas and the Judicial Attitude Toward That Reception, 1840–1859," 29 Texas L. Rev. 904 (1951).

[31]*Edwards* v. *Peoples*, Dallam 359, 360 (Tex., 1840).

[32]Texas const., 1845, art. IV, sec. 10. On Texas procedure, see Joseph W. McKnight, "The Spanish Legacy to Texas Law," 3 Am. J. Legal Hist. 222, 299 (1959).

[33]*Whiting* v. *Turley*, Dallam 453, 454 (Tex., 1842).

[34]*Long* v. *Anderson*, 4 Tex. 422, 424 (1849).

in courts, which by the ingenuity and learning of both common and civil law lawyers and judges had become so refined in its subtleties as to substitute in many instances the shadow for the substance.[35]

In the long run, the civil-law tradition was too alien and inaccessible to survive. But it did undermine the inevitability—and therefore the legitimacy—of strict common-law pleading. What resulted was a procedure that used common-law terms and some common-law attitudes, but was considerably more streamlined and rational. Peripheral Texas was, in short, free to do what other states could do only by breaking with habit and tradition. But in Texas, divergences from the common law did not *look* like reforms; they looked like civil-law survivals. In a sense they were; what survived, however, survived because it suited the needs and wants of Texas jurists.

Chunks of civil law also remained imbedded in the substantive law of Texas. Texas recognizes the holographic will—an unwitnessed will in the dead person's handwriting. Texas has also kept the community-property system; indeed, Texas gave the system constitutional recognition.[36] Texas shares these "survivals" with Louisiana, and with a number of states carved out of Mexican territory, notably California. That these institutions lived on, despite the terrific pressure for common law, indicates either that they were toughly sewn into the social fabric, or that they fulfilled some unique social function. The holographic will invited ordinary people to make wills by themselves, without consulting lawyers. The community-property system suited the facts of family life as well as or better than common-law rules of marital property; the common-law rules were themselves in process of change.

Louisiana was the only solid, durable enclave of civil law. Here American expansion collided with an entrenched civil-law population. Louisiana's brand of civil law had no particular intrinsic merits. At the time of the Louisiana Purchase it was an arcane, bewildering hodgepodge of French and Spanish law, a melange of codes, customs and doctrines of various ages. The French had settled Louisiana, but the Spanish had governed it from 1766 to 1803. Louisiana law was as baffling as the common law at its worst. Its "babel" of legislation, according to Edward Livingston, was only equaled by the "Dissonances" of the Court of Pleas, "where

---

[35]*Hamilton* v. *Black*, Dallam 586, 587 (Tex., 1844).
[36]Texas const.. 1845, art. VII, sec. 19.

American Shop keepers, French planters and Spanish clerks sit on the same bench," listening to "American Attorneys, French procureurs and Castillian Abogados," each speaking his own language.[37]

In Louisiana, too, the usual conflict developed between the native population and incoming lawyers and judges.[38] Jefferson was anxious to Americanize the government and law. He controlled the governorship and the territorial judges. But the Creole population was a continuing problem. The territorial legislature, in 1806, under some pressure to move toward common law, was willing to accept trial by jury in criminal cases, along with the writ of *habeas corpus,* but otherwise declared the civil law in force, that is, the "Roman Civil code... which is composed of the institutes, digest and code of the emperor Justinian, aided by the authority of the commentators of the civil law.... The Spanish law, consisting of the books of the *recopilación de Castilla* and *autos acordados* ...the seven parts or *partidas* of the King Don Alphonse the learned [and others]... the ordinances and royal orders and decrees [applicable to]... the colony of Louisiana"; and "in matters of commerce," the "ordinance of Bilbao," supplemented by "Roman laws," a number of named English and civil-law treatises, "the commentaries of Valin," and "the respectable authors consulted in the United States." Governor William Charles Claiborne vetoed the law. The legislature was under the control of the Creole population; and Claiborne looked on the law of 1806 as particularly dangerous.[39]

The matter, of course, did not end there. The leading Creole residents of Louisiana clamored for a code, to clarify the law, and to insure them against sudden, disruptive change in their social and economic status. They wanted familiar law in a workable form. The Digest of 1808, designed to bring order out of chaos, was influenced by drafts of the new French code, the Code Napoleon. This Louisiana code, then, was a civil-law code to the core; but in style it was new-French and not old-Spanish. Its political meaning was great. A careful student of the period in Louisiana feels that, from a long-term historical perspective, the civil code adopted in 1808 "was the political compromise on the basis of

[37]Quoted in George Dargo, *Jefferson's Louisiana: Politics and the Clash of Legal Traditions* (1975), p. 112.
[38]See, in general, Elizabeth G. Brown, "Legal Systems in Conflict: Orleans Territory, 1804–1812," 1 Am. J. Legal Hist. 35 (1957).
[39]Dargo, *op. cit.,* p. 136.

which the settled population of Lower Louisiana finally accepted permanent American rule." Essentially, the Jefferson administration accepted the code, and thereby gave up the possibility of total Americanization, in return for a speedier and less bumpy absorption of "what was essentially a colonial possession."[40] This compromise worked, and outlasted the fate of the code itself.

The supreme court of Louisiana later held (in 1817) that the code of 1808 had not driven out all of the old Spanish law. "Our civil code," said the court, "is a digest of the civil laws, which were in force in this country, when it was adopted"; those laws "must be considered as untouched," wherever the "alterations and amendments, introduced in the digest, do not reach them."[41] This unfortunate decision brought back the confusion of the days before the code, when the civil law of Louisiana was "an indigested mass of ancient edicts and Statutes ... the whole rendered more obscure by the heavy attempts of commentators to explain them."[42] At legislative request, Louis Moreau Lislet and Henry Carleton translated and published "The Laws of Las Siete Partidas which are still in force in the State of Louisiana," in 1820. The legislature also moved to recodify the basic law of Louisiana. They appointed three commissioners for this purpose. These commissioners drafted what became the famous Civil Code of 1825.

The leading figure in drafting this code was Edward Livingston. He was a New Yorker, devoted to law reform, who found

[40]Dargo, op cit., p. 173. The actual sources of the code of 1808 are far from clear; basically, the code seemed to be French, with a certain Spanish element, but there is great doubt, and much arguing among scholars, as to the precise weighting of the two. On this point, see Dargo, op. cit., pp. 155–64. Whatever the facts about the code itself, there is evidence that the courts cited Spanish authorities almost as much as they cited French ones. See Raphael J. Rabalais, "The Influence of Spanish Laws and Treatises on the Jurisprudence of Louisiana, 1762–1828," 42 La. L. Rev. 1485 (1982).

The living law of the territory, the actual legal customs of the people, is still another matter. Hans Baade has examined marriage contracts in French and Spanish Louisiana and concluded that French "legal folkways" with regard to marital property were dominant before Spanish rule; that they continued in some parts of the territory during Spanish rule; and that they popped back into full vigor throughout the colony when Spanish rule ended in 1803. Hans W. Baade, "Marriage Contracts in French and Spanish Louisiana: A Study in 'Notarial' Jurisprudence," 53 Tulane L. Rev. 3 (1978).

[41]Cottin v. Cottin, 5 Mart. (O.S.), 93, 94 (1817).

[42]Quoted in William B. Hatcher, Edward Livingston (1940), p. 247. For Livingston's role in the making of the civil code of 1825, see ch. 11, "The Codifier," pp. 245–88.

fertile soil for his talents in Louisiana. About eighty percent of the code's provisions were drawn directly from the Code Napoleon. French legal commentary was another important source. The common law had some influence, particularly on the law of obligations. The special needs of Louisiana were only one factor in the minds of the commissioners. They also wanted to prove that a pure, rational system of law was attainable in America. They rejected

> the undefined and undefinable common law.... [In England] the Judge drew his own rule, sometimes with Lord Mansfield, from the pure fountain of the Civil Code, sometimes from the turbid stream of doubtful usage, often from no better source than his own caprice.... [In Louisiana] our Code... will be progressing toward perfection.... the Legislature will not judge, nor the Judiciary make laws.... [W]e may hope to have the rare and inestimable blessing of written Codes, containing intelligible and certain rules to govern the ordinary relations and occurrences of life, the operations of commerce and the pursuit of remedies by action.[43]

As the quotation shows, the commissioners expected that the civil code would be only the first of a series. A code of practice was adopted by 1825. It was one of the most original of the codes. It blended French, Spanish, and common-law forms into a skillful, efficient whole. The common-law writs which were retained did not have to "pursue the forms, and be conducted according to the rules and regulations prescribed by the common law," as the code of 1805 had asserted. Louisiana came, then, to use a tripartite system of procedure, vaguely comparable to the compromise of Texas. The court structure was American. Some aspects of the common law were preserved, notably trial by jury in criminal cases. The rest of the system was a joining of two civil-law streams. In Texas common law dominated, in Louisiana civil law. In both cases, the blend was more streamlined and efficient than the common law, at least in its 19th-century version. Other states, less free to innovate, reached this state of development more gradually.

Once it had enacted a civil code and a code of procedure, the Louisiana legislature lost its zest for novelties. A proposed code of commerce was never adopted.[44] Livingston's codes of evidence and criminal law were too advanced for the legislature to swallow.

---

[43]Louisiana Legal Archives, vol. 1 (1937), xcii.
[44]The civil code already covered some aspects of commercial law.

The age of innovation passed. French language and French customs also slowly lost their grip. The civil-law substrate remained solid, in translation. The constitution of 1812 expressly provided that the legislature "shall never adopt any system or code of laws, by a general reference to the said system or code, but in all cases, shall specify the several provisions of the laws it may enact" (art. IV, sec. 2). This was meant to rule out passage of a general statute purporting to "receive" the common law. The gesture was probably unnecessary. The civil law, like the right to trial by "an impartial jury of the vicinage"[45] (also preserved by the constitution), was too important to the people who mattered in New Orleans. They were used to it; they did business by it. The codes survived the destruction of a distinctive French culture; they became an element of Louisiana's *legal* culture—part of the learning and lore of lawyers, part of the life and experience of consumers of law. By virtue of this fact, the social and educational costs of changing the system became far greater than the benefits that might be gained by matching the law of Louisiana to the law of its neighboring states. The "reform" elements of Louisiana's codes were based on civil law; but their goal was clear, concise, and useful law, law that a man could count on and make business predictions by, law which could be easily mastered. To the old-line residents, the common-law system was a weird and foreign chaos; they did not realize that the reform goals of Louisiana were also goals of common-law reform. What is clear is that, in the main, Louisiana's codes were not survivals, any more than was the case with the system of pleading in Texas. The codes were rather a reworking of an inherited legal culture, along paths that ran parallel to those the common law would follow.[46]

In Louisiana, it is a matter of local pride that there is a special legal tradition, different from other states. Louisiana is proud to belong to the great civil law family. Hence, it is natural, and easy, to overstate differences between Louisiana's legal culture and that of (say) Arkansas or Texas. Louisiana is part of a federal system,

[45]Louisiana const., 1812, art. VI, sec. 18.

[46]The same 1812 constitution, which forbade a change to the common-law system, declared that all laws and public records had to be in "the language in which the constitution of the United States is written" and the same for "judicial and legislative...proceedings." Louisiana const., 1812, art. VI, sec. 15. For those who did not speak French, French was a nuisance. This callous attitude toward the historic tongue of the settlers suggests obliquely that the preservation of the civil law in Louisiana owed precious little to sentiment.

and is subject to federal law. That was significant even in the early 19th century; it has grown more so with the passage of time. It shares a common economic system with its neighbors. The political system is not much different from Mississippi or Alabama. American settlers streamed in and out across the border, neither noticing nor caring, by and large, that they were crossing the frontier between civil and common law. Attitudes toward law and expectations about law, one guesses, are more or less the same in Shreveport as in Little Rock or Natchez. The cultural elements of Louisiana law were and are closer to Mississippi and Texas than to Ecuador or France. Whole raw pieces of common law—such as the trust—were eventually absorbed by Louisiana. Much new law that was added during the 19th century was not noticeably "civil law" in its content: business law, railroad law, the law of slaves. The civil law lives on in Louisiana, but mostly as lawyers' law and lawyers' process. In most other essential regards, Louisiana law has long since joined the Union.

CHAPTER III

LAW AND THE ECONOMY: 1776–1850

LAISSEZ-FAIRE AND ITS LIMITS

By reputation, the 19th century was the high noon of *laissez-faire*. Government, by habit and design, kept its heavy hands off the economy. But when we actually burrow into the past, we unearth a much more complex reality. It is certainly true that, for much of the century, opinion leaders and policy were both strongly supportive of business, productivity, growth. In particular, the first half of the century was a period of promotion of enterprise. Policy aimed—in Willard Hurst's phrase—at the release of creative energy; and that meant economic energy, enterprise energy. Government, reflecting its powerful constituencies, did what it could to help the economy grow; where this required subsidy or intervention, no overriding theory held government back.

Most government intervention, and government regulation, was carried on, in 1800 or 1830, by the states, not the federal government. This made it easy for scholars to accept a distorted picture of reality. The literature of the law never gave the states their due. Then, as now, jurists concentrated on what was most general about the law, features which could be summed up easily in textbooks, and which most concerned lawyers in their courtroom work. This left little room for (say) a Vermont statute on the licensing of peddlers. Historians, for their part, were concerned with dramatic and striking events, acted out on a national stage. Quite naturally, they emphasized the public law of slavery and the slave trade and the delicate relationship between state and federal governments. In the economic sphere, they watched the debates over tariff policy, a national banking system, and internal improvements. But an accurate picture of law and the economy requires close study of local law.

The federal government was not totally passive. There was some pressure to build big works of internal improvement; this

177

actually bore some fruit in the National Road. The federal effort was not frustrated by a *laissez-faire* philosophy; the "real issue," rather, was "between national and state action."[1] Generally speaking, it was the states that carried the day. So, it was true that the federal government owned no railroads, and that acts of Congress showed little awareness of railroads, before the Civil War. But this did not mean that the railroad effort was essentially, as in England, private. There was constant, feverish legislation in the states. The Pennsylvania Railroad was once quite literally the railroad of the state of Pennsylvania. State governments, furthermore, turned to railroad building after years of involvement with turnpikes, plank roads, ferries, and bridges.

In this half of the century, to be sure, the major theme of legal concern was not, in the main, regulatory, in the sense of hostile control. Overall, the thrust of the law was promotional, though from time to time there were serious moves to cut down the overpowerful to size. The men who held political power meant to create a sound basis for economic growth. This itself was partly a matter of ideology; partly it was a response to rampant pressure groups within each state. Indeed, Professor Harry Scheiber, in his study of the Ohio canal era, has demonstrated that strong political forces not only demanded state intervention to provide a general basis for economic growth, but demanded "equal distribution of costs and benefits among all members of the polity as well." This meant, in essence, giving every identifiable interest group (geographical ones included) its cut of the pie—its canal, railroad, turnpike, bank, bridge, patronage, county seat, or whatever.[2] If there was a golden age of *laissez-faire* at all, philosophically speaking, it came later in the century; and even then, it was never pure. Government promoted and encouraged the building of the Western railroads, not to mention the constant undercurrent of state economic legislation.

[1]Carter Goodrich, *Government Promotion of American Canals and Railroads, 1800–1890* (1960), p. 44.

[2]Harry N. Scheiber, *Ohio Canal Era: A Case Study of Government and the Economy, 1820–1861* (1969). See also Scheiber's essay, "The Transportation Revolution and American Law: Constitutionalism and Public Policy," in *Transportation and the Early Nation* (1982), p. 1; on the general question of the relationship of law and the economy, the writing of J. Willard Hurst is fundamental, especially *Law and the Conditions of Freedom in the Nineteenth Century United States* (1956); *Law and Economic Growth: The Legal History of the Lumber Industry in Wisconsin, 1836–1915* (1964); and *Law and Markets in United States History: Different Modes of Bargaining among Interests* (1982).

In the first half of the century, *franchise* was a key legal concept. The franchise was a grant to the private sector, out of the inexhaustible reservoir of state power. Historically, it meant a freedom, a release from restraint. To be sure, there was a great deal of controversy over franchises, in general and particular. But much of the controversy, particularly before 1850, centered on how to unlock the door of enterprise without destroying fundamental values or upsetting the balance of power.

There was a public right—a public duty—to lend a hand to productivity. This meant that government must provide public goods, especially transport, but also currency and credit. The monetary system was one of the irritants that led to Shays's Rebellion; a bitter struggle between debtors and creditors raged in the background as the Constitution of 1787 was debated; and the background noise profoundly affected the debate. The Constitution itself clearly showed a "strong distrust of allowing state legislatures to set money-supply policy"; rather, control of the money supply had to be "a matter of national policy."[3] Thus, the Constitution federalized the coinage of money; the states could not "emit Bills of Credit": they could not "make any Thing but gold and silver Coin a Tender in Payment of Debts."[4]

National banking policy was a subject of intense controversy. Twice, the federal government chartered a national bank. President Andrew Jackson was the sworn enemy of the second bank; and he succeeded in killing it. Both before and after this event, there was far more activity in the states; the states tried to ensure a sound supply of money and credit by creating their own banks or by encouraging private banking.[5] Pennsylvania owned one-third of the capital of the Bank of Pennsylvania, chartered in 1793. The Bank of the State of South Carolina, chartered in 1812, acted as the state's depository and fiscal agent; it was in effect the banking arm of the state itself.[6] Later on, it was not so common for states to own an outright share of banks. Instead, they enacted

[3] J. Willard Hurst, *A Legal History of Money in the United States, 1774–1970* (1973), p. 8.

[4] U.S. Const., art. I, sec. 10.

[5] The subject is exhaustively treated in Bray Hammond, *Banks and Politics in America, from the Revolution to the Civil War* (1957); see also J. Willard Hurst, *A Legal History of Money in the United States, 1774–1970* (1973). There is interesting material on bank litigation in Alfred S. Konefsky and Andrew J. King, eds., *The Papers of Daniel Webster: Legal Papers*, volume 2, *The Boston Practice* (1983), pp. 527–37.

[6] Hammond, *op. cit.*, p. 168.

programs of regulation, which on paper were often quite heavy. In either case, the banks, public and private, were deeply enmeshed in politics. The currency and credit problem seemed central to the life of the community. An unsound bank—and there were many—threatened its community with financial ruin.

States chartered their banks one by one. The chartering process was therefore a *rite de passage* in the life of every bank; at this crucial point, the state could (in theory) exert critical control by forcing clauses into the charter. There was, in fact, a good deal of variation in bank charters; and many of them had provisions which were designed to tie the hands of the bank in this or that way. For example, a Vermont law of 1833 granted a charter to a bank, to be known as The Farmer's Bank; the charter limited interest on loans to 6 percent; required every director to post bond with the state treasurer; and kept for the state of Vermont the option of acquiring 10 percent of the shares.[7]

In practice, the special charter system did not turn out to be a convenient or effective way to control the behavior of banks. The states began instead to adopt general banking laws, which would apply to any and every bank. In 1829, New York passed a safety-fund law. Under this law, banks had to contribute a portion of their capital to a general fund which would be used to insure payment of the notes of insolvent banks.[8] In 1837, Michigan passed the first free banking law, which dispensed with the need for a special charter; any group of incorporators could start up a bank, so long as they followed the statutory formula. New York passed a similar law in 1838. As we shall see, corporation law went through the same cycle of development, from special charter to general laws.

Transport, like money, was part of the economic infrastructure, the skeletal frame of economic life. As the possibility that the federal government would play a major role grew dimmer, the states and cities moved into the vacuum. After 1820, a tremendous amount of statutory law dealt with bridges, roads, ferries, and canals. Much of the work of the legislatures, in the first half of the 19th century, consisted of chartering transport companies, and amending these charters. Taking the Maryland laws of 1835–36 as a sample, we find in the first pages an amendment

[7]Acts of Vt., 1833, ch. 34, pp. 60–67.
[8]Ronald E. Seavoy, *The Origins of the American Business Corporation, 1784–1855* (1982), pp. 117–48.

to "an act for building a bridge over the Little North-East, in Cecil County, near McCauley's mill" (ch. 23), three more bridge laws, and an amendment to "the act incorporating the Annapolis and Potomac Canal Company" (ch. 37), all in January 1836; many other laws in the same session incorporated or amended the charters of road or turnpike companies, or authorized road building— for example, "An Act to lay out and open a road through a part of Frederick and Baltimore Counties," which was passed March 2, 1836 (ch. 121).

Chartering, however, was only one of the ways in which the government played a role in stimulating transport. The states and cities played a more critical role: they supported, by money and credit, internal improvements; some they constructed themselves. New York built the great Erie Canal between 1817 and 1825— 363 miles long—at a cost of a little more than $7,000,000. It was a tremendous financial success. The tolls surpassed all expectations. Even more important, the canal stimulated commerce, and served as a "great channel of westward migration." Its opening "may be regarded as the most decisive single event in the history of American transportation."[9] The Erie Canal naturally invited emulation. In the peak year of 1840, an estimated 14.19 million dollars was invested in canals in the United States.[10]

By this time, the railroad was already moving toward the center of the stage. The full flowering of the railroad era came later. But both the Pennsylvania Railroad and the Baltimore and Ohio were founded in this period; and both were supported if not controlled by government. It was the city of Baltimore which supplied the money for the B & O. Other states chose one or the other path of support for their railroads during the early, flush period of enthusiasm. In Ohio, in 1837, the state passed a general law—the "Loan Law"—promising support in the form of matching funds, to *any* internal improvement company (railroad, canal, or turnpike) that met certain standards. The law was repealed in 1842; but more than a hundred special laws, between 1836 and 1850, authorized local aid to the promoters of railroads.[11]

[9]Carter Goodrich, *Government Promotion of American Canals and Railroads, 1800– 1890*, pp. 52–55.

[10]Carter Goodrich et al., *Canals and American Economic Development* (1961), p. 209; see also the excellent study by Harry N. Scheiber, *Ohio Canal Era: A Case Study of Government and the Economy, 1820–1861* (1969).

[11]Carter Goodrich, *Government Promotion of American Canals and Railroads*, pp. 136–37; Harry Scheiber, *Ohio Canal Era*, pp. 110–11, 152.

The states granted charters; sometimes they contributed money. They also used their lawmaking power to make rules and give instructions to legal institutions, in ways that would help the entrepreneur. For example, the state had the power of eminent domain (the power to seize property for public use); but the state had to pay for whatever property it took. This requirement of "just compensation" was written into federal and state constitutions. In the first half of the 19th century, states freely lent this power to private businesses that served "public" purposes—canal or turnpike companies, very notably. The companies could then take what land they chose. This was itself a kind of subsidy; but there was more. Judicial doctrine tilted very substantially toward the companies, and not the landowners. In many places, for example, the doctrine of "offsetting" values was in effect. This meant that if a canal company took my land, worth $5,000, it was entitled to take account of the benefits I would get from the canal. If the canal would raise the value of the *rest* of my land by $3,000, this could be subtracted from my compensation. The result was "no doubt a very large involuntary private subsidy" for public undertakings.[12]

On the surface, such policies favored business, especially transport business, and disfavored the ordinary farmer and landowner, the backbone of the country. But these policies were, no doubt, genuinely popular. A few unlucky people suffered; but the great bulk of farmer-settlers had a desperate hunger for transport: bridges, ferries, canals, turnpikes, and later railroads. These were necessary to carry their goods to market, to bring settlers to their region, to stimulate business, to raise the overall value of their lands. In general, the subsidies were popular, and so was an orgy of bond-floating and shaky investment, which the states and cities indulged in like drunken sailors. The national hangover came later.

Outside of transport and finance, state regulation was rather random and planless. Not that a massive ideology dictated limits. The country was underdeveloped; most Americans no doubt felt that the state should encourage development, though perhaps they also felt that the state, like the Lord, helped those who helped

[12]Harry N. Scheiber, "The Road to *Munn:* Eminent Domain and the Concept of Public Purpose in the State Courts," in Donald Fleming and Bernard Bailyn, eds., *Law in American History* (1971), pp. 329, 364.

themselves. Economic law was practical and promotional. Trade laws were tailored to specific needs. The states continued colonial programs of quality control over export commodities. Georgia law (1791) required tobacco to be "packed in hogsheads or casks" and "stamped by some inspector legally thereunto appointed";[13] unstamped tobacco could not be legally exported. In Connecticut, by a law of 1794, bar iron could not be sold unless "stamped with the name of the manufacturer thereof, and of the town where such iron is manufactured."[14] In New York, salt was to be packed "in barrels, casks or boxes" and inspected to make sure that the salt was "free from dirt, filth and stones, and from admixtures of lime... and fully drained from pickle."[15] The New York revised statutes of 1827–28 included laws to regulate sales by auctioneers, hawkers, and peddlers and provisions for the inspection of flour, meal, beef, pork, "pot and pearl ashes," fish, "fish or liver oil," lumber, staves, flaxseed, sole leather, leaf tobacco, butter and pressed hay. Not all of these were export commodities. Some were merely staple goods.

It was an ancient task of government to regulate weights and measures and to provide standard measures for commodities. Massachusetts, for example, prescribed standard measures by statute for potatoes, onions, salt, and wood. There were also state laws that aimed at protecting consumers against false labeling and adulteration. In Massachusetts (1833), only "pure spermaceti oil"[16] could be "sold under the names of sperm, spermaceti, lamp, summer, fall, winter and second winter oils." A seller who sold "adulterated" oils under one of these names had to pay double the difference between the value of pure and adulterated oil. But no statutory machinery was set up to enforce this law. The crude penalties would be enough, it was hoped, to attract an aggrieved merchant or consumer to enforce the law on his own.

The age of conservation was a long way off; nonetheless, there were preliminary attempts to safeguard natural resources. Massachusetts in 1819 made it unlawful to take pickerel "with spears, in the night time," or to shoot these fish "at any time." This act attached a money penalty of fifty cents per unlawful

---

[13]Oliver H. Prince, comp., *Digest of the Laws of the State of Georgia* (2nd ed., 1837), p. 817 (act of Dec. 23, 1791).

[14]Stats. Conn. 1808, pp. 421–22 (act of May, 1794).

[15]Rev. Stats. N.Y. 1829, vol. I, p. 270.

[16]Laws Mass. 1833, ch. 215.

fish, payable "to and for the use of the person who shall sue for the same."[17] The usual motive was economic, rather than a love of nature. Massachusetts (1818) prohibited indiscriminate killing of birds which were "useful and profitable to the citizens, either as articles of food or as instruments in the hands of Providence to destroy various noxious insects, grubs, and caterpillars."[18] New Jersey, in 1789, restricted the picking of cranberries between June 1 and October 10, because "cranberries, if suffered to remain on the vines until sufficiently ripened, would be a valuable article of exportation."[19] By a protectionist act of 1822, Massachusetts forbade nonresidents to "take any lobsters, tautog, bass or other fish, within the harbors, streams, or waters of the towns of Fairhaven, New Bedford, Dartmouth, and Westport," and transport the catch "in smacks or vessels" of over fifteen tons, or in those of any size owned outside the Commonwealth.[20]

Public health was also a matter of some state concern, though the tools were primitive and the scope of regulation rather narrow. Quarantine laws were common, however. New York had an elaborate law in the 1820s directing ships to anchor near "the marine hospital on Staten-Island," dividing ships into classes depending on the perceived danger, and prescribing rules for clearing quarantine, including whitewashing and fumigation "with mineral acid gas" and the washing and airing of clothing and bedding. The rules were especially strict for ships coming from places where "yellow, bilious, malignant, or other pestilential or infectious fever" had existed, or if disease had broken out on board the ship.[21] State laws allowed "nuisances" to be "abated" when they were a danger to health. Land-use controls were in their infancy; but Michigan, for example, in the 1830s, authorized township boards, village governments, and the mayors and aldermen of cities to "assign certain places for the exercising of any trade or employment offensive to the inhabitants, or dangerous to the public health." Any such "assignment" could be revoked if the place or building became a "nuisance" because of "offensive smells

---

[17]Laws Mass. 1819, ch. 45. A later act subjected the operation of this law to local option.
[18]Laws Mass. 1818, ch. 103.
[19]Rev. Stats. N.J. 1821, p. 89 (act of Nov. 10, 1789).
[20]Laws Mass. 1822, ch. 97.
[21]Rev. Stats. N.Y. 1829, vol. I, pp. 425ff.

or exhalations," or was "otherwise hurtful or dangerous."[22]

When food products were regulated, the primary goals were usually economic; but sometimes public health or consumer protection were at least secondary goals.[23] Some states gave local medical societies the power to examine and license prospective doctors. Unlicensed doctors were not allowed to collect fees through regular court process. Other laws made unauthorized practice subject to fines.[24] Lastly, laws on gaming, drinking, and gambling aimed to protect public morality. In New York, no "puppet-show...wire or rope-dance, or...other idle shows" could be exhibited for profit.[25] Regulations of morality were also economic regulations, in that they defined the permissible limits of earning a living. From this point of view, too, much of the penal code was concerned with economic control: laws against theft, to take the simplest example.

Despite these examples of economic regulation, 19th-century government was no leviathan. Even in the large Eastern states, its hold over the economy was weak. Many programs must have existed only on paper. Many of the inspection laws, licensing laws, and laws about weights and measures were feeble and vapidly enforced. Two pillars of the modern state were missing: a strong tax base and a trained civil service. Without these two, and perhaps without a firmer grip on economic information, the state could not hope to master and control behavior in the market.

State government depended chiefly on the property tax. This tax was locally assessed and locally collected. It was supplemented by excise taxes—on slaves, on carriages, or on personal property in general. Hard money was scarce, and the voting public was not accustomed to the idea that they should pay to the state any appreciable chunk of their income or wealth. John Marshall, in one of his most famous lines, said that the power to tax was the power to destroy.[26] Power to destroy was not lightly conceded in the 19th century. There was a general concern for fairness and equality in

[22]Rev. Stats. Michigan 1838, p. 171.

[23]Oscar and Mary Handlin, *Commonwealth: A Study of the Role of Government in the American Economy: Massachusetts, 1744–1861* (rev. ed., 1969), p. 206.

[24]Laws N.Y. 1806, ch. 138; Laws Mass. 1819, ch. 113; Laws N.Y. 1830, ch. 126; unauthorized doctors were liable to forfeit "a sum not exceeding twenty-five dollars." See, in general, Richard H. Shryock, *Medical Licensing in America, 1650–1965* (1967).

[25]Rev. Stats. N.Y. 1829, vol. 1, p. 660.

[26]The case was *McCulloch* v. *Maryland,* 4 Wheat. 316 (1819).

tax policy,[27] but above all there was a general disdain for shelling out much in the way of cash. The level of taxation and expenditure was low. The state of Massachusetts spent $215,200, all told, in 1794. More than half of this was interest on debt.[28] Dollars went farther in those days; still, the puniest sewer district today could better that mark.

State action, then, was pinched for pennies. It had to substitute artifice for cash; hence there was heavy use of the fee system. Wherever possible, users bore the costs of state services. Litigants paid judges for their lawsuits; bride and groom paid for their marriage licenses. Local users had to pay assessments for local roads—or, if they were cash-poor, pay off their share in labor and sweat. In Mississippi, under a law of 1831, free adult males who paid less than six dollars of taxes a year had to "perform not exceeding four days labour on the roads in each year," along with "all free persons of colour, male and female, over eighteen and under forty-five years of age." Under some conditions, a man could substitute by providing horses, oxen, and plows.[29] Under a Virginia act of 1818, staves could not be exported before an inspector general and "cullers" had inspected them. The inspector general was "entitled to demand and receive" a fee of ten cents "on every thousand merchantable staves"; cullers too had to be paid their fee.[30] An elaborate Pennsylvania act of 1835 set up a similar system for meat. For "inspecting, examining and branding each tierce, barrel and half barrel of salted beef or pork," the inspectors could demand eight cents.[31]

There was no trained civil service in the modern sense. Government was not run by experts, even experts in running a government. Politics was a way to make money or use power. It was sometimes an occupation, less frequently a calling. Many politi-

[27]A clause in the Arkansas constitution of 1836 declared that "no one species of property...shall be taxed higher than another species of property, of equal value," excepting taxes on "merchants, hawkers, peddlers, and privileges" (art. VII, Revenue, sec. 2). Citing this clause, the state supreme court declared void a special tax on billiard tables, and a tax on "the privilege of keeping each stallion or jack." The right to own a billiard table or to keep a stallion was a "property right" not a "privilege"; it was unlawful, therefore, to tax these rights specially. *Stevens v. State*, 2 Ark. 291 (1840); *Gibson v. County of Pulaski*, 2 Ark. 309 (1840).

[28]Handlin and Handlin, *op. cit.*, p. 62.

[29]Laws Miss. 1831, p. 364 (act of December 16, 1831).

[30]Va. Rev. Code 1819, vol. II, pp. 197, 200.

[31]Laws Pa. 1834–35, sec. 82, p. 405.

cians were amateurs, or lawyers who were amateurs except at law. That every man could aspire to high office was part of the democratic faith; as we saw, the principle of rotation was written into some of the early constitutions. Men like Jefferson and Jackson considered high turnover no evil, but a positive virtue in government. Jackson, especially, felt that government jobs called for basic, fungible skills; any man of intelligence and honor could hold office. In fact, Jefferson and Jackson tended to appoint men of elite background and standing to higher offices, despite their egalitarian ideologies. These men were not experts, but they were educated and skillful. If there was any lack of trained men in government, the lawyers filled it. Lawyers had some education, some grasp of the machinery of government, some insight into stateways.[32]

In general, however, both the scope and administrative strength of regulation were limited. Regulation tended to be local, self-sustaining—as in the fee system—and conservative in the use of staff. Typically, administrative tasks were given to existing office-holders. When a state created an insurance commission, it might appoint the state treasurer commissioner. For simplicity of regulation, laws frequently required private citizens to stamp, mark, label, or post. Every ferry keeper in Illinois had to maintain "a post or board, on which shall be written the rates of ferriage... by law allowed."[33] Basically, the law let private citizens enforce what regulation there was. If no one brought a lawsuit, or complained to the district attorney about some violation, nothing was done. The state did not seriously try to administer, or carry through independently, what the statutes decreed.

Some types of social control, which may have worked well enough in tight, narrow seabound colonies, were strained to the breaking point after 1800. They did not suit a country of great distances, scattered population, diverse social conditions. Statutes in the Western states and territories, borrowed from the East, spoke of public markets and commodity inspection. Probably these programs never came to life; they were dead words on paper. In the rest of the country, the gap between book law and living law was perhaps only slightly less real. When culture and technology

[32]See, in general, Sidney H. Aronson, *Status and Kinship in the Higher Civil Service* (1964).

[33]Francis S. Philbrick, ed., *Pope's Ill. Digest, 1815*, vol. I (1938), p. 264.

posed demands that government was too poor and too weak to respond to, the private sector took over. Historically, government controlled money and credit, and government built and ran highways, ferries, bridges, and canals. In the 19th century, the commercial and landowning public wanted more and more of these improvements. The economy had an unquenchable thirst for infrastructure; but at the critical time, the power of government fell short of the demand; and control of the infrastructure passed into private hands. *Laissez-faire*, it may turn out, was more powerful as practice than as theory, even in the 19th century.

THE BUSINESS CORPORATION

A corporation, in the jargon of lawbooks, is an artificial person. This means that it is a legal entity, which, like a person, can sue and be sued, own property, and transact business. Unlike natural persons, the corporation can survive the death of any particular member or members. Its life begins with a charter; and it dissolves when its charter expires. An unlimited, or perpetual, charter is a definite possibility; and in fact is the normal case for 20th-century corporations.

The charter is a grant of authority from the sovereign, which specifies the powers, rights, and duties of the entity. In an American state in the 1980s, anyone who fills out a simple form, and pays a small fee, can receive articles of incorporation and embark on corporate life. In the early 19th century, however, the legislature granted charters by statute, one by one. Every charter was in theory tailor-made to the case at hand.

In the colonial period, this system was not at all inappropriate. Corporations were uncommon before 1800. And few of those which existed were business corporations. Almost all of the colonial corporations were churches, charities, or cities or boroughs.[34] New York City was a chartered corporation.[35] In all of

---

[34]In England, only the crown had the right to incorporate. In the colonies, royal governors, proprietors, and in some cases legislative bodies issued charters. Actually, not many colonial cities and towns were technically corporations at all. It did not seem to make much difference in the way these municipalities behaved.

In 1778, Governor Livingston of New Jersey tried to issue a charter himself without legislative approval; but that was an isolated incident. It was generally recognized after the Revolution that the legislature was the branch of government that made corporations. John W. Cadman, Jr., *The Corporation in New Jersey: Business and Politics, 1791–1875* (1949), p. 4.

the 18th century, charters were issued to only 335 businesses. Only seven of these were during the colonial period; 181 were issued between 1796 and 1800.[36] Banks, insurance companies, water companies, and companies organized to build or run canals, turnpikes, and bridges made up the overwhelming majority of these early corporations. A mere handful, notably the New Jersey Society for Establishing Useful Manufactures (1791), were established for manufacturing purposes.

In the 19th century, the situation began to change. In the first place, more and more charters were issued each year. And while most charters in the first half of the century were still connected with finance and transport, a small but growing minority had more general commercial or industrial aims. In Pennsylvania, 2,333 special charters were granted to business corporations between 1790 and 1860. Of these about 1,500 were transportation companies; less than two hundred were for manufacturing.[37] Joseph S. Davis has pointed out that

> The English tradition that corporate powers were to be granted only in rare instances, never deeply intrenched here, was opposed by a strong and growing prejudice in favor of equality—a prejudice which led almost at once to the enactment of general incorporation acts for ecclesiastical, educational, and literary corporations. Partiality in according such powers was to be expected of the English crown, but it was a serious charge to lay at the door of democratic legislatures.... Not least important, the physical ease of securing charters was far greater in the new states than in England.... Legislatures were not overworked and did business free of charge and with reasonable promptness.... Finally, the practice in creating corporations for non-business purposes, though it did not lead promptly to granting freedom of incorporation to business corporations, undoubtedly smoothed the way for special acts incorporating business associations.[38]

On the colonial corporation in general, see Joseph S. Davis, *Essays in the Earlier History of American Corporations* (1917).

[35]See, in general, Hendrik Hartog, *Public Property and Private Power: The Corporation of the City of New York in American Law, 1730–1870* (1983).

[36]Joseph S. Davis, *Essays in the Earlier History of American Corporations*, vol. II (1917), p. 24.

[37]Louis Hartz, *Economic Policy and Democratic Thought: Pennsylvania, 1776–1860* (1948), p. 38.

[38]Davis, *op. cit.*, vol. II, pp. 7–8.

Until about the middle of the century, the corporation was by no means the dominant form of business organization. Most commercial enterprises were partnerships. They consisted of two or three partners, often related by blood or marriage. The partnership was "used by all types of business, from the small country storekeepers to the great merchant bankers."[39] But as the economy developed, entrepreneurs made more and more use of the corporation, especially for transport ventures. The corporate form was a more efficient way to structure and finance their ventures. The special charter system was clumsy and cumbersome. It was a waste of the legislature's time as well—or would have been, if in fact each charter was carefully scrutinized, and its clauses cut to order for the particular case. In fact, except for projects of special importance, charters became stylized, standardized, matters of rote. They were finally replaced, as we shall see, by general incorporation laws.[40]

Early charters had many features which, from the standpoint of 20th-century corporation law, appear odd or idiosyncratic. Eternal life was not the rule. In the early 19th century, charter terms of five, twenty, or thirty years' duration were quite common. In New Jersey, every manufacturing company (except one) had a limited term of life before 1823; perpetual duration remained rare before the Civil War.[41] In Maryland, a general law of 1839 limited corporate life (for mining or manufacturing companies) to a maximum of thirty years.[42] Early charters often departed from the principle of one vote for each share of stock. It was not the rule in Maryland, for example, until after 1819. In New Hampshire, under the charter of the Souhegan Nail and Cotton Factory (1812), each of the fifty shares of capital stock was entitled to a vote, but no member was entitled to more than ten votes, no matter how many shares he owned.[43] The 1836 charter of a Maryland company, incorporated to build a turnpike from Hagerstown to the Pennsylvania border, allocated votes as follows: "for every share ... not exceeding three, one vote each; for any number of

[39] Alfred D. Chandler, Jr., *The Visible Hand: The Managerial Revolution in American Business* (1977), pp. 36–37.

[40] The movement from special charter to general incorporation laws in New York is treated in Ronald E. Seavoy, *The Origins of the American Business Corporation, 1784–1855* (1982).

[41] John W. Cadman, *The Corporation in New Jersey, 1791–1875* (1949), p. 366.

[42] Joseph G. Blandi, *Maryland Business Corporations, 1783–1852* (1934), p. 56.

[43] Laws N.H., vol. 8, 1811–20 (1920), p. 149.

shares greater than three and not exceeding ten, five votes; for any number of shares greater than ten, and not exceeding fifty, seven votes; for any number of shares greater than fifty, and not exceeding one hundred, ten votes; and for every additional hundred shares above one hundred, ten votes"; thirty votes was the maximum for any shareholder.[44] Some charters restricted the number of shares any individual might hold in any one corporation. In Pennsylvania, after 1810, bank charters usually prohibited the transfer of bank stock to "foreigners."[45] In 1822, a bank charter in New Jersey required the new corporation to use some of its capital to aid the fisheries at Amboy.[46] Limited liability—now considered one of the main objects of incorporation—was not universal in the 19th century. Bank stock did not possess this great boon in New York, for example. In Connecticut, limited liability was common for manufacturing companies before the 1830s; but in some charters—for example, that of the Mystic Manufacturing Company of 1814—the stockholders were to be "responsible in their private capacity," if the corporation became insolvent.[47]

But the main line of development was clear. Gradually, these variations were leveled out, and the practice moved in the direction of a kind of common law of corporations, whose basic contours were set by business custom and the needs of entrepreneurs. Between 1800 and 1850, the essential nature of the corporation changed. No longer was the business corporation a unique, *ad hoc* creation, vesting exclusive control over a public asset or natural resource in one group of favorites or investors. Rather, it was becoming a general form for organizing a business, legally open to all, and with few real restrictions on entry, duration, and management. Business practice led the way. The living law on proxy voting, general and special meetings, inspection of books, and the transfer of stock, gradually created demands (which were granted) for standard clauses in corporate charters; and ultimately these norms were embodied in the statute and case law of corporations.

There were many detours along the way before the law reached a stage in which there was simple access to the corporate form, open to all. Something must be said about state partnership in

[44]Laws Md. 1835–36, ch. 321, sec. 4.
[45]Hartz, *op. cit.*, p. 255.
[46]Cadman, *op. cit.*, p. 68.
[47]*Resolves and Private Laws, Conn., 1789–1836*, vol. II (1837), p. 851.

corporate affairs, about the anticorporation movement, and about the fate of rival forms of business organization.

State partnership in corporate enterprise seemed natural in the early 19th century. In the first place, many corporations were chartered to do work traditionally part of the function of the state. These jobs included road building, banking and the digging of canals. Secondly, since each franchise was a privilege and favor, the state had the right to exact a price,[48] which might include strict controls or even profit sharing. Thirdly, state participation was a good way to help out an enterprise. It was a way of priming the pump, a way of supporting vital enterprise that would in turn enrich the economy. Fourth, public participation enhanced public control: if the state owned stock, and its men sat on the board, they could make sure the company acted in the public interest. Fifth, state investment could bring money into the treasury. If the dreams of the enterprise came true, big dividends would flow into public coffers. Pennsylvania, for example, not only owned stock in its banks, but, after 1806, invested in turnpikes, bridge companies, canal companies, and finally in railroads. States and cities both engaged in railroad boosting. Between 1827 and 1878, New York State lent, leased, or donated $10,308,844.77 for construction of sixteen railroads.[49] Some of these loans turned very sour in the aftermath of the panic of 1837. The New York constitution of 1846 severely restricted state aid to private corporations. The railroads then turned to the cities and towns with "astonishing success." Cities and towns were passionately eager to induce the lines to build routes that went through their communities; a railroad line, they felt, meant access to markets, rising land values, and general prosperity. Most commonly, the cities bought stock in the railroads. The city of Buffalo, for example, subscribed $1,000,000 for stock in the Buffalo & Jamestown Railroad. A few towns bought bonds; a few donated money outright; and in 1842, the city of Albany guaranteed, by endorsement, $100,000 worth of bonds of the Mohawk & Hudson.[50]

Pennsylvania experimented with mixed public and private enterprises. At one stage in the state's marriage with its railroads,

[48]Sometimes quite literally. The charter of the Bank of Philadelphia (1803) required the bank to pay a bonus of $135,000 to the state. The bonus practice was not abolished in Pennsylvania until 1842. Hartz, *op. cit.*, pp. 54–56.

[49]Harry H. Pierce, *Railroads of New York: A Study of Government Aid* (1953), p. 15.

[50]Pierce, *op. cit.*, pp. 18–19.

in the 1830s, Pennsylvania furnished locomotives; private companies supplied the other cars. Before 1842, the state of Maryland chose ten of the thirty directors of the Baltimore & Ohio; the city of Baltimore chose eight. In New Jersey, the "monopoly bill" of 1832 granted exclusive transport franchises in exchange for gifts of stock to the state. The state's shares carried a higher priority for dividends than other shares—one of the earliest instances of preferred stock. For years, New Jersey profited nicely from its railroad investments; the income helped lower the taxes that had to be levied on residents.

State participation in enterprise was, as it turned out, only a passing phase. There was periodic outcry that the state had no business meddling in the sphere of private capital. These voices were weak at first. The business cycle strengthened them; during periods of crashes, panics, and depressions, state investments often went seriously awry. This led to disillusionment with the whole idea of state participation. States and cities, nearly bankrupted in the years after 1837, were tempted to sell off their assets for cash. In 1844, a referendum in Pennsylvania approved sale of the Main Line to private interests. As it happened, the sale was not consummated until 1857. The Pennsylvania Railroad then bought the line for cash and railroad bonds. In exchange the state gave the railroad all tracks and equipment of the line, and exempted it "forever, from the payment of taxes upon tonnage or freight carried over the said railroads; and... on its capital stock, bonds, dividends or property, except for city, borough, county, township, and school purposes." This extraordinary boon was declared unconstitutional one year later, in the great case of *Mott* v. *Pennsylvania Railroad*.[51] Pennsylvania's Chief Justice Ellis Lewis wrote a strong opinion denying that the state had any right to commit "political suicide" by giving up the power to tax. Legislative authority was not for sale. Lewis also felt that the public had to exert some control over the legislature, to keep it from pawning its sovereignty. Alas, faith in the "fidelity of the legislature" was often misplaced:

> Limitations of power, established by written constitutions, have their origin in a distrust of the infirmity of man. That distrust is fully justified by the history of the rise and fall of nations.[52]

[51] 30 Penn. State 9 (1858).
[52] *Ibid.*, p. 28.

This typical American fear was the source from which the system of checks and balances grew. It was a fear of unbridled power— the power of large landholders and dynastic wealth, and, most notably, the power of government. An influential segment of the public was willing to try many techniques to prevent concentration of authority and to offset the corrosive effect of money and power. The triumph of the corporation as a form of business association was therefore neither painless nor noiseless. The corporation was an object of great controversy in the first half of the 19th century. Partly because of the historic meaning and role of corporations, people in 1800 identified corporations with franchised monopolies. Corporations were creatures of state, endowed with breath for the sole purpose of holding franchise or privilege, that is, some power or right that no one else could lay claim to. Most corporations were transportation monopolies, banks, insurance companies—aggregations of "capital," representing the "few" against the "many." Unlike farm and industrial enterprise, they did not *produce* any product (so people thought). They were in a sense parasitic, and yet unduly powerful. Hence, multiplicity of corporations seemed to present grave dangers to the health of the body politic. James Sullivan, attorney general of Massachusetts, warned in 1802 that "The creation of a great variety of corporate interests . . . must have a direct tendency to weaken the power of government."[53]

The word "soulless" constantly recurs in debates over corporations. Everyone knew that corporations were really run by human beings. Yet the metaphor was not entirely pointless. Corporations did not die, and had no ultimate limit to their size. There were no natural bounds to their life or to their greed. Corporations, it was feared, could concentrate the worst urges of whole groups of men; the economic power of a corporation would not be tempered by the mentality of any one person, or by considerations of family or morality. People hated and distrusted corporations, the way some fear computers today, which are also soulless, also capable of joining the wit, skill, and malevolence of many minds.

In theory, the special charter system was a strong mode of corporate control. But the demand for charters was too great. By the 1840s and 1850s, it would have swamped the legislatures, if the process had not become so routine. Even so, state session laws

[53]Quoted in Handlin and Handlin, *op. cit.*, p. 260.

bulged with special charters. Valuable time was spent in the drudgery of issuing, amending, and extending hundreds of charters. In the rush, there was little time to supervise those charters which perhaps needed supervision. Since even a radical routinization was not the answer, the legislatures took the next logical step, delegation: that is, the passage of general acts. The legislature could save itself time; could make effective law for all corporations, in one carefully considered law; and could turn the corporate form into a freely available right, rather than a privilege of the few.

Even in the late 18th century a few general laws were passed, which applied to churches, academies, and library societies. A New York law of 1811, "relative to incorporations for Manufacturing purposes," is usually credited as the first general law for *business* corporations. Under this law, "any five or more persons who shall be desirous to form a company for the purpose of manufacturing woollen, cotton, or linen goods, or for the purpose of making glass, or for the purpose of making from ore bar-iron, anchors, millirons, steel, nail-rods, hoop-iron and ironmongery, sheet copper, sheet lead, shot, white lead and red lead," and who filed a certificate with some standard information in the office of the secretary of state, became, for "the term of twenty years next after the day of filing such certificate," a "body corporate and politic, in fact and in name."[54]

Other corporation acts picked up the New York plan. These laws were general in the sense that they applied to all corporations in a particular field—manufacturing, banking, or insurance. Typically, too, the laws did not provide an exclusive method of starting a corporation. They left the door open for private charters, if the incorporators preferred. In fact, the early general laws were not particularly effective. When they imposed rules of any bite at all, the business community ignored them and took the private-charter route. At most, entrepreneurs would incorporate temporarily under a general law, until they could extract a private charter from the legislature. To put teeth into the general laws, the New York constitution of 1846 took a somewhat more drastic step. It restricted special charters to "cases where in the judgment of the Legislature, the objects of the corporation cannot be attained under general laws."[55] As it turned out, the legislature was quite

[54]Laws N.Y. 1811, ch. 47.
[55]N.Y. const., 1846, art. 8, sec. 1. See Seavoy, *op. cit.*, pp. 177–88.

accommodating in making such judgments. At the close of the period, then, the special charter was still dominant. But the handwriting was on the wall. The Louisiana constitution of 1845, a bellwether in many ways, contained a much stronger clause: "Corporations shall not be created in this State by special laws except for political or municipal purposes."[56]

It was no accident to find clauses about charters in state constitutions. When Chief Justice Lewis spoke of the infirmity of man, he meant man in government as well as private man. There were rich and unscrupulous incorporators, and they were not always unwilling to use influence (or money) to put legislators in a pliant mood. There were enough actual scandals to weaken public confidence in elected officials. To win the war against the great agglomerations, it was felt necessary to put restraints on the legislatures too. Under the New York constitution of 1821, the "assent of two-thirds of the members elected to each branch of the legislature" was needed for passage of any bill "creating, continuing, altering, or renewing any body politic or corporate."[57] A similar provision appeared in Delaware's constitution of 1831. Delaware little dreamed it would some day be a snug harbor for out-of-state corporations; its constitution added sternly that no act of incorporation "shall continue in force for a longer period than twenty years, without the re-enactment of the Legislature, unless it be an incorporation for public improvement."[58]

In all the debates and controversies, of course, corporations never lacked for defenders. When a two-thirds provision, like New York's, was proposed in the New Jersey convention of 1844, one delegate remarked he was "a friend to corporations. They have done more to increase the prosperity of our State than anything else. Let the legislature grant all that may apply, if the object is to benefit the community." Proponents of the two-thirds rule had "ventured to show their teeth at these little monsters, but if they believe them to be such dangerous creatures as they have represented them to be, they had better come manfully up to the work and strangle them at once, than to keep up this continued snapping at their heels."[59] The proposal was defeated.

[56]La. const., 1845, art. 123. This provision was copied in Iowa the following year. Iowa const., 1846, art. 8, sec. 2.

[57]N.Y. const., 1821, art. 7, sec. 9.

[58]Del. const., 1831, art. 2, sec. 17.

[59]*Proceedings of the New Jersey State Constitutional Convention of 1844* (1942), pp. 537–38, 539.

The movement against corporations could never muster the strength or consensus to strangle them, as opposed to snapping at their heels. Yet no issue was more persistent, perhaps, in the period between 1815 and 1850, than the issue of public control over corporations. In the famous case of *Dartmouth College* v. *Woodward* (1819),[60] the United States Supreme Court faced the issue squarely. By the terms of the federal Constitution, no state could impair the obligation of a contract. But what was a "contract"? In *Dartmouth College*, the court decided that a corporate charter was "a contract made on a valuable consideration," a "contract for the security and disposition of property." Consequently, no legislature could change the terms of any charter which a previous legislature had granted; to do so would "impair" the charter.[61]

Dartmouth College was no business corporation; but the court, and the newspaper-reading public, well understood that the decision went beyond any question of the charters of colleges. News of the decision evoked a great howl of protest. Many contemporaries (and their intellectual descendants) felt that the *Dartmouth College* case was a blow to popular sovereignty; it took away from "the people and their elected representatives" a "large part of the control over social and economic affairs." That was one way of looking at the case. The court and its defenders saw it differently. The purpose of the decision was to secure property interests, and to protect ownership and management rights from shifting, temporary winds of public opinion. A climate of legal stability promoted economic growth, while doing simple justice.

Dartmouth College had a far less sweeping effect on the law of corporations than one might have guessed. In the actual decision, Joseph Story wrote a concurrence, which, perhaps offhandedly, suggested a simple way to avoid the impact of the rule. If the legislature, Story said, really wanted to alter corporate charters, it ought to reserve the right to do so when it issued them. If it

[60]4 Wheat. 518 (1819). An important precursor was *Fletcher* v. *Peck*, 6 Cranch 87 (1810). This case came out of the so-called Yazoo land scandals in Georgia. The Georgia legislature entered into a corrupt land-grant deal. The next legislature repealed the grant; but, meanwhile, some of the land had passed into the hands of out-of-state investors who were not part of the original tainted deal. The United States Supreme Court, under John Marshall, sided with the buyers of the land. The grant of land by the legislature, said Marshall, was a "contract"; what one legislature gave, the next could not take back. See C. Peter Magrath, *Yazoo, Law and Politics in the New Republic: The Case of Fletcher v. Peck* (1966).

[61]See Charles Grove Haines, *The Role of the Supreme Court in American Government and Politics, 1789–1835* (1944), p. 419.

did, then the right to alter the charter would, legally speaking, be part of the "contract" between the state and the corporation; and when the legislature passed a law changing the terms of the charter, that would be no "impairment." In later years, charters normally contained a standard clause (put in at the insistence of legislatures) reserving to the state the right to alter, amend, and repeal. This right was also a common feature of general incorporation laws. Finally, the right was inserted in state constitutions. The New York constitution of 1846 provided that "all general laws and special acts" about corporations "may be altered from time to time or repealed" (art. 8, sec. 1).

Corporations were rare before 1800; hence the case law on corporations was thin. As corporations multiplied, so did their litigation. The prior law was not germane to many of the new situations they faced. The rights and duties of stockholders in a factory or bank were hardly comparable to the problems of members of some academy or church; and the powers of management posed different questions in these polar types of corporation. The law of corporations was, therefore, thoroughly revamped, so much that for all practical purposes, it was created brand-new in the 19th century.

At first, the courts treated corporate powers rather gingerly. They adhered to the "general and well settled principle, that a corporation had no other powers than such as are specifically granted; or, such as are necessary for the purpose of carrying into effect the powers expressly granted."[62] This "principle" followed logically from the concept of a corporation as an occasion for aggregating capital toward a single venture or purpose—a bridge, a factory, a bank. Chief Justice Roger Taney built on this concept in the famous case of the *Charles River Bridge* (1837).[63] This case stood for the proposition that charters were to be strictly construed; it was best to keep the powers of corporations, like those of government itself, within narrow boundaries. Courts recognized, of course, that a certain latitude in interpretation might be necessary; for the sake of "public prosperity," it was a good idea to give enterprises some leeway in "acting and counteract-

---

[62]Joseph K. Angell and Samuel Ames, *A Treatise on the Law of Private Corporations Aggregate* (2nd ed., 1843), p. 66.

[63]*Proprietors of the Charles River Bridge* v. *Proprietors of the Warren Bridge,* 11 Pet. 420 (1837). On the background and meaning of the case, see Stanley I. Kutler, *Privilege and Creative Destruction: The Charles River Bridge Case* (1971).

ing."[64] Hence, like the federal government, corporations could enjoy some powers that were merely "implied," but not literally spelled out in their charters.

In the long run, the creative draftsmanship of private citizens— the people who actually wrote the texts of the charters—helped to bury the idea of strict construction. Business practice led the way; the charters reflected what was fact: the growing scope and flexibility of enterprise. The logic of economic growth, invisible to most contemporaries, was drawing up law for itself. What the draftsmen devised, the courts accepted, and legislatures only weakly resisted. The old controls on corporations, meant to reduce their power or their economic role, either disappeared or became innocuous.

But while one kind of restriction faded, another was in process of birth. The business corporation, unlike most earlier corporations, was an economic venture. Law had to be devised to govern the relationship of officers, directors, shareholders, and creditors. Some of this law was hammered out in the cases. Joseph Story, for example, is credited with inventing the so-called trust-fund doctrine. It stemmed from *Wood* v. *Drummer* (1824).[65] Stockholders of the Hallowell and Augusta Bank, of Maine, which was winding up its corporate existence, declared dividends amounting to seventy-five percent of the capital stock of $200,000. The bank thus became a hollow shell, especially since not all of the capital stock had actually been paid in. The plaintiffs held bank notes that became worthless. Story held that it was wrong for the stockholders to distribute the capital to themselves in such a way as to defraud the bank's creditors, that is, the holders of the bank notes. The capital stock of banks was "to be deemed a pledge or trust fund for the payment of the debts contracted by the bank." Creditors could "follow" the funds "into the hands of any persons, who are not innocent purchasers," and recover it from them. This gave the plaintiffs a right to recover from the stockholders, who had lined their pockets with the money from the bank. Later cases repeated the rule, and extended it to analogous situations. Meanwhile, the courts slowly built up a body of rules about the internal life of corporations and their relations to the outside world.

The triumph of enterprise was probably inevitable; but the corporate form was not the only possibility. A New York statute

[64] Angell and Ames, *op. cit.*, p. 162.
[65] 3 Mason C.C. Rpts. 308, Fed. Cas. No. 17,944 (1824).

of 1822, later widely copied, introduced the limited partnership into American law, in part based on a French business form, the *société en commandite*. In a limited partnership, some members ("general partners") stood fully responsible for partnership debts. Limited (or "special") partners, however, were liable "no further than the fund which he or they have furnished to the partnership stock."[66] A limited partnership (with its "one or more sleeping partners") was "supposed to be well calculated to bring dormant capital into active and useful employment."[67] (The words are Chancellor Kent's.) As we have seen, most commercial enterprises were partnerships of one form or another before the middle of the century.

Another form of enterprise was the Massachusetts or business trust; this was an unincorporated association that carried on business using the structure of a trust. Managers (trustees) held title to the property of the trust. Instead of stockholders, there were "beneficiaries"; instead of capital stock, the owners held certificates of beneficial interest. A "trust government," something like a charter, spelled out the powers and duties of the managers.

Still another business form in common use was the joint-stock company. It resembled a partnership, but its capital, unlike that of a partnership, was divided into transferable shares.

It was by no means certain that a corporation, as that term was understood in 1800 or 1820, was the best way to raise and manage money for enterprise. Early American land companies, studied by Shaw Livermore, made use of a great variety of business forms. Speculative land companies, even before 1800, showed "all the various states of complexity in modern business organization beyond the partnership"; yet they were not incorporated. Livermore has argued that these associations were the "true progenitors of the modern business corporation."[68] In other words, the general corporation did not evolve from the special charter system; rather, it reflected the richness of business practice in private associations, operating without charters. These associations could be compared to the later, full-blown business corporations, because functionally they were so much alike. The argument is that the old law of

[66]See Edward H. Warren, *Corporate Advantages Without Incorporation* (1929), pp. 302 ff.

[67]James Kent, *Commentaries on American Law* [cited hereafter as Kent, *Commentaries*], vol. III (2nd ed., 1832), p. 35.

[68]Shaw Livermore, *Early American Land Companies: Their Influence on Corporate Development* (1939), p. 216.

corporations provided nothing but words and forms, like rubble from which a new bridge is built; the architecture and the plans derived from current business practice and economic drive. That the triumphant business form, as it ultimately emerged, was a "corporation," not some mutation of the partnership or Massachusetts trust was due to almost random factors, which tipped an unimportant balance. Similarly, in the 20th century, before the Uniform Commercial Code, the dominant form of installment sale was different in different states. In some places, it was called a conditional sale; in some, a chattel mortgage; in Pennsylvania, a bailment lease; in England, a hire-purchase contract. Where one form was dammed up by an unfavorable doctrine or statute, practice flowed freely into another channel. The triumph of the corporation over its rivals was the same phenomenon a century before. The overriding need was for an efficient, trouble-free device to aggregate capital and manage it in business, with limited liability and transferable shares. But in a sense the argument over origins is merely an argument over words. French law was not the "progenitor" of the limited partnership; charters of towns, colleges, and hospitals were not the "progenitors" of railroad charters; land syndicates were not the "progenitors" of general corporation laws. All these were merely models and occasions. The theory of legal history is that the architect of contemporary law is always contemporary fact. History does not supply decisions—only raw materials and plans.

CHAPTER IV

THE LAW OF PERSONAL STATUS: WIVES, PAUPERS, AND SLAVES

MARRIAGE AND DIVORCE

In England, ecclesiastical courts had jurisdiction over marriage and divorce, and the church had an important role in family law. The United States had no such courts, and, after the early 19th century, no established churches. Family law was thoroughly secular in the United States. Marriage, in legal theory, was a contract—an agreement between a man and a woman. The law, of course, did not forbid or even discourage religious ceremonies. And moral and religious ideas were, as always, powerful influences on the law of marriage and divorce. But American law recognized two secular forms of marriage: the civil ceremony, which had been well-known during the colonial period, and the so-called common-law marriage, which was probably an American innovation.

The concept of a "common-law marriage" is often misunderstood. People today often use the phrase loosely. It is one way to describe a man and a woman who live together without the slightest pretense of marriage. The legal meaning is very different. In law, a common-law marriage, in states that recognized this form of marriage, was as valid as any other kind—as valid a marriage as one that started off with a civil or religious ceremony. But it was completely informal. Its essence was a "verbal contract," that is, an agreement by a man and a woman to consider themselves husband and wife, followed by cohabitation. The origins of this form of marriage are fairly murky. Probably there was no such institution in England. Chancellor Kent, and some other writers, felt that the common law did not require any "peculiar ceremonies" in order for a marriage to be valid. The presence of a clergyman, though a "very becoming practice," was unnecessary; the "consent of the parties is all that is required."[1]

Kent and other judges of the early 19th century probably misread the English authorities. But the common-law marriage did not pop up because some judges made mistakes in reading old cases. It had a more solid basis in the social context: the intellectual climate, and the felt needs of the population. Joel Bishop, writing in 1852, advanced this explanation: in England, only Episcopalian clergymen were authorized to perform marriages. The Puritan dissenters had "fled to these western wilds for the single purpose of escaping from what they regarded as oppression and moral contagion flowing from those churches." They would not have tolerated any requirement that they import an "Episcopal ecclesiastic...paying him tithes, simply that he might become an invited guest at their weddings. Though the American colonies were not all settled by puritans, the spirit of this suggestion will apply to most of them."[2] This factor, Bishop felt, explained why some states came to accept the idea of a common-law, informal marriage.

In any event, there was a shortage of clergymen of every faith. Most of the population lived outside the cities; and many parts of the country were thinly populated. More important, there were large numbers of ordinary people who owned houses and farms, and who had a stake in the economy, and therefore in the legal system. There were, apparently, couples who lived together after makeshift ceremonies, or no ceremony at all. These couples raised flocks of children. The doctrine of common-law marriage allowed the law to treat these "marriages" as holy and valid.

Bishop, a shrewd observer of law and morals, felt that the early settlers were inclined to make a virtue of necessity, or at least come to terms with it. Despite their "pure morals and stern habits," the settlers could not tolerate a strict adherence to the English marriage laws (or their American imitations), which did not suit American conditions. The stringent marriage laws of Pennsylvania, for example, were "ill adapted to the habits and customs of society"; a "rigid execution of them," remarked Chief Justice John Bannister Gibson in 1833, "would bastardize a vast majority of the children which have been born within the state for half a century."[3] Hence the need for the common-law marriage.

---

[1]Kent, *Commentaries,* vol. II (2nd ed., 1832), pp. 86–87.
[2]Joel Bishop, *Commentaries on the Law of Marriage and Divorce* (1852), p. 130.
[3]C. J. Gibson, in *Rodebaugh v. Sanks,* 2 Watts 9, 11 (Pa., 1833).

The laxity of its form did not escape opposition. Some people denounced it as a "strange and monstrous crossbreed between a concubinage and a marriage." There were other problems, too. An informal marriage was, most likely, also a fairly secret marriage; common-law marriage thus might lead to disputes over property rights, to public scandal, and to the perils of bigamy. In *Grisham* v. *State* (1831),[4] the highest court of Tennessee refused to validate the concept of common-law marriage. John Grisham, a widower, and Jane Ligan, a widow, had agreed to cohabit as man and wife; they swore an oath, before witnesses, to that effect. They were indicted and convicted of "lewd acts of fornication and adultery...to the great scandal of the...good and worthy citizens." The law, said this court, was the "guardian of the morals of the people"; so saying, the court upheld this conviction. But in most states, the guardian bowed to the inevitable and accepted informal marriage, overcoming doubts and ignoring costs.

England had been a "divorceless society," and remained that way until 1857. There was no way to get a judicial divorce. The very wealthy might squeeze a rare private bill of divorce out of Parliament. Between 1800 and 1836 there were, on the average, three of these a year. For the rest, unhappy husbands and wives had to be satisfied with annulment (no easy matter), or divorce from bed and board (*a mensa et thoro*), a form of legal separation which did not entitle either spouse to marry again. The most common "solutions," of course, when a marriage broke down, were adultery and desertion.[5]

In the colonial period, the South was generally faithful to English tradition. Absolute divorce was unknown, divorce from bed and board very rare. In New England, however, courts and legislatures occasionally granted divorce. In Pennsylvania, Penn's laws of 1682 gave spouses the right to a "Bill of Divorcement" if their marriage partner was convicted of adultery. Later, the governor or lieutenant governor was empowered to dissolve marriages on grounds of incest, adultery, bigamy, or homosexuality. There is no evidence that the governor ever used this power. Still later, the general assembly took divorce into its own hands. The English privy council disapproved of this practice, and, in the 1770s, dis-

[4]10 Tenn. 588 (1831).
[5]See Gerhard O. W. Mueller, "Inquiry into the State of a Divorceless Society: Domestic Relations Law and Morals in England from 1660 to 1857," 18 U. Pitt. L. Rev. 545 (1957).

allowed legislative divorces in Pennsylvania, New Jersey, and New Hampshire. The Revolution, of course, put an end to the privy council's power.[6]

After Independence, the law and practice of divorce began to change; but regional differences remained quite strong. In the South, divorce continued to be unusual. The extreme case was South Carolina. Henry William Desaussure, writing in 1817, stated flatly that South Carolina had never granted a single divorce.[7] He was right. There was no such thing as absolute divorce in South Carolina, throughout the 19th century. In other Southern states, legislatures dissolved marriages by passing private divorce laws. The Georgia constitution of 1798 allowed legislative divorce, on a two-thirds vote of each branch of the legislature—and after a "fair trial" and a divorce decree in the superior court. This left the judges unsure of their exact role in the process.[8] The legislature later resolved these doubts; it passed a law reserving to itself exclusive right to grant divorces. Between 1798 and 1835, there were 291 legislative divorces in Georgia. The frequency curve rose toward the end of the period. Twenty-seven couples were divorced legislatively in 1833—for example, Green Fuller and Susannah Fuller, whose "matrimonial connection, or civil contract of marriage," was "completely annulled, set aside, and dissolved"; so that the two would "in future be held as distinct and separate persons, altogether unconnected by any mystical union or civil contract whatever."[9]

North of the Mason-Dixon line, courtroom divorce became the normal mode, rather than legislative divorce. Pennsylvania passed a general divorce law in 1785, Massachusetts one year later. Every New England state had a divorce law before 1800, along with New York, New Jersey, and Tennessee. Grounds for divorce varied somewhat from state to state. New York's law of 1787 permitted absolute divorce only for adultery. Vermont, on the other hand, allowed divorce for impotence, adultery, intolerable severity, three years' willful desertion, and long absence with presumption of death (1798). Rhode Island allowed divorce for "gross misbehaviour and wickedness in either of the parties, repugnant to and in

---

[6]Nelson M. Blake, *The Road to Reno: A History of Divorce in the United States* (1962), pp. 34–47.

[7]Henry W. Desaussure, *South Carolina Eq. Rpts.*, vol. I, p. liv; vol. II, p. 644.

[8]See Oliver H. Prince, comp., *A Digest of the Laws of the State of Georgia*, vol. II (2nd ed., 1837), p. 187.

[9]Laws Ga. 1833, pp. 82–83.

violation of the marriage covenant."[10] In New Hampshire, it was grounds for divorce if a spouse joined the Shaker sect—not an unreasonable rule, since the Shakers did not believe in sexual intercourse.[11]

This efflorescence of divorce laws must reflect real increase in demand for legal divorce. The size of the demand doomed the practice of divorce by statute. Like corporate charters, private divorce bills became a nuisance, a pointless drain on the legislature's time. At the end of the period, some states still granted legislative divorce; but others had abolished them. Later in the century, private divorce laws became extinct.

So much was structural. What was the source of this sudden desire for a simpler way to divorce? The divorce rate in the 19th century, of course, was the merest trickle in comparison to the rate in more recent times. Still, it was noticeable, and it was growing; to some self-appointed guardians of national morals, it was an alarming fire bell in the night, a symptom of moral dry rot, and a cause in itself of still further moral decay. President Timothy Dwight of Yale, in 1816, called the rise in divorces "dreadful beyond conception." Connecticut faced "stalking, barefaced pollution"; if things went on, the state would become "one vast Brothel; one great province of the World of Perdition." The "whole community," he warned, could be thrown "into a general prostitution."[12]

This apocalyptic vision never really came to pass. Nor was the rising divorce rate so obviously a sign that the family was breaking down. The family was indeed changing. There were new strains on marital relationships. William O'Neill put it this way: "when families are large and loose, arouse few expectations, and make few demands, there is no need for divorce." That need arises when "families become the center of social organization." At this point, "their intimacy can become suffocating, their demands unbearable, and their expectations too high to be easily realizable. Divorce then becomes the safety valve that makes the system workable."[13] Moreover, a divorceless state is not a state without adultery, prostitution, fornication. It may be, rather, a place sharply divided between zones of official law and zones of unofficial behavior. A

[10]Blake, *op. cit.*, p. 50.
[11]See *Dyer* v. *Dyer*, 5 N.H. 271 (1830).
[12]Quoted in Blake, *op. cit.*, p. 59.
[13]William L. O'Neill, *Divorce in the Progressive Era* (1967), pp. 6–7.

country with rare or expensive divorce is a country with two kinds of family law, one for the rich and one for the poor. The United States had its rich and its poor; but, unlike England, enormous numbers of people owned property and had some stake in society. Easy divorce laws grew out of the needs of the middle-class mass. The smallholder had to have some way to stabilize and legitimize relationships, to settle doubts about ownership of family property. It was the same general impulse that lay behind the common-law marriage. Divorce was simplest to obtain and divorce laws most advanced in those parts of the country—the West especially—least stratified by class.

Divorce was, then, genuinely popular. Even in Timothy Dwight's day, there were plenty of writers and jurists who did not agree with his fire-eating words. Zephaniah Swift, who wrote at the end of the 18th century, thought it morally wholesome that Connecticut's laws should recognize absolute divorce. The alternative was divorce from bed and board—legal separation. This, he felt, was an "irresistible temptation to the commission of adultery," suitable only to those with "more frigidity or more virtue than usually falls to the share of human beings." Liberal divorce laws, on the other hand, were "favourable...to the virtue, and the happiness of mankind."[14]

Since there was strong opinion on both sides, it was only natural that neither side got its way completely. Divorce laws were a kind of compromise. In general, the law never recognized full, free consensual divorce. It became simpler to get a divorce than in the past; but divorce was not routine or automatic. In form, divorce was an adversary proceeding. A divorce decree was, in theory, a reward for an innocent and virtuous spouse, victimized by an evil partner. Defendant had to be at fault; there had to be "grounds" for the divorce. Otherwise, divorce was legally impossible. Eventually, of course, the collusive or friendly divorce became the normal case. By the time divorce reached the courtroom, both partners wanted it, or at least had given up on the marriage; in any event, the real issues had all been hammered out beforehand. What went on in court became a show, a charade, an afterthought.

The collusive divorce did not dominate the dockets until later in the century. But it was not unknown, say, in 1840. Collusion

[14]Zephaniah Swift, *A System of the Laws of the State of Connecticut* (1795), vol. I, pp. 192–93. Bishop called the divorce *a mensa et thoro* a "carbuncle on the face of civilized society," a "demoralizing mock-remedy for matrimonial ills." Bishop, *op. cit.*, pp. 217–18.

was probably most common in states with strict divorce laws, like New York, where adultery was the only practical grounds. Chancellor Kent observed, from his experience as a trial judge, that the sin of adultery "was sometimes committed on the part of the husband, for the very purpose of the divorce."[15] This must have been extreme behavior; since perjury probably bothers many people less than adultery, collusion no doubt flourished in the courts of New York.

FAMILY PROPERTY

At common law, elaborate rules governed the property rights (and duties) of married women. These rules, however, were mainly deducible from one grand "principle of the common law, by which the husband and wife are regarded as one person, and her legal existence and authority in a degree lost or suspended, during the continuance of the matrimonial union."[16] Essentially, husband and wife were one flesh; but the man was the owner of that flesh.

> The husband, by marriage, acquires a right to the use of the real estate of his wife, during her life; and if they have a child born alive, then, if he survives, during his life, as tenant by the curtesy. He acquires an absolute right to her chattels real, and may dispose of them.... He acquires an absolute property in her chattels personal in possession.... As to the property of the wife accruing during coverture, the same rule is applicable.[17]

Actually, customs and practices—and legal doctrine—were more complex than appears from this quotation. The law distinguished between types of property; and courts of equity had for a long time softened the husband's dictatorial control, by allowing a father or other relative to establish a separate estate for the woman, through a premarital settlement or by way of a trust. In England, such settlements were common. Marriage settlements were accepted as valid by the courts, and a rich body of law grew up about them. They were, of course, practically speaking, confined to the wealthy, landed classes.

In the United States, these English doctrines and practice had

[15]Kent, *Commentaries*, vol. II (2nd ed., 1832), p. 106.
[16]*Ibid.*, p. 129.
[17]Chief Justice Zephaniah Swift, in *Griswold* v. *Penniman*, 2 Conn. 564 (1818). A lease is an example of a "chattel real." The term "coverture" means marriage.

been recognized and, to some extent, followed. Not every colony or state had courts of equity; this was a complication. The status of married women in colonial times is a matter of some dispute. It was once widely assumed that colonial law, compared to English law, was quite liberal; it tended to treat married women much more as free souls. This began a tradition which perhaps never quite died out. Other scholars, more recently, have questioned the picture of an enlightened colonial past. At the very least, the case has not been proven.[18]

In any event, there is no doubt that legal change took place in the period of independence. The beginnings were modest. In 1787, Massachusetts, recognizing that "sometimes...husbands absent themselves from this Commonwealth, and abandon their wives...who may be thereby reduced to great distress," by statute gave the deserted wife authority to petition the court for the right to sell land, "as if she was sole and unmarried."[19]

Essentially, the English system was tolerable, in its home territory, only for upper-class landowners, and even then only because of elaborate tricks and bypasses, which softened its impact. Plantation owners of the South were also able to adapt to the law of settlements and trusts. But these devices were far too intricate for the average person to handle, even the average landowner, and even when aided by the average lawyer. There were piecemeal reforms, and also private acts, to take care of particular situations—the legislature could give "feme sole" status to a married woman whose husband had abandoned her, making it possible for her to sell or mortgage her land.[20]

Major reform came with passage of so-called married women's property acts. The first of these, a crude and somewhat tentative version, was enacted in 1839, in Mississippi (another example of reform that began on the legal periphery).[21] The early statutes

---

[18]For a discussion of the issues, see Marylynn Salmon, "The Legal Status of Women in Early America: A Reappraisal," 1 Law and Hist. Rev. 129 (1983); on the use of marriage settlements, see Marylynn Salmon, "Women and Property in South Carolina: The Evidence from Marriage Settlements, 1730 to 1830," 39 William and Mary Q., 3rd ser., 655 (1982).

[19]*The Perpetual Laws of the Commonwealth of Massachusetts* (1788), p. 362 (act of Nov. 21, 1787).

[20]See Richard H. Chused, "Married Women's Property Law: 1800–1850," 71 Georgetown L. J. 1359, 1370 (1983), for examples in Alabama.

[21]On the Mississippi statute, see Elizabeth G. Brown, "Husband and Wife—Memorandum on the Mississippi Woman's Law of 1839," 42 Mich. L. Rev. 1110 (1944).

on married women's property did not give married women full legal equality; they attacked the problem bit by bit. Four of the five sections of the Mississippi act regulated the rights of married women to own and dispose of slaves (the husband retained "control and management of all such slaves, the direction of their labor, and the receipt of the productions thereof").[22] In Michigan, for example, a statute of 1844 merely exempted the wife's earned or inherited property from liability for her husband's "debts and engagements." Still, there was a strong trend at work; New York passed its first law in 1848; and by 1850, about seventeen states had granted to married women some legal capacity to deal with their property.[23]

Real changes had occurred in the social and economic position of women between 1800 and 1845. A few bold and militant women spoke out for women's rights; they made themselves heard, for example, during the debates on the New York law of 1848. But the real fulcrum of change was outside the family and outside the women's movement. It lay in the mass ownership of property, in the increased activity of women in managing property, and in the felt needs of an active land market. There was a dramatic increase in the number of women with a stake in the economy. There was also, as has been stressed before, a dramatic increase in the number of *men* with a stake in the economy. This too was important in the drive to reduce the archaic disabilities of the married woman. The disabilities were anomalies in a market society, where the dominant actors were smallholders, and the clarity of land titles a central value.

A key factor, then, was the breakdown, in the United States, of the kind of legal pluralism so characteristic of England, where the classic common law was primarily geared toward the needs of a tiny minority, the landed gentry. In the United States, the middle-class family was deeply engaged in the ordinary, working legal system. English land-law practices were too cumbersome, technical, and expensive for this class to bear. Moreover (and this was critical), the tangle of rules and practices was potentially an im-

---

[22]Laws Miss. 1839, ch. 46.

[23]There is a growing literature on these statutes, stimulated by the new interest in women's history. Two books deal with New York: Peggy Rabkin, *Fathers to Daughters: The Legal Foundations of Female Emancipation* (1980); Norma Basch, *In the Eyes of the Law: Women, Marriage, and Property in Nineteenth-Century New York* (1982). The study by Richard H. Chused, "Married Women's Property Law," cited above, has material from Maryland.

pediment to the speed and efficiency of the land market. The statutes spoke of rights of husband and wife, as if the main issue was the intimate relations between the sexes. Feminist leaders worked for passage of these laws, a fact which also tends to point toward these laws as reforms in the politics of family.

But the evidence suggests that the real point of the statutes was somewhat more modest. They were meant to rationalize more cold-blooded matters, such as the rights of a creditor to collect debts out of land owned by husbands, wives, or both. Most litigation over married women's property was not litigation between spouses, or within the family at all. In almost no case did a husband sue his wife or vice versa. The typical cases, both before and after the married women's property acts, therefore, were about the family's external relations, not its internal life. Passage of these laws did not signal a revolution in the status of women; rather, they *ratified* and adjusted a silent revolution. A curious fact provides striking, though indirect confirmation of this point: the statutes concerned that most basic of institutions, the family, and seemed to work radical change; yet the debates were only modest and fitful. Newspapers made almost no mention of the laws. Little agitation preceded them; great silence followed them. It was the silence of a *fait accompli*.[24]

ADOPTION

Another innovation in family property law was the invention of an American law of adoption. England was not only a divorceless society; it was a society without adoption laws as well. A child was natural-born or nothing. In the United States, similarly, there were no provisions for adoption; and the first general adoption law, it is usually said, was a Massachusetts law passed in 1851.

In point of fact, this was not really the first (Alabama had a law in 1850); and there were many adoptions tucked away in the

[24]On this point, see Kay Ellen Thurman, *The Married Women's Property Acts* (LL.M. thesis, University of Wisconsin Law School, 1966). In fairness, it must be said that the new literature tends to give the women's movement more credit for the passage of the acts than the text does here; most recent writers agree that many and complex forces lay behind the new laws. See Linda E. Speth, "The Married Women's Property Acts, 1839–1865: Reform, Reaction, or Revolution?," in D. Kelly Weisberg, ed., *Women and the Law: The Social Historical Perspective*, vol. 2 (1982), p. 69.

pages of the statute books. Adoptions, in other words, like divorces, were often effected one at a time, by legislative act. The wave of general laws, which started around 1850, replaced this rather clumsy system.

There is something of a literature on the development of American adoption law;[25] this literature lays stress, quite naturally, on changes in the nature of family life, in the role of children and their parents, and their relationships to each other. But the point of adoption, as a *legal* device, is not love, but money; nobody needs formal adoption papers or a court decree to love a child desperately; inheritance of property from a "father" or a "mother" is another matter. Adoption is not a requirement among the landless poor. Thus the felt need for general adoption laws is yet another reflex of the master fact of American law and life: the enormous bulk of the landed middle class.

POOR LAWS AND SOCIAL WELFARE

In every period, society makes some attempt to care for its weaker members; its institutions insure at least some of its people against some social risks. Law and order are themselves devices of social insurance. They guard property owners against physical attacks on their wealth. Debtor protection laws keep merchants and landowners from falling too far in the social scale too fast. The family takes care of small children until they can care for themselves. Church groups, the extended family, and the web of personal friendships provide relief for many more of the helpless. All this was true in the 19th century, but with much greater reliance on private institutions. The poor laws were residual. Paupers were the people at the absolute bottom of the social ladder, those who had nowhere to go, and no one but government to turn to. Even so, the poor laws probably worked best in small towns and rural areas. The failures of the welfare system became glaring when its creaking institutions faced a large class of transients or the urban landless poor.

Few have had a kind word to say about 19th-century poor laws.

[25]See, for example, Jamil Zainaldin, "The Emergence of a Modern American Family Law: Child Custody, Adoption and the Courts, 1796–1851," 73 Northwestern U. L. Rev. 1038 (1979).

But their weaknesses have to be understood in context. To contemporaries, it was hard to think of any real alternatives. There
was private charity, of course; but it never quite filled the bill.
Some people, to be sure, wanted to abolish poor relief completely,
on the grounds that it did more harm than good. But this view,
too, never prevailed. For want of anything better, the colonial
poor laws stumbled on, after 1776, at first without much change.
The basic principle was local rule. The poor were to be supported
by and in their own community. They were a charge on that
political subdivision in which they were "settled." As expressed in
the New York law of 1788: "Every city and town shall support
and maintain their own poor."[26] The administrative unit was local:
the city, town, township, or county, or some combination of these.[27]
Centralized state administration was a century away.

A fortiori, the federal government had nothing to do with the
poor laws. It played a minute role in social welfare. The exceptions
were few and revealing. On February 17, 1815, after the great
earthquake in New Madrid, Missouri, Congress passed an act to
help those whose lands had "been materially injured by earth-
quakes." These sufferers were allowed to locate "the like quantity
of land" in other parts of the public domain in Missouri Territory.[28] This act, one notes, did not extract a cent of hard cash
from the treasury. The federal government was short of money,
but long on land. It gave away geese, not golden eggs.

Even at that, there were few federal land grants for welfare
purposes. Only after long and bitter debate did the federal government assign land to the Kentucky Deaf and Dumb Asylum
(1826). Dorothea Dix lobbied vigorously for land grants to aid
the insane. Yet President Franklin Pierce vetoed such a bill in
1854, partly because he felt it was inappropriate for the federal
government to act as "the great almoner of public charity,
throughout the United States."

In some instances, the federal government was more lavish,
and its authority was not questioned by states' righters. A law of
1798 imposed a payroll tax on the wages of sailors. The money

[26]Quoted in David M. Schneider, *The History of Public Welfare in New York State,
1609–1866* (1938), p. 112.
[27]Fern Boan, *A History of Poor Relief Legislation and Administration in Missouri*
(1941), pp. 22–23.
[28]3 Stats. 211 (act of Feb. 17, 1815).

was to be used to support hospitals for sick and disabled seamen.[29] Veterans of national wars were entitled to pensions and bonuses of land. Neither veterans nor sailors, of course, were pariahs. They were in the same category as the victims of the New Madrid earthquake: their deprivations, people felt, were in no way their own doing. These beneficiaries were respectable people, voters, the family that lived next door. Veterans' benefits, indeed, had a double meaning. The unspoken premise and promise was that men who could expect help from a grateful nation would be that much more likely to enlist.

The public was relatively generous to others who were also clearly blameless—the sick, the old, the deaf and dumb, the insane. Kentucky established a state home in the 1820s for those "who, by the mysterious dispensation of Providence, are born deaf and of course dumb." The law called on all "philanthropic citizens" to "promote an object so benevolent and humane," and backed up its words with a cash appropriation. Kentucky also established a public asylum for the insane. Massachusetts set up a state reform school in 1847, for young offenders.[30] This was an early example of special treatment for the young, of a kind which became more prominent later on.

The township pauper, on the other hand, particularly if he was a stranger in town, had no such claim on public sympathy. He or she was likely to be labeled an idler, a profligate, a weakling. Communities bitterly resented the money they had to pay for support of this sort of people. The argument was made that the whole system of relief should be abandoned, since "distress and poverty multiply in proportion to the funds created to relieve them." The dole, in other words, was counterproductive; it tended to "impair that anxiety for a livelihood which is almost instinctive";

[29]Henry W. Farnam, *Chapters in the History of Social Legislation in the United States to 1860* (1938), pp. 232–34.

[30]Sophonisba P. Breckinridge, *Public Welfare Administration in the United States* (2nd ed., 1938), pp. 98, 99, 101, 113. The treatment of dependent children, however, seems by modern standards barbaric. Orphans were liable to be sold as apprentices. But there was little else to be done with homeless boys and girls. A master was at least supposed to teach his apprentice to read and write. Girls learned to cook and sew. Boys worked, and learned a trade, in exchange for meals and a home. In 1794, for example, ten New York boys from the almshouse were "bound to Andrew Stockholm & Co. at the Cotton Manufactury." Schneider, *op. cit.*, p. 181. On the founding of houses of refuge for wayward children, in the 1820s, see Robert M. Mennel, *Thorns and Thistles: Juvenile Delinquents in the United States, 1825–1940* (1973), p. 50.

giving out money could "relax individual exertion by unnerving the arm of industry." These are quotes from an influential New York report, published in 1824.[31] Poor relief was not, in fact, abolished; but it was widely felt that the laws should be punitive, even harsh. They were meant to deter, to make poverty unpalatable, to make relief come bitter and dear.

How the poor laws actually worked has not been so carefully researched as one would like. Perhaps they were not so bad as pictured. History does not record routine acts of kindness. The abuses, however, scream from the record. And, indeed, the indications are alarming. A substantial body of law bore on the question whether a pauper was "settled" in this or that county or town. "Settlement" fixed responsibility for the pauper's upkeep. Under a New Hampshire law of 1809, which was not atypical, a town might support a pauper even if he was not technically "settled" there. The creditor town then sued the town of settlement to recover its costs.[32] Towns and counties often fought out the question of "settlement" in court, to decide who bore these costs, the receiving or the shipping jurisdiction.

A legal concept begins its career as smooth and as perfect as an egg; if the concept has important economic or social consequences, and leads to contention among interest groups, litigation may batter and bruise it out of shape. Dozens of reported cases turned on the concept of settlement. In one volume alone of the *Connecticut Reports* (volume VII, for 1828–29), four cases on poor relief were reported. The town of Litchfield sued the town of Farmington over support of a pauper named Asabel Moss and his family. The town of Reading sued the town of Weston "for supplies furnished to *Harriet,* the wife, and *Sally* and *Lucinda,* the minor children, of Samuel Darling." The keeper of the county jail in Norwich sued the town of Norwich "to recover for support furnished by the plaintiff, to *James Hazard* and *John Blake,* prisoners in such gaol." In the same volume, the town of Plainfield sued a putative father, one Hopkins, "for the maintenance of a bastard child." And these were appellate cases only—the visible tip of the iceberg. After decades of litigation, the whole settlement concept became one of the most intricate known to the law.

The right of one township to recover from another was supposed to remove the bite from the concept of settlement; a person

[31] *Report of the Secretary of State on the Relief and Settlement of the Poor,* New York Assembly Journal, Feb. 9, 1824.
[32] Laws N.H. 1809, ch. 36.

without settlement would not necessarily starve. But lawsuits have always been expensive. Since the concept and facts of settlement were in constant dispute, no town could predict the precise outcome of a difficult case. An action for reimbursement, then, must have been a town's last, desperate resort to get its money back. Far better to have no paupers to begin with. Moreover, a pauper, if he stayed long enough, might gain a valid settlement in town. In many states, it was a crime to bring a pauper into a new county. Paupers, as in colonial days, were "warned out" to prevent them from gaining a settlement. Sometimes, they were escorted to the county or township line and dumped over the border. In extreme cases, paupers were passed on from place to place, "sent backwards and forwards ... like a shuttlecock, without end."[33]

Local authorities were constantly at pains to keep down the costs of relief. Under a law of Indiana Territory (1807), by no means unique, overseers of the poor in each township had the duty "to cause all poor persons, who have, or shall become a public charge to be farmed out at public vendue, or out-cry, to wit; On the first Monday in May, yearly and every year, at some public place ... to the person or persons, who shall appear to be the lowest bidder or bidders."[34] In 1845, Emaley Wiley bought all of the paupers of Fulton County, Illinois, for $594.[35] Obviously, this system of farming out the poor tended to drive the level of care down to the very bottom; it encouraged the worst penny-pinching, if not outright starvation tactics. In many places, it must have been an engine of sheer exploitation, feeding on the labor of the poor.

There were plenty of contemporary critics who were aware of the inhumanity of this system, and who saw that it failed to get at the roots of poverty. The medicine was not working; paupers seemed to be multiplying in the land. Josiah Quincy's report of 1821, on the pauper laws of Massachusetts, issued blunt words of warning. The "pernicious consequences of the existing system" were "palpable" and increasing.[36] The report called for a radical

[33]Quoted in Martha Branscombe, *The Courts and the Poor Laws in New York State, 1784–1929* (1943), p. 102.
[34]Francis S. Philbrick, ed., *The Laws of Indiana Territory, 1801–1809* (1930), pp. 308–9.
[35]Sophonisba P. Breckinridge, *The Illinois Poor Law and Its Administration* (1939), p. 63.
[36]Quoted in Breckinridge, *Public Welfare Administration in the United States*, p. 32.

restructuring. It rejected *outdoor* relief (support for the pauper in his own home), and the auction system, and strongly urged adoption of what came to be called *indoor* (that is, institutional) relief. The New York report on the welfare laws, which was quoted earlier, and which was published in 1824, agreed with Quincy; indoor relief was the better way. The almshouse or poorhouse was the answer—more efficient, and a chance to provide moral education, not to mention putting the poor to work. Best of all, the government would save money:

> It is believed that with proper care and attention, and under favorable circumstances, the average annual expense *in* an almshouse, having a convenient farm attached to it, will not exceed from 20 to 35 dollars for the support of each pauper, exclusive of the amount of labour he may perform; while *out* of an almshouse, it will not be less than from 33 to 65 dollars, and in many instances where the pauper is old and infirm, or diseased, from 80 to 100 dollars, and even more.[37]

The poor farm was not a new invention; but these two reports helped give the idea fresh popularity. In 1824, New York passed a comprehensive act "to provide for the establishment of county poorhouses." This act, a "historic step," established the "principle of indoor relief"; it made the county poorhouse "the center of the public relief system." It also introduced some wholesome reforms; it "advanced the principle of county responsibility for all poor persons lacking settlement," and prohibited "removals of indigent persons across county lines."[38] Of course, this law could not and did not guarantee that poor farms would be efficient or humane, despite the hopes of its sponsors. As was true of prison reform, well-meant changes sometimes merely centralized the horror. By 1838, some county homes were reported to be in a state of inhuman squalor.[39]

The root of the problem was not structural. It lay in society's indifference. The mass of the public feared and distrusted vagrants. Even men of good will were blinded by the fantasy of "sturdy beggars," that is, the able-bodied poor, men unwilling to earn an honest living. Reform movements fed on a few noisome scandals, emphasized the failures of the old system, and called

[37]*Ibid*, p. 43.
[38]Schneider, *op. cit.*, p. 236.
[39]*Ibid.*, pp. 244–45.

for fresh approaches. But reformers lacked the will to follow through, and no concrete interest group stood to gain from a thorough reform of public welfare. Thus, even when reform succeeded in changing formal law, the new programs did not work as they were supposed to; old evil habits soon reappeared. From poor laws to poor farms to AFDC, there is a single sad lesson on what powerlessness can mean in this country.

SLAVERY AND THE BLACKS

The most visible American pariah, before the Civil War, was the black slave. As we have seen, an indigenous system of law grew up to govern the "peculiar institution" of slavery.[40] What was at first a law for the servant class developed deeper and deeper overtones of color. The slave laws then became laws about the fate of a race.

No feature of American life has been so marked with blood and failure as the confrontation of white and black. Yet in 1776, liberals had some reason to be optimistic. The air rang with hopeful speeches on the inherent rights of man—rights which seemed to apply to the black man as well as the white. There was wide agreement, too, that the slave trade was an abomination and had to be destroyed. A society was formed in Pennsylvania in 1784 "for promoting the abolition of slavery, and the relief of free negroes, unlawfully held in Bondage, and for Improving the Condition of the African Race." In New York in 1785, John Jay and Alexander Hamilton helped organize a "Society for the Promotion of the Manumission of Slaves and Protecting such of them that have been or may be Liberated."[41] Before the end of that century, Northern states took definite steps to rid themselves of slavery. A Pennsylvania law of 1780, "for the gradual abolition of slavery," recited its belief that all "inhabitants of the ... earth," were "the work of an Almighty Hand," even though different "in feature or complexion." To "add one more step to universal civilization by removing as much as possible the sorrows of those who have lived in undeserved bondage, and from which by the assumed

---

[40]See, in general, Kenneth M. Stampp, *The "Peculiar" Institution: Slavery in the Ante-Bellum South* (1956).

[41]Merrill Jensen, *The New Nation* (1950), pp. 135–36.

authority of the Kings of Britain, no effectual legal relief could be obtained,"[42] the statute provided for registration of all slaves held in Pennsylvania, and forbade the creation of any new slaves. The statute also took steps to assimilate the legal condition of black servants to that of indentured whites.

Even the South felt some of this moral fervor. Quaker and Methodist leaders were dead set against slavery. A distinguished and respected minority in the South, including such political leaders as Jefferson, Washington, and Madison, were disturbed by the "peculiar institution," and hoped it would disappear. St. George Tucker, one of the most eminent of Virginia lawyers, wrote a *Dissertation on Slavery; with a Proposal for the Gradual Abolition of It, in the State of Virginia* (1796). "Abolition" was not yet a curse word in the South. Some slaveowners actually set their slaves free. Southern legislatures had for some time indulged in passage of private acts of manumission. In 1782, Virginia passed a general, and permissive law, allowing owners manumission rights. Maryland, in 1790, authorized owners to set slaves free by their last will and testament.

It was, for the blacks, a false dawn only. Slavery was not destined to wither away. The Constitution of 1787 never mentioned the word "slavery," but slavery was an issue in the Constitutional debates; and the final document tried to deal with slavery in a way that would offend neither North nor South. On the question of fugitive slaves, the Constitution was relatively firm. A fugitive slave "shall be delivered upon Claim of the Party to whom [his] Service or Labour may be due" (art. IV, sec. 2). A similar provision appeared in the Ordinance of 1787, though slavery itself was outlawed in Northwest Territory. In the South, it became clearer and clearer as the years went on that the legal rights of man stopped at the color line. The cleavage between North and South did not dissolve; on the slavery question, it deepened and darkened.

On paper at least, slavery law grew more severe between the Revolution and the Civil War. The slaveowning South dug in its heels. Slavery had become an essential pillar of the labor system, particularly in the plantation South; it was a pillar of the Southern social system too. In some ways, economic motives seem too flaccid

---

[42]*Statutes at Large of Pennsylvania from 1682 to 1801*, vol. X, 1779–81 (1904), pp. 67–68; see, in general, Arthur Zilversmit, *The First Emancipation: The Abolition of Slavery in the North* (1967).

to explain the Southern passion about race. The slave system was a way of life. And slaveowners, in the course of time, felt more and more threatened, more beleaguered. The South became, in a way, a kingdom of fear—fear of the influence of free blacks, fear of the North, fear of abolitionists. But above all, race war was the fear. Race war, said De Tocqueville, "is a nightmare constantly haunting the American imagination," both North and South.[43] In the South, laws were passed to crush any possible slave revolt, and to punish disobedience and rebellion with brute force. Slaves could not legally own guns. Penalties for actual insurrection were particularly harsh—in many states, death. Free persons who incited rebellion were not spared. Incitement to insurrection by free persons became a capital crime in Alabama in 1812; in 1832, the state authorized the death penalty for those who published or distributed literature which might tend to arouse slave rebellion.[44]

Southern states moved, too, to tighten the law of manumission. Even in the 1780s manumission was more common in progressive Virginia than in South Carolina. But after 1805, any slave who tarried in Virginia, for more than a year after manumission, might legally be "apprehended and sold by the overseers of the poor of any county...in which he or she shall be found."[45] This cruel law was sometimes softened by private statutes. In 1814, for example, a special act allowed an old black, George Butler, to remain in Virginia with his family, who were still slaves. By the 1830s, petitions for this sort of private act were common enough to warrant a general law on the subject. In the new law (1837), the legislature washed its hands of the matter and referred individual cases to the courts.[46]

It was fortunate that exile laws were not strictly enforced. Free blacks had nowhere to go. Northern states did not greet them with open arms, to put it mildly. By an Illinois statute of 1829, any "black or mulatto person" who wanted to settle in Illinois had to show the county court of his county "a certificate of his or her freedom"; and had to post a thousand-dollar bond "conditioned that such person will not, at any time, become a charge to said

[43] Alexis de Tocqueville, *Democracy in America* (J. P. Mayer and Max Lerner, eds., 1966), p. 329.
[44] Farnam, *op. cit.*, p. 187.
[45] Laws Va. 1805, ch. 63, sec. 10.
[46] Laws Va. 1836–37, ch. 70.

county, or any other county of this state, as a poor person, and
...shall...demean himself, or herself, in strict conformity with
the laws of this state, that now are or hereafter may be enacted."[47]
A Tennessee law put it bluntly: "No free person of color shall
remove from any other State or territory of the Union into this
State to reside here and remain in the State twenty days."[48] The
city of Cincinnati tried to enforce a law requiring blacks to post
a five-hundred-dollar bond (1829). Blacks petitioned for relief;
white mobs took to the streets; riots ensued; afterwards, more
than a thousand blacks moved to Canada.[49]

There was, of course, another side to this picture: the growing
abolition movement and the stubbornness of the North toward
the various fugitive-slave laws. A federal law supplementing the
Constitutional mandate was passed in 1793. In the 1820s, there
was strong resistance in the North against attempts to enforce it.
Fugitive slaves figured in some celebrated cases, in the decades
after 1820; these cases generated enormous heat, exacerbated
relationships in a more and more tenuous union, and fed the
appetite of a growing body of constitutional law. The 1850 fugitive-slave law added fuel to the fire, gave impetus to the so-called
Underground Railway spiriting fugitives to Canada, and set off
a course of legal wrangling that reached a climax in the *Dred Scott*
case.[50]

The Southern states, for their part, defended their institution
with great vigor. Legal limits and restraints on manumission were
one sign. Strict laws made it impossible for slavery to diminish.
Some control over manumission was, in context, understandable.
Otherwise, when a slave became too old or too sick to be productive, an owner might be tempted to set her free and shift the

[47]Rev. Laws Ill. 1829, p. 109.

[48]Tenn. Code 1858, sec. 2726.

[49]Leon F. Litwack, *North of Slavery: The Negro in the Free States, 1790–1860* (1961),
pp. 72–73.

[50]Russel B. Nye, *Fettered Freedom: Civil Liberties and the Slavery Controversy, 1830–
1860* (1963), pp. 257–78. On the enforcement issues under the fugitive-slave laws,
see Robert Cover, *Justice Accused: Anti-Slavery and the Judicial Process* (1975); Paul
Finkelman, *An Imperfect Union: Slavery, Federalism, and Comity* (1981), deals with
the tangled issues of the extraterritorial effects of slavery in a federal union which
was half slave and half free. The full meaning of the *Dred Scott* case is explored
in Don E. Fehrenbacher, *The Dred Scott Case: Its Significance in American Law and
Politics* (1978).

There had been enforcement problems under the laws against the slave trade
as well. See Warren S. Howard, *American Slavers and the Federal Law, 1837–1862*
(1963).

cost of food, medicine, and clothes to the state. Or an insolvent master might manumit his slaves to thwart his creditors. Still, the *political* sins of emancipation no doubt stood uppermost in legislative minds. The South did not want the free black mass to grow. As early as 1800, South Carolina law declared it an abuse to set free any depraved or dependent slaves. Emancipation could not take place unless and until "five indifferent freeholders living in the neighborhood" were satisfied that the slave had good character and could support himself. By 1820, South Carolina cut off all emancipations except by will, and only as a reward for meritorious service. The final step, outlawing *all* manumission, occurred reluctantly and late: in 1858 in Arkansas; in 1860 in Maryland and Alabama.[51] Soon afterwards, the civil war dealt with the issue once and for all.

The "issue," however, was not full equality for blacks. That was nowhere conceded. For most free blacks, life was no bed of roses; whites never treated them as equals. The free black population was not inconsiderable. All Northern blacks were free; almost 60,000 free blacks lived in Virginia, 25,000 in Baltimore alone. Free blacks were a negligible part of the population only in the newer slave states, such as Mississippi. But law for free blacks was a kind of modified law of slavery. The free black (as John Hope Franklin put it) was "quasi-free."[52] As of 1830, only four states, all in New England, allowed free blacks the same right to vote as free whites. Many Northern states—for example, Illinois—did not allow intermarriage between black and white. As we saw, free blacks were unwelcome as immigrants in many Northern states.

In slave states, there were extreme disabilities. In Maryland (1806), a free black could not own a dog. In Georgia, free blacks could not own, use, or carry firearms, dispense medicine, set type, or make contracts for repairing buildings. They could not deal in agricultural commodities without permission. They could not acquire land or slaves in Savannah and Augusta; in some Georgia cities, they could not operate restaurants and inns. Under some criminal laws, there were special punishments for free black offenders, more severe than those imposed on whites who committed the same crime.[53] Free blacks, as a Virginia legislator said,

---

[51]Farnam, *op. cit.*, pp. 199–200.

[52]John Hope Franklin, *From Slavery to Freedom: A History of American Negroes* (2nd ed., 1956), ch. 14.

[53]W. McDowell Rogers, "Free Negro Legislation in Georgia before 1865," 16 Ga. Hist. Q. 27 (1932).

had "many *legal* rights but no constitutional ones."[54] They had some formal rights, in other words, but these did not really guarantee any freedom from oppression. The free black, in the words of a notorious Georgia case, "resides among us, and yet is a stranger. A *native* even, and yet not a citizen. Though not a *slave*, yet is he not free.... His fancied freedom is all a delusion ... (S)ociety suffers, and the negro suffers by manumission."[55]

Even the formal rights were subject to constant attrition. The South saw the black man as black; whether he was slave or free was almost incidental. The free black was a danger to the state. As we have seen, newly freed slaves were usually required to leave the state. Immigration of free blacks was also outlawed—in Virginia as early as 1793. Later, Virginia appropriated money to help send free blacks to Africa. The status of free blacks who stayed in the state was not too many steps above that of the slave. After 1830, law often frowned on giving an education to blacks, free or slave. The Georgia penal code made it a crime to "teach any slave, negro, or free person of color, to read or write, either written or printed characters."[56] In South Carolina, it was already unlawful in 1800 for "any number of slaves, free negroes, mulattoes, or mestizoes, even in company of white persons, to meet together for the purpose of mental instruction or religious worship, either before the rising of the sun or after the going down of the sun." White fraternizers were highly unwelcome. By an 1834 law in South Carolina, a white man who gambled with a black, slave or free, was liable to be whipped "not exceeding thirty-nine lashes." In New Orleans, in 1835, the city council adopted an ordinance which allocated the city's cemeteries one-half to whites, one-fourth to slaves, one-fourth to free blacks. In 1841, an ordinance required separate burial registration lists for whites and blacks.[57]

William Goodell, an antislavery writer, stated wryly that American slavery might be added "to the list of the strict sciences. From a single fundamental axiom, all the parts of the system are logically and scientifically deduced." The axiom was that the slave was property, that he had "no rights."[58] To be sure, the slave was a

---

[54]Quoted in John H. Russell, *The Free Negro in Virginia, 1619–1865* (1913), p. 122.

[55]Lumpkin, J., in *Bryan v. Walton,* 14 Ga. 185, 202, 205 (1853).

[56]Laws Ga. 1833, p. 202.

[57]Roger A. Fischer, "Racial Segregation in Ante-Bellum New Orleans," 74 Am. Hist. Rev. 926, 933 (1969).

[58]William Goodell, *The American Slave Code in Theory and Practice* (1853), p. 105.

"person," for purposes of the criminal law, and indeed, the slave was more answerable for some of his crimes than free whites. But in other regards, he was a commodity. He could not vote or hold office; he could not contract or own property; he was bought and sold like a bale of cotton. The case reports of slave states are full of wrangles about sales, gifts, mortgages, and bequests of slaves. In a case from Kentucky, one of the parties took "a negro boy" to the races at New Orleans, and bet him on the horse Lucy Dashwood.[59] The slave, moreover, could not marry, under white man's law, or in a way that white man's law would recognize as binding. There were, of course, slave "marriages"—stable and lasting unions; strong, well-knit family groups[60]—but they were never recognized by law. The family could be, and often was, broken up by sale, gift, or transfer of a parent, spouse, or child. Some scholars have seen a deep contrast between the law and practice of slavery in the United States and Latin America. The Latin American slave was allowed to marry; to the Church, he was a soul, to be treated as a soul; he was, at worst, only more or less a chattel.[61] American law was on the surface more rigorous; it reflected a harsher theory about slaves, a harsher attitude. Of course, the laws governing slavery—the slave codes of the South— were not responsible for social attitudes. On the contrary, race feelings, whatever their psychic or economic background, helped write the codes.

The slave was a capital asset, and belonged to the land. A law of colonial Virginia (1705), as we have seen, declared slaves to be real estate, not personal property. Kentucky in 1798, and Louisiana Territory in 1806, had similar laws.[62] In those jurisdictions, this meant that, in essence, a single set of rules applied to transfer

---

[59]*Thomas* v. *Davis*, 7 B. Mon. 227 (Ky., 1846). The horse won the race.

[60]See Herbert G. Gutman, *The Black Family in Slavery and Freedom, 1750–1925* (1976), pp. 9–17. These marriages, moreover, often began with a ceremony. On the plantation of James Henry Hammond, in South Carolina, the master conducted weddings, gave gifts to the bride and groom, and punished slaves who were unfaithful to their husbands or wives. Drew Gilpin Faust, *James Henry Hammond and the Old South: A Design for Mastery* (1982), p. 85.

[61]For this thesis, much discussed and much criticized, see Stanley M. Elkins, *Slavery: A Problem in American Institutional and Intellectual Life* (1959); Herbert S. Klein, *Slavery in the Americas: A Comparative Study of Virginia and Cuba* (1967).

[62]Farnam, *op. cit.*, p. 183. The study of the slave as property (in the technical, legal sense) has been much neglected. But see Thomas D. Morris, "'Society Is Not Marked by Punctuality in the Payment of Debts': The Chattel Mortgages of Slaves," in David J. Bodenhamer and James W. Ely, Jr., eds., *Ambivalent Legacy: A Legal History of the South* (1984), p. 147.

and inheritance of the estate as a whole—that is, the same rules covered both the plantation and farm, and the slaves who worked in the fields and in the house. In these jurisdictions, for example, widows had dower rights in their husbands' slaves. Virginia repealed its law in 1792, perhaps because it was technically cumbersome. Nonetheless, the law remained sensitive to connections between slaves and the land. A Virginia statute of 1794, for example, prohibited the sale of slaves to satisfy the master's debts, unless all other personal property had been exhausted. Legally, land could not be levied on until *all* the personal property had been sold to pay debts. Under this statute, then, the slaves were halfway between land and personalty, in regard to creditors' rights. And after 1823, slaves owned by a child, who died before twenty-one, were treated as if real estate, for purposes of settling the dead child's estate.

Slaves themselves had little claim on the law for protection. A South Carolina judge, in 1847, put the case bluntly. A slave, he said, "can invoke neither *magna charta* nor common law.... In the very nature of things, he is subject to despotism. Law as to him is only a compact between his rulers."[63] The Louisiana Black Code of 1806 (sec. 18) declared that a slave "owes to his master, and to all his family, a respect without bounds, and an absolute obedience, and...is...to execute all...orders." The Texas penal code of 1856 recognized the power of the master "to inflict any punishment upon the slave not affecting life or limb...which he may consider necessary for the purpose of keeping him in...submission."[64]

On the other hand, some slave rights were written into law. Ten Southern codes made it a crime to mistreat a slave. The law of six states required the master to provide suitable food and clothing for his slaves. The Black Code of Louisiana of 1806 made "cruel punishment" a crime (except "flogging, or striking with a whip, leather thong, switch or small stock, or putting in irons, or confining such slave"). Under the Louisiana Civil Code of 1825 (art. 192), if a master was "convicted of cruel treatment," the judge could order the sale of the mistreated slave, presumably to a better master.[65] And a black who was held as a slave, illegally, had the right to sue for his freedom.

[63] Wardlaw, J., in *Ex Parte Boylston*, 2 Strob. 41, 43 (S. Car., 1847).
[64] Quoted in Farnam, *op. cit.*, p. 184.
[65] But in an interesting case, *Markham* v. *Close*, 2 La. 581 (1831), the Louisiana court refused to allow a third party to bring a civil suit to compel the sale of a

How real were these rights? Did they mean much in practice? There is evidence that at least some Southern courts honestly enforced the law in cases on the rights of slaves that came before them. There are decisions on record in which courts punished slaveowners for acts of cruelty that passed the boundaries of custom and law. The highest state court of Alabama, in 1843, upheld the conviction of William H. Jones, indicted for murdering a slave girl Isabel. Jones, it was charged, "did ... feloniously, wilfully and of his malice aforethought, cruelly, barbarously and inhumanly beat and whip" the girl to death.[66]

There is evidence of fairness—and also evidence of diversity, as between different slave states, and different decades of the 19th century—but the question is what to make of this evidence. Appealed and reported cases had to be exceptional. Only especially blatant incidents, or perhaps situations where the black man was exceptionally tenacious, or had a champion, were at all likely to come to court, in the first place; appeal was no doubt even rarer. The rights of slaves were narrow, and not often invoked. Yet these rights gave Southern law an appearance of justice, an appearance of fairness, which the slaveholding class valued greatly. At the same time, there was no way the enforcement of rights could threaten the real social order. Had these rights been widely used, or used beyond the limits of Southern toleration, they would not have survived, even on paper.

As it was, a slave who wanted his day in court faced formidable barriers. No slave could testify against his master. In some states, no black could testify against a white man at all. In "free" Indiana Territory, for example, by a law of 1803:

mistreated slave. A certain D. K. Markham, probably out of the kindness of his heart, alleged that the defendant had acted cruelly toward his slave. The slave, Augustin, had run away and been recaptured. There was testimony that he was then lashed "severely," his "back and hips very much cut and skinned. The weather being warm, the wounds smelled badly"; the slave was so severely hurt that he could not sit or lie. But because the master had not been actually *convicted* of cruelty, the court held it was powerless to order Augustin to be sold.

[66]*State v. Jones,* 5 Ala. 666 (1843). Between 1830 and 1860, there were thirteen reported appellate cases in which a master's conviction for homicide or attempted homicide of a slave was upheld. A. E. Keir Nash, "A More Equitable Past? Southern Supreme Courts and the Protection of the Antebellum Negro," 48 N. Car. L. Rev. 197, 215 (1970). Nash's work has been criticized for its dependence on appellate cases; see Michael S. Hindus, *Prison and Plantation: Crime, Justice and Authority in Massachusetts and South Carolina, 1767–1878* (1980), pp. 130, 135. Nash has defended his work in "Reason of Slavery: Understanding the Judicial Role in the Peculiar Institution," 32 Vanderbilt L. Rev. 7 (1979).

> No negro, mulatto or Indian shall be a witness except in the
> pleas of the United States [i.e., criminal cases] against negroes,
> mulattoes, or Indians, or in civil pleas where negroes, mu-
> lattoes or Indians alone shall be parties.[67]

Forty-three years later, in 1846, the law was still on the books.
This fact drew caustic remarks from a select committee of the
Indiana Assembly:

> The track of the foot, the nail of the shoe, the bark of the
> dog, or the bray of the donkey, may be given in evidence to
> ferret out villainies; but the negro . . . though acquainted with
> the villain, and cognizant to the villainy, for no reason than
> because he is a negro, is not even permitted to develope
> corroborating circumstances.[68]

On countless occasions, the rule must have frustrated justice.
In 1806, the chancellor of Virginia, George Wythe, together with
a black servant, died after drinking from a pot of coffee. The
coffee had been laced with arsenic. The finger of suspicion pointed
toward Wythe's great-nephew; he was arrested for murder. A
black cook could have given evidence against him. But the court
was unable to hear this testimony; and the nephew went
free.[69]

On the other hand, when it came to controlling the slave population, society and law were willing to dispense with the niceties.
The black criminal codes were clear and severe. Slave punishment
was largely corporal. Fines and imprisonment meant nothing—
slaves were penniless, and were already unfree. Slaves who transgressed were whipped—thoroughly, soundly, and often. In the
local courts of South Carolina, convicted blacks were whipped in
94.7 percent of the cases; only 10 percent were jailed (most of
these, of course, were also whipped). One out of twelve received
more than 100 lashes.[70]

Some laws authorized even stronger bodily penalties. Under a
Mississippi law of 1822, if any "Negro or mulatto" gave "false
testimony," he was to be nailed by the ear to the pillory for one
hour; then the ear was to be cut off; then "the other ear to be

[67]Francis S. Philbrick, ed., *Laws of Indiana Territory, 1801–1809* (1930), p. 40.
Mulatto was defined as a person with "one fourth part or more of negro blood."
[68]Quoted in Emma Lou Thornbrough, *The Negro in Indiana* (1957), p. 122.
[69]See William Draper Lewis, ed., *Great American Lawyers*, vol. I (1907), pp. 84–85.
[70]Michael S. Hindus, *Prison and Plantation*, p. 145.

nailed in like manner," and after one hour cut off.[71] For serious crimes, the codes often imposed the death penalty. Burning grain or stealing goods were capital crimes for slaves in Georgia (1806). Under the codes, arson by slaves was frequently made a capital crime. Attempted rape of a white woman was punishable by death in Georgia and Louisiana in 1806, in Kentucky in 1811, in Mississippi in 1814 and 1822, Tennessee in 1833, Texas in 1837, South Carolina in 1843.[72] As we noted, the law looked very severely on slave insurrection. Under the North Carolina Code of 1854, any slave "found in a state of rebellion or insurrection," or who agreed to "join any conspiracy or insurrection," or who persuaded others to join, or who "knowingly and wilfully" helped or encouraged slaves in a "state of rebellion," was liable to the death penalty. Slaves could be convicted, too, of the usual crimes for which white men were liable; and slaves were probably punished with special severity, even when the law did not specifically so provide. Between 1800 and 1855, 296 slaves were executed in South Carolina.[73]

A dead slave was a capital loss for his master. This put at least *some* natural check on the cruelty of masters. It was irrational, economically speaking, to harm a slave. Unfortunately, not everybody is rational. (It is also irrational to wreck a car, or beat a wife in a drunken rage; but people do it nonetheless.) Economic rationality also had its dangers. A master was tempted to hide the crimes his slaves committed, to keep them from dying on the gallows. To avoid this collusion, states gave compensation to owners of slaves put to death. A law of Alabama of 1824 provided that the jury, trying a slave for a capital offense, should also "assess the value of the slave"; the owner was entitled to claim up to one half this amount.[74] Virginia appropriated $12,000 in 1839 to pay owners "for slaves executed and transported."[75]

---

[71]Laws Miss. Adj. Sess. 1822, p. 194 (act of June 18, 1822, sec. 59). In addition, there would be thirty-nine lashes on the "bare back, well laid on." Note that the punishment applied to free blacks as well as to slaves.

[72]Farnam, *op. cit.*, pp. 184–85.

[73]Hindus, *op. cit.*, p. 103. The number of whites executed is unknown; but almost surely the rate of execution was far less.

[74]Laws Ala. 1824, p. 41. The law also levied a tax—"one cent on all negroes under ten years, and two cents on all negroes over ten and under sixty"—to provide a compensation fund. The slaveowner had to employ "good and sufficient counsel" to defend the slave, and was forbidden from concealing a slave "so that he or she cannot be brought to condign punishment."

[75]Laws Va. 1839, ch. 3.

Court records in the South reveal a good deal about social control of the slave population. In the day-to-day cases, there was little attention to procedural niceties, though this was almost surely true of routine prosecutions of whites as well. For special problems, the South evolved special procedures. In some states there were "slave patrols," which roamed the countryside, looking for erring blacks. If a stray black in Georgia could not show a pass (or "free papers") the patrol might "correct" him on the spot, "by whipping with a switch, whip, or cowskin, not exceeding twenty lashes."[76]

Equally important, if not more so, was what Michael Hindus has called plantation justice.[77] Basically, the master's will, uncontrolled by formal rules, was law for the slave. He was judge and jury; he tried "cases," passed sentences, and had them carried out in his little world. From the slaveowner's law there was no appeal, except in the most desperate, deviant cases—and only rarely then. Anyone with praise for Southern justice, at the level of formal courts, has to bear in mind what plantation justice was like.

Slave law, in short, had its own inner logic. Its object was repression and control. Everything tended toward that end. The South shut every door that could lead to black advancement or success—slave or free. The South deprived and degraded its blacks, then despised them for what they were; at the same time, the South was afraid of the monster created in its midst. Slavery was a coiled spring. In the end, it was a trap for whites as well. The whites, of course, had the upper hand; but even they paid the price in the long run. Slavery was one of the irritants that brought on a great civil war. Hundreds of thousands died, victims in a sense of the South's "peculiar institution."

---

[76]Prince, *Digest of the Laws of Georgia* (2nd ed., 1837), p. 775 (law of 1765).
[77]Hindus, *op. cit.*, p. 117.

CHAPTER V

AN AMERICAN LAW OF PROPERTY

THE LAND: A NATIONAL TREASURE

Land law was the kernel and core of common law. More exactly, real-property law was the core. Real property meant more than land; the term applied to that cluster of privileges and rights which centered on land, or on the exercise of power which had a focus in some point in space. In medieval England, rights to real property meant jurisdiction as well as ownership. The lord of the manor was a little sovereign as well as an owner of houses, land, and growing crops. Only people with land or land rights really mattered: the gentry, the nobles, the upper clergy; land was the source of their wealth and the source and seat of their power. Well into modern times, power and wealth were concentrated in the hands of great landlords. The social system turned on rights in land.

Clearly, American conditions were quite different. There was no landed gentry. The land was widely held. But in America, too, land was the basic form of wealth.[1] This was especially true in the West, where land was fertile and particularly abundant. After

[1]Nor did ownership of land have the same relationship to power that it did in England. It was, however, true that in many jurisdictions the right to vote depended on ownership of property. This has to be understood in context. After all, most adult white males *did* own land; property qualifications apparently nowhere excluded even half the potential voters; and in some states—South Carolina, Virginia, perhaps New York—very few men were affected at all. Willi Paul Adams, *The First American Constitutions* (1980), pp. 198–207. The property qualification was gradually eliminated; by 1850 it was practically speaking gone. It had its defenders, of course. Chancellor Kent argued in 1821 that New York needed it, for the Senate at least, as a "security against the caprice of the motley assemblage of paupers, emigrants, journeymen manufacturers, and those undefinable classes of inhabitants which a state and city like ours is calculated to invite." L. H. Clarke, *Report of the Debates and Proceedings of the Convention of the State of New York* (1821), p. 115. But this was a rear-guard, losing struggle.

1787, the vast stock of public land was at once a problem and a great opportunity. The federal government claimed title to millions and millions of acres. The Louisiana Purchase brought in millions more. As the frontier moved toward the West, American society faced a central issue: in what way to map, settle and distribute this almost limitless treasure of land.

How the federal government disposed of its land is a story of staggering detail.[2] The issue was as persistent as issues of war, slavery, and the tariff. The public-land question touched every other national issue—fiscal policy, veterans' benefits, the spread or containment of slavery, population diffusion, and the political strength of factions and regions. Federal law determined the very shape of the land. The act of May 18, 1796, "for the Sale of the Lands of the United States, in the territory northwest of the river Ohio, and above the mouth of [the] Kentucky river,"[3] created the office of surveyor general. Public lands were to be surveyed "without delay" and divided into townships of six miles square. Half of the townships were to be further divided into sections; each section contained one square mile, that is, 640 acres. Under later acts, sections were further divided into half-sections, and tracts of 160, 80, and 40 acres. In any event, the land had to be surveyed before it was sold, and the units of sale were strict rectangular plots. No chain of title could escape federal land policy, any more than the lots and farms could ignore the merciless, invisible grids stretched over the land at government order. The law of 1796, and its later versions, made us a nation of squares.

Once land was surveyed, it was disposed of. Public-land law flowed from one basic choice. The government did not choose to manage its land as a capital asset, but to get rid of it in an orderly, fruitful way. A whole continent was sold or given away—to veterans, settlers, squatters, railroads, states, colleges, speculators, and land companies. On the surface, one sees in this policy the powerful influence of free enterprise and *laissez-faire*. The government possessed a resource of incalculable value; but it was firm public policy to denationalize it as soon as possible. True, the land was sold for cash, and the government certainly wanted the money; but not to make itself powerful or to increase the size

[2]See, in general, Benjamin H. Hibbard, *A History of the Public Land Policies* (1939); Paul W. Gates, *History of Public Land Law Development* (1968); Everett N. Dick, *The Lure of the Land* (1970); Paul W. Gates, "An Overview of American Land Policy," 50 Agricultural History 213 (1976).

[3]1 Stats. 464 (act of May 18, 1796).

and scale of the public sector. And, in any event, divestment was the goal.

Yet never the whole goal, or the whole policy. The reason for getting rid of the land was not so much an ideology of weak government as it was a means of strengthening the dominant form of land tenure, and affirming the basic postulate of American social structure. The ideal was a country of free citizens, small-holders living on their own bits of land. Where strict market principles seemed to clash with this goal, the principles were forced to yield. Government was never merely a passive umpire of the market; it did more than chop the land into units and market it. It used land as a lever of policy. And this, too, was not a question of philosophy, but of concrete interests, demands, and needs, pressing in politically on Washington.

Nor was the federal government totally supine, spending its wealth in land like some sort of spendthrift, without any checks and controls. The government, for example, fought stubbornly to keep mineral rights out of private hands, dreaming of the gold and silver that might be hiding in the ground out West. The Ordinance of 1785 reserved to the government "one-third part of all gold, silver, lead and copper mines." The law of 1796 held back from sale "every...salt spring which may be discovered."[4] In 1807, Congress provided that lead-bearing lands should be leased, not sold.[5] Local administration of this law was peculiarly ineffective, but the government kept to its policy. Land grants in general were gifts on condition. They were used to advance national policy—to encourage colleges and railroads, for example; or to provide incentives for the draining of swamps; or simply to give new states a sort of dowry. Unfortunately, national land programs never worked as they were meant to work on paper. Field administration was the weak point: feeble, incompetent, corrupt.[6] Where national policy was more or less consistent with the economic self-interest of local residents, the policy worked more or less well. But when policy collided with self-interest, Washington's arm was never long enough or steady enough to carry through.

In general, for most of the 19th century, there was little deviation from the basic theme of divestment. All along, however, subsidiary decisions had to be made. Would public land be sold

[4] 1 Stats. 464, 466, sec. 3 (act of May 18, 1796).
[5] 2 Stats. 445, 446, sec. 2 (act of March 3, 1807).
[6] See, in general, Malcolm J. Rohrbough, *The Land Office Business: The Settlement and Administration of American Public Lands, 1789–1837* (1968).

in great blocks to wholesalers, or in small pieces to actual settlers? Should the land be sold in such a way as to raise the most money for the treasury? Should farmers or veterans be given some preference, or should the man with cash on hand always call the tune? On these points, the federal government was pushed now in this, now in that direction, by regional and other interests.

To begin with, the act of 1796 clearly called for sales of large tracts of land. This policy, however, was politically dangerous. It raised the bogeyman of land monopoly, and seemed to favor dealers and speculators over farmers. In any event, the land sold badly. To encourage sales, the government sharply reduced the minimum unit of sale to half-sections, quarter-sections, eighty-acre tracts, and then finally (in 1832) to forty-acre tracts.[7] The price of public land weakened, too. The act of 1796 had fixed a minimum price of two dollars an acre—much higher than the price at which huge blocks had earlier been sold. For a while, the price held firm. Between 1800 and 1820, public land sold at or near the two dollar price; during sieges of speculative fever, the price went even higher. Yet the Western states and territories insisted all along that the price must come down.

An important law of 1820 tried to meet these Western demands, while reforming the methods of sale. Under earlier acts, the government had sold its land on credit. By 1820, settlers owed the federal government about $21,000,000. Periodically, Congress passed laws giving its debtors some relief; an act of 1816, for example, gave land claimants in Mississippi Territory two years and eight months more to pay what they owed.[8] Still, many settlers forfeited their lands. The act of 1820 reduced the minimum price to $1.25. At the same time, it put an end to sales on credit. Every buyer had to make "complete payment" at the time he bought his land.[9]

The act meant to vest land and power in the hands of smallholders, without giving up the hope of making some money off sales of public land. But the votes and voices of settlers, real and potential, outshouted the greed of the government. These votes and voices also molded national policy toward squatters on public land. Settlers (and speculators) streamed into the West far ahead of the formal date of sale, sometimes even ahead of the official

[7]Hibbard, op. cit., p. 75.
[8]3 Stats. 300 (act of April 24, 1816).
[9]3 Stats. 566 (act of April 24, 1820).

survey. Theoretically, no one could gain a good title to the land until it was surveyed and sold. But a series of laws gave piecemeal preference (pre-emption rights) to actual settlers, even illegal settlers, or recognized and ratified state policies on pre-emption.[10] Finally, in 1841, Congress passed a general pre-emption law. The head of a family who had settled "in person" on land and "improved" it had first choice or claim to buy the land, up to 160 acres, at the minimum government price.[11] Somewhat naïve safeguards against abuse were written into the act. Big landowners were excluded from participation. No one was allowed to squat in the same state or territory as his former residence. But the most important aspect of the law was its general concept. It removed the last shred of pretense that the squatters were acting either illegally or immorally.

THE LAW OF PRIVATE LAND

Land-law reform was well under way even before the Revolution. After the Revolution, legislatures carried on the work of dismantling the feudal past. Economic thinkers of the day saw no reason to treat land differently from any other commodity; and holders of political and social power—big and small landowners, and speculators—stood to gain, in general, from a free, mobile market in land. Primogeniture, dead in most of New England, vanished from the South by 1800. Gradually, the rules of inheritance of land were assimilated to rules of inheritance of money and goods. The statute makers swept feudal tenures—most of them were not living law in this country—clean off the books. "The title of our lands," wrote Jesse Root proudly in 1798, "is free, clear and absolute, and every proprietor of land is a prince in his own domains, and lord paramount of the fee."[12]

In the first generation, statutes and court cases brushed aside many obnoxious or ill-fitting English doctrines. One casualty, for example, was a common-law rule that when two or more persons held interests in land, they were presumed to be joint tenants, not tenants in common. The difference between the two forms of co-ownership was technical, but not unimportant. If two per-

[10]E.g., 5 Stats. 412 (act of February 18, 1841) (Tennessee).
[11]5 Stats. 453, 455, sec. 10 (act of September 4, 1841).
[12]Jesse Root, *Reports* (Conn., 1798), Intro., xxxix.

sons owned land in common, each had a separate, distinct, undivided share. Each could sell, give away, or divide his interest. A
joint tenancy carried with it the right of survivorship; if one tenant
died, the other automatically succeeded to the property. A joint
tenancy, then, was a sort of last-man club in land. It was suitable
for family lands; less so, for lands of people dealing at arm's length
with each other in the market. The change in presumption was
defended in terms of the probable intention of the parties: "In
ninety-nine cases out of a hundred, of persons purchasing land
together, they would prefer not to be joint tenants, but tenants
in common. The law ought therefore to follow what is the common
wish of parties."[13] If this presumption was in fact correct, it was
because land purchasers meant to treat land as a commodity, as
a marketable good.

Changes in land law were generally of this quality. They were
in the first place empirical. They strove, to a marked degree, to
follow the "common wish of the parties." But the common wish
of parties reflected the rapid, volatile quality of dealings in land.
Land not only could be traded on the market; it *was* traded, openly
and often. In land lay the hope of national wealth, and the hope
of countless individuals for private fortune. As soon as land could
be cleared of native inhabitants, and properly surveyed, it was
traded with speed and fury. Speculation in raw land was almost
a kind of national lottery. Even when genuine settlers arrived,
built houses, and planted crops, the turnover was still exceedingly
rapid. Farmers themselves were speculators who gambled on the
rising price of land. Many farmers who had worked their land
for a while were eager to sell out (at a profit) and move on to a
newer frontier.

The 19th century was full of talk about respect for property,
for vested rights, and so on. But the property that was respected
most was productive property, property put to use, property that
was dynamic rather than static. The very meaning of property
changed—from a "static agrarian conception entitling an owner

[13] 1 Am. Jurist 77 (1829). Another doomed doctrine was the doctrine of "tacking," in the law of mortgages. In English law, a third mortgagee might get the
jump on a second mortgagee by buying the interest of a first mortgagee and
"tacking" that interest to his own. This doctrine was "very generally exploded" in
the United States. Chancellor Kent reported hearing Alexander Hamilton himself,
in 1804, "make a masterly attack upon the doctrine, which he insisted was founded
on a system of artificial reasoning, and encouraged fraud." Kent, *Commentaries*,
vol. IV (2nd ed., 1832), p. 178.

to undisturbed enjoyment, to a dynamic, instrumental . . . view."[14] We have already seen the impact of this new view on the law of eminent domain. Now, in the 19th century, this conception, which fit the interests of the landowning mass like a glove, worked massive, major changes in the law of land and related areas of American law.

In a climate of active trading, the law of conveyancing had to undergo a sea change. In the United States, everyman (and later, everywoman) was or might be a conveyancer. The elaborate forms of English law were clearly unsuitable. Legal sophistication was a scarce resource. What was acceptable or tolerable to a small upper class of landlords was intolerable in the great American mass market. Vestigial modes of tenure and conveyancing survived in some parts of the country, particularly the plantation South. But even in South Carolina, a court of equity showed genuine surprise that Alicia H. Middleton and Sarah Dehon of Charlestown had executed "deeds of feoffment, with livery of seisin," in 1836, instead of using more streamlined forms.[15] In the rest of the country, the enormous demand meant that land documents had to become simple and standard. They had to be mass-produced at minimal cost for mass use. At exactly that point of time when conveyancing skills became rare, draftsmanship in fantastic quantity was needed. There were, of course, plenty of lawyers. But there were not half enough *if* every land transfer needed careful counseling and delicate architecture. And the lawyers who practiced in small towns or on the frontier could not cope with the jigsaw puzzles of English land law.

In many ways, reform was clean and swift. The old conveyance of feoffment, with livery of seizin—the turf and twig—clearly had to go. It was little used; and the New York revised statutes of 1827–28 expressly abolished it.[16] Deeds had to be in writing, but were valid if they followed simple, rational form. Out of the welter of available models, lawyers in the republic worked out two basic types of deed. The *warranty deed* grew out of the old deed of bargain and sale, with covenants of warranty. The *quitclaim deed* developed from the common-law release.[17] A warranty deed was used to make a full transfer of land from one owner to another.

---

[14]Morton J. Horwitz, *The Transformation of American Law, 1780–1860* (1977), p. 30.

[15]See *Dehon* v. *Redfern,* Dudley's Eq. Rpts. (S. Car. 1838), 115.

[16]Kent, *Commentaries,* vol. IV (2nd ed., 1832), pp. 489–90.

[17]A. James Casner, ed., *American Law of Property,* vol. III (1952), p. 223.

The seller guaranteed that he had and could transfer good title. The quitclaim deed made no such promises. It simply transferred whatever rights the transferor had, good or bad; and was so understood. People used quitclaim deeds to give up or pass on cloudy or contingent rights to land. The historical origin of both kinds of deed was still clearly visible in wording and form; but they were drastically shortened and streamlined. It would be too much to say that their use was within the grasp of an average layman. But they were accessible to lawyers of some training and experience, and to shrewd land dealers as well. They were available in popular form books, and in various versions of *Every Man His Own Lawyer*, or books with similar titles, which sold thousands of copies in America. Using these books, a businessman or lawyer could try to make deeds on his own. He could copy down the forms and fill in the blanks.

Both land practice and statutes worked toward simplicity in the law of real property. In old England, land actions (lawsuits over land) were a frightful jumble of technicality. There was plenty of American technicality, too, but it was a pale shadow at best of the English mess. Joseph Story grew almost ecstatic at the efficiencies of the action of ejectment, which tested title to land, "on the picturesque banks of the Hudson, the broad expanse of the Delaware and Chesapeake, the sunny regions of the South, and the fertile vales and majestic rivers of the West."[18] In fact, ejectment was most popular at the fringes of the country. In 1821, when Story wrote, Massachusetts, Maine, and New Hampshire still did not share the national passion for ejectment. These states, instead, used "writs of entry for the trial of land titles." The writs had been "disembarrassed...of some troublesome appendages and some artificial niceties," but were still, by comparison, archaic.[19]

A federal system is legally a decentralized system; and this was true of land law as well, outside the public domain. There was therefore a lot of local diversity. Massachusetts might retain its traditions; and so long as these were not *too* irrational—so long as they did no harm to the land market—these traditions could survive. The states also had different economic needs, different quantities of legal skill, different geographical features. They shared many innovations. But the land law of no two states was

[18]Joseph Story, "An Address Delivered Before the Members of the Suffolk Bar," Sept. 4, 1821, in 1 Am. Jurist 1, 17 (1829).

[19]*Ibid.*, p. 17.

identical. There was no central authority to make codes, and no central codes of law; so, despite all the labor of simplification, there were bound to be great amounts of complexity left in the land law.

Parts of the older land law survived because they were familiar and useful. Parts hung on (in the books at least) precisely because they were too irrelevant to be worth abolition. Much of the English law of tenures and estates was nominally in effect. American lawyers spoke of fee simple and life estates, terms of years, easements, covenants, and profits. This much was part of the marrow of American law. But the strange wonderland of executory devises, powers of appointment, contingent remainders, shifting and springing uses, though not formally abolished, lay asleep, like Rip Van Winkle. This ancient body of learning had little to do with the general land market. When, in the 1820s, there arose a thoughtful, pragmatic movement to reform the law, the reformers lopped away three elements of the land law: first, doctrines and institutions that seemed to do positive harm; second, those which, whatever the impact, appeared to be "tyrannical" or "feudal"; third, those that had to be purged as part of a general cleanup, a general rationalizing, a general codification. These three prongs were especially visible in New York's important revision of property law in 1827–28—a summing up of a full generation of reform.

Rules of *capacity* were among those most thoroughly revamped in the course of the 19th century. Ideally, every adult should be able to own and deal in land. The property rights of married women, as we have seen, were ultimately modernized. In common law, aliens could not, for reasons of policy, inherit land. The rule, and the bias against aliens, seemed somewhat out of place in America. The provisions against aliens "originated in ages of barbarism, out of the hatred and jealousy with which foreigners were regarded ... [To] those [aliens] who are actually resident amongst us, the best policy" would be "to encourage their industry by giving them all reasonable facilities in the acquisition of property."[20] There was, on occasion, plenty of xenophobia in America; one need only cite the Alien and Sedition laws, in the late 18th century. But in a country where hundreds of thousands played the land market, much as some of their descendants might play the stock market, there was no room for the old ban on alien landholding. An

[20] 1 Am. Jurist 87–88 (1829).

expanding population meant rising land prices; this called for an open-door policy for aliens and incentives for certain kinds of investment by noncitizens.

Local compromises began to replace the absolute disability of aliens. As early as 1704, a South Carolina act, praising resident aliens for "their industry, frugality and sobriety," for their "loyal and peaceabl[e]" behavior, pointed out that they had acquired "such plentiful estates as hath given this Colony no small reputation abroad, tending to the encouragement of others to come and plant among us," and granted them full rights to acquire property by gift, inheritance, or purchase.[21] An Ohio law (1804) made it "lawful" for aliens who became "entitled to have" any "lands tenements or hereditaments" by "purchase, gift, devise or descent," to "hold, possess, and enjoy" their lands, "as fully and completely as any citizen of the United States or this state can do, subject to the same laws and regulations, and not otherwise."[22] Federal pre-emption and homestead laws also gave rights to resident aliens.

Against the "tyrannical" and "feudal," legislators slashed away with might and main. Primogeniture, as we noted, fell by the wayside. The fee tail was another casualty. When a man held land in fee tail, it descended from generation to generation to the heirs of the body, that is, to lineal descendants. No one could sell such a "fettered inheritanc[e]," as Kent called it,[23] because the land belonged to the tenant's children, and his children's children thereafter. As a matter of fact, as far back as the 15th century, tenants in tail had been able to sell their land, free of the claims of unborn generations, through tricks of conveyancing which "barred" the entail. But this was no job for an amateur. In a nation of amateurs, the fee tail was offensive; since it did not work even in England, there was no point in preserving it. It was abolished in Virginia in 1776, in New York in 1782. Not every state carried abolition through to a neat and logical conclusion. In some places,

[21]*Statutes at Large of South Carolina*, vol. II (1837), pp. 251–52 (act of Nov. 4, 1704). To qualify, however, an alien had to take an oath to the crown "on the Holy Evangelists, or otherwise according to the form of his profession."

[22]Laws Ohio 1803–4, p. 123 (act of Feb. 3, 1804). The American experience brought about a redefinition of the very meaning of citizenship and allegiance. These were essentially a matter of free choice, not the result of an inborn, permanent, perpetual status. See James H. Kettner, *The Development of American Citizenship, 1608–1870* (1978). The usefulness of this idea of "volitional allegiance" in a country trying to build population and stimulate the land market is obvious.

[23]Kent, *Commentaries*, vol. IV (2nd ed., 1832), p. 12.

the fee tail survived in a weak and fossilized form; any attempt to create a fee tail was treated automatically as a life estate followed by a plain fee simple. But even in those states the fee tail was never of any significance.

In general, fear of land monopoly and land dynasties haunted the lawmakers. New York state was particularly sensitive on this score, perhaps because of the long shadow cast by the estates on the Hudson. Even Chancellor Kent, certainly no radical, saw a clear connection between republican government and free transfer of land:

> Entailments are recommended in monarchical governments, as a protection to the power and influence of the landed aristocracy; but such a policy has no application to republican establishments, where wealth does not form a permanent distinction, and under which every individual of every family has his equal rights, and is equally invited, by the genius of the institutions, to depend upon his own merit and exertions. Every family, stripped of artificial supports, is obliged, in this country, to repose upon the virtue of its descendants for the perpetuity of its fame.[24]

This attitude, and those like it, underlay the New York revision of property laws of 1827–28. This famous enactment can properly be called a code. It arranged, changed, and simplified great parts of the law of property. The English law of perpetuities was tightened. A more severe limit was placed on the time that land could be tied up within a family. Under the English rule, future interests in property were void for "remoteness of vesting." The New York rule made future interests invalid if they unduly "suspended" the "power of alienation." The difference between the two concepts was technical, and, in most cases, inconsequential. But the New York version of the rule expressed one dominant aim of land law reform: to keep the land market open and mobile. For the same reason, the code frowned on the creation of trusts of land. Trusts were only allowed for a few, specific purposes— for example, for the benefit of a minor. Here the dangers seemed slight, the utility obvious, and the trust would come to a predictable natural end.

The legislature watered down the more radical New York innovations in later years. Others were misconstrued or mishandled by the courts. The judges' hostility was not just blind reaction.

[24]*Ibid.*, p. 20.

There were flaws in the draftsmanship of the code. The novelty of its schemes bred confusion and encouraged litigation. Also, some of its provisions mistook the direction in which economy and society would go. Chancellor Kent had been skeptical from the start; the trust provisions of the code, he felt, could not work. The desire to "preserve and perpetuate family influence and property," he noted, was "very prevalent with mankind," and was "deeply seated in the affections."[25] Trusts would probably not wither away. "We cannot hope," he wrote, to "check the enterprising spirit of gain, the pride of families, the anxieties of parents, the importunities of luxury, the fixedness of habits, the subtleties of intellect." The law, he predicted, would bring wholesale evasion: the "fairest and proudest models of legislation that can be matured in the closet" could not prevail against the "usages of a civilized people."[26] Time has proved Kent to be correct, on the whole, and a far better sociologist than his cohorts. Wealth grew; new fortunes were created; and among the super-rich, the dynastic urge soon reared its ugly head. There was no political force strong enough to withstand the aristocracy of money, at least in its minor aspirations. Land baronies were dead for good; but later on, the long-term trust became popular again among the very rich, as a dynastic device not tied to land, and to an extent even Kent would have found astounding; it is still growing today.

Land-law reform had, on the whole, made the law of real property more serviceable. But as old problems were solved, new ones emerged. There were chronic difficulties in determining title. Government surveys, for all their defects, made it possible to identify the physical aspects of the land. But title is a concept more elusive than longitude, more nebulous than a tree stump or a stream. Title became as vexatious and intractable a subject as the abolished law of tenure. Nobody planned it that way. But sometimes the chain of title had defective or mysterious links. It depended, perhaps, on the terms of some vast, ambiguous grant—from the federal government, or the King of Spain, or some long-dead proprietor. Or it had to take into account the patents (grants) of American state governments, possibly equivocal, possibly corrupt. There were types of rights in land unknown to England. Georgia continued its headright system until past 1800.[27] Raucous

---

[25]*Ibid.*, p. 19.

[26]*Ibid.*, p. 313.

[27]Milton S. Heath, *Constructive Liberalism: The Role of the State in Economic Development in Georgia to 1860* (1954), pp. 84–92.

squabbles, arising under state and federal pre-emption laws, and the law and practice of local land offices, were meat and bread to Western lawyers. The very marketability of land added to the general confusion. Federal and state governments floated land scrip and bounty warrants, to veterans, for example. Some issues were freely transferable; some fluctuated on the market, like modern stocks and bonds. These land certificates, passing from hand to hand, gave rise to a whole new body of law, a whole new body of controversies.

Especially in the West, local officials were weak and corrupt. The effect on land titles was devastating. Forgery and fraud, if we can believe the stories, were epidemic. Since land was the soul of trade, this meant that there was weakness in the quality control of a staple commodity. Public weakness and private greed were a formidable combination. Joseph Story was struck by the land law of Kentucky, its "subtle and refined distinctions," its labyrinth of titles. "Ages will probably elapse," he wrote in 1829, "before the litigations founded on it will be closed." To outside lawyers, "it will forever remain an unknown code, with a peculiar dialect, to be explored and studied, like the jurisprudence of some foreign nation."[28] And Kentucky was not an old conservative society, but a new state at the legal periphery. Its problem was not archaic law, but the unrestrained clash of interests. The same tangle of titles occurred time and time again: in Missouri, in Illinois, in California. With one hand, government labored to create a rational land system. It provided for survey and recording of land interests. It did all it could to further orderly exploration and settlement. But at the same time, government would not and could not resist political pressures; would not and could not correct its weakness in the field. The result was constant tension between chaos and order.

The goals of policy in Kentucky were much the same as in other states: an orderly system of settlement, and clean, clear ways to register and keep track of land. But Kentucky also attempted to do justice to—or coddle—the "actual settler" (and voter). The courts heard endless disputes over questions of priority and validity of claims. Had A or B raised a crop of corn on the land or built a cabin? And which had done it first? Where were the bound-

---

[28]Joseph Story, in 1 Am. Jurist 20 (1829). On the Kentucky land title problem, see Mary K. Bonsteel Tachau, *Federal Courts in the Early Republic: Kentucky, 1789–1816* (1978), ch. 8.

aries between vague, overlapping claims, claims impossible to rationalize, even without human error and barefaced lies? In one case, reported in 1799, a Kentucky court heard a witness say that a certain Berry "blazed a white ash or hickory" to mark his claim, "but which of them he can not be certain, and cut the two first letters of his name and blacked them with powder, and... sat down at the foot of a small sugar tree and chopped a hole with his tomahawk in the root of it.... [A]t the place where Berry made his improvement the branch [of a river] made a bend like a horse shoe." Where was the ash or hickory now? "Cut down, but the stump remained," in a "very decayed state." The sugar tree was still standing, and identifiable; the tomahawk mark was "still perceivable"; presumably the horseshoe bend could still be found. None of these was exactly an unambiguous sign.[29] This kind of evidence could be easily invented, or contradicted. In many of these cases, it was a struggle for the family home, the farm, the very livelihood. In some, the land was of baronial size, or a mighty city had grown up on top of it; thus vast fortunes hung in the balance. Some of the greatest American trials, in terms of cost, time, and acrimony, have been trials over title to land.

Free alienability of land was always an aim of the land law, but not as an end in itself. The goal of public policy was economic growth, a rising, spreading population, a healthy, aggressive middle class. This usually meant free trade in land; but sometimes the market principle had to give way. Devices and doctrines to protect smallholders (a politically potent class) came to permeate the law. One such device was the mechanic's lien. On the surface it seemed to have a different thrust; but this was misleading. Essentially, the mechanic's lien gave special remedies and preferences to "mechanics," artisans who labored on buildings or made improvements to land. If the landowner failed to pay the "mechanic," the "mechanic" could enforce his claim directly against land and improvements.[30]

The mechanic's lien was a purely American invention. It can be traced back to 1791. In that year, commissioners, in charge of building the new capital city of Washington, D.C., suggested a lien to "encourage master builders to contract for the erecting and finishing of houses." Maryland, the relevant state, passed necessary legislation. Pennsylvania was the next state to enact a form

---

[29]*McClanahan* v. *Berry*, Hughes' Ky. Rpts., vol. 1 (1799), pp. 323, 327–28.
[30]See Farnam, *op. cit.*, pp. 152–56.

of the lien. Its first law (1803) applied only to certain kinds of "mechanic," and only to certain sections of the city of Philadelphia. Gradually more and more states adopted broader and broader versions of the lien. By the end of the period, the mechanic's lien was a sweeping security device. In Illinois, in 1845,

> Any person who shall... furnish labor or materials for erecting or repairing any building, or the appurtenances of any building... shall have a lien upon the whole tract of land or town lot... for the amount due to him for such labor or materials.[31]

The mechanic's lien was a pro-labor statute, but not in the New Deal sense. The "mechanics" of the lien law were not poor urban workers; they were suppliers and artisans. The law protected labor, in the early 19th-century sense of the word: those who added tangible value to real assets. The law preferred their claims over those of general creditors. Not least of all, the lien was intended to *help* the landowner, in an age when cash, hard money, liquid capital was short. The law promised a safe and immovable form of collateral to those who supplied materials and labor. The lien was a kind of bootstrap finance (the phrase is Willard Hurst's), almost a subsidy, almost a kind of government credit to encourage building and improvement of land.

The ideal of the small freeholder, backbone of the nation, lay at the root of another American innovation, the homestead exemption. The exemption defined certain kinds of property (the "homestead"), and immunized this property from the fangs and claws of creditors. The homestead exemption first appeared in Texas, before Texas was admitted to the Union. The legislature expanded the doctrine steadily until, in 1839, up to 50 acres of land or one town lot—when these constituted a family's "homestead"—tools, books, livestock, feed, and some household furniture were immune from seizure for debt. The idea was attractive, and spread from the periphery toward the center. The first adoption was in Mississippi (1841). By 1848, Connecticut, Wisconsin, and Michigan, along with some of the Southern states, had enacted one form or other of the homestead exemption. By the time of the Civil War, all but a few states had done the same.[32]

[31]Rev. Stats. Ill. 1845, p. 345.
[32]Farnam, *op. cit.*, pp. 148–52. The Texas constitution of 1845 specifically mentioned the right of the legislature to pass a homestead act. The Wisconsin constitution of 1848 specifically instructed the legislature to pass a "wholesome" exemption law.

On the surface, the homestead exemption and the mechanic's lien seem contradictory. One law made home and farm a sanctuary against creditors; the other gave creditors a sharp new legal tool to use against home and farm. In practice, there was little conflict. The small farmer did not use hired workmen on a scale that exposed him to the lien laws. Economic interests protected by the two acts did not usually collide. And both acts were in a sense developmental. The homestead law, in Texas, was specifically meant to encourage immigration. It sought, indirectly, to mobilize labor and capital toward the prime job of the times: building population, and enriching the land—precisely the aims of the mechanic's lien. To new settlers, the homestead exemption promised a haven of safety in a boom-and-bust world. The mechanic's lien got their homes built; and, if a crisis came, it gave a preference to productive laborers against mere lenders of money—middlemen, who, in 19th-century thought, were more or less parasitic; they did not produce goods or add to the nation's stock of wealth.

BOOM AND BUST: THE LAW
OF MORTGAGES

Lien and exemption laws were enormously important because of the pervasive, ruinous force of the business cycle. Crisis struck the economy with shock waves at regular and irregular intervals. Volcanic eruptions and disruptions in prices caused deep insecurity among debtors, creditors, and merchants. The money system was disastrously weak; credit information was primitive. No man was safe unless he held silver and gold, and these metals were rare indeed. The law reflected a desperate search for security—how to protect one's own assets and how to get recourse against the other man's. Since land was so large a part of the national wealth, land law was very sensitive to the business cycle. Legislatures, courts, and the business community shaped security devices in land with one eye to the volatile nature of land values.

The prime instrument of land security, then as now, was the mortgage. Mortgage means, literally, "dead pledge." A mortgage is "dead" to the creditors, since the borrower stays in possession of the land and keeps whatever it produces, over and above the debt; by contrast, a pawnbroker takes his pledges "live." The mortgage was an old, old legal device, in constant adjustment to fresh reality.[33] Its development in modern times bears the scars of the never-ending struggle between debtor and creditor. In 19th-century America, there were definitely classes of debtors or borrowers, though not always clearly marked off from the lenders. Still, there was constant pressure to reform the law in the direction of debtors' rights—to abolish imprisonment for debt, for example. There was also pressure for political change (widening of the suffrage), and for economic programs (inflation and easy money). Creditors too exerted influence. And it was not always clear which policy benefited debtors or creditors. A strong mortgage law, giving creditors strong rights, was as necessary for debtors as for creditors, if only to make capital flow into real-estate investment. In many states (Wisconsin, for example), the homestead exemption did not cover a purchase-money mortgage. This was a large hole in the law, but apparently vital for farmers and homeowners. Most men had no capital security except the land itself; yet only a fool would lend money to a man to buy land without this security.

Debtors were, on the whole, inconsistent men, but for understandable reasons. They took one attitude during good times and another during bad. In good times they needed money to buy land and to build and raise crops; they were willing to promise the moon, hoping that land values would go up and lighten their debts. During bad times promises turned sour, debts became mountainous, and debtors looked about for avenues of escape.

Legislatures, particularly in the West, found debtor relief politically irresistible. On the other hand, businessmen and creditors were not without resources. They appealed, sometimes successfully, to the law for protection. Quite early, they found that the courts, free from the pressures of frequent election, were willing to take what struck them as a longer and sounder view of economic policy than the legislatures. Creditors too were expert at evasion. Where there was an economic demand for their product, formal law was almost helpless against this demand. Law, at least in the United States, has often lacked both the means and the will to impose strong economic regulation. Those who dealt in the mar-

---

[33]Much of mortgage law was developed in or through courts of equity. This made some technical adjustments necessary in those jurisdictions which had no chancery courts. Pennsylvania, for example, substituted, through the action of *scire facias sur mortgage* (1705), a common-law mode of foreclosure for the usual procedures in equity. *Scire facias sur mortgage* was a writ, used when the mortgagor lapsed into default, requiring him to "show cause" why the mills of the law should not begin to grind, foreclosing the mortgage.

ket have been clever at inventing small-scale, half-visible ways of getting around some obnoxious rule. Legal history has demonstrated time and again that there is more than one way to skin a cat. There is no mystery in the process. The clash of interests naturally produces inconsistent, half-enforced, largely symbolic rules and doctrines. Particularly does this happen in a decentralized system, where the losers in one forum merely proceed to the next.

The outline history of mortgage law is instructive.[34] Over the years a costly and complicated system of *equitable foreclosure* had evolved, partly to give the debtor some protection. Its essential feature was the debtor's "equity" or right to redeem his lost land. Draftsmen then invented a clause to undo this "equity." The debtor would agree, in advance, that if he defaulted, his creditor could sell the land without going to court. As early as 1774, a New York statute specifically ratified this practice, though with some procedural safeguards. In some Southern states, however, courts reached a different conclusion; they held that no one could legally grant such a power of sale to a mortgagee. Mortgages then began to name third persons ("trustees") to exercise the power of sale, in case of default. The "deed of trust," then, acted as the functional equivalent of the Northern mortgage with power of sale.

A mortgage armored with a power of sale was an effective instrument of credit. But while the courts accepted the power of sale, and the deed of trust (undercutting the old equity of redemption), new laws were passed that had the opposite effect. The year 1819 was a year of panic. A New York statute of 1820 gave a year of grace to hard-pressed land debtors. It was not clear whether this type of law applied to mortgages at all. The question was decided one way by a court in New York, another way by Tennessee, which had adopted a similar law. The panic of 1837 produced a fresh crop of redemption statutes. Illinois's law (1841) specifically applied to "mortgaged lands." It gave the mortgagor, in essence, one year to redeem his property. It further provided that no mortgaged land could be sold at foreclosure sale, to any bidder, for less than two-thirds the appraised value of the land. This too was an attempt to salvage something from the land-debtor's equity. The *New York Journal of Commerce* spoke in disgust

[34]See Robert H. Skilton, "Developments in Mortgage Law and Practice," 17 Temple L. Q., 315 (1943). This excellent article is the source of much of the discussion of mortgage law in this chapter.

of this kind of law as "dishonest and knavish." "More than all defalcations of individual swindlers," it "attests the almost hopeless depravity and corruption of the age."[35] The law applied to existing, as well as to future, mortgages. Indeed, that was the point of it: to relieve the debtors of Illinois who were crushed by the fall in prices and values. In the famous case of *Bronson* v. *Kinzie*,[36] the United States Supreme Court struck down the Illinois statute as an impairment of the obligation of contracts. A storm of protest arose in Illinois, but the burden of inertia had now shifted; creditors were once more in the saddle. *Bronson* precipitated a second crisis: a confrontation between the legislature, responsive to the debtors, and the courts, defending stability and creditors' rights. Ultimately, it was conceded that the legislature could validly impose a redemption right on future mortgages, regardless of what creditors wished. The courts' impact, though great, was not decisive: still, courts were able to force a delay, to exact a compromise from the legislatures that were too "ultra" on the debtors' side.

SUCCESSION: WILLS AND TRUSTS

In a market economy, property is freely bought and sold, and freely transferred by way of gift. Most gift transactions take place within the family. Few property owners make major gifts during their lifetime; but when they die, they take nothing with them; everything now must be given away. Almost the entire stock of private wealth turns over each generation, by last will and testament, or through the intestacy laws, or by some gift in the shadow of death. Only public, corporate, and dynastic property is immune from this law of mortality.

Colonial probate law and practice had a certain flexibility. There were early attempts to administer the estates of the dead without hard and fast rules, treating each case as required by the family situation. These tendencies were abandoned. A rather tight network of rules grew up, more or less on English models. These rules made up in efficiency and certainty what was lost in flexibility. But flexibility and individualized handling of estates was a

---

[35]Quoted in Charles Warren, *The Supreme Court in United States History* (rev. ed., 1935), vol. II, p. 102.

[36]1 How. 310 (1843). For an attempt to measure the impact of the Illinois relief laws, see George L. Priest, "Law and Economic Distress: Sangamon County, Illinois, 1837–1844," 2 J. of Legal Studies 469 (1973).

luxury that a mass society, with mass ownership of wealth, thought it could not afford.

American probate laws were never slavish imitations of the English laws.[37] To be sure, there was a good deal of copycatting in the law of wills. There were two key English statutes. The statute of frauds (1677) had required a written, witnessed will for real estate. The Wills Act (1837) covered both realty and personality. The two statutes differed, slightly, in other details. After 1837, American states tended to follow one or the other of these models, or a mixture of both. Statutory rules for the formal execution of a will distinctly hardened. With few exceptions, American states imposed the same formal requirements on wills of land and on testaments of personal property.[38]

A formal, standard, precise law of wills was vital to the property system. The Ordinance of 1787 authorized wills of land, "provided such wills be duly proved." This was a clear departure from English law. In England, a person could introduce a will into court, to prove a claim to ownership of land, even though the will had never gone through probate. And even if it had, that fact did not bind the court trying title to land. The Ordinance of 1787, and the practice that grew up under it, gave much more weight to the probate *process*.[39] There was colonial precedent for this practice.[40] But it is best understood in the context of post-Revolutionary land law. Land instruments had to be rational, simple, and standard; land procedures had to be objective, and routine. The will, like the deed, was a fundamental instrument of transfer. Probate was to the will what recording was to the deed. Transitions were smoother, records were more exact, and title was less clouded, if all wills were funneled through probate.

Because of their importance to land titles, the wills themselves have been carefully preserved in many counties. They exist in an unbroken line from the beginnings of county history to the present. An occasional title searcher disturbs their dust. An occasional genealogist tunnels into the caves, in search of a lost forefather.

[37]The Massachusetts double share for the eldest child was given up in 1789.

[38]In a group of Southern and Western states, and states where civil law influence was strong (Texas, Louisiana), holographic wills were also valid. These wills, if entirely handwritten by the testator, required no witnesses.

[39]William W. Blume, "Probate and Administration on the American Frontier," 58 Mich. L. Rev. 209, 233 (1959).

[40]See Thomas E. Atkinson, "The Development of the Massachusetts Probate System," 42 Mich. L. Rev. 425, 448 (1943).

Historians have generally neglected them; but from these old wills, stiff and stereotyped as they are, the voice of social history speaks out. One finds in them an occasional fact of rare beauty, some aspect or insight of the era, trapped in county archives as if in amber. John Randolph of Roanoke freed his slaves by will, "heartily regretting" that he ever owned slaves. He bequeathed to these "old and faithful servants, Essex and his wife Hetty ... three-and-a-half barrels of corn, two hundred weight of pork, a pair of strong shoes, a suit of clothes, and a blanket each, to be paid them annually; also, an annual hat to Essex, and ten pounds of coffee and twenty of brown sugar." Benjamin Franklin left to his daughter "The King of France's picture, set with four hundred and eight diamonds." It was his wish that "she would not form any of those diamonds into ornaments, either for herself or daughters, and thereby introduce or countenance the expensive, vain and useless pastime of wearing jewels in this country."[41]

Wills are ambulatory, that is, they can be revoked or replaced by the testator up to the moment of death. In the 19th century, the deathbed will was more common than in later, more calculating times.[42] Perhaps partly for this reason, many 19th-century wills were human documents, more poignant and direct than 20th-century wills tend to be. The typical will, of course, did little preaching and betrayed little sentiment. Only the wealthy, by and large, made out wills. Even at the very end of the period, probably less than five percent of the persons who died in the typical county, in any one year, left wills that passed through probate.[43] Even fewer of those who died intestate, that is, without wills, left estates that were formally administered. All in all, more than ninety percent of the population passed on without benefit of probate.

Willmakers tended to be landowners, men (and some women) of substance. Their estate plans (to use a modern term) nearly always disposed of their land within the family. Men were at special pains to provide for the interests of wives, sisters, and daughters.

[41]Virgil M. Harris, *Ancient, Curious, and Famous Wills* (1911), pp. 370, 414.

[42]In earlier times and in England, wills were even more likely to be deathbed documents; see Wilbur K. Jordan, *Philanthropy in England, 1480–1660* (1959), p. 16, on 16th-century wills; for some colonial data, see James W. Deen, Jr., "Patterns of Testation: Four Tidewater Counties in Colonial Virginia," 16 Am. J. Legal Hist. 154, 167–68 (1972).

[43]Some probably wrote out a will, but left so small an estate it made no sense to probate the will.

It was not usual to give women actual control over land. Before
the Married Women's Property Acts, property left to a woman
might pass out of the testator's bloodline, might even fall prey to
creditors of the woman's husband. Among the wealthy, then, there
was a definite tendency not to make outright gifts (of land in fee
simple) to women. Rather, property was *settled* on women; or left
in trust; or given to women in the form of lesser "estates": life
interests for daughters, estates during widowhood for a surviving
wife. Almost forty percent of a group of New Jersey wills, in the
period 1810–13, which contained gifts to a widow, gave her an
estate measured by the duration of her widowhood.[44] In New
York City, seven out of twelve wills probated, in the summer of
1843, contained some sort of nonfee disposition.[45]

One has the impression that more of the population stood
outside the formal system of succession in New York in 1840 than
in Massachusetts Bay two centuries before. In the early colonial
period, probate was cheap, accessible, and relatively informal. In
the 18th century, probate was more elaborate and costly; only the
well-to-do made use of it. At some point, perhaps about 1800, the
curve reached a peak and slowly changed direction. From then
on participation in the probate process gradually increased, along
with national literacy and wealth. In absolute terms, the number
of nonfee dispositions (trusts, settlements, chains of future interests) certainly increased, in the 19th century—at least as fast as
the population and probably much faster.

Trust litigation was fairly sparse in the early 19th century. Except for marriage settlements, living trusts were probably not common. Most trusts were short-term, "caretaker" trusts, created to
protect some weaker member of the family: married women, minors, incompetents. Frequently, too, a man would set up a trust
to avoid passing property on to a bankrupt son or son-in-law.
Thomas Jefferson left the residue of his estate to his grandson,
Thomas J. Randolph, and two friends, in trust for Jefferson's
daughter. Her husband, Thomas M. Randolph, was insolvent.
The trustees were to hold the estate "in base fee, determinable
on the death of my said son-in-law"; at that time, the estate would
vest in the daughter and her heirs. This arrangement would "pre-
clude the rights, powers and authorities" that would otherwise

[44]N.J. Archives, 1st series, vol. XLI (vol. 12 [1949], Calendar of Wills, 1810–
13).
[45]New York, Surr. N.Y. Cnty., Will Bk. No. 88, pp. 2–65 (July–Sept. 1843).

devolve on the son-in-law "by operation of law." In this way, the estate was guarded against the creditors of Jefferson's son-in-law.[46] In a Pennsylvania case, *Ashhurst v. Given* (1843),[47] the deceased left to his son Samuel Given, a kind of trusteeship over the estate, consisting of an "undivided half part of the Kidderminster estate, including the factory buildings, dwelling-house, water-powers... machinery and fixtures." Samuel was to manage the estate for the benefit of his children, paying himself a "reasonable support out of the trust fund." Through this circuitous scheme, the testator hoped to provide for the family, without exposing the estate to "those debts which he [Samuel] contracted in an unfortunate business."

A second, rarer, use of the trust device might be called dynastic. Through trusts and settlements, a testator who wished could bind an estate within his family for as long as the law would permit. How long was that? There was a limiting doctrine, called the rule against perpetuities. The rule, which had reached full flower in England by 1800, was at least nominally in force in the United States. The New York revision of 1827–28 modified the rule, and made it even more stringent. The New York statutes on trusts were, as we have seen, antidynastic. Only caretaker trusts were intended to survive the onslaught of reform, although the point was blunted by later amendments. Neither in New York, nor in Michigan, Wisconsin, and Minnesota, which borrowed the code, were the rules to stamp out the dynastic trust ever fully carried out.

The draftsmen of the New York code had a specific image in mind, a specific type of dynasty. They were thinking of the great English landed estates. Under a settlement or long-term trust, such an estate was "tied up" in a family in two senses: no current member of the family had the right to sell his interest, nor could anybody, including the trustee, treat land and improvements as market commodities; land and family were tied tightly together. New York had some estates of this type; they were also known in the plantation South. But a new type of trust was developing, which was dynastic in a different sense. Some great merchant families were wealthy in capital assets other than land—factories, banking houses, ships, and stocks and bonds. Particularly in Boston, rich men in the early 19th century began planning dynastic

[46]Harris, *op. cit.*, p. 398.
[47]Watts & Serg. 323 (Pa., 1843).

trusts that were fundamentally different from the baronial land trusts. These long-term trusts needed flexible management; the assets were not meant to be preserved as such; it was taken for granted that the trustees would change the portfolio as their business sense dictated.

Massachusetts law proved quite permissive to these mercantile dynasties. In the famous *Harvard College* case (1830),[48] the court enunciated a standard of investment for trustees which came to be known as the "prudent investor" rule. It freed the trustee from rigid restrictions on trust investment. The rule in other jurisdictions was that a trustee could invest only in government bonds or first mortgages on land. From 1830 on, the trustee in Massachusetts could manage and invest more freely; he could shift assets about, buying whatever was "prudent"; he could, for example, buy sound corporate stocks. The rule was the Magna Charta for a Boston phenomenon, the private, professional trustee. This shrewd Yankee figure, manager of other people's fortunes, first appeared in Boston around 1820. For several decades, until the rise of trust companies, he managed the wealth of the Brahmins. The *Harvard College* case set him loose from restraints that were suitable only for caretaker trusts managed by nonprofessionals. Some old firms of private trustees, grown rich and indispensable, still survive on Boston's State Street, with a century or more of prudence in their files. They are still able to compete for a corner of the business which, in general, the trust companies captured after the Civil War.[49]

Hostility to dynastic trusts was understandable in this country. It was not so much distrust of the rich as distrust of any arrangement that locked assets up and kept them off the market. The Massachusetts solution was to broaden the power of trustees, so that they too could trade in the market. The rule did not take hold in other states; but in Pennsylvania, for example, where the stricter investment rule prevailed, the legislature passed hundreds of private laws giving trustees and other fiduciaries power to sell land in specific instances. In *Norris* v. *Clymer*[50] it was argued that the legislature had no power to pass this kind of law. Chief Justice Gibson disagreed. He was impressed by a "list of nine hundred

[48]*Harvard College* v. *Amory,* 26 Mass. (9 Pick.) 446 (1830).

[49]See Lawrence M. Friedman, "The Dynastic Trust," 73 Yale L. J. 547 (1964).

[50]2 Pa. Stats. 277 (1845). The statute at issue was an act of March 2, 1842, authorizing trustees under the will of Joseph Parker Norris to sell lands from his estate, despite the provisions of the will.

statutes" already passed, similar to the one at issue, and the possibility that "ten thousand titles" depended on acts of the type. Nothing horrified the mind of the times quite so much as the unsettling of titles.

There is also a kind of dynastic trust that is not based on family: the long-term charitable trust. It has had a curiously checkered career in this country.[51] Charities, so goes the maxim, are favorites of the law. The favor was not always very obvious. In the early 19th century, charity was associated with privilege, with the dead hand, with established churches, with massive wealth held in perpetuity. None of these were particularly popular.

The key English statute was the statute of charitable uses, passed in the waning years of Queen Elizabeth I. In New York, this ancient statute was not in effect; and the revisions of 1827–28 did not restore it. Virginia and Maryland did not recognize the charitable trust at all. Some states enacted "mortmain" laws. These, based on an English statute, tried to cut down deathbed gifts to charity; only a will made more than thirty days before death could leave money to charity. Charity, by law, began at home. A faint odor of anti-Catholicism also hung over these laws—the fantasy of the evil priest, extorting ransom for the Church as the price of absolution.

Attitudes of hostility toward charity weakened, but only slowly. A charitable trust was the subject of the *Harvard College* case. John McLean, the deceased, had left $50,000 to trustees; after the death of his wife, one half of the trust was to be paid to the Massachusetts General Hospital, the other half to Harvard College, to be "exclusively and forever appropriated to the support of a professor of ancient and modern history." A college endowment, whose corpus was made up of stocks and bonds, and which supported a professor of history, was not as frightening as a barony or church. One sign of the turning tide was the great case of *Vidal* v. *Girard's Executors* (1844).[52] The banker Stephen Girard had died childless, leaving behind an enormous estate. His complex, quirky will called for creation of a school, Girard College, and provided American legal history with more than a century of litigation. The question in *Vidal* was whether charitable trusts were valid at all. Specifically, did courts of chancery have inherent powers to administer charitable trusts, without special permission in the form of a statute?

[51]See, in general, Howard S. Miller, *The Legal Foundations of American Philanthropy, 1776–1844* (1961).
[52]2 How. 127 (1844).

This was a crucial question, since the English statute and its imitations were missing in most states. To uphold the charitable trust,
which it did, the Supreme Court reversed a prior line of cases.
New York, Virginia, Maryland, and some followers, continued to
constrict the charitable trust. In other states, *Vidal* encouraged a
fresh look at the social utility of nonprofit dynasties.

INTELLECTUAL PROPERTY: PATENTS AND COPYRIGHTS

The Constitution (art. 1, sec. 8) gave Congress power "to promote
the progress of science and useful arts, by securing for limited
times to authors and inventors the exclusive right to their respective writings and discoveries." This was the formal source of
federal power over patents and copyrights.

In English law, a patent was a monopoly grant, an exclusive
right to make and deal in some item of trade. Patents had been
occasionally and individually granted by the colonies. For example, South Carolina passed an "Act for the due Encouragement
of Dr. William Crook," who had devised a "Composition" of "Oyl
or Spirit of Tar, which with other Ingredients will preserve the
Bottoms of Vessels from the River-Worm, and also the Plank from
rotting" (1716).[53] Monopoly was in bad odor by 1776, except for
the special case of the patent, which served as an incentive for
technical innovation. The first patent act (1790) gave patent power
to the secretary of state, the attorney general, and the secretary
of war, "or any two of them." They were to issue a patent if they
felt "the invention or discovery [was] sufficiently useful and important."[54] The first American patent was for a process of "making
Pot and Pearl Ashes." Only sixty-seven patents were granted under this first patent act, which was replaced in 1793.[55] In the new
act, the secretary of state, with the approval of the attorney general, had power to issue patents valid for fourteen years. The
federal government did not independently investigate patents under this law.[56]

[53]Bruce W. Bugbee, *Genesis of American Patent and Copyright Law* (1967), p. 76.
[54]1 Stats. 109–10 (act of April 10, 1790).
[55]Floyd L. Vaughan, *The United States Patent System: Legal and Economic Conflicts
in American Patent History* (1956), pp. 18–19; *Two Centuries' Growth of American Law,
1701–1901* (1902), p. 392.
[56]*Two Centuries' Growth of American Law, 1701–1901* (1902), p. 393; 1 Stats. 318
(act of Feb. 21, 1793).

By 1836, 9,957 patents had been issued, and the rate was accelerating. An important handful of these were inventions of immense importance to business. A major patent act was passed in 1836. It established a Patent Office, headed by a commissioner of patents, within the Department of State. The commissioner was to grant patents only when the subject of the patent had not been previously "invented or discovered," when the applicant was the actual inventor of the device, and when the article was "sufficiently useful and important" to deserve a patent. In case of doubt, a board of "three disinterested persons," appointed by the secretary of state, would decide the issue of patentability. One of the three was to be an expert in "the particular art, manufacture, or branch of science to which the alleged invention appertains."[57]

A fundamental question haunted patent law. To grant patents liberally might encourage innovation; but each patent was a little monopoly, and monopoly was undesirable. The liberal policy won some early victories in court. In *Earle* v. *Sawyer* (1825),[58] the question was whether a patent could be granted for a certain "new and useful improvement in the machinery for manufacturing shingles." The "improvement" consisted mostly of using a circular instead of a perpendicular saw. It was objected that "the combination itself is so simple, that, though new, it deserves not the name of an invention." Joseph Story, on circuit, brushed this objection aside. To be patentable, an object must simply be "new." That was the heart of the matter; a "flash of mind" or "genius" was not necessary.[59] The act of 1836, however, tightened the requirements for a patent grant. This turn of the wheel was a judgment that the disincentive costs of monopoly could well outweigh the incentive benefits of patents.

Between 1783 and 1786, every state but Vermont passed a copyright law at the urging of Congress. The first federal Copyright Act became law in 1790. An author might gain "sole right and liberty of printing, reprinting, publishing and vending" a "map, chart, book or books," for fourteen years, renewable for one additional term of fourteen years. The author had to deposit a printed copy of his work with the clerk of the federal court in his district, before publication. Another copy had to be delivered

---

[57]5 Stats. 117, 119, 120 (act of July 4, 1836).

[58]Fed. Cas. No. 4247 (C.C. Mass., 1825).

[59]The "flash of mind" requirement did not stay permanently buried; it was resurrected later on in patent law. See below, part III, ch. IV, p. 437.

within six months to the secretary of state as well.[60] In 1831, the original term was extended to 28 years. By this time, the act covered musical compositions, designs, engravings, and etchings as well as maps, charts, and books.[61]

In the case law of copyright, *Wheaton* v. *Peters* (1834) was a landmark decision.[62] Curiously, this was a lawsuit by one reporter of Supreme Court decisions, Henry Wheaton, against another, Richard Peters. The Supreme Court here ruled on copyright aspects of its own opinions. Richard Peters had reprinted the decisions reported by his predecessors, without offering to pay. Wheaton did not have a statutory copyright, and he lost the case. The Supreme Court held that there was no common-law right of literary property. An author's sole source of protection was the federal copyright statute. There was therefore only one source of copyright law, relatively uniform and simple. As in the law of patents, there was a tension between the (monopoly) rights of creators and the free-market interests of the business public. In *Wheaton* v. *Peters,* the Supreme Court leaned away from the monopoly aspects of copyright, by confining copyright to the terms of the federal statute.

An allied field—trademark law—was relatively undeveloped in this period. No trademark infringement case was decided in the United States before 1825.[63] Joseph Story granted the first injunction for trademark infringement, in 1844, to protect the makers of "Taylor's Persian Thread." Congress provided neither guidance nor any machinery of registration. Legal protection for designers of trademarks had to be forged in the rough mills of the courts. The economy was still deeply rooted in land and its produce. Intellectual property, despite the name, was not valued for intellectual reasons at all, but because of mercantile and industrial applications. As such, this property was not a central concern of the law until the full-blown factory age.

[60] 1 Stats. 124 (act of May 31, 1790).
[61] Richard Rogers Bowker, *Copyright: Its History and Its Law* (1912), pp. 36–37; a more modern treatment of the subject is Lyman R. Patterson, *Copyright in Historical Perspective* (1968), pp. 180–212.
[62] 8 Pet. 591 (1834).
[63] *Two Centuries' Growth of American Law* (1901), p. 435.

CHAPTER VI

THE LAW OF COMMERCE AND TRADE

A FEDERAL QUESTION: ADMIRALTY
AND GENERAL COMMERCE

By all contemporary accounts, American commercial law was deeply and persistently in debt to England. New developments in English case law traveled across the Atlantic almost with the speed of the clipper ships. Theoretically, even national sovereignty was not a barrier. The law of admiralty, marine insurance, commercial paper, and sale of goods was not, in theory, merely English law, but an international body of rules. "The marine law of the United States," wrote Chancellor Kent, "is the same as the marine law of Europe. It is not the law of a particular country, but the general law of nations."[1]

These words should be taken with a grain of salt. But they contained much truth as well; and, what is more important, they reflected the opinion of leading American lawyers. Trade was in fact international. American settlement in 1776 was strung out narrowly along the coast. Commerce was, in large measure, ocean commerce; the customs and documents of trade were also those of ocean commerce. The received law of admiralty and ocean trade was part of the stock in trade of a developing country with its door to the sea. Law was a vital segment of the infrastructure. But American commercial law soon developed its own substance and style.

The Constitution federalized admiralty jurisdiction; it put an end to state admiralty courts, and to Congress's own creature, the "Court of Appeals in Cases of Capture," which had been set up under the Articles of Confederation. This Court heard appeals from state decisions in prize cases—cases mostly about ships seized

---

[1]Kent, *Commentaries,* vol. III (2nd ed., 1832), p. 1.

as British by American privateers.[2] Under the Constitution, the judicial power of the United States extended to all "Cases of admiralty and maritime Jurisdiction" (art. III, sec. 2). But how broad was that grant of jurisdiction? What did the clause mean? What situations did it cover, and what areas of law?

English precedent was not entirely unequivocal. Some judges and statesmen read the English tradition to mean that admiralty power reached only those waters within the "ebb and flow of the tide."[3] The "ebb and flow of the tide" was perhaps a good enough criterion in England, an island nation. England had no Great Lakes and no Mississippi River. To use the same test in the United States was not, however, merely a case of blind imitation of the past. Those who defended the tidewater concept, in America, were those who took a narrow view of admiralty power; they wanted to keep federal jurisdiction within narrow limits, and expand the scope and reach of state law. Chancellor Kent warned that a broad admiralty power would injure the right of trial by jury (admiralty courts used no jury). Expansion would also divest the state courts "at one stroke, of a vast field of commercial jurisdiction." Justice Story consistently defended the tidewater concept as "the prescribed limit," which courts were not "at liberty to transcend." Justice William Johnson spoke in 1827 of the "silent and stealing progress of the admiralty in acquiring jurisdiction to which it has no pretensions."

But as population moved toward the interior, lakes and rivers became arteries of commerce as important as turnpikes and roads. The tidewater concept now came in for serious re-examination. In 1833, in *Peyroux* v. *Howard*,[4] the Supreme Court discovered what one judge later called an "occult tide," invisible to the naked eye, but strong enough to bring the Mississippi at New Orleans into the nets of federal admiralty power. In 1845, Congress passed an act that gave district courts jurisdiction over "matters of contract and tort" concerning "steamboats and other vessels of twenty tons burden and upwards, enrolled and licensed for the coasting trade," and operating on "lakes and navigable waters." The act

[2]Henry J. Bourguignon, *The First Federal Court: The Federal Appellate Prize Court of the American Revolution, 1775–1787* (1977).

[3]On admiralty power, see Milton Conover, "The Abandonment of the 'Tidewater' Concept of Admiralty Jurisdiction in the United States," 38 Oregon L. Rev. 34 (1958); Note, "From Judicial Grant to Legislative Power: The Admiralty Clause in the Nineteenth Century," 67 Harv. L. Rev. 1214 (1954).

[4]7 Peters 324 (1833).

was vague, the wording clumsy. But this act, and a collision on Lake Ontario between the schooner *Cuba* and the propeller *Genesee Chief*, provided the occasion for the great case of the *Genesee Chief* (1851).[5] The Supreme Court, through Chief Justice Taney, finally got rid of the tidewater rule, as a limit on admiralty jurisdiction. Federal power unequivocally reached all public navigable waters.

Admiralty cases were staples of the docket of all the federal courts. The federal judges became adept at handling matters of admiralty law, and Joseph Story, characteristically, was a master. His opinions swarmed with erudition (quotations from Latin sources, references to Richard Zouch, the laws of Oleron, and other mysteries of the maritime past). But admiralty law was not a game; it was, among other things, a branch of foreign policy. Decisions on prize law, neutrality, and the embargo were its meat and drink. The docket cast up cases like *Brig Short Staple and Cargo* v. *U.S.*, decided by the Supreme Court in February term, 1815; the brig had been seized "for having violated the embargo laws of the United States, by sailing to a foreign port."[6] In an 1814 case, a vessel, the *Cordelia*, on its way to Surabaya, was boarded by a British officer, who warned the ship not to put in at any port in Java. The shipmaster obeyed, and sailed for Philadelphia. The ship was insured; its policy covered, among other risks, "unlawful arrests, restraints, and detainments." But the Supreme Court held that the policy did not reach the *Cordelia's* situation. "The right to blockade an enemy's port ... is a right secured to every belligerent by the law of nations." The restraint therefore was not "unlawful."[7]

The federal courts also decided many cases of maritime commerce. In *De Lovio* v. *Boit* (1815), Joseph Story, on circuit, held that a policy of marine insurance was a "maritime contract."[8] This gave federal courts jurisdiction over the matter. But the jurisdiction was concurrent, not exclusive, that is, it had to be shared with state courts. The pages of New York's state reports, in the early 19th century, fairly bristle with cases on marine insurance.[9] But

[5]*The Propeller Genesee Chief* v. *Fitzhugh*, 12 Howard 443 (1851).

[6]*Brig Short Staple and Cargo* v. *U.S.*, 9 Cranch 55 (1815). The shipowners admitted the fact, but claimed, in justification, that an armed British vessel had captured her and forced her into port.

[7]*M'Call* v. *Marine Insurance Co.*, 8 Cranch 59 (1814).

[8]7 Fed. Cas. No. 3776 (C.C.D. Mass., 1815).

[9]On the law and practice of marine insurance, see Julius Goebel, ed., *The Law Practice of Alexander Hamilton*, vol. II (1969), pp. 391–778.

in the partnership between state and federal power, the federal presence was definitely growing, a process that led to the *Genesee Chief*. One clear goal of the trend was centralization of foreign policy. But there was also a strong domestic motive. The Supreme Court, along with other important political factions, believed that the country should be governed as a single large free-trade area. Commerce should flow smoothly across state borders; no robber barons should extract toll on the way.

The issue came to the fore in the mighty case of *Gibbons* v. *Ogden,* decided by Marshall's court in 1824.[10] New York had given to Robert R. Livingston and Robert Fulton the exclusive right to navigate "all the waters within the jurisdiction of that State, with boats moved by fire or steam." Ogden operated a steamboat line between New York and New Jersey, under license from Livingston. Gibbons owned two steamboats, which he ran between New York and Elizabethtown, New Jersey. Ogden got an injunction against Gibbons. On appeal, the Marshall court voided the New York act and struck down the monopoly. The decision rested on two bases. In the first place, Congress had passed certain acts, licensing ships that plied the coasting trade; arguably these laws "pre-empted" or shoved aside the state's overlapping legislation. The second basis was the clause of the Constitution that gave Congress power to regulate interstate commerce. *Gibbons* v. *Ogden* did not flatly hold that the commerce power was exclusive, that is, that the states had no residuum of power over commerce that crossed state lines. And the federal license laws made the case a bit more ambiguous than otherwise, and blunted its thrust. Perhaps the court really wanted it that way. Still, to some unplumbed extent, federal power over commerce—a dormant giant in regard to domestic trade—cut down, by its very existence, the power of the states to pursue independent policies on trade.

The Supreme Court also moved to unify the commercial law of the country. It hoped that a single body of law would emerge under federal hegemony. *Swift* v. *Tyson* (1842)[11] decided that fed-

---

[10] 9 Wheat. 1 (1824).

[11] 16 Pet. 1 (1842). The precise question was whether the Judiciary Act of 1789 required the court to follow state law. Section 34 of the Act directed federal trial courts to follow "the laws of the several states" except where the case presented a federal question. Did "laws" mean only statutes or did it include common-law doctrines? Not the latter, said the court, at least in cases of "contracts and other instruments of a commercial nature." The doctrine of *Swift* v. *Tyson* later expanded to cover all sorts of diversity cases in federal court; but the original holding was

eral courts, in ordinary commercial cases, had the right to apply the "general" law of commerce, even if this was different from the law of the state in which the court was sitting, and even if no "federal question" was presented, and the case came to a federal court solely because plaintiff and defendant were residents of different states. The actual question in the case came out of the law of negotiable instruments. What were the rights of a person to whom a bill of exchange was endorsed? If he did not buy the bill with fresh money or goods, but took it to satisfy an old debt which the endorser owed him, was he a "holder in due course"? (A "holder in due course" had much greater rights than a non-holder.) The law of New York, where the bill had been accepted, at least arguably said no, he was not a holder; the general view, in commercial law, was yes. But the law of commerce, Story said, speaking for the court, was and ought to be international—not the "law of a single country only, but of the commercial world." The parochial view of New York thus could not prevail.

SALE OF GOODS

The law of sales of goods developed rapidly in the first half of the 19th century. Many, if not most, of the leading cases were English. They were adopted in the United States with some rapidity. Two strains of law—contract and the law merchant—each with a somewhat different emphasis, acted as parents of the law of sales. The law merchant was suffused with what one might call the psychology of market overt. In market overt ("open market"), goods were as freely transferable as bills, notes, and paper money. A buyer of goods in market overt acquired full rights to the goods. If he bought in good faith and for value, his claims were superior to those of any prior owner, even if the goods had been stolen. At one time, every shop in London was considered a market overt; but by the 18th century the doctrine in the literal sense had gone into decline. Chancellor Kent condemned it as a barbarous survival; in any event, it never took root in the United States.[12]

In common-law countries, the law merchant was subtly altered

---

plainly influenced by the idea that commercial law had no room for strictly local doctrine. The *Swift* case has been treated in two monographs by Tony A. Freyer, *Forums of Order: The Federal Courts and Business in American History* (1979); and *Harmony and Dissonance: The Swift & Erie Cases in American Federalism* (1981).

[12] *Wheelwright* v. *Depeyster*, 1 Johns. R. 471, 480 (N.Y. 1806).

in the direction of principles of contract. This meant that rules at least *appeared* to be less rigid and objective, and that the "intention of the parties" was emphasized. The law of sales grew up about the concept of *property* or *title* to goods. Title was an invisible rope which tied a chattel to its original owner until title legally "passed" to a buyer. Title was a concept of intention: in broad theory, it passed when it was intended to pass. But the rules of title were not as neutral as they appeared on the surface; they leaned in the direction of sellers' rights, as against buyers'. English and American cases agreed that title could pass without either payment or delivery, if so intended. This meant that the buyer bore risk of loss at an early stage of the bargain. In a well-known English case, *Tarling* v. *Baxter* (1827),[13] the parties bought and sold a haystack. The buyer agreed not to remove the hay until he paid for it. The seller drew a bill of exchange on the buyer, payable in one month; the buyer accepted the bill. The bill was then negotiated to a good-faith purchaser. Meanwhile, a fire destroyed the haystack completely. The buyer was, naturally, unwilling to put out good money in exchange for some smoldering ashes; but the court held that he had to. Title to the haystack had passed; therefore, it was the *buyer's* haystack that had burned. On the other hand, if the buyer went bankrupt or failed to pay, so that right to repossess, rather than risk of accidental loss, was at issue, the courts invented a shadowy security interest that did not "pass" so quickly.

These and other doctrines were gradually woven into a tight, logical fabric of rules. In operation, in the actual reported cases, courts applied these rules more flexibly than one might guess from the way they were formulated in the abstract. As a total package, they were rather too elegant (and too unknown except to lawyers) to have had much effect on the real-life market. But whatever their practical import, one may ask why commercial law should have moved away from classic "mercantile" principles, even on paper, in the heyday of the market economy. The answer may lie in the difference between a market economy and a merchant's economy. Commercial law was once the province of a small in-group of merchants; in a typical transaction, both buyer and seller were middlemen, who understood the business background and were familiar with documents and customs. In the early 19th century, the law concerned itself more with the needs and activities

[13]6 Barn. & C. 360 (1827).

of ultimate buyers and sellers. It shifted its emphasis to favor manufacturers and producers, a class vaguely correlated with sellers rather than buyers.

Even so, American commercial law, on paper, had a certain Adam Smith severity, a certain flavor of the rugged individual. American lawyers liked to contrast the stern simplicity (real or imagined) of the common law with the paternalism (real or imagined) of civil law. In California, just after statehood, a minority group of San Francisco lawyers petitioned the legislature, asking that "the Legislature ... retain, in its substantial elements, the system of the Civil Law." The judiciary committee of the California Senate denied their request; the committee extolled the virtues of the common law, specifically in commercial law. The common-law doctrine, said the report, "is *caveat emptor* ... In other words, the Common Law allows parties to make their own bargains, and when they are made, holds them to a strict compliance"; the civil law, on the contrary, with its dangerous doctrine of implied warranty, "looks upon man as incapable of judging for himself, assumes the guardianship over him, and interpolates into a contract that which the parties never agreed to. The one is protective of trade, and a free and rapid interchange of commodities—the other is restrictive of both." The committee ascribed almost magical qualities to the common law. English and American commerce "whitens every sea, woos every breeze.... Its merchants are princes—its ships palaces.... The Commerce of Civil Law countries ... creeps timidly along a few familiar shores ... sluggish in its progress, and unprofitable in its results. It is not fostered by the quickening influence of English and American law ... the spirit of life is not in it—it is dead."[14]

This is almost certainly sheer rhetoric, with a dash of patriotic self-delusion. It is doubtful that majestic capitalism would have smothered in its crib without the rule of *caveat emptor*.[15] It is doubtful whether specific doctrines of commercial law were cause, effect, or condition of American capitalism; or all or none of these. It is true that *caveat emptor* was loudly proclaimed in some American cases. In *McFarland* v. *Newman* (1839),[16] a Pennsylvania case,

[14]Report of Feb. 27, 1850, reprinted in appendix to 1 Cal. Rpts. 588, pp. 595, 597.

[15]See Walton Hamilton, "The Ancient Maxim Caveat Emptor," 40 Yale L. J. 1133, 1178–82 (1931).

[16]9 Watts 55 (Pa. 1839).

one Newman bought a horse from McFarland. The horse "had a defluxion from the nose at the time of the bargain," but Mc-Farland "assured Newman it was no more than the ordinary distemper to which colts are subject." In fact, the horse had glanders. In a crisp, biting opinion, Pennsylvania's John Gibson reversed a lower-court decision for the buyer. "He who is so simple as to contract without a specification of the terms, is not a fit subject of judicial guardianship." The civil-law rule would have made the seller liable; but this rule was obnoxious to the health of the economy. It "would put a stop to commerce itself in driving everyone out of it by the terror of endless litigation."

Not every case on record was so favorable to the rule of *caveat emptor*.[17] In South Carolina, at least one judge called *caveat emptor* a "disgrace to the law." In the case in question, decided in 1818, barrels of blubber were sold as "oil." The judge adopted the civil-law rule: "A sound price requires a sound commodity."[18] This case, however, was regarded as exceptional. Most decisions in most states in the first half of the 19th century agreed with Gibson's formulation of the rule. But although common-law courts refused to *imply* warranties, they showed a marked tendency to read *express* warranties into a seller's words, at the slightest provocation. Often, these "express" warranties were much the same as those which the namby-pamby civil law "implied."

In the 20th century, warranty means a promise of quality, which is enforceable regardless of intention or fault. A supermarket is liable to its customer if she takes sick from adulterated soup, even though the soup company sealed the soup can before it ever reached the supermarket shelf. In Gibson's day, warranty was still strongly colored with its historical meaning, which restricted recovery to open, blatant deceit. The civil-law rule—that a sound price requires a sound commodity—*seems* more consonant with market principles, because it carries out the reasonable intention of honest parties. Gibson's language hid a paradox. *Caveat emptor*, though individualistic, defeated contractual intent. It is best seen as another attempt to accommodate law to the conditions of a broadly based market. The Gibson rule on warranties favored sellers, to be sure. But more significantly, it enhanced the finality of bargains. It made it harder for parties to drag into court their harangues over warranty and quality. This is what Gibson had in

---

[17]See *Baker* v. *Frobisher*, Quincy 4 (Mass. 1762).
[18]*Barnard* v. *Yates*, 1 Nott & M'Cord 142 (S. Car. 1818).

mind when he spoke of the "terror of endless litigation." A clear, harsh rule, he felt, was necessary. Otherwise, the courts might be overburdened with cases, the canals of commerce clogged.

Rules about bills, money and notes made up the law of negotiable instruments, a somewhat different mix of law merchant and common law. The key concept in this field was negotiability. Paper money has this quality in the highest degree. Money is "bearer paper"; it can be transferred from hand to hand. A check is also negotiable, though by endorsement. A negotiable instrument, when validly transferred, cuts off "equities" between the original parties. In other fields of law, a buyer of rights or goods steps into his seller's shoes. A buyer of land rises no higher in right than his seller; if there were charges, claims, liens, or doubts about title that clouded the rights of the seller, they follow the land into the buyer's hands, and haunt him there. But a good-faith buyer of a check takes fresh, unobstructed title.

The colonies, as we have seen, had enacted liberal assignment statutes, so that the law of negotiable instruments was in some ways more advanced than in England. This liberality continued. A Georgia statute of 1799 declared that "All bonds, and other specialties, and promissory notes, and other liquidated demands ...whether for money or other things...shall be negotiable by endorsement in such manner and under such restrictions as are prescribed in the case of promissory notes."[19]

The reference to "other things" was significant. Today, only instruments payable in money can claim to be negotiable. But the chattel note was widely used and recognized in colonial times. In the tobacco colonies and states, notes were commonly made payable in tobacco. After Independence, and well into the 19th century, chattel notes were common in the West, where hard money was in chronically short supply. In a Wisconsin case (1844), a note had been made payable in "five thousand three hundred and seventy-five lbs. of lead."[20] An Ohio case (1827) dealt with a note payable in "good merchantable whiskey." The court refused to treat it as negotiable.[21] Chattel notes were undesirable because

[19]Prince, *Digest of the Laws of Georgia* (2nd ed., 1837), p. 426 (act of Feb. 16, 1799, sec. 25); Frederick Beutel, "The Development of State Statutes on Negotiable Paper Prior to the Negotiable Instruments Law," 40 Columbia L. Rev. 836, 848 (1940).

[20]*Garrison* v. *Owens*, 1 Pin. 471 (1844).

[21]*Rhodes* v. *Lindly*, 3 Ohio Reports 51 (1827).

they were hard to standardize. Negotiable instruments do their job best when they are as simple and formal as possible. A check is a bare, unvarying document; it is completely stereotyped in looks and in wording. Chattel notes were tolerated only because money was so scarce; or where (as in the tobacco states) a certain chattel, like wampum or cowrie shells in other cultures, was a recognized medium of exchange. These were transient conditions, however. By the end of the period, courts were regularly holding that no chattel note could be truly negotiable; only money instruments had that quality.

Throughout the period, there was no satisfactory national currency. Gold and silver were rare. Private bank notes constituted the circulating medium of exchange. Credit depended on these bank notes and on personal promissory notes. The law of bills and notes was a vital part of the economic system for this reason; as the pale of settlement moved west, the law of negotiable instruments went with it. Law reports were thick with cases on bills and notes. The bill of exchange was an instrument used in commerce, mostly by merchants and bankers; it produced most of its case law in the East. The promissory note, on the other hand, was everywhere. Case law confirms the guess that basic aspects of the law of bills and notes were part of the living law. People were familiar with some simple, general rules about promissory notes, and endorsements of notes, just as they are more or less familiar with the rules about checks today.

In the 19th, as in the 20th century, the economy sailed on a sea of credit. Credit, however, was a high-risk matter in an age of radical business cycles, an age without Dun and Bradstreet, without computerized credit-services,[22] an age without public insurance of money and deposits. It was a life-and-death matter to know your debtor, and whether he was solvent. The law saw to it that a creditor could rely on the validity of a circulating note, provided it conformed on its face to the simple requirements of negotiability. The solvency of the maker was another matter. The more endorsements of sound, solid citizens a note might bear, the more the note could be counted on. Endorsements were a form of credit guarantee. It was often the case that people signed notes as an "accommodation"—that is, for nothing—in order to lend their name or credit to someone else. An "accommodation" party,

[22]By the 1840s, there was some rudimentary credit rating.

naturally, tended to resent it if the maker of the note failed, and endorsers were called to account. These failures were all too frequent. The country was large, and there were many ways for a debtor to escape from his debts. In a great, young, runaway economy, subject to violent outbursts of boom and bust, fortunes were easily made and unmade. During the downswings, banks drowned in a sea of debt, leaving behind heaps of worthless paper. Makers and endorsers failed or dodged their obligation; the sureties sometimes tried to wriggle out through tiny cracks in the law or the practice. Many cases, then, turned on the rights and obligations of sureties who signed for another. In general, the case law was lenient to them; unless the creditor swiftly and sternly pursued his rights, courts had a tendency to let the surety go. And if the creditor took any action that might be harmful to the surety—for example, if the creditor gave his debtor extra time to pay, without consulting the surety—then the surety was considered released.[23]

The *note* was paper of a thousand uses. It was a "courier without luggage": one scratch of the pen, and it moved swiftly and easily into the stream of commerce. Simplicity and ease of travel meant a great deal in a nation of continental size, whose population moved restlessly from place to place. New types of negotiable instruments developed, borrowing the virtues of the old. Municipal and corporate bonds were drawn into the orbit of negotiability. Banks launched the negotiable certificate of deposit—so popular today—before 1850. The bank check had been in use for at least a century, but had never been of much consequence. Ultimately, it became the people's instrument of payment, just as the note was the people's instrument of credit. In Story's treatise on promissory notes and other commercial paper (1845), the check was important enough to merit a chapter of its own.[24] Some of these new developments came by way of England. Some changed radically in the United States. The bill of lading, in England, was a document of ocean freight. In the United States, the name and doctrine came to be used for railroad documents too.

Much of this law was, and had always been, judge-made. Business practice provided norms; and courts tended to ratify what business did. The statute book played an important but secondary

[23]See, for example, *Clippinger* v. *Creps*, 2 Watts 45 (Pa. 1833).
[24]Joseph Story, *Commentaries on the Law of Promissory Notes* (1st ed., 1845), pp. 614–45.

role in developing the law. But on other aspects of the law of commercial paper, and on questions of currency and banking, public policy spoke with a louder voice. The rise and fall of the two Banks of the United States has already been mentioned. There was always tremendous pressure for policies that would stimulate lending. Cash was always in desperately short supply. Entrepreneur, industrialist and smallholder alike needed credit. Public debates over monetary policy, as usual, invoked political and economic principle; but, regardless of abstract principle, that policy usually won out which seemed to promise the highest payoff to those with political and economic power.

BANKRUPTCY AND INSOLVENCY

Bankruptcy law was another branch of commercial law with intense economic significance. The Constitution gave Congress the power "to establish uniform laws on the Subject of Bankruptcy throughout the United States." But Congress did not accept this clear invitation to establish a national system. Before the Civil War, only two federal bankruptcy acts were passed. The first, in 1800, lasted two and a half years.[25] The second, in 1841, was repealed with even more indecent haste.[26]

Charles Warren has said that "desire for bankruptcy legislation and depression have always been coupled in our history."[27] Panic and commercial failure were the backdrop for the first act, the law of 1800. It followed closely the scheme of the contemporary English statute. Only creditors could initiate bankruptcy proceedings, and only "traders" (merchants) were liable to be put through bankruptcy. (Actually, some merchants used the law to get rid of their debts by inducing friendly creditors to push them into bankruptcy.) The law was bitterly criticized in Congress. Thomas Newton, Jr., of Virginia, denounced it as "partial, immoral...impolitic ...anti-Republican."[28] The law was administratively inconvenient. In some parts of the country, it was awkward to travel long distances to reach the federal court. Some rich debtors abused the law; they canceled their old debts and contracted new ones, in

[25]Act of Apr. 4, 1800, 2 Stats. 19, repealed Dec. 19, 1803, 2 Stats. 248.
[26]Act of Aug. 19, 1841, 5 Stats. 440, repealed Mar. 3, 1843, 5 Stats. 614.
[27]Charles Warren, *Bankruptcy in United States History* (1935), pp. 21–22.
[28]Quoted in Warren, *ibid.*

ways that caused a certain amount of public scandal. But these incidents were not really the causes of the downfall of the law; they were merely used as fuel for the fires of repeal. The main opposition came from those congressmen who spoke for agriculture and the debtor class.

In the second bankruptcy act, too, a creditor could force into bankruptcy only members of the commercial class: "all persons, being merchants, or using the trade of merchandise, all retailers of merchandise, and all bankers, factors, brokers, underwriters, or marine insurers, owing debts to the amount of not less than two thousand dollars." But the act, significantly, opened another door: "all persons whatsoever" might file a petition for voluntary bankruptcy. The act was passed, somewhat belatedly, in the wake of the shattering economic crisis of 1837. The act marked something of a shift in emphasis, as the debate over passage made clear. Earlier bankruptcy laws had been drafted primarily to protect the creditors of an insolvent man; the point was to make sure that everyone with cargo in a sinking ship was fairly and equitably treated. The act of 1841 was at least equally interested in the other goal of a bankruptcy law: to wipe clean the debtor's slate. During debate, the proposed law was frequently denounced as not truly a bankruptcy law, but rather an "insolvency law." The term referred to state laws, which emphasized debtor relief rather than fair treatment of creditors. Debtor relief was certainly a major result of the act. Charles Warren, who studied its operation, reported that 33,739 persons took advantage of the law; $440,934,000 in debt was canceled; a mere $43,697,357 was surrendered by the debtors.[29] One of the factors that doomed the law was in a sense its very success. Economic revival, and the rapid discharge of hundreds of debtors, removed some of the sense of urgency; the "reduction in the incidence of distress quickly eased the pressure for a permanent bankruptcy system."[30]

The collapse of the federal law was in many ways a misfortune. Such a law could have ensured fair, uniform division of assets among creditors. But it was too much to hope for a long-lasting federal law, if only because of the "cankering jealousy of the general government with which some of the states are so deeply affected."[31] In between federal laws, the states did not leave the

[29]Warren, *ibid.*, p. 81.
[30]Peter J. Coleman, *Debtors and Creditors in America: Insolvency, Imprisonment for Debt, and Bankruptcy, 1607–1900* (1974), p. 24.
[31]1 Am. Jurist 49 (1829).

subject untouched. In the broadest sense, few legal relationships led to more ceaseless agitation and enactment than the relationship between debtor and creditor. In the process, the debtor-creditor law gained political passion, but lost moral affect. Bankruptcy had originally a punitive ring. It was at one time a crime, later a disgrace. But in the mercantile era, the triumph of the merchant meant the triumph of a cool neutrality toward debt.

One symptom of changing attitudes was the abolition of imprisonment for debt. This was a humanitarian gesture, of course; but it was particularly appealing in the new age. As William E. Nelson has pointed out, bankruptcy and insolvency laws are "sensible arrangements in an industrialized society"; a man does not lose his productive capacity when bankrupt, but he does when he sits in jail. Land, on the other hand, can remain productive even though the owner is in prison; but when a man goes through bankruptcy he is stripped of his land or most of it. The end of imprisonment for debt, therefore, and the rise of bankruptcy and insolvency, reflected economic change, bringing change in modes of social control over debtors.[32]

Imprisonment for debt was not only cruel; it was also inefficient. Imprisonment for debt decayed considerably before it was formally done away with. By the end of the 18th century, in New England, few debtors actually spent much time in prison—less than two per cent spent a year or more; many were released after one day. The concept of a "prison" was also rather loose. Many debtors were only nominally in jail. Often they were allowed to roam about the city, or to work by day, and return to the prison by night. This situation was expressly authorized by statutes, some of colonial age. For example, a New Hampshire law of 1771, "for the Ease and Relief of Prisoners for Debt," gave imprisoned debtors the "liberty" of the prison yard, and established these limits at "within one hundred feet of the walls of the Prison," on posting of bond.[33] This and similar ameliorations did not mean that imprisonment for debt was totally dead; there were pathetic cases of people who did in fact rot in jail for trivial debts, well into the 19th century. In Rhode Island, in 1830, a widow from Providence was put in jail for a debt of sixty-eight cents; in 1827 and 1828, a sick, 67-year-old laborer named Freeborn Hazard was kept in

[32]Nelson, *The Americanization of the Common Law,* p. 218.
[33]*Laws N.H. Province Period, 1745–1774* (1915), pp. 548, 549–50 (act of Jan. 17, 1771).

prison for four months and later recommitted for a debt of one dollar and costs of $3.22. Nonetheless, abolition was, in part, a ratification of pre-existing social change. The very idea of imprisonment for debt became quite intolerable. The mass basis of American law meant that imprisonment was a risk for the many, rather than the miscreant few. Hundreds of thousands played the land market; the business cycle, when it crashed, shook the economy with the primitive force of an earthquake, and brought down many small men, who were not really undeserving. For these, even one day, and even in an expansive prison, was too much. The risk was at least sporadically real. In Boston, 1,442 debtors went to jail in 1820, and another 1,124 in 1830; in Springfield, one victim was a woman of nineteen, "with a child at her breast"; she owed six to eight dollars.[34]

Many state constitutions specifically addressed the issue of imprisonment for debt. The Pennsylvania constitution of 1776 provided that "the person of a debtor...shall not be continued in prison after delivering up his Estate, for the benefit of his creditors, in such manner as shall be prescribed by law" (art. 9, sec. 16). This type of provision, of course, did not prevent debtors from going to prison in the first place. That was a later step, and the states did not usually take it all at once. In New Hampshire, for example, a law passed before 1820 restricted imprisonment to those who owed more than $13.33. In 1831, the legislature ended the imprisonment of women debtors. Finally, in 1840, the last, most general step was taken.[35] In other states, however, final, complete abolition did not become law until much deeper in the century.

For most states, if not all, to ameliorate or abolish imprisonment for debt was only one aspect of debtor relief. The states quite generally had insolvency laws, which took the place of the absent federal bankruptcy law—more or less. But these laws were patchworks, and were different from place to place and time to time. There were also stay laws and mortgage moratoria. The colonies had experimented constantly with debtor-relief laws, and the Revolution did not interrupt the process; indeed, the dislocations of the war, and the economic misery that followed, gave a strong push to debtor relief. South Carolina passed an "installment" act

---

[34]Coleman, *op. cit.*, p. 42. The widow and Freeborn Hazard are discussed at p. 89.
[35]Coleman, *op. cit.*, pp. 62–63.

in 1787. The act recited that "many inhabitants of this country before the revolution owed considerable sums of money," which they could not pay because of the "embarrassment of the war," and because of "very considerable importations of merchandise since the peace, and the loss of several crops." Under the act, debts contracted before January 2, 1787, might be paid in three installments, on March 1, 1788, 1789, and 1790. Ominously, a special section of the act imposed heavy penalties on "any person or persons [who] shall assault, beat, wound, or oppose" those who tried to carry the act into effect.[36]

The South Carolina law was a planters' relief law, on the face of it. Other states also tailored relief laws for groups of dominant debtors—farmers and landowners, typically. But the state laws were neither complete, nor uniform, nor fair. Insolvency laws and debtor-relief laws naturally followed the business cycle. Lawmaking was most shrill and frenetic in the lean years following a crash. In some states (for example, Connecticut), insolvent debtors petitioned for private acts of relief, and these were frequently granted. The volume of these added point to the demand for insolvency laws. The Rhode Island legislature received more than 2,300 petitions between 1758 and 1828.[37] Peter Coleman's research suggests that as many as one householder out of three may have been "hauled into court as a defaulting debtor" in the late 18th century, and that one out of five in the early 19th century became insolvent during his working lifetime.[38] The panic of 1819 stimulated a fresh burst of activity; everywhere there was agitation for stay laws and other forms of debtor relief; in some states, creditor interests blocked the legislation, but in others, particularly in the West, the agitation bore fruit.[39]

The typical state insolvency law gave the *debtor* the right to set the process of insolvency in motion. Some laws did, and some did not, provide for ratable division of assets among all creditors. Under some of these laws, creditors complained long and loud of unfair preferences, fraud, and great inconveniences. So much smoke suggests at least a little fire. The laws were probably poorly administered in most cases. They badly needed workable rules

[36]*Statutes at Large, So. Car.*, vol. V (1838), pp. 36, 37 (act of Mar. 28, 1787).
[37]Coleman, *op. cit.*, p. 96.
[38]*Ibid.*, p. 207.
[39]See Murry N. Rothbard, *The Panic of 1819: Reactions and Policies* (1962), pp. 24–56.

about what claims had first rights to be paid, and rules about how the rules should work. Without these, the laws were picked clean by the elemental greed of creditors and debtors. A contemporary witness (in 1829) judged state insolvency laws very harshly:

> Instead of one uniform, unbending rule for dividing the estate of an insolvent among his creditors, it is left to be disposed of by accident or caprice. One man prefers his father, brothers, and uncles, because they are his relations; another prefers his endorsers and custom-house sureties, because that is the general practice; and the business of a third is often settled by the sheriff's seizing his stock, before he has time to complete his arrangements.[40]

Moreover, there were simply too many of these laws. Businessmen did business across state lines; but insolvency law stopped at the borders. "There should not be one law at New York and another at Philadelphia, one law at Charleston and another at New Orleans."[41] And yet there was.

Insolvency laws were under an almost continual legal cloud. They were politically and economically important. Even before the Civil War, it had become quite usual that laws of great heat or conflict were drawn into court and their constitutional pedigree questioned. As a rule, state courts upheld their own insolvency laws. The judges generally were similar in background to the legislators who enacted these laws, and they understood the reasons why. But insolvency laws raised a ticklish federal question. Did the bankruptcy clause of the Constitution pre-empt the field? In 1819, in *Sturges* v. *Crowninshield*,[42] John Marshall's court held otherwise. The case, however, embodied a deft and typical Marshall compromise. A New York insolvency law of 1811 was the subject of the case. The court threw it out, as an impairment of the obligation of contracts, insofar as it discharged contracts and debts entered into before the act had been passed. State insolvency laws were not held illegal *per se*. But they would have to meet the court's exacting standards; they must not impair legitimate business expectations retroactively; they must not strangle the instruments of credit.

State insolvency laws heavily favored debtors. Yet the same legislatures who passed these laws passed lien laws; and were

[40]1 Am. Jurist 45 (1829).
[41]*Ibid.*, p. 36.
[42]4 Wheat. 122 (1819).

attentive to certain forms of creditors' rights, in lean years as well as in fat. State governments were poor; they could make only limited use of subsidy and tax. But they did have power to bind and to loose, to create legal rights and impose legal duties. Sometimes this power could serve in place of direct intervention with money. To attract the capital that debtors so desperately desired, obviously there had to be aid to creditors; but of course not too much. Some tension, some vacillation was thus inevitable. Similarly, debtors had to be relieved in times of crisis—but again, not to such an extreme as to do permanent damage to the economy. At any moment, the law of insolvency, and creditors' rights, reflected the results of this ambivalence, this push and pull of interests.

CONTRACT

The 19th century was the golden age of the law of contract.[43] As late as Blackstone, contract occupied only a tiny corner of the temple of common law. Blackstone devoted a whole volume to land law, but a few pages at most to informal, freely negotiated bargains.[44] In the 19th century, contract law, both in England and America, made up for lost time. This was a natural development. The law of contract was a body of law well suited to a market economy. It was the general branch of law that made and applied rules for arm's-length bargains, in a free, impersonal market. The decay of feudalism and the rise of a capitalist economy made the law of contract possible; in the age of Adam Smith it became indispensable. After 1800, the domain of contract steadily expanded; it greedily swallowed up other parts of the law. Land law remained vitally important, of course. But land dealings were more and more treated contractually. Special rules still governed deeds, leases, and other kinds of conveyance; but these documents were now called "contracts" and were subjected to many general doctrines of contract law.

---

[43]On the meaning and role of contract law in the 19th century, see in general, Lawrence M. Friedman, *Contract Law in America* (1965); Morton J. Horwitz, *The Transformation of American Law, 1780–1860* (1977), ch. 6. For developments in England, see Patrick S. Atiyah, *The Rise and Fall of Freedom of Contract* (1979).

[44]He devoted somewhat more space to doctrines of commercial law, which were of course also concerned with economic exchange.

The amazing expansion of the contract clause also illustrates the voracious appetite of the concept of contract. The Constitution forbade states from impairing the obligation of a contract. But what was a contract? The Supreme Court gave broad and un-expected answers. A legislative land grant, a college charter, even a legislative exemption from tax: all were included in the con-cept.[45] In part, these cases used the notion of contract as a met-aphor. The state was duty-bound to support a broad, free market; to do so, business had to be able to rely on the stability of ar-rangements legally made, at least in the short and middle run. The contract clause guaranteed precisely that kind of stability, or tried to. The root notion of the growing law of contract was bas-ically the same. Freely made bargains would be honored and, if necessary, enforced. There would be no *ex post facto* tampering with bargains, for whatever reason.

Contract as a branch of law can best be called residual; it dealt with those areas of business life not otherwise regulated. Its car-dinal principle was permissive: agreements should be given what-ever effect parties meant them to have. But the search for "assent" was a search for objective reality, not merely for subjective inten-tion. A contract was defined as a "meeting of the minds," but this phrase must not be taken too literally. The law emphasized the document itself, if there was one, and the plain meaning of its words, just as it did in land law or the law of negotiable instru-ments, and probably for similar reasons. For example, a rule, which came to be called the parol-evidence rule, shut off any evidence that might contradict the terms of a written document (at any rate, a final document, as opposed to a draft or a prelim-inary version). As Theophilus Parsons explained, "the parties write the contract when they are ready to do so, for the very purpose of including all that they have finally agreed upon, and excluding everything else." If evidence of "previous intention" or earlier conversations were allowed, "it would obviously be of no use to reduce a contract to writing, or to attempt to give it certainty and fixedness in any way."[46] In *Mumford* v. *M'Pherson* (New York, 1806), the buyer of a ship claimed that the seller promised, orally, that "the ship was completely copper-fastened." The bill of sale con-

---

[45]Respectively, *Fletcher* v. *Peck,* 6 Cranch 87 (1810); *Dartmouth College* v. *Woodward,* 4 Wheat. 518 (1819); *Piqua Branch of the State Bank of Ohio* v. *Knoop,* 16 How. 369 (1853).

[46]Theophilus Parsons, *The Law of Contracts,* vol. II (3rd ed., 1857), p. 57.

tained no such promise. The parol-evidence rule prevented the buyer from winning his case; where a contract "is reduced to writing," said the court, "everything resting in parol becomes thereby extinguished."[47]

Another major principle of contract law was its insistence on a true bargain between the parties. One party must have made an offer, which the other must have literally accepted. And offer and acceptance had to be glued together with a mysterious substance called *consideration*. Consideration was a term of many meanings; it signified, among other things, the *quid pro quo*, the exchange element of the contract. "The common law ... gives effect only to contracts that are founded on the mutual exigencies of men, and does not compel the performance of any merely gratuitous engagements."[48] But it was an element whose presence and "adequacy" were not to be measured by the court. If one man exchanged ten dollars in consideration for a tract of land worth (apparently) vastly more, the law was not supposed to interfere. For purposes of the law of contract, price as fixed by the parties was conclusive proof of objective market value. As in sales law, where courts believed themselves bound by *caveat emptor*, contract courts insisted that no inquiry could be made into the price and the terms of the bargain. On the other hand, mere "moral" obligations, with no element of exchange, could not be enforced in court. When one part-owner of a brig, the *Sea Nymph*, promised to buy insurance for the brig, and forgot, and the ship was lost, he was not liable to the other owner. When a father gave his note to one son who was "not so wealthy as his brothers," and "had met with losses," that note too could not be enforced.[49]

As is often true, the actual run of cases, as reported, presents a more complicated picture. The results were not always as unyielding as theory insisted on. In a broad-based market, not everyone who made a contract was a hard, shrewd businessman. In some cases, the unsophisticated, the amateurs, the weak—widows and orphans—sued on or defended claims in contract. Judges were only human. In particular cases, the rigor of the rules was bent. In the long run, the rules of consideration, and the other rules which insisted on holding people to their bargains, all of

[47]*Mumford* v. *M'Pherson*, 1 Johns. R. 414 (N.Y. 1806).
[48]Theron Metcalf, *Principles of the Law of Contracts* (1874), p. 161.
[49]*Thorne* v. *Deas*, 4 Johns. R. 84 (N.Y. 1809); *Fink* v. *Cox*, 18 Johns. R. 145 (N.Y. 1820).

which seemed to be made of the toughest stone, were worn down somewhat by the slow drip-drip of life situations.

In general, the law of contract was not as technical as land law or civil procedure. It had little jargon of its own. Its rules were few, and departed less from common sense than the rules of other fields of law. Contract law asked for very little; agreements, to be enforced, had to have a definite shape, but the law of contract was itself relatively passive and amorphous. There was therefore little need for trans-Atlantic differences. Of all the staple fields, contract was perhaps the most similar on both sides of the water. It was also to a large degree the province of the judges. Few statutes intruded upon it.

Of these few, the old statute of frauds (1677) was perhaps the most notable. The statute listed certain classes of contracts which could not be enforced unless they were in writing and signed by the party "to be charged therewith," or his agent. Those contracts that had to be in writing included land contracts, contracts "to answer for the debt, default, or miscarriage" of another person; and contracts for the sale of goods above a minimum value (fifty dollars in New York). The states adopted the statute almost verbatim.[50] In one sense, the statute of frauds was hardly a statute at all. It was so heavily warped by "interpretation" that it had become little more than a set of common-law rules, worked out in great detail by the common-law courts.

The statute of frauds has been criticized as an anachronism. This venerable law has now celebrated its three-hundredth birthday, still under attack as empty formality. Formality it is, but not quite empty. To require land contracts, in 1800 or 1850, to be in writing, was not unreasonable; nor was it out of tune with the way land law was developing. An orderly land market (people thought) required orderly form: simple, standard deeds, duly recorded. In the state of the market, oral land deals were an abomination. What was valued was not form for form's sake, but useful form. The statute of frauds survived; other formalities, which had no purpose or place, disappeared from the law of contract.

Among them was that ancient device, the seal. Early contract law paid great homage to the seal. Sealed documents were spe-

[50]There were some local variations. In New York, contracts that offended the statute were "void" rather than (as in England) merely unenforceable. Rev. Stats. N.Y. 1836, vol. II, p. 70. This difference was not of much moment.

cially treated and favored in the law; the seal, for example, "imported" consideration, which meant that a sealed document needed no further proof of consideration. In the United States, few people actually owned and used a seal; and literacy was high enough to undercut the need for this device. Strictly speaking, a seal meant an impression in wax; but in some states, any scrawl or scroll on paper was good enough. In New York, Chancellor Kent was insistent on the traditional method, wax and all.[51] But this was probably because he was an enemy of the seal, and wanted to kill it with strictness.[52] Later, state statutes were passed that undercut considerably the meaning of the seal. In New York, by the close of the period, a seal was "only... presumptive evidence of a sufficient consideration"; its effect could be "rebutted in the same manner, and to the same extent, as if [the] instrument were not sealed."[53] Ultimately, the seal vanished completely, except as an empty form. In general, sentiment and tradition had little place in commercial law; what survived was the fit and the functional.

---

[51]*Warren* v. *Lynch*, 5 Johns. R. 239 (1810).
[52]Joseph Dorfman, "Chancellor Kent and the Developing American Economy," 61 Columbia L. Rev. 1290, 1305 (1961).
[53]Rev. Stats. N.Y. 1836, vol. II, p. 328.

CHAPTER VII

CRIME AND PUNISHMENT:
AND A FOOTNOTE ON TORT

PENAL LAW AND PENAL REFORM

The American Revolution, whatever else was at issue, fed on resentment against English oppression. Like all revolutions, it was a struggle for control of the reins of power. The criminal law is one lever through which government brings power to bear on the individual citizen. The Revolutionary leaders, quite naturally, identified oppression with abuse of criminal law, and identified the rights of man with basic rights to fair criminal trial. The Bill of Rights, as we have seen, contained a minicode of criminal procedure. The late 18th century, moreover, was a period in which intellectuals began to rethink the premises on which criminal law rested. Great reformers—men like Cesare Beccaria, whose *Treatise on Crime and Punishment* was written in Italy in 1764—suggested that the premises were wrong, and argued for a more enlightened criminal law.[1]

Reform ideas left an imprint on the early state constitutions. Section 38 of the liberal Pennsylvania constitution of 1776 imposed on "the future legislature" a duty to "reform" the "penal laws." Punishment must be made "in some cases less sanguinary, and in general more proportionate to the crimes." Enlightened opinion was in revolt against bloodthirsty criminal codes. The Bill of Rights outlawed cruel and unusual punishment. "No wise legislature," said the New Hampshire constitution of 1784, "will affix the same punishment to the crimes of theft, forgery and the like, which they do to those of murder and treason.... [A] multitude of sanguinary laws is both impolitic and unjust. The true design

---

[1]Marcello T. Maestro, *Voltaire and Beccaria as Reformers of Criminal Law* (1942), pp. 51–72.

280

of all punishments being to reform, not to exterminate, mankind" (art. I, sec. 18).

Of course, these were mere exhortations. Real penal reform has never been easy to achieve. The legislature of Pennsylvania did not match action to words for ten full years. In 1786, the death penalty was abolished for robbery, burglary, and sodomy. In 1790, a new, more conservative constitution omitted the clause on penal reform, and the act of 1786 was repealed. But in 1794, Pennsylvania enacted an important, innovative law about murder. The statute stated that the "several offenses, which are included under the general denomination of murder, differ... greatly from each other in the degree of their atrociousness." The statute then proceeded to distinguish between two different "degrees" of murder. Murder "in the first degree" was murder "perpetrated by means of poison, or by lying in wait, or by any other kind of wilful, deliberate, or premeditated killing, or which shall be committed in the perpetration, or attempt to perpetrate, any arson, rape, robbery, or burglary." All other murder was murder in the second degree. Only murder in the first degree was punishable by death.[2] This idea of degrees was borrowed, first in Virginia, then in Ohio (1824), New York (1827), and Missouri (1835). Some states (for example, Missouri) also divided manslaughter into degrees.

The agitation in Pennsylvania was part of a wider movement to reduce the number of capital crimes, reform the penal code, and, if possible, get rid of the death penalty altogether.[3] According to the new penology, the proper goal of criminal law was deterrence of crime and rehabilitation of the criminal. Death was dubious as a general deterrent, and as an agent of rehabilitation, impossible. It had no place, then, in a rational system of law. These propositions were put forward with great vigor, but they probably never commanded the agreement of a majority of articulate people. Many, then as now, put the case strongly on the other side— people like the "citizens of Albany," who, by petition in 1842, asked the New York legislature not to do away with the death penalty for murder:

> The Penalties inflicted by human law, having their foundation
> in the intrinsick ill-desert of crime, are in their nature vin-

[2]On the statute in general, see Edwin R. Keedy, "History of the Pennsylvania Statute Creating Degrees of Murder," 97 U. Pa. L. Rev. 759 (1949).

[3]See, in general, David B. Davis, "The Movement to Abolish Capital Punishment in America, 1787–1861," 63 Am. Hist. Rev. 23 (1957).

> dictive as well as corrective.... Beyond all question the mur-
> derer deserves to die.... Death is the fitting penalty for murder;
> fitting because, in addition to its correspondence with the
> enormity of the crime, it must needs be more efficacious than
> any other, in preventing its repetition ... God has revealed to
> us His will, both through the laws of reason and conscience,
> and in his written word, that the murderer should be put to
> death.[4]

Judging by the results, neither side carried the day. The penal
codes changed (quite dramatically in some instances), but the death
penalty was not fully abolished in the majority of the states. In
1800, Kentucky restricted it to murder. Thomas Jefferson proposed, in 1779, that Virginia abolish the death penalty except for
murder and treason. Rape was to be punished by castration; a
woman guilty of sodomy was to have a hole bored through her
nose; people who maimed or disfigured would be maimed and
disfigured themselves, preferably in the "same part." Virginia
never adopted this odd proposal; but the legislature did in fact
abolish the death penalty in 1796 for all crimes except murder
(and crimes by slaves).[5]

Total abolition was another question. Edward Livingston had
no provision for capital punishment in the penal code he wrote
for Louisiana; but the code was never enacted. In 1837, Maine
passed a statute which *almost* went the whole distance. A man
under sentence of death would be placed in the state prison, in
"solitary imprisonment and hard labor." He could not be executed
for one year. The whole record of his case had to be certified to
the governor; and the death sentence would be carried out only
if the governor issued a warrant, under the great seal of the state,
"directed to the Sheriff of the County wherein the State Prison
shall or may be situated, commanding the said Sheriff to cause
execution to be done."[6] In 1845, Michigan became the first state
to abolish capital punishment completely, followed by Wisconsin.
All other states kept the death penalty, but they drastically short-

[4]*Memorial to the Legislature,* N.Y. Senate Documents, vol. 4, 1842, Doc. No. 97,
pp. 21–39.

[5]Kathryn Preyer, "Crime, the Criminal Law and Reform in Post-Revolutionary
Virginia," 1 Law and History Review 53, 58–59, 76 (1983). New Jersey also cut
down on the death penalty in 1796; see John E. O'Connor, "Legal Reform in the
Early Republic: The New Jersey Experience," 22 Am J. Legal Hist. 95, 100 (1978).

[6]Laws Maine 1837, ch. 292.

ened their list of capital crimes. In South Carolina, 165 crimes carried the death penalty in 1813. By 1825, only fifty-one, by 1838, only thirty-two, and by 1850, only twenty-two crimes remained in this group.[7]

Most states did not make much use of the death penalty, either before or after they reduced the number of crimes nominally subject to this penalty. There were important differences by race and by region. South Carolina hanged many more people than Massachusetts; and many more blacks than whites. And even though hanging was not an everyday affair, still there *were* hangings; and they were public events that took place in broad daylight, before morbid or festive crowds. A hanging was an occasion, a spectacle. People eagerly watched the trip to the gallows; and they listened eagerly to the condemned man, when, as sometimes happened, he made a last speech in the shadow of the gallows.

Liberal reformers and humanitarians had led the movement to abolish the death penalty; but they also made a strong practical argument for squeezing the blood out of criminal law. The death penalty, so to speak, was a case of overkill. Capital punishment was ineffective because it was not, and could not be, consistently applied. Its deadly severity distorted the working of criminal justice. A jury, trapped between two distasteful choices, death or acquittal, often acquitted the guilty. The New Hampshire constitution of 1784, criticizing "sanguinary laws," voiced a fear that "where the same undistinguishing severity is exerted against all offences; the people are led to forget the real distinction in the crimes themselves, and to commit the most flagrant with as little compunction as they do those of the lightest dye" (part I, art. 18). In South Carolina, the typical defendant in a homicide case was either acquitted or found guilty only of manslaughter. In one district, thirty-three men were tried on murder indictments between 1844 and 1858. Eighteen were acquitted, ten found guilty of manslaughter; only five were convicted of murder. In Phila-

[7]Jack K. Williams, *Vogues in Villainy: Crime and Retribution in Ante-Bellum South Carolina* (1959), p. 100. In general, there were more capital crimes in the South than in the North. Some of the difference is accounted for by the special, severe laws relating to slaves and free blacks. Perhaps more is to be accounted for by the special, archaic, patriarchal nature of the Southern legal system. For the thesis that finds the differences rooted, in part, in differences in legal culture, see Michael S. Hindus, *Prison and Plantation: Crime, Justice, and Authority in Massachusetts and South Carolina, 1767–1878* (1980); and Edward L. Ayers, *Vengeance and Justice: Crime and Punishment in the Nineteenth-Century American South* (1984).

delphia, between 1839 and 1845, there were 68 indictments for first degree murder; 40 defendants were tried; the jury found 25 of them guilty. Of those convicted, only a few were sentenced to death.[8]

This gap between indictment and conviction, and between conviction and sentence, probably prevailed in most parts of the country. The problem was not harsh punishment in itself, but formal harshness compared to what the moral sense of the community allowed. Severe penal codes are often instruments of repressive policy, imposed by the rulers on the ruled. In the United States, however, there was a greater degree of overlap between the rulers and the ruled than in England. This led to much looseness in the actual use of penal measures.[9] Moreover, a group may be less severe on its own forms of deviance than on the deviance of outsiders, particularly outsiders whom the group regards as inferior. Juries in America were more tolerant of violations of game laws than the king and his servants would have been; on the other hand, the slave codes, which dealt with a class outside of power, were more bloody in theory and deed than the ordinary law of crimes.

A system of criminal justice is more than rules on paper. It is also a plan for distribution of power among judges, jurors, legislators, and others. In American legal theory, jury power was enormous, and subject to few controls. There was a maxim of law that the jury was judge both of law and of fact in criminal cases. This idea was particularly strong in the first, Revolutionary generation, when memories of royal justice were fresh. In some states the rule lasted a long time, and in Maryland, the slogan was actually imbedded in the constitution.[10] But the rule came under

---

[8]Williams, *op. cit.*, p. 38; Roger Lane, *Violent Death in the City: Suicide, Accident and Murder in 19th Century Philadelphia* (1979), pp. 68–69.

[9]This is not to say that the British system was not itself quite loose in certain regards. In 18th-century England, there were many capital crimes; but justice was frequently tempered with a kind of mercy; and indeed it can be argued that a system of this sort, which is *potentially* extremely cruel and bloody, but which allows appeals for mercy to the grace and favor of the rulers, makes for tight, efficient, repressive social control. Douglas Hay, "Property, Authority and the Criminal Law," in Douglas Hay et al., eds., *Albion's Fatal Tree: Crime and Society in Eighteenth-Century England* (1975), p. 17.

[10]Md. const., 1851, art. 10, sec. 5. It was a common provision that juries were judges of fact and law in "prosecutions or indictments for libel," for example, N.J. const., 1844, art. 1, sec. 5.

savage attack from some judges and other authorities. There was fear that the rule, if taken seriously, would destroy the "chances of uniformity of adjudication." It also threatened the *power* of judges. By the end of the period, many states, by statute or decision, had repudiated the doctrine.[11]

In any event, it is not easy to tell what the maxim meant in practice. Juries did not divide their verdicts into separate bundles of fact and of law. The maxim did recognize explicitly that the jury held ultimate power to make decisions about crime and criminal law. Juries were not afraid to exercise this power. In South Carolina, according to Jack K. Williams, "the same jury which would change a murderer's indictment to manslaughter would condemn a common thief to the gallows without hesitation," if so inclined.[12] On the other hand, the jury could be quite cavalier about the letter of the law, not to mention the facts of the world. In *State* v. *Bennet* (1815), a South Carolina jury found as fact that the goods John Bennet had stolen were worth "less...than twelve pence," even though all the witnesses had sworn they were "of much greater value." This "pious perjury" let the jury find Bennet guilty of petty larceny, rather than grand larceny, which would have sent him to the gallows. The appeal court affirmed the jury's right to do as it pleased.[13] This same process had made some of the crimes on England's long list of capital crimes less fierce than they seemed. This type of behavior has been called jury lawlessness; but there is something strange in pinning the label of "lawless" on a power so carefully and explicitly built into law. Jury power meant that a measure of penal "reform" could take place without formal change in legal institutions. Jerome Hall has suggested that, as social attitudes toward criminals and crime begin to change, the changes first appear in the administration of criminal justice; penal "reform"—enacted laws and new rules—follows as a "ratification of practices" already developed.[14]

But it is not easy to get an accurate picture of how the justice system worked. Most of the surviving literature does not deal with

[11]See Francis Wharton, *A Treatise on the Criminal Law of the United States* (4th ed., 1857), pp. 1115–25; William Nelson, *Americanization of the Common Law* (1975), ch. 9.

[12]Williams, *op. cit.*, p. 39.

[13]*State* v. *Bennet*, 3 Brevard (S. Car.) 514 (1815).

[14]Jerome Hall, *Theft, Law and Society* (2nd ed., 1952), p. 140.

the day to day, humdrum operations of trial courts. Only recently has research begun to push aside the dust and muck and examine court records in the raw. Most offenders, and almost everybody charged with petty crimes, were dealt with in a great rush, and quite summarily. Only serious offenses went to the jury. Juries tended to convict: Michael S. Hindus's figures show that 71.5 percent of South Carolina defendants (1800–1860), and 85.9 percent of Massachusetts defendants (1833–1859) were found guilty. In South Carolina, too, there was much greater slippage at earlier stages: of all cases presented to the grand jury, only 30.9 percent were eventually convicted; in Massachusetts, the figure was 65.8 percent.[15]

The criminal justice system was, on the whole, not the professional business it is today. Almost nobody involved in criminal justice was a full-time expert on the subject. There were no detectives, probation officers, public defenders, forensic scientists; even the district attorney probably worked at his job part-time; the jurors were of course total amateurs. Today, the system is highly professionalized; this means, among other things, that the police and prosecutors filter out the weakest cases, and toss them out early in the process. Much less of this screening is left to judge and jury. In 1800, or 1850, there was nothing organized or bureaucratic about any part of the system. This even applied to what happened after conviction; the only way to get out of prison early (except through a break-out) was to appeal to the governor for a pardon. The governor in some states pardoned with a lavish hand; but in making his decisions, he did as he pleased and took advice from whomever he pleased.

Today, most people charged plead guilty to the charges brought against them, or to some lesser crime. The guilty plea accounts for as many as 90 percent of all convictions, in some places. This was not so in the 19th century. But the guilty plea was already a significant factor, and becoming more so. In New York State, in 1839, there were guilty pleas in a quarter of the cases, and this percentage rose to about half by the middle of the century.[16] A guilty plea puts an end to the proceedings; when a defendant

---

[15]Hindus, *op. cit.*, p. 91. In Marion County, Indiana, in the period 1823–1850, the ultimate conviction rate was more like South Carolina than like Massachusetts: for "all indictments, the prosecution secured convictions at a rate only slightly better than one of every three defendants." David J. Bodenhamer, "Law and Disorder on the Early Frontier: Marion County, Indiana, 1823–1850," 10 Western Hist. Q. 323, 335 (1979).

[16]Raymond Moley, *Politics and Criminal Prosecution* (1929), pp. 159–64.

pleads guilty, there is no trial, by jury or otherwise. Hence a rising rate of guilty pleas means a falling rate of trials.

Undoubtedly, the behavior of defendants reflected changes in the organization of criminal justice, though many of these changes are fairly obscure. One, however, is both obvious and important: the rise of the police. The police, as an important element in the system, appeared only toward the end of our period. At best, criminal justice trembled on the brink of professionalism. Private prosecution, more or less in the English style, apparently survived in Philadelphia well into the 19th century.[17] In Boston, a police force appeared in 1838, under Mayor Samuel Eliot; before that, there was the usual haphazard collection of constables and night watchmen; these did not and could not hope to cope with "the incendiary, burglar, and the lawlessly violent."[18] New York's police force, strongly influenced by the Metropolitan Police of London, emerged in 1845.[19] Big cities soon began to build on these models. But in the South, and in rural areas, there was no professional enforcement at all.

The development of police forces ultimately brought about dramatic changes in public crime-fighting. But the early police were much different from the modern police. They were hardly "professional." They took no exams, and had no schooling for their job. What brought about urban police was not so much a felt need to ferret out silent, secret crime as fear of urban disorders—riots, in short. Today, we are accustomed to the idea that the state has a monopoly of violence. But this was not always so, at least not literally. The state was weak and lax, for the most part; when it needed more muscle, it recruited private citizens to help it out. The Western "posse," familiar to every movie fan, was a survival from the days when a sheriff or other officer simply rounded up able-bodied men to help him out. The line, in short, between riot and disorder on the one hand and law enforcement on the other was at one time far from distinct.[20] Today the line is sharp; and the building of the wall of separation between public

[17]Allen R. Steinberg, "The Criminal Courts and the Transformation of Criminal Justice in Philadelphia, 1815–1874" (Ph.D. thesis, Columbia University, 1983).

[18]Roger Lane, *Policing the City: Boston, 1822–1885* (1967), p. 34.

[19]On the rise of the police, see Wilbur R. Miller, *Cops and Bobbies: Police Authority in New York and London, 1830–1870* (1977); Samuel Walker, *Popular Justice: A History of American Criminal Justice* (1980), pp. 55–64.

[20]On this point, see Pauline Maier, "Popular Uprisings and Civil Authority in Eighteenth-Century America," 27 William and Mary Q. 3rd series, 3 (1970).

and private force is one of the great master trends in criminal justice.

But the old, archaic, preprofessional system was not immediately replaced by a thoroughly modern one, despite the founding of a police force here and there. In hindsight, we can see a clear, steady trend; the path to be followed had the smooth, paved surface of inevitability. It did not look that way at the time. Control still remained in the hands of amateurs, especially members of juries. And the jury system certainly had its faults. Outcomes were to say the least unpredictable. There were ways to control juries— the law of evidence, as we mentioned, was one. We have described how a system of checks and balances, in the trial process, grew almost cancerously. It reached its high point (or low) in the system of criminal justice. Here judge was played off against jury, state against citizen, county against state, state against federal government. Every master had to submit to another master. The system had benefits, of course. But from the standpoint of any particular group, it also had a major defect: one could never be sure that policies of criminal justice, however well formulated, would be actually carried out.

Hence it is not surprising that the private use of force did not die out with the coming of the police. On the contrary, it had ferocious powers of survival. There were periodic outbursts of lynching and vigilantes in almost every state. These cracks in law and order were no accidents. The degeneracy (or overvigor) of judge, jury, state, or national authority sometimes reached the point where justice (as defined by vigilantes) demanded that "the public" take the law into its hands. Vigilantes and lynch mobs, in other words, were pathologies of a system with too many checks and balances for public opinion. Vigilantes were especially vigorous in the South. Here the legal culture nurtured them. Lawlessness was a way of life; violent crime was common; men habitually walked the streets carrying guns; the elites placed heavier value on the code of honor (including the duel) than on resort to law. Vigilantes were the logical negative of the governor's power to pardon. The pardoning power was itself one kind of check and balance; the mob was another. In Montgomery, Alabama, for example, a vigilante group called the Regulating Horn sprang up in the 1820s. The men blew horns to summon the rest of the group. They gave suspects a hearing on the spot. If they found a man "guilty," they tarred and feathered him and rode him out of town on a rail. Violence can be an addictive habit; with success came excess: the Regulating Horn lost legitimacy, and community tolerance evaporated. After that, they were doomed to fail.[21]

In South Carolina, the abolitionists were the prime target of vigilantes in the 1840s. Here mob rule luxuriated in the cleft between official, national doctrine and opinion in the local community. The abolitionists were guilty of no crime, except that they offended Southern opinion. The Southern slave patrols, on the other hand, were in a way a kind of legitimized lynch law. There was no precise Northern equivalent. But the South was not the only region of bloodshed. Riots, mock law, and mob violence were a dark stain on the whole country, crossing every border, entering every state. Between 1830 and 1860 "at least 35 major riots occurred in the four cities of Baltimore, Philadelphia, New York, and Boston."[22] It was out of a climate such as this that the demand rose for urban police.

The strength of the idea of checks and balances was also one of the factors that impelled penal law toward codification. The leaders of the Revolutionary generation felt strongly that there had to be safeguards against the political or oppressive use of criminal justice—the offenses King George was blamed for. This was also an attitude underlying the Bill of Rights; and the attitude by no means died out in the Republic. The rules of criminal justice should be open, transparent, easy to know. Criminal law should not be scattered through hundreds of books, in obscure little pieces and fragments. It should be a single, clear-cut body of rules. Codification, as the Puritan magistrates found, is sometimes a means of controlling authorities. The same theory was behind codification of penal law in Europe, after the shock waves of the French Revolution.

The common law was supposed to rest on the community's moral consensus, as it percolated through the collective mind of the judges. Courts had invented and elaborated doctrines of crime at common law, just as they had elaborated other sorts of doctrine. But the idea of a common-law crime came to look dangerous: a possible instrument of oppression. Common-law decisions were

[21]Jack K. Williams, "Crime and Punishment in Alabama, 1819–1840," 6 Ala. R. 1427 (1953).

[22]Richard Maxwell Brown, "Historical Patterns of Violence in America," in Hugh D. Graham and Ted R. Gurr, eds., *Violence in America: Historical and Comparative Perspectives*, vol. I (1969), pp. 45, 54.

in a sense retroactive; and judges were less subject to public control than legislators. Statutory rules, on the other hand, were prospective only; and they were enacted by the people's representatives. The way the king's judges had behaved, in England and in the colonies, made it easy to disapprove of the power of judges to invent and define new crimes. There were instances on record where the concept was used in this country, too. In *Kanavan's case* (Maine, 1821), the defendant dropped the dead body of a child into the Kennebec River.[23] No statute covered the case explicitly; but the highest court in Maine affirmed the man's conviction. An appeal court in Tennessee sustained an indictment for "eavesdropping" in 1808.[24] But the concept of the common-law crime was in retreat during the whole of the 19th century.

There were special reasons to object to the power of *federal* judges to invent new crimes. One reason was widespread fear of a powerful central government. The concept of common-law crime was exploded, soon and totally, on the federal level. The case was *United States* v. *Hudson and Goodwin* (1812);[25] defendants were indicted for "a libel on the President and Congress of the United States, contained in the Connecticut Courant of the 7th of May, 1806, charging them with having in secret voted $2,000,000 as a present to Bonaparte, for leave to make a treaty with Spain." No statute covered such an "offense" against the federal government. The Supreme Court held that no federal court was "vested with jurisdiction over any particular act done by an individual in supposed violation of the peace and dignity of the sovereign power. The legislative authority of the Union must first make an act a crime, affix a punishment to it, and declare the court that shall have jurisdiction of the offense." If federal prosecutors and judges could define crimes for themselves and punish them, enormous (and in this instance, unwelcome) power would accrue to the central government.

Codification was something of a curb on the power of the judges; but it only went part of the way. Judges lost the power to invent new crimes; but the common law still *defined* the precise meaning and application of old crimes, like rape or theft. The strong, sometimes freewheeling power of judges to interpret the laws remained. The judges developed and used *canons of construction*—rules of interpretation—that maximized their discretion and

[23] 1 Greenl. (Me.) 226 (1821).
[24] *State* v. *Williams*, 2 Overton (Tenn.) 108 (1808).
[25] 7 Cranch 32 (1812).

authority. One such canon declared that penal statutes had to be narrowly construed, that is, limited to the smallest possible compass their language would bear. The canon made some sense; otherwise, retroactive, judge-made criminal law could be brought in through the back door, so to speak. Only those acts ought to be crimes which were plainly so labeled. Courts should not widen the coverage of a penal law beyond the unvarnished meaning of its words. Criminal law had to be known and knowable, without subtlety and artifice:

> The law to bind (the prisoner) should first be *prescribed;* that is, not only willed by the legislature, but should also be announced, and clearly and plainly published, that every citizen, if he would, could learn its meaning and know the measure of its punishment.

This was said by counsel at the trial of one Timothy Heely of New York, charged with stealing a lottery ticket. The statute made it a crime to steal a "public security." The court agreed with counsel that a state lottery ticket was not a public security, and let Heely go.[26] The canon of strict construction, in theory, gave expression to the idea that judges were humble servants of the law, the people, and their elected representatives. But there was no short-run control over whether courts used the canon or avoided it. Hence its application was in fact if not in theory a matter of discretion. And what was or was not a strict or narrow construction was itself a difficult question, which gave still more discretion to the courts.

THE SUBSTANTIVE LAW OF CRIMES

In English law, treason had been a complex, protean concept, used to suppress all sorts of persons or groups defined as enemies of state. It was treason to levy war on the kingdom; it was treason, too, to violate the king's (unmarried) eldest daughter. It was treason to alter or clip coins; or to color "any silver current coin... to make it resemble a gold one."[27] When war broke out, the colonists seized this terrible weapon for themselves. New York, for example, passed a fire-breathing law in 1781: anyone who preached, taught, spoke, wrote, or printed that the king had or

---

[26]*People* v. *Heely,* New York Judicial Repository, 277 (1819).
[27]4 Blackstone, *Commentaries,* 90.

ought to have dominion over New York thereby committed a "Felony without Benefit of Clergy," punishable by death or by banishment.[28]

When the war ended, passions cooled. Maryland, Massachusetts, New York, Pennsylvania and Vermont all provided, in their early constitutions, that the legislature had no power to attaint any person of treason.[29] The federal Constitution radically restricted this king of crimes: it defined its content, once and for all, and hedged in treason trials with procedural safeguards. Treason against the United States "shall consist only in levying War against them, or in adhering to their Enemies, giving them Aid and Comfort. No Person shall be convicted of Treason unless on the testimony of two Witnesses to the same overt Act, or on Confession in Open Court" (U.S. Const., art. 3, sec. 3).

Treason was a special crime, with unusual political significance. The shrinking law of treason mirrored a prevailing theory of criminal law. A total state, even a semitotal state, has trouble distinguishing between treason and ordinary crime. In the Soviet Union, for example, it is a crime against the state, severely punished, to deal in currency or to steal factory property (which is all state-owned). The United States took a strikingly different path. It shrank the concept of state crime to an almost irreducible minimum. The men who drafted penal codes were willing to accept a lot of slippage in enforcement, to protect the innocent and (even more) to keep the government in check. No doubt much of this liberality was only on paper. The Sedition Law of 1798, passed by a nervous, partisan federal government, was (to modern eyes) a shocking encroachment on the freedom of political speech; passage of this law showed, once again, that historical fears of central government were far from groundless.[30] But the theory that government should not be too strong in the criminal department did leave its mark; in particular, it helped determine how government was structured, and what resources government had to do its job.

Not that the criminal law was unimportant in the United States. By any measure, the *number* of acts defined as criminal grew stead-

[28]J. Willard Hurst, "Treason in the United States," 58 Harv. L. Rev. 226 (1944); see also Bradley Chapin, *The American Law of Treason: Revolutionary and Early National Origins* (1964).

[29]Hurst, *op. cit.*, p. 256.

[30]See, in general, James Morton Smith, *Freedom's Fetters: The Alien and Sedition Laws and American Civil Liberties* (1956).

ily from 1776 to 1850, despite the decline in the use of the common-law crime. The classic crimes (theft, murder, rape, arson) remained on the books. There were great numbers of economic crimes, and laws defining public morality; and new ones were constantly added. The revised statutes of Indiana of 1831—a fair sample—made it a crime to allow epsom salts "to remain unenclosed and exposed to the stock, cattle or horses of the neighborhood." It was a crime in Indiana to "alter the mark or brand" of domestic animals; to sell retail liquor without a license; to ferry a person across a creek or river for money, within two miles of any licensed ferry. It was a crime, too, to keep "either of the gaming tables called A.B.C., or E.O. Tables, billiard table, roulette, spanish needle, shuffle board, [and] faro bank." It was an offense, punishable by fine, to "vend any merchandize which may not be the product of the United States, without having a license." Profane swearing was a crime; so was "open and notorious adultery or fornication." Major statutes often included, as a final clause, a provision punishing violation or frustration of the policy expressed.

One usually thinks of a crime as an act which offends some deep-seated moral sense. But crime can also be neutrally defined, as any behavior punished at public expense and through criminal process. An unpaid seller, or a person who slips on the ice, sues the buyer or landowner at her own expense, and on her own initiative. The costs of punishing a murderer are socialized, partly because violence is thought to be a danger to everyone, not just the victim's little circle of family and friends. Murder was once privately enforced. But private justice is either too ineffective, or, conversely, too effective, giving rise to feuds and wholesale bloodshed. Public prosecution does away with private vengeance. Regulatory and economic crimes are enforced at public expense and initiative, but for rather different reasons. If a man sells ten baskets of defective strawberries to ten different people, it would not pay any one buyer to sue the seller. The lawsuit would eat up far more money than could possibly be recovered. If the sheriff and district attorney—public servants, paid by the state—have power to enforce the rules, they might deter the seller far more effectively. This is quite apart from whether or not selling spoiled strawberries is considered especially immoral or not. Criminal process, then, can act as a kind of crude, undifferentiated administrative agency. This (largely inarticulate) conception was one of the reasons for the flowering of regulatory crimes. Economic crimes never gave trial courts much work. They never captured the imagination of the public. Criminal provisions of regulatory laws were not always even *meant* to be rigorously enforced. They were meant more as a last resort, as a threat to persistent and flagrant violators. When administrative justice developed in later generations, some of these "crimes" actually disappeared from the books.

The *relative* rise of the economic crime, on the statute books, was probably an external sign of a real change in the center of gravity of the criminal law. If crime was sin—fornication, blasphemy—before the Revolution, it gradually shifted to concern for protection of private property and furtherance of the community's economic business. What little we know about actual enforcement suggests the rapid decline of prosecutions for victimless crime—perhaps as early as the 18th century—and its replacement in center stage by crimes against property. This was, for example, decidedly the case in England. William E. Nelson's research, in Massachusetts, corroborates this notion. Nelson found that prosecutions for fornication, Sunday violation, and the like declined dramatically after the Revolution; prosecutions for theft, on the other hand, rose. By 1800, more than forty percent of all prosecutions in seven counties studied were for theft, only seven percent for offenses against morality.[31] The criminal was not pictured any more as a sinner against God, but as a social danger, a person who invaded the property rights of others. The dominant use of criminal law, then, in this period, was as defender of an economic and political order, and much less as guardian of a code of sexual and social behavior. The wheel would turn once more, but only later.

[31] William E. Nelson, "Emerging Notions of Modern Criminal Law in the Revolutionary Era: An Historical Perspective," 42 N.Y.U. L. Rev. 450 (1967); for some comparable English data, see Lawrence M. Friedman, "The Devil Is Not Dead: Exploring the History of Criminal Justice," 11 Ga. L. Rev. 257 (1977); on the date of the shift in the colonies, see Hendrik Hartog, "The Public Law of a County Court: Judicial Government in Eighteenth-Century Massachusetts," 20 Am. J. Legal Hist. 282, 299–308 (1976).

THE CRIME OF PUNISHMENT:
THE AMERICAN PRISON

The typical jail of 1776 was a corrupt, inefficient institution—a warehouse for the dregs of society. Men and women were thrown into common cell rooms. Administration was totally unprofessional. Dirt and ordure were everywhere. Discipline was lax; yet brutality went unchecked. Oddly enough (to the modern mind), these jails were not primarily places where people were sent to be punished. Imprisonment was a rare form of sanction in the colonial period. Most people who sat in jail were waiting for their trials. Many of the rest were debtors.

After the Revolution, the old methods of punishment declined, and the prison took on new importance. There was less emphasis on whipping, and on shaming; and, of course, the decline of the death penalty created a vacuum that the prison now filled. There were also new theories to explain where crime came from. The "sources of corruption," as David Rothman has put it, "were external, not internal."[32] Society—bad company, the rot of cities—were the causes of crime. Hence the rehabilitation of the criminal demanded a kind of radical surgery: removal from the evil context. This meant, of course, imprisonment.

As prisons were then constituted, they could hardly be expected to improve the inmate in any way. To do the job, radical new structures were needed. As early as 1767, Massachusetts law authorized imprisonment at hard labor. The Pennsylvania Constitution of 1776 mentioned "visible punishments of long duration," and called for construction of "houses" to punish "by hard labour, those who shall be convicted of crimes not capital." In 1790, the Walnut Street prison, in Philadelphia, was remodeled as a showplace for an enlightened policy. Its chief novelty was a "penitentiary House" (the name is significant) containing sixteen solitary or separate cells:

> Each cell was 8 feet long, 6 feet wide, and 10 feet high, had two doors, an outer wooden one, and an inside iron door. ... Each cell had a large leaden pipe that led to the sewer,

[32]David Rothman, *The Discovery of the Asylum: Social Order and Disorder in the New Republic* (1971), p. 69.

and thus formed a very primitive kind of a closet. The window
of the cell was secured by blinds and wire, to prevent anything
being passed in or out.[33]

Some convicts in the prison worked in shops during the day;
but the convicts in the solitary cells did not work at all. This lonely
asceticism would presumably lead the prisoners of Walnut Street
to rethink their lives, and meditate on self-improvement. But it
was soon conceded that there was a need for hard labor; isolation
alone was too cruel, led to madness, and did not work.

In New York, the north wing of Auburn prison was remodeled
in 1821 to conform to advanced principles of penology. In the
Auburn system, the prisoners worked together during the day-
time and slept in solitary cells at night. The Cherry Hill prison in
Philadelphia (1829) was another innovation in prison styles.[34]
Cherry Hill was built in the form of a grim fortress, surrounded
by walls of medieval strength. Great stone arms radiated out of
a central core. Each arm contained a number of individual cells
connected to tiny walled courtyards, one to a cell. The prisoners
lived in cell and courtyard, utterly alone, night and day. Sometimes
they wore masks. Through peepholes, the prisoners could listen
to religious services. In both Auburn and Cherry Hill, absolute
silence was imposed on the prisoners—a punishment perhaps
more inhumane than the flogging and branding that were supposedly supplanted.

Regimentation and uniformity were key planks of the new penology. Thus some of the state laws were remarkably detailed. When
Massachusetts converted its state prison to the Auburn system in
1828, its statute carefully provided that

> each convict shall be allowed, for his yearly clothing, one pair
> of thick pantaloons, one thick jacket, one pair of thin pan-

[33]Orlando F. Lewis, *The Development of American Prisons and Prison Customs, 1776–
1845* (1922), p. 27. The developments described in this section took place over
time, and rather raggedly; more slowly, in general, in the South than in the North.
So, for example, in a Tennessee County in the period before 1820 we find many
examples of corporal punishment—whipping and branding—and even the pillory. See Cornelia Anne Clark, "Justice on the Tennessee Frontier: The Williamson
County Circuit Court, 1810–1820," 32 Vanderbilt L. Rev. 413, 440 (1979).

[34]See, in general, Negley K. Teeters and John D. Shearer, *The Prison at Philadelphia: Cherry Hill* (1957); for New York, W. David Lewis, *From Newgate to Dannemora: The Rise of the Penitentiary in New York, 1796–1848* (1965). See also Adam
J. Hirsch, "From Pillory to Penitentiary: The Rise of Penal Incarceration in Early
Massachusetts," 80 Mich. L. Rev. 1179 (1982).

taloons, one thin jacket, two pairs of shoes, two pairs of socks, three shirts, and two blankets, all of a coarse kind.

The daily ration was part of the law, down to an allowance of "two ounces of black pepper" per hundred rations.[35] All this detail was part of the regimen, and was perhaps meant to symbolize careful administration and the meticulous care used in translating theory into practice.

What were the penitentiaries really like? Charles Dickens visited Cherry Hill on his American tour, and was horrified. "Those who devised this system of Prison Discipline," he remarked, "and those benevolent gentlemen who carry it into execution, do not know what it is that they are doing." This "dreadful punishment" inflicts "immense...torture and agony" on the prisoners. It was a "slow and daily tampering with the mysteries of the brain...immeasurably worse than any torture of the body." The silence, Dickens felt, was "awful.... Over the head and face of every prisoner who comes into this melancholy house, a black hood is drawn; and in this dark shroud...he is led to the cell....He is a man buried alive."[36]

But not everybody agreed with Dickens. Visitors saw, perhaps, what they wanted to see. One of the enthusiastic visitors was no less than Alexis de Tocqueville, who, together with Gustave de Beaumont, published a book on the American system of punishment in the 1830s. Beaumont and de Tocqueville admired the rigor and discipline of the penitentiary. It was both "moral and just. The place which society has assigned for repentance, ought to present no scenes of pleasure and debauch." They praised the stark regimentation, the bare, unyielding routine—and even the food, which was "wholesome, abundant, but coarse": it supported the "strength" of prisoners, without unnecessary "gratification of the appetite." American prison life, they admitted, was "severe." And they pointed out a paradox: "While society in the United States gives the example of the most extended liberty, the prisons ...offer the spectacle of the most complete despotism."[37]

But this was not, perhaps, a paradox at all. Here was a society

[35]Mass. Laws 1828, ch. 118, secs. 14, 15.
[36]Charles Dickens, *American Notes* (1842), pp. 118, 121.
[37]Gustave de Beaumont and Alexis de Tocqueville, *On the Penitentiary System in the United States and Its Application to France* (1833).

embarked on what seemed at the time a radical experiment: popular government. All obvious forms of authority had been dethroned. There was no monarchy, no established church, no aristocracy. Instead there was only law. Essentially, people were supposed to govern themselves; the law entrusted them with power. Those unworthy of the trust had to be removed from society. One rotten apple spoils the barrel. Criminals betrayed the American experiment; the penitentiary regime was what they needed—and deserved.

The modern reader is more likely to agree with Dickens than with Beaumont and de Tocqueville. The classic penitentiary seems indescribably cruel. Indeed, there were prisoners who went insane in their cells. Administration also quickly degenerated. The success of the penitentiary depended on absolute control, on solitary confinement, on total discipline. Honest guards and wardens were essential, too. But after a few years, strait-jackets, iron gags, and savage beatings were a way of life at Cherry Hill. Even in the relatively well-run Massachusetts State Prison, the silent system was abandoned in the 1840s.[38]

What went wrong? Society in the 19th century, fearful of moral failure, committed to a dour theory of deterrence, intensely suspicious of power, niggardly with regard to public enterprises, never had the will to carry out its theories to their logical conclusion. What little vigor and talent were available expended themselves on theory, on legislation and, occasionally, on administration at the apex of the system. The central problem was administrative failure: not enough skill, and money, and care, to make the ideal real. This was the vice from top to bottom. Local jails—county and city—were scandals; and what is more, archaic scandals. The great new prisons were wrecked in the war between the aims of reformers and the anarchic indifference of everybody else. The real power in the country did not belong to reformers. It belonged to the rest of the public, people who wanted criminals safely behind bars, out of sight. It was, indeed, this interest that explains why prison reform was possible at all. Before the Walnut Street reforms in Philadelphia in 1790, the good citizens of the city had to suffer the sight of shaven-headed men working the streets,

---

[38]Hindus, *Prison and Plantation*, p. 169. In the prison, iron collars and leg irons were sometimes used to prevent escapes; and recidivists were tattooed with the letters "MSP." Also, anybody was entitled to visit the prison, after paying a twenty-five-cent admission fee. This practice, which brought in a fair amount of money, was not abolished until 1863. *Ibid.*, pp. 168–70.

heavily guarded, in "infamous dress ... begging and insulting the inhabitants, collecting crowds of idle boys, and holding with them the most indecent and improper conversations."[39] Reform at least got convicts off the streets. The prisoners of Walnut Street lived like monks, out of sight and out of mind.

Once prisoners were removed from their midst, the public lost interest, in both senses of that word. The new penitentiaries were expensive; they were big, strong buildings, and they needed a lot of cells if prisoners were to be kept silent and alone. The money was simply not forthcoming. Some of the Southern states tried to make money out of the penitentiaries by turning them into factories. When this failed to produce enough profits, they leased the penitentiaries out to private businessmen. Kentucky did this as early as 1828; later, so did Alabama, Texas, Missouri, and Louisiana.[40]

In the end, prisons, like poorhouses and insane asylums, continued to serve primarily as storage bins for deviants. Beatings and strait-jackets, like the well-meant cruelty of solitary confinement, were visited on a class of men (and a handful of women) who had no reason to expect good treatment from the world, no hope of changing that world, and no power to do so. Their interests were represented by proxies in outside society; and their fate was determined by the strength and persistence—never great—of those proxies who stood for reform. Each failure merely paved the way for another wave of misguided and misplaced reforms.

A FOOTNOTE ON TORT

A tort is a civil, that is, a noncriminal, wrong; it is any one of a miscellaneous collection of misdeeds that lay the basis for a suit for damages. One type of action, for negligence, has come to outweigh all the others in importance. The lesser torts include assault and battery, trespass to land, and libel and slander.

All in all, tort law was not a highly developed field in 1776, or for a good many years thereafter. Not a single treatise on the law of torts was published before 1850, on either side of the Atlantic. Negligence was the merest dot on the law. Blackstone's *Commen-*

[39] Orlando F. Lewis, *op. cit.,* p. 18.
[40] Ayers, *Vengeance and Justice,* p. 68.

taries had almost nothing to say about the concept. Nathan Dane's *Abridgement,* in the 1820s, treated the subject quite casually. Negligence was a kind of residual category—those torts which could not "be brought conveniently under more particular heads." Only one or two of his examples of negligence had much empirical significance: "If the owner of a ship, in the care of a pilot, through *negligence* and want of skill, sinks the ship of another, this owner is liable."[41] Indeed, well into the 19th century, Morton Horwitz has argued, the negligence concept was quite different from its later form. It referred, by and large, to failures to perform a specific duty—often a contractual one.[42] It was not defined as a failure to measure up to a general standard of care, the behavior of the reasonable man.

The explosion of tort law, and negligence in particular, has to be attributed to the industrial revolution—to the age of engines and machines. Mainly, this branch of law is about personal injuries. In preindustrial society, there are few personal injuries, except as a result of assault and battery. Modern tools and machines, however, have a marvelous capacity to cripple and maim their servants. From about 1840 on, one specific machine, the railroad locomotive, generated, on its own steam (so to speak), more tort law than any other in the 19th century. The railroad engine swept like a great roaring bull through the countryside, carrying out an economic and social revolution; but it exacted a tremendous toll—thousands of men, women, and children injured and dead.

Existing tort law was simply not designed to deal with accidents of this type. It had been devised with other situations in mind. American law had to work out some fresh scheme to distribute the burden of railroad accidents among workers, citizens, companies and state. Because the job was new, the resulting law was also new. There was some continuity in phrasing, but this was in a way misleading. Tort law was new law in the 19th century.

There is considerable controversy about the origins and functions of the developing law of torts. One view is that the new rules were rules with a single, distinct purpose: to encourage the growth of young businesses, or at least not put obstacles in their way. Or, to be more accurate, the new rules were rules that judges and others might *think* of as proenterprise. The rules, in short, put

[41]Nathan Dane, *A General Abridgement and Digest of American Law,* vol. III (1824), pp. 31–35.

[42]Morton J. Horwitz, *The Transformation of American Law, 1780–1860* (1977), p. 87.

limits on enterprise liability. This was the thrust of the developing law of negligence; and there were parallel developments in other branches of law—compensation for public taking of property, and nuisance law, for example.[43]

The most famous (or infamous) new doctrine was the fellow-servant rule. This was the rule that one servant (employee) could not sue his master (employer) for injuries caused by the negligence of another employee. In the law of agency, the principal is generally liable for negligent acts of his agent:

> If an inn-keeper's servants rob his guests, the master is bound to restitution. . . . So likewise if the drawer at a tavern sells a man bad wine, whereby his health is injured, he may bring an action against the master.[44]

But this general rule was never extended to the factory and to railroad workers. The reason was most notably expressed in the leading American case, *Farwell* v. *Boston & Worcester Railroad Corporation* (1842).[45] Farwell was a railroad engineer, working for a wage of $2 a day. A switchman allowed a train to run off the track. Farwell was thrown to the ground "with great violence"; and one of the wheels of the car crushed his right hand. He sued the railroad, claiming the switchman was negligent. Chief Justice Lemuel Shaw of Massachusetts wrote a brilliant opinion denying recovery. Shaw argued that the workman who takes on a dangerous job must be held to have assumed the ordinary risks of the job. In theory, the wage rate included an adjustment for the added danger. Since that was so, the risk must be left on the person who had, for a price, voluntarily taken it on. The injured workman was thus thrown back on his own resources, or, if he had none, left to the tender mercies of the poor laws. The economic impact

---

[43]This thesis is expounded by Horwitz, *op. cit.*, supra. On the background and early history of negligence law, see also Robert L. Rabin, "The Historical Development of the Fault Principle: A Reinterpretation," 15 Ga. L. Rev. 925 (1981).

[44]1 Blackstone, *Commentaries*, p. 430. On the rise of the fellow-servant rule, see Lawrence M. Friedman and Jack Ladinsky, "Social Change and the Law of Industrial Accidents," 67 Columbia L. Rev. 50, 51–58 (1967); an alternative view is in Comment, "The Creation of a Common Law Rule: The Fellow-Servant Rule, 1837–1860," 132 U. Pa. L. Rev. 579 (1984).

[45]45 Mass. (4 Metc.) 49 (1842). The rule was first enunciated in *Priestley* v. *Fowler*, 3 M. & W. 1 (Ex. 1837), an English case, which did not, however, arise out of an industrial setting. *Murray* v. *South Carolina R.R.*, 26 So. Car. L. (1 McMul.) 385 (1841) was decided one year before *Farwell*, and reached the same result; but it was never so frequently cited as the opinion of Chief Justice Shaw.

of railroad accidents was thereby socialized (or ignored), relieving the roads of one possible heavy cost; or so an enterprise-minded judge might have thought.

The fellow-servant rule had far-reaching consequences. An employee could not sue his employer for negligence unless his injuries were caused by the employer's own personal misconduct, not those of the fellow servants.[46] But in factories and mines and on railroads, any negligent conduct was likely to be conduct of a fellow servant. Factory and railroad owners and managers were not usually at the work site at all; and every year, corporate masters employed a higher percentage of the work force. In the years after *Farwell*, state after state adopted the fellow-servant rule. The doctrine of contributory negligence, which grew up in the first half of the 19th century, added another barrier to plaintiffs who sued in tort. If an injured party was negligent herself, however slightly, she could not sue on the basis of defendant's negligence. Since most plaintiffs were individuals, and most defendants companies, the impact of the doctrine is quite obvious. Contributory negligence applied to passenger injuries as well as to injuries to workers. This made it doubly useful to the railroads.[47]

[46]The injured worker could also sue the negligent worker, of course; but this was a hollow right, because the fellow servant was almost certain not to have much money.

[47]The law of torts was never quite so harsh and unyielding as its formal rules may have made it appear. Almost from the very first, juries, judges, and legislatures took away with their left hand some of what had been built up with the right. The full sweep of this countertrend appeared most clearly only after 1850. See below, part III, ch. VI.

CHAPTER VIII

THE BAR AND ITS WORKS

THE BAR

The bar has always suffered from a certain degree of unpopularity. During the Revolution, it is said, lawyers became even more unpopular than before. If so, it was not for lack of heroes. Many lawyers were loyalists, to be sure; more than two hundred of these, perhaps, eventually left the country.[1] About 40 percent of the lawyers in Massachusetts were loyalists.[2] But, on the other side, almost half of the signers of the Declaration of Independence and more than half of the members of the Federal Constitutional Convention were lawyers. Jefferson, Hamilton, and John Adams, patriots without blemish, were lawyers.

The two groups might have canceled each other out in the public mind. If they did not, one must search deeper for causes of unpopularity. Some lawyers, not Tories themselves, defended the Tories against state confiscation laws between 1780 and 1800. Alexander Hamilton built a career by working for these unpopular clients. Yet even this fact does not carry one very far. Broader social forces were undoubtedly at work. Economic depression followed the end of the war. Clamor against lawyers was a tide that rose and fell with the business cycle. In Massachusetts, during Shays's Rebellion, there were uprisings against courts and lawyers; the lawyers seemed too zealous in the oppression of debtors. It was a common lay opinion that the law was all tricks and technicalities, run by unscrupulous men who built legal careers "upon

---

[1]Charles Warren, *A History of the American Bar* (1911), p. 213. Some lawyers afterwards returned. For a case study of the career of a lawyer who wavered in his allegiance, left the country, lived in exile, and ultimately came back to a successful practice (Peter Van Schaack), see Maxwell Bloomfield, *American Lawyers in a Changing Society, 1776–1876* (1976), pp. 1–31.

[2]Gerald W. Gawalt, *The Promise of Power: The Emergence of the Legal Profession in Massachusetts, 1760–1840* (1979), p. 37.

the ruins of the distressed."[3] "Lawyers," wrote St. John Crèvecoeur in 1782, "are plants that will grow in any soil that is cultivated by the hands of others; and when once they have taken root they will extinguish every other vegetable that grows around them. The fortunes they daily acquire in every province, from the misfortunes of their fellow citizens, are surprising! ... They are here what the clergy were in past centuries.... A reformation equally useful is now wanted."[4]

At various points in history, the lawyer has been labeled a Tory, parasite, usurer, land speculator, corrupter of the legislature, note shaver, panderer to corporations, tool of the trusts, shyster, ambulance chaser, and loan shark. Some of his bad odor is due to his role as hired hand. The rich and powerful need lawyers and have the money to hire them. Also, lawyers in the United States were upwardly mobile men, seizers of opportunities. The American lawyer was never primarily a learned doctor of laws; he was a man of action and cunning, not a scholar. He played a useful role, sometimes admired, but rarely loved. The role, of course, was shaped by concrete circumstances. A revolution is an attack upon a specific government; and the government in turn means specific men, in this case the local agents of the tyrant king, many of them lawyers. Later, with the rise of Jeffersonian and Jacksonian democracy, the leading political party opposed the idea of government by experts. This was a point of view that implied either some limits on the power of the bar, or opening the bar to all or more comers.

Under the pressure of American practical politics, it would have been surprising if a narrow, elitist profession grew up—a small, exclusive guild. No such profession developed. There were tendencies in this direction during the colonial period; but after the Revolution the dam burst, and the number of lawyers grew fantastically. It has never stopped growing. In Massachusetts, in 1740, there were only about 15 lawyers (the population was about 150,000). A century later, in 1840, there were 640 lawyers in the state—ten times as many in ratio to the population. It was after the Revolution that the big push came.[5]

[3]Quoted in Oscar Handlin and Mary Handlin, *Commonwealth: A Study of the Role of Government in the American Economy: Massachusetts, 1774–1861* (rev. ed., 1969), p. 41.

[4]*Letters from an American Farmer* (1904), pp. 196–97.

[5]Gawalt, *op. cit.*, p. 14. In 1790 there were 112 lawyers; in 1800, 200; in 1810, 492. Some of these were practicing in what became the state of Maine; but none-

This kind of growth would have been impossible if the profession had real control over entry. In fact, the doors to the profession were at all times relatively open. Control over admission to the bar was loose, to say the least. Legal education was not very stringent. The bar became a great avenue of social advancement. Young men entered the profession for reasons not very different from those which attract them today. "Law," wrote young James Kent, "is a field which is uninteresting and boundless." It was "so encumbered with voluminous rubbish and the baggage of folios that it requires uncommon assiduity and patience to manage." Yet he pushed ahead, because law, despite its faults, "leads forward to the first stations in the State."[6]

Maxwell Bloomfield sampled death notices of lawyers, carried in the *Monthly Law Magazine*, around the end of the period. He found a rich diversity of family backgrounds. There were forty-eight in his sample. Among their fathers were three doctors, five merchants, eleven ministers, ten farmers, two mechanics, two soldiers, eleven lawyers, and four judges.[7] Careers in law were a vehicle through which some poor men's sons reached wealth and position. Others, of course, tried and failed. The American myth was not that everyone succeeds, but that everyone had a fighting chance to succeed. And there was enough truth in this—enough stories of the trip from log cabin to riches—to make the law an attractive career for ambitious young men.

The bar was open to almost everybody in the formal sense; but this did not mean that there were no barriers of class or background. The Jackson ideology should not be taken necessarily at face value. Mobility at the bar did not mean, for one thing, that the bar was not stratified. In the 20th century, there is tremendous social distance between a Wall Street partner and the lawyers who scramble for a living at the bottom of the heap. Studies have shown that lawyers from wealthy backgrounds are far more likely to reach the heights than lawyers from working-class homes. In 1800

theless, the number of lawyers in the Massachusetts counties grew steadily and dramatically in ratio to the population. There were also substantial increases in the number of lawyers practicing in Virginia; see E. Lee Shepard, "Breaking into the Profession: Establishing a Law Practice in Antebellum Virginia," 48 J. Southern Hist. 393, 405 (1982).

[6]Quoted in William Kent, *Memoirs and Letters of James Kent, Ll. D.* (1898), p. 16. See, in general, E. Lee Shepard, "Lawyers Look at Themselves: Professional Consciousness and the Virginia Bar, 1770–1850," 25 Am. J. Legal Hist. 1 (1981).

[7]Maxwell Bloomfield, "Law vs. Politics: The Self-Image of the American Bar (1830–1860)," 12 Am. J. Legal Hist. 306, 313–14 (1968).

or 1850, there were no large law firms. But there were rich lawyers and poor lawyers in those years; there were lawyers who represented well-to-do clients and rich merchants; and there were those who squeezed out a living handling petty claims in petty courts. Some of the best, most famous lawyers came up the hard way; but all in all, good social background was important then too. A person with Jefferson's background got the right education and contacts more easily than a poor man's son. He was more likely to *become* a lawyer, more likely, too, to reach the top of the bar. Of 2,618 trained lawyers who practiced in Massachusetts and Maine between 1760 and 1840, 71.4 percent, or 1,859, were college-trained. There is evidence, indeed, that the bar, after the first Revolutionary generation, drew even more heavily than before upon children of professionals, as compared to children of farmers or laborers. Between 1810 and 1840, it seems, more than half the lawyers, who were college graduates and were admitted to the bar in Massachusetts, were sons of lawyers and judges; before 1810, the figure was about 38 percent. The percentages of lawyers from a farming or laboring background declined slightly at the same time.[8]

Gerard Gawalt's figures for Massachusetts also show great variation in income and property holdings among lawyers. A typical income seemed to be something less than $1,000 a year, in 1810 or 1820. But Lemuel Shaw probably grossed more than $15,000 in private practice in the late 1820s.[9] This was an enormous sum for the day—the equivalent of several hundred thousand in purchasing power in the 1980s. Daniel Webster, who of course was one of the most famous lawyers of the period, usually earned over $10,000 a year after 1825; in 1835–36, he earned over $21,000 in fees.[10]

There were many styles and types, then, of law practice. We have already mentioned that colorful subspecies, the frontier or Western lawyer. No frontier town was too raw and muddy for lawyers. They were out to seek their fortunes in land and litigation, sometimes even in genteel larceny. Politics had an irresistible appeal for Western lawyers, as one road to fame or to fortune,

[8]Gerard W. Gawalt, *op. cit.*, pp. 140, 171–72.

[9]Leonard W. Levy, *The Law of the Commonwealth and Chief Justice Shaw* (1957), p. 17; Gawalt, *op. cit.*, pp. 109–15.

[10]Alfred F. Konefsky and Andrew J. King, eds., *The Papers of Daniel Webster. Legal Papers*, Vol. 2: *The Boston Practice* (1983), pp. 122–23.

or both. Many began their careers in the West as politicians who had wangled a job in the territories. Some took up one public office after another. Lewis Cass, born in New Hampshire, in 1782, received a "classical education of a high order"; taught briefly in Wilmington, Delaware; and crossed the Alleghenies in 1799, at the age of seventeen, "on foot, carrying his knapsack and seeking, unaided, and without the help of wealth or power, a new home in the wilderness of Ohio."[11] In Marietta, Ohio, he learned law in a law office. Then he became a general, a politician, and governor of Michigan.

Some lawyers wandered from town to town, almost like itinerant peddlers, until they found the right opening for their talents. David Davis, Lincoln's friend, later a justice of the United States Supreme Court, was born in Maryland. He attended Yale, studied law in a Massachusetts office, and arrived in Pekin, Illinois, in 1835. A little while after, he moved to Bloomington. George Grover Wright (1820–96), who became president of the American Bar Association in 1887, was born in Indiana, in 1820, the "son of a poor man." He settled in Keosauqua, Iowa, in 1840, where, it is said, his stagecoach from Keokuk broke down.[12] Joseph G. Baldwin (1815–64), whose vivid word-pictures of frontier justice have earned him a small but honorable place in American literature, was born in Virginia, read Blackstone, settled in Dekalb, Mississippi, moved to Gainesville, Alabama, stayed put for eighteen years, then moved on to a newer frontier—San Francisco. He had been appointed to the supreme court of California before he died.[13]

A taste for the frontier was not limited to sons of the poor. Almost all of the thirty-six members of Harvard's law class of 1835 were natives of New England and the Middle Atlantic States, mostly middle class and above. One-third of them (twelve) ended their careers in another part of the country: Michigan, California (two), Ohio (two), Louisiana (two), South Carolina, Tennessee, Georgia, Illinois, and Missouri.[14] No doubt the idea of seeking a fortune in the West was romantically appealing; but the main reason for this shifting about was not wanderlust but ambition.

[11]William T. Young, *Sketch of Life and Public Services of General Lewis Cass* (1853), pp. 18–19.

[12]James G. Rogers, *American Bar Leaders* (1932), p. 47.

[13]William A. Owens, Introduction to Joseph G. Baldwin, *The Flush Times of Alabama and Mississippi* (1957).

[14]Charles Warren, *History of the Harvard Law School*, vol. III (1908), pp. 11–12.

Still, it was not so easy to scratch out a living in new soil. Some lawyers, to be sure, found a quick niche, stayed put, watched their rude villages grow up to cities, and became themselves rich and respectable. If they lived long enough, they wrote colorful "recollections" of bench and bar for local historical journals and lawyers' magazines. Their practice took patience, luck, and skill. They did not bother asking what was or was not fit work for a lawyer. Whatever earned a dollar was fair game. Some, indeed, had to leave the practice for a while, or for good, to make ends meet. John Dean Caton, later chief justice of Illinois, arrived in Chicago in 1833 with fourteen dollars in his pocket. He found a few lawyers there but little business. A "very good lawyer," Russell E. Heacock, who had practiced downstate, found the going so rough in Chicago that he "built a log carpenter's shop at the corner of State and South Water street, where he worked at the trade which he had learned before he studied law. He also held the office of justice of the peace."[15]

Some lawyers came West as agents for Eastern land speculators, then later struck out on their own. Their main legal business was the land—buying it and selling it for others, searching titles, making deeds. Land was the backbone of practice. It was also a medium of payment. Michael Stoner hired young Henry Clay, in 1801, to "prosecute a claim...to five hundred acres of Land." Clay would pay all the costs; if he won, he was to receive one fourth of the winnings.[16] Another staple of the lawyer's practice was collection work. Lawyers dunned and sued, both for local people and for Easterners who held debts in the form of promissory notes. The lawyer usually paid himself from the proceeds—if he collected. Indiana attorney Rowland, collecting two notes in 1820 for E. Pollard, one "for 100 dollars in land-office money," the other for $100.37, "payable in leather to be delivered four miles from Bloomington," was to "receive the customary fees when the money is collected, and if it is never collected then a reasonable fee for [his] trouble."[17] As this example shows, hard money was at all times scarce; a lawyer who got his hands on some cash would cast around for the most profitable investment. So, some frontier

---

[15]John Caton, *Early Bench and Bar of Illinois* (1893), p. 2.
[16]James F. Hopkins, ed., *The Papers of Henry Clay*, vol. I (1959), pp. 59–60.
[17]*Pollard* v. *Rowland*, 2 Blackf. 20 (Ind., 1826); see, for a general picture of Western practice, William F. English, *The Pioneer Lawyer and Jurist in Missouri* (1947), pp. 65–80, 94–119.

lawyers added to collections and land speculation the high-risk venture of lending out money at interest. For nonresidents, the Western lawyer searched titles, paid taxes, and in general looked after the absentee's affairs. He might also scramble for a share of petty criminal work.

Courtroom clients were a shifting if not shiftless lot. House counsel was unknown, though in time successful lawyers and affluent clients did enter into occasional retainer agreements. Almost all lawyers, then, were constantly seeking new business and were in constant need of advertisements for themselves. There was no prohibition against advertising in the literal sense, and lawyers reached out for the public through notices ("cards") in the newspapers.[18] Word of mouth was probably a more effective way to attract good clients. The flamboyance, tricks, and courtroom antics of 19th-century lawyers were more than a matter of personality; this behavior created reputation; and a courtroom lawyer who did not impress the public and gain a reputation would be hard pressed to survive.

Since many lawyers had no settled relations with definite clients, and since so much of practice was litigation, their lives were spent in close contact with other lawyers, as colleagues, friends, and friendly enemies. Riding on circuit was a hard but rewarding school of experience, a school whose most famous alumnus was Abraham Lincoln. As John Dean Caton described it, in its Illinois version, lawyers traveled

> with the judge ... on horseback in a cavalcade across the prairies from one county seat to another, over stretches from fifty to one hundred miles, swimming the streams when necessary. At night they would put up at log cabins in the borders of the groves, when they frequently made a jolly night of it....
>
> This circuit practice required a quickness of thought and a rapidity of action nowhere else requisite in professional practice. The lawyer would, perhaps, scarcely alight from his horse when he would be surrounded by two or three clients requiring his services.... It is surprising how rapidly such practice qualifies one to meet ... emergencies.[19]

Typically, the lawyer traveled light; he took with him a few personal effects, a change of linen, a handful of lawbooks. In

[18]Daniel H. Calhoun, *Professional Lives in America: Structure and Aspiration, 1750–1850* (1965), pp. 82–83.

[19]Caton, *op. cit.*, p. 51.

some cases, a young lawyer, too poor to buy a horse, trudged along the circuit on foot.[20]

It was not only country lawyers who went on circuit. The Supreme Court bar, mainly recruited from Pennsylvania, Maryland, and Virginia, was also an itinerant group. Peter S. DuPonceau, of Pennsylvania, described the life of these lawyers:

> counsel ... were in the habit of going together to Washington to argue their cases. ... We hired a stage to ourselves in which we proceeded by easy journies. ... we had to travel in the depth of winter through bad roads in no very comfortable way. Nevertheless, as soon as we were out of the city, and felt the flush of air, we were like school boys in the playground on a holiday. ...
>
> Our appearance at the Bar of the Supreme Court was always a scene of triumph.[21]

But any kind of settled practice—even debt collection—was an enemy of the personal, itinerant style. The circuit-riding era slowly passed on; it was colorful and romantic, and hence its importance was easy to exaggerate. Even in outlying counties, settled office-work began to take hold before the Civil War.[22]

In any event, the Eastern and Southern statesman-lawyer was a far cry from the dusty rider of the plains. Some, like Jefferson, were great squires who studied law as a gentleman's pursuit. In the North, too, there were lawyers from elite backgrounds. They formed a small but sophisticated bar of commerce, together with some upwardly mobile colleagues. These lawyers advised the great mercantile houses on matters of marine insurance and international trade. Yet they too were basically courtroom lawyers, in practice on their own, like their poor Western cousins. Alexander Hamilton had a general practice in the late 18th century, and frequently appeared in court. He was "a very great favorite with the merchants of New York." Many questions of marine insurance went to court and Hamilton had an "overwhelming share" of this business.[23] According to one estimate, about five hundred lawyers

---

[20]John W. McNulty, "Sidney Breese, the Illinois Circuit Judge, 1835–1841," 62 J. Ill. State Historical Society 170 (1969).

[21]Charles Warren, *History of the American Bar,* p. 256.

[22]Daniel H. Calhoun, *Professional Lives in America* (1965), pp. 59–87.

[23]The quotations are from Chancellor Kent, in William Kent, *Memoirs and Letters of James Kent* (1898), p. 317. On Hamilton's career, there is abundant material in

practiced in New York City in 1830, when the city had a population of about 200,000.[24] Almost all of these men were solo practitioners. There was a handful of two-man partnerships, but no firms of any size. In a few of these partnerships, the partners began to specialize. George Washington Strong and John Wells formed a partnership in 1818; the two partners soon agreed on a rough division of labor. One was a better advocate in court; the other preferred to stay in the office and prepare necessary papers and briefs.[25]

At least three embryo partnerships of old New York were ancestor firms of large "factories" of law on Wall Street. One of these, forefather of the Cravath firm of New York, has been carefully traced by Robert T. Swaine.[26] To Swaine we owe a valuable picture of the practice of R. M. Blatchford, one of the founding fathers, in the years 1826–32, when he was still practicing alone. Blatchford's practice was exceptional but probably not unique. It was, in a way, far more like its Wall Street descendants than like the work of Blatchford's contemporaries in small towns, or out West, or at the petty criminal courts of New York. Blatchford in 1826 had become American financial agent and counsel for the Bank of England; this connection brought him "a great deal of business from English solicitors whose clients had American investments." He became counsel, too, to the second Bank of the United States. Blatchford went to court once in a while; but most of his work was as an adviser. When he formed a partnership with his brother, in 1832, he again dropped out of litigation. The early years of this brotherly firm were spent in large measure on "office practice—advising on legal problems and drafting legal documents affecting industry, trade and finance. . . . There were many loan transactions, commercial and on real estate mortgages, much of the latter business coming from English clients, who also sent occasional marine insurance and other admiralty matters. There was also much collection business for City merchants and for English exporters."

the various volumes of *The Law Practice of Alexander Hamilton*. Vol. I (1964) and vol. II (1969) were edited by Julius Goebel; vols. III (1980), IV (1980), and V (1981) by Julius Goebel and Joseph H. Smith.

[24]Henry W. Taft, *A Century and a Half at the New York Bar* (1938), p. 7.

[25]Taft, *op. cit.*, p. 22.

[26]Robert T. Swaine, *The Cravath Firm and Its Predecessors, 1819–1948*, vol. I (1946).

Blatchford was active as a professional trustee, and probated estates of wealthy clients. Later, as industry grew, there were cases where businesses needed loans "too large for a single lender." Here there developed a practice of pledging or conveying the security to a trustee, "for the joint benefit of a group of lenders. Blatchford developed a business as trustee in such transactions— the forerunner of the modern corporate trust. In the '30s there also appeared a form of investment security as a means of attracting British capital to America of the same general nature as the modern investment trust. In this field, too, Blatchford was active, both as a trustee and as a lawyer. Out of that activity grew the North American Trust & Banking Company litigation which was in the New York courts from 1841 to 1858 and was one of the Blatchford firm's principal matters after ... 1854."[27]

Blatchford was one kind of wave of the future. Few lawyers could afford to stray so far from litigation. Courtroom advocacy, both East and West, was the main road to prestige, the main way to get recognized as a lawyer or a leader of the bar. It was surely the only way for a lawyer, as a lawyer, to become famous. Daniel Webster was a celebrity; Blatchford was not. Webster, the courtroom lawyer, lives on in literature and in folklore. Chancellor Kent, who was learned and influential, but whose courtroom delivery was "most shocking,"[28] is remembered only by specialists and scholars.

Eloquence in court gained attention, and attention gained clients. There was a ready audience too. In the days before radio and television, the public appreciated a good trial and a good courtroom speech. In the provinces, when the court arrived at the county seat, court day was an occasion; trials and courtroom business broke up the monotony of life. In the rather dull society of Washington, ambassadors, congressmen, and the wives of politicians crowded into the Supreme Court galleries to hear the giants of the bar hold forth. "Scarcely a day passed in court," Story wrote in 1812, "in which parties of ladies do not occasionally come in and hear, for a while, the arguments of learned counsel. On two occasions, our room has been crowded with ladies to hear Mr. [William] Pinkney, the present Attorney General."[29] Speeches at

---

[27]Swaine, op. cit., pp. 14–15.
[28]Diary of George T. Strong, quoted in Taft, op. cit., p. 102.
[29]Quoted in Charles Warren, The Supreme Court in United States History, vol. II, p. 467.

the bar went on for hours, sometimes for days. Alexander Hamilton supposedly spoke for six hours before the New York supreme court in Albany, in a case of criminal libel in 1804.[30] The federal Supreme Court was described in 1824 as "not only one of the most dignified and enlightened tribunals in the world, but one of the most patient. Counsel are heard in silence for hours, without being stopped or interrupted."[31]

Some of these marathon speeches became famous. Daniel Webster argued for four hours in *Dartmouth College* v. *Woodward* (1818),

> with a statement so luminous, and a chain of reasoning so easy to be understood, and yet approaching so nearly to absolute demonstration, that he seemed to carry with him every man of his audience.... Now, and then, for a sentence or two, his eye flashed and his voice swelled into a bolder note... but he instantly fell back into [a] tone of earnest conversation.

The judges listened, we are told, with rapt attention. At the end of his formal argument, Webster added his famous peroration: "Sir, you may destroy this little institution; it is weak; it is in your hands..." At the words, "It is, sir, as I have said, a small college. And yet there are those who love it—"

> the feelings which he has thus far succeeded in keeping down, broke forth. His lips quivered; his firm cheeks trembled with emotion; his eyes were filled with tears, his voice choked... he seemed struggling to... gain... mastery over himself.

At that point, according to one biographer, John Marshall's eyes were "suffused with tears"; and when Webster sat down, there was "a deathlike stillness" in the room; it lasted for "some moments; every one seemed to be slowly recovering."[32]

Unfortunately, these tears may be purely legendary; and even the text of Webster's famous speech is suspect. But there is no doubt about the oratorical athletics. The great courtroom masters really poured it on. The prose is far too purple for 20th-century tastes; but it was no doubt often effective. Old Horace Binney,

---

[30]Julius Goebel, Jr., ed., *The Law Practice of Alexander Hamilton,* vol. I (1964), p. 793.

[31]Quoted in Charles Warren, *The Supreme Court in United States History,* vol. I, p. 467.

[32]Quoted in George T. Curtis, *Life of Daniel Webster,* vol. I (1872), pp. 169–71. A lawyer who worked with Webster in New Hampshire described him as "a born actor... touring the courts with him... was like being on a caravan." Irving H. Bartlett, *Daniel Webster* (1978), p. 10.

looking back at the bar of his youth (he wrote in 1866), saw the great lawyers in a romantic light: flamboyant, oratorical, anything but businesslike and gray. There was Theophilus Parsons, before the turn of the century: "Socratic in his subtlety," but "careless" of dress: "his purple Bandana handkerchief curled loosely over his neckcloth." William Lewis, born in 1745, appeared in court with a "full suit of black" and a "powdered head."

> His first attitude was always as erect as he could make it, with one hand insinuated between his waistcoat and his shirt, and the other lying loose upon his loin; and in this position, without any action but that movement of his head, he would utter two or three of his first sentences.... Then, with a quick movement, and sometimes with a little jerk of his body, he would bring both his hands to his sides, and begin the action. And it was pretty vehement action from that time to the conclusion; his head dropping or rising, his body bending or straightening up, and his arms singly or together relieving his head.... His voice ... was deep, sonorous, and clear to the last ... not sweet, but ... a fine working voice for a court-room.[33]

Judges, too, were in a sense oratorical. Charges to the jury, in the early part of the period, sometimes ran on at enormous length. The judges expatiated on subjects far distant from the business at hand. Inflammatory speeches to grand juries, as we noted, helped bring on the crisis between Federalist judges and Republicans in office. In time, the free-flown speeches of the judges were curbed; and what one might call the oratorical style of law practice died down, though it never died out. The style was essentially suited for small elites and small communities, and for generalist, courtroom lawyers. The rise of big business and the Wall Street style of practice spoiled the monopoly held by the oratorical style. Law-office law meant a different relationship with clients, different ways of getting and keeping business. Then, too, the sheer mass of business had an effect; as dockets became swollen, there had to be an end to the leisurely pace of litigation. After the Webster days, hard-pressed courts, even had they wanted to, could not listen to long speeches and still get on with their work.

[33]Horace Binney, *The Leaders of the Old Bar of Philadelphia* (1866), pp. 17, 38–40.

ORGANIZATION OF THE BAR

The English distinctions of grade—between attorneys, counselors, barristers, and sergeants—exerted a certain fascination, but failed to leave a permanent mark on the American bar. A few colonies had recognized a graded bar; some—New Jersey and Massachusetts—held on to a distinction between two classes of attorneys for a number of years after Independence. The statutes of the Northwest Territory also briefly distinguished between attorneys and "counsellors." Only "counsellors," more exalted than ordinary attorneys, could appear before the highest court. This gradation (1799) lasted only a few years, even on paper.[34] New York distinguished between attorneys and counselors between 1829 and 1846; Virginia distinguished between solicitors, who practiced in equity, and the ordinary attorneys of the common-law courts. The distinction had no great significance; a common-law attorney could easily and quickly, with a few additional formalities, get for himself the solicitor's right to practice in equity court.[35] Soon Virginia did away with this small formal distinction too.

The graded bar was thus a rather transient phenomenon. The old established bar did struggle to keep their guild small and elite. They did not succeed. By the early 19th century, the bar was, formally speaking, an undifferentiated mass. There were rich and poor lawyers, high ones and low; but all were members of one vast sprawling profession. The few primitive bar clubs, associations, and "moots"[36] did nothing to provide real cohesion or self-control. The bar was very loose, very open. Nobody controlled it at the top, or from within. Requirements for admission to the bar were lax.[37] In New England and New York, during the late colonial period, the lawyers themselves had a great deal of power, formal or informal, over admission to the bar. But then the courts took

[34]Francis S. Philbrick, ed., *Laws of Indiana Territory, 1801–1809,* cxcii–cxciii.
[35]Alfred Z. Reed, *Training for the Public Profession of the Law* (1921), p. 80.
[36]See Charles Warren, *A History of the American Bar* (1911), p. 203. In Massachusetts, the associations of the bar, under rules of court of 1810, gained a significant power, which they had long desired. Recommendation from the county bar association became a prerequisite for admission to the court of common pleas and the Supreme Court. These rules lasted about one generation. Gerard W. Gawalt, *op. cit.,* pp. 116–17.
[37]The best treatment is Reed, *op. cit.,* pp. 67–103.

over; thereafter only they could prescribe qualifications and handle applications. This was a symptom of loss of professional cohesion. The courts' rein was bound to be looser than that of the practicing bar; courts had less interest in keeping fee schedules high and the supply of lawyers low.

At the time of the Revolution, there was no uniform mode of admission to the bar. In Massachusetts, each county court admitted its own attorneys; the high court theoretically controlled all admissions in South Carolina; in Rhode Island, Delaware, and Connecticut local courts admitted lawyers; but admission to one bar gave an attorney the right to practice in all. After the Revolution, New York (1777) and the federal courts (1789) switched to the Massachusetts system. This then became the "dominant system in the north-eastern conservative section of the country." In the 1830s, the Delaware method became more popular. The lawyer who could get himself admitted, even by the most slipshod local court, was a fully licensed member of the bar of the state, and could practice before any court.

Requirements for admission were also not uniform. A few states were uncommonly strict. In New Hampshire, between 1805 and 1833, the federated county bars required five years of preparation for admission to the lower courts in the case of applicants qualified to enter Dartmouth (but they did not have to know Greek). Three years was the term for college graduates. Two years further practice was required for admission to the superior court. New York, between 1829 and 1846, by rule of court, demanded seven years of preparation for the right to practice as an "attorney" before the supreme court, "toward which there might be counted up to four years of classical study pursued after the age of fourteen."[38] It took three years more of practice to become a "counsellor." This kind of rigorous time-serving was rapidly discarded in most other states. In 1800, fourteen out of the nineteen states or organized territories prescribed a definite period of preparation for the bar. In 1840, only eleven out of thirty jurisdictions did so. In Massachusetts, a statute was passed in 1836 which obliged the courts to admit anyone of good moral character who had studied law three years in an attorney's office. A person who did not meet this requirement could take his chances on an examination. In

[38]Reed, *op. cit.,* p. 83. The New Hampshire rule was continued by order of court to 1838. On admission to the bar in Virginia, see Charles T. Cullen, "New Light on John Marshall's Legal Education and Admission to the Bar," 16 Am. J. Legal Hist. 345 (1972).

the 1840s, a few states eliminated *all* requirements for admission to the bar, except good moral character. One was Maine (1843); another was New Hampshire (1842), reversing its former stringency. At this point, then, it was hard to make the case that law was a learned, difficult, exclusive profession.

Yet these rules (or lack of rules) must not be taken too literally. Laymen did not practice law, even in New Hampshire and Maine in the 1840s. New Hampshire and Maine were extreme only in frankness. Rules of admission and preparation were probably nowhere rigorously administered. In some states—particularly in the West—"examination" in court of lawyers-to-be was almost a farce, if we can believe a mass of anecdotes. Gustave Koerner, who had immigrated from Germany, began to practice in the 1830s, in Illinois; he reported that his examination was very informal, lasted about half an hour, consisted of a few perfunctory questions; then everyone adjourned for brandy toddies.[39] Salmon P. Chase had almost as perfunctory an examination in Maryland, in 1829. The judge wanted him to "study another year"; but then Chase begged for a favorable ruling, because he had "made all ...arrangements to go to the Western country and practice law"; the judge relented and swore him in.[40] John Dean Caton's experience was quite similar. Caton was admitted to the Illinois bar in 1833. He rode down to Pekin, Illinois, on horseback, one October day; there he introduced himself to Judge Samuel D. Lockwood. Caton told the judge he was practicing in Chicago, but needed a license. They went for a walk after supper; it was a "beautiful moonlit night." Suddenly, near a "large oak stump," Lockwood began asking questions. This was the examination, to Caton's surprise. There were some thirty minutes of questions; then the judge said he would grant the license, but that Caton still had "much to learn."[41]

Theories of Jacksonian democracy have been used to explain why the bar let down its bars on admission. But basic social facts pushed the profession in the same direction. Government control of occupations was, in general, weak and diffuse. Geographical and social mobility was high. There were many jurisdictions; no one of them could really define standards for itself; and the weak-

[39]Jack Nortrup, "The Education of a Western Lawyer," 12 Am. J. Legal Hist. 294, 301 (1968).

[40]J. W. Schuckers, *The Life and Public Services of Salmon Portland Chase* (1874), p. 30.

[41]John Dean Caton, *Early Bench and Bar of Illinois* (1893), pp. 170–71.

ness of one was the weakness of all, as was true of substantive law as well (the later histories of divorce law and corporation law are examples). Besides, a factotum profession, within the grasp of ambitious men of all sorts, was socially useful. The prime economic fact of American life, as we have said, was mass ownership of land and (some bits of) capital. It was a society where many people, not just the noble or the lucky few, needed some rudiments of law, some forms or form-books, some know-how about the mysterious ways of courts or governments. It was a society, in short, that needed a large, amorphous, open-ended profession.

In many ways, then, loose standards were inevitable. Perhaps they even enhanced the vigor of the bar. *Formal* restrictions tended to disappear; but the market for legal services remained, a harsh and sometimes efficient control. It pruned away deadwood; it rewarded the adaptive and the cunning. Jacksonian democracy did not make every man a lawyer. It did encourage a scrambling bar of shrewd entrepreneurs.

LEGAL EDUCATION

A lawyer was a man with legal training, or some legal training and some legal skill. Even at the low point of professional self-government, no one practiced law without some pretense at qualification. Most lawyers gained their pretensions by spending some time, in training, in the office of a member of the bar. The basic mode of training, in short, was a kind of apprenticeship. For a fee, the lawyer-to-be hung around an office, read Blackstone and Coke and a miscellany of other books, and copied legal documents. If he was lucky, he benefited from watching the lawyer do his work, and do it well.

Apprenticeship was useful to everybody: to the clerks, who picked up some knowledge of law, at least by osmosis; and to the lawyers, who (in the days before telephones, typewriters, word processors, Xerox machines and the like) needed copyists and legmen badly. Legal education, in the sense of organized school training, grew up out of the apprenticeship method. To begin with, some lawyers were conscientious about their clerks, anxious to give them proper training. Some became in effect popular teachers. Theophilus Parsons, in Massachusetts, was so much in demand, shortly after 1800, that a special rule of court, aimed at him, restricted law offices to a maximum of three students at any one time.[42] Lemuel Shaw, too, was a popular and diligent teacher. He drew up rules to govern the conduct and training of his students. The students were to report each Monday on their previous week's reading. They were also encouraged to "enter into free conversation" with Shaw "upon subjects connected with their studies, and especially in reference to those changes and alterations of the general law which may have been effected by the Statutes of the Commonwealth and by local usage, and in respect to which therefore little can be found in books."[43] Shaw's office became almost a small private school for lawyers. A few lawyers, with a flair for teaching, took the next logical step; they practiced less and less and spent more time with their clerks. Leonard Henderson of North Carolina, a future chief justice of the state, advertised in 1826 in the *Raleigh Register* that he had "four offices for the reception of Law Students" and was on the verge of opening a fifth. "I shall not," he promised, "deliver formal lectures, but will give explanations whenever requested, examinations will be frequent, and conversations held on law topics," most usually "at table after meals." Henderson fixed the fee for "instruction and boarding, exclusive of washing and candles," at $225 a year.[44]

The first law schools grew out of these specialized law offices.[45] They used much the same techniques as the offices. The earliest such school was founded in Litchfield, Connecticut, by Judge Tapping Reeve, probably in 1784. It proved successful, and grew rapidly in size. Eventually, it gained a national reputation, and attracted students from all over the country.[46] In 1813, fifty-five students were in attendance. In the late 1820s, the school felt the keen effects of competition; it went into decline and closed its doors in 1833. More than a thousand students had been "graduated" from Litchfield by that time.

The Litchfield school taught law by the lecture method. Its lectures were never published; to publish would have meant to perish, since students would have lost most of their incentive for

[42]Frederic Hathaway Chase, *Lemuel Shaw, Chief Justice of the Supreme Judicial Court of Massachusetts* (1918), p. 37.

[43]*Ibid.*, p. 123.

[44]Quoted in Robert H. Wettach, ed., *A Century of Legal Education* (1947), p. 15.

[45]The fullest account of the rise of American legal education is Robert Stevens, *Law School: Legal Education in America from the 1850s to the 1980s* (1983), but, as the title suggests, it concentrates mostly on a later period.

[46]Alfred Z. Reed, *Training for the Public Profession of the Law* (1921), p. 130.

paying tuition and going to class. The lecture plan was modeled on Blackstone's *Commentaries,* but the Litchfield lectures paid more attention to commercial law, and little or none to criminal law. Daily lectures lasted about an hour and a quarter or an hour and a half. The full course took fourteen months, including two vacations of four weeks each. Students were required to write their notes up carefully, and to do collateral reading. Every Saturday there was a "strict examination" on the week's work. During the later years of the school, "optional moot courts and debating societies" were in operation.[47]

The Litchfield school spawned a number of imitators in a number of states. Some were popular; most lasted only a short time. Some students combined school with apprenticeship. Robert Reid Howison of Fredericksburg, Virginia, began to read law books on his own, at 18, in 1838. He began, naturally, with Blackstone, but plowed ahead through any number of texts. In fall, 1840, Howison took a course of lectures at a law school run by Judge John T. Lomax in the basement of his house in Fredericksburg. The next spring, Howison spent three weeks in the office of the clerk of court in Fredericksburg, copying documents. He was then examined and admitted to the bar.[48]

Ultimately, university law schools replaced the Litchfield type as the major alternative to office training. But legal training at universities was slow to get started, and well into the 19th century there were no "law schools" as such at universities. A few colleges taught law as part of their general curriculum. The first American chair of law was at William and Mary College, where, at the behest of Thomas Jefferson, George Wythe was appointed professor of "Law and Police." St. George Tucker, who later held this chair, published an American edition of Blackstone in 1803, with copious notes and additions, to be used as a kind of textbook for students. Professorships were also established, in the late 18th and early 19th centuries, at the University of Virginia, the University of Pennsylvania, and the University of Maryland. Some of these were not meant for lawyer training at all. James Wilson projected a series of lectures at Pennsylvania (1790) "to furnish a rational and useful entertainment to gentlemen of all professions." David

[47]Reed, *op. cit.,* p. 131.

[48]W. Hamilton Bryson, *Legal Education in Virginia, 1779–1979, A Biographical Approach* (1982), p. 10.

Murray Hoffman's lectures at Maryland and James Kent's at Columbia produced works which enriched legal literature. But these early experiments were mostly in the tradition of Blackstone, that is, they were lectures on law for the general education of students, and not law training strictly speaking.

The Harvard Law School was a somewhat different animal, and it proved more permanent than the lectureships at this or that college. Out of funds left to Harvard by Isaac Royall, a chair of law was set up in 1816. The first professor was Isaac Parker, chief justice of Massachusetts. Parker, in his inaugural address, spoke of law as a "science," one "worthy of a place in the University," and "worthy to be taught, for it cannot be understood without instruction."[49] At Harvard, there were already separate faculties in theology and medicine. Parker expected, or hoped for, a professional, independent law school too. It would live with Harvard College but be clearly distinct from it. A major gift, from Nathan Dane, helped bring this hope to fulfillment. Dane had written a most successful lawbook, *A General Abridgement and Digest of American Law*. In England, in the 18th century, Charles Viner had written a popular abridgement of English law, and used the proceeds to endow a chair in law, which Sir William Blackstone filled. Dane followed the Vinerian precedent; he gave $10,000 to support a professorship. Dane specifically urged that the professor's "residence at Cambridge shall never be required as a condition of his holding the office; believing the best professors will generally be found among Judges and lawyers, eminent in practice in other places conveniently situated, and who, while professors, may continue their offices and practice generally; also thinking law lectures ought to increase no faster than there is a demand for them. Clearly, their great benefit will be in publishing them."[50] Dane himself suggested a candidate for the first Dane professor: Joseph Story. Story was indeed only a part-time professor, out of sheer necessity; when he accepted the post, in 1829, he was a justice of the United States Supreme Court.[51]

The Harvard Law School, at least during the Story period, was

[49] Quoted in Charles Warren, *History of the Harvard Law School*, vol. I (1908), p. 301.

[50] Quoted in Warren, *op. cit.*, p. 420.

[51] Isaac Parker resigned as Royall professor in 1827. The subsequent holders of this chair—first John Ashmun, then Simon Greenleaf—were in regular full-time attendance.

extremely successful; by 1844, 163 students were in attendance, an unheard-of number.[52] Those who completed their course earned an LL.B. The fame and skill of the professors undoubtedly acted as a drawing card. Students who could afford it must have preferred life at Cambridge to the typical sort of office apprenticeship, with its dreary routine. As the oldest and most successful law school, Harvard became the model for all newer schools. It was a pure and rigorous model, as Story wished it to be. It defined the province of law school and legal training severely. Politics and the study of government were put to one side;[53] common law, rather than the study of statutes, was stressed.

Within this narrow domain, the school produced a rich crop of scholarship. Ultimately, the law faculty turned into a veritable treatise-writing machine. Story wrote *Commentaries* on an amazing variety of subjects: promissory notes, equity jurisprudence, the conflict of laws, agency, bailments, bills of exchange, partnership. Simon Greenleaf wrote a popular treatise on evidence. The law school also began to amass a major law library. The catalogue for the academic year 1846–47 claimed that the law-school library owned 12,000 books.[54] The success of Harvard demonstrated that professional training at a university could satisfy the needs of budding lawyers as well as office training could. Yet Harvard did not succeed in raising the *period* of training for the bar above the statutory minimum. And the main path to practice still went through apprenticeship, for the overwhelming majority of lawyers. Apprenticeship influenced Harvard, in this period, more than Harvard influenced general legal education.

THE LITERATURE OF THE LAW

The common law, as it developed over the years, was embodied in reported cases—opinions of high-court judges. What was not reported was barely law. In England, *reporters* (some skillful and accurate, others less so) privately prepared many volumes of cases.

---

[52]Reed, *op. cit.*, p. 143. On the later vicissitudes of Harvard, see below, part III, ch. XI, pp. 612–18.

[53]By way of contrast, James Kent, in his *Introductory Lecture to a Course of Law Lectures* (1794), pp. 19–23, proposed to "begin with an Examination of the nature and duties of Government in general ... The Political History of the United States ... a summary review of the Law of Nations."

[54]*Centennial History of the Harvard Law School: 1817–1917* (1918), p. 94.

There were no American reports to speak of in the colonial period.[55] By and large, the practicing lawyer had to rely on English reports, or on secondhand knowledge of English cases, gleaned out of English treatises. He knew the local statutes, to be sure, and the local practice of his court. Some lawyers prepared, for themselves, collections of local cases. Occasionally, manuscript volumes of cases circulated among lawyers. This practice was certainly followed in the Republican period. Eleven manuscript notebooks, covering the period 1792 to 1830, have been recovered and reprinted for the small state of Delaware alone.[56]

But manuscripts could not satisfy the hunger of lawyers for cases, in an expanding legal system. In 1789, Ephraim Kirby published a volume of *Connecticut Reports*. In the preface, Kirby voiced the hope that a "permanent system of common law," and an American one at that, would emerge in the country. This hope was soon realized. It was more than a matter of patriotism and pride. After all, lawyers wanted reports and were willing to pay for them. In 1790, Alexander Dallas published a volume of "Reports of Cases Ruled and Adjudged in the Courts of Pennsylvania, Before and Since the Revolution." The earlier cases, from 1754 on, were "kindly furnished by Mr. Rawle"; sitting judges helped Dallas by giving him notes on their current cases. Dallas, like Kirby, professed a patriotic aim; he hoped that his reports would "tend to show the pure and uniform system of jurisprudence that prevails in PENNSYLVANIA." In the second volume, Dallas added cases from the United States Supreme Court, which was then sitting at Philadelphia. In this volume, quietly and unobtrusively, began that magnificent series of reports, extending in an unbroken line down to the present, that chronicles the work of the world's most powerful court.

William Cranch, chief justice of the circuit court of the District of Columbia, was the Supreme Court's next reporter. Cranch's first volume appeared in 1804, bright with the hope (as a newspaper put it) that a "code of Common Law" would grow "out of our own Constitutions, laws, customs and state of society, independent of that servile recourse to the decisions of foreign Judicatures to which, since our revolution, we have been too much

---

[55]Some colonial reports were printed later; Josiah Quincy's *Massachusetts Reports* (1761–1771), for example, was published in 1865. Recently, a fair number of volumes of colonial reports have been edited by scholars, sometimes with valuable introductory matter and notes.

[56]Daniel J. Boorstin, ed., *Delaware Cases: 1792–1830* (3 vols., 1943).

accustomed."[57] In his preface, Cranch added another theme, quite characteristic of the times. Reports, he said, were essential to "a government of laws." The "least possible range ought to be left to the discretion of the Judge. Whatever tends to render the laws certain, equally tends to limit that discretion; and perhaps nothing conduces more to that object than the publication of reports. Every case decided is a check upon the Judge." Cranch was succeeded by another able reporter, Henry Wheaton, later famous as a diplomat and scholar of the law.[58]

More and more state reports were also issued. Nathaniel Chipman published *Reports and Dissertations* in Vermont, in 1793. Jesse Root published his *Connecticut Reports* in 1798. By 1810, reports had appeared in New York, Massachusetts, and New Jersey as well. Some of these had official status—for example, George Caines's reports of the supreme court of New York, beginning in 1804. Many early reporters were judges who collected their own opinions and those of their colleagues. Other judges worked closely with their reporters, helping them bring out full, accurate work. Chancellor Kent had a close relationship with William Johnson, whose New York reports were very popular at the bar. Caines acknowledged his debt to "Their Honors on the bench [who]... have unreservedly given their written opinions...the whole bar has frankly and generously afforded their cases, and every other communication that was wished or desired. To these aids the clerk of the court has added an unlimited recurrence to the papers and pleadings his office contains."[59] Rhode Island was the last state to fall in line. The first volume of Rhode Island cases, reported by J. K. Angell, did not appear until 1847.

Some early reports were far more than slavish accounts of the judges' words. Like the great English reports, they were guidebooks for the practitioner. Some reporters added little essays on the law to the oral and written courtroom materials they collected. Chipman filled out his book with "dissertations," including a "Dissertation on the Negotiability of Notes." The full title of Jesse Root's first volume of *Connecticut Reports* (1798) gives some indication of the contents:

[57]Quoted in Charles Warren, *The Supreme Court in United States History,* vol. 1 (rev. ed., 1935), p. 289n.
[58]See, in general, Elizabeth F. Baker, *Henry Wheaton, 1785–1848* (1937).
[59]George Caines, preface, *Reports* (1804).

> Reports of Cases adjudged in the Superior Court and Supreme Court of Errors. From July A.D. 1789 to June A.D. 1793; with a Variety of Cases anterior to that Period, Prefaced with Observations upon the Government and Laws of Connecticut. To Which is Subjoined, Sundry Law Points Adjudged, and Rules of Practice Adopted in the Superior Court.

But Root's "cases" were not full verbatim reports. Frequently they were little more than brief notes, recounting some point of interest in a trial or appellate case. The following is one "report," *Bacon* v. *Minor,* given in its entirety:

> Action of defamation; for saying that the plaintiff had forged a certain note. Issue to the jury. Daniel Minor was offered as a witness and objected to, on the ground that he was a joint promissor in said note, and is sued for speaking the same words. By the Court—Not admitted being interested in the question.[60]

Eventually, appointed officials replaced private entrepreneurs as law reporters. Official reports tended to be fuller and more accurate than unofficial reports, but they were also much more standardized. Caines remarked that his "exertions have been reduced to little more than arranging the materials received, and giving, in a summary manner, the arguments adduced." What was lost in style was gained in authenticity.

The ultimate influence of the reports can hardly be measured. They enabled the states to put together their own common law, as independent of the common law of England, or of other states, as they liked. At the same time, the reports made it possible for states to borrow more freely from each other. Big states and famous judges were considered more authoritative, and were cited more frequently than small states and small judges. New York's reports carried high prestige, especially the opinions of Chancellor Kent. Lemuel Shaw in Massachusetts was another great name. At first, few state cases could be decided on the basis of local precedent alone. And, in practice, local decisions, even when they were available, were not exclusively relied upon. The sense of the judges was that the common law was a single great language of law; one did not move out of step unduly or without good cause. Many courts still had the habit of citing English cases, more or

[60]That is, the testimony was not allowed on the grounds that Minor had a financial stake in the matter litigated. The case is 1 Root 258 (1791).

less frequently. In the first volume of Saxton's chancery reports (New Jersey, 1830–32), well over half the citations were English— more than fifty years after Independence. State reports made English doctrines more digestible, giving them a local habitation and a name. Yet, basically, the case reports were building blocks for an indigenous system of law—indeed, for a system of systems, each state on its own.

With few exceptions, official reports contained only *appellate* opinions. Occasionally, newspapers covered important or lurid trials; a few trial transcripts appeared as pamphlets. A few especially succulent grand-jury charges, by noted judges, were privately printed.[61] The best courtroom oratory was also published. In 1844, an enterprising publisher brought forth the arguments by Horace Binney and Daniel Webster in the noted case of the will of Stephen Girard.[62]

A body of jurisprudential and practical literature also began to appear in the republic. Publishers brought out English works in "American editions"; often, the editor added footnotes to bring these books up to date and to point out American innovations. A fourth American edition of Joseph Chitty's *Practical Treatise on the Law of Contracts* was published by J. C. Perkins in 1839, with "copious notes of American decisions to the present time." St. George Tucker, scholar and jurist of Virginia, published a five-volume Blackstone, in 1803. This was an important work in its own right; its thoughtful "Appendices" discussed government, law, and Virginia jurisprudence. John Reed published a *Pennsylvania Blackstone* in 1831, in three volumes. Reed retained the general plan of Blackstone (that "invaluable treasure of correct information, clothed in the most pure and classical style"),[63] and large chunks of the original (in quotation marks); but Reed also rewrote extensively and added much new material, in order to form "in a connected view, an elementary exposition of the entire law of Pennsylvania, common and statute." Gradually, more and more treatises were written that owed little or nothing to English models, except in the most general way.[64]

---

[61]For example, Alexander Addison, *Charges to Grand Juries of the Counties of the Fifth Circuit in the State of Pennsylvania* (1800); an 1806 grand-jury charge of Chief Justice Parsons of Massachusetts is reprinted in 14 Am. Jurist 26 (1835).

[62]See Entries, Catalogue of the Law School of Harvard University, vol. II (1909), p. 1084.

[63]Preface, p. iv.

[64]See, in general, ch. xiii, "Early American Law Books," and ch. xx, "American Law Books, 1815–1910," in Charles Warren, *A History of the American Bar* (1911).

With some exceptions, American legal literature was (and is) rigorously practical. Books were written for the practicing lawyer. The object to be served was his search for the dollar, not his intellectual curiosity. Systematic legal theory was studiously ignored by most writers as well as by the bar. Legal theory has never been a strong suit in common-law countries. There was, of course, a notable literature of political theory, and the law can lay some claim, not wholly farfetched, to the writings of Thomas Jefferson, James Wilson, and the *Federalist Papers*. Some education in government was part of the general training of the better lawyers. Many general treatises on law devoted space to politics, natural law, and the sources and aims of the law.[65] James Sullivan, in his *History of Land Titles in Massachusetts*, published in 1801 in Boston, saw fit to add to his book some "General Observations on the Nature of Laws in General, and those of the United States in particular."[66] The rest of the book was a conventional treatment of the American law of real property.

Even before 1800, some American lawyers struck out on their own. Zephaniah Swift published his *System of the Laws of Connecticut* in 1795–96. In 1810, he wrote a *Digest of the Law of Evidence in Civil and Criminal Cases* and a *Treatise on Bills of Exchange and Promissory Notes*. His books were informative and as readable as their subjects would allow. He propounded no grand theories; but was content, as he said in the *Evidence*, "to arrange the subject in a plain but systematic manner."[67] Swift was not afraid to criticize as well as arrange. For example, he attacked the American rule that the plaintiff (in discovery proceedings) was bound by the defendant's disclosures and might not contradict them. "This practice," he said, "must have been adopted at an early period, without due consideration."[68] Characteristically, Swift's criticism did not flow from any systematic theory of justice or law, clearly articulated. Criticism was always piecemeal and pragmatic. Later

[65]The first volume of Blackstone's *Commentaries* had also dealt with these general subjects.

[66]James Sullivan, *The History of Land Titles in Massachusetts* (1801), pp. 337–56. Emory Washburn (1800–1877), who became a judge, governor of Massachusetts, and then professor of law at Harvard, published a number of works in legal history, notably *Sketches of the Judicial History of Massachusetts, 1630–1775* (1840). On Washburn's career, see Robert M. Spector, "Emory Washburn: Conservator of the New England Legal Heritage," 22 Am. J. Legal Hist. 118 (1978).

[67]Zephaniah Swift, *Digest of the Law of Evidence in Civil and Criminal Cases* (1810), preface, p. x.

[68]*Ibid.*, p. 120.

treatises had the same general features. Among the most popular or durable were the *Treatise on the Law of Private Corporations Aggregate* by Joseph K. Angell and Samuel Ames (1832); Simon Greenleaf's treatise on *Evidence* (1842); Henry Wheaton's *Elements of International Law* (1836); and Theodore Sedgwick's *Treatise on the Measure of Damages* (1847). A more general work was Timothy Walker's *Introduction to American Law* (1837). The book was designed for students, was enormously successful, and went through many editions. Nathan Dane's *General Abridgement and Digest of American Law*, in eight volumes (1823–24; a supplemental ninth volume was published in 1829), has already been mentioned. The "abridgement" was a loosely organized work; this had also been true of the earlier English "abridgements." As literature, it had little to recommend it. In a contemporary's view, Dane "had no graces of style, either native or borrowed; neither did he ever seek for any."[69] But lawyers bought the abridgement for their working libraries; and Dane made enough money to become a patron at Harvard.

Even less pretentious were works at the other end of the spectrum of generality—local practice manuals and helpful guides of one sort or another, for particular jurisdictions. William W. Henning's *The New Virginia Justice* (1795), a guide for justices of the peace, represented a numerous genre, with many English and colonial ancestors. The book was vaguely designed for lay judges—perhaps for fledgling lawyers too. It quoted statutes, set out simple legal forms, and digested some relevant cases. Similar works appeared in other states. John F. Grimké (1752–1819) wrote *The South Carolina Justice of the Peace* in 1788 and the *Duty of Executors and Administrators* in 1797. Esek Cowen wrote a *Treatise on the Civil Jurisdiction of Justices of the Peace in the State of New York* in 1821; this was a guide for the perplexed (lay) justice, perhaps also (Cowen hoped) "useful to the man of business," and even to Cowen's "brethren of the profession." Still lower on the literary scale were simple form-books and guides for the laymen, works with the ubiquitous title *Every Man His Own Lawyer*, or books with names like the *Western Clerks' Assistant* or *The Business Man's Assistant*. This last was a compendium of "useful forms of legal instruments," together with tables of interest, currency information, "laws, instructions and forms necessary for obtaining a patent," and

---

[69]"Biographical Notice of the Honorable Nathan Dane," 14 Am. Jurist 62, 67–68 (1835).

"agreements for constructing railroads." It claimed to have reached its 33rd thousand at the time it was reprinted in Boston in 1847 by one D. R. Butts, "assisted by an attorney." Richard Henry Dana (1815–82), best known as the author of *Two Years Before the Mast* (1840), wrote a manual on the law of the sea called *The Seamen's Friend*, in 1841.

Legal periodicals were few, and even fewer had much of a life span.[70] Before 1830, twelve periodicals were founded. *The American Law Journal and Miscellaneous Repository* was one of these, published in Philadelphia in 1808, but it expired within a decade. Most of its pages were devoted to case reports and digests of statutes; but there was also some secondary writing on legal subjects. Periodicals of this type competed weakly with the reports; they reprinted key decisions and other primary sources of law. Better reporting put most of them out of business. In 1810 only one periodical was actually in existence; this was also true in 1820. In 1830 there were five. *The American Jurist and Law Magazine* (1829–42), founded by Willard Phillips, was one of the five. More pretentious and successful than most, it contained scholarly essays on points of law, case notes, historical notes, and question-and-answer materials. Prominent members of the Boston bar, including Joseph Story, often contributed to the journal.

By common consent, the two most significant figures in American legal literature in the first half of the 19th century were James Kent and Joseph Story. Both were erudite teachers and judges. Both had enormous reputations in their day. Both have since suffered a decline in prestige, and an irretrievable decline in their readership. In their day, their reputations went further than any other legal scholars in America. No one on the Continent had ever heard of James Sullivan or Zephaniah Swift. But Joseph Story was a name that won respect even from continental jurists. And when Kent's *Commentaries* were published, George Bancroft said: "Now we know what American law is; we know it is a science."[71]

Joseph Story was born in 1779 and died in 1845.[72] In 1811, at the age of thirty-two, he was appointed to the United States Su-

---

[70]On the periodicals of this period, see Maxwell Bloomfield, "Law vs. Politics: The Self-Image of the American Bar (1830–1860)," 12 Am. J. Legal Hist. 306, 309–19 (1968).

[71]Quoted in Warren, *op. cit.*, p. 543.

[72]See Mortimer D. Schwartz and John C. Hogan, eds., *Joseph Story* (1959); Gerald T. Dunne, "Joseph Story: The Germinal Years," 75 Harv. L. Rev. 707 (1962); Gerald T. Dunne, *Justice Joseph Story and the Rise of the Supreme Court* (1970).

preme Court. Contrary to expectations, since he was nominally a
follower of Jefferson, he became John Marshall's strong right arm
on the court. In 1829, he was named Dane professor at Harvard.
He did not resign from the court. As Dane professor, however,
he wrote his series of *Commentaries,* published between 1831 and
1845. He was a man of vast, almost ponderous erudition. According to his son,

> He was well versed in the classics of Greece and Rome....
> He was a good historical scholar; and in the sciences and
> mechanic arts, he had attained to considerable proficiency.
> He was omnivorous of knowledge.... No legal work ap-
> peared, that he did not examine.[73]

Story was not one to wear his erudition lightly. In his seminal
work on the conflict of laws (1834), which systematized a new field
(at least in the United States) out of virtually nothing, one page
(360) has three lines of French and six of Latin, and quotes from
Louis Boullenois, Achille Rodemburg, P. Voet, J. Voet, C. d'Ar-
gentre, and U. Huberus, names that the American lawyer would
find totally mysterious.

Story's erudition was not always so blatant; and this particular
subject matter had hardly been treated by writers in English.
Learning did not interfere with the main line of Story's argument,
which proceeded clearly and stoutly, even gracefully at times. Story's erudition was organic; it involved his whole attitude toward
law. He was a scholar and a traditionalist; he had reverence for
the law and for the past. As he saw it, law was completely a product
of history, of the historical dialectic of ideas. Without deep, total
understanding of its history, it was foolhardy to try to interfere
with the law and its modes of operation. Story fully agreed with
Sir Edward Coke that the common law was reason personified;
that it was not the parochial product of English or American
experience, but a branch of the great, ancient tree of human
wisdom. He was, in a sense, a legal pantheist. He saw divinity in
Roman law as well as in common law. But for that very reason,
he worshiped the law of his state and his nation; he saw them as
connected with mighty currents of law that swept through human
history; the precise development of one's own legal institutions
was a specific adaptation of great general principles. In his treatise
on *Equity Jurisprudence* (1835), Story asked:

[73]Schwartz and Hogan, *op. cit.,* p. 202.

Whether it would, or would not, be best to administer the whole of remedial justice in one Court, or in one class of Courts, without any separation or distinctions of suits, or of the form or modes of proceeding and granting relief.

One might have guessed that a Massachusetts lawyer with a profound knowledge of European law would have no difficulty in seeing that law and equity should properly be joined.[74] But Story does not commit himself. He begins by quoting Francis Bacon: all nations have some equivalent of equity, at least in the broad sense of the word. Bacon thought it might be harmful to mix law and equity in one and the same institution. Six lines of Baconian Latin follow. Then Story refers to the civil law, where "the general, if not the universal, practice is the other way."

> But whether the one opinion, or the other, be most correct in theory, it is most probable, that the practical system, adopted by every nation, has been mainly influenced by the peculiarities of its own institutions, habits, and circumstances; and especially by the nature of its own jurisprudence, and the forms of its own remedial justice.... The question...never can be susceptible of any universal solution.[75]

James Kent, the second major figure of American legal literature, was born in New York in 1763. He went to Yale, then read law, and became a member of the New York bar in 1785. Like Story, Kent had a distinguished career on the bench. He served as chancellor of New York from 1814 to 1823. He was forced into premature retirement by provisions of the New York constitution of 1821 that fixed a maximum age—sixty—for judges. In retirement, Kent wrote his masterpiece, *Commentaries on American Law,* in four volumes, published between 1826 and 1830. The bar received this work with enthusiasm from the moment it came out. Kent continued to bring out fresh editions until his death in 1847. The work was so popular that more editions continued to appear after Kent's death, with new editors. The 12th edition (1873) was edited by young Oliver Wendell Holmes, Jr.

Nobody reads Kent any more (or, for that matter, Story; or even Blackstone). Perry Miller found Kent a "bore"; he was re-

---

[74]Massachusetts, it will be recalled, had no separate courts of equity; and such a thing was of course unknown to Continental law.

[75]Joseph Story, *Commentaries on Equity Jurisprudence,* vol. I (1836), pp. 34–36.

pelled by Kent's "stiffly neoclassical rhetoric"; Kent's "treatment of almost all areas" he thought "platitudinous."[76] But it is possible to read Kent and find him quite enjoyable. Kent intended his huge work to be the national Blackstone. To a considerable degree, he succeeded in this aim. Like Story, he was cautious and erudite. But he had little of Blackstone's smugness and self-satisfaction, and little of Story's stultifying pedantry. The style is at all points clear, the exposition transparent. Occasionally, Kent even turns a decent phrase or two. He had a sure and impressive grasp of the whole fabric of American law. His jurisprudential thought was not original or profound; but his attitude toward the living law was pragmatic, hard-boiled, and often shrewd.

Too much emphasis has been placed on Kent's conservatism. His biographer subtitled his book "A Study in Conservatism."[77] To be sure, Kent was not on the left, even in his day. He fought doggedly in New York against repeal of the property qualification for voters; he lost this fight. History is cruel to losers. Kent was old-fashioned, in a sense, but he was never romantic or naive. He had no use for the obsolete, no aversion to productive change. No American, except a dyed-in-the-wool Tory, could have been thoroughly committed to the legal *status quo*. This would have meant denouncing American law in general, and defiling the American revolution. Kent was no Tory of this stamp. His love for the American way emerges constantly in his discussions of the law. On dower, for example, he remarks that, "In this country, we are, happily, not very liable to be perplexed by such abstruse questions and artificial rules, which have encumbered the subject ... in England to a grievous extent."[78]

Kent is often put in the camp of enemies of codification. But he had praise for the American law of "crimes and punishments. ... The law ... has become quite simple in its principles, and concise and uniform in its details. Our criminal codes bear no kind of comparison with the complex and appalling catalogue of crimes and punishments ... in England."[79] He had a deep respect for property rights, but a tremendous concern for enterprise as well. He loved law as an instrument both of security and of mobility.

---

[76]Perry Miller, *The Legal Mind in America: From Independence to the Civil War* (1962), p. 92.

[77]John T. Horton, *James Kent, A Study in Conservatism, 1763–1847* (1939).

[78]Kent, *Commentaries*, vol. IV (2nd ed., 1832), p. 52.

[79]*Ibid.*, p. 544.

He had no sentimental attachment to tradition, if it interfered with the "stability and energy" of property. He wanted law to serve the cause of economic growth, to protect institutions that worked. What was conservative, perhaps, was his pessimism. He was profoundly skeptical about human nature. This made him suspicious of some kinds of reform; he often doubted whether basic human behavior patterns could be changed merely by tinkering with statutes. Many lawyers shared his belief. Many drew different political conclusions from similar premises. But there was no disputing Kent's clarity, his common sense, his skill in expounding the law. The *Commentaries* deserved to be what they became from the moment of publication: a best seller of American law.

PART III

American Law to the Close
of the 19th Century

CHAPTER I

BLOOD AND GOLD: SOME MAIN THEMES
IN THE LAW IN THE LAST HALF
OF THE 19TH CENTURY

THE NEW ERA

The years of the last half of the 19th century were crowded with events and evolutions. The most dramatic outer happening was the Civil War, when the country tore apart along the jagged line between North and South. Hundreds of thousands of soldiers died between 1861 and 1865. The century also ended with a war— a "splendid little war," compared to the blood and devastation of the Civil War; and when this war, with Spain, came to an end, the country owned an overseas empire.

In many ways, wars fundamentally disrupt the operation of the legal system. The Civil War was fought on American soil. It was an unusually violent episode, and it did unusual violence to the ordinary administration of justice. It was also a constitutional crisis. It was followed by a period of martial law and domestic upheaval in the South. The war required enormous effort—armies had to be raised and equipped; unprecedented problems had to be solved. All this meant a dramatic escalation in the role of the national government. This too was reflected in many ways in every part of the law.

It is not hard to argué that American law, between 1850 and 1900, underwent revolutionary change. In many fields, the law or the practice looked entirely different at the end of this period, compared to the beginning. There was, in short, rapid, unprecedented change; but often change came about because of the cumulative effect of tiny events, each one insignificant in itself. And some of these changes continued trends established earlier in the century.

337

Between 1850 and 1900, the population swelled; the cities grew enormously; the Far West was settled; the country became a major industrial power; transportation and communication vastly improved; overseas expansion began. New inventions and new techniques made life easier and healthier; at the same time, the social order became immeasurably more complex, and perhaps more difficult for the average person to grasp. New social cleavages developed. The North-South cleavage was bandaged over in the 1860s and 1870s. The black man was put back in a subordinate place. When the blood of the Civil War dried, the Gilded Age began. This was the factory age, the age of money, the age of the robber barons, of capital and labor at war. And the frontier died. The pioneer, the frontier individualist, had been the American culture hero, free, self-reliant, unencumbered by the weakness that inhered in the cities. The frontier had been a symbol of an open society; opportunity was as unlimited as the sky. In 1893, Frederick Jackson Turner wrote his famous essay, "The Significance of the Frontier in American History." He traced the influence of the frontier on American character and institutions; but as he wrote the essay, Turner also announced that the frontier was dead.

What really passed was not the frontier, but the idea of the frontier. This inner sense, this *perception* of change, was perhaps one of the most important influences on American law. Between 1776 and the Civil War, dominant public opinion exuberantly believed in growth, believed that resources were virtually unlimited, that there would be room and wealth for all. The theme of American law before 1850 was the release of energy, in Willard Hurst's phrase. Develop the land; grow rich; a rising tide raises all boats. By 1900, if one can speak about so slippery a thing as dominant public opinion, that opinion saw a narrowing sky, a dead frontier, life as a struggle for position, competition as a zero-sum game, the economy as a pie to be divided, not a ladder stretching out beyond the horizon. By 1900 the theme was: hold the line.[1]

Many trends, developments, and movements provide at least indirect evidence of some such basic change in legal culture. One

[1]We are speaking only of the United States, and only relatively. It was probably also true *after* 1870 that, compared to other societies and other periods, Americans were still a "people of plenty" and that the sense and reality of abundance profoundly shaped the national experience. David M. Potter, *People of Plenty* (1954). On the nature of law in this period in general, see Morton Keller, *Affairs of State: Public Life in Late 19th-Century America* (1977), ch. 9.

piece of evidence was the increasing propensity of Americans to join together in organized interest groups. The United States became a "nation of joiners." De Tocqueville had already noted in his travels a magnificent flowering of clubs and societies in America. "Americans," he wrote, "of all ages, all stations in life, and all types of disposition are forever forming associations... religious, moral, serious, futile, very general and very limited, immensely large and very minute."[2] But organization in the last half of the 19th century was more than a matter of clubs and societies. Noticeably, there developed groupings which centered around economic interests—labor unions, industrial combines, farmers' organizations, occupational associations. These interest groups jockeyed for position and power in society. They molded, dominated, shaped American law.

A group or association has two aspects: it defines some people in, and some people out. People joined together in groups not simply for mutual help, but to exclude, to define an enemy, to make common cause against outsiders. Organization was a law of life, not merely because life was so complicated, but also because life seemed to be a competitive struggle, jungle warfare over limited resources, a game in which if railroads won, farmers lost, or if labor won, employers lost.

The consequences were fundamental. At first, this was a country wide open for immigration; by the end of the period, Congress had passed Chinese exclusion laws, and there were demands for literacy tests; ultimately, in 1924, the country adopted a quota system.[3] Resources, in 1800, looked inexhaustible; by 1900, it seemed clear that natural resources could be chopped, burned, and eroded past recovery; extinction threatened many birds and animals; a conservation movement was already under way. Government, in 1840, was boosting railroads; in 1880, it was trying to control them, or pretending to try. In general, before the Civil War, leaders of opinion looked at government, and law, as ways to unleash the capacity of the nation. After the war, government's role began slowly to change to that of regulator and trustee. There was bitter opposition, of course, to this new-minted role. Much of the opposition was couched in ideological terms. But the fundamental issues were issues of economic and political strength.

[2]Arthur Schlesinger, "Biography of a Nation of Joiners," 50 Am. Hist. Rev. 1 (1944); Alexis de Tocqueville, *Democracy in America* (J. P. Mayer and M. Lerner, eds., 1966), p. 485.

[3]Maldwyn A. Jones, *American Immigration* (1960), pp. 247–77.

The Revolutionary generation had been suspicious of *any* governmental power. The generation of the Gilded Age was still suspicious of imbalance of power. But significant segments of the public saw danger from outside government as well: danger not only from the tyranny of the state, but also from the tyranny of the trusts, or big business in general, or (conversely) from the "dangerous classes" or the urban proletariat. American optimism was balanced by a growing pessimism that the charmed life of America might come to an end unless people mounted a major battle against creeping decay.

Of course, none of these changes took place overnight. There had been unions and farm groups and big companies before the Civil War. What changed was scope and scale and intensity. The stakes were high. American law was an essential instrument or weapon in economic struggle. Classic English law was a law of and for an elite. In America, more and more people had a stake in the system. This meant that law was necessary, and accessible, to a broad and diverse middle class; that law could serve as a social instrument of great power. Hence the struggle to control the operations of law. Each session of an American legislature was a cockpit of contention between interests. In the Midwest, in the early 1870s, the organized farmers had their day. Their legislation (the Granger laws) merely paid railroads and grain elevators back for what *they* had done to farmers when *they* were at the helm. Or so the farmers thought. Less dramatically, in the 1890s, there was a great rush to pass occupational licensing laws: for plumbers, barbers, horseshoers, lawyers, pharmacists, midwives, and nurses. These laws cemented (or tried to cement) the economic position of the people that lobbied for them in the first place: the organized trade group. It is naive to think of these laws as hostile regulation, or as laws passed by legislators sincerely devoted to the "public interest."

The struggle against industrial combines—the dreaded trusts—was part of the general struggle for a "fair share" of the economy, as the various interest groups viewed it. It was not a struggle to keep free enterprise pure. It would be a mistake to read much economic theory into the passage of the Sherman Anti-Trust Act (1890). Small business, farmers, independent professionals, all feared the *power* of the trusts; antitrust laws were an attempt to use law to cut that power down to size. Regulation, trust-busting, licensing, labor legislation: all these were part of the same general battle of all against all, a battle for security, wealth, prestige, authority, for all the social goods. The power of the state—the law, in short—was both a means and an end in the battle: a way to achieve social goods, and a charter of the dominance of one set of norms and values. The ideal of individual autonomy still remained strong. The farmer, for example, still valued his independence. But he sought government intervention precisely for this reason: to counterbalance those mighty forces (railroads, for example) that held him in their grip and threatened that very independence.

The railroads, of course, fought back. Thus the typical outcome of contention in the legislative chamber was some sort of compromise. No one group was ever absolute. Law was made by hammering out bargains, some explicit, some not. Since power was not evenly distributed, some bargains were more one-sided than others. And of course some groups were so weak, so unorganized, or so oppressed that they were in effect chased away from the bargaining table. Nobody spoke very loudly for the interests of black sharecroppers, or "tramps," or prisoners, or the desperately poor.

Different legal institutions were valuable in different ways and to different groups. Because there were so many power centers, so many little fiefdoms and bailiwicks, so much checking and balancing, groups could pick and choose among parts of the system for leverage and for veto power. In some states, labor was relatively strong in the legislature; hence management turned to the courts. Other groups and individuals also tried their hand at this game. In this period, judicial review reached a stage of fresh power, or—in the view of some critics—bizarre excess. Some of the most prominent, or notorious, decisions had a quite conservative cast. Social Darwinism had its converts on the bench. This was also the period of the equity receivership, and the period when the labor injunction was born. It was the period, too, in which lawyers themselves felt the urge to organize, to cement their positions, to move ahead. It was therefore an age in which lawyers and judges invented fresh myths and disguises to protect their roles.

Quite naturally, in this period, since social change was so deep, legal culture changed along with it; and every significant field of law was profoundly reworked by social forces. Some changes were swift, and the rite of passage plain to see. Other changes took place obscurely, in the dull dishwater law of the dockets. But each hard little nugget of new doctrine had its point of origin in some concrete, living issue. However much judges liked to clothe doctrine in history and in the costume of timeless values, doctrine was still at bottom flesh and blood, the flesh and blood of real, contemporary struggles over goods and positions and authority.

ORGANIC LAW

The Civil War was a profound constitutional crisis. The Union broke apart in 1861; but the Constitution survived. In fact, the idea of the Constitution was never really attacked. The Confederate states adopted their own constitution, suspiciously like the federal Constitution in many details. It provided for a Supreme Court; but this court in fact never sat, in fact was never organized.[4] The end of the Civil War proved, not that American government was stable and permanent, but that crisis and change could be accommodated within the aging language of that one and only Constitution, somewhat amended from time to time.

The Constitution did not look much different, on paper, in 1900 from the way it looked in 1800. The major novelties were the three Civil War amendments, the thirteenth, fourteenth, and fifteenth. These were rammed down the throats of the Southern states. Ratification was so highhanded that over a century later there are still a few diehards who argue that the process was illegal, and even dream that these clauses may somehow go away. These were crucial amendments in making the Civil War victory permanent. The thirteenth amendment abolished slavery. The fifteenth amendment guaranteed the right to vote to all citizens, regardless of "race, color, or previous condition of servitude." The fourteenth amendment has had the most marvelous career of the three. It was the longest of the amendments; most of its language was tied to specific consequences of the Civil War. But some of the language was broad and sweeping. All persons born or naturalized in the United States were "citizens of the United

---

[4]William M. Robinson, Jr., *Justice in Grey: A History of the Judicial System of the Confederate States of America* (1941), pp. 437–57; see, in general, Charles R. Lee, Jr., *The Confederate Constitutions* (1963).

States and of the State wherein they reside." No state could "abridge" their "privileges or immunities." No state could deprive any "person" of "life, liberty, or property, without due process of law"; nor could a state deny "to any person within its jurisdiction the equal protection of the laws."

What was the "original understanding"?[5] Did these clauses work some kind of revolution? Did they fundamentally change the power relationship between the states and the federal government? Specifically, were they intended to engraft some kind of *laissez-faire* theory onto the country's organic law? Were they meant to give Congress, or the courts, some undefined power to supervise the social and economic activities of local governments? Or were they nothing more than expanded guarantees of rights for blacks? Whatever the draftsmen meant at the time, it is certainly true that the Fourteenth Amendment turned out to have marvelous powers of germination. The innocent words "due process" made up one magic phrase. "Equal protection of the laws" was another. In the last two decades of the century, state courts, and some federal courts, used the due-process clause as a hook on which to hang a sweeping authority: no less than the authority to declare void offensive and unreasonable state laws. In some famous and infamous cases, the courts made the clause seem the very voice of economic reaction. When a state passes a law to regulate or prohibit some activity, the law at least can be *said* to take away "liberty," or "property," from people who would otherwise carry on that activity. If the law is "unreasonable," the court can at least *say* that this deprivation was without "due process of law."

This use of the clause was foreshadowed in Justice Joseph Bradley's dissent, in the famous *Slaughter-House* cases (1873).[6] Louisiana had passed a statute, in 1869, that gave a monopoly to the Crescent City Live-Stock Landing and Slaughter-House Company; Crescent City had the exclusive right to slaughter cattle in New Orleans. The law threatened to drive all other butchers out of business; they went to court to fight off the law. A bare majority of the Supreme Court held what would have been self-evident two generations before: that the Constitution had nothing to say about

[5]See, in general, Harold M. Hyman and William M. Wiecek, *Equal Justice under Law: Constitutional Development, 1835–1875* (1982), ch. 11.
[6]16 Wall. 36 (1873).

the killing of intrastate pigs. Bradley, however, argued that the law was "onerous, unreasonable, arbitrary and unjust"; that a law which "prohibits a large class of citizens from ... following a lawful employment previously adopted" deprives them of "liberty" and "property."

In the course of time, Bradley's ideas won more converts on the Court. In *Chicago, Milwaukee and St. Paul Railway Company* v. *Minnesota* (1890),[7] Minnesota had established a railroad and warehouse commission, and had given it power to fix freight rates. The commission ordered the railroad to reduce freight rates from three cents a gallon to not more than two and a half cents a gallon on milk transported from Owatonna, Faribault, Dundas, Northfield, and Farmington, to St. Paul and Minneapolis. This half-cent a gallon made legal history. The Supreme Court, speaking through Justice Samuel Blatchford, struck down the Minnesota statute creating the commission:

> The question of reasonableness of a rate of charge for transportation by a railroad company ... is eminently a question for judicial investigation, requiring due process of law for its determination. If the company is deprived of the power of charging reasonable rates for the use of its property, and such deprivation takes place in the absence of an investigation by judicial machinery, it is deprived of the lawful use of its property, and thus, in substance and effect, of the property itself.[8]

Two aspects of the case are worth noting: first, the conservative tenor of the decision as far as the *economy* is concerned; second, its radical tenor as far as *judicial power* is concerned. Both aspects drew fire from the great American left-of-center, which was at war with the court off and on until the later New Deal period. Undeniably, *some* major constitutional decisions, both state and federal, were both conservative in result and radical in method. The number of these cases can be easily exaggerated. On the whole, federal courts threw out only a minority of the state regulatory statutes that came before them for review. On the other

[7]134 U.S. 418 (1890).

[8]*Ibid.*, p. 458. Interestingly enough, Justice Bradley dissented in this case. One effect of the case was to weaken the authority of *Munn* v. *Illinois*, 94 U.S. 113 (1877), which had upheld an Illinois statute fixing maximum charges for grain elevators.

hand, some legislatures may have lost enthusiasm for social legislation because of the doctrines or realities of judicial review. It is impossible to say for sure.

Toward the federal government, the court was more deferential. After *Marbury* v. *Madison,* there was no clear-cut example of a case striking down a federal law until the *Dred Scott* case in 1857,[9] which destroyed the Missouri Compromise. The Court's experience with this case and with the *Legal Tender* cases[10] was not calculated to encourage overuse of this powerful weapon. But the Melville W. Fuller court, between 1889 and 1899, did declare five federal acts unconstitutional, along with thirty-four state acts and four municipal ordinances.[11]

Heavy use of the fourteenth amendment occurred only at the very end of the 19th century. In the first decade of the amendment, the United States Supreme Court decided only three cases, in the next decade, forty-six. After 1896, "the flood burst. Between that date and the end of the 1905 term of court, two hundred and ninety-seven cases were passed upon under the amendment—substantially all under the 'due process' and 'equal protection' clauses."[12] These figures do not tell the whole story of the impact of the court on the legal and economic systems. The impact, unfortunately, cannot be measured, as we mentioned already. But whatever that impact, clearly the Supreme Court had developed a dangerous appetite for power. From then on, it was like a man-eating tiger; everyone in its shadow had to cope with its awesome and lethal tastes.

[9]*Dred Scott* v. *Sandford,* 60 U.S. 383 (1857). There is a huge literature on this case. See Stanley I. Kutler, ed., *The Dred Scott Decision: Law or Politics?* (1967); and Don Fehrenbacher, *The Dred Scott Case: Its Significance in American Law and Politics* (1978).

[10]*Hepburn* v. *Griswold,* 75 U.S. 603 (1870), which ruled that the Legal Tender Acts, passed during the Civil War, were invalid, was overruled in the *Legal Tender* cases, 79 U.S. 457 (1871).

[11]These figures are from William F. Swindler, *Court and Constitution in the 20th Century: The Old Legality, 1889–1932* (1969), p. 344. The worst was yet to come. The Edward D. White court invalidated twenty-two state statutes in a single year (1915); the William H. Taft court's finest hour was 1926, when twenty statutes fell. *Ibid.,* p. 345.

[12]Edward S. Corwin, *The Twilight of the Supreme Court: A History of Our Constitutional Theory* (1934), p. 77.

STATE CONSTITUTIONS

The United States Constitution was a steadfast rock compared to the state constitutions. These were on the whole far more brittle. A few states have gone through their history with a single constitution (though perhaps liberally amended). No state had a *coup d'état*. But almost every state convened a constitutional convention, at least once in the period, to draft a new constitution. Some conventions labored in vain. A convention was held in Springfield, Illinois, in 1862: it produced a constitution that was massively rejected at the polls.[13] But particularly in the South, there was a great deal of molting of constitutions. Each Southern state typically had a Reconstruction constitution.[14] This came to be denounced as a carpetbag charter, when the wheel of politics turned, and a new constitution was then adopted. The Arkansas constitution of 1868 restricted the right to vote or hold office of leaders of the "late rebellion." In 1874, when the older elites were restored to power, a new constitution was adopted. This constitution, among other things, dropped the elaborate franchise provisions of 1868. It provided that "no power, civil or military," should ever interfere "to prevent the free exercise of the right of suffrage"; and that no law would make the right to vote dependent on "previous registration of the elector's name" (Ark. const. 1874, art. III, sec. 2; Ark. const. 1868, art. VIII, secs. 3, 4, 5).

There was great diversity in state constitution making. Region differed from region, state from state; but some clear patterns emerged. For one thing, state constitutions grew longer and bigger. Most of the states had come to feel that public order demanded more of a constitution than a bare frame of government; and particularly that legislatures could not always be trusted to act honestly and in the public interest. Restrictions and controls on lawmaking had already appeared in the years before 1850; now the trend grew stronger. The new constitutions tried to con-

[13]Emil J. Verlie, ed., *Illinois Constitutions* (1919), p. xxvii.
[14]The Federal Reconstruction Acts—14 Stats. 428 (act of March 2, 1867), 15 Stats. 2 (act of March 23, 1867) and 15 Stats. 14 (act of July 19, 1867)—made restoration of civil government dependent on approval of the fourteenth amendment, and on adoption of a constitution, with full suffrage for blacks, ratified by Congress and by an electorate from which Confederate leaders were excluded.

trol the problem of bad laws through their own, overriding superlaws, which took the form indeed of antilaws—that is (constitutional) laws against (legislative) laws. Moreover, the trend toward the inflation of constitutional texts continued. Indeed, it was almost out of hand.

Louisiana takes some sort of prize for fickleness and inflation. By 1847, it had already gone through two constitutions; before 1900 it added five more, in 1852, 1864, 1868, 1879 and 1898 (six, if one counts as a separate charter the revised constitution of 1861, which carried Louisiana out of the Union). The constitution of 1879 was already obese; that of 1898 was grotesque. It ran to 326 articles. It fixed the yearly salary of the governor at $5,000 and the lieutenant governor's pay at $1,500 (art. 68, art. 70). It put a limit on the "clerical expenses" of state officials; the state treasurer, for example, was not to spend more than $2,000 a year. Twenty-eight separate articles dealt with the government of the city and parish of New Orleans. The jurisdiction of state courts was specified, to the last jot and tittle. One article created a "Railroad, Express, Telephone, Telegraph, Steamboat and other Water Craft, and Sleeping Car Commission" (art. 283). The article then went on to enumerate the commission's powers, in elaborate detail. Buried in the mass of specifics were provisions of sharper bite— cutting off, in effect, the black man's right to vote. But the detail was so gross, and so stultifying, that the constitution was bound to fail, or, if it survived, to need constant bandaging through amendments. In fact, this constitution was amended twenty-six times before 1907. The twenty-fifth amendment (1906) authorized, among other things, an appropriation for the Southern University at New Orleans, but of no more than $10,000 a year.

As before, states freely borrowed constitutional clauses from each other, either from important recent constitutions, or (in the West) from the home state of the settlers. Some major issues were, and had to be, thrashed out each time afresh. But settled matters, dead issues, and convenient ways of saying things were freely borrowed. Settled, of course, did not mean unimportant; for example, each new state copied a Bill of Rights from older states, in a fairly stereotyped form. More than half of the Oregon constitution of 1859 can be traced to the Indiana constitution of 1851. Other bits were modeled on clauses from the Iowa, Maine, Massachusetts, Michigan, Ohio, Illinois, Connecticut, Wisconsin, and Texas constitutions. The Wisconsin constitution of 1848 bor-

rowed, without much thought, provisions against long-term agricultural leases and feudal tenures. These came from New York
and reflected the Hudson Valley problem and the antirent disorders—problems with no real counterpart in Wisconsin. The
Nevada convention of 1864 was based on California patterns. This
was no wonder; all but two of the delegates had moved to Nevada
from California.[15] The Colorado constitution of 1876 was a model
and a debating point for those Rocky Mountain states—Idaho,
Wyoming, Montana—with similar problems of eminent domain,
taxation of mining industries, and water rights.[16]

The trend toward curbing legislative power was strong in the
1850s. Rhode Island, by an amendment of 1854, took the pardoning power away from the legislature and gave it to the governor. State after state decided that their legislature could meet
less often and still get their business done. State after state decided
to limit the power of legislatures to make law and spend money.
Maryland, in 1851, increased the governor's term from one to
four years. At the same time, a biennial legislature was told not
to establish lotteries, grant divorces, use the credit of the state for
the special benefit of private persons or corporations, appropriate
money for internal improvements, or contract debts for more than
$100,000.[17] Small issues, such as the legislative divorce, were only
symptoms. There was a general rejection of the idea of an elastic,
living constitution, at least on the state level. The real issue was
fear of abuse: fear of corruption in the legislature, and the corrosive effects of great power.

Actually, most constitutional conventions were called to deal
with major problems—railroad or bank regulation, or the suffrage problem. Reapportionment was another frequent issue—
the attempt to shift political power from the east end of a state
to the west, or from lowland to highland. The Iowa convention
of 1857 was convened, after a referendum, partly because the
"people of Iowa were anxious to repeal the restrictions upon banking."[18] The Southern conventions of the postwar 1860s were called

---

[15]*Official Report of the Debates and Proceedings in the Constitutional Convention of
the State of Nevada, 1864* (1866), p. xvi.

[16]Gordon M. Bakken, "The Impact of the Colorado State Constitution on Rocky
Mountain Constitution Making," 47 Colo. Magazine, No. 2, p. 152 (1970).

[17]Fletcher M. Green, *Constitutional Development in the South Atlantic States, 1776–
1860* (1930), pp. 285–86.

[18]*Debates of the Constitutional Convention of the State of Iowa,* vol. I (1857), p. ii.

to accept the results of losing the war. The Southern conventions of the 1870s were called to undo these constitutions, and to make sure the white man won the peace. At the Nevada convention of 1864, there were furious debates about taxation of mines and mining enterprise. Some issues turned out to be so divisive that the convention turned them over to popular referendum. This was done with a controversial banking provision, in Wisconsin in 1848, and with the women's-suffrage issue, thirty years later, in Colorado.

The constitutions of the 1870s, in general, went a long way in restricting the power of the legislature. In the third Illinois constitution, adopted in 1870, the judiciary was revamped; the governor's power was increased; the legislature was put under greater controls. The constitution outlawed many kinds of "local or special laws"; the legislature was not to use this vehicle to grant divorces, change rates of interest on money, provide for "the sale or mortgage of real estate belonging to minors or others under disability," make laws to protect fish or game, or grant "to any corporation, association, or individual the right to lay down railroad tracks," among other things. There were twenty-three of these prohibitions in all. Moreover, "in all other cases where a general law can be made applicable, no special law shall be enacted."[19] Later states copied this list, or similar lists, and often added new restrictions. In the 1889 constitution of North Dakota, the twenty-three specific prohibitions had grown to thirty-five.[20]

Behind the Illinois constitution was fear of gross economic power, so gross it could buy and sell an upper and lower house. The constitution reflected the fears and interests of the farmers of the state. It was the first of the midwestern Granger constitutions. These 1870s constitutions typically provided for tighter regulation of railroads and warehouses. The aim was to provide some sort of countervailing force to balance the great lobbies. A special article (art. XIII) of the Illinois constitution, seven sections long, dealt with regulation of grain elevators and warehouses. In another section, the general assembly was specifically told to "correct abuses and prevent unjust discrimination in the rates of freight and passenger tariffs on the different railroads in this State."[21]

[19] Ill. const., 1870, art. IV, sec. 22.
[20] N. Dak. const., 1889, art. II, sec. 69.
[21] Ill. const., 1870, art. XI, sec. 15.

Nebraska, in 1875, was so bold as to empower its legislators to establish "maximum rates of charges" for railroads.[22] Legislatures were supposed to work for the public interest; they were not to pass narrow, selfish laws, not to act as tools of railroads and banks. Constitutions in other parts of the country also mirrored this point of view. The Pennsylvania constitution of 1873 took many a leaf from Illinois's book. It outlawed free passes on railroads, and attempted to work out a fair and rational way to tax these companies.[23]

Control of railroads was also an issue in California, in the brawling, bitter convention of 1878–79.[24] A large and voluble bloc of radicals, called Kearneyites, after their leader Dennis Kearney, clashed repeatedly with more moderate delegates. But the end result was not notably different from, say, Illinois's or Nebraska's constitution. Agitation over Chinese labor and immigration was one special feature, however. The debates were rabidly racist in tone. The Chinese, said one delegate, were "unfit for assimilation with people of our race"; to mix with them would produce "a hybrid of the most despicable, a mongrel of the most detestable that has ever afflicted the earth." Behind the oratory was fear of the Chinese impact on wage scales. The Chinese

> have disorganized our labor system, brought thousands of our people to wretchedness and want, degraded labor to the standard of brute energy, poisoned the blood of our youth, and filled our streets with the rot of their decaying civilization. ... [The Chinese] is a sinewy, shriveled human creature, whose muscles are as iron, whose sinews are like thongs, whose nerves are like steel wires, with a stomach case lined with

[22]Neb. const., 1875, art. XI, sec. 4.

[23]Rosalind L. Branning, *Pennsylvania Constitutional Development* (1960), pp. 101–5. The specter of the mighty railroads lurked behind some apparently unrelated provisions of this constitution. One section, for example, denied to the legislature the power to authorize "investment of trust funds by executors, administrators, guardians, or other trustees in the bonds or stock of any private corporation." The clause was proposed by George W. Biddle, a Philadelphia lawyer and delegate. Biddle charged that the legislature had once passed, in indecent haste, a law which in effect made it legal for fiduciaries to buy fourth mortgage bonds of the Pennsylvania Railroad. It was his desire—the convention agreed with him—that such things should never again be allowed to happen to the money of widows and orphans. See Lawrence M. Friedman, "The Dynastic Trust," 73 Yale L.J. 547, 562 (1964).

[24]Carl B. Swisher, *Motivation and Political Technique in the California Constitutional Convention, 1878–79* (1930).

brass; a creature who can toil sixteen hours of the twenty-
four; who can live and grow fat on the refuse of any American
laborer's table.[25]

Fear of the foreigner, distrust, xenophobia, sexual paranoia
were thus added to the powerful, rotting sense of economic insecurity. Only one or two delegates—spokesmen of industry—
defended the Chinese. The convention was strongly in favor of
turning its invective into law. A proposed ban on "Asiatic cool-
ieism" would have made it illegal for any corporation, or the state,
to hire a Chinese to do any work. That the convention showed
any restraint at all was at least partly because the delegates were
aware of the distant but powerful federal Constitution, which
would have curbed the most extreme proposals.

New Western states, in the late 1880s and the 1890s, drew up
constitutions that reflected suspicion of big business. The Washington constitution (1889) outlawed free railroad passes, and ad-
jured the legislature to "pass laws establishing reasonable maximum
rates of charge for the transportation of passengers and freight
and to correct abuses." It prohibited corporations from issuing
watered stock. Another provision of this constitution declared that
"monopolies and trusts shall never be allowed in this state." Corporations were not to join together to fix prices, or limit output,
or regulate "the transportation of any product or commodity."[26]
Particularly in the West, organized labor began to make an impact
on fundamental law. Colorado, in 1876, ordered the general assembly to "provide by law for the proper ventilation of mines, the
construction of escapement-shafts and other such appliances as
may be necessary to protect the health and secure the safety of
the workmen therein"; law was also to "prohibit the employment
in the mines of children under twelve years of age."[27] Idaho, in
1889, prohibited the "employment of children under the age of
fourteen (14) years in underground mines."[28] Provisions on labor
relations were absent from the New York constitution of 1894.
But this constitution was forward-looking in other respects—in

[25]*Debates and Proceedings of the Constitutional Convention of the State of California*,
vol. 1 (1880), pp. 632–33 (remarks of John F. Miller, December 9, 1878).
[26]Wash. const., 1889, art. XII, secs. 18, 22. "The legislature shall pass laws,"
the text went on, "for the enforcement of this section," if necessary by declaring
corporate charters forfeit.
[27]Colo. const., 1876, art. XVI, sec. 2.
[28]Idaho const., 1889, art. XIII, sec. 4.

its emphasis on a professional, bureaucratic civil service (in which appointments and promotions "shall be made according to merit and fitness to be ascertained, as far as practicable by [competitive] examinations") and in its new interest in conservation (the "forest preserve as now fixed by law...shall be forever kept as wild forest lands").[29]

A different kind of conservation pervaded Southern consti-. tutions in the last part of the century. Race relations were the key. These constitutions were obsessed with the preservation of white supremacy. Blacks had to be kept in their place, legally and socially. The constitutions of the 1870s had taken away restraints on the right of "rebels" to vote. Later, when the North, the federal government, and the judiciary had evidently lost whatever taste they once had for racial equality, the South proceeded to make white supremacy a matter of fundamental law. As early as 1870, the Tennessee constitution provided that no school aided by the state "shall allow white and negro children to be received as scholars together" (art. XI, sec. 12). This constitution also prohibited the "marriage of white persons with negroes, mulattoes, or persons of mixed blood, descended from a negro to the third generation" (art. XI, sec. 14). The South Carolina constitution of 1895 had a similar clause. Ominously, this constitution contained a long paragraph on the penalties of lynching, including damages of "not less than two thousand dollars," assessed against the *county* in which the lynching took place (art. VI, sec. 6).[30] Southern constitutions also set out systematically to deprive the black man of his vote. The Mississippi constitution of 1890 set up a poll tax of two dollars. It also required (after January 1, 1892) that "every elector shall...be able to read any section of the constitution of this State; or...be able to understand the same when read to him, or give a reasonable interpretation thereof" (art. 12, secs. 243, 244). Local officials would know how to use these provisions. The Louisiana constitution of 1898 contained the famous grandfather clause: all males entitled to vote on January 21, 1867, their sons and grandsons, and naturalized persons and their sons and grandsons, were excused from the onerous "educational or property qualification" of the constitution (art. 197, sec. 5). This meant that only blacks faced these hurdles, and local registrars were only too eager to

[29]N.Y. const., 1894, art. V, sec. 9; art. VII, sec. 7.

[30]The amount could, of course, be recovered by the county from those actually at fault.

enforce these rules. The number of black voters declined in the Southern states, in some cases by 90 percent or more. Law and terror made a most effective combination.

The Utah constitution of 1895 may be taken as a summary of the state of the constitutional art toward the close of the century. It balanced the old and the borrowed against the particular and the new. Bitter conflict between Mormon and gentile left its traces on provisions outlawing polygamy and plural marriages, in the emphasis placed on religious freedom and separation of church and state, in the abolition of the probate system through which, it was thought, Mormon elders helped perpetuate their power. Western radicalism was reflected in other provisions. The legislature was ordered to prohibit women and children from working in the mines, to restrict convict labor, and to prevent "political and commercial control of employees" by their masters (art. XVI, sec. 3). The new conservation motif was also present: "The legislature shall enact laws to prevent the destruction of and to preserve the forests on the lands of the State" (art. XVIII, sec. 1). Most of the rest of the constitution (bill of rights and all) was boiler plate. The constitution as a whole was long, detailed, and diffuse. It set out the salaries of seven state officials, headed by the governor at $2,000 a year. It thus provided ample fodder for litigants and courts to feed upon.

There was all the more fodder in that many constitutions did *not* change, and all constitutions dragged along old matters from prior versions without re-examination. There *was* a high turnover in state constitutions; but many undramatic provisions were altered only at high cost and at a snail's pace. Some constitutions (for example, Delaware's in 1897) went into great detail about the number and organization of courts, jurisdiction, civil procedure, and appeal practice. In such states, court reform proceeded very slowly. Many provisions which seemed valuable when enacted became nuisances later on. In Michigan, for example, no general revision of the statute laws was constitutionally possible after 1850. Before 1850, a single man had revised the Michigan statutes; this struck many politicians in Michigan as too much concentration of power. Their solution to the problem lasted long after the problem had ended, and became a problem in its own right.[31] Michigan also found itself in acute political and financial embarrassment in

[31]See W. L. Jenks, "History of Michigan Constitutional Provision Prohibiting a General Revision of the Laws," 19 Mich. L. Rev. 615 (1921).

the 1950s, partly because the constitution did not allow the state to contract any sizable debts, a provision left over from the 19th century.

More often, fossil constitutional clauses led to elaborate circumlocution. Many of the new constitutions prohibited "local" legislation. At the time, this seemed like an important reform. It struck a blow at logrolling, venality, inefficiency. If local legislation were permitted, the legal system might fragment into something like the Holy Roman Empire, and every town and village would have its own rules. On the other hand, different parts of the state—and different cities—might *need* special legislation. Legislatures were not allowed to pass laws that applied only to one town or city; but they were allowed to put municipalities into classes, and to pass laws for all members of the class. This turned out to be an excellent loophole. The legislature could, and often did, set up classes that in fact had only a single member; in Wisconsin, a law of 1893 defined cities with more than 150,000 population as cities of the first class. There was only one: Milwaukee.[32] More blatantly, Ohio passed an act in 1891, to authorize village councils to float improvement bonds; but the act was restricted to villages which, according to the 1880 or "any subsequent federal census," had a "population of not less than three thousand three hundred and nine nor greater than three thousand three hundred and twenty." Another act, of the same year, purported to "provide a more efficient government for cities having a population of not less than 33,000 and not more than 34,000 inhabitants." This kind of pinpointing, however, ran considerable judicial risk.[33]

On the whole, however, it was fairly easy to circumvent the rule against local legislation. To say "big cities" (or "cities of the first class") rather than "Chicago" (a forbidden word) was hardly much of a burden. But when, as in Wisconsin, it was a constitutional limit on debt that had to be evaded, the evasion was *not* so free of cost. The state could not float its own bonds; the constitution outlawed "public debts" except for "extra-ordinary expenditures," and even these could not exceed $100,000 (art. 8, sec. 6). Obviously, this limitation was hard to live with in the 20th century.

[32]Laws Wis. 1893, ch. 312. See *State ex rel. Risch* v. *Board of Trustees of Policemen's Pension Fund*, 121 Wis. 44, 98 N.W. 954 (1904).

[33]Laws Ohio 1891, p. 74 (act of Mar. 4, 1891); Laws Ohio 1891, p. 77 (act of Mar. 5, 1891). A later version of this latter law, covering all cities with between 27,000 and 34,000 population, was upheld as sufficiently general in *State ex rel. Monnett* v. *Baker*, 55 Ohio St. 2, 44 N.E. 516 (1896).

To get around the law, the state used various devices. Ultimately, it hit on the device of the so-called "dummy corporation." Improvements, such as university dormitories, would be built by these corporations on state land; the corporation would lease the land from the state, then lease it right back to the state university. The university agreed to pay rent, including rent sufficient to retire the loan, which had been made from the bank to finance part of the construction. The device was upheld in 1955 as valid, and not a violation of the state constitution.[34] But the debt probably carried higher than normal interest, because it was not directly backed by the state's own credit. The fact that these nuisance clauses survived meant that they had *some* lingering political strength or attractiveness—enough to allow a kind of veto power, since it took relatively little force to block any change in so rigid a structure as a state constitution. Moreover, legislators sometimes feel they cannot get rid of a useless prohibition, because the public would misinterpret what they did. To repeal the constitutional limit on debts of state may be like repealing the adultery laws; it looks like a vote in favor of sin. It was not until 1969 that Wisconsin pulled the teeth of this archaic limitation.[35]

Judicial review of state statutes was a rare, extraordinary event in 1850; it was a common occurrence in 1900. What happened in the state courts paralleled what happened in the federal courts. The taste for power was intoxicating to some of the state tribunals. The figures speak out loud and clear. In Virginia, for example, up to the outbreak of the Civil War, the state's high court had decided only thirty-five cases in which the constitutionality of a law or practice was questioned. Of these, the court declared only four unconstitutional. Between 1861 and 1875, "a dozen or more laws or practices were declared unconstitutional."[36] The Alabama supreme court went so far as to declare an entire constitution, the constitution of 1865, null and void. But the real spurt in judicial review came at the end of the century. In Minnesota, the supreme court declared nineteen laws unconstitutional in the

[34]*State ex rel. Thomson* v. *Giessel,* 271 Wis. 15, 72 N.W. 2d 577 (1955).

[35]An amendment to art. 8, sec. 7, adopted in 1969, authorized the state to "contract public debt...to acquire, construct, develop...land, waters, property, highways, buildings...for public purposes," subject to certain limitations.

[36]Margaret V. Nelson, *A Study of Judicial Review in Virginia, 1789–1928* (1947), p. 54.

1860s. Only thirteen statutes fell in the next fifteen years. But between 1885 and 1899, approximately seventy state statutes were struck down, with a decided bunching in the last few years of the century.[37] In Utah, between 1896 and 1899, twenty-two statutes were reviewed by the Utah supreme court. Exactly half of these were declared to be mere parchment and ink.[38]

It would be an exaggeration to call the state high court a third chamber of the legislature. But such a court was a force to be reckoned with. The explosion of judicial review did not rest on the due-process clause alone or on other clauses borrowed from federal law. Due-process cases grew voluptuously; but many dramatic cases of judicial review turned on clauses with no federal counterpart at all. The wordy, excessive texts of the state constitutions were made to order for an aggressive judiciary. Technical controls over sloppy, corrupt, and selfish legislation were written into the constitutions; these too played into the hands of litigants and courts. In Indiana, for example, not a single statute in the 19th century failed because it violated the right of free speech. Eight statutes were void because they were ex post facto or because they were guilty of "impairing the obligation of contract." But eleven statutes could not meet the test that "No act shall ever be revised or amended by mere reference to its title, but the act revised, or section amended, shall be set forth and published at full length."[39]

Another fruitful clause for judicial review was the clause that provided that "Every act shall embrace but one subject... which subject shall be expressed in the title." The quoted version is from Indiana, and cost nine statutes their lives in the 19th century.[40] As early as 1798, as part of the backlash against the Yazoo shenanigans, the Georgia constitution provided that no law might contain "any matter different from what is expressed in the title." The New Jersey constitution of 1844 added to this a requirement that every law could "embrace but one object."[41] A year later the Louisiana constitution picked up the clause. It soon became quite

---

[37]These figures are from Oliver Field, "Unconstitutional Legislation in Minnesota," 35 Am. Pol. Science Rev. 898 (1941).

[38]Martin B. Hickman, "Judicial Review of Legislation in Utah," 4 Utah L. Rev. 50, 51 (1954).

[39]Ind. const., 1851, art. IV, sec. 21. Oliver P. Field, "Unconstitutional Legislation in Indiana," 17 Ind. L.J. 101, 118, 121 (1941).

[40]Field, op. cit., p. 120.

[41]Ernst Freund, Standards of American Legislation (1917), pp. 154–55.

common. It fit neatly into the general reform of legislative procedure which, along with restrictions on the legislature's power, formed a striking aspect of constitution-making in the last half of the 19th century. The clause was by no means senseless. It was designed, as Thomas Cooley explained,

> *first* to prevent *hodge-podge,* or "log-rolling" legislation; *second,* to prevent surprise or fraud upon the legislature by means of provisions in bills of which the titles gave no intimation, and which might therefore be overlooked and carelessly and unintentionally adopted; and *third,* to fairly apprise the people... of the subjects of legislation that are being considered, in order that they may have the opportunity of being heard thereon.[42]

Whether the clause actually had these effects is another question. It did give the judiciary another meat ax to butcher legislation. In most instances, to be sure, courts upheld the statutes that were attacked under the clause. But the power was there; it had to be reckoned with. Litigants could use the clause to delay, to thwart, sometimes to defeat legislation. Courts, too, could use the clause, in a number of ways, to get at real abuses in the legislative process, or as a mere device to further ends quite different from those which Cooley mentioned.

In *State* v. *Young,* an Indiana case of 1874, the legislature had passed an act entitled, "An act to regulate the sale of intoxicating liquors, to provide against evils resulting from any sale thereof, to furnish remedies for damages suffered by any person in consequence of such sale, prescribing penalties, to repeal all laws contravening the provisions of this act, and declaring an emergency." The ninth section of the act imposed a five-dollar fine on any person "found in a state of intoxication." This section, the court ruled, was unconstitutional. The title "points to the sale of intoxicating liquors," not the "intemperate use of such liquors." Hence the punishment of drunks was a "matter not expressed in the title," and the act was void.[43]

How courts made use of constitutional technicality is strikingly illustrated by a bizarre West Virginia case, *Rachel Cutlip* v. *Sheriff of Calhoun County.*[44] The county seat of Calhoun County had once

---

[42]Thomas M. Cooley, *A Treatise on Constitutional Limitations* (5th ed., 1883), p. 173.

[43]*State* v. *Young,* 47 Ind. 150 (1874).

[44]*Rachel Cutlip* v. *Sheriff of Calhoun County,* 3 W. Va. 588 (1869).

been located at Arnoldsburg, West Virginia. In 1867, the legislature passed "An Act locating the county seat of Calhoun County." The first section of the act put the county seat "at the farm of Simon P. Stump, on the Little Kanawha river." The third section of the act authorized the board of supervisors "to sell any county property at Arnoldsburg." The next legislature unceremoniously repealed this act. Later, Rachel Cutlip was indicted for murder in the circuit court of Calhoun County, sitting at Arnoldsburg. She argued that she had been "unlawfully detained," that all the proceedings were invalid, that there was in fact *no* county seat in Calhoun County, and that the circuit court, meeting in what it imagined to be the county seat, had no real power to indict her. It was not a frivolous argument. The act of 1867 eliminated Arnoldsburg as county seat. The next statute got rid of Simon Stump's farm as county seat. Through ignorance or inadvertence, it failed to put the county seat back at Arnoldsburg. The court had no wish to let Rachel Cutlip go free. Nor did they want to leave Calhoun County in a state of nature. They reached, in despair, for the West Virginia constitution. The title of the law in 1867 referred only to a change in the location of the county seat. Another section authorized sale of county property at Arnoldsburg. This, said the court, was a different "object" altogether, not expressed in the title of the law. Hence, the statute of 1867 was never valid, and the county seat had never really moved away from Arnoldsburg.

This can be described as crabbed, misbegotten, petty technicality. But it served, at least arguably, a useful purpose. It gave the court an excuse to intervene. The court patched up the job that the legislature had badly or corruptly done, and sternly reminded the other branch that the court took standards of performance, as prescribed by the constitution, quite seriously.

This was a legitimate role. Far more controversial were cases that seemed to have a sinister goal: to "annex the principles of *laissez faire* capitalism to the Constitution and put them beyond reach of state legislative power."[45] An early and startling example, where judicial review seemed to run wild, was *Wynehamer* v. *People* (New York, 1856).[46] New York had passed a prohibition law;

---

[45]Edward Corwin, *The Twilight of the Supreme Court* (1934), p. 78. The quote actually referred to the work of the United States Supreme Court.
[46]13 N.Y. 378 (1856).

Wynehamer declared it unconstitutional. The road to this surprising conclusion led through the due-process clause. The court pointed out that stocks of liquor had been, before the law was enacted, undeniably "property" in the "most absolute and unqualified sense." Afterwards, "intoxicating liquors" were "laid under" the ban, "the right to sell them ... denied, and their commercial value ... thus annihilated." The law was a clear deprivation of property rights, then, and without due process of law.

The precise holding of *Wynehamer* never won much of a following. Free enterprise in liquor, lottery tickets, gambling, and sex never appealed much to 19th-century judges. The case would be nothing more than a historical curiosity, except that its daring use of the due-process clause later became so popular. Activist courts fed on this kind of food, particularly after constitutional theorists made the idea intellectually palatable.[47] In *Matter of Jacobs* (1885),[48] the New York Court of Appeals held unconstitutional "An act to improve the public health, by prohibiting the manufacture of cigars and preparation of tobacco in any form, in tenement-houses." The law, said the court, in self-righteous indignation, "interferes with the profitable and free use of his property by the owner or lessee of a tenement-house who is a cigarmaker." It "trammels him in the application of his industry and the disposition of his labor, and thus, in a strictly legitimate sense, it arbitrarily deprives him of his property and of some portion of his personal liberty." Of course, it was claimed that the law had a valid purpose—to "improve the public health." But the court took it on itself to assess this claim; and was quite willing to dismiss it as a sham, even though the legislature, a co-ordinate branch of government, had in theory aired this question thoroughly and come to the opposite conclusion. The law had, in fact (said the court), "no relation whatever to the public health."

In *Godcharles* v. *Wigeman* (1886),[49] the Pennsylvania court confronted a statute, enacted in 1881, which required all businesses "engaged in mining coal, ore or other mineral ... or manufacturing iron or steel ... or any other kind of manufacturing," to pay their employees "at least once in each month," and to pay in cash

---

[47]See, in general, Clyde Jacobs, *Law Writers and the Court* (1954); Arnold M. Paul, *Conservative Crisis and the Rule of Law: Attitudes of Bar and Bench, 1887–1895* (1960).

[48]98 N.Y. 98 (1885).

[49]113 Pa. St. 431, 6 Atl. 354 (1886).

or legal tender, not in "other paper"; the law also forbade the companies from overcharging in company stores.[50] Enraged, the court declared the statute "utterly unconstitutional and void." It was an attempt "to do what, in this country, cannot be done, that is, prevent persons who are *sui juris* from making their own contracts." The law was "an insulting attempt to put the laborer under a legislative tutelage, which is not only degrading to his manhood, but subversive of his rights as a citizen of the United States." The court did not bother to cite any clause, from either state or federal constitutions, in defense of its action. (Perhaps the "utterly void" was a self-evident category.) In *Ritchie* v. *People,* an emanation of the Illinois supreme court in 1895,[51] the law under attack limited the labor of women in "any factory or workshop" to eight hours a day and forty-eight hours a week. This, said the court, was a "purely arbitrary restriction upon the fundamental rights of the citizen to control his or her own time and faculties." Perhaps the high-water mark of the mentality of *Ritchie* and similar cases was *Lochner* v. *New York,* decided by the Supreme Court in 1905.[52] New York had passed an elaborate labor law regulating work conditions in bakeries. Among other things, it established maximum hours. No employee could be "required or permitted to work in a biscuit, bread or cake bakery or confectionery establishment more than sixty hours in any one week." This statute, said the court, violated the due process clause of the fourteenth amendment. The case inspired Oliver Wendell Holmes, Jr. to write a famous dissent; but to no avail.

Cases such as these evoked, quite naturally, a good deal of liberal outrage. Labor groups and social reformers had struggled and lobbied for protective legislation. They learned soon enough that getting their programs enacted was winning a battle, not winning a war. Courts had the power to destroy the legislation, sometimes on the flimsiest legal basis, sometimes, as in *Godcharles,* with apparently no basis at all. Out of these cases arose the reputation of courts as fortresses of dark and deep reaction. Conservatives, of course, took the opposite point of view; the courts were acting as bulwarks of traditional liberty. Only the courts seemed to understand that there were "unforeseen dangers," hid-

[50]Laws Pa. 1881, no. 173, p. 147. One point of the law was to prevent companies from paying their workers in slips of paper redeemable only at the company store.
[51]155 Ill. 98, 40 N.E. 454 (1895).
[52]198 U.S. 45 (1905).

den costs, that lurked in legislation which, though seemingly beneficial, actually ran "counter to the broad general basis of Anglo-
Saxon civilization."[53] The court's political reputation did not turn
around decisively until the days of the Warren court, in the 1950s.

Neither praise nor blame were entirely deserved. The cases
cited were famous, horrible examples. There was a great wave of
social legislation in the last two decades of the century; basically,
the courts let it pass undisturbed. Some courts were even outspo-
kenly friendly to these laws. Constitutional madness was not distributed evenly across the country; the Illinois supreme court, for
example, was exceptionally hostile to labor laws. What was nationwide was the *threat,* the *possibility* of a court contest. The test
case became an accepted part of the life cycle of major legislation.
This cloud, hanging over the fate of specific laws, may have been
the major effect of judicial review.

What caused the outburst of judicial review? Limitations and
controls over legislative acts had been written into state constitutions. Who would enforce them? Either no one or the courts.
High courts had good reputations for integrity and craftsmanship.
They had the technical skill to oversee legislative behavior. They
could criticize and correct draftsmanship and parliamentary process when these were contradictory. It was tempting for the courts
to cross over from procedure to substance. And the demand for
the product was there. When a power bloc was thwarted in one
branch of government, it naturally turned to another. If the legislatures were populist or Granger, there was always one last hope
for a railroad or mining company: the courts.

Of course, courts might have resisted the temptation, and many
of them did. But a significant proportion of the judges leaped to
the bait. Judges, after all, were members of the same society as
their litigants. They shared the general outlook that American
life was a zero-sum game. Their business was the rule of law, legal
tradition, adjudication. Legislation, whatever its subject, was a
threat to their primordial function, molding and declaring the
law. Statutes were brute intrusions, local in scope, and often short-
sighted in principle or effect. They interfered with a legal world
that belonged, by right, to the judges. Particularly after 1870,
judges may have seen themselves more and more as guardians of
a precious and threatened tradition. The world about them seemed
to be growing more turbulent and unsettled. The clash of inter-

[53]Frederic J. Stimson, *Popular Law-Making* (1910), p. 238.

ests, the warfare of classes, brutally destroyed time-honored values. The judges read their constitutions as instruments of caution, delay, and honest doubt; they read them as instruments that preserved historic truths about democratic society and right reason; they read them as middle-class texts, embodying middle-class values, striving toward middle-class goals.

The power that the courts assumed was not used solely in the service of the rich and the powerful. In some blatant cases, to be sure, judges used constitutional doctrine to strengthen the hand of big business at the expense of organized labor. They allowed themselves to be persuaded that organized labor was dangerous and un-American, that it threatened the balance of society. But the judges were, by and large, almost equally afraid of the sinister un-American trusts. The constitution, as they interpreted it, did not prevent the licensing of barbers, plumbers, doctors, and lawyers; did not prevent farmers, artisans, and professional men from uniting to form strong, solid middle-class groups; did not protect giant industrial combines from the righteous wrath of the people. They were suspicious of labor legislation, but they tended to allow legislatures to outlaw oleomargarine, in the interests of sturdy farmers, and they generally supported campaigns against prostitution, lottery tickets, alcohol, and vice. Their taste for power was general, but the prejudices of the judges—predominantly old-American, conservative, middle-class—dictated where the effects of the power would fall.

The worst thing about this power was that it was randomly and irresponsibly exercised. It could be neither predicted nor controlled. Judges did not declare *all* social laws unconstitutional, only a small minority of them. Nor were *all* statutes challenged in court. The court had no way to pull cases onto its docket. A private litigant had to be willing to finance the case. Even then, the court might evade or avoid the constitutional issue. Judicial review was slow at best. One scholar studied 172 Indiana cases in which the court declared laws unconstitutional. On the average, the statutes were slightly under five years old when they fell. In fifty cases, the statutes had been on the books for more than five years. Seventeen statutes were struck down after ten years or more of apparent validity; in one case the elapsed time was 42 years.[54]

[54]Oliver P. Field, "Unconstitutional Legislation in Indiana," 17 Ind. L.J. 101, 108–9 (1941). The figures include cases up to 1935. But the conclusions hold reasonably well for the 19th century. Field cites a case in 1879, voiding a statute of 1861; a case in 1880 overturned a law of 1855. *Ibid.*, pp. 116–17.

On balance, over the whole range of American history, there is a strong argument that judicial review has been eminently worth while; but its benefits have been by no means without cost. The main effect may have been preventive, keeping down the rate of legislative change. All in all, in the 19th century, the costs, not the benefits, of judicial review may have weighed in the balance most heavily.

THE WEST

At the end of the century, the frontier—according to Turner and others—was officially dead. But in 1850, by all accounts, it was very much alive. After the Mexican War (1848), the United States squeezed out of Mexico another gigantic domain, sparsely settled, to add to the gigantic empire, stretching to the Oregon coast, which came with the Louisiana Purchase. A steady stream of settlers made the dangerous land-crossing; some were looking for land to farm in Oregon; some were Mormons making the trek to the promised land in Utah; many, after gold was discovered in California, were looking for wealth and adventure.

At the end of the rainbow was California, a beautiful land, mild and fertile, on the brink of the ocean. But California was not an easy destination. It was a kind of land island, sealed off from the rest of the country by a parched, blazing desert, and by a line of high, jagged mountains crowned with perpetual snow. The land crossings, in the middle of the century, before the transcontinental railroad was completed, form one of the great sagas of American history. Thousands of settlers—men, women, children—made the slow crawl from the pale of society to the Pacific rim. Many died along the way.

For most of the distance, they were outside any formal institutions of law and order. Yet the wagon trains and emigration companies were surprisingly lawful in behavior. There is a persistent story—or myth—that the pioneers administered "crude but effective justice on their overland journeys"; that they had courts and trials, and followed procedures as regular as conditions permitted. Lafayette Tate, who murdered a man on the overland trail, in June 1852, just east of the Rockies, was caught, tried by a makeshift jury, and a makeshift judge, prosecutor and defense counsel, convicted, sentenced, and quickly hanged. But these instances of "law" were probably rare; this kind of overland justice has probably been unduly romanticized.[55] On the other hand, John Philip Reid argues that the pioneers showed remarkable respect for certain postulates of living law. Out in the trackless wilderness, hundreds of miles from police, courts, and judges, the fundamental rules of property and contract were followed, just as they were in Illinois or Massachusetts.[56]

This is no paradox. The travellers were transients; they were moving along a path they had never gone on before, and would never travel again. As Reid points out, under these circumstances, and in the midst of strangers, there was hardly an opportunity for new "customs" to develop. The "law" that prevailed was "the taught, learned, accepted customs" of the people; it was part of the baggage they brought with them.[57] Even more important, perhaps, was the influence of peers and of destinations. Behind them, in the East, were courts, judges, police; ahead of them, at the end of the road, were the same. They were in an interlude, a halfway point, between two points of law. Under these conditions, old habits do not break; old fears of punishment and revenge do not snap in two.

When the pioneers reached their promised lands, they confronted once more a kind of legal frontier. The United States had already absorbed millions of acres of land first governed more or less by civil law—in Florida, Texas, and the Mississippi Valley. Now came California, New Mexico, Arizona, and other enormous tracts of new land; in all of this, too, civil law had held at least nominal reign. In most of it, the struggle between the two legal systems was brief; the outcome was never much in doubt. American lawyers and judges poured in along with other American settlers. In Utah, for example, Spanish-Mexican law never really had any force. The immigrants were Americans, who "tacitly" brought common law with them to an empty country.[58]

In California, however, and particularly in New Mexico, there lived substantial numbers of Spanish-speaking residents. In New

[55]David J. Langum, "Pioneer Justice on the Overland Trails," 5 Western Hist. Q. 420 (1974).

[56]John Phillip Reid, *Law for the Elephant: Property and Social Behavior on the Overland Trail* (1980).

[57]Reid, *op. cit.*, p. 362.

[58]See the remarks of Emerson, J., in *First National Bank of Utah* v. *Kinner*, 1 Utah 100, 106–7 (1873).

Mexico, judges frequently cited civil law, sometimes approvingly.[59] California was not so close a case. The gold rush brought a cataclysmic inflow of population. The new residents were mostly Americans, all totally ignorant of civil law. Spanish-Mexican law had its spokesmen—members of the existing San Francisco bar vigorously defended it; but the more influential majority felt otherwise. The "Common Law of England" (insofar as not "repugnant" to the United States Constitution and the laws and constitution of California) was formally adopted in 1850 as the "rule of decision in all the Courts of this State."[60]

The civil law left some legacies behind. One was a muddled collection of land grants, which plagued the land law of California and New Mexico for decades. The civil-law tradition influenced many specific doctrines and institutions—the community property system, for example.[61] Civil law background may have inclined Western states to be hospitable to codes and procedural reform, but other explanations are equally persuasive. Idaho was a code state, too, without the slightest shadow of civil-law influence.

Many frontier traits, familiar from earlier generations, were repeated in the far West: the mixture of old and new in the substantive law; the code-making habit; a legal profession composed predominantly of young hustlers. The nature of the land itself sometimes made legal change almost a necessity. Some Western states—Texas and California—were rich in resources and had some excellent farmland. But most of the West was bleak, arid, mountainous. Landscape strikingly affected water and resource law. The common-law rule for water was the so-called doctrine of riparian rights. Every landowner, in other words, along the banks of a river had equal right to take water; and no one owner could take so much that the stock was depleted. This made sense in rainy England and in the rainy American South and East. The Western states quite generally discarded this doctrine in favor of the prior appropriation doctrine, which was more or less first-

[59]In *Chavez* v. *McKnight,* 1 Gildersleeve (N.M.) 147, 150–51 (1857), the judge cited "Escriche" writing "under the head[ing] of Mujer Casada" (married woman), a reference to the work of Joaquin Escriche y Martin (1784–1847); the judge spoke of the "humane regard" and "wise and just policy" of the civil law toward married women.

[60]Laws Cal. 1850, ch. 95.

[61]On the civil law legacy, see also pp. 167–76, above.

come-first-served. There was never enough water to give every landowner who fronted on a river an equal shake. The Western doctrine "encouraged entrepreneurs to scramble for water, quickly construct works, and apply the asset to the industry of the region." It "recognized the environmental limitations of the water supply" and "gave certainty to users in terms of title."[62] Significantly, the new doctrine was completely in effect only in the wholly arid states; California and Texas, with their double climates, had mixed systems of water law too.[63]

Two famous Western institutions were the miners' codes and the vigilante movement. The miners' codes were little bodies of law adopted as binding customs in Western mining camps. The miners' courts and codes had a certain similarity to the claim clubs of the Midwest. These had been organizations of squatters who banded together to control the outcomes of public land auctions, and who also drew up rules and procedures for recording and judging their own land claims. These clubs flourished in Wisconsin in the late 1830s, in Iowa through the 1840s. There is some slight evidence of connection between the claim clubs, miners' groups in the Midwest (near Galena, Illinois, and in southwestern Wisconsin), and the miners' codes of the Far West. These last were at least as old as the California gold rush, and were also found in other parts of the West—in Gregory Diggings (Colorado) in 1859, in the Black Hills of Dakota Territory in the 1870s, and in Nevada. Many codes were reduced to written form. They set up rough but workable rules and processes for recording claims, for deciding whose claim was first, for settling disputes among claimants, and for enforcing decisions of miners' "courts." The Gregory Diggings ruled itself through its little legal system two years before Colorado Territory was formally organized. The mining code served the function, well known in American legal history, of a makeshift judicial and political order, where settlement had run past borders of legitimate government. The Gregory code was copied by other mining districts. As business increased, "judges" handled a wide range of disputes. The Colorado territorial legislature in 1861 and 1862 ratified, with a broad sweep, the system of local claims and judgments rendered by these informal courts.

[62]Gordon M. Bakken, *The Development of Law on the Rocky Mountain Frontier: Civil Law and Society, 1850–1912* (1983), p. 71.

[63]See Walter P. Webb, *The Great Plains* (1931), pp. 431–52; Betty E. Dobkins, *The Spanish Element in Texas Water Law* (1959).

A squatter, or his assignee, or any person whose title rested on a "decree or execution, of any of the so-called Provisional Government Courts, People's or Miners' Courts," could bring actions of trespass, ejectment, and forcible detainer (except against the United States government itself.)[64]

More flamboyant, and at the same time more sinister, was the vigilante movement. This was not exclusively a western phenomenon; but the West was the heartland of the movement. Two famous examples were the San Francisco Vigilance Committees, of 1851 and 1856. These committees were "businessmen's revolutions" directed against corrupt, inept local government. Most favorably viewed, they were sincere attempts by "decent" citizens to use self-help in order to curb violence and misrule in San Francisco. The city was turbulent; gold-hungry hordes had swollen its population. The first committee began its work by arresting and trying a "desperate character" named Jenkins. He was convicted and hanged from a heavy wooden beam on a small adobe house left over from the Mexican period.[65] The Second Vigilance Committee was more powerful than the first. It even presumed to seize and try David Terry, a justice of the California supreme court; it hanged some unsavory local characters; it defied local, state, and national governments; in general, it held San Francisco in the grip of a benevolent despotism. "The safety of the people," said the *San Francisco Bulletin,* which spoke for the vigilantes, "is above all law."[66] The "trials" run by the Vigilance Committees were highly irregular; but they never quite descended to barbarism, and they would not have been totally unrecognizable to a lawyer. Best of all, the movement in San Francisco had the decency to die a natural death.

Vigilante justice was older than the gold rush; but San Francisco gave it new life and inspired imitation. There were twenty-seven vigilance committees in California in the 1850s. In 1858, there was a vigilance committee in Carson Valley, Nevada. There were vigilantes in Denver, Colorado, from 1854 to 1861. Wyoming had

[64]Ovando J. Hollister, *The Mines of Colorado* (1867), pp. 75 ff.; pp. 359–63; Laws Terr. Colo. 1861, p. 249; Laws Terr. Colo. 1862, p. 69.

[65]Alan Valentine, *Vigilante Justice* (1956), pp. 54–58. On American vigilante movements in general, see Richard Maxwell Brown, "The American Vigilante Tradition," in Hugh D. Graham and Ted R. Gurr, eds., *Violence in America: Historical and Comparative Perspectives* (1969), p. 154.

[66]Quoted in A. Russell Buchanan, *David S. Terry of California* (1956), p. 43.

vigilantes too—beginning with "two lethal movements in the wild railroad boomtowns of Cheyenne and Laramie," in 1868–69.[67]

In the 1860s, the vigilantes of Montana rode high. In the words of their chronicler, Thomas Dimsdale, they brought "swift and terrible retribution" to the "ruffians and marauders" of the Territory—men like Captain J. A. Slade, who was condemned by the vigilantes of Virginia City and strung up on the gate posts of a corral while his wife raced madly from their ranch to try (in vain) to save him.[68] The Montana vigilantes were, in general, a rougher bunch than the boys of San Francisco. They had less regard for the niceties of trial. Sometimes they avenged crimes never committed or hanged the wrong man by mistake. For the sake of law and order, vigilantes were quite willing to put up with a bit of slippage in those places where, as Dimsdale put it, regular justice was "powerless as well as blind."

To the vigilantes, as this quotation makes clear, formal justice was too slow; or, in other cases, formal justice was an invited guest who had not yet arrived. Willard Hurst has suggested that vigilantism was not really a "pre-law phenomenon," a "groping towards the creation of legal institutions," but more accurately a "reaction against the corruption, weakness, or delays" of the established legal order.[69] From one point of view, the vigilantes did no more than put together a makeshift criminal justice system, just as the miners put together a makeshift property code, in accordance with their customs and needs.

But there is another side to the story. The vigilantes were also reacting to a code that was simply not to their liking. It was not that justice was weak, but that it reached the wrong results. Dimsdale complains about juries that refused to convict, about "sympathy" for offenders; he whines about drunkenness, the use of "strong language on every occasion," about persistent Sabbath-breaking, and the pervasive presence of vice: "women of easy virtue" were seen "promenading" about, catering to the inordinate

[67]Brown, *op. cit.*, pp. 162–63.

[68]Thomas Dimsdale, *The Vigilantes of Montana, or Popular Justice in the Rocky Mountains* (1953), pp. 13, 16, 194 ff. The book was originally published in 1866. Dimsdale was an Englishman who arrived in Virginia City in 1863 and taught school. He was the first superintendent of public instruction in Montana Territory. *Ibid.*, intro., ix.

[69]Willard Hurst, "The Uses of Law in Four 'Colonial' States of the American Union," 1945 Wis. L. Rev. 577, 585.

desire of the miners "for novelty and excitement."[70] His vigilantes
were not blind justice, but the code of Montana's elites; it was
"popular justice," to be sure, but antipopular as well.

In any event, social control, like nature, abhors a vacuum. The
"respectable" citizens—the majority, perhaps?—in Western towns
were not really lawless. Quite to the contrary, people were accustomed to the rule of law and order; these were the same people
who, on the wagon trains described by Reid, paid scrupulous
attention to property and contract. They were Americans; they
were unwilling to tolerate too sharp a break in social continuity;
they reacted against formal law which was too slow, or too corrupt,
for their purposes, or which had fallen into the hands of the less
respectable. Vigilantes were the products of a culture clash, in
small communities—which were, moreover, communities of transients and strangers.

There may have been another, subtler factor at work. The men
of the mob had the satisfaction, grim though it was, of a justice
that lay literally in their hardened hands; they pulled on the ropes
themselves, not through surrogates. Regular courts would never
have been so swift. To many people, punishment is twice as satisfying when it works with white-hot immediacy, when the arguments and doubts of a trial do not disturb its naked emotions.

Just as some look on the vigilantes and the miners' codes as
bloodthirsty and antidemocratic, so others, quite the contrary, saw
in these institutions the outcroppings of genuine popular justice,
an Anglo-Saxon inheritance as old as Teutonic folkmoots, transplanted here to fresher soil. This was, by and large, a 19th-century
idea. The historian H. H. Bancroft advanced this point of view.
The frontier thesis of Frederick Jackson Turner also pictured the
Westerner as nature's democrat, a noble breed, dying along with
the buffalo, the Indian, the whooping crane.

Benjamin Shambaugh, writing in 1902, similarly idealized the
Midwestern claim clubs. He saw them as "fountains of that spirit
of Western Democracy which permeated the social and political
life of America during the 19th century."[71] Modern scholarship

[70]Dimsdale, *op. cit.*, pp. 9, 12.

[71]Benjamin F. Shambaugh, *History of the Constitutions of Iowa* (1902), p. 65. He
added that the members were men who "in the silent forest, in the broad prairies,
in the deep blue sky, in the sentinels of the night, in the sunshine and in the storm,
in the rosy dawn...must have seen and felt the Infinite," a rather florid way of
saying that the pioneers rarely went to church. *Ibid.*, p. 24.

has been more hard-headed, much less lyrical about the claim clubs.[72] These tight little organizations were hardly fountains of Western democracy; they were little cartels, which tried to protect early claimants from later, more innocent arrivals; they also tried to force the government to sell land at the lowest possible price. Miners' groups, too, were less democratic than guildlike and protectionist. The romance of the West, the drama of the landscape, has long overwhelmed historical fact. The land was harsh and empty; this gave opportunity, to be sure, to the occasional rogue and outlaw, and to the genuine free spirit; it was easy for a few to slip free of civilization in the endless vastness of the West. The land encouraged courage; yet curiously enough, it also fostered dependency. Out West, men wanted freedom; but they also wanted subsidies for railroads; and since the sky was so unyielding, and drops of water so scarce, they wanted tax money spent to help them irrigate their lands. What traveled west, more important than form, was the general legal culture, the general ways of thinking about law. This included a notion quite the antithesis of primitive democracy. The notion was: organize or die; and it was the theme of American law, East and West, in the last half of the 19th century, in every area and arena of life.

[72]See, for example, Allan G. Bogue, "The Iowa Claim Clubs: Symbol and Substance," 45 Miss. Valley Hist. Rev. 231 (1958).

CHAPTER II

JUDGES AND COURTS: 1850–1900

THE JUDGES

After the middle of the century, the popular election of judges was more and more accepted as normal. Every state that entered the union after 1846 provided that the voters would elect some or all of their judges. The California constitution of 1849 made the whole system elective, from the supreme court down to justices of the peace. In the year 1850 alone, seven states changed laws to provide for more popular election of judges. In 1850, both the Michigan and Pennsylvania supreme courts turned elective.[1]

In only a few states were judges still appointed—Maine and Massachusetts, for example, and, of course, the federal government. In Connecticut the legislature chose judges, but, in 1856, the term of office was changed to eight years; before that, judges had served during "good behavior," which meant, in practice, for life. The traffic did not entirely go one way, that is, toward the elective principle. Some Southern states returned to the appointive system during Reconstruction. Texas, between 1866 and 1876, went from an elective to an appointive supreme court and back. Mississippi abolished its elected high court of errors and appeals under the constitution of 1868. The new supreme court consisted of three judges appointed by the governor and confirmed by the senate. Mississippi did not return to an elective system until 1910.

In the long run, the elective system did not have results so earthshaking, for good or bad, as proponents had hoped and opponents feared. In the first place, elections did not become quite as partisan as they might have. Some lawyers had warned of the grave dangers to the polity that might come from making

[1]Evan Haynes, *The Selection and Tenure of Judges* (1944), pp. 100, 116, 127; Kermit L. Hall, "The Judiciary on Trial: State Constitutional Reform and the Rise of an Elected Judiciary, 1846–1860," 45 The Historian 337 (1983).

judges run for office; hostile politicians would grub about in the reports, find an unpopular decision, and use it politically to ruin a sitting judge. But as it turned out, most sitting judges who ran again won again, regardless of party. There were some striking exceptions, however. Michigan's most illustrious judge, Thomas M. Cooley, was defeated for re-election in 1885; the main reason was a "Democratic Deluge" that "submerge[d] even the mountain tops"; labor was opposed to him, and his close connection with the railroads cost him dearly with some voters.[2] Chief Justice Charles B. Lawrence of Illinois was defeated because of the wrath of the Grangers in 1873.[3] Sometimes it was enough that a judge stood for a particular party or position. In 1861, Chief Judge John C. Legrand and Judge William B. Tuck, of the court of appeals of Maryland, were defeated for re-election by two judges who ran on a ticket of stern loyalty to the Union.[4]

The elective principle may have had some subtle effect on decision-making, or on the form in which opinions were cast. There were jurists who saw this as an additional danger. Partly for this reason, they continued to oppose the election of judges. The elective principle undermined the idea that no one but lawyers had the right to determine the proper outcome of cases, and that strictly legal principles were the only tools that belonged in the toolshed of judges. The defeat of Chief Justice Lawrence looked like a case where "a herd of dissatisfied farmers have put an ignorant demagogue in the seat of an able and upright judge."[5] These words were written by an editor of the *Albany Law Journal*, in 1873, at a time when a new—and futile—attempt was made to overturn the elective principle in New York. The writer added:

> The people are the worst possible judges of those quali-
> fications essential to a good judge. They could select an or-
> ator, an advocate or a debater, as his qualities are palpable
> and salient; but the qualities of a judge are peculiar, and are
> seldom appreciated by cursory and general notice. That un-

[2]Lewis G. Vander Velde, "Thomas McIntyre Cooley," in Earl D. Babst and Lewis G. Vander Velde, eds., *Michigan and the Cleveland Era* (1948), pp. 77, 92.

[3]James E. Babb, "The Supreme Court of Illinois," 3 Green Bag 217, 234 (1891).

[4]Carroll T. Bond, *The Court of Appeals of Maryland, a History* (1928), p. 159. Maryland at least was spared the embarrassment of fighting on the Union side with secessionist judges. To a certain extent, the federal government was in this fix. Chief Justice Taney, author of the *Dred Scott* decision, lived until 1864. His wartime conduct was a thorn in Lincoln's side.

[5]8 Albany L.J. 18 (July 5, 1873).

common, recondite and difficult learning; that power and turn of mind and cast of character called the "judicial," are likely to go unremarked by the nonprofessional observer. To him the effective advocate seems best fitted to fill the judicial office; but experience has proved that the best advocate is not likely to prove the best judge, as the two functions exact diverse qualifications.

But the chief objection to an elective judiciary is the effect it has upon the office; its dignity; its just weight; its hold upon the general confidence.

While it may be true that the selection of candidates for judges is generally left to the legal members of the [party] conventions, it is equally true that these legal members are not usually such a class of lawyers as is competent to do anything so important as the making of a judge—young, ambitious men, more familiar with the management of ward caucuses or town meetings than with the conduct of a cause in court.

The elective principle, at least, made a contribution to the withering away of impeachment. There were few removals after 1850, except for good and sufficient (that is, nonpolitical) cause. Federal impeachment proceedings were exceedingly rare. The House judiciary committee recommended impeachment for John C. Watrous, district judge for Texas, in 1853. Supposedly, he practiced law while on the bench, and heard cases in which he had a financial stake. No action was taken against him. Between 1872 and 1875, four federal judges were investigated on grounds of irregular conduct; all of them resigned under fire.[6] Few state judges, too, were ever impeached. In 1852, Chief Justice Levi Hubbell of Wisconsin was accused of a wide range of offenses, from partiality, and improper conduct of trials, to taking a bribe. Hubbell was irascible and partisan. There was evidence of "shoddy standards" in his work, but the senators seemed to demand (and did not get) extraordinary proofs of misconduct; Hubbell was not removed.[7]

In the Gilded Age, in the fetid atmosphere of the Tweed ring, the lower New York bench distinguished itself for corruption. "The stink of our state judiciary is growing too strongly ammoniac and hippuric for endurance," wrote George Templeton Strong in his diary. This stench from the courtroom was one of the stimuli that led to formation of the New York City Bar Association, in

[6]Joseph Borkin, *The Corrupt Judge* (1962), pp. 201, 253–54.
[7]Alfons J. Beitzinger, *Edward G. Ryan, Lion of the Law* (1960), pp. 32–39.

1870. Two of the most notorious of the judges were George G. Barnard and Albert Cardozo, justices of the supreme court. Cardozo, whose son Benjamin ultimately redeemed the family name, handed out receiverships to relatives and friends. Strong wrote: "I think Nature meant Cardozo to sweep the court room, not to preside in it.... He would look more natural in the dock of the Sessions than on the Bench of the Supreme Court."[8] In 1872, because of their "gross abuse of...powers," their venality, their improper conduct, charges of impeachment were drawn up against Barnard and Cardozo. Cardozo resigned; Barnard was impeached and forever barred from public office.[9]

A more political use of the threat of impeachment drove "carpetbag" judges off the bench in the South after Reconstruction collapsed. In South Carolina, the one black supreme court justice, Jonathan Jasper Wright, was harassed from his post in 1877. Despite the smoke of propaganda, the charges against these Southern judges have never been fully proven. The carpetbag judges, black and white, suffered the fate of history's losers. They were probably no more corrupt than Southern white judges of the same time and culture. Moses Walker, from Ohio, served with some distinction on the Texas supreme court.[10] Albion W. Tourgée,[11] a carpetbag judge, later drew on his Southern experience to write a series of novels. One of these, A Fool's Errand (1879), was sensationally successful. Tourgée's liberal views on black-white relationships were far ahead of his times. Late in his life, he worked on the briefs in Plessy v. Ferguson, before the case went up to the Supreme Court. Tourgée was an exceptional man; yet his case suggests the danger of accepting too quickly the orthodox Southern view that carpetbag judges were stupid and corrupt.

Controversy also surrounded the reputations of the territorial judges. Territorial judges were strictly appointive. These were patronage jobs, and eager claimants badgered President after President for appointment. Some were political hacks, ill-paid, ill-prepared for their jobs, almost invariably nonresidents, whose sole claim to office was whatever made them successful at patronage

[8]A. Nevins and M. Thomas, eds., The Diary of George Templeton Strong, vol. 4 (1952), pp. 264–65.

[9]History of the Bench and Bar of New York, vol. I (1897), p. 199.

[10]James R. Norvell, "The Reconstruction Courts of Texas, 1867–1873," 62 Southwestern Historical Q. 141, 160–61 (1958).

[11]His career is described in Otto H. Olsen, Carpetbagger's Crusade: The Life of Albion Winegar Tourgée (1965).

in Washington. Some of these judges hardly had the decency to set foot in their jurisdictions; some resigned after a short term in office, going after more lucrative game. Some, like the wandering frontier lawyers, took jobs in one territory after another. Samuel Chipman Parks of Illinois, for example, was a judge in three territories in a row: Idaho (1863), New Mexico (1878), and Wyoming (1882).[12]

A territorial judgeship was not a genteel post, like that filled by the wig-wearing judges of England, or even the quiet black-robed dignitaries of the Eastern bench. For fair reasons or foul, local residents were often hostile to these judges, sent in by Washington. One hears about "sage-brush districting"—legislatures that carved up judicial districts in such a way as to exile an unpopular judge to the barren wastelands. The legislature of New Mexico, according to the *Santa Fe Post*, sent Chief Justice Joseph G. Palen in 1872 "to the hottest locality over which they had jurisdiction," regretting only "that their jurisdiction is so limited."[13]

A few of these judges became famous or notorious. Kirby Benedict served as chief justice of New Mexico Territory in the 1850s and 1860s. The territorial secretary of state complained, in a letter to President Lincoln, that Benedict "visits the gambling Hells and drinking saloons and with a swagger and bluster defiles his judicial robes." Perhaps he was driven to drink. As a new judge, in 1854, Benedict had to ride circuit through a vast desert country; hostile tribesmen hid in its arid canyons. Benedict gave as good as he got: he denounced his accuser as a "moronic maniac, an egotist, a general mischief-maker."[14] Lincoln reappointed Benedict; but President Johnson removed him from office as a drunkard. Benedict practiced law for a while, then was disbarred.

But it would be wrong to label all of these judges as incompetents and eccentrics. Their worst sin, perhaps, was politics. Federal judges served for life; but the justices of territorial supreme

---

[12]Earl S. Pomeroy, *The Territories and the United States, 1861–1890* (1947), p. 136.

[13]*Ibid.*, p. 57. For other examples of "sage-brushing," see John D. W. Guice, *The Rocky Mountain Bench: The Territorial Supreme Courts of Colorado, Montana, and Wyoming, 1861–1890* (1972), pp. 59, 81.

[14]Letter of W. F. M. Arny to Lincoln, Dec. 19, 1863; letter of Benedict to Edward Bates, Jan. 3, 1864, printed in Aurora Hunt, *Kirby Benedict, Frontier Federal Judge* (1961), pp. 165, 166. On the administration of justice in New Mexico Territory, see Arie W. Poldervaart, *Black-Robed Justice* (1948).

courts were appointed to four-year terms and could be fired at any time. This thrust territorial courts into "perhaps the wildest political scramble in American history." The phrase is from John Guice's study of these courts in three Western states. But Guice's research led him to respect these Rocky Mountain judges: on the whole, they were "civilizers, builders, and makers of law who contributed substantially to the territories and to the nation as a whole."[15]

Western judges often had to be made of tougher stuff than their Eastern counterparts. The barren, empty lands bred or harbored a certain amount of lawlessness; the vast anonymity of the West attracted killers and thieves. This was the world of Judge Isaac Parker, the hanging judge, first appointed by President Grant, who ruled over the Western Arkansas District from his seat in Fort Smith. Parker's realm included Indian Territory. It was the "land of the six-shooter." Parker did not shrink from stern duty, as he saw it. He began his regime of law and order by condemning six men, who were hanged on September 3, 1875. Before his career was over, in 1896, seventy-nine men, many of them native Americans or blacks, had put on the black hood and mounted the gallows. Superstitious men thought that the restless ghosts of the dead haunted the gallows at night.[16]

The United States Supreme Court stood at the apex of the federal pyramid, at the farthest remove from Judge Parker. All of the justices were lawyers, and on the whole, all had some stature. Compared with earlier justices, the late 19th-century appointees were, on the average, older men. Young countries tend toward young leaders; older, more settled countries seem to gravitate toward older leaders. Joseph Story had been named to the Court at thirty-two; William Strong, of Pennsylvania, was confirmed in 1870 at the age of sixty-two, the first man over sixty to be ap-

[15]Guice, *The Rocky Mountain Bench*, pp. 48, 152. John Wunder's study of the justices of the peace in the Pacific Northwest in the late 19th century comes to a similar conclusion: "Justices have been regarded . . . as uneducated, illiterate personages with no legal training and no access to written law; in fact, local judges were sometimes learned in the law." They were a stable, established group; and Wunder feels they did a creditable job on the whole. John R. Wunder, *Inferior Courts, Superior Justice: A History of the Justices of the Peace on the Northwest Frontier, 1853–1889* (1979), p. 170; on the territorial justices of Nebraska, see Michael W. Homer, "The Territorial Judiciary: An Overview of the Nebraska Experience, 1854–1867," 63 Nebraska History 349 (1982).

[16]On Parker see Glenn Shirley, *Law West of Fort Smith: A History of Frontier Justice in the Indian Territory, 1834–1895* (1957); J. Gladston Emery, *Court of the Damned* (1959).

pointed.[17] The experience of the later justices was somewhat more national than the earlier judges. Robert Trimble, appointed in 1826, was the first Supreme Court justice with prior experience in the lower federal courts. State courts were the main source of Supreme Court justices throughout the 19th century. But many justices had some federal service in their background.[18]

Appointments to the Court were as political as those to any lower court. Presidents appointed old cronies, famous politicians, deserving members of the cabinet; they appointed men because they were Southern or because they were not Southern, as the case might be. Occasionally, nominees were rejected for political reasons. President Grant nominated Attorney General E. R. Hoar, who had made too many enemies in the Senate. His name languished in the Senate, and he was finally turned down.[19] Most nominations, however, went through Congress unopposed or with little opposition.

Judges of the Supreme Court had politics in their background or were politically active. Some never lost the habit. David Davis, among others, had political ambitions. Davis was a serious contender for the presidential nomination in 1872 and was elected to the Senate from Illinois in 1877. Chief Justice Chase lusted after the Democratic nomination for president in 1872. Joseph P. Bradley cast the deciding vote on the Electoral Commission that made Rutherford B. Hayes president in 1877.[20]

Despite the politics of the appointment process, the judges' own

[17]Cortez A. M. Ewing, *The Judges of the Supreme Court, 1789–1937* (1938), pp. 66ff.

[18]*Ibid.*, p. 100.

[19]Grant next tried Edwin Stanton, who had been a member of Lincoln's cabinet. Stanton was confirmed but dropped dead before assuming office. Two other Grant nominees were withdrawn because of newspaper outcry or senatorial reluctance.

[20]The election of 1876 was inconclusive. Both parties claimed victory for their candidate. Samuel Tilden, the Democratic candidate, was one electoral vote short of a majority; but electoral votes from Florida, Louisiana, South Carolina and Oregon were in dispute. To settle the matter, Congress established an Electoral Commission of fifteen, five Senators, five Representatives, and five judges. Seven of these were Democrats, seven Republicans and the fifth judge was to be chosen by the other four judges. This was Bradley. The Commission gave Rutherford Hayes *all* the disputed electoral votes, 8–7. Bradley voted with the majority, and Hayes was elected. Bradley always claimed his work on the Electoral Commission was as pure as the driven snow: "So far as I am capable of judging my own motives, I did not allow political, that is, party, considerations to have any weight whatever in forming my conclusions." Quoted in Charles Fairman, "Mr. Justice Bradley," in Allison Dunham and Philip Kurland, eds., *Mr. Justice* (1956), pp. 69, 83.

nose for politics, and numerous errors of ambition and prejudice, the Supreme Court had an unblemished record of honesty; and it crafted its decisions with care. The prestige of the Court ebbed and flowed, but the long-range trend was, as far as one can tell, steadily rising. The judges bore tremendous responsibilities, and had life tenure. Their political independence probably enhanced their prestige. The judges survived the *Dred Scott* case, the *Civil Rights* cases, the *Slaughter-house* case, the *Income Tax* case, and the thousand crises, large and small, that pounded upon their heads. Their written opinions were always sleekly professional. Increasingly, people who could never have read a single opinion seem to have accepted the legitimacy of the Court. The Supreme Court by 1900 was more than a century old. It was a fixed and traditional part of an accepted system of government. The canonization of the Supreme Court, or at least its beatification, was not a fast or automatic process. *Dred Scott* and after were relatively dark days. Yet, at some point—roughly, in the last half of the century—the Court reached a position of high, almost unassailable prestige. Perhaps the Court was an accurate mirror of upper middle-class thought. The Court vacillated between nationalism and localism; so did the country. And the Court fulfilled a valuable function, or seemed to: it was the forum for sober second thoughts. The Supreme Court (so, too, many of the state courts) tended to smooth over the dips and eddies of wide swings of opinion. At least this was a claim that could be plausibly made.

The size of the Court fluctuated until the 1870s. Lincoln and Grant were not above a genteel sort of court-packing. Lincoln did some unpacking, too; he allowed three seats to stay empty. John A. Campbell, of Alabama, had resigned; two other justices had died, one a Southerner. Lincoln held the seats open until it was clear that the South would not voluntarily return.[21] During the Civil War, Congress by law gave the Court its largest size: ten members. Congress played with these numbers during Reconstruction, at the time of its tug of war with President Johnson. A law of 1866 provided that no vacancy should be filled until the membership of the Court sank to seven. This looked suspiciously like a plan to keep Andrew Johnson from filling any vacancies, although the evidence now appears weaker than was previously supposed.[22] During the Grant administration, finally, Congress

[21]Carl B. Swisher, *Stephen J. Field, Craftsman of the Law* (1930), p. 113.
[22]See Stanley I. Kutler, *Judicial Power and Reconstruction Politics* (1968), pp. 48ff.

settled on what has since become the sacred number—nine.

The Court was, in general, blessed by a number of long tenures. This gave the Court great stability, perhaps even too much. Unionists considered Taney's long life a great curse (he was eighty-seven when he died, in 1864). Robert C. Grier stayed on the Court three years after a stroke had left him somewhat befuddled. It is not certain that he understood, in late 1869, which side he was voting for in the *Legal Tender* cases. A delegation from the Court, including Stephen Field, then asked him gently to resign. Field's own career was the longest in the nineteenth century. He was appointed in 1863, at the age of forty-six, and he served for thirty-four years, eight months, and twenty days, longer than anyone before. In his last year on the Court, in 1897, his mind failed noticeably; at times he lapsed into a "dull stupor." Justice John Marshall Harlan was sent to talk to Field, and persuade him to resign. Harlan reminded Field of his mission to Grier; but Field, his eyes "blazing with the old fire of youth,... burst out; ... 'a dirtier day's work I never did in my life.'"[23]

When Taney finally died, in 1864, Lincoln appointed Salmon P. Chase, formerly his secretary of the treasury, as chief justice. Chase was a disappointment to the administration; in 1870, he was one of the five-man majority in the first *Legal Tender* case. The Court held that paper-money laws, passed during the Civil War, were beyond the power of Congress. What was ironic was that Secretary Chase had been an architect of the policy which Chief Justice Chase now repudiated. But Secretary Chase had been a Republican in the midst of a war; Chief Justice Chase in 1870 was a Democrat, confronting problems of peacetime finance. One year later, after two new appointments by President Grant, the decision was reversed. The incident shows both how much the president could control the Supreme Court, and also ultimately how little. The mighty power to appoint was balanced by the fact that, once confirmed, a judge was free to go his own way, and often did.

No later chief justice had the stature of Marshall or Taney; but outstanding men sat on the Court after the war: Samuel Miller, Stephen Field, Joseph Bradley, John Marshall Harlan. They served during the first golden age of judicial review, a period in which high court judges demanded a share of the power of government,

[23]Quoted in Swisher, *op. cit.*, p. 444; see also John S. Goff, "Old Age and the Supreme Court," 4 Am. J. Legal Hist. 95 (1960).

and found the basis for this power in the 14th amendment. It was also an age in which open disagreement in the Court was more visible. Dissenting opinions had been rare on the Marshall court. Peter V. Daniel (1841–1860) was a persistent dissenter. He wrote almost as many dissents and special concurrences as majority opinions.[24] Samuel F. Miller dissented 159 times, and Stephen Field 233 times, in the course of their careers. John Marshall Harlan (1877–1911) entered no less than 380 dissents.[25]

Still, the ordinary case was unanimously decided, unlike cases on the Warren and Burger courts. More than seventy cases are reported in Volume 71 of the United States Reports, drawn from December term 1866. All except five were unanimous decisions. In one of these, the famous case of *Ex parte Milligan*, there was indeed a separate opinion; but it was a concurrence, that is, it agreed with the result but not the majority's reasons. In four other cases, there were dissents; but in two of these, the dissenters merely recorded the fact that they dissented; they did not file a written disagreement. On the other hand, the famous test oath cases, *Cummings* v. *Missouri* and *Ex parte Garland*, elicited a long dissent.[26]

It was the difficult, controversial cases that drew blood, in other words. But most of the work of the Supreme Court was not made up of such cases. A slowly increasing minority of cases turned on constitutional issues. A growing number arose under important federal statutes. Still, there were many cases in the Supreme Court about commercial contracts, or land titles, or the like. These were cases that entered the federal courts on diversity grounds, that is, because the parties were citizens of different states. Typically, there was no federal issue in them at all. The Court's sheer burden of work rose constantly. Between 1862 and 1866, the Court handed down 240 decisions; between 1886 and 1890, 1,125—and this without relief from the arduous burden of traveling on circuit.[27] The work load meant that the leisurely days of long oral argument

[24]John P. Frank, *Justice Daniel Dissenting* (1964), p. 181.

[25]Karl ZoBell, "Division of Opinion in the Supreme Court: A History of Judicial Disintegration," 44 Cornell L.Q. 186, 199 (1959).

[26]The number of dissents and concurrences rose with the years; but rather slowly. In Volume 168, reporting cases from October term, 1897, there were forty-three unanimous opinions, five dissents and two concurrences without opinion; and only three dissents and one concurrence with separate written opinion.

[27]Charles Fairman, *Mr. Justice Miller and the Supreme Court, 1862–1890* (1939), p. 62.

were over. Only so much time could be allotted to each case, even the important ones.

By common consent, the golden age of *state judges* was also over, by 1870. A golden age is a tricky concept. What was golden about the judges had been measured on a scale of judicial skill and judicial craft. The great judges—Lemuel Shaw, John Bannister Gibson, John Marshall—were builders of institutions and molders of doctrine; moreover, they had style.

There is no doubt that the next generation of judges had a somewhat different approach to their craft. Ironically, controversy about activist judges was very great in this age of silver or brass. Some state judges after 1860 were famous men in their time, and men of vigor and imagination: Edward Ryan of Wisconsin, Oliver Wendell Holmes, Jr., of Massachusetts, Thomas Cooley of Michigan. Holmes was perhaps the greatest master of the English language ever to sit on an American court. But his fame rests mostly on his later career, as a justice of the Supreme Court. Of the state-court judges of the period, Roscoe Pound thought that only one stood out "as a builder of the law since the Civil War"—Charles Doe.[28] Doe was chief justice of New Hampshire from 1876 to 1896. He was a man who, in the words of his biographer, believed that "judicial power was grounded upon the logic of necessity and the function of the court [was] to furnish a remedy for every right."[29] In a number of significant cases, Doe disregarded formalities, ignored niceties of pleading, and shrugged off the burden of precedent. He believed judges should sometimes make law, and make it openly.

What most marked off Doe from his contemporary judges was a matter not of substance but of style. Doe stood out because he denied the dominant theory of the legitimacy of judges. The judges who invented and first used the labor injunction were making law. When a judge reworked doctrine, and knew it, he was making law. Yet the late 19th-century judges stressed very strongly that they did not make law. Precedent, the Constitution, principles of common law—these were the rulers; the judge was only an instrument, a vessel. Hence a judge should not *seem* to be creative. There were ample reasons why the judges assumed so docile a

---

[28]Roscoe Pound, "The Place of Judge Story in the Making of American Law," 48 Am. L. Rev. 676, 690 (1914).

[29]John P. Reid, *Chief Justice: The Judicial World of Charles Doe* (1967), p. 300.

posture. For one thing, it provided magnificent camouflage. It disclaimed responsibility for unpopular opinions. It was one reason why judges, even though elected, did not stand so naked before the partisan public as, say, governors and congressmen did. The flight into technicality and impersonality was only apparently a flight toward a more humble, self-effacing role. A doctor does not humble himself when he claims that the principles of medicine determine what he does. The judges claimed that they were professionals; their job was too difficult for the layman, too pure for the politician. They claimed the expert's privilege of monopoly control of their business and insisted that what they did, like all experts' work, was value-free. These were valuable postures of self-defense.

Of course, there were many variations between court and court. Styles of decision, literary merit, and craftsmanship were not uniform; neither was there a single conception of the judicial role. Again, the number of dissents is a rough index of differences in judges' conceptions of that role. Their is no doubt that dissents, in general, were more frequent in the period after the Civil War, on state high courts, than beforehand. But not every state had a similar propensity toward dissent. In Missouri, in 1885, there were 275 reported unanimous opinions and 57 cases with dissents or specially concurring opinions (mostly dissents). On the other hand, the Vermont supreme court, in 1890, decided seventy cases unanimously; there was one dissent, and that one lacked a written opinion. In New York's Court of Appeals, in 1888, about one case in ten carried with it a dissenting opinion.[30]

Karl Llewellyn has called the years of the late 19th century years of the formal style, in contrast to the grand style of Marshall, Gibson, and Shaw.[31] Much of the crispness and flair had gone out of the printed reports. It is certainly true that many high court opinions, in the late 19th century, make tortuous reading; they

[30]In general, dissents and concurrences were not the rule in any court. A study of sixteen state supreme courts, for the period 1870–1900, found that over 90% of the reported decisions were unanimous; there were concurring opinions in 2.7% of the cases, and dissents in 6%. Lawrence M. Friedman, Robert Kagan, Bliss Cartwright and Stanton Wheeler, "State Supreme Courts: A Century of Style and Citation," 33 Stan. L. Rev. 773, 787 (1981).

[31]Karl N. Llewellyn, "Remarks on the Theory of Appellate Decision and the Rules or Canons About How Statutes Are to Be Construed," 3 Vanderbilt L.R. 395, 396 (1950); The Common Law Tradition: Deciding Appeals (1960), pp. 35–39. See below, ch. 11, pp. 623–24.

are bombastic, diffuse, labored, drearily logical, crammed with unnecessary citations. There are many reasons for this difference in style. Reports were fuller, and were not carefully edited. The work load was too great to allow time for pruning and polishing. But style also reflected the training and philosophy of the judges.

Who were these judges? On the whole, they were fairly conservative men, educated in traditional ways, and they lived out their careers in a general environment that exalted the values of American business (though not necessarily *big* business). They tended to be jealous of their judicial and economic prerogatives. High-court judges were no cross section of the country. They represented old America. The bench was lily-white and mostly Protestant; there was a tendency toward dynasties—the Tuckers in Virginia, for example. In New Jersey, every chief justice from 1776 to 1891, with only one exception, was Presbyterian. Most associate justices had also been Presbyterians, many of them elders in their churches. Nearly all of the judges with a college education were products of Princeton.[32] As of 1893, of forty-eight judges elected to Virginia's highest court, only three had been "born outside of the...limits of Virginia."[33] From 1860 to 1900, virtually every Vermont judge was a native; only occasionally did a son of Connecticut or New Hampshire creep in. The fifteen supreme court judges of Minnesota between 1858 and 1890 were all Protestants, and primarily from good, solid middle-class backgrounds.[34]

For judges of this stamp, formalism was a protective device. They were middle-of-the-road conservatives, holding off the vulgar rich on the one hand, the revolutionary masses on the other. The legal tradition represented balance, sound values, a com-

[32]John Whitehead, "The Supreme Court of New Jersey," 3 Green Bag 493, 512 (1891). Whitehead adds that, except for Chief Justice Hornblower, "a small, delicate, slender man," the judges were "of good size, well-proportioned, strong, and vigorous." The trial bench of Boston, 1880–1900, was equally monolithic: there were 14 judges, all men, every one born and raised in New England. Six were Harvard alumni. Robert A. Silverman, *Law and Urban Growth: Civil Litigation in the Boston Trial Courts, 1880–1900* (1981), p. 38.

[33]S. S. P. Patteson, "The Supreme Court of Appeals of Virginia," 5 Green Bag 407, 419 (1893).

[34]Robert A. Heiberg, "Social Backgrounds of the Minnesota Supreme Court Justices: 1858–1968," 53 Minn. L. Rev. 901 (1969). In the West, of course, the situation was the reverse of the East. In states like Washington, or Wyoming, none of the judges were or could have been natives of the state.

mitment to orderly process. The judges, by habit and training, preferred to work within the comfortable confines of legal tradition; there were, of course, still great opinions (great in the sense of consequential); but, in a generation of bulging law libraries, creativity no longer required the style of the judges of the "golden age," who invented whole areas of law in a few majestic brush-strokes. "Formalism," thus, was less a habit of mind than a habit of style, less a way of thinking than a way of disguising thought.

Still, when all this is conceded, it might still be true that the judges (particularly of the lower courts) *were*, by and large, lesser men than the judges of the first generation—they were elected, not elite. America of 1880 was an ambitious, industrial society, run by businessmen and politicians. Most high court judges were simply successful or ambitious lawyers; relatively fewer were liberally educated gentlemen, from good families, with a sense of style and *noblesse oblige*; fewer were the children of the well-to-do or younger sons of New England ministers. The results showed in their craft, if not necessarily in doctrines and results.

JUDICIAL ORGANIZATION

The late 19th century was not a period of radical innovation in judicial organization; but important changes did take place of a more gradual nature. The typical state system was still a pyramid of courts, imperfectly manned and badly paid at the bottom.[35] No administrator ran, controlled, or co-ordinated the judicial system. No one could shift judges about as needed from a crowded to an empty docket or monitor the flow of litigation or set up rules to tell the courts how to behave. Higher courts weakly and partially controlled lower courts through the power to reverse decisions— but only in the event of an appeal. There was, however, more of a tendency to keep totally separate the lines between trial and appellate courts. At one time, almost all high court judges did some trial work; and almost all high courts were also in some

---

[35]Where the fee system was in effect, some lower court judges were paid only too well. The Pennsylvania constitution of 1873 (art. V, sec 12) specifically provided that Philadelphia magistrates "shall be compensated only by fixed salaries."

degree trial courts. In the late 19th century, this was less and less the case.

In many states, high court judges were busier than ever before. State courts, like the United States Supreme Court, often had to scramble to keep up with their load. The Illinois supreme court wrote 150 opinions in 1854 and 295 in 1889–90.[36] The federal courts, too, increased their business. In 1871, the United States district courts disposed of 8,187 criminal cases; in 1900, 17,033. In 1873, these courts disposed of 14,527 civil cases; in 1900, 22,520. There were 52,477 civil cases pending in the district courts in 1900.[37]

There is no mystery behind the increase in the work load of appellate courts. The villain was nothing more than simple population growth, and perhaps economic growth as well. To solve the problem, the states hit on various mechanisms. Some states added a third tier to the pyramid of courts. They set up intermediate appellate courts. So, for example, Illinois divided the state in 1877 into four districts, each with a three-judge court (two of these in crowded Cook County). Texas established a court of criminal appeals in 1891. Under the Missouri constitution of 1875, a special appellate court was created for the city of St. Louis; another court of appeals, for Kansas City, was established in 1884, and the two courts then handled appeals from lower courts in the rest of the state as well.[38]

Many states increased the number of high court judges—Minnesota, for example, from three to four, then to five. California, in 1879, tried an interesting and productive experiment; it allowed its supreme court to divide itself, like an amoeba, into separate segments ("departments"); only especially difficult or important

[36]James E. Babb, "The Supreme Court of Illinois," 3 Green Bag 217, 237 (1891).
[37]American Law Institute, *A Study of the Business of the Federal Courts* (1934), Part 1, Criminal Cases, p. 107; Part 2, Civil Cases, p. 111.
[38]Roscoe Pound, *Organization of Courts* (1940), pp. 227–31. At the time of the Civil War, in eleven states the highest court was still a wanderer—required or expected to sit at least once a year in various parts of the state. Before 1900, five of these—Maryland, Michigan, Missouri, Georgia, and Illinois—had settled down permanently at the state capital. Pound, *op. cit.*, p. 199. On the creation of intermediate appellate courts, and other devices to solve the problem of overload at the level of the highest court, see Robert Kagan, Bliss Cartwright, Lawrence Friedman and Stanton Wheeler, "The Evolution of State Supreme Courts," 76 Mich. L. Rev. 961 (1978).

cases would be decided *en banc,* that is, by the whole court. In some states the supreme court could farm out cases to "commissioners," whose decisions could be (and usually were) accepted by the court as its own. Kansas, in 1887, authorized the governor, "by and with the consent of the senate," to appoint three citizens of Kansas, "of high character for legal learning and personal worth," to be "commissioners of the supreme court." They would "aid and assist the [supreme] court...in the disposition of the numerous cases pending in said court" (Laws 1887, ch. 148). In 1895, Kansas created two "courts of appeal," one for the north and one for the south part of the state, "inferior to the supreme court and superior to all other courts in the state" (Laws 1895, ch. 96). And a constitutional amendment of 1900 (to art. III, sec. 2) increased the size of the supreme court from three to seven; the court could "sit separately in two divisions."[39]

In some states, the supreme court's burden was lightened, to a certain extent, by limiting the court's jurisdiction. The West Virginia constitution of 1872 (art. VIII, sec. 3) confined the appellate jurisdiction of the Supreme Court of Appeals to criminal cases, constitutional cases, "controversies concerning the title or boundaries of land" or the "probate of wills," civil cases "where the matter in controversy, exclusive of costs," was "of greater value, or amount than one hundred dollars," and a miscellaneous category, including cases "concerning a mill, roadway, ferry, or landing." In Illinois, in 1877, the appellate (intermediate) courts became last-stop courts of appeal for contract and damage cases where the amount in controversy was less than one thousand dollars, exclusive of costs. The supreme court still heard criminal cases, and "cases involving a franchise or freehold."[40]

The federal system was improved, in 1869, when Congress provided a circuit judge for each of the nine circuits. Each Supreme Court justice continued to be assigned to a circuit, as before, but it was recognized that he could not and would not do much of the circuit's work. The Civil War, Reconstruction, and the post-Civil War amendments gave added importance to the federal system. The Removal Act of 1875 put tremendous power into the federal-court system. From then on, any action asserting a federal right could begin in a federal court; or, if begun in a

[39]The courts of appeal were abolished in 1901.
[40]Laws Ill. 1877, pp. 70–71.

state court, could be removed to the federal courts. The act "opened wide a flood of totally new business for the federal courts."[41] Finally, Congress enacted major reform in 1891; an act of this year set up a circuit court of appeals for each circuit, to act as an appellate court, and provided for an extra circuit judge. Supreme Court justices under this act still each belonged to a circuit, and could sit there, but almost none ever did.[42]

Beyond these changes, political leadership seemed to have little interest in making court organization more rational. Lay politicians did not want a czar for the courts of their states. Muddled and overlapping jurisdiction was perfectly acceptable; the alternative—a strong chief justice with power to run his system—was not. In some states, to prevent any possibility of judicial leadership, the legislature downgraded the office of chief justice. In Ohio, in 1852, the chief justice was nothing more than "Judge of the Supreme Court having the shortest time to serve."[43] Many state constitutions had similar provisions.[44] Obviously, this system resulted in "a periodical rotation" in office, and precluded "any continuity of development of the administrative side of the court's work." In 1900, however, no less than seventeen of the thirty-eight states with an elected supreme court had this or a similar provision.[45] In some states, even clerks of court were elected— an absurdity from the standpoint of administrative coherence.[46]

The high courts were busy institutions. They were particularly involved in the economy. About a third of the decided cases, in the period 1870–1900, were cases of debt and contract; another 21 percent dealt with issues of real property law. About 10 percent were tort cases; another 10 percent criminal cases; 12.4 percent were on questions of public law (tax, regulation of business, eminent domain and similar matters); 7.7 percent on issues of family law and family property (divorce, inheritance, administration of

[41] Felix Frankfurter and James M. Landis, *The Business of the Supreme Court: A Study in the Federal Judicial System* (1928), p. 65.

[42] 26 Stats. 826 (act of March 3, 1891).

[43] Laws Ohio 1852, p. 67 (act of Feb. 29, 1852).

[44] Neb. const. 1875, art. VI, sec. 6. In Wisconsin, const. 1848, art. VII, sec. 4, as amended, 1889, the judge longest in service was chief justice.

[45] Pound, *op. cit.*, p. 169.

[46] For example, Va. const. 1850, art. VI, sec. 19: "The Voters of each county ... in which a circuit is held shall elect a clerk of such court, whose term of office shall be six years."

estates).[47] Yet it seems likely that these courts heard proportion-
ately less and less of the significant disputes in business and personal life. The costs of law were simply too high. Perhaps a
deliberate social choice lies behind this fact. Society, in a sense,
had decided to allow the price of full trial to rise to encourage
the development of alternatives. In this sense, the history of the
great American courts is also a history of those events that passed
them by.

Issues of inclusion and exclusion are important for understanding the trial court systems too. The court system—slow, expensive,
relatively technical, despite the pruning and reform of generations—could not possibly meet the needs generated by economic
and social change, at least not if courts followed the formal, official
plan. The American legal system faced demands from industry
and commerce and from an enormous middle class of consumers
of law. These demands could be met by new practices, new legislation, new forms of freedom and control. But not by long, costly
trials. The focus of creativity lay outside the courtroom. Formal
court systems could not hold day-to-day power over any important
segment of the economy—at any rate, not by means of ordinary
litigation, and through cases heard on appeal. Judge-kings might
reign; they could not rule. The business of running economy and
society had to drain out into other hands.

Yet, on the trial court level, the judicial system *did* make a real
contribution; the economy and polity could not run without it.
This was a low-key contribution, to be sure. In the first place, the
judicial system *worked*. It provided stability and certainty. Not, to
be sure, the stability and certainty of formal rationality; but a
creditor knew, in general, that he could collect on debts without
bribery or incompetence; that courts would be open and functioning in every season. The corruption in some courts (New
York's, for example) should not obscure the basic honesty and
competence of the trial court system.

In some ways, the trial court system was in crisis. There are
many complaints that courts could not keep pace with demand.
They were fixed in size and limited in staff; legislatures simply
did not add enough new judges and courts to fill the need. Delays

[47]Robert A. Kagan, Bliss Cartwright, Lawrence M. Friedman, and Stanton
Wheeler, "The Business of State Supreme Courts, 1870–1970," 30 Stan. L. Rev.
121, 133–35 (1977).

piled up. Litigants had to wait long periods to get their cases tried. What made the situation tolerable was simply that courts were not indispensable, either for ordinary social control or for settling most disputes that arose in society. There were great cases on the dockets. But routine commercial disputes stayed away. Most cases filed in trial court never actually went to trial. They were settled along the way. The legal business of business mostly bypassed the courts. The judges were professionals, lawyerly lawyers; there was no guarantee that they would understand the nature of a business dispute and handle it properly even if the judges had had enough time. In any event, full-scale litigation was slow, costly, disruptive. Time only accentuated these failings of the courts. The crowded dockets, the long delays, were symptoms of two contradictory phenomena: first, that there were matters that only courts could decide; and, equally, that here was an institution too marginal to be worth a heavy investment by society.

Yet in another sense the trial court system functioned well, and in a way that had profound impact on society. At the lower levels, courts processed a fantastic number of small cases. Debts were collected, divorces granted, mortgages foreclosed. Not many scholars have paid attention to the work of the bottom courts. One exception is Francis W. Laurent's study of the local courts of Chippewa County, Wisconsin: the courts handled hundreds of cases of domestic relations, debt collection, insurance, mortgage foreclosure, petty criminal actions, and the like.[48] Big city courts also handled a staggering volume. The municipal courts of Boston, at the very end of the century, "entertained the problems of about 20,000 plaintiffs a year."[49] The vast majority of the "cases" were utterly cut-and-dried. Debt collection was the main theme: grocers, clothing stores, doctors, asking the court to make their debtors pay.

The great volume of cases could only be handled through radical routinization. In probate, mortgage, divorce, and commercial

[48] Francis W. Laurent, *The Business of a Trial Court: One Hundred Years of Cases* (1959). On the flow of business through the courts of St. Louis, see Wayne V. McIntosh, "150 Years of Litigation and Dispute Settlement: A Court Tale," 15 Law & Society Rev. 823 (1981); and for a picture of the courts at work in a rural California county toward the end of the century, Lawrence M. Friedman, "San Benito 1890: Legal Snapshot of a County," 27 Stan. L. Rev. 687 (1975).

[49] Robert A. Silverman, *Law and Urban Growth: Civil Litigation in the Boston Trial Courts, 1880–1900* (1981), p. 144.

law, courts developed or used standardized procedures, almost as perfunctory—and essential—as procedures in parking-ticket cases in the 1980s. This was assembly-line justice; and the losers, overwhelmingly, were the little people: the men and women who owed money on a piano or a sewing machine; the tenants who could not pay their rent; the patient who never took care of the doctor bill. On the surface, it looks as if the law "responded to the cold-blooded interests of merchants."[50] But there was another side to the law. The courts held out the promise of help to small merchants whose customers did not pay. This promise of help must have made it somewhat easier and cheaper to extend credit to great masses of people. Thus, "millions had a chance to buy goods and services they could not have obtained otherwise."[51] This economic advantage came, of course, at a heavy price.

[50]Lawrence M. Friedman, "Law and Small Business in the United States: One Hundred Years of Struggle and Accommodation," in Stuart W. Bruchey, ed., *Small Business in American Life* (1980), pp. 304, 314.
[51]*Ibid.*

CHAPTER III

PROCEDURE AND PRACTICE:
AN AGE OF REFORM

MR. FIELD'S CODE

1848 was a year of revolution in Europe. In the United States it was the year in which New York passed an "act to simplify and abridge the Practice, Pleadings, and Proceedings of the Courts."[1] This was a full-blown Code of Civil Procedure, radically new in appearance at least. The code is often called the Field Code, after David Dudley Field, who played a vital role in its enactment. The Field Code, more than any other statute on the subject, acted as a catalytic agent of procedural reform in the United States.

New York had adopted a new constitution in 1846. One clause called for the "appointment of three commissioners, to revise, reform, simplify, and abridge the rules and practice, pleadings, forms and proceedings of the courts of record of this State" (art. VI, sec. 24). The state got more than it bargained for, perhaps. One of the original commissioners, Nicholas Hill, Jr., resigned in 1847, horrified because his colleagues were willing to recommend changes "so purely experimental, so sudden and general, and so perilous." David Dudley Field (1805–94) was appointed in his place. From his early days at the bar, Field had been seized with the vision of codification and law reform. In 1839 he wrote an open letter on reform of the judicial system. He later harangued a legislative committee on the subject. From 1847 on, he was the heart and soul of the movement.[2]

Stylistically, no greater affront to the common-law tradition can be imagined than the 1848 code. It was couched in brief, gnomic,

[1]Laws N.Y. 1848, ch. 379.
[2]Henry M. Field, *The Life of David Dudley Field* (1898), pp. 42–56. Mildred V. Coe and Lewis W. Morse, "Chronology of the Development of the David Dudley Field Code," 27 Cornell L.Q. 238 (1941).

Napoleonic sections, tightly worded and skeletal; there was no trace of the elaborate redundancy, the voluptuous heaping on of synonyms, so characteristic of Anglo-American statutes. It was, in short, a code in the French sense, not a statute. It was a lattice of reasoned principles, scientifically arranged, not a thick thumb stuck into the dikes of common law. The substance of the Field Code was almost as daring as its style. The heart of the code was its sixty-second section, which declared:

> The distinction between actions at law and suits in equity, and the forms of all such actions and suits heretofore existing, are abolished; and, there shall be in this state, hereafter, but one form of action, for the enforcement or protection of private rights and the redress or prevention of private wrongs, which shall be denominated a civil action.

Taken literally, this was the death sentence of common-law pleading. It was meant to put an end to all special pleading, forms of actions and writs, and to close the chasm between equity and law; it was meant to destroy at one blow the paraphernalia of this most recondite, most precious, most lawyerly area of law.

Like many other revolutions, the upheaval of 1848, in the legal communes of New York, was not completely a bolt from the blue. The Field Code had a number of distinguished intellectual forefathers. In England, Jeremy Bentham, who died in 1832, had savagely attacked the "ancestor-worship" of the common law. Bentham put his vigorous pen at the service of legal rationality. Lawyers in Bentham's circle preached hard for reform of the common law, particularly procedure. In 1828, Henry Brougham spoke for six hours in the House of Commons, eating a "hatful of oranges as he went, calling for law reform," and ending with a dramatic plea: "It was the boast of Augustus...that he found Rome of brick, and left it of marble; a praise not unworthy of a great prince. ...But how much nobler will be the Sovereign's boast...that he found law dear, and left it cheap; found it a sealed book—left it a living letter; found it a patrimony of the rich—left it the inheritance of the poor; found it a two-edged sword of craft and oppression—left it the staff of honesty and the shield of innocence."[3] In response to Brougham's speech, Parliament appointed

---

[3]Quoted in Brian Abel-Smith and Robert Stevens, *Lawyers and the Courts: A Sociological Study of the English Legal System 1750–1965* (1967), p. 19; see also Robert W. Millar, *Civil Procedure of the Trial Court in Historical Perspective* (1952), p. 43. Millar's book is a richly detailed, if technical, account of American civil procedure.

a commission to consider procedural reform, and passed some reform statutes in the early 1830s. In the United States, the Field Code had a precedent of sorts in the codes drawn up by Edward Livingston in Louisiana. The Louisiana codes were not relevant, technically speaking, since Louisiana was a more or less civil-law state; the fusion of law and equity in Texas could also be explained away on the grounds of civil-law contamination. In some other states, notably Massachusetts, commissions had issued reports calling for improved and simplified procedure. Colonial practice had been much simpler than English practice and colonial habits had never been wholly extinguished. As we have seen, a number of states had taken up procedural reform; Georgia's experiment had been quite radical for its day. Undoubtedly, precedents and examples were important. But most of all, the time was ripe. Code pleading was an idea whose day had finally come.

Not that code pleading was an immediate and unqualified success. Ironically, the code had particular trouble in New York itself. In 1849 the Field Code was re-enacted, but much wounded by amendments and supplements. The new act contained 473 sections. An act of July 10, 1851, again substantially amended the code. This act in turn was frequently amended. In 1870, the legislature appointed a new commission to revise the code; it reported a fresh version in 1876, of monstrously inflated size—"reactionary in spirit . . . a figure of Falstaffian proportions among the other codes," its principles "smothered in details."[4] By 1880, the New York procedural codes (including the code of criminal procedure) contained no less than 3,356 sections.[5] This was a far cry, indeed, from the simplicity and artlessness that the original code had proclaimed as its goal. In the 1890s, New York's procedure was still considered so imperfect that a strong movement grew up at the bar to reform it still further.

The courts, too, showed a certain hostility and resistance to change. The conventional wisdom has it that many judges manhandled the code. One extreme example, perhaps, was Judge Samuel Selden, who remained convinced that law and equity were categories of the real world. He simply could not grasp the idea

Also useful is Charles M. Hepburn, *The Historical Development of Code Pleading in America and England* (1897). On the general background, see Charles M. Cook, *The American Codification Movement: A Study of Antebellum Legal Reform* (1981).

  [4]Hepburn, *op. cit.*, p. 130.
  [5]Alison Reppy, "The Field Codification Concept," in Alison Reppy, ed., *David Dudley Field Centenary Essays* (1949), pp. 17, 34–36.

of merging the two: "It is possible to abolish one or the other," he wrote, in an 1856 decision, "but it certainly is not possible to abolish the distinction between them."[6] Chief Justice John Bradley Winslow of Wisconsin wrote in 1910 that the "cold, not to say inhuman, treatment which the infant code received from the New York judges is matter of history."[7] But the historical record is not quite that clear; very little is known about the behavior of trial-court judges, though the fate of the code was really decided there. Certainly the code could not destroy the habits of a lifetime, nor, by itself, transform what may have been deeply imbedded in a particular legal culture. But the stubbornness of the judges was a short-run phenomenon, to the extent it occurred. The real vice of the code probably lay in its weak empirical base. The draftsmen derived their basic principles from ideas of right reason, rather than from a careful study of what actually happened in American courts, and what functions and interests courts and their lawsuits served.

The Field Code, as such, did not make much headway in the East. Even in New York, the draftsmen of the code thought of it merely as a temporary draft; the full text, completed a few years later, was too much for the legislature to swallow. Further west, the situation was dramatically different. The ink was hardly dry on Field's Code when Missouri adopted it into law (1849). In 1851, California, a new state, at the uttermost limit of the country, enacted the Field Code. Before the outbreak of the Civil War, the Field Code had been adopted in Iowa, Minnesota, Indiana, Ohio, Washington Territory, Nebraska, Wisconsin and Kansas.[8] Nevada adopted the code in 1861, and by the turn of the century, so had the Dakotas, Idaho, Arizona, Montana, North Carolina, Wyoming, South Carolina, Utah, Colorado, Oklahoma, and New Mexico.

Why the West? Supposedly, the Western bar was young and open-minded; technical training in common-law pleading was not common coin among these lawyers. Stephen Field, David Dudley Field's brother, was a prominent California lawyer, and may have helped advance his brother's cause. In Missouri, an attorney named

[6]J. Selden, in *Reubens* v. *Joel,* 13 N.Y. 488, 493 (1856); see Charles E. Clark, "The Union of Law and Equity," 25 Columbia L. Rev. 1 (1925).

[7]Quoted in Clark, *op. cit.,* p. 3.

[8]Kentucky and Oregon also adopted the code, but maintained the separation of law and equity. Iowa reintroduced the distinction in 1860. Millar, *op. cit.,* p. 54. Later, Arkansas adopted the Kentucky model.

David Wells had been agitating for years for the abolition of the distinction between law and equity. Both states had some remnants of civil law in their background; both entered the Union with a history of land controversies and a full docket of land-grant problems. These land claims were hard to analyze in terms of the distinction between "legal" and "equitable" matters; as to these claims, the distinction was meaningless and procedurally disruptive.

Western states were also more eclectic in general than states of the older East. The glitter of the Field Code may conceal the extent to which some Eastern states (Massachusetts, for example) were working toward procedural reform in their own way, in accordance with what the bar considered the inherent logic of their own institutions. The New York name had no magic in Massachusetts. Some states rejected the Field Code as unsuitable, or too advanced, or as the product of a different culture. Dean Henry Ingersoll of the University of Tennessee, writing in the Yale Law Journal in 1891, decried the "attempt of one State to adapt a Code of Procedure prepared for an entirely different social and business condition." In North Carolina, one of the few Eastern states to adopt the code, he felt the experiment (which he blamed on blacks and carpetbaggers) had been a disaster:

> During...Reconstruction...the legal practice of the State was reconstructed by the adoption of the New York Code of Civil Procedure, with all its penalties and high-pressure machinery adapted to the conditions of an alert, eager, pushing commercial community. Rip Van Winkle was not more surprised on returning to his native village after his long sleep than were the lawyers of the old "Tar-heel State."... This new-fangled commercial machine...was as well adapted to their condition as were the light driving buggies of the Riverside Park to the rough roads of the Black mountains, or the garb of the Broadway dandy to the turpentine stiller.... North Carolina had about as much use for the system as she had for a clearing-house, a Central Park or a Stock Exchange. The clamors of the bar soon brought about...amendment ...and left [the code]...a great cumbrous piece of machinery without driving-wheels, steam-chest or boiler, propelled along by the typical slow oxteam.[9]

[9]Henry H. Ingersoll, "Some Anomalies of Practice," 1 Yale L.J. 89, 91, 92 (1891).

Actually, it is dubious whether systems of procedure fit particular cultures so snugly as Ingersoll seemed to think; or whether North Carolina was really so primitive or so idiosyncratic as not to need procedural reform. Ingersoll's diatribe mostly meant that lawyers could attack code pleading more easily when it was possible to identify it with an alien, and in this case, a hated culture. In his statement, there may lurk a small grain of truth: procedural reform was most necessary, or at least most desirable, in commercial states. In a business economy, business needs as rational and predictable a common context as it can possibly get. An orderly, rational law machine was infinitely preferable to the chaos of common-law pleading. Business wanted the machine to turn out swift, nontechnical, predictable decisions, based on the facts, not on the accidents of writs and forms of action. Classical pleading was a sort of slow, gentlemanly ritual dance. Its aim was to isolate pure "issues" of law or fact. But these issues often turned out to be mere by-products of pleading, hence, in a sense, purely hypothetical. Old procedure and excess technicality survived the longest in parts of the law where society had less of a sense of the value of mass-producing results. The jury trial of a murderer is a unique, unstandardized event, the exact legal opposite of a garnishment or a parking ticket.

But where business was unavoidably dependent on the courts, procedure was radically and successfully simplified. This process was not obvious because the development was quiet, almost invisible. Just as a mass market led to mass production of commodities, so a mass market led to mass production of law. The system stamped out, like so many iron nails, its tiny but numberless outputs. Their importance lay in their cumulative effect—small debts collected, garnishments achieved, instruments neatly recorded. These legal outputs generally depended on the validity of pieces of paper invented by businessmen and business lawyers. Where the courts accepted these documents (as they usually did), business could safely ignore the grand debate over codes and procedure, debates about the esthetic shape of the legal system, that raged in upper circles of the bar. These great debates—whether law emanated from the spirit of the people or not, whether the common law would lose its soul if it was codified completely—meant little or nothing to people engaged in making and losing money, day by day.

In the earlier part of the 19th century, law reform probably did command wide support from the businessmen or merchants.[10] They saw that law was cumbersome and unfeeling; they sensed that it was necessary to redirect the law, to strip it of excesses, before they could make use of it efficiently. David Dudley Field promised the businessman that law would become his willing tool. And so it did, but not in the way that Field imagined. The industrialists of the Gilded Age did not use law and lawsuits to solve ordinary business disputes. They used law to collect and record, as a tool of mass production. In the grand struggles of robber barons, too, lawyers used law as a weapon; the barons battled each other in court, showering each other with a blizzard of writs and injunctions. And in the big constitutional cases, business tried to bend, delay, or prevent the rise of the welfare state. The reformers never succeeded in their Utopian aim of creating a simple, rational system of law. To this extent, their dreams went sour. But the failure was not on the technical level; reformers were frustrated by concrete interest groups, and the uses groups made of legal process.

The bar in some states opposed code pleading with gusto. But code pleading in the long run probably had a good effect on lawyer's practice. One of the root ideas of the code was fact-pleading, so simple and rational that the average citizen would not need a lawyer. This was a completely visionary goal. Yet procedure became, on the whole, much less technical. In a small way, this perhaps helped free lawyers from the drudgery of learning how to plead and appeal. Procedural reform may have indirectly smoothed the way for the rise of the "office" bar—counselor-lawyers who never set foot in court. Or, perhaps, the rise of the "office" bar meant that traditional rules and skills of pleading became ever rarer, and hence had less and less support from leaders of the bar.

By 1900, the Field Code was widely adopted, copied, modified. Field's reforms had earned, moreover, the supreme compliment of close study in England, mother country of the common law. Field's work influenced the English Judicature Act of 1873. English reforms, in turn, had American consequences. The Connecticut Practice Act of 1879, for example, drew "in considerable measure upon the English reforms," and was, on the whole, "a

[10]See, in general, Lawrence M. Friedman, "Law Reform in Historical Perspective," 13 St. Louis U.L.J. 351 (1969); Maxwell Bloomfield, *American Lawyers in a Changing Society, 1776–1876* (1976), chapter 3 (on William Sampson).

distinct advance over the codes which had emanated from ... New York."[11]

In short, before the 19th century was over, almost all states had reformed their procedures at least somewhat. Only a minority—New Jersey, Delaware, Illinois—clung tenaciously to old-style pleading. Yet no state had carried its reform as far as Field would have liked. In every state, the union of law and equity remained imperfect. For one thing, the federal Constitution, and state constitutions, had provisions preserving the right of trial by jury; courts felt that they had to pay attention to the historical distinction between law and equity since only in "law" was there a jury right to be preserved. On balance, the union of the two systems was a triumph for equity; from equity, the new procedure derived some of its most striking traits: greater freedom in joinder of parties, a liberal attitude toward the rights of defendants to put forward counterclaims, more suppleness in general in the use of judicial remedies. Even those New England states which had never granted full equity powers to their courts—Maine, New Hampshire, Massachusetts—granted these powers after the Civil War. In fact, many striking legal developments, between 1850 and 1900, made creative use of tools of equity. Courts put bankrupt railroads in receivership and virtually ran the roads; they forged out of the injunction a terrible sword to use in industrial disputes. Injunction and receivership were both old, trusty tricks of equity, rapidly and vigorously reshaped. This was, after all, a period of activist judges; equity, free from the jury's fetters, was made to order for a judge with a taste for power.

COURT PROCEDURE IN COURT

Despite the Field Code, questions of procedure continued to claim a high proportion of the attention of appellate courts. Upper courts had the power to control lower courts and juries with a tight hand, at least as far as the formal record was concerned. Between 1870 and 1900, there are persistent complaints that some state supreme courts behaved as if their chief function was to reverse decisions of their lower courts for technical errors. A piece

[11]Robert W. Millar, *Civil Procedure of the Trial Court in Historical Perspective* (1952), p. 55.

in a law journal in 1887 expressed the view that the Texas Court of Appeals "seems to have been organized to overrule and reverse. At least, since its organization that has been its chief employment." As evidence, the article cited an amazing fact: during the twelve years of the court's existence, it had reversed 1,604 criminal cases, and affirmed only 882—a margin of almost two to one. In one volume of reports, there were five reversals to every single affirmance.[12]

This was Roscoe Pound's "hypertrophy," most marked in criminal cases, and carried over from the earlier part of the century. At least on paper, tighter rules about the conduct of trials continued to tame the lower-court judges. Judges had once been in the habit of giving oral instructions to the jury. They told the jury about the law in frank, natural language. But this practice died out—or was driven out. The instructions became solemn written documents, drafted by the lawyers. Each side drew up statements of law; the judge merely picked out those that were (in his judgment) legally "correct." In any event, the instructions were technical, legalistic, utterly opaque. They were almost useless as a way to communicate with juries; the medium conveyed no message.[13] Each instruction had to be framed with great care, so as not to give the upper court a chance to find reversible error. At one time, too, it was standard for judges to comment on the evidence, to tell the jury quite openly what the judge thought about the witnesses, and what their testimony was worth. In Missouri, for example, this practice was stamped out by 1859.[14]

Appellate procedure also remained very technical and complex, throughout the 19th century. After reading cases in the last part of the century, Roscoe Pound was "tempted to think that appellate procedure existed as a system of preventing the disposition of cases themselves upon their merits."[15] Here too, the Field Code tried to bring in a radical new order; it swept away all the cumbersome rules, the distinctions between writs of error

---

[12]Note, "Overruled Their Judicial Superiors," 21 Am. L. Rev. 610 (1887).

[13]See, for examples in criminal cases, Lawrence M. Friedman and Robert V. Percival, *The Roots of Justice: Crime and Punishment in Alameda County, California, 1870–1910* (1981), pp. 186–187.

[14]Henry F. Luepke, Jr., "Comments on the Evidence in Missouri," 5 St. Louis U.L.J. 424 (1959); on the role of the jury in 19th century law in general, see Note, "The Changing Role of the Jury in the Nineteenth Century," 74 Yale L.J. 170 (1964).

[15]Roscoe Pound, *Appellate Procedure in Civil Cases* (1941), p. 320.

and appeals in equity, and replaced them with a single form of
review, which it called an "appeal." Some noncode jurisdictions
(Alabama in 1853, Pennsylvania in 1889) also abolished the writ
of error, and brought in a simpler form, which they too called an
appeal.[16]

But in general, record worship did not die out. It seemed to
retain a stranglehold on appellate review; it was as if upper courts
tried, not cases, but printed formulae, and tried them according
to warped and unreal distinctions. Again, excesses in behavior
were most striking in criminal appeals. Harwell, the defendant in
a Texas case decided in 1886,[17] had been arrested and convicted
for receiving stolen cattle. The Texas court reversed, because,
among other things, the jury found the defendant "guity" instead
of "guilty." In 1877, the same court reversed a conviction because
the jury carelessly wrote, "We, the jury, the defendant guilty,"
leaving out the word "find."[18] The same court, however, mag-
nanimously upheld a conviction of "guily" in 1879,[19] proving that
a "t" was less crucial than an "l" in the common law of Texas.

It is not easy to account for this behavior. Perhaps appeal courts
were simply too busy for perspective. They relied less on long
oral arguments than on written briefs. They spent their lives looking at formal records, and may have come to believe in them too
much. Again, the profession took itself (as always) very seriously.
A judge may consider very significant an error which an outsider
would find trivial at best. Stylistically, this was a period of conceptualism, of dry legal logic. The bench, as we have suggested,
was peopled with lesser men; rules were their one excuse for
power. Some procedural excess may have stemmed from a good
idea gone bad: a fumbling attempt to govern, standardize, and
rationalize trials, appeals, and written arguments. Appellate reports sometimes complained about the sloppy or misdirected work
of lawyers and lower-court judges. This was particularly true in
the early years of a state or territory. It seems clear that some
appeal judges took seriously the job of riding herd on lower courts,
lawyers, and juries, and set a high value on at least minimal regularity in procedure. The law commonly allowed litigants who lost

[16]Pound, *op. cit.*, PS, pp. 260–61.

[17]*Harwell* v. *State*, 22 Tex. App. 251, 2 S.W. 606 (1886); see also *Taylor* v. *State*,
5 Tex. App. 569 (1877); *Wilson* v. *State*, 12 Tex. App. 481 (1882).

[18]*Shaw* v. *State*, 2 Tex. App. 487 (1877).

[19]*Curry* v. *State*, 7 Tex. App. 91 (1879).

in municipal courts or justice-of-the-peace courts to take their cases to the regular trial courts. There the litigant would get a trial *de novo* (that is, the court would do the whole trial over, including the evidence and the finding of facts).[20] This shows a certain lack of respect for the craftsmanship of basement courts. Record worship showed a similar disrespect for trial courts.

On the other hand, it is easy to exaggerate the amount of record worship. The legal literature is full of horror stories, but rather short on facts and figures. One rarely hears about the cases—and there must have been many—in which the trial court *did* act unfairly; and yet the appeal court let things lie. Consistently, more cases were affirmed than reversed: 60 percent or more, in most jurisdictions. This hardly suggests a gleeful perversity on the part of high courts.

At the trial court level, criminal procedure was harder to reform than civil procedure. The constitutions themselves put limits on reform by enshrining certain practices in bills of rights. There was, for example, no way the federal government could abolish use of the grand jury in serious criminal cases.[21] Moreover, there was probably less impetus for reform. Suspicion of government died hard. People were not so anxious to relax rules of criminal procedure, for fear of unleashing the full power of government. Of course, textbook procedure was not the same as living procedure in court. The legal guarantees of fair trial hardly worked at all for ignorant, timid, or unpopular defendants. Kangaroo-court justice, the blackjack, police harassment, the Ku Klux Klan, vigilante justice, and the lynch law of the 1880s and 1890s in the South were as much a part of the living law of criminal procedure as record worship was. The two phenomena may even be connected. The vigilantes and the lynch mobs demanded quick, certain law and order (as they defined these); they did not trust the regular courts in either respect. The devilish inversions of procedure, perpetrated by vigilantes and lynch mobs, acted as a kind of countervailing force: a balance, of sorts, to the power of upper courts to bind and loose for reasons that looked irrational below.

---

[20]See, for example, *Hurtgen* v. *Kantrowitz*, 15 Colo. 442, 24 Pac. 872 (1890).

[21]By the 5th amendment: "No person shall be held to answer for a capital, or otherwise infamous crime, unless on a presentment or indictment of a Grand Jury." On this institution in general, see Richard D. Younger, *The People's Panel: The Grand Jury in the United States, 1634–1941* (1963).

The law of evidence remained complex. Simon Greenleaf, in his treatise on evidence (first published in 1842), had once praised the "symmetry and beauty" of this branch of law. A student, he felt, "would rise from the study of its principles convinced, with Lord Erskine, that 'they are founded in the charities of religion, in the philosophy of nature, in the truths of history, and in the experience of common life.'" A more realistic critic, James Bradley Thayer, of Harvard, writing in 1898, felt, on the other hand, that the law of evidence was "a piece of illogical ... patchwork; not at all to be admired, or easily to be found intelligible."[22] It was still largely a gloss on trial by jury, and its amazing complexity—John H. Wigmore spun ten volumes out of it in the twentieth century— had no counterpart outside of the common law. Indeed, Thayer reported that even English lawyers were surprised "to see our lively quarrels over points of evidence." In the United States, objections to evidence were presented as "exceptions, a method never common in England and now abolished there, which presents only a dry question of law—not leaving to the upper court that power to heed the general justice of the case which the more elastic procedure of the English courts so commonly allows; and tending thus to foster delay and chicane."[23]

The law of evidence remained consistent with its immediate past. It was founded in a world of mistrust and suspicion of institutions; it liked nothing better than constant checks and balances; it was never sure whether anyone, judge, lawyer, or jury, was honest or competent. On the other hand, a few of its more restrictive rules were mitigated. The old rule that an interested party could not testify was abolished. England took this step in 1843, Michigan in 1846, and other states followed over the next thirty years. The rule that disqualified the *parties* to a lawsuit was only a special case of the rule; it too was abolished. Connecticut may have been the earliest to do so, in the late 1840s; other states followed, though some of them rather slowly; Illinois took this step in 1867.[24] The states then, however, passed laws which prevented a survivor from testifying about transactions with a dead person: "If death has closed the lips of the one party, the policy

---

[22]The Greenleaf quote, and Thayer's comment, are in James B. Thayer, *A Preliminary Treatise on Evidence at the Common Law* (1898), pp. 508–09.

[23]Thayer, *op. cit.*, pp. 528–29.

[24]Rev. Stats. Conn. 1849, Title 1, ch. 10, sec. 141: "No person shall be disqualified as a witness...by reason of his interest...*as a party* or otherwise" (emphasis added); Laws Ill. 1867, p. 183.

of the law is to close the lips of the other."[25] The list of exceptions to the hearsay rule also kept swelling. In general, then, more categories of evidence became admissible; but there were also more rules.

CODIFICATION AND REFORM

Field's Code of procedure was only one part of a larger, bolder plan to codify the whole common law. The smell of feudalism still oozed from the pores of the common law. To men like Jeremy Bentham and his followers in England, and David Dudley Field, Edward Livingston, and others in America, the common law was totally unsuited for an Age of Reason. It was huge and shapeless. Common-law principles had to be painfully extracted from a jungle of words. "The law" was an amorphous entity, a ghost, scattered in little bits and pieces among hundreds of case-reports, in hundreds of different books. Nobody knew what was and was not law. Why not gather together the real principles of law, put them together, and build a simple, complete and sensible code? The French had shown the way with the Code Napoleon. Louisiana was at least something of an American demonstration. In 1865, Field published a general Civil Code, divided into four parts. The first three dealt with persons, property, and obligations; the fourth part contained general provisions. This scheme of organization ran parallel to that of the great French code; like that code, Field's Code tried to set out principles of law exhaustively, concisely, and with great clarity of language. But New York would have none of it. Till the end of his long life, Field continued to press for adoption in his state. He never succeeded. New York did enact a penal code, which went into effect in 1881; but the civil code was repeatedly turned down, the latest snub occurring in 1885.

The codification movement is one of the set pieces of American legal history. It has its hero, Field; its villain is James C. Carter of New York,[26] who fought the idea of codification with as much vigor as Field fought for it. Codification was wrong, Carter felt,

[25]*Louis's Adm'r* v. *Easton*, 50 Ala. 470, 471 (1874); see John H. Wigmore, *A Treatise on the Anglo-American System of Evidence*, vol. 1 (2nd ed., 1923), pp. 1004–05.

[26]On Carter (1827–1905), see the essay by George A. Miller in *Great American Lawyers*, Vol. 8 (1909), pp. 3–41.

because it removed the center of gravity from the courts. The legislature—the code-enacting body—was comparatively untrustworthy; it was too passionately addicted to the short run. "The question is," he wrote, whether "growth, development and improvement of the law" should "remain under the guidance of men selected by the people on account of their special qualifications for the work," or "be transferred to a numerous legislative body, disqualified by the nature of their duties for the discharge of this supreme function?"[27] Codes impaired the orderly development of the law; they froze the law into semipermanent form; this prevented natural evolution. Carter was impressed by the teachings of the so-called historical school of jurisprudence, founded by German jurists in the early 19th century. They taught Carter that laws were and ought to be emanations from the folk wisdom of a people. A statute drafted by a group of so-called experts was bound to be an inferior product, compared to what centuries of evolution, of self-correcting growth, could achieve. The courts apply to private disputes a "social standard of justice" which is "the product of the combined operation of the thought, the morality, the intellectual and moral culture of the time." The judges know and feel this, because "they are a part of the community." The "social standard of justice grows and develops with the moral and intellectual growth of society.... Hence a gradual change unperceived and unfelt in its advance is continually going on in the jurisprudence of every progressive State."[28] This point of view, of course, was useful not only in fighting codification; it was also a handy club to use against much of the social and economic legislation of the late 19th century. These too were doomed to failure; they were hasty intrusions, and they contradicted the deeper genius of the law.

Field saw codification in a different light. The laws were "now in sealed books, and the lawyers object to the opening of these books." Lawyers "as a body never did begin a reform of the law, and, judging from experience, they never will."[29] The closed books had to be opened. Progress demanded no less. The two great antagonists were in many ways one in their basic point of view. Legislative patchwork was as offensive to Field as to Carter, as

[27]James C. Carter, *The Proposed Codification of Our Common Law* (1884), p. 87.
[28]James C. Carter, *The Provinces of the Written and the Unwritten Law* (1889), pp. 48–49.
[29]Titus M. Coan, ed., *Speeches, Arguments, and Miscellaneous Papers of David Dudley Field*, vol. III (1890), pp. 238, 239.

offensive as the patchwork common law. The codes that Field had in mind would be the work of experts—jurists like Field himself. The legislature would simply take the codes and give them its stamp of validity. The codes, then, would be the product of a legal elite; they would be subtle and flexible, as the common law should have been, but was not, since the common law had become (unfortunately) a prisoner of history, bound up in the narrow self-interest of old-fashioned men. Carter and Field, then, agreed about ends, disagreed about means. They both valued flexibility in the law; liked a businesslike rationality; distrusted the role of nonexperts, of laymen, in the making of law. Carter preferred common-law judges, as philosopher-kings, and looked on codes as straitjackets. Field took the opposite view.

In the last third of the century, ideas like those of Carter and Field were, so to speak, in the air. They were similar, in some respects, to the ideas of Christopher Columbus Langdell, who led the reform of legal education at Harvard, starting in 1870. Langdell felt strongly that the common law was a science, that it contained within itself a precious core of basic principle. Legal education should find and teach this essence, as refined in the crucible of experience, and with the legislative warts removed. Langdell shared Carter's basic concept of law; yet his idea of a legal principle was much like that of Field, only implicit, evolutionary, more subtly dynamic.

The Civil Code—and Field's codes on other branches of law—were not total failures. Like the Code of Civil Procedure, they found greater acceptance far from home. Dakota Territory enacted a civil code in 1866; Idaho and Montana also made a code part of their law. The chief victory, however, was California, which enacted a civil code in 1872. This was, however, not a blanket adoption of Field's code. Its provisions were thoroughly revised and reconstituted, in the light of California's own prior statutes and cases.[30] California also adopted a penal and a political code.

Codification found a home in Georgia as well. The legislature appointed three commissioners in 1858 to prepare a code "which should, as near as practicable, embrace in a condensed form, the Laws of Georgia." The code was to embody the "great fundamental principles" of Georgia's jurisprudence, and "furnish all the information, on the subject of law, required either by the citizen or the subordinate Magistrate." The code was divided into

[30]See Arvo Van Alstyne, *The California Civil Code* (1954), p. 11.

four parts—"the Political and Public Organization of the State," then a civil code ("Which treats of rights, wrongs, and remedies"), a code of practice, and a penal code. The Georgia code did not purport to make new law, or to "graft upon our system any new features extracted from others, and unharmonious with our own." It merely attempted to clarify and restate, to "cut and unravel *Gordian knots*," to "give shape and order, system and efficiency, to the sometimes crude, and often ill-expressed, sovereign will of the State." The code ran to some 4,700 sections. It was adopted in 1860 as the law of Georgia.[31]

The success of the codes in the West was due to reasons that by now are familiar. These were sparsely settled states in a hurry to ingest a legal system. A few had something of a civil-law tradition. In none of the Western states did the bar have a strong vested interest in the continuance of old rules, especially rules of pleading. Codes were a handy way to acquire new law, a way of buying clothes off the rack, so to speak. But once the codes were on the books, the results fell far short of the hopes. What happened afterwards would have brought Field to the rim of distraction. Courts and lawyers were not used to codified law; they tended to treat some of the code provisions in accordance with ingrained common-law habits and prejudices. In some cases, the codes' provisions were construed away; more often, they were simply ignored. Nor did the legislature keep its hands off the codes; they tended to let stand the broad statements of principles (they made little difference anyway), but they added all sorts of accretions. It is hard to resist the conclusion that the codes had almost no impact on behavior, either in court or out. Law in action in California did not seem much different from law in action in noncode states, in any way that the codes would help to explain.

The codes did focus attention on some of the drawbacks of common law. The codes are the spiritual parents of the Restatements of the Law—black-letter codes of the 20th century, sponsored by the American Law Institute, but meant for persuasion of judges, rather than enactment into law. Both codes and restatements were reforms that did not reform. In the 19th century, law was constantly and vigorously changing; every new statute was in a sense a reform; so was every new doctrine and ruling. The drafters of codes were interested in reform in a special sense.

[31] *The Code of the State of Georgia,* prepared by R. H. Clark, T. R. R. Cobb, and D. Irwin (1861), pp. iii, iv, vii, viii.

They wanted to perfect an existing system. They wanted to make it more knowable, harmonious, certain. Drastic shifts in allocation of political or economic power, through law, were not to their purpose.

Behind the work of the law reformers was a theory of sorts: that legal system is best, and works best, and does the most for society, which most conforms to the ideal of legal rationality—the legal order which is most clear, orderly, systematic (in its formal parts), which has the most structural beauty, which most appeals to the modern, well-educated jurist. This theory was rarely made explicit, and of course never tested. It was in all probability false, since it is hard to see how society can be changed by reforms which only rearrange law on paper. One child labor act or one homestead act had more potential impact than volumes of codes.

In fact, paper changes were in a way the main point of law reform: law reform was, basically, those changes in law which could be agreed upon by leaders of the bar, and which were not socially or politically sensitive. Only these could be put forward as the program of the bar, without arousing public animosity. A uniform wage-and-hour law, or a tax code, could never be presented as something blandly, incontrovertibly good. Law reform became prominent as the public-service work of the legal profession; it was useful for the lawyer's tarnished image. But service to the whole public is sometimes the same as service to nobody. No doubt the public (and most lawyers) hardly suspected that "law reform" had such limited goals, and such minor potential impact; law reform generally masqueraded as a vital social movement. In any event, law reform could be used by lawyers to justify their own monopoly of practice; it could pass for one of the social services that every profession is supposed to perform.[32]

This, at least, was the character of late 19th-century law reform. It was a program of the upper or organized bar. The bar association movement began in the 1870s; and by the 1890s, the American Bar Association, and the local organizations, were pushing vigorously for reform and unification of American law. But even the "law reform" that came out of these efforts was fairly meager, at least up to the end of the 19th century. Codification on a uniform basis was extremely difficult in a federal union. As far as most branches of law were concerned, each state from Maine to

[32]See, in general, Lawrence M. Friedman, "Law Reform in Historical Perspective," 13 St. Louis U.L.J. 351 (1969).

the Pacific was a petty sovereignty, with its own brand of law. The American Bar Association left most of the law alone; it concerned itself with fields of law whose implications crossed state lines: the law of migratory divorce, for example, and commercial law, both of which were notoriously nonuniform.

On the surface, reform efforts resulted in solid achievements in standardizing commercial law. Arguably, the need·was great. The United States was, or had become, a gigantic free-trade area; businessmen needed fair, uniform laws of commerce to take advantage of this huge, rich domestic market. Moreover, many differences in detail, in the state laws, had no particular basis in culture or opinion; the laws were functionally the same, with little quirks here and there, and small technical differences. Uniformity could not be achieved through the courts, not even the federal courts, though these courts did in fact make an effort;[33] the job demanded legislation. In the last decade of the century, the ABA threw its weight behind a uniform law movement. States were encouraged to appoint commissioners who would meet and consider the problems. The first major effort of the commissioners on uniform state laws was a Negotiable Instruments Law, modeled after the English Bills-of-Exchange Act (1882), and with something of a nod to the California code. The NIL was to become one of the most successful of all the so-called uniform laws. It had been widely enacted by 1900; and it won almost universal acceptance before it was swept away by the Uniform Commercial Code in the 1950s and 1960s.

There were other triumphs of uniformity, however, which are easy to overlook, because they did not come out of the formal movement for uniform laws. The Interstate Commerce Act of 1887, the Sherman Act of 1890, the Bankruptcy Act of 1898, were all in a real sense responses to demands, whether commercial or political, for a single national authority. The "national" scope of legal education and legal literature was another impulse toward uniformity, at least as far as legal culture is concerned, and particularly after Langdell purged Harvard of the lecture method

---

[33]The federal courts, under the doctrine of *Swift* v. *Tyson*, were supposed to apply general law, not the law of particular states, in cases between citizens of different states. See above, pp. 261–62; Tony A. Freyer, *Harmony and Dissonance: The Swift & Erie Cases in American Federalism* (1981); on other efforts by the federal courts in this direction, see Tony A. Freyer, "The Federal Courts, Localism, and the National Economy, 1865–1900," 53 Bus. Hist. Rev. 343 (1979).

and launched the case method on its way. Not that all members
of the legal profession were trained and socialized in the same
way; but the profession was stratified more by social class and
training than along geographical lines.

Publishers continued to spew forth an incredible profusion of
legal materials: cases by the thousands; statutes in every state,
every year or every other year; regulations, rulings, ordinances,
and local customs on a scale that dwarfed the imagination. Tricks
of research made this fabulous diversity somewhat more tractable.
In the last quarter of the century, the West Publishing Company,
of St. Paul, Minnesota, began a profitable business based on taming the dragons of case law. The states published their decisions
very slowly; West published them fast, and bound them up into
regional reporters (Atlantic, Northeast, Northwest, Southern,
Southeast, Southwest, and Pacific). *The Northwest Reporter,* which
included Minnesota, was the first; it began to appear in 1879.
West ultimately indexed the cases with a naïve but effective "key-
number" system. Very soon, the little pop-art key of this private
company became an indispensable tool of the lawyers. *The Century
Edition of the American Digest,* which West published beginning in
1897, gathered together every reported case (it claimed there were
more than 500,000 of them) indexed, classified, and bound into
fifty volumes, from "Abandonment" through "Work and Labor."
Each ten-year period since then, West has published a *Decennial
Digest,* harvesting the cases for that decade; in between, it markets
advance sheets and temporary volumes. The Citator system also
began in the late 19th century. The Citator, published for individual states, then for regional groupings, helps the lawyer find
out the later history of a reported case. All this is expressed in
dry numbers and letters; but from these the reader can tell who
cited the case, on what point, and whether it was approved, disapproved, or "distinguished." The Citator began as gummed labels for lawyers to paste in their personal or office copies of reports.
Then it graduated to bound volumes. These red books, thick and
thin, useful but unloved, became as familiar to lawyers as West's
little keys.

Nothing remotely comparable was ever done, unfortunately,
for the even more chaotic system of statute law; Frederic Stimson
published *American Statute Law* in 1881, a thick volume which gave
the gist of the statutes, but it was nothing but a palliative. Until
very recently, enacted law was still an uncharted sea, fifty times

over; it was waiting for some hero with an index. Nobody, until the computer came on the scene, proved up to the task.

In a federal system, the diversity of American law was deep-seated and ineradicable, despite a common heritage, despite the oneness of the economy, despite the tools (telephone, telegraph) that developed to bridge distances, despite the West system of reporters and digests. The older the state, the more volumes of reports bulged on its shelves. Each state built up its own body of laws, and, as time went on, had less and less need to grub around elsewhere for precedent, or pay attention to its neighbors, and hardly any need at all to look at mother England. The West system did not cure these local diseases. The same was true of statutes; borrowing was common, but each state had its own codes and revisions. There were regional groupings, to be sure. "Legislative precedent" can be traced as it traveled across the country. California acted as a focal point for Western legislation and case law; Nevada, its desert satellite, drew on it heavily. The Southern states worked out local solutions (if that is the word) to mutual problems of race relations; the smaller New England states modeled their railroad commissions on that of Massachusetts; states of the great plains had common problems of agriculture, freight rates, grain storage, railroad regulation; they all borrowed answers from each other. In general, what kept the dialects of law from becoming mutually unintelligible was their community of experience. The states traveled similar economic and social journeys, and the law went along.

That people and goods moved freely across state lines was the most important fact of American law. It meant that a competitive market of laws existed in the country. If a New Yorker had money, and wanted a divorce, she went to another state. If the corporation laws of his state were too harsh to suit an entrepreneur, New Jersey was willing to accommodate, and later on, Delaware. The states could act as "laboratories" of social legislation, to use a later euphemism; but this was only half the story. The states acted also as competing sellers of jurisprudence in a vast federal bazaar. A kind of Gresham's law was in operation: easy laws drove out the harsh ones. Experiments in the "laboratories" would not work so long as neighbor states refused to go along. New York's hard divorce laws remained nominally in force; but they were at least partly nullified by the divorce mills, notably (in the 20th century) in Nevada.[34] Legislators hesitated to pass advanced labor laws for fear of driving out business; there always seemed to be other states which were only too eager to attract runaway businesses by offering low-wage shelters. Big national companies could not be controlled by regulation in any one particular state; the national railroad nets laughed at the efforts of a Rhode Island or a Connecticut. The only solutions were voluntary moves toward uniformity or strong federal control. The first had no real muscle behind it. The second was the ultimate solution.

As of 1900, the American legal system was, as it had been, a system of astonishing complexity. Much had been streamlined and simplified; but the sheer number of separate sovereignties, and the inherent jumble of the common-law system, meant that there was plenty of complexity (useful and useless) left to complain about. Diversities as old as the 17th century still survived here and there. Local circumstances, local economic needs, local turns of events, local legal cultures—these helped preserve some diversities, and helped create new ones. Legislation was not uniform; each state had its own set of statutes. English influence was down to a trickle; but Massachusetts, conservative in lawyer's law, was a port of entry for a few last pieces of English doctrine, which landed at Boston and were transshipped farther West. No two states had the same economy, society, or history; no two had the same mix of peoples. Yet, these differences among states cannot easily explain all the differences in the laws. Why Illinois should have a more backward civil process than Missouri is not easy to explain by reference to concrete social forces. Centrifugal and centripetal forces were both strong—and complex—currents running through American law.

[34]In the 20th century, Nevada made a career, so to speak, out of legalizing what was illegal elsewhere, especially in its big neighbor, California. Gambling was and is the most egregious example.

CHAPTER IV

THE LAND: AND OTHER PROPERTY

THE TRANSFORMATION OF LAND LAW

The dominant theme of American land law was that land should be freely bought and sold. For this reason, lawyers, judges, legislatures—and the landowning public—had gone to great pains, in the years after Independence, to untie the Gordian knots of English land law. Law had to fit the needs of a big, open country, with faith in abundance, and with huge tracts of vacant land. Land was the basis of wealth, the mother of resources and development. As the frontier moved further west, land law followed at a respectable distance. The land itself was transformed from wilderness to farm or industrial land; from vacant sites to towns to cities; so, too, the land law passed through phases of development. A state like New York had needs quite different from Wyoming. But differences in land and resource law, though never eliminated, tended to diminish over time. Colonial history in a way repeated itself; relatively rude, relatively simple land law, in the new settlements, changed to more complex, more sophisticated law, chiefly because more sophisticated law became more and more relevant to conditions.

For example, there was never much question that American law would absorb the concept of the *fixture*, with its attendant rules. A *fixture* is an object attached to the land, which is legally treated as part of the land. This means that sale of the land is automatically sale of its fixtures. A building is par excellence attached to the land, yet in Wisconsin in the 1850s a court decided in one case that a barn in Janesville, in another, the practice hall of the "Palmyra Brass Band," were mere chattels, and therefore severable from the land.[1] These were flimsy, temporary buildings;

[1] Lawrence M. Friedman, *Contract Law in America: A Social and Economic Case Study* (1965), p. 34.

the cases simply recognized what was a local and transient condition.

Inherited doctrines did not last if they seemed to clash with the needs of the American economy. Much of the law of property was still vigorously proenterprise—for example, the doctrine of nuisance, which, in the late 19th century, increasingly protected entrepreneurs in their use of land, as against private homeowners.[2] A similar point can be made about the fate of certain ancient easements. In England, it was settled doctrine that "uninterrupted enjoyment" could give a landowner an easement of light and air. In other words, a landowner whose land had always had a pleasant, open view had a right to keep things that way; he could block the owner of an adjoining plot of land from putting up a building that would impair this easement. Especially in towns and cities, this doctrine was out of place—or so the courts thought—in a country bent on economic growth, trying to promote, not curb, the intensive use of land. Chancellor Kent thought the rule did not "reasonably or equitably apply ... to buildings on narrow lots in the rapidly growing cities in this country." "Mere continuance of ... windows," according to a Massachusetts law (1852), did not give an easement "of light and air" so as to keep an adjoining landowner from building on his land.[3] By the late 19th century, every state except three had rejected this easement.[4]

In contrast, the doctrine of adverse possession was eagerly embraced in the United States. Under this doctrine, if a person occupied land that belonged to somebody else, and did it openly and notoriously, and for a certain number of years, the title shifted to the occupier, and the old owner lost his rights.[5] Western states, in particular, passed laws encouraging acquisition of title through adverse possession. They shortened the period of time it took for adverse possession to ripen into title. The traditional period had been twenty years; this telescoped into five in the Nevada territorial laws of 1861.[6] The occupant, to prove possession, had to

[2]Paul M. Kurtz, "Nineteenth Century Anti-Entrepreneurial Nuisance Injunctions—Avoiding the Chancellor," 17 William & Mary L. Rev. 621 (1976).

[3]Kent, *Commentaries*, vol. III (2nd ed., 1832), p. 446n; Laws Mass. 1852, ch. 144.

[4]Christopher G. Tiedeman, *An Elementary Treatise on the American Law of Real Property* (1885), sec. 613, pp. 475–76.

[5]Possession also had to be "hostile," that is, inconsistent with the true owner's claims. A tenant, for example, who leases land and pays rent, is in possession, but his possession is not "hostile," and does not threaten the landlord's title.

[6]Laws Terr. Nev. 1861, ch. 12, sec. 5.

show a house, a fence, a pastoral or pasturage use, or some other sign that he had exploited the land. Quite a few court cases turned on the question of what was sufficient possession.

On the surface, the doctrine of adverse possession seemed to favor settlers against absentee owners. Western land law seems to support this explanation. On the other hand, there is evidence that points in another direction. In some states, starting with Illinois in 1872, an adverse claimant could not gain good title unless he paid taxes on the land while the period of possession was running. This requirement too was most prevalent in Western states. An adverse claimant was not supposed to be merely a squatter. He should be someone who honestly thought he had a claim to the land. (Such a person would quite naturally pay taxes.) The tax provision suggests that the popularity of the doctrine was still another response to the chaos of land titles. It was easy for a person to think—wrongly—that he had good title to the land he was farming. If he stayed in possession long enough, the doctrine cured the mistake. The statute, said Chief Justice Gibson of Pennsylvania, in 1845, "protects the occupant, not for his merit, for he has none, but for the demerit of his antagonist in delaying the contest beyond the period assigned for it, when papers may be lost, facts forgotten, or witnesses dead."[7] On the other hand, the doctrine itself was a cloud on titles; one could search county records till Kingdom come without finding any record of adverse possession.

THE PUBLIC LAND

Public lands continued to be a major topic of controversy in the second half of the century. The idea that the great federal treasure of land should be used to raise money was all but dead. The clamor for free land reached its climax in the famous Homestead Act of 1862; and government continued to use land heavily as a kind of subsidy. The Morrill Act of 1862 gave away a vast tract of land to the states: 30,000 acres for each Senator and Representative the state was entitled to under the 1860 census. The land was to be used to establish "Colleges for the Benefit of Agriculture and

[7]*Sailor* v. *Hertzogg*, 2 Pa. St. 182, 185 (1845).

Mechanic Arts.''[8] In 1850, after much debate, the federal government also began to make land grants to help build railroads.
The economic advantages, for most sections of the country, out-
weighed any lingering scruples about the right of the national
government to support internal improvements.

The first major land grant concerned a proposed railroad from
Chicago to Mobile. (It ultimately became the Illinois Central Railroad.) The law, passed in 1850,[9] gave to the states of Illinois,
Alabama, and Mississippi alternate sections of land for six miles
on either side of the future line of tracks; the state would sell off
the land and use the proceeds to build the road. Ungranted sections of land were to be sold by the United States government at
not less than $2.50 an acre ("double the minimum price of the
public lands").[10] Later acts—for example, the law of 1862 in aid
of the Union Pacific—short-cut the process by giving the alternate
sections directly to the railroad instead of to the states.[11]

In theory, the government lost nothing and got a railroad free,
that is, without spending any cash. Government land, sandwiched
between sections of railroad land, would fetch a double price,
because the presence of a railroad would surely drive up its value.
But even this notion was abandoned in the 1860s. The railroads
of the 1860s had to run through the far West—through endless
grasslands, over great mountains, past deep forests, and across
huge deserts. This domain was almost empty of people. The government price, understandably, had to be lowered. Moreover, the
railroad grants conflicted with the spirit of the Homestead Act;
after 1871, for a variety of reasons, the government made no
more land grants to railroads. By this time, whatever harm or
good would result from the policy had mostly been done. The
exact amount of land granted to the railroads is in some dispute;
even a conservative estimate would put it at more than 130,000,000
acres.[12]

[8] 12 Stats. 503 (act of July 2, 1862); Paul W. Gates, *History of Public Land Law
Development* (1968), pp. 335–36.

[9] 9 Stats. 466 (act of Sept. 20, 1850); see Gates, *op. cit.*, pp. 341–86.

[10] 9 Stats. 466 (act of Sept. 20, 1850). The government retained the right to
transport its property and troops "free from toll." Some of the land on either side
of the road was bound to be already occupied or taken; the statute therefore made
provision for the granting of substitute lands to make up these deficiencies.

[11] 12 Stats. 489 (act of July 1, 1862).

[12] Robert S. Henry, "The Railroad Land Grant Legend in American History
Texts," 32 Miss. Valley Hist. Rev. 171 (1945).

The Homestead Act was the climax of a long political struggle. The homestead concept itself was a logical extension of trends in public-land policy. A vocal, sharply focused interest group worked (on the whole successfully) to defeat the other great general goal of land policy—raising revenue for the government. As this policy faded, the land-grant principle, which confronted the settlers with a less diffuse and greedier adversary, was the only rival of the homestead policy.

Until 1861, the homestead proposal was entangled in the sectional and slavery crisis. There were strong champions of a homestead bill in Congress, like Galusha Grow of Pennsylvania, but there was also bitter opposition; President Buchanan vetoed a homestead bill in 1860. The outbreak of the Civil War removed many opponents from Congress. In 1862, the bill became law, and the government became formally committed to the policy of granting land, free, to the pioneers, described by Grow as the "soldiers of peace," the "grand army of the sons of toil," as those who struggled against the "merciless barbarities of savage life," and who had "borne [the] eagles in triumph from ocean to ocean."[13]

The provisions of the act were simple. Heads of families, persons over twenty-one, and veterans (but not those who had "borne arms against the United States or given aid and comfort to its enemies") were eligible, subject to certain exceptions, to "enter one quarter section or a less quantity of unappropriated public lands." Claimants had to certify that they wanted the land for their own "exclusive use and benefit" and "for the purpose of actual settlement." After five years of settlement, the government would issue a patent for the land. An actual settler who qualified could, however, buy up the land at the minimum price (generally $1.25 an acre) before the end of the five-year period.[14]

The Homestead Act assumed that a supply of productive land stood waiting for the settlers. Special laws provided for the disposal of less desirable land—swamp land (1850), and desert lands (1877). These lands were commercially useless, and the government threw in extra inducements for reclamation. The swamp lands went free to the states, which, however, could sell them off to be drained. The desert land laws allowed individual claimants

---

[13]Galusha Grow, quoted in Benjamin Hibbard, *A History of the Public Land Policies* (1924), p. 384.

[14]12 Stats. 392 (act of May 20, 1862).

more acres than they could acquire through the Homestead Act; but the claimant had to irrigate his holdings. In addition, the federal government gave each new state a dowry of land as it entered the union. The states therefore held a considerable stock of land—swamp land; land under land-grant college laws; dowry lands at statehood. The states sold these lands on the open market. Wisconsin, for example, when it was admitted to the union, received public land from the federal government to be sold to raise "a separate fund to be called 'the school fund.'" The state disposed of its school lands at cheap prices and very favorable terms and used the proceeds to lend money at interest to farmers who needed money, thus (it was thought) killing two birds with one stone. The panic of 1857, however, wrecked the farm-loan system. As debtors went into default, it became clear that the program had been fearfully mismanaged. The state lost heavily on its investments.[15] Many states similarly frittered away their Morrill Act lands in the 1860s. In a number of states, the state's "school lands" generated a tangled, almost forgotten mass of law about claims, terms, and priorities, a wonderland of complexity which bears witness to the insufficiency and greed of public-land law.

The basic problem was that the public-land laws were hopelessly inconsistent. Some land was free for settlers; other land was for sale. The government proposed to sell some land to the highest bidder; proposed using other land to induce private enterprise to build railroads; gave other land to the state to fund their colleges. Administration of land laws was notoriously weak. The homestead principle, if that meant giving land free to the landless poor, was weakest of all, and the first to go. The government continued to sell land for cash; and the best land was "snapped up" by speculators. As Paul Wallace Gates describes it, settlers arriving in Kansas between 1868 and 1872

> were greeted with advertisements announcing that the choicest lands in the state had been selected by the State Agricultural College, which was now offering 90,000 acres for sale on long-term credits. The Central Branch of the Union Pacific Railroad offered 1,200,000 acres for prices ranging from $1 to $15 per acre; the Kansas Pacific Railroad offered 5,000,000 acres for $1 to $6 per acre; the Kansas and Neosho

[15]The Wisconsin School Land Act in operation has been explored by Joseph Schafer, "Wisconsin's Farm Loan Law, 1849–1863," in *Proceedings, State Historical Society of Wisconsin, 68th Ann. Meeting, 1920*, p. 156.

Valley Railroad offered 1,500,000 acres for sale at $2 to $8 per acre; the Capital Land Agency of Topeka offered 1,000,000 acres of Kansas land for sale; Van Doren and Havens offered 200,000 acres for $3 to $10 per acre; T. H. Walker offered 10,000 (or 100,000) acres for $5 to $10 per acre; Hendry and Noyes offered 50,000 acres, and even the United States government was advertising for bids of approximately 6,000 acres of Sac and Fox Indian lands.[16]

All of this choice land, in government or private hands, was unavailable to the homesteader. These heavy sales of Western land were a sign, then, of the failure of the Homestead Act. In addition, those who drafted the act seemed to have in mind the rich and well-watered land of the Middle West. Immense tracts of land in the further West were simply not fit for family farms; they were more suited to grazing and ranching.[17] Particularly after 1880, many people made use of the commutation privilege of the Homestead Act—the right to short-cut the homestead period by paying the regular price for the land. From 1881 to 1904, 22,000,000 acres were commuted, twenty-three percent of the total number of homestead entries for this period. This was the "means whereby large land holdings were built up through a perverted use of the Homestead Act." A Senate document later recorded that "not one in a hundred" of these commuted lands was "ever occupied as a home.... They became part of some large timber holding or a parcel of a cattle or sheep ranch." The commuters were "usually merchants, professional people, school teachers, clerks, journeymen working at trades, cow punchers, or sheep herders." Typically, these commuters sold their land immediately after title vested.[18]

So ignoble a failure casts doubt on the idea that aid to the actual settler was ever really the guiding principle of public land law. Land law took the form of exalting the yeoman farmer; it used him for slogans and propaganda. The law itself served more com-

---

[16]Paul W. Gates, "The Homestead Law in an Incongruous Land System," in Vernon Carstensen, ed., *The Public Lands* (1963), pp. 315, 323–24.

[17]Similarly, the Southern Homestead Act of 1866, which aimed to open public land in the South to freedmen and refugees, "turned out to be a resounding failure, partly because the lands set aside under it were of the poorest quality, and partly because the freedmen lacked the necessary means to support themselves while working to clear the land and cultivate a crop." Martin Abbott, *The Freedmen's Bureau in South Carolina, 1865–1872* (1967), pp. 63–64.

[18]Hibbard, *op. cit.*, pp. 386–89; Paul W. Gates, *History of Public Land Law Development* (1968), pp. 387ff.

plicated interests: businessmen, speculators, merchants, lawyers, in addition to farmers and settlers. The Homestead Act itself, and the public-land law in general, were complex and contradictory because of the multiplicity of interests that had a voice in enactment and administration. The unending maze of case law, legislation, regulations, public-land-office rulings, and decrees testify and owe their confusion to the same basic fact.

Toward the end of the century, the change in national attitude associated with the death of the frontier began to make its mark on public-land law. The underlying trait of policy, in the beginning, had been a kind of roaring optimism. The public domain was looked on as an inexhaustible treasure. Whether land was to be sold or given away, used to create new centers of population or fund a school system, government's function was to divest itself of this primary form of wealth as soon and as equitably as possible.[19] In the last years of the 19th century, the psychological horizon darkened. The national domain was visibly vanishing. Out of a new sense of scarcity, and a muted pessimism, the seeds of the conservation movement grew. Yellowstone National Park was established in 1872 "as a public park or pleasuring-ground for the benefit and enjoyment of the people."[20] A law of 1891 gave the President authority to "set apart and reserve ... public lands wholly or in part covered with timber or undergrowth, whether of commercial value or not, as public reservations." President Harrison took prompt action, and set aside, by proclamation, about 13,053,440 acres. President Cleveland added a vast new area, evoking a storm of protest from Western Congressmen and Senators, who saw threats to mining and lumbering.[21]

In the states, there were parallel developments. A law of New York State, in 1892, established "the Adirondack Park," to be "forever reserved, maintained and cared for as ground open to the free use of all the people for their health or pleasure, and as forest lands necessary to the preservation of the headwaters of the chief rivers of the state, and a future timber supply."[22] The New York constitution of 1897 declared the preserves "forever" wild. Conservationists made halting attempts to stop the slaughter

---

[19]The chief exception—mineral lands—merely underscores this point: it was recognized much earlier that these resources were finite and irreplaceable.
[20]17 Stats. 32 (act of Mar. 1, 1872).
[21]Gates, op. cit., pp. 567–69.
[22]Laws N.Y. 1892, Vol. 1, ch. 707.

of wildlife. Fish and game laws, too, were passed in increasing numbers. New Hampshire, for example, created "a board of commissioners on fisheries" in 1869. This later became a full-fledged fish and game commission, with power, for example, to close any restocked waters against fishing "for a period not exceeding three years." As of 1900, New Hampshire statutes forbade anyone to "hunt, kill, destroy, or capture any moose, caribou, or deer," except between September 15 and November 30. It was illegal to use dogs to hunt these animals. There was a season, too, for sable, otter, fishers, gray squirrels and raccoons, and an absolute prohibition on killing beaver. There were protective laws for many birds, too, including a ban on killing any "American or bald eagle."[23] After 1900, Americans could not foul their nest with quite so much impunity or legitimacy. The engines of pollution, however, also grew more powerful: the growth of industry, cities, and population, and the taste for consumption of natural products.

In the cities, too, there was an upsurge of interest in beautification, parks, and boulevards. The first great public park was Philadelphia's Fairmount Park (from about 1855), followed soon afterwards by New York's Central Park. The "green boulevard" soon became a feature of city landscapes. Illinois passed an elaborate statute on parks in 1871.[24] Cities and states began to use their powers of eminent domain as a way to *expand* the public sector, as a means of preserving natural beauty, and expanding parks and boulevards, not merely as a tool to encourage economic growth.[25] Meanwhile, some towns and cities began to regulate, or even prohibit, billboards.[26]

A conservation mentality of another variety colored the growth of new tools of land-use control. Fashionable neighborhoods, with "good" addresses, developed in Eastern cities. These enclaves of

[23]N.H. Stats. 1901, chs. 130–32.

[24]Christopher Tunnard and Henry H. Reed, *American Skyline* (1956), pp. 108–110; Rev. Stats. Ill., 1877, ch. 105.

[25]Generally speaking, too, the courts (and legislatures) in the years after the Civil War changed their general attitude toward eminent domain doctrines; in the early period (see above, p. 182), doctrines tilted toward the taker of the lands; now more protection tended to go toward the landowner whose lands were taken. See *Pumpelly* v. *Green Bay Company*, 80 U.S. 166 (1871).

[26]At first, these ordinances did not always find a friendly reception in the courts. In *Crawford* v. *City of Topeka*, 51 Kan. 756, 33 Pac. 476 (1893), a billboard ordinance was voided as "unreasonable." The court could not see how "the mere posting of a harmless paper upon a structure changes it from a lawful to an unlawful one."

wealth generated a demand for legal devices to protect property values and to maintain prevailing patterns of segregation by income and class. A leading English case, *Tulk* v. *Moxhay* (1848),[27] launched the doctrine of the equitable servitude or covenant. This was a useful doctrine for preserving the amenities, in new subdivisions or neighborhoods. *Parker* v. *Nightingale* (Massachusetts, 1863)[28] brought the doctrine to America. The heirs of Lemuel Hayward had sold lots in Hayward Place, Boston, under the express condition that they would allow only buildings "of brick or stone, of not less than three stories in height, and for a dwelling house only." Forty years later, in 1862, James Nightingale, who owned one of the lots, leased his land to Frederick Loeber, who opened a "restaurant or eating-house." Crowds of "noisy and boisterous persons" disturbed the decorum of Hayward Place. The neighbors brought an action to try to keep their neighborhood free of businesses. Legally, their problem was this: they were strangers to the transaction; they had an agreement, to be sure, but it ran to Hayward and his heirs, not to Nightingale or Loeber. The court, as in *Tulk* v. *Moxhay,* vaulted over this objection. The original covenant was binding, in equity, on behalf of the "parties aggrieved." By the original scheme, "a right or privilege or amenity in each lot was permanently secured to the owners of all the other lots." The law came to recognize that the "free changing of property and the shifting of titles" could work "hardship"; the "continued use of property in a particular locality for the same purpose was a very important element in the value and desirability of an investment . . . in the building of new towns of great promise, and in the building of great houses in old towns."[29] Long before zoning laws, therefore, the equitable covenant was a kind of functional equivalent—a legal tool to buttress neighborhood values against the encroachments of urban change.

[27]2 Phil. 774, 41 Eng. Rep. 1143 (Ch., 1848).
[28]6 Allen (88 Mass.) 341 (1863).
[29]Henry U. Sims, *A Treatise on Covenants Which Run with Land* (1901), preface, v.

PROPERTY LAW AND THE DYNASTS

The New York property codes, from the late 1820s, were adopted, as we have seen, by Michigan, Wisconsin, and Minnesota. Later Western codes—the Dakotas, Arizona—also absorbed chunks of property law whose ultimate source was New York. The New York codes had abolished a lot of deadwood and revised many aspects of the law of property. The codes revamped the law and lore of *future interests*—those interests in property other than present, possessory rights. The old law of future interests had served the landed estates. With a slight twist, the law turned out to serve the needs of new dynasts, whose money was tied up not in landed estates, but in trusts.

The details of the rebirth of future interests are not important and, in any event, are almost beyond the layman's patience or comprehension. Essentially, what happened was this: in some rare but important cases, rich men established trusts (by will or deed), to be invested for their children, and distributed to grandchildren (or collateral relatives). Meantime, the principal was safe, and the estate remained an entity, intact. The role of the law of future interests was to regulate relationships among remote beneficiaries, to determine what kinds of dynastic arrangements were permissible, and how long they might last. Now it was the New York reforms that, in the end, had to be reformed. And the ghosts of the old English doctrines of contingent remainders, springing uses, determinable fees, and other mysteries, began to haunt the law courts. An American master, John Chipman Gray, a Bostonian and a law teacher, made the rule against perpetuities his particular province. His treatise on the subject, first published in 1888, is still (in revised form) in print.

Alongside of the law of future interests, a law and practice of trust administration grew up. Most trustees were amateurs—relatives or friends appointed by will, or in a trust agreement. A few (almost exclusively in Boston) were professional managers. After the Civil War, a new institution appeared: the corporate trust company. In 1871, for example, a charter was issued in New York to the Westchester County Trust Company. The company had power to invest trust money "in public stocks of the United States," in securities of New York State, in "bonds or stocks of any incorporated city," and in corporate securities up to $10,000.[30] Toward the end of the century, some states began to formalize the law of trust investment by enacting "legal lists"—lists of authorized investments for trustees to put trust funds in without running the risk of complaints by beneficiaries. Massachusetts, and a few other states, gave their trustees more autonomy. The leading decision in Massachusetts was the famous *Harvard College* case (1830).[31]

The *Harvard College* rule—the rule of the prudent investor—was indeed more suitable to the dynastic trust. But this kind of trust was relatively rare, a fact which perhaps kept the Massachusetts doctrine from spreading. The other line of authority, the more restrictive line, had in mind protection of people who were legally or factually helpless—the proverbial widows and orphans. This was almost the only type of trust outside the major commercial centers; and even in the East it was the dominant form. In Pennsylvania, the constitution of 1873 forbade the legislature from authorizing the investment of trust funds "in the bonds or stocks of any private corporation."[32]

There were a number of quite startling developments in the law of trusts. One was the so-called spendthrift trust doctrine. A spendthrift trust was a trust which tried to lock up the beneficiary's interests totally: beneficiaries could not sell, give away, or mortgage their rights in the trust; and no creditor of a beneficiary could reach or attach a beneficiary's interests before money actually passed into the beneficiary's hands. There was no such thing, in other words, as the right to garnish an interest in a spendthrift trust, or put a lien on it. John Chipman Gray, in the first edition of his tedious little book, *Restraints on the Alienation of Property*, attacked this extraordinary doctrine as illogical and against the weight of precedent. Yet Massachusetts, Gray's home state, ignored the logic, and boldly adopted the doctrine, in *Broadway Bank* v. *Adams* (1882).[33] Gray wrote an angry preface to his second edition: the spirit of "paternalism," he said darkly, "the fundamental essence alike of spendthrift trusts and of socialism," was abroad in the land. But the spirit of the spendthrift trust was

[30]Laws N.Y. 1871, ch. 341. See James G. Smith, *The Development of Trust Companies in the United States* (1928); Lawrence M. Friedman, "The Dynastic Trust," 73 Yale L.J. 547 (1964).

[31]*Harvard College* v. *Amory*, 26 Mass. (9 Pick.) 446 (1830); see above p. 253.

[32]Pa. Const. 1873, art. III, sec. 22. A similar provision appears in Alabama (1875), Colorado (1876), Montana (1889), and Wyoming (1889).

[33]133 Mass. 170 (1882).

neither socialism nor paternalism: it was the dynastic urge of the rich, coming to the forefront and finding a doctrinal home in the state whose capital was Boston.

The rule against perpetuities was the rule that set final limits to a dynast's dreams of immortality. The rule, which developed over the course of two centuries, reached the dreaded form familiar to generations of suffering law students by about 1800. The rule had to do with the length of time trusts or chains of future interests could last. No interest was good, unless it "vested" no later in the future than "lives in being," plus twenty-one years. One could postpone "vesting" as long as a set of lifetimes lasted— lifetimes of persons born before the estate in question was established—plus an additional period of about one generation. The practical effect of the rule was to limit dynasties to no more than seventy-five or one hundred years, at the outer limit. The New York property laws of the late 1820s had been more ruthless and restrictive. Their version of the rule was copied in California, Michigan, and Wisconsin, among other states. The common-law rule was in at least nominal effect elsewhere.

For much of the 19th century, the *charitable trust* had not been favored in the law. These trusts suffered from fear of the dead hand, particularly the dead hand of the Church. New York's property laws severely limited creation of charitable trusts. When Samuel Tilden, lawyer and almost-President, died, he left millions of dollars to fund a public library in New York City. But the New York courts (1891) held the Tilden trust invalid, and handed the money over to his heirs. The case finally galvanized the legislature into action. In 1893, a statute removed the shadow of invalidity from charitable trusts in New York.[34]

Charitable trusts were also invalid or much restricted in those Midwestern states which had borrowed New York's property laws (Michigan, Minnesota, Wisconsin), and in a cluster of Southern states centering on Virginia. In these Southern states, there were perhaps long memories and old hatreds flowing from the Reformation. A number of states also enacted "mortmain" statutes, which restricted gifts to charity in wills; such gifts could not be made too soon before death (thirty days in some states). The Pennsylvania version was passed in 1855.[35] These statutes were

---

[34]*Tilden* v. *Green,* 130 N.Y. 29, 28 N.E. 880 (1891); James B. Ames, "The Failure of the 'Tilden Trust,'" 5 Harv. L. Rev. 389 (1892); Laws N.Y. 1893, ch. 701.

[35]Laws Pa. 1855, ch. 347, sec. 11.

no doubt influenced by the fantasy of the evil priest who preyed on the fears of the dying, persuading them to impoverish their families and enrich the Church instead.

These prejudices were a long time in vanishing. What finally weakened them was the changing nature of charitable trusts, and indeed of American wealth. The age of the great foundations was still far in the future; but part of the public had already begun to lay moral claim to conscience money from barons of finance, oil, and steel. When the Tilden trust failed in New York, no dead hand became richer; but the city itself was the poorer.

Some states had come sooner to the realization that the charitable trust was beneficial, and had never thrown serious obstacles in its path. Indeed, Massachusetts courts had put new life in the doctrine of *cy pres* (law-French for "so near"), a doctrine essential to the health of a long-term charity. This doctrine was used to save charitable gifts whose original purpose had failed or became impossible. Rather than give money back to the heirs, a court of equity would apply it to a purpose as near as possible to the original one. In *Jackson* v. *Phillips* (1867),[36] the doctrine was applied to the will of Francis Jackson of Boston. Jackson had died in 1861, leaving money to trustees, partly to be used to "create a public sentiment that will put an end to Negro slavery," partly for the benefit of fugitive slaves. By 1867, slavery had been legally ended; these objects could not be literally carried out. Jackson's relatives therefore claimed the money for themselves. But the court refused to dismantle the trust. Instead, the court directed a "so-near" use of the fund—for welfare and education work among New England blacks and among freed slaves. The court did not invent the doctrine—it was old in England—but it received a new and vigorous lease on life, as an adjunct of the law of dynastic charities, just as the Massachusetts rule on trust investment was an adjunct of the law of dynastic trusts in general.

The law of *wills* had always been receptive to terms and doctrines imported from England. Some of the American statutes, for example, were remolded in the light of the English Wills Act (1837). The general trend, despite the holographic will in the West and South, was toward more formality in the execution of wills, for the sake of property records if nothing else. Informal, oral wills ceased, practically speaking, to count. This does not mean that the law of wills remained implacably formal and rigid.

[36] 96 Mass. 539 (1867).

In general, courts loosened their rules of interpretation of wills. They moved away from fixed canons of construction, and stressed what the testator actually meant; his intention was the "pole star," the "sovereign guide" of interpretation.[37] This attitude was appropriate in a country of general, though hardly sensational, literacy, diffuse property ownership, and low standards of legal (and lay) draftsmanship. The cases reflected tension between the desire of courts to carry out the testator's wishes and the need for certainty, sound routine, and rough predictability.

Between 1850 and 1900, more ordinary people developed the habit of making wills; and more estates went through probate. One study of wills compared a sample of 1850 wills in Essex County, New Jersey, with those of 1875 and 1900. In 1850, in Essex County, less than five percent of those who died left testate estates; only about eight percent had estates of any sort. By 1900, roughly fourteen percent of the dying population left estates that went through probate; eight percent were testate. Fewer of the probated wills were "deathbed" or last-illness wills in 1900. In 1850 at least a quarter of the wills were executed less than a month before death; in 1900 less than a fifth. The wealthier testators at least were more sophisticated about draftsmanship in 1900 than in 1850; they were more likely to cover, in their wills, such simple contingencies as what to do if a beneficiary died before the testator did.

Interestingly, the earlier the will in Essex County, the more likely it was to leave property in trust or in the form of a legal life estate. This was especially true of gifts to or for women: 73.3 percent of the 1850 wills made these nonoutright gifts, but only forty percent of the 1900 wills. The change came about partly because of the greater social independence of women, partly because more middle-class people made out wills, partly because of changes in the legal status of married women. Many 1900 testators were women, some of them women in simple circumstances— Mrs. Mary Duffy, who signed her will by mark and left everything to her husband; Grace Creamer, whose pathetic will, executed on her dying day, left everything to her newborn, illegitimate child. The earlier wills, by and large, directed the executors to sell off the property; in the uncertainties of the 1850s, the safest course seemed to be to tell the executor to collect, and liquidate, the

---

[37]James Schouler, *A Treatise on the Law of Wills* (2nd ed., 1892), p. 500.

estate. Only later did sophisticated wills contemplate an estate that would continue, under careful management, with retention of its assets until market conditions dictated otherwise.[38]

LANDLORD AND TENANT

The concept of tenancy has meant different things, depending on whether the tenant held farm land, commercial property, or a city apartment, and on what terms. In New York, pitched battles in the 1840s marked the beginning of the end for one of the last remnants of a kind of feudal tenancy in America. Economic and social conditions had made the New York landed estates an anachronism. The American dream was for each household to hold land in fee simple. Farmers looked with horror on the idea of a permanent class of tenants with no right ever to own their land. The New York constitution of 1846, after the downfall of the patroons, outlawed feudal tenures and long-term agricultural leases. Meanwhile, exemption and homestead laws, in almost all the states, protected the farmer's basic holdings of land, animals, and tools from seizure for debt. Distress for rent—the landlord's right to extract delinquent rent directly from the land—was, in many states, abolished.[39]

The American lease was, in general, no longer a document of tenure; even for agricultural lands, it was basically a commercial contract. Most farm families were freeholders; but there were plenty of tenant farmers, absentee landlords, and sizeable leaseholds, even in the North. In Illinois, there were large "frontier landlords," whose tenants paid in shares of crops or, more rarely, cash. One of the most notorious was William Scully, of Ireland, an alien and absentee landlord; on his vast prairie holdings in the 1880s there was considerable unrest.[40] On the other hand, the leasehold, protean and flexible, was for many young farmers the first step up the ladder of farm success; and for old farmers, it

[38]This discussion was based on Lawrence M. Friedman, "Patterns of Testation in the 19th Century: A Study of Essex County (New Jersey) Wills," 8 Am. J. Legal Hist. 34 (1964).

[39]Laws N.Y. 1846, ch. 274.

[40]Paul W. Gates, *Frontier Landlords and Pioneer Tenants* (1945).

was a way to transfer land to their sons to manage, without giving up complete control.

That characteristic Southern arrangement, the cropping contract, was quite different. There had been cropping contracts in the North and South before the Civil War. But only after the war did the cropping system become a cardinal feature of the South's economic system. The legal attributes of sharecropping developed along with its changing social meaning. In 1839, the North Carolina supreme court held that a landlord had no rights in the crop *before* the tenant actually gave the landlord his share. There was no statutory lien, and the right to distress for rent had been done away with; hence creditors of the tenant were free to levy on the crop, without interference from the landlord.[41]

In 1874, the legal relationship looked different to the court. A cropper was now said to have "no estate in the land"; the estate "remains in the landlord." The cropper was only a "laborer receiving pay in a share of the crop."[42] There was room for dispute about who was or was not a "cropper." In the case that inspired these words the tenant was held *not* to be a cropper, even though he received his horses, his corn and bacon, his farming utensils and his feed from the landlord. There were indeed arrangements, in which farmers were actual tenants, paying "rent" in a share of the crop; and there were also farm workers who were paid in crop shares.[43]

But sharecropping itself was much more common—over 50 percent of the small farms in the South—than either of these arrangements. The basic document was a contract in which the cropper (usually black, usually illiterate) agreed to work the land. A typical contract (executed in 1886, in North Carolina) gave the cropper half the crop, in exchange for his promise to work "faithfully and diligently," and to be "respectful in manners and deportment" to the owner. The owner provided "mule and feed for the same and all plantation tools and Seed to plant the crop," and advanced "fifty pound of bacon and two sacks of meal per month and occationally Some flour," to be paid out of the cropper's share.[44]

Thus the cropper was a worker, not an owner; his status was

[41]*Deaver* v. *Rice,* 20 N. Car. 431 (1839).

[42]*Harrison* v. *Ricks,* 71 N. Car. 7 (1874).

[43]Roger L. Ransom and Richard Sutch, *One Kind of Freedom: The Economic Consequences of Emancipation* (1977), pp. 90–91.

[44]*Ibid.,* p. 91.

halfway between a kind of serfdom and the autonomy of ownership. By statute in 1876, North Carolina clarified the landlord's rights. All crops were "deemed and held to be vested in possession" by the landlord and his assigns at all times. It was the sharecropper now who owned nothing, until his share was actually turned over to him.[45] These cases and statutes affirmed the landlord's superiority—against the village merchant and outside creditors as well as against the tenant. The land tenure system, and the leases and leaselike arrangements, reflected and reinforced, as far as possible, the real world of power relationships in the South.

MORTGAGES

Throughout the century, the mortgage remained the primary mode of financing land. Particularly in the West, when land was bought and sold, promissory notes were executed, secured by mortgages on the property. Since land was the chief asset of the chief class of the population, the mortgage was a basic instrument of credit and finance. It was also one of the major subjects of case law and statute. West's *Century Digest,* covering all cases reported to 1896, has more than 2,750 pages of cases on mortgages. The mortgage was used by farmers to raise money for more land, to buy agricultural machinery, even to cover personal expenses. In some parts of the country, farmers tended to borrow to the limit of their equity; in good years, when land prices were rising, they simply borrowed more. One swarm of locusts, one drought, one "panic" of the 19th century breed, was enough to wipe out the security, sweep the farm into court, and replace an economic problem with a legal one. It is no wonder, then, that the law tended to swing with the business cycle. Legislatures expanded or contracted the redemption period, according to whether times were good or bad. In 1886, Washington state changed a six-month period to a full year; in a period of upswing (1899), Michigan, perhaps as an incentive to investment, passed a statute which gave the debtor six months after sale to redeem; the period had previously been two years and three months.[46]

[45]Laws N. Car. 1876–77, ch. 283, sec. 1.

[46]Robert H. Skilton, "Developments in Mortgage Law and Practice," 17 Temple L.Q. 315, 329–30 (1943).

No wonder, too, that voters in agricultural states constantly agitated for government loans, cheap mortgage money, tough rules on foreclosure, easy rules on redemption. One incident may give some idea of the politics of mortgage law. In the early 1850s, many Wisconsin farmers bought stock in railroad companies. Since they had no ready money, they pledged their lands as security. The interest due on the mortgage—usually eight percent—was to be paid out of the railroad's future dividends. The railroads then used, or misused, the farmers' notes and mortgages to seduce Eastern investors to sink money into railroad finance. In the panic of 1857, the Wisconsin railroads collapsed. The farmer-mortgagors were left high and dry with worthless stock; their mortgages were in the hands of Eastern bankers.

The legislature, responsive to pressure from the farmers, passed a series of laws, trying every which way to repudiate the mortgages and prevent a wave of foreclosures. The legislature used various techniques. One law stripped the notes and mortgages of negotiability, so that the farmers could raise the defense of fraud, before friendly local juries in foreclosure suits. In a line of cases, beginning in 1858, the Wisconsin supreme court declared all these statutes unconstitutional, one by one, citing the *Dartmouth College* doctrine and the court's own sense of justice and sound economics.[47] The court felt that the bite of foreclosure was bitter, but not half so bitter as a policy that would dry up the money market and choke off investment in the state. And it was this sense that in the long run preserved the tensile strength of the law of mortgages—the need for mortgage investment acted as a brake on liberalization of mortgage and foreclosure law.

THE DECLINE OF DOWER

Common-law dower had once been an admirable way to provide for a widow's twilight life. Dower was a peculiar kind of estate. For one thing, it attached to land only. For another, dower was a mere life estate (in one-third of the late husband's dowable property). The widow had no right to sell the land; and she had no rights over the "remainder," that is, no right to dispose of the land after her death, by will or otherwise. The land remained, in

[47]The story is told in Robert S. Hunt's fine study, *Law and Locomotives: The Impact of the Railroad on Wisconsin Law in the Nineteenth Century* (1958).

short, in the husband's bloodline. The most remarkable feature of dower was that a husband could not defeat the right by selling his land or giving it away. Over all land he owned, or had owned, hung the ghostly threat of "inchoate dower." This potential claim followed the land through the whole chain of title, until the wife died and extinguished the claim.

As a protection device, dower had severe limitations. If the husband's wealth consisted of stocks and bonds, or a business, dower did the wife little good. Dower had other faults, too. It was superior to claims of the husband's creditors, which was good for wives but sometimes bad for business. And dower was an annoying cloud on titles. Long years after a transaction was over, the widow of some previous owner might rise up to haunt a buyer in good faith. That this last danger was the real fly in the ointment seems clear from the story of the rise and fall of dower. The Midwest, poor in everything *but* land, showed impatience with this ancient institution. Indiana abolished it, at least in name, in 1852. In its place, Indiana gave the widow a cut from her husband's personal property, and one-third of his real estate "in fee simple, free from all demands of creditors."[48] The same statute abolished "tenancies by the courtesy" (usually spelled *curtesy*), the corresponding estate for husbands (which had, however, this peculiarity: it vested only if the couple ever had a child born alive), and gave the husband symmetrical rights in his wife's estate. The Kansas laws of the Civil War period gave the widow the right to elect her dower, or, "as she may prefer," to choose to come under a statute which gave her an absolute share (one-half) of her husband's estate, both real and personal.[49] The absolute share was always to her advantage, unless her husband died insolvent, in which case dower was better. In a statute of *this* sort, the policy of protection took precedence over the policy of clear titles.

[48]Rev. Stats. Ind. 1852, ch. 27, secs. 16, 17. If the land was worth more than $10,000, the widow could have only one quarter of it, as against the husband's creditors; and if the land was worth more than $20,000, one fifth.

[49]Kans. Stats. 1862, ch. 83. For these and other early developments, see Charles H. Scribner, *Treatise on the Law of Dower*, vol. 1 (2nd ed., 1883), p. 48.

A TANGLE OF TITLES

As before, so also after 1850, the traumatic weakness of land titles had a pervasive effect upon the land law. It played a role, for example, in the decline of dower. It hastened the decline of the common-law marriage, and stimulated the increasing formality of wills. As fast as institutions developed to make land more marketable and to improve the quality of titles, other events seemed to conspire to undo the good and make the situation worse. The vagueness of railroad, school, and land grants, for example, created serious problems of title in some of the Western states. In California and New Mexico, a legacy of confusion was inherited from the Mexican period. Congress established for California a three-man commission to unsnarl titles flowing from Mexican grants (1851). Every claimant whose "right or title" to land "derived from the Spanish or Mexican government" was to present his claim to the commissioners, together "with such documentary evidence and testimony of witnesses as the said claimant relies upon."[50] The board completed its work by 1856; but litigation continued for years afterwards in the federal courts. The board handled something over eight hundred cases; 604 claims were confirmed, 190 rejected, nineteen withdrawn. But the California landowner had to wait, on the average, seventeen years after filing his petition before his title was finally confirmed.[51] The course of events in New Mexico was even more protracted. As late as 1891, Congress passed an act "to establish a Court of Private Land Claims," to untangle Mexican land grants in New Mexico, Arizona, Utah, Nevada, Colorado and Wyoming.[52]

Floating land scrip was another source of confusion. Scrip had been issued for a number of purposes: under the Morrill Act, for example, the scrip stood as evidence of the state's entitlement to college-aid land. Congress passed a miscellaneous group of statutes creating other scraps of scrip. One such law was for the benefit of Thomas Valentine, a land claimant from California; he lost his fight for a three-square-league ranch near Petaluma, but

---

[50] 9 Stats. 631 (act of March 3, 1851).
[51] W. W. Robinson, *Land in California* (1948), p. 106.
[52] 26 Stats. 854 (act of March 3, 1891).

got Congress to pass a private relief act in 1872. In exchange for a release of his claims to the ranch, Valentine received scrip for 13,316 acres of public land. Some he used, and some he sold:

> Speculators got some, hiking the price, to peddle along with other types of scrip. In time Valentine scrip became too high-priced to be used on admittedly public lands, and scrip own-ers had to look for forgotten islands—"sleepers"—areas over-looked by government surveyors and with questionably held titles.[53]

Many doctrines of land law contributed to the weakness of titles. Adverse possession was one such doctrine. Poor administration of the land laws was another chronic cause of doubtful titles. "Tax-titles" were notoriously weak. These were interests in land created when local government sold off property for delinquent taxes and issued a deed to the purchaser. The laws on the subject were complicated, and so difficult to comply with that, in the words of a contemporary treatise, "the investigator of titles always looks with suspicion upon a title that depends upon a tax-deed."[54] Leg-islatures constantly had to intervene to make good the faulty work of local officials. In the Iowa laws of 1880, for example, fifty-nine separate acts were passed to legalize defective actions of officials. Many related to land transactions. One act, for example, recited that swamp lands had been sold without the county seal, as the law required, and without the clerk's signature; since "doubts" had "arisen" about these deeds, the deeds were "hereby legalized and made valid" (ch. 180).

What made the situation worse was the sheer volume of land transactions. Deeds, mortgages, transfers, were counted in the thousands, then in the hundreds of thousands. The crude system of land registration could barely cope with the volume. Private solutions preceded public solutions to the problem. Title com-panies sprang up to check titles for a fee and to ensure landowners against mysterious clouds that might arise to befuddle their in-terests. The Real Estate Title Insurance Company of Philadelphia, chartered in 1876, seems to have been the pioneer. The prede-cessor of New York's Title Guaranty & Trust Company was char-tered in 1883 (Laws N.Y. 1883, ch. 367). In Chicago, the great

[53]Robinson, *op. cit.*, p. 179.
[54]Christopher G. Tiedeman, *An Elementary Treatise on the American Law of Real Property* (1885), p. 580.

fire of 1871 destroyed the public records. Four private abstract companies saved their records: indexes, abstracts, maps, and plats. These companies later formed a title-guarantee company; a merger in 1901 created the Chicago Title & Trust Company, which came to dominate the business in Chicago.[55]

One proposal that held out hope for a comprehensive cure of diseases of title was the Australian system, called *Torrens* after its inventor, Sir Robert R. Torrens. In the standard American method of recording, the documents—deeds, mortgages, land contracts—are deposited and noted in a public-record office. The office acts as little more than a warehouse with indexes. When land goes into Torrens, however, the state of the title is examined, and a certificate of title issued. Land brought into Torrens undergoes a scathing, one-time baptism of law; in the process, it is cleansed of its sins, all those "faint blemishes" and "mysterious 'clouds'" which "so darkly and portentously hang" over real estate, even when "hitherto not visible to the naked eye."[56] After this initial trauma, the land emerges as fresh and free of taint as a newborn baby. From that point on, title is in effect insured by the state. A contract, not a deed, becomes the instrument of transfer; and title and guaranty are at all times simply and efficiently kept up to date.

Illinois was the first state to pass a title-registration statute, in 1895; Massachusetts, Ohio, and California had statutes before 1900. The state bar association and the Chicago real-estate board supported a Torrens system for Illinois; but there was bitter opposition, too; and the title guarantee companies were not happy to see a governmental competitor. The Illinois law called for a referendum in any county that wanted to embark on Torrens; Cook County (Chicago) did so want, and after one false start— the Illinois supreme court declared the first Torrens act unconstitutional—a valid act was passed, in 1897, and put into effect.[57] The system was optional, however, even in Cook County. The public, legal and lay, was torpid and indifferent. Besides, Torrens had a serious drawback: the *first* land registration for any parcel of land was expensive. In 1899, there were only 155 applications

[55]Pearl J. Davies, *Real Estate in American History* (1958), pp. 35–36.
[56]John T. Hassam, "Land Transfer Reform," 4 Harv. L. Rev. 271, 275 (1891).
[57]Theodore Sheldon, *Land Registration in Illinois* (1901), pp. 1–3.

to register land under the Torrens system in Cook County.[58] As of 1900, then, title registration was at best a hope, at worst a missed opportunity.

INTELLECTUAL PROPERTY: PATENTS, COPYRIGHTS, AND TRADEMARKS

After the act of 1836, which established the Patent Office, Congress made few major changes in administration of patent law. Patents themselves multiplied like weeds. Between 1836 and 1890, 431,541 were granted.[59] The number increased each year. So did the volume of patent litigation. The patent office refused many applications; but even when it granted a patent, its patent was no guarantee of validity. The patent did not mean, in itself, that the device truly deserved to be patented, or that it would stand up in court. Patent litigation was frequent, complex, and fruitful of doctrine and controversy. In an infringement suit, it was a good defense to allege that the patent was invalid to begin with and should never have been granted. A few law firms built their fortunes on patent litigation, as they learned to deal with these intricate, technical cases. After the Civil War, there were the beginnings of a specialized patent bar; and a few lawyers, notably George Harding (1827–1902), became rich and prominent, principally through arguing patent cases in federal court.[60] The path of a patent was truly a rocky one. According to one authority, between 1891 and 1904, 30 percent of all patents adjudicated in the circuit courts of appeal were declared invalid; another 41 percent were held not to be infringed. Only 19 percent were pronounced to be both valid and infringed.[61] This meant, as it had for a generation or more, that outside the Patent Office, the federal courts sat as another many-headed commissioner of patents.

The courts played a creative role, too, in the sculpturing of doctrine. An industrial society rests on pillars of fresh technology.

[58]Richard R. Powell, *Registration of the Title to Land in the State of New York* (1938), p. 145.

[59]Chauncey Smith, "A Century of Patent Law," 5 Quarterly J. of Economics 44, 56 (1890).

[60]See Albert H. Walker, "George Harding," in *Great American Lawyers*, vol. VIII (1909), pp. 45–87.

[61]Floyd L. Vaughan, *The United States Patent System* (1956), p. 199.

The patent monopoly was in some regards an anomaly, in an expansive, free-market economy. But like corporate franchises, land grants, and high tariffs, the patent was a subsidy as well, an incentive to economic growth. As was true of these other incentive systems, public opinion was of two minds about it. The original law no doubt had in mind the small inventor, working through the night in his study or laboratory. There were such people, but they came to be a minority of American inventors; and in general, they were precisely those who could not bear the costs of patent litigation, or fight off the patent pirates.

Toward the end of the century, the courts seemed to become keenly aware that a patent could be used to stifle competition. They became quite stingy with preliminary injunctions against infringement. The only foolproof way to protect a patent, then, was to engage in long, costly litigation. This policy was hard on the small inventor; on the other hand, it cut down the use of patents in restraint of trade. Some courts apparently felt that too many patents were granted; they were afraid that no "standing room for an inventor" was left, no "pathway open for forward progress."[62] Patents were, potentially, another tool of the trusts. This attitude, this fear, was part of the sense of economic constriction, the general terror of small horizons, so marked in the late 19th century.

As early as 1850, Justice Samuel Nelson, speaking for the United States Supreme Court, enunciated a doctrine that cut down the number of potentially valid patents. The case turned on whether a patent for a new doorknob was valid. The only novelty, it seemed, was that the doorknob was made out of porcelain. A patent, said Nelson, required "more ingenuity" than that of "an ordinary mechanic acquainted with the business."[63] In 1875, a case in the Supreme Court concerned a patent on a plan for preserving fish "in a close chamber by means of a freezing mixture, having no contact with the atmosphere of the preserving chamber." The Court held the patent void. The scheme had no novelty, made no advance over prior art; it reminded Justice Noah H. Swayne, speaking for the Supreme Court, of a technique that had been used by undertakers (though indeed not for fish), and of what every man knew about ice cream.[64] In 1880, Swayne let loose a

[62]*Two Centuries' Growth of American Law,* p. 396.
[63]*Hotchkiss* v. *Greenwood,* 52 U.S. (11 How.) 248, 267 (1850).
[64]*Brown* v. *Piper,* 91 U.S. 37 (1875).

striking phrase—"a flash of thought"—to describe what a patent needed to be truly valid.[65] The "ordinary mechanic"—a kind of blue-collar version of the "reasonable man" in the law of torts— was the negative model; the positive concept was the "flash of genius," which alone gave merit to a patent. In general, the courts tried to hew to the middle of the road in developing patent law. They tried to restrict the patent to genuine novelty, to individual skill: they fought against corporate mass production of small improvements.

Entrepreneurs, however, had their own approach; they could hardly have been fond of the chaos of patent law. As early as 1856, manufacturers of sewing machines formed a patent pool.[66] Large companies learned how to stretch out their monopoly by manipulating patents. Bell Telephone bought a German patent, vital for the technology of long-distance telephoning. It waited until *its* telephone patent had almost expired, then pressed ahead with the German device. This gave it control of the telephone industry even after its first basic patent had passed into the public domain. Under the umbrella of the patent monopoly, companies divided up markets, licensed out the nation in segments, and chained whole counties or states to particular vendors of a patented good.

Patent law illustrated the tendency of law to expand the concept of property—to protect whatever had a real market, including intangibles. In a similar vein, the law of copyright grew steadily. In 1856, the copyright statute was amended to include dramatic productions; in 1865, to cover photographs and negatives.[67] In 1870, the copyright (and patent) laws were substantially revised, and now a "painting, drawing, chromo, statue, statuary, or model or design for a work of the fine arts" could also come under their wing.[68]

The expansion of trademark law was even more remarkable. This whole branch of law started from a few scattered judicial opinions; none in the United States seems to have been earlier than 1825. The first injunction in a trademark or trade-name case was granted in 1844, as we saw, to protect the makers of "Taylor's Persian Thread."[69] From this acorn grew a mighty oak. The trademark has a crucial role in a mass-production economy based more

[65]*Densmore* v. *Scofield,* 102 U.S. 375, 378 (1880).
[66]Vaughan, *op. cit.,* p. 41.
[67]13 Stats. 540 (act of March 3, 1865).
[68]16 Stats. 198, 213 (act of July 8, 1870).
[69]*Two Centuries' Growth of American Law,* p. 436.

or less on free enterprise. Products compete jealously for the consumer's dollars; but many kinds of goods pour out of factories identical except for package and name. The 1870 law that codified patent and copyright law applied to trademarks, too. But the Supreme Court, in 1879, thought that the patent power did not extend to trademarks, and, finding no warrant for the law in the commerce clause either, they declared the law unconstitutional as to trademarks.[70] The gap was partially filled by state statutes. Courts continued, however, to play a creative role, inventing concepts, expanding them, contracting them, sitting in judgment on their own creations.

Trademark litigation was acrimonious and, like patent litigation, relatively frequent. Business ethics in the 19th century were not simon-pure; case law records the activity of many jackals of commerce who tried to make off with values that inhered in another man's product. Some cases also began to develop an independent concept of unfair competition, to supplement the protective armor of a trademark. A man named Baker, for example, who made chocolate, could not so act as to make people think that his product was the famous Baker's Chocolate. He could not imitate the shape, label, and wording of the original product, whether or not he was technically "infringing" a trademark.[71]

Toward the end of the century, too, the union movement encouraged use of union labels on union-made goods, and tried to get laws to protect their rights in such labels. A Minnesota statute (1889) declared it "lawful for associations and unions of workmen" to adopt "for their protection labels, trademarks and advertisements," asserting that the goods were union-made. Imitations were unlawful, and could be enjoined.[72] Illinois had a similar law; the Cigar Makers' International Union, for example, put a "small blue plaster" in each box of cigars, certifying that the cigars were union-made, and not the product of "inferior, rat-shop, coolie, prison or filthy tenement-house workmanship." The state court upheld the law, in a case against a cigar-dealer who had simply copied the label.[73] Each firm, union, and trade group was engaged in marking out its little claim on the economy, and protecting this claim from encroachments of a tough and hostile world.

[70]Trade-Mark Cases, 100 U.S. 82 (1879).
[71]*Walter Baker and Co.* v. *Sanders,* 80 Fed. Rep. 889 (C.C.A. 2nd 1897).
[72]Laws Minn. 1889, ch. 9.
[73]*Cohn* v. *Illinois,* 149 Ill. 486 (1894).

CHAPTER V

ADMINISTRATIVE LAW AND
REGULATION OF BUSINESS

THE COMING OF THE BUREAUCRATS

In hindsight, the development of administrative law seems mostly a contribution of the 20th century. American historiography has always been biased toward the big federal agencies. The creation of the Interstate Commerce Commission, in 1887, has been taken to be a kind of genesis. The ICC, to be sure, was the first great independent regulatory commission—on the federal level. But there was a great deal of administration, and administrative law, in the 19th century in a wider sense. The Post Office, to take an obvious example, was a large, functioning, federal bureaucracy. There were agencies attached to the office of the commissioner of patents, the General Land Office, and the Pension Office of the Department of Interior. This last, the Pension Office, handled massive amounts of work (often badly). It made a multitude of small decisions affecting the lives of many people every day of its official life. In 1891, the Pension Office was reported to be the "largest executive bureau in the world." It had a work force of more than 6,000. In 1898, 635,000 cases were pending for adjudication.[1]

Before 1887, also, there were many administrative agencies attached to state and local government. State railroad commissions preceded the ICC by many years. Agencies regulating warehousing, grain elevators, and railroad freight rates were a regular feature in the Midwest during the Granger period. Most states had some sort of functioning insurance or banking commission before 1870. Locally, there were boards of health and bodies to administer school affairs.

[1]Leonard D. White, *The Republican Era: 1869–1901* (1958), pp. 211, 214.

The administrative agency was the child of necessity. Big government and positive government meant a government which divided its labor among specialists and specialized bodies. The period between 1850 and 1900 is considered the climax of *laissez-faire*—the age of social Darwinism, and the businessman's earthly kingdom in the United States. There is, to be sure, a good deal of truth in this notion. On the other hand, to a certain extent, it was merely the period in which businessmen made the loudest noise, some of it defensive. The legal culture had been for some time the culture of modern rationalism, the culture of instrumentalism. The ultimate tests of law and government were pragmatic. Traditional authority had always been weak in the United States; and though the legal system had vast tensile strength, and vast legitimacy, it was by no means supported, as some systems have been, by supernatural or metahuman grace.[2] This meant that levers of power were fair game for anybody who could grab them and make them do his bidding. Social Darwinism and the doctrine of *laissez-faire* were desperate attempts by the rich and powerful to persuade other groups to let go—for the ultimate good of society. The argument worked somewhat, and for a certain period of time. But never perfectly.

Meanwhile, a huge, tumultuous, middle-class population, anxious for security if not power, made more and more demands on and through government. The country was enormous; its product was enormous; its technology was enormous; and slowly its government too became enormous, in response to demands from various publics. Mass transport and communication increased the potential size of interest groups, created powerful agencies which needed control, and made social control technologically that much more feasible.

Control: the word is the key. In a society of mass markets, mass production, and giant enterprises, the individual shrinks into relative insignificance. What she eats and wears is made in some distant factory; there is no *personal* control over safety, over quality. When she rides in a train, or even walks along crowded city streets, her bodily security is in the hands of strangers. Moreover, the great aggregations—in business, for example—themselves exercise more and more power, and visibly so. To the general public, it seems as if the only source of control is that system called law.

---

[2] A kind of natural-law aura hovered about the Constitution and the Bill of Rights, even in the late 19th century; this was important but exceptional.

And the agencies of control are, more and more, administrative: that is, bodies of civil servants charged with a continuous, steady, rational job of monitoring some segment of business or of life.[3]

Traditional agencies of government could not regulate big business or keep the infrastructure tame. Courts were simply not good regulators. They were passive and untrained. Kansas created a "court of visitation" in 1898 to regulate railroads, fix freight rates, classify freight, "require the construction and maintenance of depots, switches, side-tracks, stock-yards, cars"; regulate crossings and intersections; require safety appliances; and in general ride herd on railroads. The law was declared unconstitutional, which prevents one from knowing whether this plan would have been an evolutionary dead end.[4] Clearly, ordinary courts were not geared to the task of overseeing enterprise. And, in the age of steel rails and telegraphs, town and county authorities were equally futile and ineffective. The cure was, at first, statewide control. When the states could not meet the demands of their constituents, these constituents embarked on federal adventure. The process was repeated in many areas of law. In welfare, for example, first came local poor laws, run by country justices and squires of the community. When this system was felt to be obsolete, states centralized their welfare administration. When the states could no longer handle the job (much later, to be sure), the federal government stepped in. This did not take place until the age of the New Deal, in the 1930s. For many kinds of economic regulation, the process ran its course much faster; railroad regulation reached its federal stage in 1887. Elementary education, on the other hand, only crossed the federal threshhold in the 1960s, and rather timidly at that.

[3]Jonathan Lurie points out, too, that there developed what might be called "the field of nonpublic administrative action undertaken by private voluntary associations, wielding considerable power in the name of public policy." His example: commodity exchanges, like the Chicago Board of Trade. *Public* administrative regulation, when it ultimately came, was imposed on this pre-existing corpus of administrative practice and behavior. Jonathan Lurie, "Commodities Exchanges as Self-Regulating Organizations in the Late 19th Century: Some Parameters in the History of American Administrative Law," 28 Rutgers L. Rev. 1107 (1975).

[4]Laws Kans. Spec. Sess. 1898, ch. 28; the statute was voided in *State ex rel. Godard* v. *Johnson,* 61 Kans. 803, 60 Pac. 1068 (1900).

REGULATING THE INFRASTRUCTURE: BANKS, INSURANCE, AND RAILROADS

These differences in pace were not accidental, of course. It was the most vital—and most threatening—sectors of the economy that first came on to be regulated: transport and money, railroads, banks, insurance companies. It was not merely the fact that these were essential services; transport and money represented power, or the danger of power. In the United States, an important segment of public opinion had always feared and distrusted all concentrations of power. And in the case of the railroads, for example, there were specific, powerful interest groups that considered themselves aggrieved.

The national currency had been in a chronic state of disrepair before the Civil War. After Jackson, there was no national banking at all. The states regulated currency and banking; but regulation was confused, halting, and in general ineffective. The federal government entered the banking picture during the war; there was a desperate wartime need for central control of fiscal and monetary systems. The Legal Tender Act was a wartime measure; after the war, it provided the occasion for one of the Supreme Court's most spectacular flip-flops, first a decision that the law was invalid, then a quick change of mind (following a change in personnel).[5] In 1863, during the war, Congress established a national banking system; in 1865 Congress placed a ten percent tax on the notes of state banks. The national bank notes provided far more uniformity, certainty, and stability in currency than was possible under the prior system. But the state banks, as banks, did not by any means fade from the picture. They remained—and so did state banking regulation.

Insurance companies, too, were an early subject of regulation.[6] Fire insurance, after the Civil War, became more and more ac-

---

[5]The cases were *Hepburn* v. *Grisword*, 75 U.S. 603 (1869), overturned by the *Legal Tender* cases, 79 U.S. 457 (1870). The backgrounds of the Legal Tender act and the national banking law are exhaustively treated in Bray Hammond, *Sovereignty and an Empty Purse: Banks and Politics in the Civil War* (1970); see also David M. Gische, "The New York City Banks and the Development of the National Banking System, 1860–1870," 23 Am. J. Legal Hist. 21 (1979).

[6]A comprehensive study of insurance law in one state is Spencer L. Kimball, *Insurance and Public Policy: A Study in the Legal Implementation of Social and Economic Public Policy, Based on Wisconsin Records 1835–1959* (1960).

cepted as a business necessity. Life insurance spread more slowly. There were even, at one time, moral objections: life insurance seemed a distasteful bet on life and death. But by the end of the century, this too was an important form of insurance.[7] Insurance claims were a friction point, where aggregated capital met the ordinary (or semiordinary) person on a plane of inequality. Some companies tried every trick in the book to weasel out of paying off claims. No doubt many claims were fraudulent as well. Insurance litigation, then, was relatively frequent. And hardly any subject was more often the subject of statute than insurance.

The development of insurance commissions followed a well-marked path. The first commissions were not independent bodies; their commissioners were state officers who held down other jobs as well. The Massachusetts commission of 1852 consisted of the secretary, treasurer, and auditor of the state. The commission's job was to receive statements from the companies, abstract the data, and present the results to the legislature. Wisconsin first established an Insurance Department in the office of the secretary of state; in 1878, an independent Insurance Department was created, headed by an appointive insurance commissioner. In New York, the comptroller had had some powers over insurance companies before 1859, when an Insurance Department was established along the lines of the Banking Department. In almost all states, then, separate "commissions" or "departments" grew out of embryonic boards in which new labors were piled upon old officers. At first, state government was too poor, too weak, and too listless to support strong, well-financed, independent regulation. An "independent" commission, in most states, was not even independent in the financial sense; the typical commission was supported by fees extracted from the companies.

The urge to regulate, however, was cumulative and persistent. In 1873, twelve states had "some form of institutionalized insurance regulation"; in 1890, seventeen states; in 1905, twenty-two.[8] Early commissions were usually advisory or exhortatory; they built up their bureaucratic traditions, and gained power and skill, unevenly but definitely. The power came from a steady inflation of insurance laws. The states passed laws that outlawed discrimination in rates, curbed "unfair" marketing practices, tried to safe-

[7]See Viviana A. Rotman Zelizer, *The Development of Life Insurance in the United States* (1979).

[8]Morton Keller, *The Life Insurance Enterprise, 1885–1910* (1963), pp. 194, 197.

guard the solvency of the companies, harnessed foreign insurance companies, and insisted on financial reserves. The volume and scope of this legislation grew to fantastic proportions. The Massachusetts law to "Amend and Codify the Statutes Relating to Insurance," passed in 1887, contained 112 closely packed sections of text.[9]

Rococo excess in the size of a statute does not mean that the statute is successful in controlling its subject. Bulk may mean almost the opposite: a frantic and hopeless attempt to control, after prior laws had repeatedly failed. Or complexity may mean that interest groups, at war with each other, have staked many and various claims on the subject matter; a long, complex law is the text, then, of an elaborate treaty, full of loopholes, special benefits, and compromise. Interest groups were in general eager to resort to legislation. These groups, like business firms, took literally the sermons that they should compete with each other; but they did not see why competition should be confined to the market; they competed in the halls of the legislatures, and in the courts as well.

Most authorities agree that insurance regulation, in this period, was not exactly a triumphal success. In New York, for example, corruption ate away at the heart of the Insurance Commission. The legislature was moved to investigate insurance regulation in 1870, 1872, 1877, 1882, and 1885. Many administrators, if not corrupt, were halfhearted and ineffectual. James F. Pierce, appointed commissioner in 1890, did not believe (he said) that his department should "erect over the lawfully appointed custodians of the people's funds another custodian who should intermeddle in their corporate administration."[10] This creed, or something like it, so delighted some companies that they were willing to buy it for cash. On the whole then, despite progress in tightening the reins, the state had by no means made itself master over insurance companies, at least not before 1900.

Partly, this was because no coherent economic theory underlay regulation. Regulation sprang, to a great extent, from fear and mistrust of the financial power of the companies, and the sense that the companies were cheating the public. These opinions did not easily translate into concrete and effective programs. Since the demand for regulation was diffuse, regulation was weak; the companies, which had vital interests at stake, gained great leverage

[9]Laws Mass. 1887, ch. 214.
[10]Quoted in Keller, *op. cit.*, p. 203.

over the content of the law and the work of everyday administration. Morton Keller points out that "the structure of supervision was at its friendliest when dealing with the technical details of the business"—taxation, investment, reserves, dividend policy. These were matters which the public hardly understood, at least not in any detail. On the other hand, policyholders had a real stake in the insurance policy itself—the contract of insurance. They also knew whether claims were paid or not, or paid promptly or not. This was therefore "a subject of fruitful and alert legislative concern." States passed nonforfeiture laws, mitigated the rules and clauses that made policies void if an applicant made false or misleading statements, and even controlled the methods of marketing insurance.[11]

Despite the volume of insurance regulation, it was still the *railroad* that dominated discussion and activity in administrative law, between 1850 and 1900, just as the railroad dominated corporation law and tort law. By 1850, states had turned to general statutes regulating railroads, and had given up the effort to slip special clauses into individual charters. In any event, in much of the country the first, promotional phase was over; this was a period in which railroads consolidated their lines and extended existing nets of track. During the development stage, the most influential voices were those of the promoters and their supporters in the community—people who wanted railroads built, almost at any cost. Once the roads were in operation, dominant public opinion seemed to shift from docility to hate. Railroads created markets, made towns bloom in the wilderness, lured farmers into planting particular crops, drew settlers from one place to another. People invested their lives and their future in the towns and markets that grew up along the lines. The railroads became enemies, then, not only because of iniquity, but also because they seemed to hold power of life and death over those who lived along the way. The farmers, who had mortgaged themselves to buy railroads, felt that they had created a Frankenstein monster in their midst. Besides, the railroads were corrupt, excessively capitalized, overloaded with debt, controlled by out-of-state interests, monopolistic. Among themselves they were vicious and quarrelsome. They were weak in the infant skills of public relations, but big in manipulation of state governments, in the black arts of lobbying, and the seduction of men in public office. They cheated

[11]Keller, *op. cit*, p. 200.

each other, their contractors and their stockholders. They floated great balloons of debt that burst during panics and crashes, ruining the greedy, hopeful people who sank money into stocks and bonds. They were deeply immersed in local politics; and they were at the mercy of the business cycle, and the prices of cotton, coal, wheat, tobacco, and corn. In the space of one short generation, they changed from engines of salvation to smoking black devils.

The history of railroad regulation was as complex as the history of public opinion on the subject of railroads. Conditions in different parts of the country affected the form and function of regulatory statutes, which ranged from severe to toothless, even on paper. The country's first railroad commission was established in Rhode Island, in 1839; it "stemmed from the necessity of imposing upon rival and warring railroads convenient connections and reasonable joint fares, freights, and services."[12] A New Hampshire commission was created in 1844.[13] Its main function, however, was to help railroads buy needed land along their routes. The statute gave the commissioners roughly the same powers and functions as those of the old commissioners of roads and highways. But the commissioners did have the duty to look over the railroads once a year, check their condition and management, and inspect "all books, papers, notes, records, bonds, and other evidences of debt, and all property, deeds and bills of sale," to see if the railroads were obeying all relevant laws. Connecticut established a commission which, in the 1850s, had the right to inspect the physical equipment of the railroads and to recommend needed repairs; safety on the roads was one of this law's major aims.[14] Maine's commission of 1858 was very much like Rhode Island's.

A new era began in 1869. In that year, Massachusetts established its own, and stronger, commission. There were three commissioners, one of them Charles Francis Adams, Jr. The commission had "general supervision of all railroads," with the right to examine them and keep abreast of their obedience to law. Whenever the commissioners felt that a company was derelict in this regard, or needed to make repairs, or if the commission felt that a "change in its rate of fares for transporting freight or passengers," or in its "mode of operating its road and conducting

[12]Edward C. Kirkland, *Men, Cities and Transportation: A Study in New England History, 1820–1900,* vol. II (1948), p. 233. Kirkland is the source for much of the following discussion of the New England commissions.

[13]Laws N.H. 1844, ch. 93.

[14]Conn. Stats. 1854, pp. 759–60.

its business" was "reasonable and expedient," the commissioners were to so inform the company. They were also to make annual reports to the legislature.[15] The other New England commissions were gradually remolded to fit the Massachusetts pattern, and the influence of the Massachusetts law was felt as far away as California.[16] The New England railroad commissions gained power and influence under the benevolent guidance of Massachusetts. But they were still able only to suggest and persuade; they had no power to fix rates or make major changes on their own. Even under later commissions, the distribution of function between court, legislature, and commission was never completely unscrambled; neither the legislatures nor the courts abdicated their right to tinker with railroad law. The railroads remained at all times influential. An extreme case was New York, which created a commission in 1855; the commissioners, paid off by the railroads, recommended that their office be abolished, and this was done in 1857.

In the Midwest, the so-called Granger laws, passed in the 1870s, took a far more radical attitude toward railroad regulation than anything attempted in New England. An Illinois law of 1871 established a Railroad and Warehouse Commission with authority to ascertain whether railroads and warehouses complied with the laws of the state. If the commission found that any laws had been violated, it had power to "prosecute ... all corporations or persons guilty of such violation."[17] By an act of April 15, 1871, the legislature flatly laid down maximum railroad rates. Class A roads— all railroads whose gross annual earnings, per mile, were ten thousand dollars or more—were to charge no more than two and one-half cents a mile for passengers (half fare to children under twelve).[18] The Granger movement was a farmers' revolt. Its legislative program aimed to bring under control the farmers' symbiotic enemies—railroads, warehouses, and grain elevators. But the legislation which was actually passed in Illinois, Iowa, Wisconsin, and Minnesota probably owed more to merchants and businessmen than to the farmers themselves. The goal of these laws was to control the railroads, in the interests of local users

[15]Laws Mass. 1869, ch. 408.
[16]Gerald D. Nash, *State Government and Economic Development: A History of Administrative Policies in California, 1849–1933* (1964), p. 160.
[17]Laws Ill. 1871, pp. 618, 622 (act of Apr. 13, 1871, secs. 1, 11).
[18]Laws Ill. 1871, p. 640 (act of Apr. 15, 1871).

and shippers. The merchants were nettled by freight rates they considered exorbitant and discriminatory. Their effect on the regulatory laws was profound. The Illinois law, it has been said, was "not so much the product of spontaneous indignation on the prairies as a monument to the strategic talents of the Chicago Board of Trade."[19]

The Grangers, in fact, came in on the tail end of a whirlwind that was already blowing full storm. In Wisconsin, in 1864, Milwaukee merchants had pressed successfully for a statute to force the railroads to deliver bulk grain to any elevator designated by the shippers, as long as it had adequate sidetracks.[20] Wisconsin farmers had been badly burnt in ill-advised schemes in promotion of railroads; it "was to be a long time before they regarded railroad men as anything but scoundrels.... They prepared the ground for the growth of the Grange."[21] In Iowa, from the 1860s, railroad regulation bills were introduced in almost every session, before there ever was a Granger movement. Iowa laws of 1868, granting lands to the railroads, carried with them a poisonous rider, reserving to the legislature the right to prescribe "rates of tariff."[22]

In the legal world of decentralized power, so characteristic of America, struggle for and against important laws does not end with enactment. As often happens, there was a second round, in the courts. Here the Grangers and their commissions won some famous victories, capped by the great (if transient) case of *Munn* v. *Illinois* (1876).[23] In *Munn,* the Supreme Court broadly upheld Illinois's package of Granger laws; specifically, regulation by commission of railroads, warehouses and grain elevators. These businesses, said the court, were "clothed with a public interest." Hence they could not claim immunity from public supervision. Again, as quite typical, there was a third round: actual administration. The Granger commissions were something of a failure in operation, perhaps partly because they were more weakly thought through than lobbied for. The right of legislatures to make rates

---

[19]Lee Benson, *Merchants, Farmers, and Railroads: Railroad Regulation and New York Politics, 1850–1887* (1955), p. 25; see also George H. Miller, *Railroads and the Granger Laws* (1971).

[20]Frederick Merk, *Economic History of Wisconsin during the Civil War Decade* (1916), p. 371.

[21]Robert S. Hunt, *Law and Locomotives* (1958), p. 64.

[22]See Earl S. Beard, "The Background of State Railroad Regulation in Iowa," 51 Iowa J. of Hist. 1, 17–22 (1953).

[23]94 U.S. 113 (1876).

was a famous victory; but the process itself was stiff and arbitrary. The roads were congenitally prone to financial troubles; it was easy for them to blame their troubles on mismanagement by commissions. The railroads and their friends turned their talents and money once more to legislative action. Wisconsin's proud and famous "Potter Law," of 1874, one of the most radical of the laws to tame the railroads, lasted a mere two years; with a turn of the political wheel, and the election of a legislature more sympathetic to the roads, the Potter Law was cast into outer darkness.[24]

Regulation by commission did not die, however. The strength of farmers and merchants ebbed, but never vanished. The idea that railroads were overmighty subjects, and had to be controlled, became a commonplace of American law. Such naked market strength could not be tolerated without some sort of watchman. The idea spread South and East. The South suffered from freight and passenger rates that were higher than those in the North. The behavior of the Southern Railway and Steamship Association, dominated by Albert Fink, gave great offense to farmers and shippers. Virginia established an advisory Railroad Commission in 1877, similar to the Massachusetts Commission; so did South Carolina in 1878; in 1879, Georgia established a three-man commission, with power to fix rates. In New York, railroad rate wars in the 1870s ended in a trunk-line pool of 1877; the New York railroads set up their own private administrative agency, and imported Albert Fink from the South to run it. Under the pooling arrangement, there were rate differentials favoring Philadelphia and Baltimore; the New York Chamber of Commerce, outraged, turned Granger, and exacted from the legislature the right to investigate the railroads. The result was the Special Committee on Railroads to Investigate Alleged Abuses in the Management of Railroads Chartered by the State of New York, commonly known as the Hepburn Committee. It reported its findings in a blaze of publicity in 1880. The Hepburn Committee helped crystallize opinion to the point where the legislature, in 1882, established a railroad commission, though with many compromises.[25]

But what, on the whole, did railroad commissions accomplish? Some were venal and impotent, like the first New York commission or the second California commission. This commission rode

---

[24]Robert S. Hunt, *Law and Locomotives* (1958), pp. 98–103, 140–42.
[25]See Lee Benson, *Merchants, Farmers, and Railroads: Railroad Regulation and New York Politics, 1850–1887* (1955), chs. 6–8.

into being in a surge of radical thought, but in 1895, a gloomy critic thus summed up its work:

> The curious fact remains that a body created sixteen years ago for the sole purpose of curbing a single railroad corporation with a strong hand, was found to be uniformly, without a break, during all that period, its apologist and defender.[26]

Even the noncorrupt commissions, of the New England type, disappointed the little man's hopes. As in the case of the insurance commission, the problem was partly one of political leverage. The forces that wanted strong control made up a large, diffuse group. The railroads were few and mighty. Campaigns for railroad laws tended to get results when farmers and shippers were organized and when they collectively made the most political noise. But these campaigns depended on wobbly, transient coalitions. All the passion went toward *passage* of these laws. After enactment, passion died down. Commissions had to live with their railroads every day. They had to chastise them but not kill them. In practice, this meant that commissions learned—if not already so disposed—to be gentle and sympathetic with their railroads. This habit, once acquired, was hard to break. And on each daily decision that affected a railroad, the railroad exerted its moral and economic pressures; farmers and shippers were unaware, unrepresented, apathetic. Moreover, not all farmers and shippers had the same interests. There was no coherent program on the demand side; thus no coherent outcome was supplied.

The state commissioners were, in any event, bound to fail in a federal system. Their power extended only to the borders of their state. Particularly after the Civil War, railroad entrepreneurs sewed together small railroads to make big interstate nets. How much control could Rhode Island ever hope to exert over railroads that passed through its territory? The Supreme Court drove home the point that state commissions were impotent. In *Wabash Railway* v. *Illinois* (1886)[27] the court held that states could not lawfully regulate commerce if it came from or was destined for a point outside the boundaries of the state. Only the federal government had this

---

[26]S.E. Moffet, "The Railroad Commission of California: A Study in Irresponsible Government," 6 Annals 469, 476 (1895). The "single railroad corporation" was the Central Pacific, later part of the Southern Pacific.

[27]118 U.S. 557 (1886).

[28]See I. L. Sharfman, *The Interstate Commerce Commission*, vol. 2 (1931).

right.[28] *Wabash* was a railroad case. The decision of the Court threw out an Illinois statute against discriminatory freight and passenger rates. Decisions of this sort gave an added push to the campaign, already strong, for a federal railroad commission. This was the Interstate Commerce Commission, which was enacted into law in 1887.[29]

This famous statute was controversial in its day, and has continued to produce a literature of historical disagreement. One thing is clear: it would be wrong to look at the ICC, naïvely, as the triumph of Grangerism on the federal level. The law paid lip service to the principle of strict control over railroads. And, of course, antirailroad agitation was a vital part of the political background. But some scholars feel that the railroads themselves were "ready and anxious to have federal railroad legislation—on their terms." For some railroad men, this was simply a way of bowing to the inevitable. Others felt that government backing could help curb what they thought of as dangerous, excessive competition. John P. Green, a vice-president of the Pennsylvania Railroad, stated in 1884 that "a large majority of the railroads in the United States would be delighted if a railroad commission or any other power could make rates upon their traffic which would insure them six per cent dividends, and I have no doubt, with such a guarantee, they would be very glad to come under the direct supervision and operation of the National Government."[30] One of the first commissioners of the ICC was no less a figure than Judge Thomas M. Cooley of Michigan, high priest of constitutional limitations. Cooley was by no means as simple and one-sided a prorailroad spokesman as he has been pictured;[31] still the commission was not radical by any means. It was meant as much to placate public opinion as to rule the roads in the sense that a fire-eating Granger might have liked.

Nor was the text of the act particularly fierce. The law gave the ICC no express power to set railroad rates, though it did declare (sec. 1) that "All charges...shall be reasonable and just." The commission, however, took a rate-making function upon itself, until the Supreme Court in the late 1890s stripped away this

[28]24 Stats. 379 (act of Feb. 4, 1887).

[30]Quoted in Gabriel Kolko, *Railroads and Regulation, 1877–1916* (1965), p. 35, an important revisionist history of the ICC.

[31]See Alan Jones, "Thomas M. Cooley and the Interstate Commerce Commission: Continuity and Change in the Doctrine of Equal Rights," 81 Political Science Q. 602 (1966).

power, saying that "there is nothing in the act fixing rates. Congress did not attempt to exercise that power.... The grant of such a power is never to be implied."[32] This left the commission relatively naked. It could do little more than punish past transgressions against the Commerce Act. The Supreme Court also emasculated the fourth section of the act, which prohibited railroads from discriminating against short hauls in fixing rates. The Court, with its practiced eye, read into the act a proviso that rate discrimination was not illegal, if it was necessary to meet competition (1897). The case concerned the Alabama Midland Railway. The commission found the railway in violation of the statute. The road charged $3.22 per ton "on phosphate rock shipped from the South Carolina and Florida field" to Troy, Alabama, for example, but only $3.00 per ton to carry this product to Montgomery, Alabama, a longer distance—in fact, the route to Montgomery ran through Troy. Troy suffered too on shipments of cotton and other goods. No matter; the court found that there was heavier competition to Montgomery than to other cities; hence, there was an adequate reason to lower prices to that point. The railroad's traffic managers were not "incompetent," nor were they "under the bias of any personal preference for Montgomery." They were, in short, economic men; and they set their rates by considering the workings of the market. For these reasons, the railroad's pricing was legal.[33]

But was this reasoning sound? Was it really the intent of Congress (and the country) to write this brand of liberal economics into the Commerce Act? Justice John M. Harlan, who dissented, felt that the Court's decisions had made the commission "a useless body for all practical purposes." Those purposes were political purposes; and the shippers who fought for the law had not intended the free market to continue in all its pristine purity. Yet, whatever the original understanding, what the Supreme Court

[32]J. Brewer, in *ICC v. Cincinnati, New Orleans and Texas Pacific Rr. Co.*, 167 U.S. 479, 494 (1897). In *Smyth v. Ames*, 169 U.S. 466 (1898), the Court reviewed a Nebraska statute, in which the legislature imposed rate cuts of almost 30% on railroad charges within the state. The Court struck down the law. See Stephen A. Siegel, "Understanding the *Lochner* Era: Lessons from the Controversy over Railroad and Utility Rate Regulation," 70 Va. L. Rev. 187, 224ff. (1984); Eric Monkkonen, "Can Nebraska or Any State Regulate Railroads? *Smyth v. Ames*, 1898," 54 Nebraska History 365 (1973).

[33]*Interstate Commerce Commission v. Alabama Midland Railway Co.*, 168 U.S. 144 (1897).

held *became* the law, at least unless and until Congress chose to act otherwise. In these cases, the Supreme Court boldly asserted power over the commission's undertaking, and, in effect, threw down the gauntlet to Congress. The Court had the last, sometimes the only, say.

Still, it would be wrong to assert that the Court had crippled the act. In some respects, the act was born to be crippled. Congress was only half-serious about taming the railroads; it was in deadly earnest only about public opinion. The act was "a bargain in which no one interest predominated except perhaps the legislators' interest in finally getting the conflict...off their backs and shifting it to a commission and the courts." And the real flaw in the act was not that it leaned toward this interest or that; but that it failed to choose between the interest groups, and that its policy was inconsistent, incoherent, inherently ambiguous.[34] Moreover, once the movement for enactment had run its course, Congress showed no great enthusiasm for putting back in the act any teeth that the Court pulled out. As Mr. Dooley said about Theodore Roosevelt and the trusts, the ICC was supposed to stamp the "heejoous monsthers" under foot, but "not so fast" or so much.[35]

The history of railroad regulation could be paralleled in the regulatory history of other public utilities. The same process occurred, the same kinds of compromise took place. In 1855, for example, Massachusetts passed a general incorporation law for gaslight companies. The law included a proviso that if a city already had a gas company, no new one could be incorporated unless the established company had earned an annual dividend of seven percent on its capital stock for a number of years. This invitation to monopoly was withdrawn in 1870, and, during the 1880s, gas companies began to feel the bite of competition. It was not to their liking. A law of 1885 established a Board of Gas Commissioners; under this law, the companies yielded to the yoke of regulation, but in exchange for protection of their monopoly position.[36]

This was the general compromise of public-utility law—regulation in exchange for a sheltered market. Competition was the "life of trade" only for other people; business generally welcomed

[34]Stephen Skowronek, *Building a New American State: The Expansion of National Administrative Capacities, 1877–1920* (1982), pp. 148–49.

[35]Quoted in William Letwin, *Law and Economic Policy in America: The Evolution of the Sherman Antitrust Act* (1965), p. 205.

[36]I. R. Barnes, *Public Utility Control in Massachusetts* (1930), pp. 14–15.

state control, provided the control was not unfriendly, and provided it carried with it protection for their little citadels of privilege. This is the key to understanding why some forms of government intervention, chiefly on the state level, grew so phenomenally during the last half of the 19th century. The statute books swelled like balloons, despite ideological sound and fury about individualism, social Darwinism, free enterprise, Horatio Alger, and the like, from pulpit, press, and bench. Every group wanted, and often got, its own exception to the supposed iron laws of trade.

Indeed, it misrepresents the temper of the times to think in terms of ideology—either for or against *laissez-faire*. In the days before the Civil War, as Charles McCurdy has argued, there was a great deal of cooperation between the state and private enterprise—in the building of roads, canals, and railroads, most notably. In the postwar period, consensus about the issues of state aid had largely broken down; and the various actors in the struggle over law disagreed about drawing the line between the sphere of government and the sphere of free enterprise. Everybody drew a different line, but largely in accord with his own economic interests. Ideology came afterwards, as icing on the cake.[37]

OCCUPATIONAL LICENSING: AND THE PULL OF PUBLIC HEALTH

A case in point was *occupational licensing*, which absolutely burgeoned in this period. The basic idea was not entirely new. The gateways into legal practice had historically been subject to control. Colonials had licensed auctioneers and peddlers. Some licensing laws, of course, were frankly and solely designed to produce revenue. Some licensing legislation was, moreover, harsh and discriminatory, a defense mechanism of local merchants against outsiders. Wisconsin's statutes, as of 1898, required every prospective peddler to make a "written application...to the secretary of state," revealing whether he intended to travel on foot, or with "one or more horses or other beasts of burden." The peddler's

---

[37]Charles W. McCurdy, "Justice Field and the Jurisprudence of Government-Business Relations: Some Parameters of Laissez Faire Constitutionalism, 1863–1897," 61 J. Am. Hist. 970 (1975); see also David M. Gold, "Redfield, Railroads, and the Roots of 'Laissez Faire Constitutionalism,'" 27 Am. J. Legal Hist., 254 (1983).

license fee ran from $30 up, depending on mode of travel; a peddler who intended to go by bicycle paid $30; to use a vehicle drawn by two or more horses cost $75. The peddler could not ply his trade in any town without this license, plus whatever fees the local community chose to levy, up to $50 a day.[38] These were stiff amounts—almost prohibitive. The point was to protect local merchants and drive away these pesty competitors, if at all possible. Laws of this kind were not new; but it was significant how they flourished during this age of (alleged) rampant *laissez-faire*. The small-town merchants were protectionist to the core.

The more familiar kind of occupational licensing blossomed in the late 19th century and reached some sort of climax in the period from 1890 to 1910. The health professions led the way. In Illinois, for example, a law of 1877 required a license for the practice of medicine. In 1881, a board of pharmacy was set up; afterwards, no one could "retail, compound or dispense drugs, medicines or poisons," or "open or conduct any pharmacy," except a registered pharmacist. In the same year, the state subjected to regulation "the practice of dentistry." A board, consisting of "five practising dentists," was charged with enforcement of the dentist's law. By this time, the idea had become quite popular. In 1897, Illinois created a State Board of Examiners of Architects. In 1899, the statutes added midwives, coal miners, and veterinarians, and also chiropractors and osteopaths ("those who desire to practice any ...system or science of treating human ailments who do not use medicines internally or externally").[39] Most of the licensed occupations were, by common consent, "professions" or subprofessions, and not just trades; but by no means all. Many states in the 1890s licensed plumbers, barbers, and horseshoers. A New York law licensing transportation ticket agents was passed, only to be declared unconstitutional in 1898.[40]

Undertakers, embalmers, and funeral directors were another group that heard the siren song of licensing. They too were struggling to define for themselves, and to protect, an area of exclusive business competence. They had many rivals. Doctors embalmed the dead. Clergymen controlled funerals. Many undertakers were part-time funeral directors who sold coffins and caskets as the mainstay of their business. In the late 1880s, Hudson Samson,

[38]Wis. Stats. 1898, secs. 1571, 1572.
[39]Laws Ill. 1877, p. 154; 1881, pp. 77, 120; 1897, p. 81; 1899, pp. 273, 277.
[40]*People ex rel. Tyroler v. Warden*, 157 N.Y. 116, 51 N.E. 1006 (1898).

president of the Funeral Directors' National Association of the United States, prepared a model legislative act for licensing embalmers. At the same time, Samson tried to uplift the artifacts of professional funerals. (In 1889, he designed a "special eight poster, oval-decked funeral car"; in 1898, a magnificent hand-carved wooden drape hearse.) It was all part of one general movement, to give tone and economic strength to the occupation, in short, to "professionalize" these doctors of the dead. Samson wanted a law to regulate "the care and burial of the dead the same as there is for the practice of medicine." In 1894, Virginia passed the first licensing law. The statute established a "state board of embalming," consisting of five members, to be appointed by the governor. Each member of the board had to have at least "five years' experience in the practice of embalming and the care of and disposition of dead human bodies." The board would control the profession and grant licenses. Thereafter, only registered embalmers could practice the "science of embalming." By 1900, some twenty-four states had passed similar legislation.[41]

The statutes in this new wave of licensing laws had certain characteristics in common. Their justification rested primarily on the developing concept of the state's police power—its power to safeguard the public health and safety. But the real motivation, or part of it, was economic. Trade groups were anxious to control competition. Typically, these were occupations with strong unions or strong trade associations; but they did not face large and powerful economic institutions as employers or consumers. Barbers, for example, were strongly unionized; but the ultimate employers were that large, diffuse group of people who want or need a haircut. Hence, licensed occupations were in a different position from ordinary industrial labor, or the farmer, or the businessmen. Their goals were the same as those of unions, farm groups, trade associations, and trusts. But their tactics in the economic battle had to be somewhat different.

The Virginia embalmers' law was typical. In occupational licensing laws, the state "board," which had power to decide who was fit to be a doctor, barber, nurse, or plumber, was effectively a private group, a clique of insiders. Its aim was to drive out marginal competition, to raise the prestige of the trade, and to

[41]The material on the embalmers is from Robert W. Habenstein and William M. Lamers, *History of American Funeral Directing* (1955), pp. 365, 369, 457–501; the Virginia law was Laws Va. 1893–94, ch. 625.

move toward the status of a self-perpetuating guild, made up of respectable professionals. By and large, the courts accepted these aims as readily as the legislatures did. Few licensing statutes were challenged in court; fewer still were overturned. Society, locked in struggle over the right of industrial labor to organize, nonetheless handed over monopoly power to middle-class professionals and artisans with hardly a murmur of protest from the courts. This fact helps us to understand the inner meaning of "freedom of contract" and other constitutional shibboleths, which courts sometimes used to overthrow social or labor legislation. The judges were themselves middle-class; they could easily empathize with professionals and artisans. Their constitutional antennae were much more sensitive when they picked up vibrations of class struggle or proletarian revolt, things which they barely understood and desperately feared.[42]

Most licensing laws had an easy time at the capital too. The lobby of plumbers, or pharmacists, or architects, was small but vocal, and no one spoke for the consumer. The statutes proceeded, however, from simple cases to more difficult; from doctors, that is, to plumbers and barbers. The justification was the same for all of the occupations just mentioned: safeguarding public health. This was a simple, obvious argument in the case of doctors, and had a lot of general appeal. For barbers, the argument was a trifle strained; for horseshoers, fairly desperate. The health argument, however, was needed to enroll neutrals in the legislature and convince judges that some public interest was at stake. The Illinois law of 1897, "to insure the better education of practitioners of horseshoeing, and to regulate the practice of horseshoers in the State of Illinois,"[43] put a veterinary surgeon on the horseshoers' board—immunized, no doubt, by his four blacksmith colleagues—and also provided that apprentices must attend lectures on the anatomy of horses' feet. In this case, the Illinois court was not impressed; but a Minnesota court, upholding a statute on barbers, spoke of the threat of "diseases spread...by unclean and incompetent barbers."[44]

Health was a powerful argument, in any case. Laws on public

[42]See, in general, Lawrence M. Friedman, "Freedom of Contract and Occupational Licensing 1890–1910: A Legal and Social Study," 53 Cal. L. Rev. 487 (1965).

[43]Laws Ill. 1897, p. 233.

[44]These cases are, respectively, *Bessette* v. *People*, 193 Ill. 334, 62 N.E. 215 (1901); *State* v. *Zeno*, 79 Minn. 80, 81 N.W. 748 (1900).

health and sanitation increased spectacularly toward the end of the century. Again, motivations were mixed. No one, or almost no one, could object to a law that outlawed rancid cheese and watered milk. On the other hand, control of the quality of food products meant a lot to the more respectable dairies and cheese-makers. They stood to gain if the state drove out marginal pro-ducers and raised public confidence in their products. Farmers and dairymen conducted a vendetta against "butterine" or oleo-margarine, both on the state and national levels. Many states en-acted laws against oleo. In some states there were stringent laws against passing the product off as butter. In 1885, Pennsylvania outlawed oleo altogether. In the 1880s, too, the federal govern-ment slapped a tax on the sale of oleomargarine. This battle was more purely economic than other struggles against the sour, the putrid, the diseased. But in the aggregate, the tremendous volume of "health" laws, snowballing between 1850 and 1900, meant that free-enterprise theory had failed significantly to win and hold its true believers. Good goods should, ultimately, drive out bad ones in the market, or batter down their price. But many people—not to mention the producers of good goods—were not willing to wait so long. Times, too, had changed. The progress of science made a growing circle of people aware that danger lurked in food and water. The discovery of germs, invisible, insidious, hidden in every spot of filth, had a profound effect on the legal system. To a much greater extent than before, goods—including food—were pack-aged and sent long distances, to be marketed impersonally, in bulk, rather than to be felt, handled, and squeezed at the point of purchase. This meant that a person was dependent on others, on strangers, on far-off corporations, for necessities of life; society was more than ever a complex cellular organism; these strangers, these distant others, had the capacity to inflict catastrophic, ir-reparable harm.

Science, which revealed the existence of unknown dangers, also provided the promise, or hope, of making the dangerous safe. Water and food could be sterilized; dirty streets could be scrubbed; light and air could be let into factories. By the time of the Gilded Age, there was not much moral or economic force left in the excuse that industry needed total protection, from seedling to tree. A dip into the Massachusetts session laws of 1887 demon-strates how much legislation was passed which, in substance or form, touched on issues of public health. One law required sellers of arsenic, strychnine, and other poisons to keep records of their sales, open to inspection by the police. Another act stated that killed poultry could not be sold unless "properly dressed, by the removal of the crop and entrails when containing food." This law was given over to city boards of health for enforcement. A few pages on, factories with five or more employees were ordered to be kept free "from effluvia arising from any drain, privy or other nuisance," and told to provide "water-closets, earth-closets, or privies" for employees. Another law created a State Board of Registration in Dentistry. Another law required factories to be ventilated, and still another was "an Act to Secure Uniform and Proper Meal Times for Children, Young Persons and Women Employed in Factories and Workshops."[45]

This was an industrial state, and its health laws reflected the strength of organized labor and its allies. There were no factory acts in the Arkansas session laws of 1881. But one act regulated "the Practice of Medicine and Surgery"; another made the sale of poisons unlawful, unless labeled as such, and required the keeping of records; another established a State Board of Health.[46] The crush of health laws was earlier and heavier in the Northeast, slower and later in the South; but the overall direction was unmistakable.

Statutory protection of social interests—meaning, basically, the private interests of fairly large groups—was a cumulative process. Lien laws and homestead provisions were still in force; and, if anything, their provisions were strengthened. In the settled parts of the country, however, they had reached a kind of plateau by the time of the Civil War. The new health laws became law after the war, indeed, most rapidly at the end of the century; mine and factory safety laws were also passed at this time. Homestead exemptions were primarily for the benefit of the farmer. The new laws reflected the rise of the cities, the growth of heavy industry, the slow passing of rural America. Iowa, for example, passed a coal-mine inspection law in 1880; the governor was to appoint an inspector, who would check ventilation and safety conditions in mines, among other things.[47] John F. Dillon, reporting as president

[45]Laws Mass. 1887, chs. 38, 94, 103, 137, 173, 215.
[46]Laws Ark. 1881, pp. 41, 107, 177.
[47]Laws Iowa 1880, ch. 202.

of the American Bar Association in 1892, was struck by how much of "recent legislation" related to "matters concerning the public health and safety, and particularly the safety of operatives and laborers."[48] He noted that Ohio now required guardrails or hand-rails on bridges, viaducts, culverts, and handrails for stairways in hotels and factories; Ohio and New York regulated scaffolding, ropes, blocks, pulleys, and tackles used in building. Georgia com-pelled seaside hotelkeepers to maintain lifeboats. Rhode Island, in an "Act for the Prevention of Blindness," required midwives and nurses to report to health officers any inflamed or reddened eyes among newborn babies. Ohio strengthened its laws on factory inspection, and regulated the manufacture of explosives. Rhode Island and Colorado "joined the long list of other states in pro-hibiting the sale or gift of cigarettes to minors" and forbidding minors "to smoke or chew tobacco in public places." And so it went.

Most of the health laws were, in form, criminal statutes. That does not necessarily mean that they were the product of moral outrage, though sometimes indeed they were. But enforcement through private initiative had been largely discredited. In theory, the upsurge of concern about health did not really require fresh doctrine. The law of warranty could have been strengthened by the courts; private causes of action were available against people who sold shoddy goods; these prior rules might have been woven into a strict and expansive law of products liability—a develop-ment which actually took place in the 20th century. Yet, who would or could go to court over a single can of peas? Criminalization meant that the remedy had been socialized: the state had assumed the cost and the burden of enforcement.

There is no doubt about the number of laws passed. The actual impact is another question. Constant tinkering indicates some-thing less than full enforcement. In most cases, the state did little more than place people's interests or passions on record. The record suggests little real control over the quality of products, even food. Quack medicines, some consisting mostly of alcohol, or hideously dangerous drugs, mislabeled, or underlabeled, were brazenly peddled; the patent-medicine industry wielded enor-mous power over newspapers, which had grown dependent on their revenues from ads. During the Spanish-American War, there

48*Report, 15th Ann. Meeting A.B.A.* (1892), pp. 167, 177–8, 183.

was a scandal over "embalmed beef"—rotten meat allegedly served to the troops who were fighting in Cuba. At the end of the period, intense agitation arose for stronger food laws. The agitation proves, if proof was needed, that existing legislation was almost useless. To be sure, it was a crime at common law knowingly to sell bad food; and there were statutes, like that of Pennsylvania (1860), which made it a misdemeanor to "sell...the flesh of any diseased animal, or any other unwholesome flesh, knowing the same to be diseased or unwholesome." But no real machinery backed up these laws. Increase in the demands for consumer protection came faster than increase in the efficiency of enforcement, or in administrative mechanisms for carrying through on policy.

Consumers were unorganized; yet, they gradually forced the government to take action. Some of the pressure was direct. Some was indirect: sales resistance, after repeated food scandals, hurt companies in their pocketbooks and frightened them into accepting or actually asking for control. In 1883, Congress passed a law forbidding the importation of adulterated tea. In 1890, a federal statute authorized inspection of "salted pork and bacon intended for exportation"; the law also forbade the import of diseased meat and adulterated food products. The next year, Congress passed a meat inspection law, covering "all cattle, sheep, and hogs which are subjects of interstate commerce, and which are about to be slaughtered at slaughter-houses, canning, salting, packing or rendering establishments."[49] New state food laws were also passed toward the end of the century. By 1889, twenty-three states had laws against the adulteration of drugs. Massachusetts, Michigan, New Jersey, and New York had more general statutes. Each year there was fresh legislation. In Minnesota, in 1889, laws were passed forbidding the sale of adulterated baking powder; regulating the manufacture of vinegar; requiring local boards of health to appoint inspectors to "inspect all cattle, sheep, and swine slaughtered for human food"; preventing the sale of cigarettes or tobacco to children under sixteen; and regulating the quality and purity of milk, butter, and cheese.[50]

State laws, of course, could not reach those producers whose poison dripped across state lines. In Congress, 190 food bills were introduced between 1879 and 1906, when the Pure Food Act finally became law.[51] Those few that succeeded, as we have seen,

---

[49]26 Stats. 414 (act of Aug. 30, 1890); 26 Stats. 1089 (act of Mar. 3, 1891).
[50]Laws Minn. 1889, chs. 7, 8, 14, 247.

were mainly those that protected export markets. But pressure was building up, and it now gained a powerful ally in the reformist bureaucracy. The fight for pure food became significantly professionalized. Dr. Harvey W. Wiley, chief chemist of the U.S. Department of Agriculture, later to be one of the guiding lights behind the Pure Food law, was at work in the late 1880s and 1890s, patiently exposing food fraud and poison. USDA bulletins, published from 1887 to 1893, calmly documented the national disgrace: wines were made of alcohol, sugar, and water; lard was adulterated; coffee was fabricated out of wheat flour and sawdust; canned vegetables sometimes contained sulfurous acid.[52] The Senate Committee on Manufactures, in 1899–1900, conducted a massive investigation of adulteration, turning a glaring spotlight on the sorry state of at least some of the country's food.

Wiley's work showed the power of bureaucracy to act as an agent of reform. Branches of government had opportunity to teach the public where its interest lay, and this meant an ability to increase the *political* strength of reform. As the civil service professionalized, this aspect of legislative history became more and more important. Cities had long since had boards of health, though not necessarily very active ones. State boards proved to be more potent. Wisconsin created a State Board of Health in 1876. It tested the state's major rivers and found them polluted. Water supplies were "discolored, odorous, and nauseous-flavored"; it was for this reason, ironically, that some people believed the water had medicinal qualities. Sewage, oil-refinery filth, sawdust, and industrial wastes were poured into the water. Underpaid and feebly buttressed by law, the board acted as an "eternal lobbyist," begging and cajoling legislatures and local government. The board's first president stated in 1876: "The people need facts: facts fortified and made cogent by figures; facts demonstrated from persistent and ever active causes." For many years, the board could do little *except* give out facts. But in the long run this proved to be a potent contribution.[53]

Tenement-house laws, too, owed a great deal of their motor force to public commissions and committees, which made full use

[51]Thomas A. Bailey, "Congressional Opposition to Pure Food Legislation, 1879–1906," 36 Am. J. Sociol. 52 (1930).

[52]Oscar F. Anderson, *The Health of a Nation: Harvey W. Wiley and the Fight for Pure Food* (1958), pp. 72–74.

[53]Earl F. Murphy, *Water Purity: A Study in Legal Control of Natural Resources* (1961), pp. 41, 74–78.

of their power to scandalize the senses and minds of the articulate public. New York had had a tenement-house law since 1867; it seemed to have little impact. Then the horrors of the tenements were brought more forcibly to the eyes, ears, and noses of the public. A ponderous federal report was issued in 1894; in 1900, Laurence Veiller, one of the tireless reformers of the late 19th century, held a tenement-house exhibition. He played on the fear and heartstrings of the public, as Jacob Riis had done in his famous book, *How the Other Half Lives* (1890). In 1900, after the exhibit, the legislature appointed a new commission to investigate; and a major law was passed in 1901.[54]

THE GREAT ANTITRUST ACT

The Sherman Antitrust Act, of 1890, was another crucial—and permanent—entry of the federal government into the world of business regulation. The Sherman Act was cut from quite different cloth than the Commerce Act. That act had created an administrative agency; whatever its defects, it had a certain hard edge of concreteness. It spoke of particular abuses and particular remedies, dealt with a particular industry. The Sherman Act was broader, vaguer, cloudier. It responded to no specific program, except the widespread, somewhat hysterical cry from the countryside to "do something" about the trusts. It was preceded by antitrust acts in some of the states. It also built on the basis of a common-law rule, never very precise, that "restraints of trade" were against public policy and were not enforceable in court.

There was a long tradition of fear of monopoly in the United States. The astonishing growth of big business after the Civil War naturally fed that fear among farmers, workers and small businessmen. After 1880, the specific bugbear was those giant combinations that came to be called the trusts. Standard Oil was apparently the first to use the trust device, in 1882, as the vehicle for merging businesses into a cohesive, permanent, yet controllable whole. A Cotton Oil Trust was organized in 1884; Linseed Oil in 1885. In 1887 came the Sugar Trust: a merger of fourteen companies, controlling 70 percent of the country's sugar refining;

[54]Lawrence M. Friedman, *Government and Slum Housing: A Century of Frustration* (1968), ch. 2; Roy Lubove, *The Progressives and the Slums: Tenement House Reform in New York City, 1890–1917* (1962).

and, in the same year, Whiskey, Envelope, Cordage, Oil-Cloth, Paving-Pitch, School-Slate, Chicago Gas, St. Louis Gas, and New York Meat trusts.

The trust device in itself did not last very long; after 1890, the holding company became a more popular method of accomplishing the same objects. But the name "trust" did not disappear so quickly; it came to be applied to any agglomeration that monopolized a field of business (or appeared to). As the trusts multiplied, a great fear arose in the public. In the late 1880s, attorneys general in some states responded by moving to "break up" some of the more egregious trusts. Michigan, Kansas, and Nebraska passed antitrust laws in 1889. The Nebraska act outlawed "any contract, agreement, or combination" to fix "a common price" for a product, or to limit the "amount, extent or number of such product to be sold or manufactured," or to divide up the profits in "a common fund." Also forbidden was "pooling" between companies and "the formation of combinations or common understanding between...companies...in the nature of what are commonly called trusts."[55]

The Sherman Act,[56] in comparison with the ICC act, or with some of the state laws, was brief and gnomic. The first section of the act declared illegal "Every contract, combination in the form of trust or otherwise, or conspiracy, in restraint of trade." The second section made it a crime to "monopolize or attempt to monopolize, or combine or conspire...to monopolize any part of the trade or commerce among the several states." The fate of such demons as the Oil Trust, the Sugar Trust, the Whiskey Trust, and the Linseed Oil Trust hung on these general words, on the zeal of the federal government in bringing suit, on the temper of the federal courts in putting flesh on statutory bones.[57] In a sense, then, the act was something of a fraud. Even its proponents thought of it as "experimental." In itself it did nothing and solved nothing, except to still the cry for action—any action—against the trusts.

Vague language in a statute is, in effect, a delegation by Con-

[55]Laws Neb. 1889, ch. 69.

[56]26 Stats. 209 (act of July 2, 1890); on the history of the Sherman Act, see William Letwin, "Congress and the Sherman Antitrust Law, 1887–1890," 23 U. Chi. L. Rev. 221 (1956); and William Letwin, *Law and Economic Policy in America: The Evolution of the Sherman Antitrust Act* (1965).

[57]And on the initiative of private persons; under the seventh section of the act, a person "injured in his business or property" by "a person or corporation" which did "anything forbidden or declared to be unlawful by this Act," had the right to sue for treble damages.

gress to lower agencies, or to the executive and the courts; it passes the problem along to these others. Such a law often buys time; it postpones resolution of a problem; it acts as a compromise between those who want sharp, specific action and those who want to stand pat. The Sherman Act did not, as some have thought, reflect, mechanically, a vanished dream of free enterprise. It was the product of a Babel of voices, and hardly reflected any coherent economic theory at all. What the solid middle class wanted, insofar as one can speak of a dominant desire, was not a law to restore pure, unrestricted competition; what was wanted was rather a giant killer, an act to cut down to size the monstrous combinations which had aggregated too much power for the country's good.

A flurry of satellite statutes followed the Sherman Act in the states. By the turn of the century, there were some 27 state antitrust laws. Ohio and Texas had tried (unsuccessfully) to use their laws to break up Standard Oil.[58] But the main event was in the federal ring. Enactment passed into history; and the work of interpretation and enforcement began. Enforcement was a fairly sometime thing. Within the federal government, attorneys general of the late 19th century were hardly a trust-busting lot. Nor did they have the money and staff to smash the combinations. Furthermore, to those who wanted a robust antitrust law, the first word from the United States Supreme Court was not encouraging. In *United States* v. *E. C. Knight Co.* (1895),[59] the government moved against the American Sugar Refining Company; this company dominated its industry and had begun reaching out its claws to acquire the stock of four Pennsylvania refiners, the only important surviving competitors. Chief Justice Fuller saw no violation of the Sherman Act. He drew a distinction between attempts to monopolize "manufacture" and attempts to monopolize "commerce." Control of "manufacture" was no part of the task of the Sherman Act, according to Fuller: to apply the act to "manufacture" might affect the "autonomy" of the states. Justice John Marshall Harlan dissented. In his view, the Court had "defeated" the "main object" of the Sherman Act. He shuddered at the power and size of the great "overshadowing combinations." There was no "limit" to their "financial" resources; their "audacity" recognized "none of the restraints of moral obligations controlling the action of individ-

[58]Bruce Bringhurst, *Antitrust and the Oil Monopoly: The Standard Oil Cases, 1890–1911* (1979), chs. 1 and 2.
[59]156 U.S. 2 (1895).

uals"; they were "governed entirely by the law of greed and self-ishness."

The conventional view is that the *Knight* case gutted the Sherman Act, that the court spoke for big business, and that Harlan's was probably the authentic voice of small businessmen, farmers, middle-class professionals. This may be an unfair reading of the case. There *was* law in the states; and *Knight* can be read as the Court's attempt to keep alive the power of states to control corporations (including out-of-state ones) that did business within their borders.[60] But as things turned out, state regulation of great enterprise was not exactly a roaring success; the Harlan view soon gained ascendancy in the Supreme Court itself. *U.S.* v. *Trans-Missouri Freight Association*[61] was decided in 1897. Here the Court, speaking through Justice Rufus W. Peckham, confronted that ancient enemy, the railroads. By a bare majority, the Court rejected the view that the Sherman Act proscribed only "unreasonable" restraints of trade. The majority now spoke of how trusts ruthlessly drove out of business the worthy "small but independent dealers," and how these men were transformed into economic robots, each "a mere servant or agent of a corporation," with "no voice in shaping the business policy of the company and bound to obey orders issued by others." In *Addyston Pipe and Steel Co.* v. *U.S.*[62] (1899), the Court continued along this road. The government had proceeded against six corporations that made and sold cast-iron pipe. The Supreme Court upheld, essentially, the government's view. The *Knight* case was distinguished to a mystery. Still, it was clear by 1900 that the courts would be an important battleground, that companies would resist the government's moves, with all the legal resources at their command. The Court was split down the middle on many issues of policy and interpretation, so that minor shifts in personnel could switch the Court from one track to another. In 1900, then, the future of the Sherman Act was quite uncertain.

[60]Charles W. McCurdy, "The *Knight* Sugar Decision of 1895 and the Modernization of American Corporation Law, 1869–1903," 53 Bus. Hist. Rev. 304 (1979).
[61]166 U.S. 290 (1897).
[62]175 U.S. 211 (1899).

CHAPTER VI

TORTS

For the 19th century, it is hard to think of a body of new judge-made law more striking than tort law. As we have seen, the law of torts was totally insignificant before 1900, a twig on the great tree of law. The common law had little to say about personal injuries brought about by carelessness—the area of law and life that underwent most rapid growth in the century. The modern law of torts must be laid at the door of the industrial revolution, whose machines had a marvelous capacity for smashing the human body.

Although many basic doctrines of tort law made their first appearance before 1850, tort law grew most explosively after that date. The first English-language treatise on the subject was *The Law of Torts, or Private Wrongs,* by Francis Hilliard, published in 1859. In 1860, Charles G. Addison's *Wrongs and Their Remedies* appeared (in England); a second edition of Hilliard came out in 1861, and a third in 1866. By 1900, there was an immense literature on the law of torts; Joel Bishop and Thomas M. Cooley had written imposing treatises on the subject; the case law had swollen to heroic proportions.

Superficially, the new law was built up out of old bricks from the common-law brickyard. And there was also an uncommon amount of transatlantic traffic. At a time when English influence on American law was dying fast, an unusual number of leading cases came out of England: *Priestley* v. *Fowler* (1837) (the fellow servant rule); *Davies* v. *Mann* (1842) (last clear chance); *Rylands* v. *Fletcher* (1868) (liability for extrahazardous activities).[1] Crosscurrents of this kind were perhaps understandable in a field left

---

[1] These cases are, respectively, 3 M. & W. 1 (1837); 10 M. & W. 546 (1842); (1868) L.R. 3 H.D. 330, affirming (1866) L.R. 2 Ex. 265.

largely to the judges. Besides, it is not quite accurate to speak of English *influence*. The industrial revolution had a head start in England; problems emerged there first, and so did their tentative legal solutions.

Every legal system tries to redress harm done by one person to another. The industrial revolution added an appalling increase in dimension. It manufactured injury and sudden death, along with profits and the products of machines. The profits were a tempting and logical fund out of which the costs of the dead and the injured *might* be paid. Moreover, the industrial relationship was impersonal. No ties of blood or love prevented one cog in the machine from suing the machine and its owners. But precisely here (to the 19th century mind) lay the danger. Lawsuits and damages might injure the health of precarious enterprise. The machines were the basis for economic growth, for national wealth, for the greater good of society.

The dilemma was first posed in railroad cases, and continued to be posed most often and most strikingly in this industry. Almost every leading case in tort law was connected, mediately or immediately, with this new and dreadful presence. In this first generation of tort law, the railroad was the prince of machines, both as symbol and as fact. It was the key to economic development. It cleared an iron path through the wilderness. It bound cities together, and tied the farms to the cities and the seaports. Yet, trains were also wild beasts; they roared through the countryside, killing livestock, setting fires to houses and crops, smashing wagons at grade crossings, mangling passengers and freight. Boilers exploded; trains hurtled off tracks; bridges collapsed; locomotives collided in a grinding scream of steel. Railroad law and tort law grew up, then, together. In a sense, the two were the same.

One basic fact of this tort-and-railroad law was that it was a law of negligence, of carelessness—the inflicting of harm, not on purpose, but because of some lapse in the standard of care. Liability for negligence was not absolute; it was based on fault. What was expected was not perfection, but the vague, subtle standard of the "reasonable man." Fault meant a breach of duty to the public, meant that the defendant had not done what a reasonable man should do. The morals were those of the ordinary person, in the new industrial world. Absolute liability was rejected; more accurately, it was never considered. In the mind of the 19th century, absolute liability might have been too dangerous; it might have strangled the economy altogether. If railroads, and enterprise generally, had to pay for all damage done "by accident," lawsuits could drain them of their economic blood. Ordinary caution became the standard.[2] The aim of the judges was to limit damages to some moderate measure. Capital had to be spared for its necessary work. This, at least, was the contemporary view.

The underlying policies of tort law did not, as a general rule, emerge explicitly from the cases; the cases did not talk policy, but the dry, dreary language of law, in the main. Occasionally, judges let down the veil and discussed the issues of context more openly. In the famous case of *Ryan* v. *New York Central Rr. Co.*, decided in New York in 1866,[3] a fire broke out in the city of Syracuse, New York, in the railroad's woodshed, because of the "careless management" of an engine. Plaintiff's house, "situated at a distance of one hundred and thirty feet from the shed, soon took fire from the heat and sparks, and was entirely consumed." Other houses, too, were burned. There was no question that the railroad was at fault, that the fire was the product of negligence. But how much should the railroad pay? The court shrank in horror from the thought of liability to people in the position of the plaintiff:

> To sustain such a claim... would subject [the railroad] to a liability against which no prudence could guard, and to meet which no private fortune would be adequate.... In a country ... where men are crowded into cities and villages... it is impossible [to]... guard against the occurrence of accidental or negligent fires. A man may insure his own house... but he cannot insure his neighbor's.... To hold that the owner... must guarantee the security of his neighbors on both sides, and to an unlimited extent... would be the destruction of all civilized society.... In a commercial country, each man, to some extent, runs the hazard of his neighbor's conduct, and each, by insurance against such hazards, is enabled to obtain a reasonable security against loss.

The railroad in *Ryan* was held not liable, precisely because the harm it caused was so great, and even though the damage could clearly be laid at the railroad's door (it was clearly at fault). The words of the court were revealing. The opinion referred explicitly to the railroad's capacity to buy and carry insurance. Insurability was important, because an insurable risk was one that could be

---

[2]See Charles O. Gregory, "Trespass to Negligence to Absolute Liability," 37 Va. L. Rev. 359 (1951).
[3]35 N.Y. 210 (1866).

spread, that *would* be spread by a careful businessman, and so would not ruin the finances of a well-run enterprise.

The *Ryan* case also reminds us that fault was only one blade of the scissors that cut away enterprise liability; the doctrine of proximate cause was another. As late as the 1870s, it was barely mentioned in the treatises; by the end of the century, it was worth a whole chapter on its own.[4] In theory, proximate cause was a concept of physical fact: did Mr. X, by his actions, cause the injury to Mr. Y, and were his actions the "proximate" cause, with no other person, event, or situation intervening? For enterprise-minded courts, proximate cause and fault were strong and supple doctrines, useful in confining liability to what the judges considered socially reasonable bounds. Courts invented others, too. There was almost certainly no conscious attempt to cut liability down to size, no conspiracy against injured workers, passengers, pedestrians. But the spirit of the age was a spirit of limits on recovery. People lived with calamity; they had no sense (as would be true in the 20th century) that *somebody* was always responsible—either the state or some private party. In the novel by Mark Twain and Charles Dudley Warren, *The Gilded Age,* written in the 1870s, there is a description of a terrible steamboat disaster. Twenty-two people died; scores more were injured. But after an investigation, the "verdict" was the "familiar" one, heard "all the days of our lives— 'NOBODY TO BLAME.'"

The traps for unwary plaintiffs were mostly in place by the middle of the century. Prominent among these were the doctrine of contributory negligence, the fellow-servant rule, and its fellow traveler, the doctrine of assumption of risk. The basic idea of contributory negligence was extremely simple. If the plaintiff was negligent himself, ever so slightly, he could not recover from the defendant. This was a harsh doctrine, but extraordinarily useful. It became a favorite method through which judges kept tort claims from the deliberations of the jury. The trouble with the jury (it was thought) was that pitiful cases of crippled men suing giant corporations sometimes worked on their sympathies. Even people who respect general rules find it hard to resist bending them once in a while, especially if the victim hauls his battered body into the courtroom, or a widow and orphans stare into the jury box. For jurors—amateurs all—every case was a one-time cause. Business

[4]Herbert Hovenkamp, "Pragmatic Realism and Proximate Cause in America," 3 J. Legal History 3, 7 (1982).

and its lawyers were convinced that juries were incorrigibly plaintiff-minded; that they were loose with other people's money; that they had a deep-dyed tendency to stretch facts to favor a suffering plaintiff. But if plaintiff was clearly negligent himself, there could be no recovery; there were no facts to be found, and a judge could take the case from the jury and dismiss it.

Contributory negligence can be traced, as a doctrine, to an English case decided in 1809. But it was rarely used before the 1850s.[5] What happened in between was the rise of the railroads. In 1840, there were less than 3,000 miles of track in the United States; by 1850, 9,000; by 1860, 30,000; by 1870, 52,000. Personal-injury cases grew as fast as the trackage. Most cases were crossing accidents. The air brake was not invented until 1868; and it was not in general use until much later than that. Before the air brake, trains simply could not slow down very quickly. They sped through the countryside, futilely clanging their bells; all too often, with a sickening noise, they crashed into cattle, other trains, or the bodies of human beings.

The doctrine of contributory negligence kept pace with crossing accidents. Plaintiff had not only to prove that the railroad was negligent; he also had to show that he was faultless himself. If he was injured at a crossing, in relatively open country, with a clear view of the train, the court could take the case from the jury with a clear conscience. Contributory negligence was a frequent issue in reported cases. Professor Malone has counted the appellate cases—and these, it must be recalled, were probably only a small fraction of the cases that began and ended in the lower courts. Between 1850 and 1860, there were only twelve reported cases in which the plaintiff collided with the doctrine of contributory negligence. Between 1860 and 1870, there were thirty-one. Between 1870 and 1880, there were fifty-eight.

Typical of these cases was *Haring* v. *New York and Erie Rr. Co.*, decided in 1852.[6] John J. Haring was "struck by the engine of the defendants, while he, with another person, was crossing the railroad in a sleigh." The railroad was plainly negligent; but the judge took the case away from the jury. "A man who rushed headlong against a locomotive engine, without using the ordinary means of discovering his danger, cannot be said to exercise ordinary care."

[5]For the story, see Wex S. Malone, "The Formative Era of Contributory Negligence," 41 Ill. L. Rev. 151 (1946).
[6]13 Barb. 2 (N.Y. 1852).

"We can not shut our eyes," added the judge, "that in certain controversies between the weak and the strong—between a humble individual and a gigantic corporation, the sympathies of the human mind naturally, honestly and generously, run to the assistance and support of the feeble.... [C]ompassion will sometimes exercise over the...jury, an influence which, however honorable to them as philanthropists, is wholly inconsistent with the principles of law and the ends of justice."

The doctrine of assumption of risk was almost as great a hurdle as contributory negligence. A plaintiff could not recover if she put herself willingly in a position of danger. So stated, the doctrine expresses a simple, harmless, even self-evident idea. It had a more sinister cast in cases of injured workmen; miners, railroad men, and factory operatives were said to assume the ordinary risks of employment merely by taking their jobs; and if the job was dangerous, the risk of injury was theirs. This was a doctrine that could easily be carried to extremes, and courts sometimes did so. In any event, its use increased in reported cases quite strikingly in the last half of the century.[7]

Assumption of risk developed hand in hand with the fellow-servant rule. Under this rule, as we have seen, a servant (employee) could not sue his master (employer), for injuries caused by the negligence of another employee. He could sue his employer for injuries if the employer caused them, personally, through negligent misconduct. This right meant very little in a factory or railroad yard. The employer was a businessman, or an abstraction—a corporation. In a crossing accident, or an accident in a textile mill, if anyone was negligent, it was most likely a fellow-servant. It was pointless for one worker to sue another worker, who was equally poor. The fellow-servant rule, then, left injured workmen without meaningful recourse to law.

The doctrine, as we saw, began with an English case, *Priestley* v. *Fowler* (1837),[8] and quickly crossed the Atlantic. "Lord Abinger planted it, Baron Alderson watered it, and the devil gave it increase," said the secretary for Ireland, in a famous remark in the House of Commons in 1897.[9] The American Alderson, of course,

---

[7]See G. Edward White, *Tort Law in America: An Intellectual History* (1980), pp. 41–45.

[8]3 M. & W. 1 (1837); see above, part II, ch. VII, p. 301.

[9]Quoted in Walter F. Dodd, *Administration of Workmen's Compensation* (1936), p. 5, n. 7. Sir Edward Hall Alderson was an English judge who further developed the doctrine.

was Lemuel Shaw, who wrote the opinion in *Farwell* v. *Boston &
Worcester Rr. Corp.* (1842).[10] And the devil, on both sides of the
Atlantic, was the concept of spoon-feeding enterprise, the blind
desire for economic growth, responsible for a good deal of 19th-
century callousness.

The doctrine did not look like the devil's work to Shaw's contemporaries. Within a few years of *Farwell*, the issue came up in
state after state. Courts eagerly swallowed the doctrine. When the
Wisconsin supreme court considered the doctrine in 1861, it treated
it as part of the American common law, as if it had been handed
down from the medieval Year Books. The fellow-servant rule,
said the court (and accurately), had been "sustained by the almost
unanimous judgments of all the courts both of England and this
country . . . [an] unbroken current of judicial opinion."[11] The rule
had at least this advantage, in its early stages: it was clear-cut and
brutally simple. The cost of industrial accidents was to be shifted
from entrepreneurs—the most productive sector of the economy—to the workers themselves.

Another restrictive device was found by rummaging about in
the toolsheds of the old common law. At common law, when a
person died, he carried to the grave all of his claims in tort. Tort
actions were "personal," it was said, and when a man or woman
died, so did their rights to sue in tort. The rule probably applied
to any action for wrongful death. To kill another man, at common
law, was a felony. The felon forfeited his property, and the victim's
family might claim a share in the forfeiture. Since this was the
case, there was some logic to the argument that the victim's family
did not need a tort action besides. Meanwhile, the criminal law
changed over the years, capital punishment was used less frequently, and the rule that forfeited a felon's goods was abolished.
The original basis for the no-tort rule was clearly gone, then, by
the early 19th century. Yet the English courts dredged it up again.
Interestingly, the case arose out of a stagecoach accident. The rule
was then applied in railroad cases, and the courts wove it once
more into the fabric of tort law.[12]

The American experience is equally enlightening. There were
clear signs in the early 19th century that American courts had

---

[10] 45 Mass. (4 Met.) 49 (1842).

[11] *Mosley* v. *Chamberlain*, 18 Wis. 700, 705 (1861).

[12] See the perceptive article by Wex S. Malone, "The Genesis of Wrongful
Death," 17 Stan. L. Rev. 1043 (1965), on which this account is mainly based.

never really accepted the rule.[13] Then, lo and behold, the rule suddenly sprang to life, in a Massachusetts railroad case, *Carey* v. *Berkshire Rr.* (1848).[14] A railroad worker was killed in an accident, and his widow ("who was poor," she alleged, and "left to provide for herself and the support of three small children") sued the railroad. The court cited the English cases and denied recovery, on the grounds that actions for personal injuries died with the person. Ten years later, a New York judge slammed the door on a claim filed by the husband of Eliza Green, whose life was snuffed out "by a collision of the cars" of the Hudson River Rail Company. "The question," he said, "has been too long settled, both in England and in this country, to be disturbed." It would "savor somewhat more of judicial knight errantry, than of legal prudence, to attempt to unsettle what has been deemed at rest for more than two hundred and fifty years."[15]

The irony was that the matter had been settled, not for 250 years, but for ten years at most in the United States. The appeal to the past was disingenuous. The fact was, death damages were hard to measure: and the courts were exceedingly leery of them. It was a horrifying prospect, apparently, to require railroads and business in general to take on the role of pensioners for widows and orphans. But as a result, in the words of one commentator, it became "more profitable for the defendant to kill the plaintiff than to scratch him."[16] Not that defendants habitually made such calculations—locomotives and their engineers did not engage in cost-benefit analysis before bearing down on plaintiffs in tort.

The courts also invented, and insisted upon, another somewhat outrageous doctrine: the immunity of charities from actions sounding in tort. This doctrine, too, could be traced to an English case, *Heriot's Hospital* v. *Ross,* decided in 1846.[17] At home in England, the case only lasted twenty years. But after its death, surprisingly enough, it rose from the grave in America. Its first important victim was James McDonald of Massachusetts, who en-

---

[13]See *Cross* v. *Guthery,* 2 Root 90 (Conn., 1794); *Ford* v. *Monroe,* 20 Wend. 210 (N.Y., 1838); see also *Shields* v. *Yonge,* 15 Ga. 349 (1854), where the fellow-servant rule was applied, but at the same time the court rejected the common-law doctrine that personal injury actions did not survive.

[14]55 Mass. (1 Cush.) 475 (1848).

[15]Bacon, J., in *Green* v. *Hudson River Rr. Co.,* 28 Barb. 9, 15 (N.Y. 1858).

[16]William Prosser, *Handbook of the Law of Torts* (3rd ed., 1964), p. 924.

[17]12 C. & F. 507 (1846).

tered Massachusetts General Hospital with a broken thighbone.[18]
He later claimed that the hospital's agent, who happened to be a
third-year student at Harvard Medical School, did not properly
set the bone. The hospital, said the court, makes no profits, pays
no dividends. It had a duty to its patients to select agents and
employees with reasonable care. Having done so, it had no further
responsibility for what these employees did.

This was in 1876; in Maryland, in 1884, a court reached a
similar result in a case brought against the Baltimore House of
Refuge, on behalf of a boy who claimed he was "maliciously as-
saulted and beaten" there.[19] Both of these cases cited the English
decision, without bothering to mention that it had been overruled.
But that hardly mattered. There is a suspicious parallel between
these cases and the early cases on the fellow-servant rule. In both
instances, the court seemed concerned with distribution of costs.
In both cases, they seemed fearful that liability would damage
defendant too badly. Some plaintiffs—perhaps some lower courts
too—looked on corporations, including charities, as a cat looks
on a canary. The appellate courts of the 19th century felt con-
strained to fight the impulse to give out money damages. Charities, like the infant railroads of the generation before, were
organizations working for the public good; and they were finan-
cially precarious. Caring for destitute victims was a task for society
as a whole, if it was a task for anybody; certainly, the loss should
not fall on these charitable defendants.

By the beginnings of the Gilded Age, the general features of
the new tort law were crystal-clear. The leading concepts—fault,
assumption of risk, contributory negligence, proximate cause—
had been all firmly launched on their careers. All had been either
invented or refined by the judges themselves. What they added
up to was also crystal-clear. Enterprise was favored over workers,
slightly less so over passengers and members of the public. Juries
were suspected—on thin evidence—of lavishness in awarding
damages; they had to be kept under firm control. The thrust of
the rules, taken as a whole, approached the position that corporate
enterprise should be flatly immune from actions for personal
injury.

Of course, courts never went so far, and never wanted to. They

[18]*McDonald* v. *Massachusetts General Hospital,* 120 Mass. 432 (1876).
[19]*Perry* v. *House of Refuge,* 63 Md. 20 (1884).

did not want to encourage carelessness; and they were never entirely without heart. Indeed, the pull in the opposite direction was always there and grew steadily stronger. Reaction to the severe rules made itself felt almost as soon as each restrictive doctrine was born. In the nagging, fuzzy manner of case law, each rule bred its counterrule. The bench was not monolithic; as time went on, some judges showed tendencies much like those that juries were supposed to have. Whole rules were eroded by sympathy; hard cases unraveled the fabric of the law. Politically, the rage of the victims counted for very little in 1840, not much in 1860; by 1890, it was a roaring force. Labor found a voice and agitated in every forum for protection. A stream of statutes chipped away at the doctrines. The rules were pawns in a political chess game; as the balance of power shifted, so did the rules. The law of torts was therefore never a perfect engine of oppression. It was an imperfect instrument from the start, showing symptoms of its own mortality. Just as there was never a perfect free market, the classic 19th-century law of torts held such brief sway that in a sense it never was.

Some of the changes were made by the judges themselves, who thus disinvented their own inventions. The doctrine of imputed negligence was one of the most offensive rules, and one of the first to go. This rule "imputed" the negligence of a driver to his passenger, and the negligence of a parent to his child, so as to prevent passenger or child from recovering in personal-injury actions.[20] Even so conservative a judge as Stephen Field thought this rule was unfair, and should be abandoned.[21] Some courts even experimented with ways to pull the teeth of the doctrine of contributory negligence. In a railroad case, in 1858, the supreme court of Illinois expressed the idea that the "more gross the negligence" of defendant, "the less degree of care" would be "required of the plaintiff." So, if plaintiff's negligence was "comparatively slight," and "that of the defendant gross," plaintiff might still recover.[22] The notion of comparative negligence found an echo in the courts of Kansas, but nowhere else. Both Illinois and Kansas courts were backtracking by the 1880s, and their doc-

---

[20]The rule applied to this situation: B hired a carriage, driven by C. The carriage collided with a carriage driven by D. Both C and D were at fault. Can B, who was injured, sue D? The doctrine of imputed negligence denied him this right.

[21]Field, J., in *Little* v. *Hackett,* 116 U.S. 366 (1885). See also *Bunting* v. *Hogsett,* 139 Pa. St. 363, 21 Atl. 31 (1891).

[22]*Galena and Chicago Union Rr. Co.* v. *Jacobs,* 20 Ill. 478 (1858).

trine disappeared, only to re-emerge with greater force in the 20th century. Yet the impulse to soften the edges of contributory negligence never died out.

Two new doctrines—last clear chance and *res ipsa loquitur* (the thing speaks for itself)—eased the burden of proving a negligence case, at least slightly. Both doctrines were English in origin; both were somewhat ingenious. In *Davies* v. *Mann*,[23] an English case of 1842, plaintiff "fettered the forefeet of an ass belonging to him" and "turned it into a public highway." Defendant's wagon, "with a team of three horses," came along "at a smartish pace," smashed into the animal and killed it. The plaintiff was obviously negligent, and strictly speaking should not have recovered for his donkey. But defendant had had the "last clear chance" to avoid the accident. The court felt that this fact, in law, canceled out the consequences of plaintiff's earlier act of fault. The plaintiff won his case, and a doctrine was launched:

> The groans, ineffably and mournfully sad, of Davies' dying donkey, have resounded around the earth.... Its ghost, like Banquo's, will not down.[24]

This was a doctrine with rich possibilities for railroad cases— for plaintiffs who wandered onto the tracks or otherwise put themselves in positions of peril. These possibilities were not lost on plaintiff's lawyers. Last clear chance did not get very far in the courts before 1900; still, it made a small, clean wound in the body of contributory negligence.

Baron Pollock in *Byrne* v. *Boadle,* an English case of 1863,[25] launched the phrase *res ipsa loquitur*—the thing speaks for itself. The plaintiff was walking past defendant's warehouse, and a barrel of flour fell on his head and injured him. Plaintiff could not prove any negligence; all he knew was that the barrel fell and struck him on the head. To the court, this mysterious falling barrel proved as inspirational as Newton's apple. "A barrel," said Pollock, "could not roll out of a warehouse without some negligence." The mere fact of the incident "spoke for itself," and made out a prima-facie case of negligence. The burden thus shifted to the defendant; he had to prove that he was in fact not at fault. Otherwise, plaintiff ought to win. This rule, too, seemed helpful in railroad

[23]10 M. & W. 546 (1842).
[24]McLean, J., in *Fuller* v. *Illinois Central Rr. Co.,* 100 Miss. 705, 56 So. 783 (1911).
[25]2 H. & C. 722 (1863).

cases—for example, in an Illinois case, of 1868, where the boiler of an engine mysteriously exploded.[26] The scope and limit of the doctrine were never quite clear; but it was definitely useful to victims of wrecks, crashes, explosions, and those pursued by all manner of falling and flying objects. It was the middle 20th century, however, so eager for theories that would make business defendants liable in tort, that really made this doctrine its own.

Vastly more important were those changes in tort law imposed by legislative act. It was in the legislatures that the voice of labor and the passenger-public sounded most forcefully. Some laws raised the standard of care imposed on tortfeasors. In Kansas, a dry, flat state, one who started a prairie fire had to bear the resulting costs, whether negligent or not. The firestarter was liable "to the party injured for the full amount of such damage."[27] Statutes as early as the 1850s imposed safety precautions on railroads; if they failed to obey, they had to take the consequences. A New York statute of 1850 made it the duty of locomotives to ring a bell when approaching a crossing. Any railroad company that failed to comply was "liable for all damages... sustained by any person by reason of such neglect."[28] A Rhode Island law of the same decade ordered "a bell of at least thirty-two pounds in weight" to be hung on every locomotive, and sounded "at the distance of at least eighty rods" from a crossing, until the engine crossed the road. Railroads had to post warning signs, too, at every crossing, "of such height as shall be easily seen," and on each side of the signboard an "inscription... painted in capital letters, of at least the size of nine inches each, 'Railroad Crossing—Look out for the Engine while the Bell Rings.'" This law also imposed liability "for all damages sustained by any person" because of a noncomplying train.[29] Other statutes required railroads to build fences, and made them liable

---

[26]*Illinois Central Rr.* v. *Phillips*, 49 Ill. 234 (1868). But the upper court reversed. The explosion did not raise a presumption of negligence. The trial court should have given an instruction about the type of evidence that would rebut this presumption.

[27]Kans. Stats. 1868, ch. 118, sec. 2. The doctrine of the *Ryan* case (p. 469, above) was also not universally accepted by the courts. In most states, wrote Thomas M. Cooley in 1879, a "negligent fire is regarded as a unity; it reaches the last building as a direct and proximate result of the original negligence, just as a rolling stone put in motion down a hill, injuring several persons in succession, inflicts the last injury as a proximate result of the original force as directly as it does the first." Thomas M. Cooley, *A Treatise on the Law of Torts* (1879), p. 77.

[28]Laws N.Y. 1850, ch. 140, sec. 39.

[29]R.I. Stats. 1857, ch. 130, secs. 3–5.

for fires caused by engine sparks. Frequently, railroads were forced to pay for any livestock that their locomotives killed. A Colorado statute of 1872 imposed liability for the death of all domestic animals; a schedule of damages was enacted, ranging from $1.50 for Mexican sheep to $37.50 for "American Work Cattle"; thoroughbred cattle and sheep, and horses, mules and asses had to be paid for "at two-thirds of their cash value." Not a word was said in the statute about negligence.[30] An interesting New Hampshire statute, dating from before the Civil War, imposed liability on railroads for any fires they caused; but on the other hand, to soften the blow, the law gave every railroad corporation "an insurable interest in all property situated on the line of such road." In theory, then, the railroad could limit its financial risk by buying fire-insurance policies for the land along its right of way.[31]

As these statutes show, big corporations, particularly the railroads, spoiled children of land grants and subsidies, felt some blows of the rod of regulation. Their immunities melted away. Toward the end of the century, the pace of safety legislation quickened. The Interstate Commerce Commission called a conference of state regulatory authorities in 1889. Safety was on the agenda; many participants urged the ICC to look to the problem of slaughter on the railroads and recommend some positive remedies. The plight of the railroad workman was the most pressing. Between June 30, 1888, and June 30, 1889, 1,972 railwaymen were killed on the job; 20,028 workers were injured. One worker died for every 357 employees; one in 35 was injured in this single year. Tort law, thanks in good measure to the fellow-servant rule, was almost useless to these workmen and their families. In 1876, in Illinois, hundreds of workmen were killed and injured; but only 24 workers recovered damages, and the total paid out by 53 railroad companies was $3,654.70. Human lives were worth less than the life of cows; the same companies paid $119,288.24 in damages for the death of livestock.[32]

There were, however, signs of change. Eighteen-ninety was not

[30] Laws Colo. 1872, p. 185.
[31] N.H. Stats. 1851, ch. 142, secs. 8–9; see *Hooksett v. Concord Rr.*, 38 N.H. 242, 244 (1859).
[32] Walter Licht, *Working for the Railroad: The Organization of Work in the Nineteenth Century* (1983), pp. 181–208. Some railroads took care of some medical expenses, and gave charity to injured workmen and their families, on a voluntary basis. But the process was "arbitrary," and done in such a way as to avoid even the appearance of "fixed rules and procedures." *Ibid.*, p. 205.

1850; labor agitation, strikes, and union activity were national political facts. In 1893, Congress imposed a clutch of safety regulations on interstate railroads: "power driving-wheel brakes," "couplers coupling automatically by impact," and "secure grab irons or handholds in the ends and sides of each car."[33] Employees injured "by any locomotive, car, or train in use contrary to the provisions" of the act were not to be "deemed ... to have assumed the risk."

There were safety regulations for other forms of transport, too. A federal statute as early as 1838 had regulated boilers on steamboats; and an elaborate act "for the better Security of the lives of Passengers on board of Vessels propelled in whole or in part by Steam" was passed in 1852.[34] Late in the century, the states began to pass laws regulating safety conditions in mines and factories. These related specially to dangerous machines, hoistways, and elevators, and often required machinery to be guarded or belted; other provisions imposed broader but vaguer standards, requiring factories and mines to provide comfort and good ventilation. Administration of safety regulations was spotty at best. But they had an effect, in the long run, on civil litigation. "Statutory negligence"—the plaintiff made out his case by showing that defendant had violated a safety statute—became an important concept in the case law. In a leading case, *Osborne* v. *McMasters* (1889),[35] a drugstore clerk sold a woman "a deadly poison without labeling it 'Poison.'" This was a criminal offense. The woman took the poison by mistake, and died. Her survivors sued, in tort. Negligence, said the court, "is the breach of legal duty." The duty can be defined just as well by statute as by common law. The fact that the statute spoke only of *criminal* penalties was immaterial.

The heyday of the rule of wrongful death was also quite brief. Lord Campbell's Act in England (1846)[36] gave a cause of action on behalf of a "wife, husband, parent, and child" who died by virtue of a "wrongful act, neglect, or default." The action lay against the person who would have been liable "if death had not

[33] 27 Stats. 531 (act of Mar. 2, 1893). The roads were given until Jan. 1, 1898, to comply, and the ICC was authorized to grant extensions.
[34] 10 Stats. 61 (act of Aug. 30, 1852).
[35] 40 Minn. 103, 41 N.W. 543 (1889).
[36] 9 and 10 Vict.; ch. 93 (1846).

ensued." Many American states copied this statute. Indeed, Massachusetts had had such a law as early as 1840, in favor of the next of kin of passengers who died on boats and railways.[37] The first Kentucky statute (1854) applied only to victims of railroad accidents and specifically excluded employees. Another section of this same law gave a general action for wrongful death, but only in cases where the defendant was guilty of "wilful neglect."[38] Many courts clung to their homemade wrongful death rules, except insofar as these were modified by statute. The statutes tended to become more general, however, or at least to fill in gaps in the older laws; Massachusetts, in 1883, finally extended protection to the families of dead railroad workers. Interestingly, the typical statute restricted recovery to widows and next of kin of the dead man; and they often put a ceiling on the amount that could be recovered—for example, $10,000 in Kansas in 1859. This trait, or quirk, seems to show that legislatures agreed with the courts that death damages could not really be measured, and that some sort of arbitrary limit had to be set. Equally, the statutory figures represented a rough sort of compromise, between giving the companies what they would have liked (no recovery at all) and giving the plaintiff an unlimited go at the jury. Ten thousand dollars, however, was no small amount in the 19th century. Very few plaintiffs in tort ever recovered this much from a jury.

The fellow-servant rule was strong medicine. It was meant to be firm and clear-cut. It demanded unswerving legal loyalty. But that is precisely what it did not get. Shaw wrote his *Farwell* opinion in 1842. In a later generation of judges, there were many who wavered or disfavored the rule. In "nearly all jurisdictions," said a Connecticut court in 1885, the "tendency" was to "limit rather than enlarge" the fellow-servant doctrine.[39] A Missouri judge, in 1891, candidly spoke of the "hardship and injustice" which the rule had brought about. In the "progress of society," "ideal and invisible masters and employers" (the corporations) had replaced "the actual and visible ones of former times." The "tendency of the more modern authorities" was to mitigate the rules, so as to

[37] Wex S. Malone, "The Genesis of Wrongful Death," 17 Stan. L. Rev. 1043, 1070 (1965). Note that this law was passed eight years before Massachusetts, in the *Carey* case (discussed earlier), denied that wrongful death actions survived at common law. The dead man in *Carey* was, alas, a worker, not a passenger.

[38] Laws Ky. 1854, ch. 964, secs. 1, 3.

[39] *Zeigler v. Danbury and Norwalk Railroad Co.*, 52 Conn. 543, 556 (1885).

place on the employer "a due and just share of the responsibility for the lives and limbs of the persons in [its] employ."[40]

There was more here than judges changing their minds. The accident rate kept increasing at a rate completely unforeseen by Shaw's generation. The railway injury rate, always high, as we have seen, doubled between 1889 and 1906. At the turn of the century, industrial accidents were claiming about 35,000 lives a year, and inflicting close to 2,000,000 injuries. One quarter of these were serious enough to disable the victim for a solid week or more. These accidents were the raw material of possible lawsuits. Litigation was costly, but lawyers took cases on contingent fees. If the case was lost, the lawyer charged nothing; if he won, he took a huge slice of the gain. The upper part of the bar looked with beady eyes at this practice, "most often met with in suits for alleged negligent injuries." Thomas Cooley thought they were beneath contempt: "mere ventures," no better than "a lottery ticket." They debased the bar, brought "the jury system into contempt," and horror of horrors, helped create "a feeling of antagonism between aggregated capital on the one side and the community in general on the other."[41] But the contingent fee had its merits. A poor man could sue a rich corporation. By 1881, the contingent fee was said to be an "all but universal custom of the profession."[42]

Neither the number of accidents nor the contingent fee system, in itself, can completely explain the rise in litigation. To justify taking risks, and to make a living, the lawyer had to win at least some of his cases. The erosion of the fellow-servant rule was a conspiracy in which juries, judges made of less stern stuff than Lemuel Shaw, and legislatures all joined in. The rule evolved along a pattern common to many rules. The courts laid it down simply and flatly, in a form intended as a final formulation. But it was not accepted as such by groups that resented the rule, and by workers and their lawyers. In a sense, strict tort rules simply did not work. The rules choked off thousands of lawsuits, no doubt. Workers and their families simply did not sue; or they settled for peanuts. Still, thousands of cases descended on the courts. Plaintiffs won some of these cases—not by any means all; but some.

---

[40]Thomas, J., in a separate opinion in *Parker v. Hannibal & St. Joseph Railroad Co.*, 109 Mo. 362, 390, 397–98, 19 S.W. 1119 (1891), quoting from *Gilmore v. Northern Pacific Railroad Co.*, 18 Fed. Rep. 866 (C.C.D. Ore., 1884).

[41]Quoted in 24 Albany L.J. 26 (1881).

[42]13 Central L.J. 381 (1881).

The more plaintiffs won, the more lawyers were encouraged to try again. Few juries and lower-court judges took as their sole duty upholding stern and salutary general principles. In Wisconsin, in 307 personal-injury cases appealed to the state supreme court, up to 1907, the worker had won nearly two-thirds in the trial court. Only two-fifths were decided for the worker, however, in the supreme court.[43] These appellate cases, of course, were merely the visible part of a huge iceberg of cases. Other states probably had a similar experience. Trial judges and juries were not playing the *Farwell* game as strictly as they might.

Doctrine, too, began to wobble. The cases opened up exceptions to the rule. One of these was the vice-principal doctrine. An employee could sue his employer in tort if the careless fellow servant who caused the injury was a supervisor or a boss, more properly compared to an employer than to a fellow servant. In one case, a railroad worker, injured by a collapsing roundhouse door, succeeded in winning by showing negligence on the part of a "master mechanic in charge of the roundhouse, foreman of the workmen, having the power to employ and discharge the hands."[44] The vice-principal concept was potentially a large hole in *Farwell*. Some states never adopted the rule, however; some states never carried it very far. In some there were exceptions to this exception; and the exceptions in turn had their own exceptions.

Other counterrules had even greater importance. Some courts accepted the rule that the master's duty to furnish a safe place of work, and safe tools and appliances, was not "delegable"; any failure opened the employer to liability. Many cases turned on this point. In one case, *Wedgwood* v. *Chicago & Northwestern Rr. Co.*,[45] the plaintiff was a brakeman. He went to "couple the cars," and was hurt by a "large and long bolt, out of place," which "unnecessarily, carelessly and unskillfully projected beyond the frame, beam or brakehead, in the way of the brakeman going to couple the cars." The trial court threw the plaintiff's case out; but the supreme court of Wisconsin disagreed: The railroad had a "duty...to provide safe and suitable machinery." Truly, this was an exception that could have swallowed up the rule, if courts had been so inclined. They never were, not quite. So the safe-tool rule grew its own exceptions—the "simple tool" rule, for example. A

[43][1907–1908] *Wis. Bureau of Labor and Industrial Statistics, 13th Bienn. Rep.*, pp. 85–86 (1909).
[44]*Missouri Pac. Ry. Co.* v. *Sasse*, 22 S.W. 187 (Ct. of Civ. Appeals, Texas, 1893).
[45]41 Wis. 478 (1877).

defective hammer or ax did not result in employer liability—another exception to an exception to an exception.

Of equal importance were modifications by statute. The rule first arose in railroad cases, and for the benefit of railroads. As the railroads became bogeymen rather than heroes, legislative changes to the rule appeared, some of which applied *only* to railroads. In Georgia, in the 1850s, a statute gave railroad employees the right to recover damages for injuries caused by fellow servants, as long as they themselves had not been negligent. Similar laws were passed in Iowa (1862), Wyoming (1869), and Kansas (1874).[46]

Small wonder, then, that the law of industrial accidents grew monstrously large. In 1894, William F. Bailey published a treatise on "The Law of the Master's Liability for Injuries to Servants"; the text ran to 543 pages. "No branch of the law," Bailey wrote in the preface, was "so fraught with perplexities to the practitioner." The law was wildly nonuniform, full of "unpardonable differences and distinctions." This meant that, by 1900, the rule had lost some of its reason for being. It was no longer an efficient device for disposing of accident claims. It did not have the courage of its cruelty, nor the strength to be humane. It satisfied neither capital nor labor. It siphoned millions of dollars into the hands of lawyers, court systems, administrators, insurers, claims adjusters. Companies spent and spent, yet did not buy industrial harmony—and not enough of the dollars flowed to the injured workmen. At the turn of the century, rumblings were already heard of the movement that led to a workmen's compensation plan. England had passed such a law. In the United States, no state enacted a compensation statute until 1911. By that time, more than half the states had abolished the fellow-servant rule, at least for railroads; and the Federal Employers Liability Act of 1908 (FELA) had done away with the rule for interstate railways.

By 1900, then, tort law had gone through a marvelous series of changes. It stood then in what might seem a state of indecision. The courts, by and large, still upheld the rights of enterprise; but they were creatures of their time, and their faith had been shaken. Very little is known about the actual operation of the tort system, except for appellate cases; and even those have rarely been studied systematically. There is some evidence that juries were not so rabid on the plaintiff's side as judges and text-writers imagined. The

---

[46]Laws Ga. 1855–56, p. 155; Laws Iowa 1862, ch. 169, sec. 7; Laws Wyo. Terr. 1869, ch. 65; Laws Kans. 1874, ch. 93.

appellate sample can be misleading. A study of reported cases, in the last quarter of the century, found about a nine to one ratio in favor of plaintiff—in cases that were actually appealed. But almost certainly actual trials were not so lopsided; a small sample of Illinois trials showed plaintiff winning 19 jury cases, and defendant winning 13.[47] Recoveries, too, were often extremely small. But the doctrinal structure was tottering; and appellate courts were becoming more "humane."[48]

One symptom of change was the way American courts reacted to the great English case of *Rylands* v. *Fletcher,* decided in the 1860s.[49] The defendants in this case had owned a mill. They built a reservoir on their land. Some old, unused mining shafts lay underneath their land. The water broke through these and flooded the plaintiff's coal mine, which lay under land close by. The English court imposed liability on the defendants, even though the plaintiff could not prove any negligence. The principle of the case, somewhat fuzzy to be sure, was that a person who sets in motion some extraordinary or dangerous process must take the consequences; it was no excuse to show he was as careful as he could be, or as careful as the reasonable man.

This was the germ of a notion far more pregnant with consequences, at least potentially, than Davies's donkey or the falling barrel. Out of it, the courts could have fashioned a doctrine of absolute liability for industrial hazards, running parallel to the piecemeal statutes on strict liability that were actually enacted. But the case had a mixed reception in America. A few courts eagerly accepted the principle. It was mentioned, approved, and applied in an Ohio case in 1899, where nitroglycerin stored on defendant's land blew up "from some cause unknown" and shattered the glass in plaintiff's factory.[50] Other courts reacted in utter panic at this alien intruder. The doctrine was too much, too soon. Oliver Wendell Holmes, Jr., writing in 1873, though he conceded that it was

---

[47]Richard A. Posner, "A Theory of Negligence," 1 J. Legal Studies No. 1, pp. 29, 92 (1972). The volume of personal injury cases in the appellate courts grew tremendously in the last quarter of the century, according to Posner's study. Almost half of these were railroad accident cases. *Ibid.,* 63, 85. See also Robert Kagan, Bliss Cartwright, Lawrence M. Friedman, and Stanton Wheeler, "The Business of State Supreme Courts, 1870–1970," 30 Stan. L. Rev. 121, 142 (1977).

[48]Gary Schwartz, "Tort Law and the Economy in Nineteenth-Century America: A Reinterpretation," 90 Yale L. J. 1717 (1981).

[49]L.R. 1 Ex. 265 (1866); upheld in the House of Lords, L.R. 3 H.L. 330 (1868).

[50]*Bradford Glycerine Co.* v. *St. Mary's Woolen Mfg. Co.,* 60 Ohio St. 560, 54 N.E. 528 (1899).

"politic" to put risks on those who engaged in "extra-hazardous employments," labeled liability without fault in general as primitive—a throwback to those ancient times before the concept of fault had evolved, when an "accidental blow was as good a cause of action as an intentional one."[51] Chief Justice Charles Doe of New Hampshire, who had a firm reputation as a liberal judge, also found the doctrine indefensible, and stoutly rejected it. Horses owned by a certain Lester Collins had been frightened by a railroad engine; they bolted, and broke "a stone post on which was a street lamp," on Albert Brown's land in front of his store in Tilton, New Hampshire. Brown sued Collins for damages. Doe took the trouble to write a long essay attacking *Rylands* v. *Fletcher*. The case would "impose a penalty upon efforts, made in a reasonable, skilful, and careful manner, to rise above a condition of barbarism. It is impossible that legal principle can throw so serious an obstacle in the way of progress and improvement." It would "put a clog upon natural and reasonably necessary uses of matter."[52] This seems rather heavy freight for a case of a damaged post. But Doe saw grave danger in the new-minted English principle. Social progress depended on the vigor and prosperity of developers, of enterprisers. To burden them with strict liability— as *Rylands* might—would slow down the human journey out of barbarism.[53]

But what *was* barbarism, after all? The American landscape had subtly altered after 1850. Smokestacks were as dense as trees in the forest. In row on row of mean houses, in crowded cities, lived hundreds of poorly paid, landless workers. Each year, accident tore through these *barrios*, extracting its tax of dead and shattered bodies, ruined lives, destitute children. A finger of shame pointed at industry. Dissatisfaction was in the air. Labor denounced the system of tort law as cruel and inefficient. It *was* inefficient, if only because it no longer worked, because too many people had lost or were losing their faith in a harsh, simple system, as the lesser of two evils. Change was clearly on the way. Insurance and risk-spreading techniques were ready; cushions of capital reserves were ready; most important, perhaps, an organized and restless working class pressed against the law with voices and votes.

[51] 7 Am. Law. Rev. 652, 653 (1873).

[52] *Brown* v. *Collins*, 53 N.H. 442, 448 (1873).

[53] See the essay of Francis H. Bohlen, "The Rule in *Rylands* v. *Fletcher*," 59 U. Pa. L. Rev. 298, 373, 423 (1911) on the meaning of the case; and on the judicial reaction to this decision.

The rules of tort law, in twilight by 1900, were like some great but transient beast, born, spawning, and dying in the shortest of time. The most stringent rules lasted, in their glory, two generations at most. Had it been worthwhile? Was that span of time so precious? Would the economy have suffered under other arrangements? It is impossible to know. There may have been some point to that short, bitter life, some virtue to the sacrifice of life and body; or then again it may all have been in vain.

CHAPTER VII

THE UNDERDOGS: 1850-1900

THE DEPENDENT POOR

The American system provided a voice and a share in the economy to incomparably more people than most of the societies of the old world; but for the unorganized and the powerless the share was niggardly indeed. The basis of politics, and law, was the pressure of interest groups; the loudest, most powerful voices won the most. Old people, transients, the feeble-minded, dirt-poor and crippled families—all these stayed by and large at the bottom of the social pit. Tort law blossomed, corporation law swelled in pride; the poor laws remained obscure, local, haphazard, backward, and cruel. There were, however, some changes, and perhaps even a measure of improvement.

There was a lot to improve. In some counties of some states, the poor, in the age of the railroad and the telegraph, were still bound out "like cattle at so much per head, leaving the keeper to make his profit out of their petty needs."[1] Or they might be sold at auction to the lowest bidder. Sometimes it was a matter of necessity to make private arrangements, since there were no reasonable alternatives. Trempealeau County, Wisconsin, in the 1870s and 1880s, boarded out its handful of "permanently demented" people; the state's asylum could not or would not hold them.[2] The auction system, in its most blatant form, was widely considered an abuse; it would eventually die out. "Indoor" relief, that is, relief inside the walls of institutions, was clearly, by 1850, in the ascendancy; "outdoor" relief was on the wane. The trend meant poor farms and poorhouses, if not more specialized institutions.

[1] Quoted in Grace A. Browning, *The Development of Poor Relief Legislation in Kansas* (1935), p. 59, n. 7. The statement quoted, from an 1899 report, actually referred to the treatment of the insane in Kansas, where they were farmed out to the counties at so much a head.

[2] Merle Curti, *The Making of an American Community* (1959), p. 285.

488

One reason for the change in policy was ideological: outdoor relief was not stigmatic enough. "Men who before had eaten the bread of industry saw their fellows receiving sustenance from the overseer of the poor.... The pauper came to look upon the aid given as his by right."[3] Many no doubt thought poorhouses would work an improvement in the quality of care; outdoor relief made moral training, medical treatment, and rehabilitation more difficult.

These high hopes were frequently disappointed. In 1850, Rhode Island made a study of its poor-law system at work. The results were harrowing. There were fifteen almshouses which spent, on the average, $51.50 per inmate per year. Some of the poor were still "vendued" to keepers who entered the lowest bid for their care. There was testimony about one keeper who beat and abused his charges: "He used to drag John Davis, an old man as much as sixty years old up stairs with a rope and kept him there in the cold for days and nights together until he died, having one of his legs frozen.... [H]e died before midnight, with no person watching with him & he lay until the sun was 2 or 3 hours high in the morning, & on a very cold morning before they came to him."[4]

But some of the public poor farms were not much better than the homes of these private keepers. Poor farms too were run cheaply, sometimes callously. In the words of one observer, they housed "the most sodden driftwood from the social wreckage of the time.... In some of the country almshouses, no clergyman comes the year round; and no friendly visitor appears to encourage the superintendent to be faithful, or to bring to light abuses that may exist."[5] The Ulster County poorhouse (New York) was in 1868 an "old, dilapidated two-story wooden structure." The rooms were small, "ceilings low, ventilation imperfect"; there were no "suitable bathing conveniences." The little wooden house for the insane contained "twenty-five small unventilated cells." The inmates were all "noisy and filthy"; several were "nearly nude." The beds were disordered and torn, and the halls littered with straw and bits of clothing. The water closet, used by both sexes, was out of repair; and the air in the room was "foul and impure."

---

[3] 10th Ann. Rpt., *Bd. of State Charities*, Indiana (1900), p. 154.
[4] Margaret Creech, *Three Centuries of Poor Law Administration: A Study of Legislation in Rhode Island* (1936), pp. 195–97, 325.
[5] Amos G. Warner, *American Charities* (3rd ed., 1919), p. 179.

In the Schoharie County poorhouse, "an insane woman was chained to the floor, and a man to a block of wood in the yard." Twenty years later, some of these hovels had been improved; some had not.[6] The poor got almost no medical care in many counties. In Michigan, in 1894, a former county physician reported the auction system still at work; many counties awarded contracts to supply medicine, give medical care, and perform surgery for the poor, to the local doctor who put in the lowest bid.[7]

Who were the people who went to the poorhouse? The intention was clear: it had to be only those who had no choice; the most desperate; men and women at the bottom of the barrel. Very few studies take a worm's-eye view of these dismal, obscure institutions. Not surprisingly, they housed unwed mothers with small children, widows, old folks with no place to turn, and, in great numbers, the mentally ill.[8] All of these were dumped into the poorhouse or poor farm, where they at least got some food, shelter, a bit of clothing. The quality of life is much harder to capture. It was surely not a country club; but whether all, or most, of the hundreds of such places were as bad as the Rhode Island or New York examples is hard to tell.

After the Civil War, some states began to reform their poor laws by centralizing administration. Massachusetts created a State Board of Charities in 1863, Illinois in 1869.[9] A Connecticut law of 1873 set up a five-member board of charities—"three gentlemen and two ladies"—appointed by the governor. The board was to visit and inspect "all institutions in the state, both public and private, in which persons are detained by compulsion for penal, reformatory, sanitary or humanitarian purposes." The board had the duty to see whether inmates were "properly treated," and whether they were "unjustly placed" or "improperly held" in the institution. The board had some vague powers to "correct any abuses that shall be found to exist," but were told to work, "so far as practicable, through the persons in charge of such institu-

---

[6]22nd Ann. Rpt., *State Bd. of Charities*, N.Y. (1889), pp. 505–11.

[7]Isabel C. Bruce and Edith Eickhoff, *The Michigan Poor Law* (1936), p. 77.

[8]Elizabeth G. Brown, "Poor Relief in a Wisconsin County, 1846–1866: Administration and Recipients," 20 Am. J. Legal Hist. 79 (1976). Another study of a poorhouse, also from the Middle West, is Eric H. Monkkonen, *The Dangerous Class: Crime and Poverty in Columbus, Ohio, 1860–1885* (1975), chs. 5 and 6.

[9]Sophonisba P. Breckenridge, *The Illinois Poor Law and Its Administration* (1939), pp. 44–5.

tions."[10] This was something less than iron discipline over charitable institutions. But the boards had the power of publicity. They could, if they wished, evoke scandal. In the late 19th century, for these areas of apathy and neglect, the enthusiasm of a small band of people, inside and outside of government—men and women like Florence Kelley, Lawrence Veiller, and others—was one of the few real forces of reform. The reformers used words, charts and pictures, as their weapons. They aimed for the sympathy of a wider public, or, more tellingly, at a public sense of social cost. They tried to show that callousness, in the long run, did not pay.

Actual improvements in welfare administration probably owed a good deal to this social-cost argument. In the 1890s, when some counties were still selling medical care of the poor to the lowest bidder, Amos G. Warner and associates noted that ten American cities, with an aggregate population of 3,327,323, spent $1,034,576.50 in one year on medical relief. Warner thought there were "three strong motives" at work: "the desire to aid the destitute, the desire to educate students and build up medical reputations, and the desire to protect the public health. The latter has often been the leading cause of public appropriations for medical charities."[11] The reformers, then, were valuable not only because they touched the heart, but because they persuaded the selfish soul as well. They played on fear of the crime, plague, and social disorder that poverty was thought to be certain to breed.

Still, reformers had to struggle against strongly held attitudes, unfriendly to public relief. These attitudes infected even public agencies. The Illinois board of charities, in 1886, voiced a common fear: the "inevitable consequences of substituting the machinery of state for the spontaneous impulses of private benevolence," would be to "paralyze" the "charitable activity" of the private sector.[12] Josephine Shaw Lowell, writing in 1890, thought that public relief was justified only when "starvation is imminent." How could one tell when this was the case? "Only by putting such conditions upon the giving of public relief that, presumably, persons not in danger of starvation will not consent to receive it. The less that

[10]Edward W. Capen, *The Historical Development of the Poor Law of Connecticut* (1905), pp. 213–14; Laws Conn. 1873, ch. 45. The power to investigate whether persons were "unjustly placed" or "improperly held" did not extend to "cases of detention for crime."

[11]Amos G. Warner, Stuart A. Queen, and Ernest B. Harper, *American Charities and Social Work* (4th ed. 1930), pp. 143–44.

[12]Quoted in Breckenridge, *op. cit.*, p. 76.

is given, the better for everyone, the giver and the receiver."[13]

Nobody, of course, asked the poor *their* opinion in this matter. The poor were thus impaled on the horns of a 19th-century dilemma: society refused to tolerate the idea of pay without work; and yet nobody in this society was supposed to starve. Relief was, in theory, available to everyone who really needed it. But this right was not to be too freely exercised. Consciously or not, relief was made so degrading and obnoxious that no one with an alternative, and some pride, would choose it voluntarily. Mostly, in fact, family and friends had to sustain the urban poor; private charity took care of some others; the public sector lagged behind. In times of depression, however, there were soup kitchens in the major cities. Some relief agencies protested that these kitchens were too indiscriminate; it was "impossible" to tell the "worthy" from the "unworthy poor."[14] Soup presumably corrupted the one but not the other. The big city machines had no such qualms. Boss Tweed of New York City personally donated $50,000 to provide the poor with Christmas dinners, in the harsh winter of 1870. He used his position in the state legislature to squeeze appropriations for charities in his city; and city funds, too, were distributed to welfare institutions. Some of this money, of course, had been extorted from the public, rich and poor. Caustically, the *New York Times* compared Tweed to a medieval baron, "who swept a man's land of his crops, and then gave him a crust of dry bread."[15] Hard times returned in the nineties; and some reform governments tried to help out the needy in new ways. Mayor Hazen Pingree of Detroit had a garden plan; the poor grew vegetables on vacant lots. San Francisco spent $3,000 a month in 1893 to help the unemployed. Some of these jobless men were put to work cleaning streets and building roads.[16]

In many states, the law of settlement and removal was reformed, and some of the worst features trimmed. Welfare law, however, continued to be obsessed with drawing a line between the worthy and the unworthy poor. Unworthy were drunks, transients, tramps, and the proverbial sturdy beggars. Worthy meant,

---

[13]Quoted in Ralph E. and Muriel W. Pumphrey, eds., *The Heritage of American Social Work* (1961), p. 223. See also Walter I. Trattner, *From Poor Law to Welfare State: A History of Social Welfare in America* (1974), pp. 86−89.

[14]Leah H. Feder, *Unemployment Relief in Periods of Depression, 1857−1922* (1936), p. 47.

[15]Quoted in Alexander B. Callow, Jr., *The Tweed Ring* (1966), p. 159.

[16]Frances Cahn and Valeska Bary, *Welfare Activities of Federal, State, and Local Governments in California, 1850−1934* (1936), pp. 201−02.

in essence. guiltless. These were the blind, children, veterans, the deaf and dumb, the epileptic. Legislatures were particularly likely to show sympathy for temporary sufferers who had fallen out of the middle class. Kansas, for example, was as stingy as any toward its destitute poor. But in 1869, it appropriated $15,000 to buy seed wheat for impoverished settlers on the western frontier; more was appropriated in 1871 and 1872. Grasshoppers scourged the western plains in 1874; in 1875, the state passed a "seed and feed" law. Townships could float bonds to provide "destitute citizens... with grain for seed and feed." Another law authorized counties to sell bonds for relief purposes. (The farmers were expected to pay the money back.) In the 1890s, the state gave away seed wheat, and sold grain and coal to farmers hurt by drought and crop failures.[17]

War veterans were another meritorious class. There had been both state and federal pensions for veterans of every American war, including, of course, the Civil War. Wounded war veterans, and their families, were singled out for special benefits in a federal pension law of 1862. The organized veterans continued to press for bonuses, pensions and bounties; after 1876, they won a number of signal victories.[18] They were a potent lobby in the states, too. Connecticut, for example, granted some tax relief to former soldiers (1869); small pensions to orphans of soldiers, up to age twelve; and incorporated, in 1864, a soldiers' orphans' home. In 1889, Civil War veterans were given job preferences for state jobs. In 1895, veterans were exempted from peddlers' licenses.[19]

There was a steady trend toward categorical programs: taking care of special classes of the poor. The government share took more and more direct forms: first, the state granted charters to private charities, then donated money to these agencies;[20] finally the state ran some institutions itself. In Massachusetts, the state lunatic hospital at Worcester was founded in the 1830s.[21] In the

[17]Grace A. Browning, *The Development of Poor Relief Legislation in Kansas* (1935), pp. 77–81.

[18]See, in general, Mary R. Dearing, *Veterans in Politics: The Story of the G.A.R.* (1952).

[19]Capen, *op. cit.,* pp. 249–55, 387–89.

[20]There were innumerable instances. See, for many examples in a general appropriation law, Laws N.Y. 1850, ch. 365. See also Jacobus ten Broek, "California's Dual System of Family Law: Its Origin, Development and Present Status," Part II, 16 Stan. L. Rev. 900, 944–49 (1964).

[21]The story of this institution is told in Gerald N. Grob, *The State and the Mentally Ill* (1966).

1840s, Dorothea Dix bravely roamed the country, pleading that something be done for the mentally ill. In New Jersey, she talked the legislature into creating an insane asylum at Trenton; it opened its doors in 1848. After 1850, other states established institutions for these neglected people. Kansas set up a hospital for the insane at Osawatomie in 1863; later, four more such hospitals were created, and in 1881, a state home for the feeble-minded. But even in states with statewide institutions, most of the insane who were not at home were at the tender mercies of county officials of the poor. The state institutions themselves were of varying quality. Government, reflecting its constituencies, was niggardly; and its span of attention was short. Neglected, some state institutions turned into snake pits. Their only advance on local institutions was that they centralized abuse.

Legislatures did, however, create or finance other kinds of "home." Particularly, there was a special effort to ease the lot of unfortunate children. Pennsylvania, in 1860, donated $5,000 to the "Northern Home for friendless children," a typical act of largess.[22] Children were a natural object of sympathy and, in the cities, homeless or abandoned children were foot soldiers for the "dangerous classes"; it behooved society to do something for these children before they were lost to decency altogether. The old apprenticeship system was not suitable in the factory age. In New York, the Children's Aid Society, founded by Charles Loring Brace in 1853, gathered up homeless children from the streets and sent them into the country—many to the Midwest—to work and build character on clean, honest, Protestant farms. No doubt some of these foster parents were cruel and exploitive; but other orphans found what were passable homes and a decent way to earn their bread. Western farm life was in any event to be preferred to street life, hunger, and an early, violent death. Up to 1892, the Children's Aid Society had "emigrated" 84,318 children; most of these (51,427) were boys.[23]

On the whole, the categorical approach was the only way to humanize welfare that had much political appeal. The approach

[22]Laws Pa. 1860, ch. 551, sec. 38.
[23]Amos Warner et al., *American Charities and Social Work* (4th ed., 1930), p. 136; Miriam Z. Langsam, *Children West: A History of the Placing-Out System of the New York Children's Aid Society, 1853–1890* (1964). In Boston, too, there was a Children's Aid Society (1864), which "maintained a home to discipline children before placing them out." Robert M. Mennell, *Thorns & Thistles: Juvenile Delinquents in the United States, 1825–1940* (1973), p. 43.

consisted of constantly pinching off a class of the more or less guiltless or worthy poor. It was therefore devastating to those left over, the unworthy or guilty poor. No programs dealt with their problems in any meaningful way. Special aid to others drained away whatever sympathy and political clout this residue could muster. It was a story to be endlessly repeated. The fate of families on relief was later matched by the fate of AFDC and public housing in the 1950s, which became more and more controversial and degraded, the more they became last-stop programs for the lowest dependents of them all.

FAMILY LAW AND THE STATUS OF WOMEN

As the factory revolution proceeded, countless thousands of women went to work in textile mills or shops. They may have merely exchanged one master for another; but in some ways work laid the foundation for the liberation of women in the eyes of the law. An economic woman was not as subservient to men as a woman totally dependent on a man for her daily bread. The right to vote, a 20th-century conquest, was only one delayed step in a series of legal emancipations, which created a new legal personality for women.[24]

For the sake of free enterprise, if for no other reason, the law presumed that adults were fully capable of buying, selling, behaving in the market. Married women's property laws, already discussed, were extended, broadened, generalized after 1850. No doubt some men felt that these laws went too far "towards clothing one class of females with strange and manly attributes," as a Wisconsin judge put it.[25] But the market and creditor's rights ultimately won out over these faintly archaic sentiments. In New York, statutes of 1860 and 1862 extended the rights of married women, giving her dominion, not just over property she owned or ac-

---

[24]There was, of course, a woman's suffrage movement in the 19th century; and it made some progress. The territories of Wyoming and Utah granted women voting rights around 1870. Congress eliminated voting rights for women in Utah, in 1887; but when Utah was admitted to the union, these rights were reinstated. By 1890, some nineteen states gave women the right to vote in elections for local school boards. Eleanor Flexner, *Century of Struggle* (1972), pp. 159–63, 176–77.

[25]Crawford, J., in *Norval v. Rice*, 2 Wis. 22, 31 (1853).

quired, but also over whatever she acquired "by her trade, business, labor or services." The courts at first interpreted this statute quite narrowly, to be sure. A case in 1878 held that the husband still had the right to sue for his wife's wages.[26] But the trend in the law was clear.

Dower, too, had been substantially revised and revamped, as we have seen. This too was generally in the interest of women's rights—though also, and perhaps more crucially, in the interests of those who traded in the market. In community-property states (California, Texas, Louisiana, and others), the husband was manager and king of the community, under the law. That is, although both husband and wife "owned" community property, the husband was vested with management and control. The law would ultimately evolve toward greater equality, paralleling social evolution; but slowly. In community property states, a wife's inheritance rights were rather secure. She automatically owned one half of the "community." When her husband died, she came into possession of this automatic half, will or no will.[27]

In the law of marriage and divorce, religion, sentiment, and morals influenced the law, along with economic and business motives. For business reasons—especially the needs of the land market—it would be helpful if marriage was a matter of record, formally created, formally dissolved. By the end of the century, most states made provision for marriage licenses, and for civil and religious ceremonies. In most states, however, the common-law marriage remained valid. Courts generally construed marriage-license laws as optional only; couples could have a formal marriage, if they wished; there was no obligation. A few states abolished the common-law marriage; or construed their statutes as killing the doctrine.[28] The concept of the common-law marriage was almost a necessity for the old slave states. Slaves had not gone through (legal) marriage ceremonies, since these were, strictly speaking, forbidden. Slave "marriages" were common-law marriages at best. An Alabama law of 1868 declared that "freedmen and women . . . living together as man and wife, shall be regarded in law as man and wife"; and their children were "declared . . .

---

[26]*Birbeck* v. *Ackroyd*, 74 N.Y. 356 (1878); Norma Basch, *In the Eyes of the Law: Women, Marriage, and Property in Nineteenth-Century New York* (1982), pp. 217–18.

[27]See Peter T. Conmy, *The Historic Spanish Origin of California's Community Property Law and Its Development and Adaptation* . . . (1957).

[28]See *Beverlin* v. *Beverlin*, 29 W. Va. 732, 3 S.E. 36 (1877).

entitled to all the rights, benefits and immunities of children of any other class."[29] In other states, it may not have been necessary to abolish the common-law marriage. It was probably dying out in practice. In an urbanizing society, a mass-communication society, the social isolation that brought the concept to life became much rarer. By 1900, "marriage" meant ceremonial marriage, for all practical purposes. The common-law concept, then, could be retained to cover the occasional hardship cases. There was little urge to abolish it; it was abolishing itself at a proper pace.

Marriage, in other words, was becoming more formal; and the state began to take a more active interest in the subject. It began to regulate more carefully *who* got married, as well as how. At common law, the age of consent had been fourteen for boys, twelve for girls. This common-law rule allowed very young marriages; Joel Bishop thought it unsuitable to the "northern latitudes"; it must have "originated in the warm climate of Italy."[30] American statutes generally redefined the age of consent, raising it to more fitting levels. In Illinois, in 1827, the ages were seventeen for men, fourteen for women. In Idaho, in 1887, the ages were eighteen and sixteen. Certainly, very young marriages were not the custom. Neither was open interracial marriage. The Southern states did not tolerate miscegenation, as one might expect. But neither did some Western and Northern states: a California statute of 1850 declared "illegal and void" all "marriages of white persons with Negroes and mulattoes."

Bigamy had always been a crime; but never a very important one. The Mormons, however, made plural marriage a national issue. This Mormon practice drew down a storm of rage, horror, disgust from pulpit, legislature, and press, vehement to a degree hard to understand today. Action followed words. In the Morrill Act of 1862, Congress moved "to punish and prevent the practice of polygamy in the territories." The Supreme Court upheld the constitutionality of this law in 1878. This was in *Reynolds* v. *United States*.[31] Reynolds, the defendant, invoked freedom of religion. The Court was not impressed. Religion did not excuse gross immorality; suppose a religion called for burning widows, or for

[29]Laws Ala. 1868, ord. no. 23, p. 175.

[30]Joel P. Bishop, *Commentaries on the Law of Marriage and Divorce*, Vol. I (4th ed., 1864), p. 127. See, in general, on state control over marriage, Michael Grossberg, "Guarding the Altar: Physiological Restrictions and the Rise of State Intervention in Matrimony," 26 Am. J. Legal Hist. 197 (1982).

[31]98 U.S. 145 (1878).

human sacrifice? Polygamy was patriarchal, and had always been confined to "Asiatic and...African peoples." There, the Court felt, it should stay.

Persecution of this kind seemed at first to have almost no effect on the Utah Mormons. In the 1880s, the Gentiles returned to the battle. President Arthur in 1881 called plural marriages an "odious crime"; James G. Blaine warned against such abominations disguised as religious practices; he repeated the line about "the claim of certain heathen tribes, if they should come among us, to continue the rite of human sacrifice."[32] The vicious and punitive Edmunds law, of 1882, put teeth into laws against polygamy; it also attempted to smash the political power of Mormon leaders. Under the Edmunds law, hundreds of Mormons were arrested, fined and jailed. The Edmunds-Tucker law, of 1887, was even more stringent. In 1890, Wilford Woodruff, president of the Mormon Church, in defeat, threw in the towel. The Church renounced polygamy. The Mormon rebellion was over; plural marriages faded into history (except for a few deviant offshoots of the main Mormon branch). No doubt, thousands of good Americans sighed with relief at the downfall of Satan.

The law of divorce was always more controversial than the law of marriage. It changed greatly in the last half of the century, both on the official level, and even more significantly in its subterranean life. The first great change was the destruction of the legislative divorce. State after state abolished it, usually by constitutional provision. By about 1880, it was virtually gone. The last holdout was Delaware, where it survived until 1897. A new constitution in Delaware at that point barred the practice. But the legislature of Delaware granted 100 divorces in the last year of this noble institution.

After the legislative divorce departed, what remained were general laws governing divorce; these turned the actual business over to the courts. The divorce statutes were somewhat variable. From about 1850 to 1870, some states adopted rather loose divorce laws. In Connecticut any "misconduct" was grounds for divorce, if it "permanently destroys the happiness of the petitioner and defeats

---

[32]Quoted in Thomas F. O'Dea, *The Mormons* (1957), p. 110. See also Ray Jay Davis, "The Polygamous Prelude," 6 Am. J. Legal Hist. 1 (1962). In Idaho Territory, anti-Mormons were in control; and an act of 1885 required all voters to swear they were not polygamists, and that they did not belong to an "order" that taught bigamy.

the purposes of the marriage relation." In Maine, a supreme-court justice could grant a divorce if he deemed it "reasonable and proper, conducive to peace and harmony, and consistent with the peace and morality of society." Divorce laws in states as different as North Carolina, Indiana, and Rhode Island were also quite permissive. Some states which did not go as far as Maine or Connecticut broadened their statutes considerably; they added to the traditional list of grounds for divorce (adultery, desertion, and impotence, for example) new and vaguer ones such as "cruelty." In the Tennessee Code of 1858, for example, divorce was available on grounds of impotence, bigamy, adultery, desertion, felony conviction, plus the following: attempting to take a spouse's life by poison; concealing a pregnancy by another man at the time of marriage; nonsupport. In addition, the court might, in its "discretion," free a woman from the bonds of matrimony if her husband had "abandoned her, or turned her out of doors," if he was guilty of cruel and inhuman treatment, or if he had "offered such indignities to her person as to render her condition intolerable and force her to withdraw."[33]

After 1870, the tide began to turn. Influential moral leaders had never stopped attacking loose divorce laws. Horace Greeley thought that "easy divorce" had made the Roman Empire rot. A similar fate lay in store for America, "blasted by the mildew of unchaste mothers and dissolute homes."[34] Theodore D. Woolsey, president of Yale University, wrote a book in 1869 denouncing the divorce laws of his state as immoral and unscriptural. It was a "sleep of justice" not to enforce the laws against adultery; this dulled the public sense of sin.[35] In Woolsey's own program, only adultery would be a valid cause for divorce. In his view, "petitions for divorce become more numerous with the ease of obtaining them"; lax laws caused the disintegration of the family, the backbone of American life. In 1881, a New England Divorce Reform League was formed. Dr. Woolsey was its president. Out of this grew a National Divorce Reform League in 1885.[36] A second edition of Woolsey's book appeared in 1882. By this time, the Connecticut law had been repealed. Maine's law fell in 1883. A more rigorous divorce law replaced it, with tougher grounds, a six-

[33]Tenn. Stats. 1858, secs. 2448–9.
[34]Quoted in Nelson Blake, *The Road to Reno* (1962), p. 91.
[35]Theodore D. Woolsey, *Divorce and Divorce Legislation* (2nd ed., 1882), p. 221.
[36]Blake, *op. cit.*, p. 132.

month wait before decrees became "absolute," and a two-year ban on remarriage of the plaintiff without court permission; as for the guilty defendant, he or she could never remarry without leave of the court.[37]

Naturally, there were two sides to the question. Militant feminists took up the cudgels for permissive divorce. A furious debate raged in New York. Robert Dale Owen, son of the Utopian reformer, went into battle against Horace Greeley. Owen, like Joel Bishop, felt that strict divorce laws, not lax ones, led to adultery. New York, rather than permissive Indiana, Owen said, was the "paradise of free-lovers."[38] Bishop bitterly condemned divorce *a mensa et thoro* (legal separation): "in almost every place where Marriage is known, this Folly walks with her—the queen and the slut, the pure and the foul, the bright and the dark, dwell together!"[39] Both men agreed, in other words, that the divorce laws had a direct impact on the level of sexual morality. But exactly this was open to question. One thing was certain: the divorce rate was rising. The number of divorces rose from 9,937 in 1867, to 25,535 in 1886, far more than population increase can explain, and despite tightened divorce laws;[40] by 1900, more than 55,000 divorces were granted each year.

How is this fact to be accounted for? There are two possibilities. Either dry rot had affected family life; or more people wanted *formal* acceptance of the fact that their marriages were dead. Those who prattled about Babylon and chastity believed in the first explanation. But the second seems far more likely. Just as more of the middle class wanted, and needed, their deeds recorded, their wills made out, their marriages solemnized, so they wanted the honesty and convenience of divorce, the right to remarry in bourgeois style, to have legitimate children with their second wife (or husband), and the right to decent, honest disposition of their worldly goods. Only divorce could provide this.

This was the middle-class need for divorce. But divorce began to spread throughout the population. A study of divorce, in two California counties, 1850 to 1890, examined the class and income status of litigants. Almost a quarter of the husbands were laborers, another 9 percent were unskilled tradesmen; 19 percent were

[37]Laws Me. 1883, ch. 212.
[38]Blake, *op cit.*, p. 90.
[39]Bishop, *Commentaries on the Law of Marriage and Divorce,* vol. I (4th ed., 1864), p. 26.
[40]Blake, *op. cit.*, p. 134.

skilled workers, 14 percent farmers, 17 percent "middle class," 15 percent upper class.[41] But why would laborers, or their wives, want divorce? Why would they be willing to put up with the cost and the fuss? Here the standard economic analysis breaks down. The middle class, to be sure, needed divorce; but as divorce became more available, it reinforced the notion that living in sin was wrong, and, what is more, unnecessary. Victorian morality was within the grasp of everyone. This was the paradox of the moral attack on divorce: the immorality of divorce depends on the sacredness of marriage; but the sacredness of marriage increased the demand for divorce. Only through divorce was respectable remarriage possible, with a regular husband or wife, and legitimate children.

Divorce law, and divorce practice, reflected changes in the family that went beyond either the economic or the moral factors mentioned. When divorce was a matter mostly for the well-to-do, men asked for, and got, custody of the children in a fair number of cases. As divorce percolated downward, it became the custom for the woman to file for divorce; this meant she was the "innocent" party, entitled to custody, alimony, and the like. The place of small children was with their mothers, it was believed. In addition, it was much less damaging to accuse a man of adultery, desertion, or cruelty than to accuse a woman. Divorce became much more a woman's remedy, at least in form. This was especially pronounced in the Northern states. In the period 1887–1906, women were plaintiffs in exactly two thirds of the divorce cases; but there was great variation among states. In Mississippi most plaintiffs were men (almost 60 percent); in Rhode Island, 78 percent of the plaintiffs were women. Western plaintiffs were overwhelmingly female, too.[42]

Divorce, as we said, became a woman's remedy; but what did it remedy? Did the state of the law (and practice) improve the lot of the deserted or mistreated wife? There is no reason to believe that it did. The image of the wife that shines through divorce law (and practice) is the image of a domestic drudge, a wife and mother but nothing else; a victim, not a partner; a dependent,

[41]Robert L. Griswold, *Family and Divorce in California, 1850–1890: Victorian Illusions and Everyday Realities* (1980), p. 25; another recent study which uses divorce records is Elaine T. May, *Great Expectations: Marriage and Divorce in Post-Victorian America* (1980).

[42]Lawrence M. Friedman and Robert V. Percival, "Who Sues for Divorce? From Fault through Fiction to Freedom," 5 J. Legal Studies 61 (1976).

not a self-propelling force. But the relationship between family law and family life is complex and difficult to read.

A related question is whether the strict laws, in most states, had any effect on family solidarity, whether they made much difference to the divorce rate. This question too is difficult to answer. At the time, it was endlessly debated. In Maine and Connecticut, there were short-term "improvements" when permissive laws were abolished; but between 1850 and 1900, the divorce rate skyrocketed everywhere. In theory, a divorce suit was an ordinary action at law, with an attacking plaintiff and a resisting defendant. In practice, few divorces were adversary cases, though a certain number of unedifying battles did take place in which bitter spouses aired their dirty linen in public. In most cases, both parties either wanted the divorce or were willing to concede it to the other. Even in states that stuck to rigid statutes, collusion became a way of life in divorce court. Divorce in New York was a scandal. Lawyers openly advertised their skill at arranging divorce. Reed's "American Law Agency," at 317 Broadway, advertised in 1882 in the *New York Sun*

> DIVORCES quietly; desertion, drunkenness; any cause, advice free.[43]

"Divorce rings" operated practically in the open. Manufactured adultery was a New York specialty. Henry Zeimer and W. Waldo Mason, arrested in 1900, had hired young secretaries and other enterprising girls for this business. The girls would admit on the witness stand that they knew the plaintiff's husband, then blush, shed a few tears, and leave the rest to the judge. Annulments, too, were more common in New York than elsewhere; they were a loophole in the divorce laws, less distasteful, though less certain, than trumped-up adultery. Friendly divorces were a simple matter in those states which allowed "cruelty" as grounds for divorce. It is hard to know exactly how much collusion there was, and when it began. Francis Laurent's figures for Chippewa County, Wisconsin, suggest a dramatic rise in friendly divorce (so to speak), in this nonurban county from the 1870s on.[44]

The migratory divorce, for people with money and the urge to travel, was another detour around strict enforcement of divorce

---

[43] Blake, *op. cit.*, p. 190.
[44] Francis W. Laurent, *The Business of a Trial Court* (1959), pp. 176–77.

law. To attract the "tourist trade," a state needed easy laws and a short residence period. Indiana was one of these states, before the 1870s. The moralists fought divorce colonies as hard as they could. Notoriety and bad publicity helped their campaign in Indiana; in 1873, the legislature passed a stricter law that shut the divorce mill down. South and North Dakota, too, had their day. Finally, Nevada became the place. In 1900, it had still not fully exploited its possibilities, though Earl Russell was one of the birds of passage who looked for divorce in this desert haven. The Earl was later indicted for bigamy in England. But the publicity only helped Nevada's business. Nevada remained quite impervious to moral arguments; its career as national divorce mill lasted longer than any other state's.

Plainly, in the late 19th century, the number of married people who *wanted* divorce was greater than before, for reasons we have explored. But the rising demand only scandalized the pious further. The last third of the 19th century was, in any event, an era of national panic over morality, eugenics, the purity of the bloodline and the future of old-fashioned white America. To prophets of doom the whore, divorce, had to be contained. The result of this clash of opinion was, as often, a stalemate—or compromise, if one prefers. It became difficult to change the laws, one way or another. Many state statutes, then, were like weird ice formations, frozen into absurd shapes, dictated by past circumstances, at that point where forces were more or less evenly balanced. The national law of divorce was a hodgepodge. South Carolina still allowed no divorces at all.[45] New York allowed divorce, practically speaking, only for adultery. Most states had a broader list. In a few jurisdictions, the innocent party might remarry, the guilty party not.[46] In some jurisdictions, the grounds were very broad—in Wyoming, for example, divorce was available for "indignities" that rendered the marriage "intolerable."[47] In the strict states, the

[45]South Carolina did, however, grant alimony under some circumstances to separated wives, even though no divorce was possible. See Michael S. Hindus and Lynne E. Withey, "The Law of Husband and Wife in Nineteenth-Century America: Changing View of Divorce," in D. Kelly Weisberg, ed., *Women and the Law*, vol. II (1982), pp. 133, 140–45.

[46]In Tennessee, a divorced adulterer or adulteress could not marry the "person with whom the crime was committed during the life of the former husband or wife." Tenn. Stats. 1858 sec. 2475.

[47]Wyo. Stats. 1899, sec. 2988; conduct by a husband that would "constitute him a vagrant" was also grounds for divorce.

compromise took this form: the moralists had their symbolic victory, a stringent law strutting proudly on the books. At the same time, enforcement of these laws was defective. A cynical traffic in runaway and underground divorce flourished in the shadows.[48] Divorce law stood as an egregious example of a branch of law tortured by contradictions in public opinion, trapped between contending forces of perhaps roughly equal size; trapped, too, in a federal system with freedom of movement back and forth, and beyond the power and grasp of any single state.

THE RACES

The war, the Emancipation Proclamation, and the 13th, 14th, and 15th amendments ended American slavery and gave the blacks the right to vote. The 14th amendment also gave them (ostensibly) the equal protection of the laws. The basic promises of Reconstruction, however, were not really kept. Until well into the 20th century, much of the history of Reconstruction was written by white Southerners, in a style unfriendly to blacks and to the radical North. Historians have only recently begun to peel away misconceptions in earnest and reconstruct Reconstruction in a more generous, balanced way.

Clearly, leaders of the old South who survived the war were in no mood for racial equality. It was a bitter enough pill that the slaves were legally free; there was no inclination to go beyond the formal status. The Black Codes of 1865, passed in almost all of the states of the old Confederacy, were meant to replace slavery with some kind of caste system and to preserve as much as possible of the prewar way of life. Mississippi led the way. Its statutes in 1865 looked to a system in which the blacks would work as laborers on farms and plantations owned by whites. It called for written contracts of labor. Any black laborer who quit "without good cause" could be arrested and taken back to his employer. The Black Codes kept some of the old disabilities of blacks. In Mississippi, blacks still could not testify in cases where plaintiff and defendant

[48]As early as 1882, a committee of the American Bar Association went to work drafting uniform legislature to get rid of fake domicile and the runaway divorce. They succeeded in inducing some states to pass their statute, but the problem did not go away. See Amasa Eaton, "Proposed Reforms in Marriage and Divorce Laws," 4 Columbia L. Rev. 243 (1904).

were white. Intermarriage between the races was strictly forbidden. Blacks could not sit on juries. The Southern states also passed stringent vagrancy laws, to keep blacks under control.[49]

The North—at least the radicals—were not ready to concede this much to the South. The Black Codes were erased; Congress enacted a strong Civil Rights Act (1866), anticipating the 14th amendment (1868); the South was put under military government. The Freedmen's Bureaus, established by Congress, were an experiment in social planning, to help blacks adapt to the white man's society and economy. Blacks were elected to Congress and held state offices. But Reconstruction did not last. The Freedmen's Bureaus practically ceased operation by 1869; they were at all times understaffed and underfinanced; and their boldest moves— for example, land redistribution on the Sea Islands of South Carolina—were frustrated by the Johnson administration's policies.[50] By 1875, the North's passion for equality had all but dribbled away. The North lost interest in black welfare; Northern racism, briefly and thinly covered over, came to the surface once more. As for the white South, it eagerly embraced the new situation. The Ku Klux Klan terrorized the blacks. Ultimately, the South saw to it that blacks did not vote or hold office. Blacks were relegated to a kind of peonage. They were to be rural workers on the white man's land. A tight network of law and practice was woven about rural blacks, who were desperately poor and largely illiterate. The network consisted of lien laws for landlords, vagrancy laws, enticement laws (which made it a crime to lure workers from their jobs, even by offering them better wages and conditions), laws against "emigrant agents," who were a kind of labor broker, and even laws that made it a crime to quit work "fraudulently." None of these laws specifically mentioned race; but they were practically speaking directed only against black workers. They resulted in a kind of serfdom. The black was tied to the soil, as he was under slavery, except that now he could also be fired.[51]

The caste-and-class system that replaced slavery included a system of legal and social apartheid. It developed inexorably in area

[49]See Laws Miss. 1865, ch. 4, ch. 6.

[50]Martin Abbott, *The Freedmen's Bureau in South Carolina, 1865–1872* (1967).

[51]William Cohen, "Negro Involuntary Servitude in the South, 1865–1940: A Preliminary Analysis," 42 J. Southern Hist. 31 (1976); Daniel A. Novak, *The Wheel of Servitude: Black Forced Labor after Slavery* (1978).

after area of southern life. C. Vann Woodward has described the strange career of Jim Crow.[52] Woodward argued that the end of Radical Reconstruction did not mean a complete, immediate system of segregation in the South. Many of the most blatant Jim Crow laws, on the contrary, belonged to the very end of the 19th century. Woodward did not claim that race relations were smooth before that, or that the black was ever welcomed into white society. He merely pointed out a period of trial and error, ambiguity, and complexity; the decisive instruments of segregation were nailed into law at a date rather later than some historians had assumed. But in South Carolina, according to Joel Williamson, where blacks could, by the letter of the law, use all public facilities between 1868 and 1889, there is evidence that few actually dared to do so. Probably the South was not of one mind or one practice on segregation; or perhaps segregation replaced a system, not of integration, but of outright exclusion.[53] In some parts of the South, the grip of Jim Crow tightened when blacks showed signs of protesting against their social and political position.

What is beyond dispute is the eruption of segregation laws near the end of the century. Georgia required separate railroad cars for blacks and whites in 1891; the state even separated white and black prisoners in chain gangs. The laws and ordinances came thick and fast. In Arkansas, by 1903, the statutes required separate "apartments" for whites and blacks in all jails and penitentiaries, and "separate bunks, beds, bedding, separate dining tables and all other furnishings" (sec. 5901); even voting was segregated— voting officials were to "conduct admittance to the voting place [so] as to permit persons of the white and colored races to cast their votes alternately" (sec. 2822). Law and social custom defined a place—a subordinate place—for blacks; those who violated the code were severely punished. Major infractions could mean death. Four blacks were lynched in South Carolina in 1876 for killing an old white couple. The Columbia *Daily Register* approved: "Civilization" was "in banishment...a thing apart, cowering in a corner"; there was a need for the "equity" of "Judge Lynch." Later

---

[52]C. Vann Woodward, *The Strange Career of Jim Crow* (2nd rev. ed., 1966).

[53]Joel Williamson, *After Slavery: The Negro in South Carolina during Reconstruction, 1861–1877* (1965), p. 287; John William Graves, "The Arkansas Separate Coach Law of 1891," 7 Journal of the West 531 (1968); on the exclusion thesis, see Howard N. Rabinowitz, "From Exclusion to Segregation: Southern Race Relations, 1865–1890," 63 J. Am. Hist. 325 (1976).

the bloodletting increased. Between 1888 and 1903, 241 blacks died at the hands of lynch mobs.[54]

The South proceeded, in fact, to ensure white supremacy on every front. Amendments to Southern constitutions took away, through one device or another, the black man's right to vote. The surviving black legislators, judges, members of Congress lost their offices. By 1900, not even many voters were left. The Constitution of South Carolina (1895) provided that a voter had to be able to read and understand the state constitution or have $300 in real property. Not many blacks could qualify. In Louisiana, the number of blacks registered to vote fell from 127,000 in 1896 to 3,300 in 1900, after the imposition of the "grandfather clause."[55] The North acquiesced. In the Senate, in 1900, Ben Tillman of South Carolina told the North, "You do not love them any better than we do. You used to pretend that you did, but you no longer pretend it." He defended the constitutional change: "We took the government away. We stuffed ballot boxes. We shot them.... With that system...we got tired ourselves. So we called a constitutional convention, and we eliminated...all of the colored people whom we could."[56]

Tillman was blunt, but probably accurate, in his assessment of Northern opinion. In 1860, there were only five states, all in New England, which permitted blacks to vote. Massachusetts was the only state to allow black men on juries. The post-Civil War amendments gave Northern blacks the vote, but did not change very much the climate of opinion. In such an atmosphere, one could hardly expect the federal courts to stand in the way of Jim Crow, or prevent the murder and oppression of America's untouchables. But in truth these courts never tried. Even the Supreme Court had a dismal record in its race cases. In 1878, the Court faced a Louisiana statute (1869) which forbade "discrimination on account of race or color" in common carriers. The court felt this law was an unconstitutional "burden" on interstate commerce. The case arose when the owner of a steamboat, bound for Vicksburg from New Orleans, refused plaintiff, "a person of color," a

[54]Clarence A. Bacote, "Negro Proscriptions, Protests, and Proposed Solutions in Georgia, 1880–1908," 25 J. Southern Hist. 471 (1959); on South Carolina, George B. Tindall, *South Carolina Negroes, 1877–1900* (1952), pp. 236–37.

[55]Thomas F. Gossett, *Race: The History of an Idea in America* (1963), p. 266.

[56]Quoted in Harold U. Faulkner, *Politics, Reform and Expansion, 1890–1900* (1959), pp. 7–8.

place "in the cabin specially set apart for white persons."[57] In 1883, the Court declared the Civil Rights Act of 1875—a public accommodations law—unconstitutional.[58] Hotels, inns, and other public places could—and did—discriminate; only after *Brown* v. *Board of Education*, in the 1950s, was there substantial change.

Plessy v. *Ferguson* (1896) was an especially dark decision. It put the Supreme Court's stamp of approval on apartheid.[59] This was another case from Louisiana. But the underlying facts were different; it was no longer a civil-rights statute that the Court confronted, but a law which called for "equal but separate accommodation for the white, and colored races," in railway carriages. The Court upheld the statute. The decision, which was 8 to 1, showed a studied ignorance (or disregard) of the realities of life in the South; according to the Court, if blacks thought such a law imposed "a badge of inferiority," that was "not by reason of anything found in the act, but solely because the colored race chooses to put that construction on it." In any event (said the Court), laws are "powerless to eradicate racial instincts or to abolish distinctions based upon physical differences." In reply, Justice John Marshall Harlan wrote a lonely but powerful dissent: "Our Constitution is color-blind, and neither knows nor tolerates classes among citizens." Brave words: but the living law was otherwise, especially after *Plessy* v. *Ferguson*.

The blacks were not the only race to feel the lash of white hatred. The shock-word "genocide," so loosely and so often used, comes embarrassingly close to describing the white man's treatment of native Americans. The tribes were driven from their lands; war and destruction were their fate. By 1880, they were no longer a military threat. They were herded onto reservations, usually land the white man did not want. Even so, treaties with the Indian tribes were constantly broken by the white man; ancient rights were trampled on; and the dominant culture had no respect for native religion, language, way of life.

In some ways, policy toward the native tribes was the opposite

---

[57] *Hall* v. *DeCuir*, 95 U.S. 485 (1878).

[58] *The Civil Rights Cases*, 109 U.S. 3 (1883). One exception to the otherwise bleak record of the Supreme Court was *Strauder* v. *West Virginia*, 100 U.S. 303 (1880). The state of West Virginia allowed only "white male persons who are twenty-one years of age" to serve on juries. The Supreme Court struck down this provision.

[59] 163 U.S. 537 (1896). Interestingly, Plessy argued also that he was not really "colored," since he had only "one-eighth African blood" and "the mixture of colored blood was not discernible in him." But the Supreme Court left to the states the power to define membership in the races.

of Southern policy toward the blacks: not segregation, but assimilation. The Dawes Act (24 Stat. 388, Feb. 8, 1887)[60] aimed at turning the natives into true Americans by splitting tribal lands into family farms, to be owned by individuals, not by tribes or clans. Natives who conformed to the act could detribalize and become American citizens in the fullest sense. But these statutes, too, which were supposed to protect the property rights of the natives, themselves spoke with forked tongue. The (not so hidden) agenda was destruction of native culture; and this policy was pursued on the reservations as well. The dominant culture looked on itself as superior—indeed, as the climax of human evolution. Cultural relativity was not a strong point of the 19th century.

In California (and in the West generally), there was virulent hatred of Asians, which manifested itself in countless ordinances and laws. A California statute of 1872 authorized school districts to establish separate schools for Chinese and Japanese. A San Francisco ordinance of 1880, aimed at the Chinese, made it unlawful to carry on a laundry in the city without the "consent of the board of supervisors," unless the laundry was "located in a building constructed either of brick and stone." Almost every San Francisco laundry was in fact in a wooden building. The Board turned down all applications of Chinese and granted all those of Caucasians. In the famous case of *Yick Wo* v. *Hopkins* (1886),[61] the Supreme Court struck down the discrimination; it was "illegal," and the public administration which enforced it was "a denial of the equal protection of the laws and a violation of the Fourteenth Amendment."

But such victories were rare. Fear of the competition of Chinese labor was one root cause of anti-Chinese feeling; and it ran deep. The hostility, wrote John R. Commons, "is not primarily racial in character. It is the competitive struggle for standards of living."[62] True enough, organized labor in the West was almost as anti-Chinese as Southern populists were antiblack. Labor, indeed, lent its support to federal restrictions on Chinese immigration. The "coming of Chinese laborers to this country," proclaimed a federal law of 1882, "endangers the good order of certain localities."[63] Everyone knew which localities were meant. This law suspended

[60]See Wilcomb E. Washburn, *The Assault on Indian Tribalism: The General Allotment Law (Dawes Act) of 1887* (1975).

[61]118 U.S. 356 (1886).

[62]John R. Commons, *Races and Immigrants in America* (1907), p. 115.

[63]22 Stats. 58 (act of May 6, 1882).

the immigration of Chinese laborers. It also provided that no state or federal court "shall admit Chinese to citizenship." The Scott Act of 1888 prohibited some 20,000 Chinese (who had temporarily left the country) from coming back. An act of 1892, "to prohibit the coming of Chinese persons into the United States," suspended immigration for another ten years, and provided that Chinese laborers were to be deported unless they applied for and obtained a "certificate of residence." A statute of 1902 made the ban on Chinese entry and Chinese citizenship permanent.[64]

Whatever the original causes, race did become part of the story: xenophobia, fear of the strange, and the eugenics fever of the 1890s. In the 1880s, riots in Rock Springs, Wyoming, ended with twenty-eight dead Chinese; then the whites in Tacoma, Washington, put their Chinatown to the torch. A blizzard of laws and ordinances, in California, testified to the hatred of Asians. A law of 1880 prohibited any corporation from employing "in any capacity any Chinese or Mongolian"; in 1882, segregated schools for Asians (there were already segregated schools for blacks) were authorized.[65] The racial minorities—blacks, Chinese, native Americans—voteless or powerless, were strangers at the pluralist table.

[64]Ronald Segal, *The Race War* (1966), pp. 205–207; 25 Stats. 476 (act of Sept. 13, 1888); 27 Stats. 25 (act of May 5, 1892); 32 Stats. 176 (act of April 29, 1902).

[65]Robert F. Heizer and Alan J. Almquist, *The Other Californians* (1971), ch. 7; on the treatment of Chinese-Americans in the courts, see John R. Wunder, "The Chinese and the Courts in the Pacific Northwest: Justice Denied?" 52 Pac. Hist. Rev. 191 (1983).

CHAPTER VIII

THE LAW OF CORPORATIONS

CORPORATION LAW: FREEDOMS AND RESTRAINTS

Law is often thought of as unfolding in slow patterns, at least before it "exploded" in the 20th century. Yet nothing could be more startling than the difference one century made in the law of the business corporation. In 1800, corporation law was a torpid backwater of law, mostly concerned with municipalities, charities, and churches. Only a bridge or two, a handful of manufacturing enterprises, a few banks or insurance companies, disturbed its quiet. The rise of the business corporation, in the 19th century, produced enormous controversy, and great quantities of law. By 1870 corporations had a commanding position in the economy. They never lost it. In the decade of the 1880s, pulpit and platform resounded with battle cries about trusts and antitrusts. The Sherman Antitrust Act was passed in 1890. In between, and afterwards, there was constant argument and change. Much of this, of course, revolved about particular kinds of corporations: banks, railroads, insurance companies. Some of it, however, concerned the corporation in general. Of the original law of corporations— from Blackstone's day—hardly a stone was left unturned. Even Chancellor Kent's law of corporations was basically transformed by 1900.

Private practices and legislation were the major makers of the law of corporations. The courts played a minor role. Corporate problems were too much of the marrow of public policy to be left to private litigation. No constitutional convention met, between 1860 and 1900, without considering the problem of the corporation. This was a 19th-century constant; it changed its form, its proponents, its antagonists, its format; but there was a numbing sameness of theme. Meanwhile, businessmen and lawyers built up corporate practice and malpractice on their own. Courts turned practice into law, when they confronted practice in litigation.

511

Sometimes the courts were ahead of other lawmakers, sometimes behind. The general trend in the law was clear: corporations could do as they wished, arrange their affairs as they pleased, exercise any power desired, unless some positive rule outside of "corporation law" made the action plainly illegal. In short, the trend was toward freedom of corporate management. In a kind of counterattack, statutes were passed circumscribing and regulating corporations in specific industries. These trends were nationwide, though new states and old states had somewhat different needs and desires. Western legislatures were still inviting, bribing, and cajoling railroads at a time when disenchantment had plainly set in in the East.

Perhaps the major event in corporation law, between 1850 and 1900, was the decline and fall of the special charter. This was, if nothing else, an advance in legal technology. It was cheap and easy to incorporate under general laws—a few papers filed, a few forms and signatures; the privilege of incorporation lay open to whoever wanted it; the legislature's time was conserved. For a generation or so, a number of states (New York, Illinois, Wisconsin, Maryland, and North Carolina) still maintained a dual system of incorporations. Special charters were possible, but they were not supposed to be issued unless the object of the corporation could not be attained under the general laws.[1] The dual system was not a particular success. In Wisconsin, for example, between 1848 and 1871, almost ten times as many incorporators went the special-charter route.[2] The Louisiana constitution of 1845 took the more radical step of forbidding the special charter altogether. One by one, other states adopted similar provisions. Alabama, in 1867, was a Southern convert: "Corporations may be formed under general laws, but shall not be created by special act" (art. XIII, sec. 1). And Congress in 1867 prohibited all incorporation laws in the territories except for general ones.[3]

In the same period, the states, burnt by experience, and distrustful of their own legislatures, began to forbid direct investment in enterprise. Cities, counties, and the states themselves had rashly piled up mountains of worthless bonds, discredited paper, high tax liabilities. By 1874, sixteen state constitutions provided that

[1]John W. Cadman, *The Corporation in New Jersey: Business and Politics, 1791–1875* (1949), p. 187.
[2]George J. Kuehnl, *The Wisconsin Business Corporation* (1959), p. 143.
[3]Gordon M. Bakken, *The Development of Law on the Rocky Mountain Frontier: Civil Law and Society, 1850–1912* (1983), p. 118.

the state could not own stock in private corporations. In twenty states, the state was forbidden to lend its credit to any corporation.

As public investment withdrew, corporations had to rely exclusively on private investors for money. The investment market was totally unregulated; no SEC kept it honest, and the level of promoter morality was painfully low. It was an age of vultures. In the 1860s and 1870s, men like Vanderbilt, Jay Gould, and Jim Fisk fought tawdry battles over the stock market, the economy, the corpses of railroad corporations. The investing public was unmercifully fleeced. To be sure, not all investors were the proverbial widows and orphans; many were grown men with a taste for easy money. They had as much larceny in their hearts as the Fisks and the Goulds, but their scale of operation was smaller, their cunning infinitely less.

The pillaging of the Erie Railroad by the robber barons, in the late 1860s, was a classic case of financial mismanagement and public corruption. The story was coldly recounted by Charles Francis Adams in his essay, "A Chapter of Erie." Adams was alarmed at what was happening—not to one railroad alone, or to the stock market, but to all of America. The best that could be said was that society was "passing through a period of ugly transition." Adams suspected far worse; the signs for the future were "ominous." The offices of the "great corporations," he wrote, were "secret chambers in which trustees plotted the spoliation of their wards"; the stock exchange was "a haunt of gamblers and a den of thieves." Modern society had "created a class of artificial beings who bid fair soon to be the masters of their creator"; they were "establishing despotisms which no spasmodic popular effort will be able to shake off. Everywhere ... they illustrate the truth of the old maxim of the common law, that corporations have no souls."[4]

In the face of this threat, legislatures seemed supine, powerless. The Goulds, the Fisks, and their corporate creatures, seemed able to buy and sell local lawmakers; through them, they controlled the law. "The halls of legislation were transformed into a mart in which the price of votes was niggled over, and laws, made to order, were bought and sold." The courts were corrupted, too. Justice was a whore of the rich. In New York, judges like George Barnard and Albert Cardozo did what the robber barons wished; they issued injunctions for a price, sold the public interest down the river out of ignorance or greed.

4Frederick C. Hicks, ed., *High Finance in the Sixties* (1929), pp. 114–16.

Inevitably, there were reactions. Many middle-class Americans no doubt agreed with Adams; corporations had to be brought under control, and kept there. In the 1870s, the decade of the Grangers, railroad regulation was a leading public issue; many states established agencies to control warehouses and grain elevators as well. Still later came the Sherman Act. These developments have already been discussed.

The law of corporations, as such, is less concerned with the economic power of corporations than with their everyday behavior. The two are of course connected. The developing law had one general goal: to fashion doctrine which would produce honest dealings between the corporation, its managers and promoters, on the one hand, and investors, stockholders and creditors, on the other; but to do so in a way that would not interfere with business efficiency. The corporation should have a free hand in the business world, and rugged honesty in internal affairs. As we have seen, the courts had begun to develop a tool kit of doctrines, even before the Civil War. There was great concern, for example, with watered stock. This was stock granted to insiders, in exchange for fictitious values—stock that the promoters or subscribers then threw on the market. Investors were cheated by watered stock, because they thought they were buying shares with a solid basis in assets or cash. The New York corporation law of 1848—on "corporations for manufacturing, mining, mechanical or chemical purposes"—declared: "Nothing but money shall be considered as payment of any part of the capital stock"; this was amended, however, in 1853, to allow a company to issue stock in exchange for "mines, manufactories, and other property necessary for... business."[5] Rules of the New York type were widely adopted, later on, in other states. There were also constitutional provisions. The Illinois constitution of 1870 stated that "no railroad corporation shall issue any stock or bonds, except for money, labor or property actually received and applied to the purposes for which such corporation was created." Also outlawed were "all stock dividends, and other fictitious increase of capital stocks or indebtedness" (Const. Ill. 1870, art. XII, sec. 13).

Under laws such as these, the grossest frauds, and most clearly watered stock, were obviously illegal. There remained gray areas of doubt. If a promoter exchanged his land, or a coal mine, or a building, for $100,000 in stock, how could one tell if the promoter

[5]Laws N.Y. 1848, ch. 40, sec. 14; Laws N.Y. 1853, ch. 333, sec. 2.

had transferred full value? The only *safe* rule was to require all
subscriptions in cash. Yet New York found this rule unduly restrictive. Courts tended to approve transactions of promoters so
long as they were done in "good faith." The concept of par value
of stock, once quite meaningful, lost its significance. As shares
changed hands in the open market, it meant very little that the
shares bore values of $100 or $1,000 on their face. Stock was
worth what it would fetch from a buyer. Par meant nothing at all
to a going concern. Values were fixed by the speculating and
investing public. Corporate capital, then, was not a fixed fund of
assets; and par did not represent an irreducible core of truth and
wealth, like the gold reserves of a bank.

In this period, the courts wrestled with problems of control of
corporate management, in occasional lawsuits brought by stockholders or others who felt victimized. At first, there were serious
procedural barriers. Technically, it was the corporation itself which
had the right to sue officers who cheated the corporation. But
precisely these officers controlled the corporation; the men who
were milking the company were the last to want to sue. The *stockholders' suit* was a class action, brought on behalf of a stockholder
plaintiff and all others in his position. The device was foreshadowed as early as the 1830s, but the Supreme Court gave it a further
push in *Dodge* v. *Woolsey*, decided in 1856.[6] The dereliction of duty
charged in *Dodge* was not one of the grand postwar piracies. It
was a technical error—paying a tax, which the stockholder claimed
was unconstitutional. In *Morgan* v. *Skiddy* (1875),[7] a New York case,
the defendants, directors of the "Central Mining Company of
Colorado," had dangled in front of the gullible public glittering
prospects of endless money from "the celebrated 'Bates lode.'" In
this case, a stockholder's suit was used as a weapon against plain
corporate fraud.

To what standard of conduct should officers and directors be
held? Case law looked to the concept of *fiduciary duty*. Officers
and directors were trustees for the corporation. This meant that
they could not engage in self-dealing; they could not buy from
or sell to the company; they were strictly accountable for any
profits they made in transactions with the company. The law of
fiduciary duties was an austere body of doctrine. Courts of chancery had applied it to trustees who managed funds for widows

[6] 59 U.S. 331 (1856).
[7] 62 N.Y. 319 (1875).

and orphans. Now it was applied, in essence, to promoters, officers and directors. The phrase "a sacred trust" has moral overtones; but the courts borrowed trust law less for its morality than as a ready-made set of propositions that seemed to fit the problem before them.

The metaphor had already been used before the Civil War. The "trust fund" doctrine meant that creditors had first claims on the assets of a corporate corpse, at least as opposed to stockholders.[8] The doctrine became more important after the war. One notable series of cases rose out of the wreckage of the Great Western Insurance Company of Illinois. The Chicago fire of 1871 had scorched the company into bankruptcy. In one case, decided in 1875,[9] a certain Tribilcock had subscribed for stock with a face value of $10,000. But all he paid was $2,000. The company's agent, he claimed, told him that was all he had to pay. When the company went under, its assignee, on behalf of the creditors, demanded the rest of the money. Justice Ward Hunt, speaking for the United States Supreme Court, wasted little sympathy on Tribilcock. The capital stock "is a trust fund...to be managed for the benefit of ...shareholders"; if the corporation dissolves, it enures to the benefit of creditors. "The idea that the capital of a corporation is a football to be thrown into the market for the purposes of speculation... is a modern and wicked invention." Subscribers had an obligation to pay in all of the money they owed; managers had no power to excuse them. This "fund" belonged to the company, and its disappointed creditors; no one had the right to "squander" it or give it away.

The tone of Justice Hunt's language was severely moral. In practice, however, the cases did not pose clear questions of good against evil. The doctrine, with its emphasis on par value as a measure of "capital," was already archaic. But it protected corporate creditors, in their injured innocence, against small stockholders like Tribilcock—who themselves were often gulled by promoters and salesmen. Also adverse to stockholders was the common provision that, until *all* of the capital (as measured by par value) was paid in, stockholders were doubly liable on their stock. This was a New York idea of 1848, widely copied elsewhere. Commonly, too, stockholders were liable for debts which the corporation owed to employees. These rules lasted through the end

[8]See part II, ch. III, p. 199, above.
[9]*Upton* v. *Tribilcock*, 91 U.S. 45 (1875).

of the century, in many of the states. In other states, however, legislatures loosened the law, to attract roving companies, looking for easy states in which to incorporate.

The "trust fund" doctrine, as metaphor, was logically weak. The corporate assets, as some courts and some writers acknowledged, were in no "true sense, held in trust" for the creditors.[10] It was also rather metaphorical to call officers and directors trustees. The term voiced a somewhat pious hope: that robber barons, big and small, might be brought to legal account. Charles Francis Adams, Jr., surveying the Erie scandals, expressed the idea that the corporate officer ought to be a "trustee—a guardian ... [E]very shareholder ... is his ward"; in the case of a railroad, "the community itself is his *cestui que trust*."[11] The Gilded Age was so morally corrupt, that the "wards themselves expect their guardians to throw the dice against them for their own property." But acts of corporate plunder "strike at the very foundation of existing society.... Our whole system rests upon the sanctity of the fiduciary relation."[12]

The courts, when they had the opportunity, tried to make the fiduciary obligation real. Directors and officers of the Arkansas Valley Agricultural Society, in Kansas, sold stock in the company to themselves, at par ($5 a share), though they had sold off thirty-six acres of fairgrounds near Wichita at a price that made each share worth ten times as much as its par value. The court made them disgorge their profits. Fiduciaries could not serve two masters. They could not "secure to themselves an advantage not common to all the stockholders."[13] Gross negligence, too, laid directors or officers open to liability. A Virginia case, decided in 1889, turned on the affairs of a "broken bank," the Farmers' and Mechanics' Savings Bank of Virginia. The president of the bank had pillaged it mercilessly and had foolishly lent large sums of money to the Washington & Ohio Railroad. The directors rarely met, and never audited the books. They did nothing, while notes payable to the bank were allowed to "sleep unprotested, unsecured, unrenewed, uncollected, and unsued on." For their negligence,

---

[10]William L. Clark, *Handbook of the Law of Private Corporations* (1897), p. 540.

[11]A *cestui que trust* (the *s* and *u* in *cestui* are silent) is the beneficiary of a trust.

[12]Hicks, *op. cit.*, pp. 26–27. Ironically, the word "trust" in business history came also to mean a villainous monopoly. Thus this high-minded concept of law turned into a bogey word, frightening voters and small children. See above, ch. V, pp. 463–66.

[13]*Arkansas Valley Agricultural Society* v. *Eichholtz*, 45 Kan. 164, 25 Pac. 613 (1891).

they were held liable to make up the bank's large losses personally.[14]

Out of such cases, a high-minded body of law could be distilled, displayed to the public, set out in treatises. How effective was it in practice? Did corporation law really exert control over the affairs of corporations? Victories were expensive; lawsuits cost money; many cases arose in the context of bankruptcy; and the worst thieves, like the president of the raped Virginia bank, were penniless, or had run away. Lawsuits were a cumbersome way to protect the innocent. Most of these lawsuits probably did too little and came too late; in any event they were useful only in arranging the affairs of a dead or plundered corporation.

More important, perhaps, were legal developments which let the corporation loose from chains forged in earlier periods. The business public wanted freedom to raise, and use, capital assets. More and more corporations were chartered, and the biggest ones got bigger and bigger. Originally the corporation was more or less a single venture, chartered for a single purpose. This concept slowly but surely died. In the last half of the 19th century, an important group of corporations became diversified "entities," dealing with many aspects of one business, or with many businesses. Like a natural person, these corporations could mobilize their power now for this purpose, now for that. A corporation could start as a railroad, gobble up a steamship line, buy timber lands, build houses, manufacture dolls, weave clothes. The largest corporations were like huge investment trusts—or like ancestral forms of the modern conglomerates, creatures with many heads and hundreds of legs, defying a single description.

The old restrictions on what corporations could or could not do were abolished or relaxed. Once, nothing was so central to the legal nature of corporations as the doctrine of *ultra vires*. The phrase means "beyond the powers"; it stood for the proposition that the corporation was a creature of limited authority. "All corporate acts which the legislature has not authorized remain prohibited."[15] The powers of a corporation had to be expressed in the charter; officials and courts were supposed to construe these charters with a narrow, jealous eye. As late as 1856, Jeremiah Sullivan Black, chief justice of Pennsylvania, stated that "A doubt-

---

[14]*Marshall v. Farmers' and Mechanics' Savings Bank*, 85 Va. 676, 8 S.E. 586 (1889).
[15]Victor Morawetz, *A Treatise on the Law of Private Corporations*, vol. II (2nd ed., 1886), p. 617.

ful charter does not exist; because whatever is doubtful is decisively certain against the corporation."[16] This attitude made it easy for a court to hold borderline corporate acts *ultra vires*. And *ultra vires* transactions, under the original version of the doctrine, were null and void; no one could enforce an *ultra vires* act against another party; the state could object to the act; so could any stockholder. This meant that a person entered into contracts with corporations at some risk. If the contract was *ultra vires*, one could never enforce it. In a Maryland case, in 1850, a company had been incorporated to conduct "a line of steamboats...between Baltimore and Fredericksburg, and the several parts and places on the Rappahannock." A certain Alexander Marshall pressed a claim in court against the company; his claim was based on improvements on the Rappahannock River, to open the river and make it navigable. These improvements were made on waters beyond Baltimore, hence not within the limits of the statutory route. The corporate undertaking (said the court) was therefore void; and Marshall was turned away without a dime.[17]

But the courts soon backed off from this extreme form of *ultra vires*. They began to "imply" powers much more freely. In 1896, the Supreme Court was willing to hold that a Florida railroad company had not exceeded its power when it leased and operated the San Diego hotel, in Duval County, Florida. A summer hotel at this seaside terminus might increase the railroad's business; to "maintain cheap hotels or eating houses...at the end of a railroad on a barren, unsettled beach...not for the purpose of making money out of such business, but to furnish reasonable and necessary accommodations to its passengers and employees, would not be...an act [such as]...to compel a court to sustain the defense of *ultra vires*."[18] Corporations were becoming indispensable. The corporate firm was the chosen form of American enterprise. *Ultra vires* was a nuisance, and an obstacle to corporate credit. The doctrine had to go.

In any event, it became irrelevant. Corporate charters were now framed so broadly that nothing was beyond its power or its reach. Only in this way were diversified businesses legally possible. Skillful lawyers who attended to corporate affairs had improved

[16]*Commonwealth* v. *Erie & No. East Rr. Co.*, 27 Pa. St. 339, 351 (1856).

[17]*Abbott* v. *Baltimore and Rappahannock Steam Packet Company*, 1 Md. Ch. 542, 549–50 (1850).

[18]*Jacksonville, Mayport, Pablo Railway & Navigation Co.* v. *Hooper*, 160 U.S. 514, 526 (1896).

the art of drafting corporate documents. The statement of purpose in the charter was now a mere form, covering anything and everything. The more "liberal" statutes ratified this change. Under the key New Jersey Act of 1896, a corporation could be formed for "any lawful business or purpose whatever."[19] Even in such sensitive areas as railroad consolidations, the law did not stand in the way of business practice and the growth of enterprise. A New York law, for example, in 1883 allowed the Poughkeepsie, Hartford, and Boston to consolidate with a connecting line in New England (ch. 514). Then, to save everybody time and trouble some states passed statutes giving blanket approval to railroad consolidation.[20]

The same story occurred in the development of holding companies. Originally, corporations were not supposed to own stock in other corporations. But such holdings were sometimes quite desirable, especially for banks and insurance companies. In 19th century law, where there was a corporate will, there was generally a corporate way, at least eventually. As early as the 1850s, legislatures began to grant piecemeal approval to some companies (by way of special charter), allowing them to own stock in other corporations. For example, Alabama (1851–52) gave the Wetumpka Bridge Company the right to own stock in other companies in the internal improvement business; Florida (1866) gave the Pensacola and Mobile Railroad and Manufacturing Company the right to own stock in the Perdido Junction Railroad Company. Pennsylvania, in 1861, allowed railroads chartered in the state to "purchase and hold the stocks and bonds" of other railroads chartered in Pennsylvania, or whose roads ran into the state. As the corporate desire grew stronger, so did the pressures on lawmakers; and lawmakers complied. In 1888, New Jersey issued a general *nihil obstat;* its law gave all corporations the privilege of owning stock in all other corporations.[21]

What came to be called the business-judgment rule was also significant. Essentially, this was a rule that let management run its own show. So long as a decision was made in good faith, and in the ordinary course of business, a stockholder could not complain if the decision turned out wrong. Constitutional law, too,

[19] Laws N.J. 1896, ch. 185, sec. 6, p. 279.
[20] For example, Ohio Stats. 1880, secs. 3379–92.
[21] See William R. Compton, "Early History of Stock Ownership by Corporations," 9 Geo. Wash. L. Rev. 125 (1940); Laws N.J. 1888, ch. 269.

developed in ways quite favorable to big business, even though some state constitutions seemed to *restrict* corporations. As "persons," corporations were under the protection of the 14th amendment, the same as flesh-and-blood people, if not more so. The idea that the 14th amendment sheltered corporate enterprise was an idea first hinted at in the 1880s. From 1890 on, it became an important constitutional doctrine. Laws which regulated business, then, faced the constitutional gamut. In the late 19th century, a striking series of cases turned the due-process clause into a kind of great wall against populist onslaughts. The wall had been built, or had seemed to be built, for the protection of blacks; by irony or design, it became a stronghold for business corporations. Many critical cases have been mentioned elsewhere: for example, cases on the power of states to fix utility rates. In a few important cases, statutes giving legislatures the power to fix rates met their doom in court, on the grounds that such laws offended against the due-process clause.

Some constitutional cases, on the rights of enterprise, turned on the so-called commerce clause—the power of Congress to regulate commerce "among the several states." Doctrine here was a mighty but sometime force. Under the clause, the federal government clearly had power to regulate interstate commerce. But it rarely used this power throughout most of the century. During periods of federal silence, could the states come in with their own regulation, or was the federal power "exclusive"? There was never a complete, general answer. In some areas, the states were supposed to have concurrent power over commerce; but state regulation was unlawful if it "burdened" that commerce. These general notions did not have, to say the least, any razorlike precision. This much was clear: cases which held federal power exclusive often wiped out the only regulation—state regulation—that was in vigorous effect. So, in *Western Union Telegraph Company* v. *Pendleton* (1887),[22] William Pendleton, of Shelbyville, Indiana, sued Western Union for damages, claiming the company had failed to deliver a telegram on time, which he had sent to Ottumwa, Iowa. He based his claim on an Indiana statute, which required companies to deliver telegrams promptly, if the addressee lived "within one mile of the telegraphic station or within the city or town in which such station is." But the Indiana statute, the Supreme Court

[22]122 U.S. 347 (1887).

thought, was an encroachment on the (unused) federal power; only Congress had authority to regulate "telegraphic communications between citizens of different states." The court, in short, guaranteed to business that there was and would be a giant free-trade area within this country. It made the country safe for big business. But it was of course business that pressed these cases forward—and which had the money and nerve and legal talent to fight to the bitter end.[23]

The main thread of the story of the commerce clause lies outside the substantive law of corporations; it is part of constitutional history. But the law of corporations was no longer a true measure of the rights and powers of corporations—or of the importance of corporate business. Corporations confronted the law at every point; they were the litigants in a larger and larger share of reported cases; they hired lawyers and made use of whole law firms; they bought and sold governments; other governments came to power for the sole public purpose of pulling their beards. Provisions relating to corporations were a staple of every state constitution after 1850. The rights and liabilities of corporations were, more and more, the real content of constitutional law. Even questions of individual rights emerged in cases with corporate litigants. *Plessy* v. *Ferguson*,[24] the 1896 segregation case, was a case about a common carrier. Plessy paid his fare on the East Louisiana Railroad, and insisted on sitting in the whites-only section, contrary to Louisiana law. In all the great cases on rate-making, labor relations, and social welfare, corporations were litigants, bystanders, protagonists, or devils.

Big business spilled over state lines. Naturally, then, multistate business was deeply interested in the relationship between federal and local law. These businesses resisted the idea that every state in which they operated could try its hand at regulation—particularly if no single guiding mind co-ordinated this multifarious regulation. True enough, each state created its own corporate jurisprudence. Economically, the lines between states were almost meaningless. Nothing separated one jurisdiction from another except a cornfield, a bridge, a short ride on a ferry, an invisible line. A corporation could be chartered in one state, and do business in another. This was both a danger and an opportunity for

[23]See Charles W. McCurdy, "American Law and the Marketing Structure of the Large Corporation, 1875–1890," 38 J. Econ. Hist. 631 (1978).
[24]163 U.S. 537 (1896).

the interstate corporation. The opportunity consisted of playing one state off against another; or migrating, like a divorce-hunting wife, to the laxest of states. For this reason, it made little difference to the giants that some states had strict corporation laws. In Massachusetts, for example, there were not supposed to be any "mechanical, mining and manufacturing" corporations with large capitalization; the limit was $500,000 until 1871, $1,000,000 until 1899. (In New York, too, there was a limit on capitalization: $2,000,000 until 1881, $5,000,000 until 1890.) Massachusetts law also made no provision for the issue of different classes of stock. Any change in the nature of the corporation's business had to be unanimously approved by the stockholders. Massachusetts directors had no power to increase the stock without stockholder permission; any new stock had to be offered to old stockholders, at par. These statutes "plainly envisaged" the corporation as an enterprise of limited scope, "simple in its capital structure," and incapable of "changing its general character" against the opposition of a single shareholder.[25]

For the big corporation, Massachusetts law was plainly out of step; and the same was true of the other tough states. But these laws were not effective. They were victims of the national free market in laws. Other states passed more friendly laws, to compete for corporate business. A cynic might even guess that easy states helped sustain tough states in high-minded resolve. There was a kind of moral division of labor, similar to what was happening in divorce law too. Massachusetts kept its attitude of rectitude, without *actually* interfering with interstate business. Business simply went elsewhere to be chartered. Such companies could then do business as "foreign corporations" in Massachusetts. The federal constitution protected them against the worst forms of discrimination.

The law set up few real barriers to the migration of headquarters. A few early cases held that a corporation could not be chartered in one state if it intended to do all of its business in another. But from an equally early date, precisely this was done, and successfully. Hence, the burden of strict statutes only fell on small companies that could not afford a far-off haven. Tough and easy states coexisted. Pennsylvania and Ohio were places to steer

---

[25] For this analysis of the Massachusetts statutes, see E. Merrick Dodd, "Statutory Developments in Business Corporation Law, 1886–1936," 50 Harv. L. Rev. 27, 31–33 (1936).

clear of in the 1890s. Connecticut, in 1891, "drove from her borders not only foreign enterprises but also her own industries"; the state enacted what William W. Cook called an "ill-advised" provision, requiring a majority of the board of directors of Connecticut companies to be residents of the state, and insisting that twenty percent of the capital stock be paid in cash. New Jersey, a poor but convenient neighbor of New York, became the "favorite state for incorporations." It succeeded in attracting big New York businesses by a combination of low taxes and easy laws. West Virginia, too, became a "Snug Harbor for roaming and piratical corporations," the "tramp and bubble companies of the country." The reason was simple: her laws were loose, and she was exceedingly cheap. Incorporation cost $6; the annual corporation tax was $50. These prices made West Virginia "the Mecca of irresponsible corporations."[26]

New Jersey's laws were an obvious threat to the power of the other states to control corporations, foreign or domestic. There was talk in some states of measures to retaliate against New Jersey, and reinstate, through controls over foreign-chartered companies, a strict regime of corporation law. There was talk—but no action.[27] Instead, still more states found the lure of easy money from chartering businesses irresistible. They cut their prices and vied with each other in passing liberal laws. They allowed non-resident directors; corporate meetings could be held outside their borders. After all, a state could make a profit even from *low* taxes, if the volume was great enough. In the late 19th century, then, a group of hungry states changed their laws at the drop of a dollar, and openly advertised for corporate business. Hundreds of corporations flew these flags of convenience. Fashions changed. Maine lost its popularity as a result of a dangerous court decision. New Jersey's corporation act of 1896 outbid all the others; it made New Jersey the "Mother of Trusts." In the first seven months of 1899, 1,336 corporations were "organized under the laws of New Jersey ... with an authorized capital of over two thousand million dollars." These included the "notorious Whiskey Trust"—the Distilling Company of America—and 61 out of 121 "in a list of the existing industrial corporations having stock and bonds exceeding

[26]William W. Cook, *A Treatise on Stock and Stockholders, Bonds, Mortgages, and General Corporation Law,* vol. II (3rd ed., 1894), pp. 1603–05.

[27]Charles W. McCurdy, "The *Knight* Sugar Decision of 1895 and the Modernization of American Corporation Law, 1869–1903," 53 Bus. Hist. Rev. 304, 336–340 (1979).

ten million dollars."[28] In 1899, another eager contender, the tiny, sleepy state of Delaware, passed its own act of welcome. It too was vastly successful. Corporations flocked to Delaware, and the phrase "Delaware corporation" passed into the English language.

No wonder that thoughtful observers, of gloomy disposition, saw no real chance of controlling these creatures, favored by chance, by the iron laws of trade, by the Constitution itself. Corporations were bound to swallow up more and more of the nation's economy. The fight against corporations became a dim, feeble rear-guard action, reflected in slow-dying legal restraints. Basically, however, the corporation had torn free of its past—it could be formed almost at will, could do business as it wished, could expand, contract, dissolve. Legal emphasis changed: first, to regulation, as we have seen; and, second, to countervailing power. Clearly, the big corporation was a permanent element of economic life. Perhaps this was not all to the bad. "A great consolidated corporation," said Charles Francis Adams in 1888, "can be held to a far stricter responsibility" than "numerous smaller and conflicting corporations."[29]

This was the time, however, when John D. Rockefeller's lawyers put a voting trust together to consolidate holdings in a number of oil companies. The *trust* became a household word. Trusts were the bogeymen of the late 1880s; but it was power, not form, that was at issue. Corporations carved up markets; they made treaties with each other; they formed huge and menacing agglomerations. The business frontier seemed as dead as the frontier of Western land. America was a society not of individuals, but of groups, of interrelationships, a seamless web. The remedies that came to mind were legislation and countertrusts. The time had come for reallocation. Other groups in society—farmers, workers, small business—formed their own "trusts," massed their own forces, demanding a larger or better share of the economic product, or, at the least, trying to hold on to their own. Aggregations in the business world inspired the growth of counteraggregations elsewhere.

---

[28]Edward Q. Keasbey, "New Jersey and the Great Corporations," 13 Harv. L. Rev. 198, 201 (1899); see also Melvin I. Urofsky, "Proposed Federal Incorporation in the Progressive Era," 26 Am. J. Legal Hist. 160, 163–64 (1982).

[29]Quoted in William W. Cook, *A Treatise on the Law of Corporations*, vol. III (5th ed., 1903), p. 2543.

A DISCORDANT ADDENDUM: THE
MUNICIPAL CORPORATION

Before Blackstone's day, there was a "law of corporations" which covered all chartered entities. Public and private, profit and non-profit companies—towns, churches, and businesses—all fit in one legal bag. The various branches of law split off and grew in different directions. The private corporation became, as we have seen, freer and more flexible. Towns and cities were not given this freedom. They remained closely regulated, and extensively controlled.

There were a few parallel developments. Cities, towns and villages were at first incorporated, one by one, by special charter. These charters were amended, recast, revised, and tinkered with piecemeal. City charters tended to be much alike, but rarely *exactly* the same, even in a single state. The powers and duties of one city differed in small, irritating, and confusing ways from its neighbors up the road. Also, the charter business became an appalling legislative burden. To mend the matter, legislatures passed general laws about cities, just as they passed general corporation laws. These statutes were influenced by an important English act on the subject, in 1835. Ohio, in 1852, was an early American example.[30] The Iowa Constitution (1846) barred the legislature from incorporating cities and towns through special acts. Most states had a more or less similar provision by 1900. Constitutions, late in the century, often divided municipalities into classes, depending on population size. Legislatures could pass laws that applied to an entire class, though they could not legislate for individual cities or towns. The Kentucky constitution of 1891, for example, set out six municipal categories. Cities with more than 100,000 population made up the first class; towns with less than 1,000 souls made up the sixth (Const. Ky. 1891, sec. 156). Often, the state's one big city stood all alone in its class. The set of first-class cities in Wisconsin, for example, had one member only in 1893:

[30]Laws Ohio, 1852, p. 223. John F. Dillon, *The Law of Municipal Corporations*, vol. I (2nd. ed., 1873), sec. 20, pp. 121–24. The English statute was "An act to provide for the Regulation of Municipal Corporations in England and Wales," 5 & 6 Wm. IV, ch. 76 (1835).

Milwaukee. This made it possible, as we have seen, for legislatures to pinpoint laws exclusively designed for their big or biggest city.

Early charters contained a quaint collection of municipal "powers"; early general statutes often did nothing more than copy those common clauses. Wisconsin cities, for example, were given the right to control the "assize of bread." This meant something to a 15th-century borough, but was Greek to Midwestern America. The "assize of bread" even cropped up in some charters as the "size of bread"; no one seemed to notice the mistake. Considering how towns and cities grew, municipal powers in the 1850s seem strangely inadequate. The Ohio statute (1852) gave cities power to abate nuisances; to regulate "the transportation and keeping of gunpowder or other combustibles"; to "prevent and punish fast or immoderate riding of horses, or driving or propelling of vehicles through the streets"; to establish markets; to provide for the measuring or weighing of "hay, wood, coal, or any other article for sale"; to prevent overloading of streets; to suppress riots, gambling, "houses of ill fame, billiard tables, nine or ten pin alleys or tables, and ball alleys." There were also powers to "regulate the burial of the dead," provide a water supply, restrain animals from running at large (including dogs), make and maintain streets and sewers, wharves, "landing places, and market spaces"; regulate vehicles for hire, taverns, and theatrical exhibitions; provide for "the regular building of houses," and make "regulations for the purpose of guarding against dangers by fire." This was a long and not unimportant list of powers; but it was a curious hodgepodge; obviously, too, it fell far short of a general grant of authority to govern. This was possibly yet another case where social change outstripped the capacity of government. But the obsolescence of city government was, in a deeper sense, perhaps deliberate. Capacity is infinitely plastic. No one really wanted to transplant to the prairies the tight reins of a medieval borough. No one expected much in the way of city government. It was boom-town law which was wanted. The Ohio statute of 1852 is once more instructive. Many sections of the law dealt with annexation of surrounding land. The cities of Ohio were not expected to rule their citizens with an iron hand; the state was careless in assigning "powers"; but cities and towns were expected, above all else, to grow and grow.

The development of general statutes was not just a matter of efficiency in handling legislative business. It marked the culmination of a change in the whole idea of the municipal corporation. New York and other cities and towns once had one-of-a-kind charters; and this fact had meaning. Each city was indeed a corporation, a separate entity—it functioned as a property owner, as an association, a community, more or less autonomous. The new law of municipal corporations was really not a law of "corporations" at all; but a law about cities and towns; a law about places which were, basically, merely parts of a large whole (the state), and were subject to its policy and control. This was the main theme of the emerging law of "municipal corporations."[31] The living reality of state control was another matter altogether. There is evidence that legislatures, even in the period of general laws, deferred quite regularly to what delegates from the localities wanted. For example, in 1892, Baltimore's representatives in the Maryland House of Delegates made 47 recommendations—all were accepted, 38 of them unanimously.[32]

Cities were complex organisms, and city finance generated huge amounts of living law. During the age of railroad optimism, cities indulged in an orgy of aid. They wanted the roads, they wanted land values to skyrocket, and only growth, growth, growth could do the trick. Short-run results were often disastrous. Many cities spent trough periods of the business cycle in a bankrupt condition, just like their railroads and banks. But still the debts grew; still more bond issues were floated. The indebtedness of cities with a population of 7,500 and more was $51,000,000 in 1860; the debt of all other local governments came to about $100,000,000. By 1890, local government owed $900,000,000.[33] No wonder that a reaction set in against this aspect of boom-town psychology. Restrictions on municipal debt began to appear in state constitutions. The Illinois constitution (1870), for example, did not allow any municipal corporation to become indebted "in the aggregate exceeding five per cent on the value of the taxable property therein" (Const. 1870, art. 9, sec. 12). Provisions like this were very much in the mainstream of American legal culture: first, insofar as they reacted to power, and abuse of power, by heaping on more checks and balances; second, in the characteristic cycle—incentives, fol-

---

[31] See Hendrik Hartog, *Public Property and Private Power: The Corporation of the City of New York in American Law, 1730–1870* (1983), ch. 14.

[32] Jon C. Teaford, "Special Legislation and the Cities, 1865–1900," 23 Am. J. Legal Hist. 189, 200 (1979). But *potentially*, the power to tax, control, and even destroy was lodged in the state.

[33] *Two Centuries' Growth of American Law,* p. 241.

lowed by laws punishing those who rose too eagerly to the bait.

The restrictions did not reach another problem: corruption in government. The shame of the cities was a byword by 1900. The Tweed ring in New York, in the decade after the Civil War, was only one of many notorious examples. William M. Tweed made an art of graft and corruption; he and his henchmen, it is said, stole more than $60,000,000. In his case, there was an ironic inversion of the usual state domination of city affairs; Tweed's influence reached up into Albany, into the legislature, and into the governor's office itself.[34] Tweed was overthrown; but this did not end the problems of New York. Reform movements came and went; at the end of the century Boss Richard Croker, a latter-day Tweed, ruled over a city which, since 1897, had been expanded to include Brooklyn, Queens, and the Bronx.

Along with the struggle for municipal reform went a quieter struggle for municipal self-rule. State reins now seemed *too* tight for efficiency and for local problem-solving. The major legal innovation, for the cities, in the last quarter of the century, was the concept usually called *home rule*. This appeared first in the Missouri constitution of 1875. Cities of more than 100,000 population had the right to frame their own charters, so long as these did not contravene the laws of the state. California adopted a home-rule provision in its 1879 constitution; as amended in 1890, home rule was available (if the legislature approved) to cities of more than 3,500 population.

One reason home rule became popular was similar to the reason why general laws were passed; it eased the legislature burden. The (nonhome-rule) New York statutes of 1873 show many examples of time-consuming trivia: "An act to provide for the regulation and licensing of scavengers in the City of New York," "An Act in relation to a sidewalk from the Village of Albion to Mount Albion Cemetery" and "An act to amend an act entitled 'An Act to authorize the construction of sewers in the village and town of Saratoga Springs'" (chs. 251, 667, 670). It did not make much sense for legislatures to spend their energy on this kind of law. Nevertheless, legislatures proved surprisingly jealous of their power. They nowhere abdicated final authority to decide what cities could and could not do. Even today, home rule is more an ideal than a working reality.

Courts, too, played something of a role in running the cities.

[34]See, in general, Alexander B. Callow, Jr., *The Tweed Ring* (1966).

Then, as now, courts were the last resort of interests and power groups politically frustrated in local affairs. In the last half of the century, cities grew enormously. So, too, did their demands on the time and attention of higher courts; as did the demands of villages, counties, and towns. John F. Dillon, in 1872, wrote the first treatise on local government law, *The Law of Municipal Corporations*. Dillon had served on the supreme court of Iowa, and had seen that "questions relating to the powers, duties and liabilities of municipalities were presented at almost every term." By 1890, a fourth edition, in two bulky volumes, appeared, reflecting, in its hundreds of pages, the vast expanse of decided cases. The expansion of judicial review had affected the law of municipal government, too. Many of the cases in Dillon were cases in which citizens or businesses attacked some action of local government— as unconstitutional or as beyond the powers of the municipal corporation.

The results of the cases, mirroring the statutes of their states, were discordantly different from the results in cases about business corporations. *Ultra vires* never died for municipalities. Charles Beach, in his treatise on public corporations, published in 1893, flatly declared that "Acts of municipal corporations which are done without power expressly granted, or fairly to be implied from the powers granted or incident to the purposes of their creation, are *ultra vires*." So too were acts of city officials which fell outside the precise literal limits of their authority.[35] Cities and villages had those powers, and those only, which were given them from above. In literally scores of cases, this authority was closely tested in court, by taxpayers and others. It was commonplace to try to reverse acts of cities or towns that had some adverse impact on a person or group. Appellate courts decided dozens of issues like that of "the validity of a sewer assessment under the sixty-fourth section of the charter of the city of Bayonne [New Jersey]."[36] The end of the period (1870–1900) was not known for the bashfulness of courts. Municipalities probably won most of the cases, especially in the lower courts; but they faced the delays of trial; and the danger of losing hung over their acts like a black cloud. Judicial review was a strong, sometimes harsh, reality. Often, it had a healthy impact. It may have forced some honesty and

[35]Charles F. Beach, *Commentaries on the Law of Public Corporations,* vol. I (1893), pp. 607–08.
[36]*Central N.J. Land Co.* v. *Mayor of Bayonne,* 56 N.J.L. 297, 28 Atl. 713 (1894).

efficiency on local government. It may have made some officials toe the line. But the costs were also high. Most litigants were only interested in themselves, their taxes, their use of land. Lawsuits were couched, of course, in general terms. One disgruntled landowner who attacked a sewer assessment might, if he won, shatter a whole scheme of urban sanitation.

CHAPTER IX

COMMERCE, LABOR, AND TAXATION

CONTRACT

The law of contract occupies a special place in American law in the 19th century. On the one hand, in theory, the century was the century of contract. The regime of contract was the hallmark of modern law. Progressive societies, wrote Sir Henry Maine in his pathbreaking book, *Ancient Law* (1861), had evolved from status to contract. These societies organized social relations through free voluntary agreement; individuals, pursuing their own ends, made their own "law," perfected their own arrangements. The dominance of contract was one of the sovereign notions of the 19th century. The Constitution itself guaranteed that the states would not "impair" the obligation of contracts. Many of the crucial constitutional cases, before the Civil War, pivoted on this clause. In the late 19th century, liberty of contract became another constitutional battle cry. The 14th amendment, as the Supreme Court and some state courts read it, protected the right to enter freely into contracts. The boundaries of this right, to be sure, were vague. But the principle—that contract deserved this kind of enshrinement—was significant nonetheless.

It was not only writers on constitutional and political theory who considered the idea of contract fundamental. Contract law was one of the basic building blocks of legal study. (It is to this day.) C. C. Langdell's first casebook (1871), a milestone in the history of legal education, was a casebook on contracts. To constitutional theorists, free contract was a pillar holding up the palace of ordered liberty; to students and teachers of law, it was the great gate to entry in the palace.

The *idea* of contract, and the *fact* of contract, may well have been as fundamental as everybody said it was. The concrete body of law *called* contract was another matter. In a way, it hardly seemed worthy of the fuss. The law of contract was essentially negative.

Its doctrines gave more or less free play to individual choice. What people voluntarily agreed on, courts would enforce. Beyond this simple principle, there were certain rules of thumb: on the formation of contracts, on the interpretation of contracts, on remedies for breach of contract. Not much of this body of law changed fundamentally between 1850 and 1900—nothing compared to the transformation of tort law, or the law of corporations. Old technicalities were dismantled long before 1850. What remained was more or less to tidy up the house of doctrine, and to express its principles as general rules.

If one looks, not to treatises, but to the actual business of the courts, it could be argued that the law of contract, after 1850, was beginning a long slide into triviality. Courts were not equipped to handle business disputes as rapidly and efficiently as a brawling capitalist economy demanded. The doctrines were attractive and necessary; the rules were flexible enough; but judges were judges, not mediators. They named winners and losers. Where parties stood in continuing business relations with each other, they preferred not to litigate at all. They worked their problems out by themselves, or went to arbitration. Moreover, judges simply lacked the right degree of business sense. They were trained in law, not in business; certainly not in the details and jargon of a thousand fields and trades. This lack was not immediately apparent. Of 206 contract cases decided by the Wisconsin supreme court, roughly in the decade before 1861, fifty-four dealt with land. Thirty-one were cases of sale; most of these concerned horses, sheep, oxen, and the cash crop, wheat, rather than manufactured goods. The thirty labor cases also arose out of simple situations. There were thirty-one cases on credit and finance, mostly about the ubiquitous bills and notes, and the sureties who signed them.[1]

So far, an intelligent judge could manage very well. He was a landowner or dealer in land himself, no doubt, and what came before him was part of his common experience. As the country industrialized, this was less and less the case. By 1905, the contract docket of the Wisconsin supreme court was very different. A few kinds of transaction were overrepresented—real-estate brokers suing for their commissions, for example. Manufacturers and major merchants had virtually disappeared from the docket, and

---

[1] This discussion is based on Lawrence M. Friedman, *Contract Law in America* (1965). Wisconsin was an agricultural state, first settled in the 1830s. Some of the trends discussed no doubt appeared earlier in New England, later in the prairie states, and in the West.

indeed, they had never been there in any quantity. It is risky to infer the business of lower courts from upper courts; but big companies were surely more likely to appeal in a commercial case than small businesses or individuals. It seems reasonable to guess that major business did not litigate contract issues in any regular way.

Between 1750 and 1850, the domain of contract law had expanded to include most of the universe of economic transactions. Even leases and deeds were treated, basically, as contracts, or as contractual in nature. Business associations became voluntary compacts, not holders of little monopolies—grants from the state. The whole of the law seemed to take on a contractual flavor. Yet, like the golden age of tort law, the golden age of contract was marvelously brief. The most familiar rules—on damages, offer and acceptance, parol evidence, interpretation of contracts—frayed noticeably between 1850 and 1900. Since business stayed out of court, what came into court tended to be marginal: special situations, unusual cases. These tempted the judge to do justice in the particular case, for the unique facts before him. Contract *law*—that is, the doctrines applied by appeal courts in actual cases, rather than the basic *regime* of contracts—was not a vital prop of the economy. The cases were one-of-a-kind. Why not warp the rules to do the right thing for *this* litigant? Most appealed cases, in any event, turned only on their facts or on questions of interpretation. Each stood on its own two feet. Moreover, statutory incursions, after 1850, significantly shrank the kingdom of contract. Every new law on the statute books, if it dealt with the economy at all, was a cup of water withdrawn from the pool or puddle of contract.

A few new doctrines were invented after 1850 which, on the surface, helped fill in gaps in classical, free-market contract law. *Lawrence* v. *Fox* (New York, 1859)[2] began the career of the so-called third-party beneficiary contract. Under the doctrine of this case, a person not actually a party to some contract could enforce it nonetheless, provided the contract was intended to benefit him. So, if A sold a horse to B, and told B, "Pay the money to my creditor, C," creditor C could sue B for the money if B refused or neglected to pay. What had stood in the way was the common law reluctance to allow the transfer of abstract rights to another

[2] 20 N.Y. 268 (1859).

(including rights to collect and to sue); the common law did not allow transferees to bring suit on the original claim or right. This was of course inconsistent with the world view of 19th-century contract. Contract had faith in the market; now almost any interests and values could be effectively transferred and sold.[3]

The law of damages for breach of contract also developed during this period, almost from nothing. It was surprisingly late that courts developed systematic rules for calculating damages, rather than throwing the whole matter to a jury. One of the leading cases was English: *Hadley* v. *Baxendale* (1854).[4] A mill had stopped its operations because of a broken crankshaft. The millowner sent for a new shaft. The shaft was delivered by "well-known carriers trading under the name of Pickford & Co." These well-known carriers, however, delivered the crankshaft late. The mill was shut down for a longer time than expected, and the plaintiffs, the millowners, lost some of their profits. The court refused to let them recover for these lost opportunities. There was no question that the carriers had breached their contract to deliver on time. But the plaintiff could only recover for the "natural consequences" of this breach; and the lost profits, said the court, did not fit in this box. The rule suited the market bias of the law of contracts: no special, personal factors should influence the rational calculus of damages. Damages had to be objective. Some mills—perhaps the more prudent ones—might have had a spare shaft.[5] Then, too, the rule of the case limited the risks carriers had to run. They were liable only for "natural" consequences—damage they could foresee and take account of. The rule was therefore a way to standardize costs and rationalize enterprise. In this regard, it can

[3]The old rule was, moreover, a rule of procedure. It seemed particularly out of date in the period of the Field Code, which allowed lawsuits to be freely brought by those who had a real interest in the outcome.

[4]9 Ex. 341 (1854). For the background and meaning of the case, see Richard Danzig, "Hadley v. Baxendale: A Study in the Industrialization of the Law," 4 J. Legal Studies 249 (1975).

[5]Another rule of damages required a person on the short end of breach of contract to show the market price before damages could be recovered; what could be collected was only the difference between contract and market. "It follows from this rule, that, if, at the time fixed for the delivery, the article has not risen in value, the vendee having lost nothing can recover nothing." Theodore Sedgwick, *A Treatise on the Measure of Damages* (2nd ed., 1852), p. 260. Only economic damages—never punitive damages—were recoverable. Breach of contract was not a wrong, not a tort.

be compared with many of the new-minted tort rules. Despite their differences, tort law and contract law were both tuned in to economic issues, as judges saw them.

The rule of *Hadley* v. *Baxendale* was eagerly adopted in the States. Indeed, it was anticipated there; in *Brayton* v. *Chase*,[6] for example, decided in Wisconsin in the same year (1854), a farmer ordered a "New York reaper," to be delivered before the first of July. The reaper came late. Brayton, the farmer, claimed he lost thereby his "large crops of winter and spring grain." But he collected no damages. Crop losses, said the court, were "too remote" a consequence of Chase's delay. They resulted "rather from the particular situation of the plaintiff than from the breach of the contract."

These doctrines were not abandoned, even as the legal climate changed. The way they were phrased made them tents rather than cages. Application was all. *Hadley* v. *Baxendale*, for example, spoke of "natural consequences." It was for the court to say what was natural and what was not. By 1900, the actual results of cases were shifting subtly away from the hard line of the 1850s. The ideal remained: rational, calculable damages, limited to the natural, foreseeable results of a breach. In general, the market measured loss. But the logic of doctrine was seriously warped in actual decisions, for reasons already mentioned. The temple of doctrine stood firm: its architects still worked on details of decoration, while the termites worked busily underneath.

NEGOTIABLE INSTRUMENTS

The law of bills, notes, checks, and certificates of deposit came from the law merchant by way of England, was modified in America, and was stabilized and somewhat Anglified by decisions and scholarly writings before 1850. This branch of law was of tremendous importance in the 19th century. Before 1864, bank notes were the chief circulating currency. Both before and after the 1860s, personal promissory notes were the chief American instrument of debt and credit. Because of its key position, the note generated endless possibilities for lawsuits and disputes. As we have seen, lawyers, particularly in the West, spent much of their time collecting debts in the form of personal paper. The law of

[6] 3 Wis. 456 (1854).

bills and notes was oil without which the machinery of business could not run. Courts after the war decided enormous numbers of cases on transfer, validity, and incidents of bills, notes and checks. This was indeed living law. The *Century Edition of the American Digest,* covering reported cases up to 1896, gave almost an entire volume over to "Bills and Notes"—about 2,700 pages, a tremendous bulk few other topics could match.

It was living law, moreover, with an ideology of change. Law was supposed to follow the custom of the business public. And in truth, the law was often supple and inventive. The bill of lading became a railroad document, shedding its saltwater past, as cases in the 1850s already attested. The certified check, a weak infant in the 1840s, barely mentioned in treatises in the 1860s, had become a lusty addition to the corpus of negotiable instruments by 1870. Business invented it, without let or hindrance from the courts. Justice Swayne, in a Supreme Court case in 1871, expressed this philosophy: "By the law merchant of this country the certificate of the bank that a check is good is equivalent to acceptance.... The practice of certifying checks has grown out of the business needs of the country.... [T]he average daily amount of such checks in use in the city of New York, throughout the year, is not less than one-hundred millions of dollars. We could hardly inflict a severer blow upon the commerce and business of the country than by throwing a doubt on their validity."[7]

Courts had more trouble with municipal and corporate bonds. Should these be treated as negotiable, the same as ordinary bills and notes? And how strictly should courts look them over before deciding whether they were valid? These were important policy questions. If negotiable, a bond once transferred cut off any defects in the original transaction. There were conflicts of interest, between the issuer, the original investors, and later ones who came to hold the bonds. These later investors were, quite often, banks and financial interests, perhaps those who invested through the Eastern money market. The original holders were, sometimes, farmer-speculators, townspeople, small-scale gullibles. In some states, statutes settled the issue in favor of negotiability. In general, the courts, too, with some vacillation, gave these bonds the magic password of negotiability. In so doing, they disregarded—in the words of Justice Robert C. Grier—the "epidemic insanity of the

[7]*Merchants' National Bank of Boston* v. *State National Bank of Boston,* 77 U.S. 604, 647–48 (1871).

people, the folly of county officers, the knavery of railroad 'speculators.'" They favored, rather, the "malleability" of the bonds, to "suit the necessities and usages of the mercantile and commercial world." The need for a free, open capital market, with no second thoughts about bond issues, was paramount. "Mere technical dogma...cannot prohibit the commercial world from inventing or using any species of security not known in the last century."[8]

The issue in the case which evoked Grier's eloquence turned on the status of bonds of Mercer County, Pennsylvania. The county issued the bonds, in order to subscribe for stock in a thievish railroad, the Pittsburgh and Erie. Some of the bonds came into the hands of a certain Hacket, "a citizen of New Hampshire," and a purchaser (in law at least) in good faith. The county wanted to renege, claiming irregularities in the issue. The Supreme Court refused. As the case indicates, courts tried to favor the good-faith purchaser for value, as much as possible, ignoring minor blemishes in the bonds themselves.

Occasionally, the swindle or scandal was so great that the legislature took a stand on bonds or notes. The farm-mortgage crisis of Wisconsin, which we have mentioned, was one of these occasions in the 1850s and 1860s. Farmers had given notes in exchange for railroad stock, secured by mortgages on their farms. The stock became worthless after the crash of 1857. Meanwhile, notes and mortgages had been sold in the Eastern money market. To save the farms from foreclosure (and prevent a voters' revolt), the Wisconsin legislature boldly attacked the negotiability of the notes. If the notes were not negotiable, despite appearances, then the farmer's "equities" survived; and the farmers could defend themselves against foreclosures by claiming fraud or mistake. An act of 1858 prohibited the holder of the note from alleging that he was a (legally) innocent purchaser. The point was obvious. The issue would go to a friendly Wisconsin jury; the farmer would win; the transaction would fail, and Wisconsin's farms would be saved. The Wisconsin supreme court, however, defied popular pressure, struck down the statute, and treated later attempts by the legislature with equal disdain.[9]

---

[8]Grier, J., in *Mercer County* v. *Hacket,* 68 U.S. 83, 95–96 (1864).

[9]See Robert S. Hunt, *Law and Locomotives; the Impact of the Railroad on Wisconsin Law in the Nineteenth Century* (1958), pp. 48–50.

In almost all states, crisis or no, statutes aided, hindered, or muddled commercial law, by tinkering with some of the rules of commercial paper.[10] The statutes ranged from a few trifling, standard provisions—postponing the maturity date of an instrument to Monday if it fell due on Sunday, for example—to sizable codes. California, for example, adopted a whole code on negotiable instruments in 1872. It consisted of 117 sections, and was copied from a code which David Dudley Field had proposed for New York. Six Western states later followed California's example. Almost every state abolished the antiquated custom of days of grace. Of the harvest of laws, some were for the specific benefit of the commercial community; others were passed for even narrower groups. Some states made usurious notes totally void, and did the same to notes given for gambling debts. This meant that no one, not even a good-faith holder, could collect on a note that suffered from these original sins. Other states protected the good-faith purchaser despite such a taint.[11] In a few states, for example Ohio, a note given for "the right to make, use, or vend a patent invention" had to bear on its face the words "given for a patent right"; and any holder of the note was "subject to the same defenses as ...the original owner"[12]—all this to help stamp out a common rural swindle.[13]

Commercial law was a field for which businessmen saw the value of uniform rules. This attitude, happily, meshed with the professional jurists' passion to "reform" law, in the direction of innocuous consistency. Business practice had helped weld (and keep) together the law of commercial paper, and the law of commerce by sea. This law carried over into the inland empire, where it worked almost equally well. But the states were free to develop variations, and they did. A report of the American Bar Association, in 1891, complained that there were "fifty different languages" of law. The businessman had a right to ask why "the meaning and effect of a promissory note" should not be "as certain

[10]See, in general, Frederick Beutel, "The Development of State Statutes on Negotiable Paper Prior to the Negotiable Instruments Law," 40 Columbia L. Rev. 836 (1940).

[11]John Daniel, *A Treatise on the Law of Negotiable Instruments*, vol. I (5th ed., 1903), pp. 223–25, sec. 197.

[12]Rev. Stats. Ohio 1880, sec. 3178.

[13]See "State Interference with Patent Rights," 16 Albany L.J. 360 (1877). These statutes were passed in the 1870s, for example, Laws N.Y. 1877, ch. 65.

and definite" in all states "as the meaning of words in an American dictionary." "Variance, dissonance, contradiction" caused "perplexity, uncertainty and damage."[14] No wonder, then, that one of the first fruits of the movement for uniformity was a commercial statute. John J. Crawford drafted a Negotiable Instruments Law, on instructions from the Conference of Commissioners on Uniformity of Laws, which met in Detroit in 1895.[15] Crawford relied heavily on the British Bills of Exchange Act (1882) and, as Professor Beutel has shown, on the California Code of 1872.[16] The NIL was the first of the "uniform laws." It was one of the most successful. The act, in general, did not pretend to bring about any changes in the general patterns of law. It was a restatement, made up of short, clean, polished sections. Most of its rules were already accepted, either as businessmen's norms or as established courtroom doctrine. It cleaned the facade of the law of commercial paper, without much more. Still, no one had asked for anything else.

THE LAW OF SALES

In general, commercial law showed a nice regard for business needs. Courts were willing to meet and accept evolution in business practice—so long as no oversensitive nerve, of politics or legal tradition, was touched. By the end of the century, however, a certain kind of argument, oriented toward consumer interests, was heard more often in court decisions. Considerations of this type, of course, interfered with the classic purity of the law. A case in point was the law of sales. It was well formulated by midcentury. It had the dignity of a separate "field" of law, thanks in part to a series of classic English cases. One key concept was "title"; title determined who bore the risk of loss. But subtle nuances of doctrine allowed sellers to keep their security interest in goods, even when the risk (and the "title") had shifted.

Overall, the case law showed some bias in favor of the seller— manufacturer or merchant. The maxim *caveat emptor* flattered the manhood and pride of the judges. In California, in 1850, as we saw, the maxim was considered one of the glories of the common

[14]"Report of the Committee on Uniform State Laws," *Report, 14th Ann. Meeting ABA* (1891), pp. 365, 371.

[15]John J. Crawford, *Negotiable Instruments Law* (1897), pref.

[16]Beutel, *op. cit.*, p. 851.

law, in contrast to the flabby solicitude of civil law. But by 1888, Edmund Bennett, in his treatise on sales, was saying the rule had "many limitations." These were cast in the form of "exceptions," but really amounted to "independent rules and principles."[17] Courts had the inveterate habit of deciding individual cases individually. The rule of *caveat emptor* was clean, abstract, general, but harsh. Also, in a mass-production market, there were limits to what a buyer could really beware of. It was one thing to examine a horse in advance of buying it, quite another to assess goods made and packaged by machines.

The concept of *implied warranty* was one of the means of sapping the vitality of *caveat emptor*. Sales by sample "implied" a warranty that the bulk would conform to the sample. When goods were sold "by description," without inspection, courts implied a warranty of "merchantability." The goods were not to be "so inferior as to be unsalable among merchants" who dealt in the article. Also, if a buyer bought for a "particular use made known to the seller," and relied on the seller's judgment to select the goods, there was an implied warranty that the goods were "reasonably fit and suitable for that purpose." When a seller, for example, sold "Wilcox's Superphosphate," a fertilizer or guano, to a farmer, the guano had to be "merchantable"; and it had to fertilize at least reasonably well. If this was not the case, the buyer had a cause of action, for breach of implied warranty.[18]

These implied warranties were especially suited to manufactured goods. Indeed, courts developed the implied warranties furthest for manufacturers; frequently, it was held that these rules did not extend to dealers. So, for example, an Illinois case of 1877, for breach of warranty on the sale of "200 barrels of mess pork," distinguished between a manufacturer and "a mere dealer in produce," who "professed to be selling for other parties."[19] For manufacturers, at least, these implied warranties almost nullified the rule of *caveat emptor*. By 1900, the *results* of the cases (if not the way their doctrines were phrased) were probably about the same as those produced by the bleeding hearts of civil law. Law had come, more and more, to favor the consumer interest. But "the consumer" was not the ordinary citizen, the people whom

[17]Edmund H. Bennett, American edition of Judah P. Benjamin's *A Treatise on the Law of Sale of Personal Property* (1888), p. 623.

[18]See *Gammell* v. *Gunby & Co.*, 52 Ga. 504 (1874).

[19]*Chicago Packing & Provision Co.* v. *Tilton*, 87 Ill. 547 (1877).

Ralph Nader champions. The consumer of 1890 or 1900 was the small merchant or farmer, who took on manufacturers in court. Courts were avidly middle class in their outlook. Their shift in emphasis meant less catering to big business, more attention to small.[20]

In the factory years, after the Civil War, goods were more and more produced in mass. Some of these goods were as small and mundane as the nails Adam Smith used as examples; others were expensive hard goods. Unless he sold for cash, the seller wanted some kind of security. He needed devices that would do for reapers, pianos, and sewing machines what the mortgage did for land. The conditional sale was one such device. Under a conditional-sale contract, title to the goods did not pass to the buyer until he paid in full. Many early contracts of this sort, judging by the facts in the cases, were "inartistically drawn." In a New Jersey case, Gustave Wetzel bought (in 1876) "one Domestic sewing machine," for $55. He paid $15 down, and gave a note "payable in installments of five dollars a month." The machine was to remain the "property" of the seller until "actually paid for in cash."[21] In some states, local decisions were unfriendly to the use of conditional-sale contracts. In these states, sellers used chattel mortgages— mortgages specially adapted for sales of personal property. In Pennsylvania, where conditional sales were void, still another device was used—the bailment lease.[22] Goods were "leased" to the buyer, who agreed to pay on installments; after he paid "rent"

---

[20]The actual history, of course, was quite complex. For example, breach of warranty, whether express or implied, is a kind of absolute liability. Fault or negligence has nothing to do with the matter. But one line of cases—*Hoe* v. *Sanborn*, 21 N.Y. 552 (1860)—seemed to veer off in another direction. The goods in that case were circular saws; the "alleged defect" was due in part to the fact that the saws were made out of unsuitable material. The judge, Samuel L. Selden, in the course of a thoughtful opinion, seemed to make the manufacturer's *negligence* an issue. Some cases followed this hint. This might have been a logical way out for those who thought that *caveat emptor* was too harsh, and *caveat venditor* unwise. Tort and warranty law might have merged. But the courts were torn between conflicting ideologies and interests, in their minds and in the outside world. The result was the kind of uncertainty in doctrine, and the kind of disparities between doctrine and result, which were mentioned in the text.

[21]*Cole* v. *Berry*, 42 N.J. L. 308 (1880).

[22]See "Bailments and Conditional Sales," 44 Am. Law Reg. 335, 336 (1896); *Goss Printing Press Co.* v. *Jordan*, 171 Pa. St. 474, 32 Atl. 1031 (1895).

for so many months, full ownership of the goods would pass to him.

Gradually these devices became standardized, routine. They cropped up as form contracts, in cases on the marketing of soda fountains, pianos, and reapers, foreshadowing the sale "on time" of automobiles, television sets, and golf clubs in the 20th century. After a while, the three security devices became almost indistinguishable. It was another example of the principle that nothing— neither small specks of technicality nor large stains of legal logic and jargon—was allowed to interfere in the 19th century with what judges or the dominant public saw as the highroad to progress and wealth. Court decisions did not create economic conditions, trends, and business practices: rather, these molded decisions and laws. There *were* differences in statutes and doctrines; consequently, security devices had different names, different blanks for buyers to fill out, different dotted lines to sign. But basically the devices all came out the same in the end. The pressures to buy and sell on credit were strong; the resistance of lawmakers was absent or transient or weak.

THE USURY LAWS

Installment sales were a triumph of marketing over small qualms and slight technicalities. The usury laws responded differently to pressure. They were an almost uncanny barometer of shifts in the political and economic demand for money.

Usury laws were part of the legal inheritance; they were of medieval origin, and fraught with moral and religious overtones. Almost every state had some kind of law placing a ceiling on interest rates. In the late 18th and early 19th century, almost for the first time, some thinkers began to question the premises on which these laws were based. Jeremy Bentham attacked them as economically unwise, and as an interference with liberty. "No man of ripe years and of sound mind, acting freely, and with his eyes open, ought to be hindered ... from making such bargain, in the way of obtaining money, as he thinks fit."[23] There were, he thought, no good reasons why government should fix the price of money, any more than it should fix the price of bread. On both sides of

[23]Jeremy Bentham, *Defence of Usury* (3rd ed., 1816), p. 2.

the Atlantic, this argument for free trade in money was heard; and it seemed to be fairly persuasive. A number of states—first Alabama, then Indiana, then Wisconsin and California—repealed their usury laws before 1860, and experimented with interest rates fixed solely by the market. There was vigorous debate about the usury laws. Much of it, in the legislature halls, rode on a high plane of rhetoric and policy. Typically, a chorus of frogs on one side quoted Jeremy Bentham and invoked the slogans of free trade; the chorus on the other side used the Bible (condemning usury) as its basic handbook.

When one peels away the layers of rhetoric, a number of striking facts emerge. By and large it was economic interest, not ideology, that called the tune. First, statutory interest rates varied tremendously from state to state. In the West, where hard money was scarce, statutes allowed far higher rates than in the East; penalties for usury tended to be softer. This suggests that states raised their rates to a point where they would not interfere *too* much with the flow of credit to farmers and dealers in land. States that abolished usury laws generally did so at the end of their territorial period, or at the very beginning of statehood. At this point in a state's career, the government dumped public lands on the market, at a relatively favorable price. Squatters and speculators needed money for cash down-payments. The land was a bargain; the money was not. It was vital to relax interest rates, and attract money from the East, even at high rates, to cash in on the bargain price of land. Some usury laws were repealed precisely in response to this kind of settler pressure. In 1849, for example, there were, in Wisconsin, a great number of squatters on government land. They needed cash desperately, to buy the land as it came on the market. The state, not surprisingly, repealed its usury laws. The following year, California, another new state, did the same. Typically, too, the free-trade period was short. At the next downswing of the business cycle (when land values fell, debts became burdensome, and foreclosures threatened), the same people who had begged for money at any price denounced as evil usurers those who had come in with satchels of money; and the legislatures thundered forth new, stringent usury laws.[24] The usury laws, in short, were as volatile as prices and credit; the high-

[24]See, in general, Lawrence M. Friedman, "The Usury Laws of Wisconsin: A Study in Legal and Social History," 1963 Wis. L. Rev. 515.

minded Benthamite debate was largely, though not wholly, a facade. In 1851, when the great need for money was over, Wisconsin repealed its repeal. And depressions, in general, caused states to toughen their usury laws, because of the clamor of debtors.

In the 1870s, a movement to repeal the usury laws appeared in the industrial East. The movement made some inroads. On the whole, though, usury was the farmer's problem for most of the century. He needed mortgage money. Later, the urban wage earner, borrowing small amounts for consumption or purchase, moved to the center of the stage. The battle cries of the Granger movement about high interest rates—and the demands for stringent laws, low rates, and government regulation of "loan sharks"—were taken over by the labor unions. But little change took place in the law before 1900. The free-trade argument against usury was dead; and the new war against city loan sharks had not reached a sharp enough focus to breed much fresh legislation.

INSURANCE

As we have seen, no business was subject to so much legal regulation as insurance. The courts took second place to the legislature here. Even litigation about claims was not very frequent, it seems, until late in the century. There were perhaps as few as one hundred reported cases on life insurance down to 1870.[25] These were of course all appellate cases, but they suggest that trial litigation was also less dense than in the next generation. Fire and marine insurance were the main subjects of these early cases. By the 1890s, appellate decisions on insurance law had mushroomed. In the *Century Digest* (1896), there were 2,808 pages densely packed with brief summaries of insurance cases. The middle class was buying more insurance, including life and accident insurance; and the great bulk of decisional material suggests an absolute increase in lawsuits on all levels. It also suggests that the companies, engaged in aggressive marketing, were inclined to contest at least some of the claims made against them.

Insurance litigation developed along interesting lines. Lawyers for the companies drafted stiff clauses to protect company inter-

[25]Morton Keller, *The Life Insurance Enterprise, 1885–1910* (1963), pp. 187ff., is the source of this statement and much of the following paragraph.

ests; yet courts and juries often found ways to stretch the language of insurance policies to allow a widow to collect life insurance, or to help a man whose house or store burned down, despite some flaw or doubt. It has been suggested that company lawyers performed an "overservice" for their clients. Their clauses, strict beyond the general norms of fairness, "exaggerating warranties to the point where they were almost one hundred percent protection against claims," were partially responsible for a "public atmosphere" against the companies; and for decisions and laws that disfavored enterprise, putting them in a position "worse...than ...any other contracting party."[26]

In claims cases, courts faced concrete human situations, and sometimes their sympathies showed. In many trials, the legal issue turned on whether what the insured stated in his application, or his policy, constituted a "warranty" or not. If the statements were "warranties," and were wrong—lies or mistakes—the policy was a mere scrap of paper. But suppose the insured had been a trifle larcenous or foolish. The loss really fell after all on his grieving family; and an uninsured business or home, burnt to the ground, seemed a high price to pay for a little bit of exaggeration or concealment. Chief Justice Ryan of Wisconsin spoke of the "crafty conditions with which fire insurance companies fence in the rights of the assured, and the subtle arguments which their counsel found upon them." The companies, he felt, acted almost as if their "single function" was to collect premiums, and not to pay claims at all.[27] Hence the concept of warranty was never allowed to dominate the issue. Courts went to great lengths to hold that misstatements were only "representations," even when the policy said in plain English that all statements were "warranties." A typical case was *Rogers* v. *Phoenix Ins. Co.* (1890),[28] where a "one-story, shingle-roof, frame building," owned by Edward and Mary Rogers, burnt down. When they applied for insurance, they said the house was fifteen years old. The policy stated that "every statement...is a warranty...and if any false statements are made, this policy shall be void." The company argued (among other things) that the house was twenty years old. The policy was therefore void. The court disagreed; the statement was a mere "represen-

---

[26]Thomas I. Parkinson, law professor and insurance executive, quoted in Keller, *op. cit.*, p. 190.
[27]Quoted in Spencer Kimball, *Insurance and Public Policy* (1960), p. 211.
[28]121 Ind. 570, 23 N.E. 498 (1890).

tation," and, since it did not "render the risk more hazardous," the policy was good, and the company should pay.[29]

Not that the companies always lost. Some of their customers *did* lie, some *did* conceal facts that increased the risk. Other litigants were blocked by language so clear that it passed the limits of interpretation; judges were willing to twist the sense of English words, but only up to a point. Case law became chaotic and complex. No one could predict how a hard-fought lawsuit would actually come out. Uncertainty invited more lawsuits. The insurance contract, especially insurance on lives, is not an enduring pact between people in continuing, multiple relations. It is drawn up for a single violent end. No one claim is worth the company's while to pay. Nor will a widow ever give up her claim on her husband's policy, if the company reneges, merely to please the company, or keep its good will. The companies usually settled or paid; but they also sometimes fought; and so, too, did survivors and insured people.

Meanwhile, states passed a torrent of statutes. Every aspect of the business was touched on by law. Some statutes plainly tried to benefit the companies, some the policyholders; some compromised the interests of the two. On balance, however, regulation was unfriendly to the companies. Wisconsin, for example, passed a law in 1870 requiring fire and marine insurance companies to keep strong reserves. The companies could not distribute profits until they had set aside "a sum equal to 100 percent of the premiums on unexpired policies."[30] A Nebraska law (1889) required companies to pay off fire, tornado, and lightning insurance, at the value asserted by the policy, which was to be "taken conclusively to be the true value," when the property was "wholly destroyed." Brokers and agents had to be licensed in Nebraska. Pages of closely knit prose in the statute books, before 1900, described the duties and obligations of insurance companies. Insurance companies were identified with two major devils: aggregated capital and foreign (that is, out-of-state) corporations (which most of them were, in any given state). This made the

---

[29]Similar results were reached by statute, for example, in Missouri: "No misrepresentation made in [a life-insurance policy]...shall be deemed material, or render the policy void, unless the matter misrepresented...actually contributed to the contingency or event on which the policy is to become due and payable, and whether it so contributed in any case, shall be a question for the jury." Rev. Stats. Mo. 1879, sec. 5976.

[30]Kimball, *op. cit.*, p. 150.

companies all the more vulnerable, and contributed to the dense texture of regulation.

The companies contested some of these laws in court. They did not often win. One estimate is that the courts, between 1890 and 1908, found only one percent of 2,000 statutes unconstitutional. *Paul* v. *Virginia* (1869)[31] was a famous earlier defeat. A Virginia law (of 1866) licensed "foreign" insurance companies. To get a license, the company had to deposit bonds with the treasurer of Virginia. Paul was agent for various New York companies (New York was "foreign" from the Virginia standpoint). The Supreme Court held that insurance was not "commerce"; thus, the federal government did not have exclusive jurisdiction. The federal government had never shown any inclination to regulate insurance. Hence the decision threw the companies back to the howling wolves in the states.

These wolves, to be sure, could often be tamed by judicious lobbying. But insurance companies were, like railroads, unusually subject to hostile, local legislation. Sometimes it took the form of laws favoring mutuals and fraternals over stock companies. The out-of-state companies had a particular cross to bear. State laws discriminated against them, taxed them more heavily than locals, sometimes tried to drive them out altogether. There was some merit to the argument that out-of-state companies were irresponsible, hard to police. But the zeal of in-state companies, eager to get rid of competition, was the real force, no doubt, behind many such laws.

The Standard Fire Insurance Policy of Wisconsin, enacted in 1895, can be taken as a symbol of how far the state was willing to go to regulate insurance. Here was a whole policy, cast in the form of a law, down to very small details—no more than 25 pounds of gunpowder could be kept on premises insured against fire; and "benzine, benzole, dynamite, ether, fireworks, gasoline, greekfire ... naptha, nitro-glycerine" were prohibited.[32] One insurance man saw in this standard policy the dragon of "socialism," which had "upreared its head" in the quiet precincts of Madison, Wisconsin. But if so, it was a strange sort of socialism. Before the policy was enacted, the insurance commissioner had talked the matter over with merchants; he had looked at and made use of a form current among companies in New York. The standard policy was a com-

[31]75 U.S. 168 (1869).
[32]Laws Wis. 1895, ch. 387.

promise. In many regards, it was quite strict with buyers of insurance. The company had the right to cancel, with five days' notice; the insured had to file burdensome proofs of loss within sixty days of his fire. The freedom of the companies was narrowed, to be sure; but regulation was balanced by standardization (business liked that); and the companies had a voice in the regulatory process. The law, then, was no total victory or defeat for either side, but a typical product of American law, splitting a subject somewhere in between, as determined by the strength or weakness of contending interests.[33]

BANKRUPTCY

The last half of the 19th century brought an old dream to reality: a national bankruptcy act. Between 1841 and 1867, there was no federal law at all. The old bankruptcy law had been repealed. The states filled in with insolvency laws, stay laws, exemption laws. In 1867, Congress passed a bankruptcy act, though by the merest hair, and over bitter opposition. The law proposed to allow both voluntary and involuntary bankruptcy. Controversially, anyone (not merely a "trader") could be forced into bankruptcy. This meant, according to the opposition, that the "free and easy but honest and true men of the West," the "farmers and merchants," could be "squeezed" into a "straitjacket" more "befitting the madmen of Wall Street." On the other hand, it could be argued that precisely the small debtor would benefit from this part of the act. Apparently, some Northern creditors hoped to use the bankruptcy law to reclaim at least a pittance from ruined debtors in the South. Only a federal law, they felt, federally administered, would stave off state laws granting stays and exemptions, and keep the prejudices of Southern juries at bay.[34]

Whatever its proponents hoped, the act was a failure in operation. It was cumbersome, badly administered, corruptly applied. The costs of proceedings consumed immense amounts of money; after lawyers and administrators took their toll, creditors were left with the crumbs. It was, of course, an age of shaky credit. The act hung like a sword of Damocles over the heads of merchants. Many were afraid some coldhearted creditor would push

[33]On the history of the standard policy, see Kimball, *op cit.*, pp. 230–32.
[34]See Charles Warren, *Bankruptcy in United States History* (1935), pp. 104ff.

them into bankruptcy. The fear was not irrational, particularly since the Supreme Court (1871) construed "insolvency" to mean not only lack of assets to pay debts, but also inability to pay debts as they came due in the ordinary course of business.[35] The panic of 1873 did not convince a doubtful Congress that the act was needed. Quite to the contrary, hard times brought a mad urge to repeal. The House killed the act in a frantic hurry (1874). The Senate, however, gave the law a reprieve. They added, too, a provision for "composition." Debtors might propose a plan for gradually settling their debts over a period of years. If a "majority in number and three-fourths in value" of the creditors accepted the plan, at a composition meeting, the plan would go into effect and be enforceable at law.[36] Other provisions, too, were designed to ease some of the problems of debtors that had arisen under the bankruptcy law. The 1874 amendments did not end criticism, however. Some of the amendments turned out maladroit, if not downright vicious. The law lasted four more years; in 1878, it was finally repealed. Once more there was no national bankruptcy act.

But the federal law was scarcely cold in its grave when a movement began to revive it. This time, revival was helped along by those segments of business and legal opinion which favored uniform, national laws of commerce and trade. Politically, farmers' influence waned; and commercial influence grew. Samuel Wagner, in a report (1881) to the American Bar Association, called for a "National Bankrupt Law." The worst fault of the prior laws had been their impermanence, he thought. The laws had been "like so many sponges"; they "wiped off a vast amount of hopeless debts," and gave everybody "a clean slate with which to start afresh"; they were temporary "physic," administered in one large dose, "brief and spasmodic efforts," quickly repealed. What was needed was a permanent, national law, "in the nature of a regimen of diet and exercise." Partly "restrictive and partly remedial," such a law might "tend to prevent rather than to cure disease," through its "even and continuous operation."[37] A young St. Louis lawyer, Jay L. Torrey, drafted a bankruptcy bill in 1890, under the stimulus of conventions of national commercial organizations, held in St. Louis and Minneapolis in 1889.[38] The Torrey bill met bitter

[35] Warren, *op. cit.*, pp. 113–14.
[36] 18 Stats., Part III, 178, 182 (act of June 22, 1874, sec. 17).
[37] Samuel Wagner, "The Advantages of a National Bankrupt Law," *Report, 4th Ann. Meeting ABA* (1881), pp. 223, 227–28.
[38] Warren, *op. cit.*, p. 134.

opposition—by Southern and Western debtors, for example. These interests preferred to trust their own legislatures, which might enact sweeping delay or debt cancellation laws. One Southern orator called the proposed law a "crushing and damnable instrumentality," an "infernal engine of ruin," the "last screw in the coffin of liberty," a plot to deliver "farmers, laborers, debtors, or small dealers" into the "soulless cupidity of a Shylock."[39] But even the South was generally in favor of *voluntary* bankruptcy.

The panic of 1893 lent arguments to both sides. Debate in Congress was sharp and prolonged. Finally, in 1898, the law was passed: "to establish a uniform system of bankruptcy throughout the United States."[40] This act was long, detailed, carefully drawn. Under the law (sec. 4a), "any person who owes debts, except a corporation," was "entitled to the benefits of this Act as a voluntary bankrupt." Involuntary bankruptcy could not be forced upon "a wage-earner or a person engaged chiefly in farming or the tillage of the soil" (sec. 4b). The act did not disturb state exemptions, "in force at the time of the filing of the petition," in the state of the bankrupt's domicile (sec. 6). The law granted special priority, over other debts, to "wages due to workmen, clerks, or servants," if "earned within three months before the date of the commencement of proceedings, not to exceed three hundred dollars to each claimant"; the law also recognized priorities granted under state law, though they ranked lower than federal priorities (sec. 64). Though no one could know it at the time, this bankruptcy act was not to suffer the fate of its predecessors. It survived the passage of time. It is still in force (with changes), and repeal is by now inconceivable. The era of "temporary physic" ended in 1898.

ADMIRALTY

Admiralty was a fairly pure body of merchant's law. The Constitution gave admiralty to the federal courts. After the *Genessee Chief* (1851),[41] federal admiralty law, as we have seen, sailed proudly on the Great Lakes as well as on coastal waters. For rules on navigation and maritime collisions, Congress still looked overseas. In 1864, Congress adopted, practically verbatim, the English code

[39]Quoted in Warren, p. 136.
[40]30 Stats. 544 (act of July 1, 1898).
[41]53 U.S. (12 How.) 443 (1851).

(1863) of navigation rules.[42] In 1890, Congress enacted the International Rules, "Regulations for preventing collisions at sea," for "all public and private vessels ... upon the high seas and in all waters connected therewith, navigable by seagoing vessels." These were rules about lights, sound signals for fog, steering and sailing rules, and distress signals. The Inland Rules (1897), which also dealt with lights, signals, steering, and sailing, applied to "harbors, rivers, and inland waters of the United States."[43]

Rules of admiralty law, in general, seemed to reflect merchants' ideas about splitting and compromising loss. In case of accident, where both sides, or neither side, was at fault, both were to share in the loss. If, for example, a ship and its cargo stood "in a common imminent peril," and the captain had to sacrifice some cargo to save the ship and the rest of the cargo, the owner of the lost goods had the right to make ship and cargo share in his loss; this ancient principle was called *general average*. The classic case was jettison—throwing cargo overboard to lighten the load. But general average was widely applied in the 19th century. In one case, fire broke out in the hold, and the crew doused and damaged part of the cargo with water. General average applied.[44] The rules of general average thus seemed, on the surface, quite different from rules of tort law, which tilted heavily toward one side of the scale.

Admiralty law was also framed in terms that looked kinder to the sailor than tort law looked to the miner, brakeman, and machinist. A sailor was entitled to "maintenance" and "cure"; that is, if he fell sick or was injured in service, he had a right to medical care, living expenses and wages, at least to the end of the voyage. Was he entitled to more—to damages for negligence? The chief cook on a steamship, sailing to Vera Cruz from New York, by way of Havana, in 1879, was ordered to fetch some ice from the ice closets, to pack the corpse of a person who died on board. On his way, in the night, he fell "through the hatch into the hold below, and received considerable personal injury." He was "cared for at the expense of the ship," and got his full wages. But he also claimed "additional compensation"—$10,000—"for his permanent injuries and consequential damages, on the ground of the negligence of the officers in leaving the hatch open through which he fell." The federal court denied this claim. They found no

[42]See Robert M. Hughes, *Handbook of Admiralty Law* (1901), p. 212.
[43]26 Stats. 320 (act of Aug. 19, 1890); 30 Stats. 96 (act of June 7, 1897).
[44]*The Roanoke*, 59 Fed. 161 (7th Cir., 1893).

warrant for the damage in the "sea laws" and in "recognized authorities on maritime law." The ship's liability was absolute, but it was also limited; negligence and contributory negligence both made no difference, either in inflating or deflating the rights of an injured sailor.[45] This was a kind of compromise strikingly like the one that factory workers ultimately settled for, some thirty years later, in the form of workmen's compensation.

Meanwhile, the Harter Act, passed by Congress in 1893, excused the "owner of any vessel transporting merchandise or property" from "damage or loss resulting from faults or errors in navigation, or in the management" of the ship, or for "losses arising from dangers of the sea ... acts of God, or public enemies," so long as the owner had exercised "due diligence" in making his ship "in all respects seaworthy and properly manned, equipped, and supplied."[46] The concept of "seaworthiness" was to prove as plastic as that of "negligence." But this long voyage lay ahead. There were strong parallels between admiralty and tort law, despite their traditional differences. Even the loss-splitting concept, so foreign to the common law, was perhaps more a difference in style than in substance. Admiralty, after all, had no jury. What the jury did secretly, in the holds and fastnesses of its chamber, admiralty judges had to do aboveboard, on open deck.

LABOR AND LAW

The labor problem—the problem of industrial relations—was practically speaking of major legal importance only after the Civil War. The basic ingredients were the factory system and the landless, class-conscious urban worker. Unrest began much earlier in Europe and went far deeper. In 1848, Europe was in upheaval; the antirent agitations of New York were feeble parodies of European revolution, and involved farmers at that. Communism, the specter that haunted Europe, did not trouble much American sleep. America had to wait some while for *its* version of class struggle. After 1860, the rich got richer and expanded their factories, mines and banks. The poor had children; and in addition, their relatives came over from the old country. The new industrial

---

[45]*The City of Alexandria,* 17 Fed. 390 (D.C.S.D. N.Y., 1883).
[46]27 Stats. 445 (act of Feb. 13, 1893, sec. 3).

system created or exploited a huge pool of workers. Many were immigrants. About half a million entered the country in 1880 alone. Most late 19th-century immigrants were peasants from southeastern Europe. They "provided an apparently inexhaustible reserve of cheap labor for mines, mills and factories."[47]

These workers in industry were poor; work and life were hard. In 1840 the average workday was 11.4 hours; in 1890 it had fallen to ten hours, but in some industries—paper manufacturing, for example—the average workday was still twelve hours.[48] Conditions in many factories and mines were appalling. Employers hired and fired at will; there was little or no job security, and the worker was trapped in a web of company rules.[49] The business cycle added special miseries. Social services were weak; sickness, broken bones, or a downturn in business added new threats to the worker's security. Many employers were callous in fact; others adopted the detached, studied callousness of social Darwinism. That the workers should remain unorganized, that business should be free from control, that the health of enterprise was the way, the truth, the consummate social good: this was the faith of the dominant class. There were also intellectuals and leaders of another stamp—men who got drunk on European radical thought or concocted a native version.

"Closed resources and freedom with insecurity," said John R. Commons, "produce in time a permanent class of wage earners."[50] He might have added: they produce disaffection. Labor problems multiplied because economic interests conflicted in a game of life that both sides were convinced was zero-sum. The era of inexhaustible growth was over; this was a world of finite possibilities. Each group had to scramble for its share; what accrued to one was subtracted from another. This attitude, we have seen, profoundly affected every aspect of the living legal system. It also rubbed social relations raw. The rich resisted socialism (everything from nationalized steel mills to unemployment compensation); the poor made war on the rich. In the postwar years, a trade-union movement grew rapidly—as rapidly perhaps as industrial combination. By the 1870s, mass labor confronted big business.

[47] Foster R. Dulles, *Labor in America* (2nd rev. ed., 1960), p. 98.
[48] W.S. Woytinsky *et al., Employment and Wages in the United States* (1953), p. 47.
[49] See Walter Licht, *Working for the Railroad* (1983), ch. 3.
[50] John R. Commons and John B. Andrews, *Principles of Labor Legislation* (rev. ed., 1927), p. 4.

In some ways, the labor history of the United States was as bloody and violent as in any industrial nation, even though there was no revolution. In 1877, strikes and riots "swept across the United States... with almost cyclonic force."[51] The major rail centers, from Baltimore west, were struck. Nineteen died, and one hundred were wounded, in a skirmish on July 26, in Chicago, between police, National Guardsmen, and a mob. At the Carnegie Steel plant in Homestead, Pennsylvania, in the early 1890s, strikers fought against Pinkerton guards. In Coeur D'Alene, Idaho, in 1892, metal miners attacked the barracks where strikebreakers lived. In the disorders that followed, five miners died, and troops were called out. Most of the violence was unplanned; it simply erupted. It was not part of union policy. Sometimes violence achieved results; sometimes—perhaps more often—it stiffened the backs of employers, and frightened the neutral middle class.

Forced to choose sides, legal institutions necessarily reflected the wants of their basic constituencies. This meant that legislatures swung back and forth, depending on the strength of interests, blocs, parties and lobbies, or compromised. The courts were more independent of short-run swings of opinion. Partly for this reason, courts could afford to indulge in principles and ideologies. These were usually on the conservative side, because the judges were solid, independent men of middle class. They were terrified of class struggle, mob rule, the anarchists and their bombs, railroad strikers, and the collapse of the social system as they knew it. When the left raged against decisions that seemed antilabor, the judges took refuge in the temple of the federal Constitution, in its regional chapels, the state constitutions, and in the half-ruined forums of the common law. These were sanctuaries where the mob (they felt) dared not enter. Theirs were not personal decisions, they insisted, but decisions under law—impersonal, classless, neutral.

The battle for labor reform was fought, first in the streets, then in the legislative halls, and then, less successfully but inevitably, in the courts. In each arena, the rhetoric was different, but the stakes were about the same. The early cases on strikes, picketing, and boycotts have evoked a good deal of historical interest. The

[51]Philip Taft and Philip Ross, "American Labor Violence: Its Causes, Character, and Outcome," in Hugh D. Graham and Ted R. Gurr, eds., *Violence in America: Historical and Comparative Perspectives*, vol. I (1969), pp. 226–28, 230–32.

cases are few, the literature fairly large. Were union activity and strikes illegal, on the grounds that they amounted to a criminal conspiracy? This point was at issue in the trial of the Philadelphia cordwainers, in 1806. This, and some later cases, did hold that striking workers could be charged with conspiracy. But in *Commonwealth* v. *Hunt* (1842), Lemuel Shaw, chief justice of Massachusetts, held to the contrary.[52] Prosecutions for conspiracy slowed down to a walk in the 1850s and 1860s. Conspiracy trials were major criminal prosecutions; they were inevitably slow and tortuous. They were embarrassed by a multitude of defendants, and subject to all the safeguards thrown up around trial by jury. Strikes were, in the abstract, perfectly legal. It was hard to prove that an illegal conspiracy had taken place, and each case stood on its own private facts. For these reasons, the doctrine of conspiracy was a poor sort of strikebreaker, and it tended to fall out of use.

More sinister and effective weapons took its place. A judge with a will could find a way. Many railroads in the 1870s, and later, were in receivership; technically, they were wards of the federal courts. This gave judges an opportunity to intervene in railway labor disputes. They did so, with a strong and mighty arm. Thomas S. Drummond, judge of the seventh circuit, made virtuoso use of contempt power to combat the strikes of 1877, against railroads that happened to be in receivership.[53] Later the judges invented, or discovered, the labor injunction, a stronger and more general piece of artillery. The injunction was an ancient, powerful, and honorable tool of courts of chancery. It had infinite possibilities and uses. Its suppleness and strength made it a deadly threat to labor. During a strike, a company might ask for a restraining order (a temporary injunction). Courts of chancery had the power to grant these orders quickly, without notice or hearing, if the court was persuaded that delay might irreparably injure the company. There was no need for trial by jury. If a union defied the order, or the injunction itself, it stood in contempt of court. Hence, officers and members could be summarily punished, even thrown into jail.

It is not clear where the labor injunction was first used. The Johnston Harvester Company asked a New York court to issue one in 1880; the defendants, claimed the company, had "com-

[52]*Commonwealth* v. *Hunt*, 4 Metc. (45 Mass.) 111 (1842); see Leonard W. Levy, *The Law of the Commonwealth and Chief Justice Shaw* (1957), pp. 183–206.
[53]See, in general, Gerald G. Eggert, *Railroad Labor Disputes: The Beginnings of Federal Strike Policy* (1967).

bined" and "enticed" workers from the factory "by means of arguments, persuasion and personal appeals." The judge saw fit to
deny this request; but injunctions were apparently issued in Baltimore and at Kent, Ohio, in 1883, in Iowa in 1884, and during
the railroad strikes of 1886. Between then and 1900, the cases
"grew in volume like a rolling snowball."[54] In 1895, the labor
injunction was sanctified by unanimous decision of the United
States Supreme Court. This was the famous case of *In re Debs*.[55]
Prosecution of Eugene V. Debs grew out of the Pullman strike of
1894. This major strike paralyzed the country's railroad lines; and
President Cleveland, in alarm, called out the troops. The attorney
general also asked for an injunction against Debs, the union leader,
calling on him to "desist...from...interfering with...the business of...the...railroads." Debs did not desist; he was then charged
with contempt, convicted, and sentenced to six months in jail. The
Supreme Court affirmed the conviction. From then on, the injunction, in the hands of a strong-minded judge, was a mighty
adversary that organized labor had to reckon with. The injunction
was swift, and it could be murderously inclusive—broad enough
in its contours to cover a total situation, outlawing every aspect
of a strike and effectively crushing it. Few courts opposed the use
of injunctions in industrial cases; but labor and its allies were
outraged. The Democratic platform of 1896 denounced "government by injunction" as a new and dangerous kind of "oppression";
the federal judges were acting as "legislators, judges and executioners," at one and the same time. Labor made an attempt to
persuade legislatures to do away with the labor injunction. But
the injunction had strong friends, too; and the attempt came to
nothing, at this time.

An injunction did not issue as a matter of course. There had
to be a threat of irreparable harm. Courts accepted the proposition that a strike was not illegal *per se*. To warrant injunction,
the strike had to fall on the illegal side of this line. Even before
the Civil War, some scattered, rather inconclusive cases, had considered what made a strike legal or illegal, and on the legal status
of other kinds of aggressive union tactics. Between 1870 and 1900,
there were many more decisions. Some tactics were clearly proscribed—the boycott, for example. "It is difficult," said Frederic
J. Stimson, writing in 1896, "to conceive of a boycott conducted

[54]Felix Frankfurter and Nathan Greene, *The Labor Injunction* (1930), p. 21.
[55]158 U.S. 564 (1895).

solely by lawful acts."[56] Picketing too had a rocky course. A few judges thought it was always illegal: "There is and can be no such thing as peaceful picketing, any more than there can be chaste vulgarity, or peaceful robbing, or lawful lynching."[57] Most courts disagreed; they saw a clear distinction between peaceful picketing and intimidation. But it was hard to know where the boundaries were; thus a union that threw up a picket line always ran a certain risk of illegality. On the other side, management tactics rarely ran afoul of the law. Companies fired workers who were active in unions; they blacklisted union leaders. Few cases challenged the blacklist; and courts failed to find any trace of conspiracy or illegality in this behavior.

Still, the labor movement made great headway in the last decades of the century. Its power was greatest in the industrial states, and its grievances were most clearly formulated there. Not all their victories were won by sheer muscle. Labor showed strength in the legislatures, too. States enacted an increasing volume of protective laws. Some states forbade the blacklist. Some outlawed the "yellow dog" contract, which forced employees to promise not to join a union.[58] Other statutes made companies pay workers in cash (as a weapon against the company store); and to pay employees weekly or fortnightly. Still others punished infringement of the union label. These protective statutes, taken together, must have had some effect on labor relations. But they were often poorly drafted, poorly administered, poorly enforced. Most grievous of all, a certain number had to run the terrible gauntlet of constitutionality. It was a test some failed to pass. The results of these cases varied from state to state. The more spectacular (and reactionary) cases have been most apt to catch the historian's eye. On the whole, labor laws were upheld; most were never even questioned. Maine, for example, passed a law in 1887, of a common type, requiring employers to "pay fortnightly each and every employee ... the wages earned by such employee to within eight days of the date of such payment." The Maine act, perhaps be-

[56]Frederic J. Stimson, *Handbook to the Labor Law of the United States* (1896), p. 223.

[57]McPherson, J., in *Atcheson, Topeka and Santa Fe Rr. Co.* v. *Gee,* 139 Fed. 582, 584 (C.C.S.D. Iowa, 1905).

[58]For example, Laws Minn. 1895, ch. 174. The Utah constitution of 1895 outlawed the blacklist; art. 12, sec. 19.

cause of a favorable Massachusetts case, was never challenged in court before 1900.[59]

But the Illinois supreme court, for one, was politically conservative, judicially activist, and intoxicated with constitutionality; in one period, labor laws fell like tenpins. In 1886, a coal-weighing act—the weight of the coal fixed the wages of the miners—was held unconstitutional; in March 1892, the court struck down a law forbidding mineowners and manufacturers from running company stores; in the same year, a new coal-weighing law failed to pass muster; in 1893, a law requiring weekly wages for workers was voided; in 1895, the court voided a law restricting the hours worked by "females" in "any factory or workshop."[60] The grounds of these decisions in Illinois and like-minded states were various. Statutes were sometimes said to be bad because they were "class legislation." Sometimes they were bad because they were infringements on a strange, cloudy concept of liberty embedded in the due-process clause. The concept included, it seemed, a rigid doctrine of liberty of contract. In some extreme cases, statutes were overthrown for no more precise reason than that they offended the spirit of the constitution. We have already cited one horrible example: *Godcharles & Co.* v. *Wigeman* (1886),[61] a Pennsylvania case. Here the court threw out a statute requiring laborers to be paid at regular intervals, and in cash, as "utterly unconstitutional and void," an "insulting attempt to put the laborer under a legislature tutelage," "degrading to his manhood," and "subversive of his rights." No clause of any constitution was cited.

There were other examples of the war of some judges on labor legislation. In 1884, New York, ostensibly "to improve the public health," prohibited the "manufacture of cigars and preparation of tobacco in any form in tenement-houses." The *Jacobs* case, a year later, held the statute void.[62] The law, said the court, was an infringement of the right to earn one's livelihood "in any lawful calling." Government interference in the economy, if not justified by the police power, could do great harm: it could "disturb the

---

[59]See E.S. Whitin, *Factory Legislation in Maine* (1908), pp. 60–61.

[60]The cases are respectively *Millett* v. *People*, 117 Ill. 294, 7 N.E. 631 (1886); *Frorer* v. *People*, 141 Ill. 171, 31 N.E. 395 (1892); *Ramsey* v. *People*, 142 Ill. 380, 32 N.E. 364 (1892); *Braceville Coal* v. *People*, 147 Ill. 66, 35 N.E. 62 (1893); *Ritchie* v. *People*, 155 Ill. 98, 40 N.E. 454 (1895).

[61]113 Pa. St. 431, 6 Atl. 354 (1886); see above, Part III, ch. I. pp. 359–60.

[62]*In re Jacobs*, 98 N.Y. 98 (1885).

normal adjustments of the social fabric...derange the delicate and complicated machinery of industry and cause a score of ills while attempting the removal of one." A California law, fairly typical, required corporations to pay workmen their wages at frequent intervals and in cash. A quartz mine, brought to task for violation, defended itself on constitutional grounds. The California court (1899) declared the statute an abomination: "the working man of intelligence is treated as an imbecile....[h]e is deprived of the right to make a contract as to the time when his wages will come due." He is not allowed to "make an agreement with the corporation that he will work 60 days" and take a "horse in payment" instead of cash. The laborer might be "interested in the corporation, or for some reason willing to wait until the corporation could pay him." The "infirmities" of the statute, which unreasonably forbade such reasonable arrangements, were "sufficient to destroy it."[63] So saying, the court swept the law off the books.

These opinions rang false even in their day. Their description of relations between workers and owners had an air of complete unreality. The extreme line they took did not prevail. For one thing, quite a few cases went the other way. And the strength of political movements was greater than the will of a few judges who stood at the fringes of respectable opinion. The judges could only call a short truce, could only hope to hold problems at bay until the country came to its senses. This never happened. The madness got worse; history—that is, the ultimate lines of force—was on the side of the judges and legislatures who took a more moderate view. There was more litigation, and more "liberal" laws. Unions, their allies, and legislatures refused to take no for an answer. Social legislation had too many branches and heads to be killed; when one law was chopped off, ten more seemed to grow in its place.

Labor law advanced along the lines where employer defenses, and conservative opinion, were at their weakest. Child labor was a case in point. It was, in fact, a terrible abuse that small children worked their lives out in factories and mines; the "bitter cry of the children" touched even hearts of stone. But the movement to abolish child labor was more than a movement to save suffering children. Organized labor was convinced that child workers depressed wage rates, that they disastrously inflated the supply of

[63]*Johnson* v. *Goodyear Mining Co.*, 127 Cal. 4, 11–12, 59 Pac. 304 (1899).

cheap labor. Adult male workers felt the same way about women in the factories. Unions strongly supported laws on the wages and hours of women, and, just as strongly, supported laws against Asians on the West Coast. The agitation in the 1870s in California against Chinese labor, the "yellow peril," was led by such radical groups as the Workingmen's party. No one was as strident for restrictions on immigration of Asians as the workmen's champions in the labor movement.

Social-welfare programs were successful, in the main, where conscience and passion could join hands with strong self-interest. Other things, too, were necessary: an efficient civil service, well-drafted statutes, and money to carry out the programs. Protective labor legislation—on child labor, women workers, factory safety, and the hours of work—grew from very little before the Civil War to an impressive web of legislation in 1900. But the trend proceeded very unevenly. The rich, highly unionized, and heavily industrialized states led the way. The South lagged badly behind. Connecticut had a primitive wage-and-hour law for children in 1842. Vermont was the last New England state to adopt some sort of child-labor law; that was in 1867.[64] Yet in 1896, Mississippi, Kentucky, Arkansas, and North Carolina, among others, still did not have any law that even purported to outlaw child labor.[65]

Child-labor laws on the books were not the same as child-labor laws enforced. New Jersey's law of 1851 outlawed factory work for children under ten; older children could work no more than ten hours a day, sixty a week.[66] Punishment for violation was a fine of $50, to be sued for "in an action of debt, in the name of the overseer of the poor." Such a law was no doubt a pious nullity. It expressed official policy; but that was all. Compulsory-education laws put life into laws against child labor. An act of 1883 raised the minimum working age to twelve for New Jersey boys, fourteen for girls; employers of young people needed a certificate, showing the minor's age, the name of his parents, and a statement, signed by the teacher, that the child had attended school. This law, too, was weak; but it at least empowered the governor to appoint an "inspector," who, at the modest salary of $1,200 a year,

[64]Lorenzo D'Agostino, *History of Public Welfare in Vermont* (1948), p. 181.

[65]Frederic J. Stimson, *Handbook to the Labor Law of the United States* (1896), pp. 74–75.

[66]This discussion of New Jersey is taken from Arthur S. Field, *The Child Labor Policy of New Jersey* (1910).

was to inspect factories (there were more than 7,000 in New Jersey) as best he could, and enforce the law.[67] In 1884, the inspector got two assistants; by 1889, he had six. In 1892, the act was amended to include provisions about women workers; the work week was set at fifty-five hours for women and persons under eighteen; fruit-canning plants and glass factories were exempted.[68] At the end of the century, children still slaved in New Jersey factories; but not so many, and not so young. A similar story could be told for other Northern states.

Constitutionally, child-labor laws had less to fear than other welfare laws. It was difficult to stretch freedom of contract, the new-minted sacred cow of the Constitution, to cover minors, who had no power to make contracts, even at common law. Married women, too, had once had contractual disabilities. This fact gave some color to arguments that the law might control the conditions under which women worked. More persuasive were reminders of the woman's role within the family, her elementary biological differences from men, coupled with Victorian sentimentality about mothers, sisters, wives. *Muller* v. *Oregon* (1908)—a Supreme Court case—decisively settled the point. A state could set valid limits on the hours that women might work.[69] "The future well-being of the race" required as much: women had to be protected "from the greed as well as the passion of man." The decision, in the eyes of the 1980s, has a patronizing, sexist ring. But in its day it was hailed by social activists, women as well as men. Before *Muller* v. *Oregon,* state cases had been of various minds on this question of women and labor. The case of Mary Maguire (1881),[70] turned on an ordinance of San Francisco under which it was a misdemeanor to hire any "female" to work, "wait" or "in any manner attend on any person" in any "dance-cellar, bar-room, or in any place where malt, vinous, or spirituous liquors are used or sold." The Supreme Court of California struck the ordinance down. A Massachusetts case (1876) upheld a law of 1874 that put a ten-hour limit on the working day of women, and a sixty-hour limit on their work week, in "any manufacturing establishment."[71] The well-known Illinois

[67]Laws N.J. 1883, ch. 57.
[68]Laws N.J. 1892, ch. 92.
[69]208 U.S. 412 (1908). See Nancy S. Erickson, "Historical Background of 'Protective' Labor Legislation: *Muller* v. *Oregon,*" in D. Kelly Weisberg, ed., *Women and the Law,* Vol. II (1982), p. 155.
[70]*In the Matter of Mary Maguire,* 57 Cal. 604 (1881).
[71]*Commonwealth* v. *Hamilton Mfg. Co.,* 120 Mass. 383 (1876).

case, *Ritchie* v. *People,* decided in 1895, reached a conclusion dia-
metrically opposed.[72]

On questions of maximum hours, labor legislation stayed
close to the shores of constitutional power. A mandatory ten- (or
eight-) hour day for all workers was believed to be beyond the
legal pale, even had it been politically feasible. The state could
regulate the labor contract only within the vague boundaries of
the police power, or if the law could be tied to some doctrine or
concept of undoubted validity. The state, as an employer, could
itself make any contract it wished with its workers, and adopt any
rule about these contracts. So New York, in 1870, restricted the
hours of its own employees. Federal eight-hour laws were passed
in 1868, in 1888 (for employees of the Public Printer and the Post
Office), and in 1892 for all "laborers and mechanics" employed
by the government, the District of Columbia, or by "any contractor
or subcontractor upon any of the public works of the United
States." But even these laws were fitfully and reluctantly enforced.[73]

Other limitations on workers' hours could be justified on social
grounds. New York, in 1888, adopted a law that street-railway
workers could not work more than twelve hours at a stretch. This
was followed, in 1892, by a ceiling on the hours of all railroad
workers. The argument (or excuse) was that an exhausted train-
man or engineer endangered the public. On this basis, enough
outside support could be mustered for passage—support that
ordinary factory labor could not yet get. That further step—
maximum hour laws for adult male workers—was not possible in
the 19th century. *Holden* v. *Hardy* (1898)[74] upheld, in the country's
highest court, a Utah law, of 1896, that limited, to eight hours a
day, the workday of "workingmen in all underground mines or
workings," in "smelters and in all other institutions for the reduction or refining of ores or metals." These were particularly
onerous and unhealthy occupations; and this case, as the century
ended, stood perilously close to the legal frontier.

[72]155 Ill. 98, 40 N.E. 454 (1895).
[73]Marion C. Cahill, *Shorter Hours* (1932), pp. 69–73.
[74]169 U.S. 366 (1898).

FEDERAL TAXATION

For most of the 19th century, the tariff, protective or otherwise, served a double function; it was a (controversial) element of economic policy; and it brought in important revenue for the federal government. Congress was most reluctant to expand the government's taxing authority. That would increase federal power, and state sovereignty was still too strong a counterforce. Even the costs of the Civil War did not at first inspire new forms of tax. Initially, the government tried to fight the war by floating bonds; Jay Cooke took up residence in Washington and lent a hand to Salmon P. Chase, who presided over Lincoln's treasury. Bond financing and greenback money did raise revenue, after their fashion. But the North lost more battles than expected; costs mounted; the war dragged on; it became clear that the struggle would be fought on an epic, not a lyric, scale. Events thus forced the government's hand. Lincoln turned to an income tax. The tax, first imposed in 1862, and amended in 1864, was mildly progressive; in its later revision, its top bracket was 10 percent. The government also imposed a death tax, and new or bigger excises on all sorts of services and goods: beer, public utilities, advertisements, perfumes, playing cards, slaughtered cattle, and railroads, for example. Despite some unfairness and bungling, these taxes brought in a good deal of money. In fiscal 1866, more than $300,000,000 was collected.

The Confederate government, on the other hand, mismanaged its finances badly. The Provisional Congress, in August 1861, imposed a direct tax of ½ percent on all property (except Confederate bonds and money). The various states, however, were allowed to pay the tax themselves. This concession proved to be a disaster; rather than collect the money from their publics, the states simply issued treasury notes or required local banks to furnish the money. The Confederate treasury became "the greatest money factory in the world." It created "wealth out of nothing" by "magic revolutions of the printing press." The result, of course, was a wild inflation. The notes "drove prices to fantastic heights. Counterfeiting...ran riot. Faith in the government vanished." The Confederacy never really undid this early mistake. Its later tax laws were inept or ill-timed; the major law of April 1863 was complex and, in part, unpopular; one feature called for payment of one-tenth of the produce of farm land as a tax in kind. The revenue question was never solved; soon Grant and Sherman made the question academic.[75]

The victorious North was anxious to return to normalcy, at least in money matters. Congress let the wartime taxes die. Indeed, the small scale of the federal government did not seem to call for severe and exotic taxes. Excise taxes, on liquor and tobacco, produced nearly ninety percent of the government's internal revenue from 1868 to 1913. Internal revenue receipts were $113,500,000 in 1873, $161,000,000 in 1893—mere pennies in today's world of hundreds of billions of dollars.[76] But government grew steadily more active; and that meant money. Meanwhile, there was jealousy and fear of the triumphant, exultant rich, the powerful trusts, and the robber barons east and west—and not merely from the far left. Political and ideological arguments, coupled with a real need for cash, won recruits for the idea of a progressive income tax—a tax that would also serve as a brake on the power of the rich. Between 1873 and 1879, fourteen different income-tax bills were introduced into Congress.

The movement reached its climax in the 1890s. The 1890s had no war for an excuse, except the Spanish-American War, which was short and profitable. But many contemporaries had a different war in mind: the battle for control of America's economy, not to mention its soul. The Eastern rich obliged by agreeing with the left on what an income tax meant: it was the archenemy, the entering wedge of socialism, the beginning of the end for America. In 1893, Grover Cleveland suggested a "small tax" on incomes "derived from certain corporate investment"; when a tax bill passed in 1894, however, he let it become law without signing. The law taxed incomes (and gains) over and above an exemption of $4,000 at the flat rate of two percent.[77] In the war of words, Ward McAllister, "leader of the Four Hundred," threatened to leave the country if the law was passed. William Jennings Bryan, rushing to the barricades, cried out that he had "never known one so mean that I was willing to say of him that his patriotism was less than two percent deep."

In the 1890s, it was not enough to pass so important a law; the

[75]For the above, see Randolph E. Paul, *Taxation in the United States* (1954), pp. 7–22.

[76]Lillian Doris, ed., *The American Way in Taxation: Internal Revenue, 1862–1963* (1963), p. 34.

[77]28 Stats. 553 (act of August 27, 1894, sec. 27).

Supreme Court still had to be convinced. William D. Guthrie of New York, risen from office boy to lion of Wall Street, determined to slay this dragon of two percent. He raised money for the lawsuit among his clients, found a willing litigant named Pollock, and launched an attack that he carried all the way to the Supreme Court itself.[78] Before the Court, an epic struggle took place. On one side was ranged a battery of prominent Wall Street lawyers— Guthrie, Joseph H. Choate, and others—on the other, Attorney General Olney, his assistant, Edward B. Whitney, and James C. Carter. The case occasioned great flights of oratory, and some dubious essays in pseudo-history, concerning the limits of the federal power to tax. In *Pollock* v. *Farmers' Loan and Trust Co.* (1895),[79] the Court at first held the tax unconstitutional, but only as it applied to income derived from real estate. On the big question, whether the whole law was unconstitutional as a "direct Tax," the Court was evenly divided, four against four.[80] The ninth judge, Jackson, was sick. The case was then reargued—with Jackson present—and this time the Court declared the whole law void, by a bare majority, 5–4.[81]

History has not been kind to *Pollock*. Professor Edward S. Corwin has called it a case of "bad history and bad logic";[82] it was surely both of these. He might have added bad law, bad politics, and bad form. The case has had one rare distinction: a constitutional amendment, passed in the 20th century, specifically undid it. At the time, of course, this could not be foreseen. Defenders and detractors alike agreed on what the decision was meant to accomplish: to make the world safe for that brand of democracy which Guthrie believed in, and Justice Field, and the rest of the

---

[78]Randolph Paul, *Taxation in the United States*, pp. 30ff; Arnold M. Paul, *Conservative Crisis and the Rule of Law* (1960), chs. 8, 9. On Guthrie's role, see Robert T. Swaine, *The Cravath Firm and its Predecessors*, vol. I, *The Predecessor Firms* (1946), pp. 518–36; Henry James, *Richard Olney and His Public Service* (1923), pp. 70–76.

[79]157 U.S. 429, 158 U.S. 601 (1895).

[80]The Constitution, art. 1, sec. 2, required "direct taxes" to be apportioned among the states by population. It had for a century or more been understood that poll taxes and property taxes, and only these, were "direct."

[81]When the Court is evenly divided, by custom it does not reveal who voted on which side. When the case was reargued, Jackson, the missing judge, voted to uphold the act. This should have given the law a 5–4 majority; in fact it lost by 5–4. There is a minor historical mystery here, since one of the other four judges in the majority must have changed his mind between the time of the two votes. No one is quite sure which judge is the guilty one. See A. M. Paul, *op. cit.*, pp. 214–17.

[82]Edward S. Corwin, *Court over Constitution* (1938), p. 188.

"sound" and wealthy people of the country. Perhaps *Pollock* deserves a bit better than it has gotten from historians. Its logic and history were weak; but its instincts were rather shrewd. The income tax *was* the opening wedge for a major transformation of American society. A journey of a thousand miles begins with a single step; and a tax whose brackets once rose as high as seven dollars out of ten may begin with a mere two percent.

STATE AND LOCAL TAX

In the 19th century, local government relied primarily on the general property tax. In 1890 this tax produced 72 percent of state revenues, 92 percent of local revenues. It has kept its primacy for local revenue, but state government later abandoned this tax,[83] and turned to other sources.

The general property tax, as its name implies, was a tax on all types of property. Essentially, it was the old real-property tax, with a tax on intangibles and personal property added. Indeed, most states at some time in the century made a constitutional point of uniformity and generality of taxes. "All taxes," said the Pennsylvania constitution of 1873, "shall be uniform, upon the same class of subjects within the territorial limits of the authority levying the tax, and shall be levied and collected under general laws" (art. IX, sec. 1). Again: "Laws shall be passed taxing by uniform rule all property according to its true value in money" (North Dakota const. 1889, art. XI, sec. 176).

A general tax was not easy to administer. It was hard enough to assess land and houses fairly; at least real estate was visible, and there were records of title. Chattels were easy to hide, and intangibles most furtive of all. The general property tax essentially reduced itself to a tax on land and buildings. A rich taxpayer could easily evade taxes on invisible assets. Meanwhile, much of the property of the less well-off was exempt from tax. Landowners who wanted to share their burden called for passage of more general taxes. But in the end, they bore most of the burden themselves.

Assessment and collection of the tax was a continual problem.

---

[83]George C. S. Benson *et al.*, *The American Property Tax: Its History, Administration and Economic Impact* (1965), p. 83. On city use of the tax, see Jon C. Teaford, *The Unheralded Triumph: City Government in America, 1870–1900* (1984), pp. 293–304.

Assessment was local, chaotic, and frequently unfair. Assessors were greatly tempted to undervalue property in their counties: why not let the burden fall on other parts of the state? Hence, on top of the layers of local officials, states began to impose "boards of equalization," first countywide, then statewide. An early state board was Iowa's: by the Iowa code of 1851 the board was "authorized and required to examine the various assessments ... and equalize the rate of assessment of real estate in the different counties," in the name of uniformity. The board could equalize "either by changing any of the assessments or by varying the rate of taxation in any of the counties."[84]

But the boards did not have adequate power to control local assessors. Indiana took the next step, in 1891: creation of a board of state tax commissioners. The board had general supervision over the tax system; but its power was "chiefly advisory," and it did not curb all the abuses that had grown up under the older system. Still, Indiana's law was "the beginning of a new administrative policy," and ultimately led to more efficient ways to assess and collect this tax.[85]

Even on paper the general property tax was never completely general. There were many exceptions and exemptions. The list of exemptions was similar to the list of property exempt from creditors, though less extensive. In the Iowa code of 1851, tax-exempt property included poultry, wool shorn from sheep, one year's crop, private libraries up to $100 in value, family pictures, kitchen furniture, one bed and bedding for each member of the family, clothes "actually used for wearing," and food.[86] In the Iowa code of 1897, much the same exemptions appeared, but with additions: "the farming utensils of any person who makes his livelihood by farming, the team, wagon and harness of the teamster or drayman who makes his living by their use in hauling for others, and the tools of any mechanic, not in any case to exceed three hundred dollars in actual value."[87] The property of charities, schools, and churches was also free from tax.

During the promotional years, railroads and other favored corporations were granted tax exemptions, too. When these com-

---

[84]Iowa Stats. 1851, secs. 481, 482. See, in general, Harley L. Lutz, *The State Tax Commission* (1918).

[85]Lutz, *op. cit.*, p. 152.

[86]Iowa Stats. 1851, sec. 455.

[87]Iowa Stats. 1897, sec. 1304, sec. 1304(5).

panies fell from grace, they had to pay their own way—in theory. There were constant battles over taxation in legislatures between 1870 and 1900; smallholders and organized labor wanted vengeance on the large corporations, and (as usual) wanted the power of big money kept in control. But revenue needs were real enough, too. To lay the foundation for more active government, states needed a broadly based, productive tax system. Where was the money to come from? The new state constitutions hamstrung legislatures in their search for money. They were not allowed to float bonds at whim or will. The lower orders of government were also squeezed. Some governmental services could be supported by fees; but this method was regressive and liable to abuse. On the other hand, business was rich and getting richer; and it had long escaped paying what looked like a reasonable share. Some states competed for incorporations with *low* taxes; but railroad tracks once laid could not run away, and the temptation was to get all one could from a captive giant.

Taxation of business proved enormously difficult. First, there were political difficulties. The wealth of enterprise excited the tax collectors' lust; but wealth was power, and business fought back. Volumes could be written about the struggles over railroad taxation alone. State governments rose and fell on the issue. Second, there were the special complexities of a federal system. Before 1850, the railroads, when they were taxed, paid the general local property tax. Afterwards, more and more states added taxes based on capitalization or gross receipts.

Interstate businesses—railroads and telegraph companies, for example—ran the risk of taxation all along their lines, as if by so many Rhenish baronies. How much taxation of "commerce" across state lines was valid? How could the property of some giant firm, sprawled across the states like a Gulliver among Lilliputians, be sliced into rational pieces and taxed? There was no uniform plan. In 1899, railroads in some parts of the country paid 17 percent of net earnings; in others, only 8.4 percent.[88] Fundamental questions of constitutional law, of conflicts of law—and politics—were often at issue. The various solutions bred intricate law. When all concerned—legislatures, state courts, and federal courts—had had their say, there was still no definitive answer, still no one definite limit to the taxes that a state could lawfully impose on an interstate tiger with one paw in the taxing *situs*. Various formulas,

[88]Emory R. Johnson, *American Railway Transportation* (rev. ed., 1907), p. 416.

of more or less sophistication, determined what part of the tiger "belonged" (for tax purposes) to Rhode Island or Texas or Washington state. Massachusetts, for example, taxed railroads and telegraph companies on that portion of their capital which bore the same ratio to total capital as tracks and lines inside the state bore to total tracks and lines. The Supreme Court, in a court test (1888), held that this method was fair.[89] But taxation of multistate commerce was one of the high court's most persistent and bothersome issues.

DEATH TAXES

The idea of death taxes fed and grew fat on fear of dynasties and the money power. Even before the Civil War, there had been some state and federal attempts at estate and inheritance taxation. A death tax was part of the Civil War package. But the real upsurge in demand came after 1885. Economists like Richard T. Ely and Edwin R. Seligman, along with such strange bedfellows as Andrew Carnegie, argued that great fortunes should be heavily taxed when the founder died. About half the states adopted some form of death tax by 1900. Generally, these taxes were not steeply progressive. Almost always, they were biased against collateral heirs and strangers to the blood: they gave spouses and children of the dead most favorable treatment. In Michigan's law of 1893, for example, the tax (on "transfers ... by will or by the intestate laws," or "in contemplation of the death of the grantor," or "intended to take effect ... at ... death") was a flat five percent on the market value of these transfers. But the rate was only one percent on gifts to "father, mother, husband, wife, child, brother, sister, wife or widow of a son or the husband of a daughter," adopted children, and "any lineal descendants"; and the first $5,000 was exempt.[90]

In 1898, the federal government re-entered the field, with a modified form of estate tax.[91] Its top rate was 15 percent, a rate that applied only to gifts from estates of more than $1,000,000, and which passed from the decedent to distant relatives, nonre-

---

[89]*Western Union Telegraph Co.* v. *Mass.*, 125 U.S. 530 (1888); Mass. Stats. 1882, ch. 13, sec. 40.

[90]Laws Mich. 1893, ch. 205; see Edwin R. Seligman, *Essays in Taxation* (6th ed., 1909), pp. 133ff.

[91]Randolph Paul, *op. cit.*, pp. 65–70.

latives, or "bodies politic or corporate." The law was part of the revenue package for the Spanish-American War, and it was repealed in 1902. All told, it brought in $22,500,000. This paltry sum was hardly enough to wound the great fortunes. Like the Civil War taxes, however, the death tax passed its constitutional test; and so did the state taxes on estates, to the horror and disgust of Guthrie and the Cassandras of Wall Street. Again, these rich and conservative men were not wholly wrong. In the future, some of their worse nightmares would come true. Tax laws would be enacted that took a substantial chunk of some large estates. But steep and progressive rates lay in the century ahead.

CHAPTER X

CRIME AND PUNISHMENT

THE MANY FACES OF CRIMINAL LAW

At one time, most lawyers were generalists, and handled criminal matters along with civil suits. Even so prestigious and prominent a business lawyer as Alexander Hamilton did criminal work. In the West, and in small towns generally, criminal law remained a staple of the practice. Later in the century, the bar in major cities became more specialized. There developed both professional criminals and a professional criminal bar. It was not necessarily a dignified bar; and it never had the prestige of that part of the bar that served big business. Some small-scale lawyers eked out a living by gathering crumbs of practice in the lower criminal courts. A few big-city lawyers made a more handsome, and sometimes less honorable, living. In New York, the "magnificent shyster," William F. Howe, flourished between 1875 and 1900. He was a member of the infamous firm of Howe and Hummel; he defended hundreds of madams, pickpockets, forgers, as well as the most notorious murderers of his day. Howe's specialty was gilded courtroom oratory, judiciously backed up by perjury, bribery, and blackmail.[1]

The leaders and money-makers of the criminal bar were always flamboyant, though not always unscrupulous. Howe and Hummel were not afraid to advertise their wares. Over their "shabby but conspicuous offices...hung not the modest shingle of a firm of counsellors-at-law but a sign thirty or forty feet long and three or four feet high...illuminated at night."[2] The organized bar, dominated by elite business lawyers, and jealous of professional

---

[1]The story of Howe and Hummel has been entertainingly recounted by Richard Rovere, in *The Magnificent Shysters* (1947).

[2]Rovere, *op. cit.*, p. 34.

prestige, stamped out the practice of openly asking for business through advertisements and illuminated signs. A criminal lawyer had no retainer business, and few repeats. This left word of mouth one of the few ways he could build a practice. A criminal lawyer, unlike the Wall Street lawyer, *wanted* publicity, wanted his name in the paper. It was for this reason that these lawyers (to this day) like to call attention to themselves. It was publicize or die. The good gray lawyers of Wall Street would have starved in the criminal practice.

Howe and Hummel were seamy caricatures; but in a curious way they illustrate a trait particularly strong in the criminal justice system: an extreme gulf between the open, public, floodlit aspects of the system, and its grubby underbelly. Criminal justice meant show trials, publicity, high drama; it was also an underground tale of corruption and routine. This was, of course, nothing new. But these traits were if anything heightened in the late 19th century.

The criminal law itself, quite naturally, underwent considerable surface change in the later 19th century. It became and remained by and large a matter of statute. The concept of the common-law crime, as we have seen, had been wiped out in federal law. The concept decayed on the state level, too. As of 1900, most states still *technically* recognized the possibility of a common-law crime. But some states had statutes that specifically abolished the concept. These statutes stated bluntly that all crimes were listed in the penal code, and nothing else was a crime. In some states, the courts *construed* their penal codes as (silently) abolishing common-law crime. Where the concept survived, it was hardly ever used; the penal codes were in fact complete and exclusive.

The living law was rather more complicated. The New York penal code (enacted in 1881) provided that "no act...shall be deemed criminal or punishable, except as prescribed or authorized by this Code, or by some statute of this state not repealed by it." This was plain abolition. Yet the penal code had a sweeping catchall clause: "A person, who willfully and wrongfully commits any act, which seriously injures the person or property of another, or which seriously disturbs or endangers the public peace or health, or which openly outrages public decency or is injurious to public morals...is guilty of a misdemeanor."[3] Obviously, prosecutors and courts could have almost as much power under this language as

[3] N.Y. Penal Code 1881, secs. 2, 675.

under the reign of common-law crime. In fact, the section was probably little used, as little as the concept of common-law crime in those states which retained it.

In *Hackney* v. *State* (1856),[4] an Indiana case, Hackney, the defendant, had been arrested for maintaining a "public nuisance"; this consisted of "keeping a ten-pin alley, and procuring for gain certain disorderly persons to meet there, rolling balls night and day, cursing, quarreling, drinking, and making great noises." Indiana had abolished the common-law crime. There was no statute on the books which said anything specific about tenpin alleys, but maintaining a public nuisance was a statutory misdemeanor. The question was, what was a nuisance? There was a body of common-law decisions defining nuisance; the court explicitly denied that these cases were relevant. The common law was not to be used, even as a source of interpretation. Instead, the court turned to an Indiana statute which defined "nuisance" as anything "injurious to health, or indecent, or offensive to the senses." This, said the court, could cover Hackney's conduct; they affirmed his conviction by the lower court.

The New York statute, and the *Hackney* case, raise the suspicion that there was more to the death of the common-law crime than meets the eye. What died was the overt, unabashed power of courts to pull out new crimes from the folkways. It was killed by that pervasive feature in American legal culture, horror of uncontrolled power. Lawmakers believed that courts should be guided—ruled—by the words of objective law, enacted by the people's representatives; nothing else should be a crime. But at the same time, the courts found covert substitutes for their lost jurisdiction. First, they benefited from vague general clauses, like the one in the New York Penal Code. Indeed, a camouflaged power was more suitable to the courts, more soothing, more protective, than a naked power at common law. Second, they allowed themselves more amplitude in interpreting the law. They rejected the extremist language of *Hackney* about common-law interpretation. But they retained the flair for "interpretation of statutes" that *Hackney* signified. There was an old maxim that courts had a duty to construe penal statutes narrowly. Courts constantly referred to this maxim; yet even this helped judges elbow their way into power. It was the judges who decided, after all, what was narrow and what was wide.

[4] 8 Ind. 494 (1856).

As we have seen, countervailing power, one of the great themes of American history, was particularly strong in criminal justice. Trial judge, appellate judge, jury, legislature stood in uneasy balance. The Constitution, the Bill of Rights, and the 14th amendment tried to strike some sort of balance between federal and state power. At least in legal theory, criminal trials were hedged about by many safeguards. A stern law of evidence kept juries honest; juries kept judges and the government in check; meticulous attention to procedure guaranteed that the citizen's liberty and life were safe from injustice. Indeed, the safeguards went too far, according to some; especially at the appellate level they passed beyond the meticulous, to the realm of the almost ridiculous: this was the "hypertrophy" of procedure that some scholars thought they saw.

The picture that emerged was one of precision, rigidity, care. Nothing was a crime unless it was clearly so engraved in the statute books. Criminal laws had to be strictly construed. There was no margin for error at the trial. Probably no field of law, however, was quite so two-faced. The ideal picture of criminal justice must be contrasted with the real criminal law, parts of which were blunt, merciless, and swift, other parts of which simply ignored whole kingdoms of crime. It was true that most appeals from criminal cases succeeded; but few were appealed—one half of one percent of total prosecutions in Chippewa County, Wisconsin; about one percent of the felony prosecutions in Alameda County, California (1870–1910). Only five percent of the cases before the Wisconsin supreme court were criminal appeals.[5]

It was an aspect of living law that the safeguards did not safeguard everybody; it was also living law that the real criminal justice system was made up of many overlapping layers, none of which resembled very closely the ideal picture of criminal justice. There were at least three of these layers: the bottom layer, in which countless thousands of petty cases were handled, rather roughly and informally; a middle layer, which disposed of ordinary cases of serious crime; and a top layer, made up of a few dramatic cases—cases where the crime was especially lurid or the defendant

[5]For the Wisconsin figures: Edward L. Kimball, "Criminal Cases in a State Appellate Court: Wisconsin, 1839–1959," 9 Am. J. Legal Hist. 95, 99–100 (1965). For Alameda County: Lawrence M. Friedman and Robert V. Percival, *The Roots of Justice: Crime and Punishment in Alameda County, California, 1870–1910* (1981), p. 262. After 1880, about 5 percent of the felony convictions were appealed, and roughly one out of seven cases in which there was a jury verdict of guilty.

prominent or unusual or both of these. It was a sensation when Professor John W. Webster of the Harvard Medical School went on trial, in 1850, for killing another professor, Dr. George Parkman, and chopping his body into pieces.[6] Cases like this made headlines in the newspapers; the public devoured every detail. They were, in short, great theater.

Everybody loves a mystery; everybody loves a courtroom drama. The great cases were also the ones in which all the stops were pulled out: juries were carefully and laboriously chosen; trials were long and crammed with detail; both sides marshaled evidence, introduced experts, battled and sparred on cross-examination; due process was meticulously observed. These were also the trials with sensational events, witnesses who wept or fainted, grisly evidence and exhibits, vast flights of purple oratory. They served, perhaps, important functions. They were "propaganda plays, plays of morality, cautionary tales." They were also the vehicle for teaching the public about law. But the public learned a curious, double message. They learned that America was scrupulous about the rights of people accused of crime. They saw that justice was real; but they also saw that it was absurd. They saw careful meticulous justice; but they also saw justice "as a ham, a mountebank, a fool."[7]

The picture was also profoundly misleading. Underneath, in the second layer, a different kind of system operated. Here thousands of cases of assault, theft, burglary, and similar crimes were prosecuted. The trial courts, as far as we can tell, were by no means kangaroo courts; but there were no long, drawn-out trials. The "hypertrophy" of due process had no role in these courts. For many defendants, there was no trial at all. The beginnings of plea bargaining can be clearly traced to this period. Defendants in increasing numbers pleaded guilty; in some cases, there was an obvious "deal"; in others, defendant simply entered such a plea, in hopes of getting better treatment. By the turn of the century, less than half of all felony defendants went to trial in some communities; in others, they were "tried," but in slapdash and routine ways, in trials that lasted a few hours or a few minutes at best. And most were convicted. In Greene County, Georgia, in

---

[6]Webster was convicted and executed, after a long trial conducted by Lemuel Shaw, Chief Justice of Massachusetts.

[7]Lawrence M. Friedman and Robert V. Percival, *The Roots of Justice* (1981), p. 259–60.

the 1870s, eight out of ten blacks were found guilty; six whites out of ten.[8]

All this was not some sort of decline from the golden age of trials (no such age ever existed), but a sign of the increasing professionalization of criminal justice. During the 19th century, the system shifted away from its almost total reliance on amateurs and part-timers. It came to be dominated more and more by full-time crime-handlers: police, detectives, prosecuting attorneys, defense attorneys who did defense work almost exclusively, judges who mostly sat for criminal cases, forensic experts of one sort or another. Later would come social workers, probation officers, and still more professionals. The system became more administrative, less adjudicative. In a system of this sort, the jury of amateurs had less place. *Routine* was not new; but the personnel who ran it, and the way it was run, dramatically altered.

Perhaps the key to the new system was the expanded role of the police. Police departments were organized in New York and a few other large cities before the Civil War; but it was only in the period after the war that the police became a universal feature of urban criminal justice. The police were divided into ranks that had a military flavor (captains, sergeants); and they wore uniforms and badges. In comparison to what went on before, the police can indeed be called professionals; but they were hardly professional in a more modern sense. Almost anybody could be a policeman—there were no requirements of training or education; departments were frequently corrupt; and politics always reared its ugly head. In Cincinnati, after an election in 1880, 219 out of 295 officers were dismissed.[9]

But the police became ubiquitous in city life; criminal justice was unthinkable without them. They made thousands of arrests, not only for major crimes, but also for those petty offenses that

[8]Edward L. Ayers, *Vengeance and Justice: Crime and Punishment in the 19th-Century American South* (1984), p. 176; Friedman and Percival, *op. cit.*, p. 173. Forty percent of the felony defendants in Alameda County pleaded guilty, in the period 1880–1910; about a fifth of the cases were dismissed or continued indefinitely; in 23 percent the jury convicted the defendant; in 16 percent the jury acquitted. On the origins of plea bargaining, see Friedman and Percival, *op. cit.*, pp. 175–81; Lawrence M. Friedman, "Plea Bargaining in Historical Perspective," 13 Law & Society Rev. 247 (1979); on implicit bargaining, Milton Heumann, "A Note on Plea Bargaining and Case Pressure," 9 Law & Society Rev. 515 (1975).

[9]Samuel Walker, *Popular Justice: A History of American Criminal Justice* (1980), p. 61.

jammed the dockets of the municipal courts, justice courts, and police courts—the third, bottom layer of the criminal justice system. Here justice was quick and informal. These were cases of drunkenness, assault and battery, domestic quarrels, disturbing the peace. The police patrolled the cities, symbolizing and maintaining the order and regularity that a modern, industrial society needed, or thought it needed. In a more sinister way, the police acted as a kind of civilian army; they exerted control in the interests of the respectable and the comfortable, against the "dangerous classes," which included those who were actually dangerous to the established order and those whose threat was largely symbolic. The police were especially hard on "tramps" and vagrants; during periods of labor unrest, in many cities they defended the interests of management's side with great vigor—protecting "scabs," breaking up picket lines, and interfering with union activities. In Buffalo, in 1892, in a strike on the streetcar lines, the police were even accused of scabbing themselves: the union claimed that officers acted as switchmen and helped move the trains. In short, the police practically acted as municipal strikebreakers.[10]

Police violence and irregularity formed part of what was virtually a fourth, unofficial layer of the criminal justice system: the irregular, illegitimate use of force and violence outside the law. To a certain extent, of course, this was force countervailing force. In the slums and tenderloins of big cities, street gangs, prostitutes, and thieves ran their American underworld, enforced their own rules, governed their own society. The policeman's force was the only kind of law that ever penetrated that jungle. Alexander S. Williams, of the New York police force, became famous in the 1870s because he "invoked the gospel of the nightstick" and organized "a strong arm squad." Patrolling the Gas House District, Williams "clubbed the thugs with or without provocation." Charges were preferred against Williams no less than eighteen times; but the board of police commissioners "invariably acquitted" him. He justified his "furious clubbing" by the observation that "there is more law in the end of a policeman's nightstick than in a decision of the Supreme Court."[11]

---

[10]Sidney L. Harring, *Policing a Class Society: The Experience of American Cities, 1865–1915* (1983), pp. 117–18. On the work of the police in the "basement" courts, see Friedman and Percival, ch. 4; there is also material on the criminal work of justices in John R. Wunder, *Inferior Courts, Superior Justice: A History of the Justices of the Peace on the Northwest Frontier, 1853–1889* (1979).

[11]Herbert Asbury, *The Gangs of New York* (1928), pp. 235–37.

The regular criminal law had, indeed, many irregular helpers. The Ku Klux Klan rode in the South, from 1867 to the early 1870s; it burned and pillaged, and punished blacks and whites who transgressed against the Klan's concept of a proper social order. The vigilantes of the West, with their brand of do-it-your-self criminal justice, were in some ways following an old American tradition. The first American vigilantes, the South Carolina reg-ulators, appeared in 1767.[12] But the movement really flourished after 1850. As we have seen, the most famous, and the models for the rest, were the two Vigilance Committees of San Francisco (1851 and 1856). Vigilante justice cropped up throughout Cali-fornia; in Colorado, Nevada, Oregon, Texas and Montana; and generally in the West. "Swift and terrible retribution is the only preventive of crime, while society is organizing in the far West," wrote Thomas J. Dimsdale, chronicler of the Montana vigilantes, in 1865.[13] All told, there were hundreds of vigilante movements. One hundred and forty-one of them took at least one human life. The total death toll has been put at 729. Virtually all of this took place before 1900, and in the West. Texas was the bloodiest vig-ilante state; and the peak decade was the 1860s.[14]

The vigilantes were not the only groups that engaged in private criminal justice. Claims clubs in the Middle West, and miners' courts in the sparse, bleak reaches of the far West, constructed their own version of property law and punished offenders. Later in the century, "Judge Lynch" presided at an all too frequent court in the South and the Border states. Mobs, in the 1890s, tortured, hanged, and sometimes burned alive black men accused of assault, murder, or rape. They sometimes snatched their victims from jail, furious at delay. Lynch mobs and vigilantes had their own sense of mission. Some of them, hungry for legitimacy, parodied the regular written law; they had their own "judges" and "juries," their own quick and summary trials. They punished crimes with-out names or without remedies, and enforced public policy as they saw it. They were responses to what some elites felt was the absence of law and order (as in parts of the West), or to the

---

[12]See Joe B. Frantz, "The Frontier Tradition: An Invitation to Violence," and Richard Maxwell Brown, "The American Vigilante Tradition," in Hugh D. Gra-ham and Ted. R. Gurr, eds., *Violence in America: Historical and Comparative Per-spectives* (1969), pp. 101 ff., 121 ff.; Richard Maxwell Brown, *Strain of Violence: Historical Studies of American Violence and Vigilantism* (1975).

[13]Thomas J. Dimsdale, *The Vigilantes of Montana* (new edition, 1953), p. 13.

[14]Richard Maxwell Brown, "The American Vigilante Tradition," pp. 128, 130.

disorganization of a defeated society (as in the South), or to the feebleness or venality of regular government. They also were a much cheaper form of punishment than tax-fed trials and long prison sentences. A newspaper writer, after a vigilante lynching in Golden, Colorado, in 1879, reported that "the popular verdict seemed to be that the hanging was not only well merited, but a positive gain for the county, saving at least five or six thousand dollars."[15]

The Southern lynch mobs were the most savage and the least excusable of all the self-help groups. Their law and order was naked racism, no more. Their real complaint against law was that the courts were too careful and too slow; that some guilty prisoners went free; and that the lesson for the rest of the blacks was not sharp enough. The lynch mobs enforced a code that no court could be expected to enforce. Western vigilantes, on the other hand, have become almost folk heroes; it is usual to regard them with sympathy, or as a necessary evil, or even as a form of popular democracy. The historian Hubert H. Bancroft lavishly praised the vigilance committees. Indeed, he loved all forms of Western justice. Vigilance, he wrote, is an "expression of power on the part of the people in the absence or impotence of law." It is "the exercise informally of their rightful power by a people wholly in sympathy with existing forms of law." It is "the keen knife in the hands of a skilful surgeon, removing the putrefaction with the least possible injury to the body politic." The San Francisco Committee of 1856, for example, was just such a surgeon: "Never before in the history of human progress have we seen, under a popular form of government, a city-full rise as one man, summoned by almighty conscience, attend at the bedside of sick law ...and perform a speedy and almost bloodless cure."[16] It was certainly true that public opinion was not overly severe on the "beloved rough-necks"; many who joined the vigilantes were leaders of their communities. Thomas Dimsdale, who wrote a very favorable book about the vigilantes of Montana, served as the state superintendent of public instruction. Some vigilantes became prominent in later life. Two governors of New Mexico had vigilante episodes in their past. It was obviously no disgrace, no impediment to success.[17]

---

[15]Quoted in Richard M. Brown, *op cit.*, p. 143.
[16]Hubert H. Bancroft, *Popular Tribunals*, vol. I (1887), pp. 10, 11, 16.
[17]Richard M. Brown, *op cit.*, p. 150.

Under some conditions, self-help law can make a persuasive case. The Donner party, in 1846, tried, convicted, and banished a man named James Reed, who had killed John Snyder in a fight. The travelers were months away from Missouri—in Mexican territory, in fact—and hundreds of miles from any court, or judge, or arm of any state.[18] The ideology of self-help was strong, too, in the 19th century; and government was stingy. It is no surprise, then, that a Wisconsin law of 1861 authorized the "organization of societies for mutual protection against larcenies of live stock." The societies were given power to choose "riders" who might "exercise all the powers of constables in the arrest and detention of criminals."[19] A similar law in Pennsylvania in 1869 incorporated the "Spring Valley Police Company of Crawford County," a "company for the recovery of stolen horses and other property." Its members were to have the same powers of arrest and detention as policemen of Philadelphia.[20] The antihorsethief movement arose "spontaneously" after the Revolutionary War. From the 1850s on, the societies sought, and got, legislative authorization. They lasted until better public police and the automobile put them out of business. In their heyday, they had more than 100,000 members.[21]

Private law enforcement was an attractive idea. A statute of 1865, in Pennsylvania, gave railroads the power to employ their own police. An act of 1866 extended this law to any "colliery, furnace or rolling-mill," thus creating the "coal and iron police." The state here authorized "a veritable private army," at the request of "powerful interests." These private police—they existed in other states as well—became anathema to the unions. They were "toughs," strikebreakers, "necessarily the enemy of organized labor."[22] But it was not until the 1930s that they were finally abolished in Pennsylvania.

[18]John W. Caughey, *Their Majesties the Mob* (1960), pp. 6–7.
[19]Laws Wis. 1861, ch. 222.
[20]Laws Pa. 1869, ch. 991.
[21]Richard M. Brown, "The American Vigilante Tradition," p. 148.
[22]J. P. Shalloo, *Private Police, with Special Reference to Pennsylvania* (1933), pp. 60, 62, 88.

THE STATUTE LAW OF CRIMES

Over the years, the criminal codes, like the dollar, became markedly inflated. Traditional crimes—treason, murder, burglary, arson, and rape—stayed on the books; new crimes were constantly added. Roscoe Pound counted fifty crimes in 1822 in the Rhode Island penal code. The number had grown to 128 crimes by 1872.[23] The revised statutes of Indiana of 1881 contained more than three hundred sections under the general heading of crimes. Instead of one section about embezzlement, there were many: embezzlement of public funds, embezzlement by officers (the crime committed when "any County Treasurer, County Auditor, Sheriff, Clerk, or Receiver of any Court, Township Trustee, Justice of the Peace, Mayor of a city, Constable, Marshal of any city or incorporated town," or any other officers and agents of local government, failed to turn over or account for funds in their trust), embezzlement by employees, by "lawyers and collectors," by railroad employees, by "innkeepers and carriers," by bailees (a "storage, forwarding, or commission merchant, carrier, warehouseman, factor, auctioneer, or his clerk, agent or employee"), by agricultural tenants, by treasurers (of state or local government), by city officials, or by fiduciaries (secs. 1942–52).

The list of crimes was long; and one wonders why certain acts were singled out for separate treatment—why, for example, there needed to be a specific section directed against anyone who "maliciously or mischievously" injured "any telegraph-pole or telephone-pole" (sec. 1956). There were great numbers of new economic or regulatory crimes, some quite trivial: shooting prairie hens or prairie chickens out of season, selling grain seed that harbored seeds of Canada thistle, swindling an underwriter, selling coal by false weight (secs. 2107, 2121, 2138, 2202). Whoever "stretches or places any net...across any creek emptying into the Ohio river in this State...in order to prevent the ingress of fish ...or their egress," was guilty of a crime, and liable to pay between $5 and $20 for each day the obstruction continued (sec. 2118). It was a crime to sell skimmed milk in Indiana; to dam up a stream and produce stagnant water; to sell "diseased or corrupted or unwholesome provisions" (secs. 2067, 2069, 2071).

There were also many sections concerned with public morality:

[23]Roscoe Pound, *Criminal Justice in America* (1930), p. 16.

sections against gambling, "bunko-steering," selling liquor on Sunday, pimping, adultery, public indecency. It was a crime to "entice" any "female of previous chaste character ... to a house of ill-fame," for the "purpose of prostitution" (sec. 1993); dealing in obscene literature was also proscribed. The statutes reflected a new, heightened interest in morals crimes, an interest which, as we will see, was characteristic of the late 19th century. It was also a crime to sell or advertise "any secret drug or nostrum purporting to be for the exclusive use of females, or which cautions females against their use when in a condition of pregnancy; or ... any drug for preventing conception or for procuring abortion or miscarriage" (sec. 1998).[24] In addition, the code referred, in the section on crimes, to more than ninety other statutory sections scattered elsewhere in the revised statutes, which also imposed criminal sanctions for this or that conduct. These were tacked on to a wide variety of statutes—on maliciously killing or injuring a "registered and tagged dog" (sec. 2649), on selling intoxicating liquors to inmates of the Soldiers' Home (sec. 2834), on violations of provisions of the "Dentistry Act" (sec. 4254), on sale of commercial fertilizers not "labeled with the State Chemist's analysis ... or ... labeled with a false or inaccurate analysis" (sec. 4897), and on violations of the Public Warehouse Act (sec. 6549).

What was true in Indiana was true in the other states as well. The steady growth of statutory crimes continued. Few were ever repealed; fresh ones were constantly added. In 1891 it became a misdemeanor in Indiana to "wilfully wear the badges or buttonaire [sic] of the Grand Army of the Republic" or other veterans' groups unless one was "entitled to use or wear the same" under the rules and regulations of the organization. Another law required road supervisors or "Gravel Road Superintendents" to cut hedges along the highways; failure to do so was an offense, and was punishable by fine. It became a felony in that year for officers of public institutions to "purchase, sell, barter or give away to any other officer ... or to appropriate to his or their own use any of the slops or offal of any of the said public institutions." Railroads had to employ flagmen at railroad crossings; for failure to comply, money penalties were prescribed.[25] About a dozen more distinct items of

[24]On the development in this period of laws against abortion, see James C. Mohr, *Abortion in America: The Origins and Evolution of National Policy, 1800–1900* (1978).
[25]Laws Ind. 1891, ch. 33, 39, 146, 150.

behavior became criminal, in 1891, and other, older crime laws were amended.

In every state, every extension of governmental power, every new form of regulation, brought in a new batch of criminal law. Each important statute governing railroads, banks, and corporations; or the marketing of milk, cheese, fruit or coal; or concerning taxation, or elections and voting; or licensing an occupation, trailed along with it at the end a sentence or two imposing criminal sanctions on violators. No doubt many of these stern laws were not criminally enforced at all; violators were rarely or never tried; appeals and reported cases practically did not exist. The full discussion of these statutes belongs more to the story of government regulation of business than to criminal justice.

These regulatory crimes should not, however, be written off completely. The multiplication of economic crimes did not mean, necessarily, that people looked on sharp business behavior with more and more of a sense of moral outrage. It meant, rather, a decision to socialize responsibility for enforcing certain parts of the law. This process began long before the Civil War (see above, Part II, ch. VII, pp. 293–94). The states, and the federal government, invoked criminal law more and more in one of its historic functions—as a low-level, low-paid administrative aid. For example, in New York, in 1898, an amendment to the penal code made it a misdemeanor to sell articles as "sterling silver" unless they consisted of 925/1000ths of pure silver.[26] The buyer's action for fraud did not disappear; the criminal sanction was basically a social supplement. Criminal enforcement was a last resort, an aid to the administrative process (repeat offenders could be threatened with criminal sanctions), and it provided a place where a cheated individual could bring his complaint. It was no substitute, of course, for sustained, efficient bureaucratic control; rather, it was a step along the way.

The Indiana statutes, as we have seen, contained many provisions on morality and vice. Not much is known about enforcement of these laws. Some of them were surely dead letters. But a characteristic of the late 19th century was the resurgence of laws about sex, morality, and so-called victimless crimes—at least on the books, if not in living law.

Colonial law, as we saw, was much concerned with sexual conduct, especially fornication. The early 19th century was a dead

[26]Laws N.Y. 1898, ch. 330.

point, a lull in the war against vice. The major concern of criminal justice was property offenses, especially theft. Adultery (for example) remained a crime; but its nature was subtly redefined. In some states it was illegal only if it was "open and notorious"; this was true of California, for example.[27] What was illegal, then, was not sin itself—and certainly not secret sin—but sin that offended *public* morality. This was what we might call the Victorian compromise: a certain toleration for vice, or at least a resigned acceptance, so long as it remained in an underground state.

The strange status of prostitution was a case in point. Prostitution, of course, was thoroughly illegal; at times, too, there were so-called brothel riots, when citizens tried to take the law into their own hands and stamp out these cesspools of vice.[28] Yet the "social evil" was a flourishing business; one contemporary in New York claimed that the city in 1866 had ninety-nine "houses of assignation" and 2,690 prostitutes, along with "waiter girls" of "bad character" by the hundreds, and "vile" barmaids to boot. A bishop of the Methodist church claimed that there were as many prostitutes as Methodists in the city.[29] Indeed, in most American cities, there was tacit acceptance of prostitution, so long as it stayed in its place, the so-called red-light districts. Some cities—New Orleans was one—even passed ordinances that defined the boundaries of these districts, districts in which illegal vice was, if not legal, at least immune from destructive raids.[30] San Antonio, Texas, even tried to collect license fees from "bawdy-houses," although the ordinance failed a court test. Licensing an illegal business was too much for the judges to swallow.[31]

By the late 19th century, the Victorian compromise began to break down. A new, intense concern with victimless crime developed. In the 1870s, societies "for the suppression of vice" sprang up every-

[27]Cal. Penal Code, 1872, sec. 266a; Ill. Crim. Code 1874, ch. 38, sec. 11 used the phrase "open state of adultery or fornication." On the history of victimless crime, see Lawrence M. Friedman, "Notes Toward a History of American Justice," 24 Buffalo L. Rev. 111 (1974).

[28]On brothel riots, see John C. Schneider, *Detroit and the Problem of Order, 1830–1880* (1980). There was a short-lived attempt, in St. Louis in the 1870s, to institute a "system of medical inspection" for prostitutes. Mark T. Connelly, *The Response to Prostitution in the Progressive Era* (1980), p. 5.

[29]Matthew Hale Smith, *Sunshine and Shadow in New York* (1880), pp. 371–72.

[30]The New Orleans ordinance even reached the attention of the United States Supreme Court, *L'Hote v. New Orleans*, 177 U.S. 587 (1900).

[31]See *Ex parte* Garza, 28 Tex. App. 381, 13 S.W. 779 (1890).

where. The Boston group, later called the Watch and Ward Society, was particularly vigorous.[32] In 1873, Congress passed the so-called Comstock Law, which made it a crime to send any "obscene, lewd, or lascivious" book in the mail—or any "article or thing designed or intended for the prevention of conception or procuring of abortion."[33] Gambling was the target of other moral reformers. Mostly, these were local struggles; on the national scene there was a furious battle over lotteries. At one time, governments used these devices widely, to raise money for new courthouses, internal improvements, and the like. But the lottery was battered by successive abolition movements; by the time of the Civil War, legal lotteries existed only in Delaware and Kentucky; there was a post-war revival, but in 1895, Congress prohibited the sale of lottery tickets across state lines; this proved to be the death blow.[34] There was also renewed interest in control of sexual behavior. The age of consent was the boundary of what was often called "statutory rape." Below this age, sexual intercourse was rape, whether the girl was willing or not. The age of consent, at common law, was 10! But California, for example, raised the age to 14 in 1889, and to 16 in 1897; ultimately, it went up to 18. This made teen-age sex a serious crime, at least on the books.[35]

Above all, liquor control was a constant fountain of law. In 1887, six states were legally dry: Iowa, Kansas, Maine, New Hampshire, Rhode Island, and Vermont.[36] The temperance movement fought hard, had many triumphs, endured many defeats, but ultimately won a stunning victory, national prohibition, in 1920. Joseph Gusfield has argued that the point of the liquor laws lay less in their real effect—less in whether or not people drank—than in whether the law, the official norm, allowed them to drink. The struggle, in short, was symbolic, not instrumental. The issue was: whose norms were dominant, whose norms should be labeled right and true: those of old-line, middle-class, Protestant America, or those of Catholics, immigrants, the working class, dwellers in cities, who drank without shame? Whether the newcomers drank more or less than old Americans mattered less than their attitude toward drink.[37]

[32]See David J. Pivar, *Purity Crusade: Sexual Morality and Social Control, 1868– 1900* (1973).

[33]17 Stats. 598 (act of March 3, 1873).

[34]John S. Ezell, *Fortune's Merry Wheel: The Lottery in America* (1960).

[35]Laws Cal. 1889, ch. 191, p. 223; Laws Cal. 1897, ch. 139, p. 201.

[36]Livingston Hall, "The Substantive Law of Crimes, 1887–1936," 50 Harv. L. Rev. 616, 633 (1937).

Much about this thesis is attractive: neat parallels can be drawn to other areas of struggle over law. Divorce, for example, comes easily to mind. To be sure, in many such struggles, morality laws had clear instrumental uses as well. The sleepy old Sunday laws, for example, came to life in part because unions wanted them enforced; they wanted a shorter work week, and Sunday laws were a useful instrument. Ministers and preachers acted as willing accomplices; labor and religion formed an odd but understandable coalition. In Philadelphia, for example, the barber's union formed a Sunday closing committee. The committee ran a campaign against barbers who would not co-operate; 239 of these were arrested in the two-year period starting December 1898.[38] In New York City, in the 1890s, when Theodore Roosevelt was president of the police board, he vigorously enforced the laws forcing saloons to close on Sundays; bakers and barbers demanded enforcement for *their* trades, too, though with mediocre results.[39] Connecticut passed a tightened Sunday law in 1897; the statute increased the fines that could be imposed for violation, and lengthened the hours of the ban. Between twelve o'clock Saturday night and twelve o'clock Sunday night all shops, warehouses, and factories had to stay closed.

Even laws about sex and vice had a strong practical base; people understood more about venereal diseases than they had at the beginning of the century; prostitution was a public health problem, as well as a matter of morals. But it would be wrong to dismiss the symbolic, ideological element of these laws. If, in regard to Sunday laws, the ministers were tools of the unions, so too were the unions tools of the ministers. The laws were never purely instrumental. The Connecticut Sunday law, for example, also outlawed sports on Sunday, which was hardly an economic matter. [40] There was real ideology here: the culture clash that Gusfield sees; and something more, perhaps. Criminal justice over the years had become, in a way, more democratic. The social base of power had broadened. Power flowed to a large, compact, middle-class mass; this class, by the end of the century, had moral as well as economic

[37]See Joseph Gusfield, *Symbolic Crusade: Status Politics and the American Temperance Movement* (1963).

[38]12 Barbers' Journal 28 (1902).

[39]Howard L. Hurwitz, *Theodore Roosevelt and Labor in New York State, 1880–1900* (1943), pp. 149–54.

[40]Laws Conn. 1897, ch. 188. The statute excepted, as was usual, "works of necessity or mercy."

strength. High-minded people believed in one society, one community, one universal moral code—a code which applied to *everybody*, even the poor, even the *lumpenproletariat*. Elites—aristocrats—tended to have a kind of bored tolerance toward the behavior of the lower orders. The triumphant middle-class expected and demanded more.

It was one thing to pass laws about morality; enforcement was quite another. The reader in the 1980s does not have to be told that the crusade against vice never quite succeeded; all the Prohibitions, of whatever stamp, had to taste the bitter fruit of failure and obloquy. But unenforceable laws were never uniformly unenforced. A symbol loses power when it is only a symbol and nothing more. The evidence suggests that blue laws and liquor laws came to life intermittently, for particular reasons in particular places. Francis Laurent has collected figures for the flow of court business in the lower courts of Chippewa County, Wisconsin. Between 1855 and 1894, sex-law prosecutions were extremely rare, but not extinct. There were five cases of incest, nine of adultery, four of fornication, one of lewd and lascivious behavior. Fifteen accusations of prostitution were brought, all within one decade. There were sixty-one prosecutions for violation of liquor-control laws; fifty occurred in one year, 1871.[41] It is hard to resist the conclusion that laws against immorality were used to "get" somebody or were invoked against some unusually flagrant or unlucky offender. One wonders who the one man was who, alone in a forty-year period, was officially lewd and lascivious. What had he done, and how was he caught? The figures also suggest that laws came to life on the occasion of a crackdown. But a crackdown was most likely to occur after scandal or when a strong organization, like the Women's Christian Temperance Union, with a firm political base, expressed a moral position. Arrests for drunkenness were high in the 19th century, and rose dramatically between 1860 and 1900, at least in one jurisdiction, Massachusetts, where the matter has been carefully studied.[42]

---

[41]Francis Laurent, *The Business of a Trial Court,* pp. 37, 122, 125.
[42]Roger Lane, "Urbanization and Criminal Violence in the 19th Century: Massachusetts as a Test Case," in Hugh D. Graham and Ted R. Gurr, eds., *Violence in America: Historical and Comparative Perspectives* (1969), pp. 361–62; see also Eric H. Monkkonen, "A Disorderly People? Urban Order in the Nineteenth and Twentieth Centuries," 68 J. Am. Hist. 539 (1981).

CRIME, CRIME RATES, INSANITY, THE GUILTY MIND

The criminal law, legitimate and illegitimate, assumes that there is a reality called crime on which law operates. Obviously, in one sense, a society chooses for itself how much crime it wants. When an act is declared criminal, all its actors are committing crime. In 1900, there was vastly more criminal law on the books than in 1850 or 1800, hence in this narrow sense more crime. But people who worry about the crime rate are thinking not of economic crime, or even morals crimes, but about the classic crimes of violence and social disruption, murder, robbery, burglary, assault. These are enforced much more systematically and with greater use of public resources than other kinds of crime. The definitions of these crimes remained more or less constant during the century, or at least constant enough for meaningful comparisons, if only the figures were at hand.

Some facts are known about crime in the real world, in the 19th century. What evidence there is suggests that the crime rate for serious crimes, at least after 1860, gradually declined.[43] Violence, murder, assaults were less of a problem in the late 19th century, and well into the 20th, than they had been before. Roger Lane's research, for Massachusetts, found a marked falling-off in jail commitments, from 333 per 100,000 population to 163, between 1860 and 1900. There are pitfalls and traps in the data; but studies in other places tend to confirm Lane's conclusions.[44] The social investment in crime-fighting increased; so, too, did the worry and the tumult. Violent crime, particularly in the cities, becomes less tolerable in an interdependent, industrial society.

[43]Roger Lane, "Urbanization and Criminal Violence in the 19th Century: Massachusetts as a Test Case," in Hugh D. Graham and Ted R. Gurr, eds., *Violence in America: Historical and Comparative Perspectives* (1969), p. 361.

[44]This is, to be sure, a vexed and difficult subject. It is discussed in Eric H. Monkkonen, *Police in Urban America, 1860–1920* (1981), ch. 2; see also Lawrence M. Friedman and Robert V. Percival, *The Roots of Justice*, pp. 27–35; Elwin H. Powell, "Crime as a Function of Anomie," 57 J. Crim. Law, Criminology, & Police Sci. 161 (1966) (Buffalo, 1854–1956); Eric H. Monkkonen, "A Disorderly People? Urban Order in the Nineteenth and Twentieth Centuries," 68 J. Am. Hist. 539 (1981); and, for cities outside the United States, Ted R. Gurr and Peter N. Grabosky, *Rogues, Rebels and Reformers: A Political History of Urban Crime and Conflict* (1976).

The city is the heart of modern society; society is governed from the city; the economy depends on city life. The city is the place where people confront strangers most continuously, where their lives, property, and health are most at hazard. A society that is heavily urban and industrial, with extreme division of labor, has little tolerance for violent crime. Crime is bad for business, and bad for the social order. The city civilizes and tames, to a certain extent; for this reason violence apparently diminished in the course of the century. But by the same token crime had not gone down fast enough for some people; the public demand for law and order, perhaps, more than kept pace with supply.[45]

Violent crimes were also the crimes of mystery and drama; the crimes that provided raw material for novels, poems, and plays; the crimes par excellence, in the public conception of crime. Pamphlets, trial transcripts, last words of condemned men, were part of American popular culture. There were hundreds of these fugitive writings: John Erpenstein, who gave his wife a bread-and-butter sandwich liberally sprinkled with arsenic, was credited with writing the "Life, Trial, Execution and Dying Confession of John Erpenstein, Convicted of Poisoning His Wife, and Executed in Newark, N.J., on March 30, 1852. Written by himself and translated from the German." The great Harvard murder mystery, the Parkman-Webster case, was naturally notorious; publishers rushed into print with transcripts and other material to satisfy the public's hunger for sensation. The Fall River tragedy—the murder of Lizzie Borden's parents in 1892—has enlivened American literature ever since.[46]

It was this type of crime, too, which evoked the raw hatred that could mold a mob and lead a man to be lynched. It was this type of crime in which trial by jury was frequent, and in which the jury was free to apply its "unwritten laws," in which justice was, in theory, tailored to the individual case. Here, too, were the cases in which the defense of insanity was invoked. Juries, to be sure, probably went

---

[45]Interestingly, the same study by Lane which suggests a decline in arrests for *major* offenses in Massachusetts suggests an equally striking increase in arrests for *minor* offenses, mainly drunkenness. This suggests a certain diminished tolerance for what is defined as antisocial behavior; Eric Monkkonen, on the other hand, in "A Disorderly People?", *supra*, found a decline in drunkenness and disorderly conduct arrests after 1860.

[46]The examples above are drawn from Thomas M. McDade, *The Annals of Murder, A Bibliography of Books and Pamphlets on American Murders from Colonial Times to 1900* (1961), pp. 35–37, 87, 311–16.

their own way; they excused men for insanity, or did not excuse them, in accordance with their own moral code and common sense, rather than the science of their time. But those scientific notions had at least a marginal and indirect effect. And in the 19th century, almost for the first time, lawyers and doctors engaged in a grand and continuing debate about the meaning of criminal responsibility and the scope of the insanity defense.

The dominant definition of legal insanity was the so-called M'Naghten rule, named after a mad Englishman; the rule was first announced, in 1843, in M'Naghten's case.[47] Simply put, a defendant could not be excused from responsibility unless he was "labouring under such a defect of reason...as not to know the nature and quality of the act he was doing; or...that he did not know what he was doing was wrong." This "right or wrong" test was a kind of pleasing platitude: it seemed to soothe the moral sense of the legal community; in any event it won rapid acceptance. In a few American states, this "right or wrong" test was supplemented by another, the "irresistible impulse" or "wild beast" test. If a man, said Chief Justice John F. Dillon of Iowa in 1868, knew that his act was wrong, but "was driven to it by an uncontrollable and irresistible impulse, arising, not from natural passion, but from an insane condition of the mind," he was not to be held responsible.[48] The idea of irresistible impulse strikes the modern ear as somewhat romantic, not to say medically absurd; but the wild-beast test was broader than the M'Naghten test alone; and some of the best psychiatrists of the day believed in irresistible impulse.[49] A third rule stood all by itself in New Hampshire. This was Chief Justice Charles Doe's rule, enunciated in *State* v. *Pike* (1869). Here the test was no test at all: the question in each case was whether the criminal act was the "offspring or product of mental disease." In Doe's view, neither delusion, nor knowledge of right and wrong, as a matter of law, should be the test of mental disease. Rather, all symptoms and "all tests of mental disease" were "purely questions of fact," within the province and power of the jury, to determine and decide.[50]

Arguments over these various "tests" were really arguments

[47]*M'Naghten's Case,* 10 Cl. & F. 200 (1843).

[48]*State* v. *Felter,* 25 Iowa 67, 82 (1868).

[49]On contemporary tests of insanity see, in general, Joel P. Bishop, *Commentaries on the Criminal Law,* vol. I (6th ed., 1877), pp. 213–29.

[50]John P. Reid, *Chief Justice: The Judicial World of Charles Doe* (1967), pp. 114–21; *State* v. *Pike,* 49 N.H. 399, 442 (1869).

over the form of stereotyped instructions, to be read to the jury. What distinguished the tests was the degree of autonomy they (apparently) gave to the jury and the degree to which they deferred to the "science" of psychiatry, then in its infancy. Whether the jury listened, or cared, or understood the rather subtle differences in wording is another question. In a few great cases, the tests acted as a dark and bloody battleground for struggles between contending schools of psychiatry. Most notable was the weird trial of Charles Guiteau, who murdered President Garfield in 1881. Guiteau's behavior, before and after (and during) the trial, was bizarre, to say the least; but probably no test, however worded, could have persuaded the jury not to send to the gallows a President's killer.[51]

The debates in some ways were signs of a heightened moral sensitivity among those concerned with the criminal law—at least a horror of putting incompetents to death or locking up in prison those who knew not what they did. But psychiatry was hardly an exact science. Some of its fashionable concepts were a threat to the very foundations of criminal law. One such concept was "moral insanity"—the idea of an insanity that affected, not the reason, but the subject's emotional and moral life. This concept, carried to its ultimate logic, would have eroded the conventional basis of criminal responsibility.[52] Then as now people found it hard to accept any doctrine which seemed to give people an excuse for gross, hateful, or heinous behavior.

Criminal law was a two-edged sword. One edge was the edge that punished "crime," in its classic sense; concern for the moral quality of acts was strongest there. The other edge was the regulatory edge, and here, if anything, moral coloring faded away. The criminal law was both more and less than the moral steward of society. Small economic crimes—shooting a deer out of season—did not require a guilty and dangerous mind like murder and rape. To get a felony conviction for crimes against property, the prosecution at common law had to show a specific intent to act illegally. Injury to property was not a crime unless it was malicious; there "had to be a definite motive of hatred, revenge, or cruelty, as well as an intent to cause the injury." In the 19th century,

[51]The story of this trial has been beautifully recreated in Charles Rosenberg's *Trial of the Assassin Guiteau* (1968).
[52]See Janet A. Tighe, "Francis Wharton and the Nineteenth-Century Insanity Defense: The Origins of a Reform Tradition," 27 Am. J. Legal Hist. 223 (1983).

this requirement loosened. It was the behavior that was dangerous and had to be stamped out; the state of the actor's mind was much less relevant. In order to protect "the wealth of the country," liability was imposed for "intentional but nonmalicious injury to property."[53] Motive or attitude thus became secondary, at least for certain property offenses. In the New York penal code of 1881, the fact that a defendant "intended to restore the property stolen or embezzled, is no ground of defense, or of mitigation of punishment."[54] The code made it a crime to destroy or injure property "unlawfully or wilfully" (sec. 654).[55] Similarly, "metaphysical difficulties" about whether a corporation could form an "intent" to commit a crime were brushed aside; originally, a corporation could not be indicted at all; and as late as the 1850s scattered cases held that corporations were criminally liable only for acts or omissions that did not require a criminal "intent."[56] It was still theoretically true in 1900 that a corporation could not be convicted of rape or treason; but most cases that tried and convicted corporations arose under statutes on economic crime—creating a nuisance, charging too much interest, breaking the Sabbath, or, as in one case, "permitting gaming upon its fairgrounds."[57]

Usually, the state must prove specifically that a person is in fact guilty of an offense, or that some action taken is legally irregular; each case starts out with a presumption of innocence. But for some crimes, the presumption of innocence or regularity was turned topsy-turvy by statute. The object was to toughen the regulatory blade of the criminal law. In the New York penal code, the "insolvency of a moneyed corporation" was "deemed fraudulent" unless "its affairs appear, upon investigation, to have been administered fairly, legally, and with care and diligence" (sec. 604). In Indiana, under a law of 1891, when a bank failed or suspended within thirty days of accepting a deposit, there was a prima-facie case of "intent to defraud" the depositor.[58] There was some nononsense toughness in liquor statutes, too. Dry states outlawed

[53]Livingston Hall, "The Substantive Law of Crimes, 1887–1936," 50 Harv. L. Rev. 616, 642 (1937).

[54]N.Y. Penal Code, 1881, sec. 549.

[55]"Wilful" was a troublesome word, however, and the requirement of "wilful" violation, common in statutes, certainly meant that the defendant could not be punished for *reasonable* mistakes of law. See Hall, *op. cit.*, p. 646.

[56]Hall, *op. cit.*, p. 647.

[57]*Commonwealth* v. *Pulaski County Agricultural & Mechanical Ass'n*, 92 Ky. 197, 17 S.W. 442 (1891).

[58]See *State* v. *Beach*, 147 Ind. 74, 46 N.E. 145 (1897).

the sale of hard liquor; but it was not easy to catch violators red-handed. So, in New Hampshire it was "*prima facie* evidence" of violation of liquor laws if the defendant "exposed" any bottles with liquor labels "in the windows of, or upon the shelves within his place of business," or if his store had a "sign, placard, or other advertisement" for liquor, or if he possessed coupon receipts showing he had paid his federal tax as a dealer or wholesaler in liquor, or if a person delivered liquor "in or from any store, shop, warehouse, steamboat... or any shanty or tent... or any dwelling-house... if any part... be used as a public eating-house, grocery, or other place of common resort." In Iowa, possession of liquor, "except in a private dwelling house," created a presumption of guilt.[59]

PUNISHMENT AND CORRECTION

In the age of Judge Lynch, it might seem strange to speak of a movement to humanize punishment and make it less barbarous. But social behavior does not need to act in an even or consistent way. The barbarism of some aspects of punishment, inside and outside the system, was balanced by a strong movement to modernize and soften the treatment of criminals.

To begin with, the use of capital punishment declined in the last half of the 19th century. Wisconsin entered statehood without any death penalty at all. Michigan abolished it in 1882, except for treason; Maine eliminated the death penalty completely in 1887, and practically speaking, it was absent in Rhode Island too. Corporal punishment (whipping and flogging) survived in a few states—in Delaware for example—as a kind of abominable relic. Elsewhere, even in the South, its legitimacy was slowly sapped. Though whipping was still legal in South Carolina up to the Civil War, a "cloud of disapproval" made public whipping of whites a rare event.[60] By 1900, except for convicts, whipping was almost extinct in the South—at least as a *legitimate* punishment; it was common, however, for prisoners, especially on the chain gang.

    [59]William C. Osborn, "Liquor Statutes in the United States," 2 Harv. L. Rev. 125, 126 (1888). Stats. N.H. 1878, ch. 109, secs. 24, 25; Iowa Code 1873, sec. 1542.

    [60]Jack K. Williams, *Vogues in Villainy: Crime and Retribution in Ante-Bellum South Carolina* (1959), p. 110.

Death itself was brought somewhat up to date, when the so-called "electrical chair" appeared in New York in 1888, to replace the hangman's noose. Polite opinion, too, rejected the old notion of public executions. In California, for example, public executions were banned in the 1850s. Still, each county hung its own prisoners; crowds of visitors sometimes climbed trees and tall buildings to peek in on the show in the yard of the local jail. Finally, in 1891, county executions were banned; all executions were to be carried out within the gloomy walls of San Quentin before the warden, a doctor, the attorney general, twelve "respectable citizens," a few relatives and friends, peace officers—and nobody else.[61]

The death penalty, of course, was a rare and dreadful punishment. Basically, the most common punishments for crime were fine and imprisonment. By and large, fines were prescribed as punishment for petty offenses and economic crimes. In the justice and municipal courts, thousands of men and women paid a few dollars for the privilege of being drunk or disorderly or for violating some municipal ordinance. If they could not pay, to be sure, they went to the local jail. For more serious crimes—manslaughter, assault with a deadly weapon, burglary, rape—the basic punishment was prison. But allowable sentences, and sentencing behavior, differed drastically, without apparent rhyme or reason in the various states.

The theory of the classic penitentiary stressed solitary confinement, hard labor, strict discipline and regimentation, and total silence. These devices, acting together, were supposed to produce reformation. They did not work; in any event, the states soon gave up the idea of following this recipe strictly. The silent system was dropped in Massachusetts as early as the 1840s.[62] Meanwhile, crowding in prisons doomed solitary confinement as well. The penitentiary scheme, as originally formulated, had clearly failed.

The failures of the prison system led to a search for new plans and new theories. The old theories had tried to treat all convicts alike. The new theories tailored (or tried to tailor) punishment and correction to the individual case. The aim was to make criminal justice more precise, more effective, and more humane. There were some men (and women) who were beyond reformation; they

[61]Friedman and Percival, *The Roots of Justice*, pp. 304–6.
[62]Michael S. Hindus, *Prison and Plantation: Crime, Justice, and Authority in Massachusetts and South Carolina, 1767–1878* (1980), p. 169.

were rotten to the core. There were others who might be saved. The new techniques tried to distinguish between these two.

A key device of the new penology was probation. In 1841, a bootmaker named John Augustus began to frequent the Boston criminal courts. In August 1841, his heart was touched by the case of a "ragged and wretched looking" drunk who was, Augustus felt, "not yet past all hope of reformation." The man swore he would not touch another drop, if he could only be "saved from the House of Correction." Augustus stepped up, went bail for the man, and brought him back to court three weeks later "a sober man." The judge, impressed as always by repentance, waived imprisonment. From this point on, Augustus began to act as a private angel and guardian of men convicted of crime. He bailed almost 2,000 convicts until his death in 1859. Other Bostonians had helped him out or gave him money; some of these carried on his work after his death. In 1878, a Massachusetts statute provided for the appointment of a paid probation officer for the Boston criminal courts. A further law authorized a statewide system in 1891. Between 1897 and 1900, Missouri, Vermont, Rhode Island, and New Jersey also enacted probation laws; Illinois and Minnesota provided for juvenile probation. Probation only came into its own in the 20th century; but the seeds had been planted by 1900.[63]

Probation was an alternative to prison. Its success depended on sifting through the facts about a man or woman convicted of crime and deciding that some were sound enough human material to deserve another chance. It focused, in short, on the offender, rather than solely on the offense. Punishment fit the criminal, not only the crime. The same was true of other reforms: the suspended sentence, indeterminate sentence, and parole. These served, too, as more professionalized substitutes for that older method of grace, the governor's pardon. (The pardon, to be sure, did not by any means die out). A judge had always had power to suspend a sentence if he felt for some reason that the trial had miscarried. But could judges suspend sentences wholesale, after trials that were scrupulously fair, simply to give the defendant a second chance? The question was litigated in a New York case in 1894.[64] The defendant, John Attridge, a "clerk in a mercantile

[63]David Dressler, *Practice and Theory of Probation and Parole* (1959), pp. 13–21.
[64]*People ex rel. Forsyth* v. *Court of Sessions of Monroe County*, 141 N.Y. 288, 36 N.E. 386 (1894).

firm," had helped himself to his employer's money. He pleaded guilty at the trial. Attridge was young and well-liked; there were a number of "mitigating circumstances." "Numerous respectable citizens" of Monroe County petitioned the court for suspended sentence. Two out of three of the judges agreed to suspend; and the highest court in the state affirmed their decision, on appeal. The power to suspend sentence, said the appeal court, was "inherent" in criminal courts.[65]

Indeterminate sentence and parole were more significant, more institutionalized reforms. An American Prison Association was formed after the civil war; and the so-called "Cincinnati Declaration" came out of the first meeting of this group; it called for sentencing reform. The earliest practical applications were in New York, in the 1870s, at the Elmira "reformatory." By law, Elmira received only young offenders, between the ages of sixteen and thirty, "not known to have been previously sentenced to a State prison," in New York or elsewhere.[66] Prisoners at Elmira were given indeterminate sentences, that is, sentences of variable (and unpredictable) length. In Elmira, the prisoners were supposed to learn trades; and, of course, the prison furnished programs of religious and moral uplift. The prisoners were divided into several "classes"; those who behaved and showed progress could move into a better class; bad prisoners moved down. The best prisoners, in the highest class, were eligible for parole. A few states copied the idea; and in 1901, New York made it mandatory for first offenders.

The indeterminate sentence was based on a simple theory. No judge was wise enough to tell when a prisoner would be "cured." Prison officials, on the other hand, had the prisoner in view every day. A criminal should be locked up as long as he was "unfit to be free." He was the "arbiter of his own fate"; he carried "the key of his prison in his own pocket." The indeterminate sentence, then, emphasized the character and background of the offender. The Illinois statute, passed in 1899, directed the warden to pay attention to "early social influences" that affected the prisoner's "constitutional and acquired defects and tendencies," among other things. Moreover, the indeterminate sentence (and parole) further

---

[65]Legal doubts about the power of courts to suspend sentence continued in the early 20th century and were only laid to rest in some states by statute.
[66]Laws N.Y. 1870, ch. 427, sec. 9.

professionalized criminal justice: they shifted power to full-time workers in the criminal justice "field."[67]

Elmira was not an unqualified success by any means. Originally, it had been a maximum-security prison, surrounded by a grim high wall. Despite remodeling and good intentions, Elmira was essentially "founded on custody and security, not on rehabilitation." Within ten years, "it was just another prison." The other systems based on the Elmira plan tended to share its defects. They suffered from neglect and "legislative starvation"; the theory of the graded system won only "perfunctory obedience." One key problem was commercialization; prisons were supposed to pay their own way through prison industry; this could hardly be reconciled with schemes of reform. Moreover, the general public had little enthusiasm for prison experiments, and an inveterate capacity for grumbling about prisons as "country clubs," "military academies" or "private schools."[68] We will return to this point.

The Elmira idea had been thought especially good for young offenders. It was shocking to treat juveniles the same as adult offenders, to lock them up together in one school for vice. Legislatures came to share this view. As early as 1825, New York set up a "House of Refuge" for juveniles. A few states tried modified forms of probation for young people in trouble. A New York law of 1884 provided that when a person under sixteen was convicted of a crime, the judge might, in his discretion, put him in care of some suitable person or institution, instead of prescribing prison or fine. Laws in Massachusetts, and later in Rhode Island (1898), authorized separate trials of children's cases. Indiana, in a series of statutes beginning in 1889, established a Board of Children's Guardians for densely populated townships. The board had the right to petition the circuit court for custody and control of a child under fifteen. Custody might last until the child came of age. The board was empowered to act when it had "probable cause to believe" that the child was "abandoned, neglected or cruelly treated" at home, or had been sent out to beg on the streets, or was truant, or "in idle and vicious association," if the parents of the child were "in constant habits of drunkenness and blasphemy, or of low and

[67]Laws Ill. 1899, p. 142; Lawrence M. Friedman, "History, Social Policy, and Criminal Justice," in David J. Rothman and Stanton Wheeler, eds., *Social History and Social Policy* (1981), pp. 203, 207–9.

[68]Miriam Allen deFord, *Stone Walls* (1962), p. 85.

gross debauchery," or if the child was "known by language and life to be vicious or incorrigible."[69]

Despite these halting moves, children in every state could still be arrested, detained, tried, and sent to prison or reformatory. There were 2,029 minors in jail in Massachusetts in 1870; 231 of these were under fifteen.[70] The first true juvenile court was established in 1899 in Cook County, Illinois (Chicago). Under the governing statute, circuit-court judges of Cook County were to designate one special judge to hear all juvenile cases. He would sit in a separate courtroom, and keep separate records; his court was to be called "the juvenile court."[71] The court had jurisdiction over dependent and neglected children as well as over delinquents. In this way, the law extended its power over young people— mostly lower class—who had been beyond the reach of prior law, and who had committed no actual crimes.

The juvenile court idea, however, had enormous appeal; from its small beginnings in Cook County, Illinois, it spread so fast and so far that within twenty years or so almost every state had some version of a juvenile court. The juvenile court was an example of the new professionalism: no jury, but (ultimately) a flock of social workers and other experts. The whole baggage of rights and rules was gotten rid of; and the emphasis was on the offender, not the offense: the individual child. (Some, indeed, had committed no offense at all.) Juvenile justice was to the minor what probation was to the adult, and more so.

Juvenile court was a reform hatched by the "child-savers" of the nineteenth century. Its paternalism, middle-class bias, and absence of due process make it seem less progressive after eighty-five years than it did to the good people of its day.[72] There were real abuses from the start; and more developed. The double stan-

[69]See Laws Ind. 1891, ch. 151.

[70]Anthony Platt, *The Child Savers: the Invention of Delinquency* (1969), p. 120. On the development of separate prisons for women, see Estelle B. Freedman, *Their Sisters' Keepers: Women's Prison Reform in America, 1830–1930* (1981).

[71]Herbert H. Lou, *Juvenile Courts in the United States* (1927), pp. 19–20; Laws Ill, 1899, p. 131.

[72]On the background of the juvenile court movement, see Platt, *op. cit. supra;* David J. Rothman, *Conscience and Convenience: The Asylum and Its Alternatives in Progressive America* (1980), ch. 6; Peter D. Garlock, "'Wayward' Children and the Law, 1820–1900: The Genesis of the Status Offense Jurisdiction of the Juvenile Court," 13 Ga. L. Rev. 341 (1979); Robert M. Mennel, *Thorns and Thistles: Juvenile Delinquents in the United States, 1825–1940* (1973).

dard was in full operation; teen-age girls who were sexually active were adjudged "delinquent" by the hundreds. But the oppressers were *not* primarily the police or upper-class reformers; they were the parents of lower-class children themselves. At least this is the evidence from the early California records (1903–1910). It was the mothers and fathers—often of immigrant stock—who threw up their hands at their unruly or incorrigible children and turned them over to the state. What these parents wanted was middle-class morality. Juvenile justice gave them access to state power to curb unruly children or, if necessary, get them off their parents' backs.

The period, then, was rich in institutional experiment. There were new theories, and new applications of theory. But the landmark places, like Elmira, were not typical of the everyday world of corrections. Elmira, though a failure, at least had high aspirations. Ordinary prisons, state and local, were starved for funds, filthy, sometimes debauched. Many prison jobs were held by ward heelers, appointed to pay off political debts. With dreary regularity, commissions reported bad news about local prisons—a dark chorus of complaints. Prisoners were whipped, starved and tortured in prisons all over the country, though not in all prisons at all times. The county jails of New Jersey were described as a disgrace in 1867. Young and old, men and women were heaped together, under conditions of "dirt, vermin, offensive air and darkness." At the state prison, on the other hand, in a perversion of the penitentiary idea, the prisoner lived in a cell measuring 7 by 12 feet—with one to four cellmates; or alone in a newer cell only four feet wide and seven feet long. In this case, he lived and ate "in a room the size of a small bathroom, with a noisome bucket for a toilet and a cot narrower than a bathtub." To bathe "occasionally," there was a "bathhouse in the yard, which was closed in bad weather."[73] In Illinois, the Cook County jail, inspected in 1869, was also "filthy and full of vermin." The county jails were "moral plague spots"; they made "great criminals out of little ones."[74]

The prisons had become, in many ways, much more lax than in the first days of the penitentiary system; in the 1870s, at Sing Sing, investigators found incredible corruption: guards sold forbidden items to prisoners; convicts were allowed to lounge about idly, or play games; the prison yard "had something of the atmos-

[73]James Leiby, *Charity and Correction in New Jersey* (1967), pp. 126–28.
[74]Platt, *op. cit.*, pp. 118–19.

phere of a village." Yet at the same time, there was incredible brutality in some prisons: prisoners were whipped and beaten; or they were tortured with pulleys, iron caps or "cages," or afflicted with the lash, the paddle, or (in the Kansas prison) a fiendish form of water torture.[75]

The story was always the same. Somehow reforms never took hold, or were perverted in practice. The fact is that convicts, like paupers and blacks, were at the very bottom of American society; powerless, their wants and needs had no American priority. On the other hand, middle-class society had a definite program, even though it was not openly expressed. People detested crime, and were afraid of it. They wanted criminals punished, and severely; even more, they wanted bad people kept out of sight and circulation. Whatever people *said*, the evidence of what they did shows that the main point was to warehouse, quarantine, and guard the "criminal class"; curing them of their criminal habits was a lesser goal. People were inclined to be skeptical, moreover, about making criminals over at all. Were criminals simply born that way? Criminal anthropologists had long explored the idea that the tendency toward crime was an inherited trait, that the criminal was a definite physical or mental type. "Intellectually and morally, criminals are for the most part weak," wrote Frederick Howard Wines, in 1895. This showed itself in "inattention, lack of imagination or the power of representation, defective memory, lack of foresight, and general aversion to mental exertion." A rich literature, dating from the 18th century, taught the physical signs of criminal personality: "The prominence of the criminal ear has been especially noted. Prisoners are said to have wrinkled faces; male prisoners have often scanty beards; many hairy women are found in prison. Redhaired men and women do not seem to be given to the commission of crime.... Convicts have long arms, pigeon-breasts and stooping shoulders." Criminals, it was commonly observed, did not blush.[76]

The average person did not know these "facts"; but people had their own common sense, no doubt, to guide them. They no doubt *knew* that the criminal was another breed, and that such people had to be removed from respectable society, for the sake of public safety. In the late 19th century, too, there was new interest in the question of eugenics. Concern for purity of morals joined hands

[75]David J. Rothman, *Conscience and Convenience,* pp. 17–21.

[76]Frederick H. Wines, *Punishment and Reformation: A Study of the Penitentiary System* (2nd ed., 1910), pp. 234–35.

with concern for purity of the blood. It is probably not too far-fetched to suspect that these attitudes reinforced the central tendency of the law of corrections, which was to quarantine the bad. What went on inside prison walls hardly mattered, so long as these walls were impermeable. If most convicts were "born criminals," there was no point in letting them loose. Better to let them rot behind prison walls.[77]

Yet, paradoxically, public unconcern sometimes was its own undoing. Legislatures (responding, no doubt, to a sense of public opinion) invariably starved the prisons for funds. Jails were jampacked, sometimes far beyond their capacity. Poor conditions within the walls frustrated any hope of rehabilitating the men and women who were locked inside; in the long run, bad conditions perhaps led to still more crime, or at the least more misery and social disorder. Sometimes, too, prisons were so crowded that the state felt obliged to make wholesale use of pardon and parole. This happened in New Jersey in the late 19th century; the ordinary outflow of prisoners "did not clear the prison fast enough."[78]

That prisoners ought to do useful work was a firm tenet of two very different groups—reformers, who wanted prisoners to improve themselves, and greedy officials, who wanted to cut costs and raise prison income. Convicts were put to work on a wide range of products, including brushes, brooms, chairs, boots, and shoes. But organized labor was a sworn deadly enemy of convict labor. The prisons were hotbeds of what unions saw as unfair competition. Manufacturers whose work force earned nonconvict wages had the same economic interest, in this case, as their workers. Labor and management united to fight against the labor of convicts. They achieved a certain success. The Illinois constitution was amended in 1886 to make it "unlawful... to let by contract ... the labor of any convict." Michigan provided that "no mechanical trade shall hereafter be taught to convicts in the State prison... except the manufacture of those articles of which the chief supply for home consumption is imported from other States or countries." Some states ruled that convict-made goods had to be specially marked. A Pennsylvania statute, passed in 1883, required these goods to be branded "convict made," in "plain En-

---

[77]See Mark H. Haller, *Eugenics: Hereditarian Attitudes in American Thought* (1963); Ysabel Rennie, *The Search for Criminal Man: A Conceptual History of the Dangerous Offender* (1978).

[78]Leiby, *op. cit.*, p. 133.

glish lettering...by casting, burning, pressing or other such process," in such a way that the brand "may not be defaced"; and the brand had to be put "in all cases...upon the most conspicuous place upon such article, or the box...containing the same."[79] For political reasons, some states tried to divert prison labor into channels that did not offend major interest groups. In Minnesota, beginning in 1892, statutes directed the state prison to acquire equipment and machinery "for the manufacture of twines known as hardfiber twines." Prison-made binding twine would be sold to farmers, "in quantities necessary for their own use." In this way, prison power would help farmers fight the National Cordage Company, which farmers felt was a vicious and domineering trust. [80]

Southern prisons were particularly disgraceful; and the campaign against prison labor made less headway there. In the South, too, convicts were still hired out on the contract system. Florida statutes specifically authorized the commissioner of agriculture (with the approval of the board of commissioners of state institutions) to "enter into contracts...for the labor, maintenance and custody of...prisoners." No labor was to be done on Sunday, or "before sunrise or after sunset on any day." The contracts could provide for "surrendering the control and custody of the prisoners to the person...contracting for their labor."[81] In Georgia, under the code of 1895, a person convicted of a misdemeanor could be sentenced "to work in the chain-gang."[82] These infamous gangs worked for counties and cities, often on the public roads. The law empowered the "authorities of any county or municipal corporation" using the gang to "appoint a whipping-boss for such convicts"; the boss was not to use his whip except "in cases where it is reasonably necessary to enforce discipline or compel work or labor by the convict."[83]

Most of the convicts leased out in the South, and almost all of the prisoners on the chain-gangs, were black; and indeed, as Ed-

[79]Laws Pa. 1883, ch. 110, sec. 2. Interestingly, "goods...shipped to points outside of the State shall not be so branded."

[80]See, in general, *20th Ann. Rpt. U.S. Commr. Labor, Convict Labor* (1905).

[81]Fla. Rev. Stats. 1892, sec. 3065.

[82]Georgia Code 1895, vol III, sec. 1039. The statute did go on to recite that the gangs were not to be employed "in such mechanical pursuits as will bring the products of their labor into competition with the products of free labor."

[83]*Ibid.*, secs. 1146, 1147.

ward L. Ayers has put it, the lease system was merely "part of a continuum of forced labor in the New South," a continuum which ran from the "monopolistic company store," through sharecropping and the peonage system, all the way to the "complete subjugation of convict labor."[84] Farming out criminals was a source of revenue to the state. In some places, large lessees subleased convicts in small or large gangs. The prisons of the South were "great rolling cages that followed construction camps and railroad building, hastily built stockades deep in forest or swamp or mining fields, or windowless log forts in turpentine flats."[85] The system was highly profitable for the states. Alabama and Tennessee made over $100,000 a year from their convict-leasing system, in the late 1880s; and there were respectable profits in Georgia, Mississippi, Arkansas, North Carolina, and Kentucky. For the convicts themselves, the picture was quite different. The dry statistical evidence suggests a system of almost unbelievable brutality. The prisoners were overwhelmingly young, healthy men when they were leased out; yet in 1870, 41 percent of Alabama's 180 convicts died; in the prior two years, there had been death rates of 18 and 17 percent; the death rate in Mississippi in the 1880s was nine times as great as in the prisons of the Northern states.[86]

The Southern lease system, racist and brutal, was yet in a way only an exaggerated form of the national system of corrections. It was heartless, in essence; it was designed to make the tax burden light. But it persisted, despite countless reform plans, and countless scandals and exposes. The only protests that seemed to do any good came from organized labor. In 1883, the Tennessee Coal, Iron, and Railroad Company hired the thirteen hundred convicts of the Tennessee penitentiary. They used the convicts partly as a lever to force free workers to agree to stiff terms of employment. In 1891, free miners set the convicts loose at the Tennessee Coal Mine Company and burned down the stockades. The next year miners battled the militia in Anderson County over the issue of convict labor. The lease system was finally abolished, in Tennessee, after this period of lobbying with fire and with blood.[87] Other Southern states abandoned or modified their leas-

---

[84]Edward L. Ayers, *Vengeance and Justice: Crime and Punishment in the Nineteenth Century American South* (1984), p. 191
[85]C. Vann Woodward, *Origins of the New South, 1877–1913* (1951), p. 213.
[86]Ayers, *op. cit.*, pp. 196–97.
[87]Woodward, *op. cit.*, pp. 232 ff.

ing system in the 1890s. The new plan was to use centralized state prison farms; by 1898, though nine states still made some use of leasing, the prison farm system had made enormous headway. The chain gang survived, however; and so did brutality and abuse.[88]

[88] Ayers, *op. cit.*, pp. 221–222.

CHAPTER XI

THE LEGAL PROFESSION:
THE TRAINING AND LITERATURE OF LAW

THE RISE OF THE LAW SCHOOL

Of the lawyers practicing in the United States in 1848, the over-whelming majority had been trained in a private law office, or had educated themselves by a course of reading. This was par-ticularly true in the West. In 1858, Abraham Lincoln wrote in a letter that "the cheapest, quickest and best way" into the legal world was to "read Blackstone's *Commentaries,* Chitty's *Pleadings,* Greenleaf's *Evidence,* Story's *Equity* and Story's *Equity Pleading,* get a license, and go to the practice and still keep reading."[1] Thou-sands of the lawyers practicing in 1900 still had come from this rough school of experience. But slowly the gap between law school and clerkship was closing. Fewer would-be lawyers studied or clerked in law offices, selling their labor cheaply or giving it free in exchange for practical experience. Of the rest, some combined clerkship with halfhearted or short attendance at a law school. A growing number simply went to school.

No state made a law degree, or a college degree, absolutely necessary for admission to the bar, either in 1850 or 1900. Yet many lawyers, even in the 1850s, did go to college,[2] and more and more students who could afford it chose law school as well. Indeed, by 1900 it was quite clear that the law schools would come to dominate legal education. It was clear, too, what kind of school: a law school affiliated with a university, public or private. Only a handful of private schools were founded after 1860; one was "Col. G. N. Folk's school, at Boone, North Carolina," established in

[1]Quoted in Jack Nortrup, "The Education of a Western Lawyer," 12 Am. J. Legal Hist. 294 (1968).

[2]Even Western lawyers. See Nortrup, *op. cit.,* above, n.1. Nortrup's article de-scribes the education of Richard Yates, who combined law-office training with a course in the law department of Transylvania (1836).

1867, which lasted some twenty-odd years.[3] Schools of the Litch-field type were almost extinct by 1900. On the other hand, after the Civil War, more and more law schools formed some sort of tie with a college or university. More than three quarters of the schools open and running in the 1890s were of this type.

Particularly in the East, law school gave the student a prestige that law-office training could not match. In the better schools, too, the student probably learned more than he learned as a clerk, and in less time. Whatever the facts, the law schools sold them-selves, slowly but surely, to the student public, as better or more efficient, or an easier road to success. There is some evidence, too, that the rise of the law schools was linked to a social change in the character of the bar—from strongly aristocratic to middle class in family background. The old established lawyers in Phil-adelphia had blocked the formation of a law department at the University of Pennsylvania in the 1830s. They wished, apparently, to preserve their private prerogative of training the bar. The revolt came from the law students themselves, "restive in the con-finement of law offices," and eager for a "less inbred program of legal studies." In 1850, George Sharswood, in response to vocif-erous student demands, reopened the university department of law.[4]

There was another factor, too. The day of the clerk was fading. The invention of the typewriter helped spell his doom. The law office of 1900 no longer needed copyists and drones in training. It needed secretaries and typists—young women, more and more, in jobs that were sealed off permanently from the professional ladder to success. The old-style clerk was obsolete.

The rise of the law schools can be chronicled in figures. In 1850, fifteen law schools were in operation; in 1860, twenty-one; in 1870, thirty-one; 1880, fifty-one; 1890, sixty-one. In the last ten years of the century, there was an enormous leap in the num-ber of schools. By 1900, 102 were open for business. In 1850, there were one or more law schools in twelve of the states; in nineteen states there were no law schools at all. In 1900, thirty-three states had law schools; only thirteen had to import school-trained lawyers from outside.[5] These were small or sparsely pop-ulated states—like New Hampshire and Nevada—or satellite states

[3]Alfred Z. Reed, *Training for the Public Profession of the Law* (1921), p. 433.

[4]Gary B. Nash, "The Philadelphia Bench and Bar, 1800–1861," in *Comparative Studies in Society and History*, vol. VII, No. 2 (1965), pp. 203, 207–8.

[5]Reed, *op. cit.*, pp. 444, 446.

like New Jersey.[6] In the academic year 1849–1850, Harvard, the country's largest law school, had a total attendance of ninety-four. Ten years later, Harvard's enrollment had risen to 166; 180 students were enrolled at Cumberland University Law School, in Lebanon, Tennessee. In the academic year 1869–70, Michigan, the country's largest law school, had 308 students; at the close of the century, Michigan again led all other law schools, with 883 students.[7] This was probably more than the total enrollment in the country's law schools in 1850. In 1870, law schools had a total student population of 1,611; in 1894, the number had risen to 7,600.[8]

Many major universities, public and private, gathered a law school unto themselves between 1850 and 1900. The University of Michigan, a public university, established a "law department" in 1859. The regents, at the very outset, voted to spend up to $100 for advertisements about the "law department," to be placed in newspapers in Detroit, Chicago, New York, Cincinnati, St. Louis, and Washington, D.C.[9] St. Louis University, in the 1840s, was the first Roman Catholic university to establish a law school. This was a short-lived venture; but other Catholic universities later turned to the training of lawyers. Notre Dame law school was founded in 1869; and Georgetown, in 1890, was one of the four largest law schools in the country. The law department of Howard University, in Washington, D.C., was the first, most successful, and most permanent of the dozen or so black law schools. It opened in January 1869 under the leadership of John Mercer Langston.[10]

The relationship of law schools to their universities was, however, a far cry from what it became in the twentieth century. The usual law degree, the L.L.B., was certainly not a postgraduate degree. Law schools did not usually require *any* college work to get in. The more pretentious law schools tightened their entrance requirements toward the end of the century; none required a full

---

[6]In 1970, seven states—New Hampshire, Nevada, Delaware, Vermont, Rhode Island, Alaska, and Hawaii—had no law school. By 1984 the list was down to three: New Hampshire, Rhode Island and Alaska.

[7]Reed, *op. cit.*, pp. 451–52. On the University of Michigan Law School, see Elizabeth G. Brown, *Legal Education at Michigan, 1859–1959* (1959).

[8]Albert J. Harno, *Legal Education in the United States* (1953), p. 82.

[9]E. G. Brown, *Legal Education at Michigan* (1959), p. 14.

[10]Maxwell Bloomfield, *American Lawyers in a Changing Society, 1776–1876* (1976), p. 328.

college education. Many "university" law schools were rather loosely connected to their parent institutions. They were by no means an organic part of the general world of higher learning and scholarship. From 1858, until he retired in 1891, Theodore W. Dwight was the dominant figure in Columbia University's law school; he ran his own show. Under arrangements solemnized in 1864, Dwight, as "Professor of Municipal Law," collected the students' tuition (fixed at $100 a year for new students). Out of these fees, Dwight paid expenses, and gave himself a salary of $6,000 a year. Any surplus was to be split fifty-fifty between Dwight and the university.[11] When Michigan decided to pay the salaries of its faculty—$1,000 a year—out of general university funds, this was a decided novelty.[12] Other "university" law schools were private schools annexed by, swallowed by, or federated with a university, which had varying degrees of success in digesting them. There are even cases of law schools that shifted allegiance from one university to another. What is now the law school of Northwestern University began its life as a department of law of the old Chicago University; in 1873, it became the "Union College of Law," connected both with Chicago and Northwestern; in 1886, this polygamy ended when Chicago University went out of business; but the school was not formally integrated into Northwestern University until 1891.[13]

Today, law school training takes, almost universally, three years. In 1850, the standard course in many law schools ran for one year only. Later in the century, a two-year program became more popular. The three-year L.L.B. was a late innovation, which began at Harvard, during the deanship of Christopher Columbus Langdell; Boston University followed suit. Prominent judges and lawyers constituted the faculty at most law schools. Full-time teachers were rare before the 1880s. The full-time teacher, too, as we shall see, was one of Langdell's innovations. Judges and lawyers were not necessarily bad teachers. Story and Greenleaf at Harvard lectured to a student body made up mostly of college graduates; and they worked up their lectures into books that were real contri-

[11]Julius Goebel, Jr., ed., *A History of the School of Law, Columbia University* (1955), pp. 57–58.

[12]On Michigan, see Elizabeth G. Brown, "The Law School of the University of Michigan; 1859–1959," 38 Mich. St. Bar J., No. 8, p. 16 (1959).

[13]James A. Rahl and Kurt Schwerin, "Northwestern University School of Law: A Short History," 55 Northwestern U. L. Rev. 131 (1960); Reed, *op. cit.*, p. 185.

butions to American legal literature. Other law schools, too, offered fairly rigorous training before the Civil War.[14]

Yet Harvard, the standard-bearer, seemed to regress toward the mean. The number of law students who were college graduates declined at Harvard after 1845. The school entered what seemed to be a period of stagnation.

> Everything about the School was stereotyped. For twenty years the language of the Catalogue as to entrance, course of study, and degree was not changed by a letter. There was no recorded faculty meeting during the entire period.... Library rules were made in theory by the Corporation, in practice by the janitor....[15]

During Harvard's dark age, which lasted until 1870, the lecture was not the prevailing method of instruction; rather the "textbook method" was used:

> from recitation period to recitation period, the students are assigned a specified portion of a regulation text-book to study, and for the most part to memorize; this is then explained by the teacher and recited on at the next period.

Part of the hour was taken up by "quizzing." This was the "more or less purely mechanical testing of the knowledge learned by the students."[16]

Neither the textbook nor the lecture method was an unmitigated evil; much depended, of course, on the man in front of the class. By all accounts, Theodore W. Dwight of Columbia was a

[14]In the late 1840s, the University of North Carolina established a professorship of law, under the direction of a high court judge, William Horn Battle. According to the university catalogue, the "department for the study of municipal law" was divided into two "classes." One, "the Independent Class," consisted of "such Students of Law as have no connection with any of the College Classes"; the "College Class" consisted of "such irregular members of College as, with the permission of the Faculty, may be desirous of joining it." The Independent Class was a two-year program, with "recitations three times a week"; the "College Class" recited once a week, and its recitations were "so arranged as not to interfere with the ordinary studies of College." The College Class took two and a half years to earn its L.L.B. "The Professor of Law and the members of the Independent Class" were not "subject to any of the ordinary College regulations." This system lasted until 1868, when the whole university closed its doors during Reconstruction. Albert Coates, "The Story of the Law School at the University of North Carolina," N. Car. L. Rev., Special Issue, Oct. 1968, pp. 1, 13, 14.

[15]Centennial History of the Harvard Law School, 1817–1917 (1918), pp. 22–23.

[16]Josef Redlich, The Common Law and the Case Method in American University Law Schools (1914), pp. 7–8.

brilliant teacher; observers such as Lord Bryce and Albert Dicey thought his school the very best imaginable. Richmond M. Pearson of North Carolina, a judge and then chief justice of the North Carolina high court, ran a private law school which lasted into the 1870s; Pearson "adopted the methods of Socrates, Plato and Aristotle"; students read their books, then came to his office twice a week, where he "would examine them upon what they read by asking them questions." Pearson also lectured, after coming in from a "walk around the hillside," chewing "a little twig from some favorite tree." At least one student thought he was "the greatest teacher that ever lived on the earth."[17]

Students' nostalgia tends toward the romantic; it is not the most trustworthy guide. In every law school, teaching was dogmatic and uncritical, except from the standpoint of the law's internal logic; in most law schools, teaching was dogmatic from any standpoint whatsoever. Law training did not convey much of a sense of connection between law and life; it did not even convey the flavor of common-law evolution. No doubt there were brilliant lectures; but there was a fundamental hollowness underneath. The methods used suited the basic aim of the schools: to equip young lawyers with rote learning, presumably of a practical nature, as quickly and efficiently as possible.

At one time, the Blackstone model had been strong in legal education—the idea of a liberal education in government, politics, ethics, and law. This tradition never completely died. In Dwight's Columbia, Francis Lieber gave lectures "upon the State, embracing the origin, development, objects and history of Political Society, on the Laws and usages of War, on the history of Political Literature, on Political Ethics, on Punishments, including Statistics, etc." As part of the curriculum, Professor Charles Nairne delivered a "course of lectures on the Ethics of Jurisprudence." Lieber attracted only a few students; nonetheless, Dwight became jealous and hostile. Lieber handed in his resignation shortly before he died, in 1872. His successor was John W. Burgess. Burgess, too, eventually left the law school; he then founded, at Columbia, a "School designed to prepare young men for the duties of Public Life," to be "entitled a School of Political Science."[18] The new field enriched the social study of man and ultimately returned to enrich the study of law. But its first effect was to impoverish legal edu-

---

[17]Quoted in Coates, *op. cit.,* pp. 9–10.
[18]Goebel, *op. cit.,* pp. 60, 89.

cation, from which it had been exiled, and which was already thin and ailing in its prison of concepts.

The stage was ripe for reform or revolution. The first shot was fired in 1870. Charles W. Eliot had become president of Harvard the year before. He appointed Christopher Columbus Langdell a professor in the law school; and in September 1870, Langdell was made dean, a position new to the school. The duties of the dean, on paper, were not very awesome; he was to "keep the Records of the Faculty," prepare "its business," and "preside at its meetings in the absence of the President."[19] But Langdell, with Eliot's backing, turned Harvard Law School upside down. First, he made it harder for students to get in. If an applicant did not have a college degree, he had to pass an entrance test. The prospective student had to show his knowledge of Latin, translating from Virgil, or Cicero, or from Caesar; he was also tested on Blackstone's *Commentaries*. Skill in French was acceptable as a substitute for Latin.

Next Langdell made it harder for a student to get out. The L.L.B. course was raised to two years in 1871 and to three years in 1876 (though the third year did not have to be spent in residence). By 1899, the school had adopted a straight three-year requirement. The old curriculum had taken up matters subject by subject, as time allowed; it paid little attention to the relationship between courses; students entered and left according to their own rhythm. Under Langdell, the curriculum was divided into "courses," each of so many hours or units apiece. Courses were arranged in a definite order; some were treated as basic, some as advanced. In 1872, Langdell instituted final examinations. The student had to pass his first-year exams before he went on to the second-year courses.

Langdell also introduced the case method of teaching law. This was his most far-reaching reform, the one for which he is most remembered. Langdell cast the textbooks out of the temple, and brought in casebooks instead. The casebooks were collections of actual case reports, carefully selected and arranged to show the principles of law, what they meant, how they developed. At Langdell's Harvard, the classroom tone was profoundly altered. There

[19]Quoted in Arthur E. Sutherland, *The Law at Harvard: A History of Ideas and Men, 1817–1967* (1967), p. 166. There is a large literature on the Langdell revolution. In addition to Sutherland, see especially Robert Stevens, *Law School: Legal Education in America from the 1830s to the 1980s* (1984); and Thomas C. Grey, "Langdell's Orthodoxy," 45 U. Pitt. L. Rev. 1 (1983).

was no lecturer up front, expounding "the law" from received texts. Now the teacher was a Socratic guide, leading the student to understand the concepts and principles hidden as essences inside the cases.[20] The teacher showed how these concepts unfolded, like a rose from its bud, through study of a series of "correct" cases over time.

There was a theory behind Langdell's method. He believed that law was a "science"; it had to be studied scientifically, that is, inductively through primary sources. These sources were the printed cases; they expressed, in manifold dress, the few, everevolving and fructifying principles which constituted the genius of the common law. Law, Langdell wrote,

> considered as a science, consists of certain principles or doctrines. To have such a mastery of these as to be able to apply them with constant facility and certainty to the ever-tangled skein of human affairs, is what constitutes a true lawyer; and hence to acquire that mastery should be the business of every earnest student of law. Each of these doctrines has arrived at its present state by slow degrees; in other words, it is a growth, extending in many cases through centuries. This growth is to be traced in the main through a series of cases; and much the shortest and best, if not the only way of mastering the doctrine effectually is by studying the cases in which it is embodied. But the cases which are useful and necessary for this purpose at the present day bear an exceedingly small proportion to all that have been reported. The vast majority are useless, and worse than useless, for any purpose of systematic study. Moreover the number of fundamental legal doctrines is much less than is commonly supposed; the many different guises in which the same doctrine is constantly making its appearance, and the great extent to which legal treatises are a repetition of each other, being the cause of much misapprehension. If these doctrines could be so classified and arranged that each should be found in its proper place, and nowhere else, they would cease to be formidable from their number. It seemed to me, therefore, to be possible to take such a branch of the law as Contracts, for example, and, without exceeding comparatively moderate limits, to select, classify, and arrange all the cases which had contributed in any important degree to the growth, development, or estab-

[20]Langdell was not the first to teach through cases. John Norton Pomeroy used a case method at New York University Law School, in the 1860s. But Pomeroy did not "shape the whole program of a leading school" with this technique. J. Willard Hurst, *The Growth of American Law* (1950), p. 261.

lishment of any of its essential doctrines; and that such a work could not fail to be of material service to all who desire to study that branch of law systematically and in its original sources.

These words appeared in the preface to Langdell's first casebook, on *Contracts,* which came out in 1871. Unlike 20th-century casebooks, it was totally bare of aids to the student—notes, comments, explanations. It consisted exclusively of the cases Langdell had culled from the mass. Most of these were English cases; a smaller number were American, chiefly from Massachusetts and New York. The West and the South, it seemed, had added nothing to the law. The material was arranged by topics; within topics, cases were in chronological order, showing the evolution of principles from darkness to light. Practically speaking, no statute was permitted to enter the harem of common law, not even the Statute of Frauds, which was so old and barnacled with doctrine that it was almost not a statute at all.

Langdell claimed an interest in the growth or evolution of law; but new-fangled reforms, which were not the work of judges, did not concern him in the least. In his *Summary of Equity Pleading* (1877), he asked the reader to "bear in mind that it is the object of these sheets to aid the student in acquiring a knowledge of the equity system as such; and with this view the writer confines himself to the system as it existed in England from the earliest times to the end of Lord Eldon's chancellorship." At least one reviewer wondered why "the study of equity pleading at Harvard University in 1877 should be limited to the system as it existed prior to 1827."[21] But from the strict Langdell standpoint, these recent changes—many of them statutory—were not part of the science of law. Even constitutional law was debauched by enactment; it was therefore an excrescence. The three-year curriculum, starting in 1876–77, did not include constitutional law at all, not even as an elective.[22] Harvard soon drew back from this extreme position, and constitutional law was let back in; but even this brief exclusion shows how far Langdell was willing to carry his logic. Besides, he needed every scrap of time. The dialogues in Langdell's classes went slowly, and covered very little ground, compared to the lecture method.

---

[21]3 So. Law Rev. (N.S.) 316, 317 (1877).
[22]Charles Warren, *History of the Harvard Law School,* Vol. II (1908), pp. 405–6.

The Langdell plan burst like a bombshell in the world of legal education. "To most of the students, as well as to Langdell's colleagues, it was abomination."[23] The students were bewildered; they cut Langdell's classes in droves; only a few remained to hear him out. Before the end of the first term, his course, it was said, had dwindled to "seven devoted men...who went by the name of 'Kit's Freshmen' or 'Langdell's Freshmen.'"[24] Enrollment at Harvard fell precipitously. Langdell's colleagues, who included the remarkable Emory Washburn, continued to teach the old way. The Boston University Law School was founded in 1872 as an alternative to Harvard's insanity. But Langdell persisted, and Eliot backed him up. The few students who stayed to listen found the method exciting. Among the faithful of "Kit's Freshmen" was a young man named James Barr Ames. Soon after graduation, Ames was taken onto the Harvard faculty. Here was another insult to pedagogical tradition. Young Ames was scholarly and intelligent, but he had never been forged in the fire of practical experience. He had never risen to high station at the bar or on the bench. No matter: to teach a science, scientists were needed, not practitioners of law.

This hiring practice was a radical break with the past; it evoked strong opposition. Ephraim Gurney, dean of the faculty of Harvard College, was one of many who were dismayed. Langdell, he wrote to President Eliot in 1883, had given him insomnia. At night he found his mind "revolving about the Law School problem." The occasion was a proposal to appoint William A. Keener to the faculty. Keener was young, a rather recent graduate, and had always had a marked academic bent. The appointment meant, Gurney thought, that the "School commits itself to the theory of breeding within itself its Corps of instructors and thus severs itself from the great current of legal life which flows through the courts and the bar." Langdell's idea seemed to be to "breed professors of Law not practitioners"; his school would divorce the study of law from "its actual administration." Both Langdell and Ames, Gurney felt, were "contemptuous" of judges, because judges did not treat "this or that question as a philosophical professor, building up a coherent system as they would have done." Langdell had an "extreme unwillingness to have anything furnished by the School

---

[23]*Centennial History of the Harvard Law School*, p. 35.
[24]Charles Warren, *op. cit.*, vol. II, p. 373.

except the pure science of the law." Students at the end of three years, Gurney thought, would enter a law office feeling "helpless," at least "on the practical side."[25]

Eliot never answered this letter; Keener got his appointment; Langdell and his followers stayed in command. Langdell must have been a charismatic teacher: that was one advantage. At any rate, he carried the day. The casebooks got written; the students trickled back to Harvard and back to class; the method spread to other schools. At first it was Langdell's disciples who carried the message to the Gentiles. James Bradley Thayer and John Chipman Gray, inside Harvard's own walls, were converted to the cause. John H. Wigmore took the case method to Northwestern; Eugene Wambaugh, to the State University of Iowa; William Keener stormed the citadel at Columbia, and carried that prize from the aging Dwight, who resigned in 1891.[26] In 1892, the law school of Western Reserve was founded, to be governed by the Harvard faith. The dean of the University of Cincinnati law school—a judge named William Howard Taft, of whom more would be heard—reported in 1896 that his "Faculty [had] decided that its wisest course would be to follow...the course and methods of study prevailing at the Harvard Law School," especially "the Case System." Cincinnati would use the "same books of select cases" that Harvard used for contracts, property, torts.[27] The new law school of the University of Chicago sent to Harvard for a dean, to get them properly started; in 1902, Joseph Beale arrived on the Midway, to organize a school governed by the "ideals and methods" of Harvard.[28] By the early 20th century, the success of the method seemed assured. In 1902, Professor Ernest Huffcutt of Cornell reported to the American Bar Association that twelve law schools had adopted the method root and branch; thirty-four others "unequivocally" clung to the "text-book system or the text-

[25]Quoted in Sutherland, op. cit., pp. 187–90.

[26]Centennial History of the Harvard Law School, p. 36; on the spread of the Harvard method, see Stevens, op. cit., pp. 60–64.

[27]Quoted in Warren, op. cit., Vol II, p. 509.

[28]Frank L. Ellsworth, Law on the Midway: The Founding of the University of Chicago Law School (1977), pp. 61ff; this represented a defeat for those forces led by Ernst Freund, who had been interested in infusing law training at Chicago with study of administrative law as well as traditional subjects. See also William C. Chase, The American Law School and the Rise of Administrative Government (1982), pp. 46–59. On the struggle over the introduction of the case method at Wisconsin, see William R. Johnson, Schooled Lawyers: A Study in the Clash of Professional Cultures (1978), ch. V.

book and lecture system"; forty-eight schools professed some sort of mixture.[29] Every major and most minor law schools ultimately swung over.

Like most revolutions, Langdell's was not an unmixed blessing. There were worms in the apple. Gurney's opinion was not unique; other lawyers and teachers thought the method too theoretical, unsuited for making sound lawyers. In actual practice and in the hands of good teachers, the method worked fairly well. It did imbue students with a craftsmanlike skill in handling materials of case law. But the vices of the method lay deep. In the most radical sense, the new method severed the cords, already tenuous, that tied legal study to American scholarship, and American life. Langdell purged from the curriculum whatever touched directly on economic and political questions, whatever was argued, voted on, fought over. He brought into the classroom a worship of common law and of the best and the brightest among common-law judges. He ignored legislation; he despised decisions that were illogical. He cloaked his views with a mantle of science. He equated law absolutely with judges' law; and judges' law, to Langdell, was formal, narrow, abstract. The textbook method had been bad enough. It too was divorced from living law, and apathetic toward issues of social policy. Langdell did not correct these evils. Instead, he purified and perpetuated them. Though many old textbook-and-lecture teachers probably had trouble retooling, others may have simply adapted old materials to new methods. After Langdell, they used the cases that lurked in the footnotes of their texts, ignoring the texts themselves.

Langdell's proudest boast was that law was a science, and that his method was highly scientific. But his model of science was not experimental, or experiential; his model was Euclid's geometry, not physics or biology. Langdell considered law a pure, independent science; it was, he conceded, empirical; but the only data he allowed were reported cases. If law is at all the product of society, then Langdell's science of law was a geology without rocks, an astronomy without stars. Lawyers and judges raised on the method, if they took their training at all seriously, came to speak of law mainly in terms of a dry, arid logic, divorced from society and life. To understand Langdell's method and, more important, to understand why it triumphed, one must see it in long-term con-

[29]Ernest W. Huffcutt, "A Decade of Progress in Legal Education," *Report, 25th Ann. Meeting ABA* (1902), pp. 529, 541.

text. In the history of legal education, two paired sets of principles were constantly in battle. A principle of vocational training struggled against a principle of scientific training. At the same time, a principle of integration with general liberal education struggled against a principle of segregation. University law schools had been weakly integrationist, and weakly and reluctantly vocational. Langdell's new method was antivocational, but strongly segregationist within the university and in the context of scholarship.

Why was Langdell's method so attractive in the long run? In some way, it suited the needs of the legal profession. It exalted the prestige of law and legal learning; at the same time it affirmed that legal science stood on its own two feet. It was an independent entity, a separate science; it was distinct from politics, legislation, and the opinions of the layman. This was a period in which interest and occupational groups fought for their places in the sun. Langdell dished up a theory that buttressed some of the legal profession's claims. Law, he insisted, was a branch of higher learning, and it called for rigorous formal training. There was good reason, then, why only trained lawyers should practice law. They deserved their monopoly of practice. The bar-association movement began at roughly the same point in time. Langdell's new method and the bar-association movement went hand in glove.

Langdell's method also promised to solve the problem of teaching law in a federal union. He handled local diversity by ignoring it entirely. There was only one common law; Langdell was its prophet. More than half of the cases in his first casebook were English. Oceans could not sever the unity of common law; it was one and indivisible, like higher mathematics.

In this regard, Langdell's method was by no means novel. The ideal had always been "national" law schools. There was a good deal of traffic across state lines; even vocational Litchfield had attracted students from all over the country. Harvard prided itself on its national scope; it even advertised in far-off places. A notice in the *St. Louis Republican,* for example, in 1848, invited law students to Harvard; the advertisement mentioned the tuition fees ($50 a term, including books), and added that "neither expediency nor the usages of society" required a large "amount of pocket-money."[30] When Michigan opened its school, too, as we have seen, it advertised in a number of cities.

A varied student body was probably a real advantage to a school.

[30]*St. Louis Republican,* Oct. 7, 1848, p. 3.

Moreover, even local boys did not always stay put. Some lawyers were rolling stones like the rest of the population. A Bostonian might go to Harvard and end up in Ohio or California. But ignoring local law was a mixed blessing at best. The unity of some parts of the common law was a fact. Langdell's abstractions, however, ignored the nature of law as a living system, rooted in time, place and circumstance. To be sure, few schools that taught local law taught it as anything better than tricks of the lawyer's trade, nuts and bolts of practical information. In one sense, Langdell's method—austere, abstract—was necessary to save legal education from degeneration. Two contradictory influences pressed against legal education. There was a constant push toward raising standards. But there was an insistent push in the opposite direction, too—toward loosening the reins, toward opening the practice to more and more people. The first pressure came from leaders of the bar, worried about income and prestige. The second pressure came from the open market.

The upper levels of the bar were of course alarmed by lax standards, by the pressures of the market. A law school required little capital to open. As demand rose, so did supply. Purists may have been shocked when the so-called Iowa Law School, in 1866, had the presumption to award twelve L.L.B. degrees. This was a mere night school, started the year before at Des Moines, by two justices of the Iowa supreme court.[31] The idea of a nighttime law school was appalling to some, but appealing to customers. Many potential students worked for a living by day, as clerks in law offices, or in factories, offices, and shops. The Columbian College of Washington, D.C., was in operation in the late 1860s. The college was deliberately set up to "reach employees in the government departments, released from their labors at three o'clock in the afternoon."[32] The movement spread to other cities. The University of Minnesota, in 1888, offered parallel day and evening sessions. In 1889–90, there were nine pure night schools, as against fifty-one day schools. In the 1890s the number of night schools doubled. In 1900 there were twenty, as against 77 pure day schools, and five schools which, like Minnesota, mixed day and night.[33]

The night schools, by and large, were rigorously "practical."

[31]Reed, *op. cit.,* pp. 396–97.
[32]Reed, *op. cit.,* p. 396; Stevens, *op. cit.,* p. 74.
[33]There was also the opportunity to study law by mail. The Sprague Correspondence School of Law, in Detroit, claimed 1,472 students in 1893. 1 Law Student's Helper 143 (1893).

They had neither the patience nor the inclination to serve a rich intellectual feast. They emphasized local practice far more than the national day schools. Their main vice was to encourage the downward mobility of legal education. Their main merit was to open the door of legal training to poor, immigrant, or working-class students. They were breeding grounds for the ethnic bar. Night schools turned out Polish, Italian, Jewish, and Irish lawyers, many of whom went back to their neighborhoods and worked with their immigrant communities. Lower-court judges and local politicians were drawn heavily from the graduates of these schools. Few found their way to Wall Street or La Salle Street. Naturally enough, these schools were resented on Wall Street and La Salle Street. For their part, these schools fought valiantly for students, money, legitimacy, recognition from the bar, and other prizes.

One such prize was the so-called diploma privilege. If a school had the diploma privilege, its graduates were automatically admitted to the bar, without any further exam. Between 1855 and 1870, Louisiana, Mississippi, Georgia, New York, Tennessee, Michigan, and Wisconsin gave the privilege to graduates of home-state law schools. In 1870, Oregon, which had no law school of its own, went so far as to give the privilege to graduates of *any* school that had this boon at home.[34] The trouble with the privilege was that it was politically difficult to discriminate between law schools in a single state; yet arguably some schools did not deserve this recognition.

The bar examination was one way to dam the infernal flow into the profession. As apprenticeship declined, and law schools became more important, supply could be controlled, in theory, by controlling the schools. Bar associations indeed began taking an interest in legal education. The schools themselves formed a trade group, the Association of American Law Schools, around the turn of the century. Both AALS and the American Bar Association went into the accreditation business. A school that lacked the approval of either or both was at a serious disadvantage in competing for students. But the standards set were a kind of lowest common denominator. Substandard legal education did not die; like stale bread or used cars, there was demand for it, and it prevailed despite attempts to drive it off the market.

---

[34] On the diploma privilege, see Reed, *op. cit.*, pp. 248–53.

THE LITERATURE OF THE LAW

By all counts, the basic literature of law, the most prolific, though hardly most artistic form, was reported case law. Hundreds of volumes of reports were in print. Year by year, month by month, day by day, more reports appeared. This fabulous collection of law was so bulky by 1900 that the Babylonian Talmud or the medieval Year Books seemed inconsequentially small by comparison. One could not, to be sure, get a complete or balanced picture of American life from their collective pages; but they touched on an amazing variety of topics. Every state published reports for at least its highest court; many states, like New York and Illinois, published reports of intermediate courts; in Pennsylvania, some county courts were also published. Every new state after 1850, out of a sense of legal independence, or merely out of habit, began to issue reports promptly after statehood. In most instances, territorial reports had also been published.

Under the California constitution, it was the duty of the state supreme court to put its decisions "in writing" and to state "the grounds of the decision."[35] There was no need for such a mandate in most states. As a matter of course, each state high court published decisions and opinions. There were many complaints in the 19th century that the case law was impossible to handle, that the volume was out of control. "What Shall be Done with the Reports?" was the title of a plaintive essay published in 1882. The author, J. L. High, was troubled by the "pernicious" effects of the "vast accumulation of reported cases." It weakened the law; the lawyer, groping his way through this "labyrinth," was bound to neglect the "underlying principle" of law, "in the search for a precedent exactly in point."[36] Alas, no reform was forthcoming. Indeed, these moans and groans now seem as naïve as complaints that twenty miles an hour was too fast for the human body to bear. Each generation taught the older one a lesson in sheer voluminousness. In 1810, there were only eighteen published volumes of American reports; in 1848, about eight hundred; by 1885, about 3,798; by 1910, over 8,000.[37] The end is by no means in

[35]Cal. Const. 1879, art. VI, sec. 4.

[36]J. L. High, "What Shall be Done with the Reports?" 16 Am. L. Rev. 429, 439 (1822).

[37]Charles Warren, *A History of the American Bar* (1911), p. 557.

sight. The National Reporter System, which began in 1879, and the digests of the West Publishing Company, helped lawyers cope a little. Even so, lawyers could hardly keep up with their own jurisdictions, let alone handle the others. Lawyers simply gave up any attempt to grasp the whole of the law or stay abreast of it. They concentrated on problems at hand, on the corners of law they dealt with day by day; and they grumbled about the expense and the confusion of law reports. Yet basically it was the lawyers' own hunger for precedent, for case law, that kept the system going as it was.

State and federal reports are important historical documents. In some ways, however, they are as hard to read as hieroglyphics. The language is stilted and formal. The "facts" are what a lower court "found," not necessarily what happened. Only the *legally* relevant is systematically reported. Even as law, reports are a strange and unreliable guide. Most cases were unimportant or ephemeral. Unfortunately, cases did not come neatly labeled wheat or chaff. The trouble with the common law was not only the *number* of cases, but the fact that books could never be safely thrown away.

The quality of writing in these cases seems to have declined after 1850, though these matters of taste are notoriously hard to measure. Karl Llewellyn called the style of Gibson, Marshall, and Shaw the "grand style"—the style that looked for "wisdom-in-result." It was based on broad principle, sweeping, magisterial, creative. This style was all but dead by 1900. It was replaced by what Llewellyn called the "formal style," which stressed order and logic in the law.[38] The style of the period was bombastic and repetitious: many case reports were filled with strings of useless citations; barren logic and bad English abounded. Llewellyn's impressions may indeed have a certain basis in fact. As the Marshalls, Shaws, and Gibsons died, or retired, comparable men did not replace them. Few high court or federal judges wrote opinions with power and persuasion. The picture was never completely dark, the work never completely drab. From 1882 on, a master stylist, Oliver Wendell Holmes, Jr., sat on the highest court of

[38]Karl N. Llewellyn, "Remarks on the Theory of Appellate Decision and the Rules or Canons about How Statutes are to be Construed," 3 Vanderbilt L. Rev. 395, 396 (1950); *The Common Law Tradition: Deciding Appeals* (1960), pp. 35–39. For Llewellyn, period-style was "a way of thought and work, not...a way of writing." But his analysis indeed fits writing style rather better in fact than it fits thought and work.

Massachusetts. But the work of the average judge in 1870 or 1900 *seems* plainly weaker than the average work of 1830.

Talent and style are not historical accidents. There were social reasons why the art declined. Judges were rushed, dockets were crowded; there was less time to polish and rework the opinions. The leisurely style of oral argument led to a leisurely style of writing opinions. All that had ended. Marshall's court had perhaps more time to ponder, to compose, to discuss, to polish its work than Fuller's. Judges in a hurry were tempted to dish up, as the opinion of the court, a scissors and paste job taken mostly from the winning lawyer's brief. The facts of judicial life may have doomed the heady sense of creativity of earlier days, the ability to work with broad, sweeping principle.

And perhaps the judges were not the men they used to be. The judges represented—or overrepresented—old-American, conservative values. Yet, on the whole, judges of 1900 were much less likely than judges of 1800 to be men of high general culture, less likely to have esthetic command of the English language. Local politicians were not apt to make great stylists on the bench. Besides, the theory of judicial decision-making had subtly altered. Formality was not only form, it was also a concept. Judges were not builders of law now, but often mere protectors of law as it was; that, at least, was the mask or disguise. Judges assuredly wielded power, sometimes great power; but they hid the power of the bench in a briar patch of legalism; they concealed their thought processes in jargon. This had two definite advantages. First, it provided a screen of legitimacy against attack from left and right. The *judges* were not responsible for unpopular decisions—it was the law and only the law that determined results.[39] The long list of cited cases—"precedents" strung out row after row in the judge's written opinion—drove this position home. Second, formalism reinforced the judges' claim of sole and ex-

[39]See, further, on this point, Morton J. Horwitz, "The Rise of Legal Formalism," 19 Am. J. Legal Hist. 251 (1975); Duncan Kennedy, "Form and Substance in Private Law Adjudication," 89 Harv. L. Rev. 1685 (1976). "Formalism" is hard to measure; and there is always a nagging doubt whether or not this is a useful way to characterize the work of the judges. Harry N. Scheiber has argued forcefully that "instrumentalism" survived and flourished in the late 19th century, despite the supposed triumph of "formalism." "Instrumentalism and Property Rights: A Reconsideration of American 'Styles of Judicial Reasoning' in the 19th Century," 1975 Wis. L. Rev. 1; see also Walter F. Pratt, "Rhetorical Styles on the Fuller Court," 24 Am. J. Legal Hist. 189 (1980).

clusive right to expound the law. The law, as he wrote it, looked technical, erudite. Everyman or everywoman could not be a lawyer or judge; they were ignorant of legal science. Langdell's theory made the same point, and was therefore most welcome to the judges.

Langdell drove the textbooks and treatises out of the temple of legal education. They lost face, but not importance. As the population of cases exploded, treatises were needed more desperately than ever. No single writer dared to restate all of American law any more. But texts and treatises of all types poured off the presses, on specific subjects, to turn a profit and help lawyers in their work. It has been estimated (perhaps conservatively) that a thousand treatises or so were published in the last half of the 19th century. Overwhelmingly now, these were American treatises, rather than American editions of British books. Blackstone by now was hopelessly out of date. There were new old favorites now—Simon Greenleaf's *Evidence*, Theophilus Parsons's *Contracts*, for example. Parsons (1797–1882) first published his treatise in 1853; supposedly, it sold more copies than any other American treatise. One admirer spoke of Parsons's "pleasing" style, his "sugar coated pills of legal lore," so easily "swallowed and assimilated."[40] When a work was popular, as Parsons's was, it was repeatedly revised, even after the author died or withdrew from the stage. Publishers hired other men to carry on under the valuable name. Samuel Williston edited the eighth edition of Parsons's *Contracts* in 1893; Oliver Wendell Holmes, Jr., edited the 12th edition of Kent's *Commentaries* in 1873.[41]

Most 19th-century treatises were barren enough reading when they first appeared, and would be sheer torture for the reader today. Charles Warren listed some thirty-seven works, written between 1870 and 1900, which he considered of prime importance.[42] The list shows mainly that there was a market for lawbooks, and writers who were willing and able to meet the profession's demands. The books were practical books on practical subjects. The busy lawyer had a voracious appetite for helpful texts which wove the authorities into neat, indexed packages. Many treatises dealt with strictly American developments in new and emerging fields

[40]Charles Warren, *History of the Harvard Law School*, vol. II, p. 312.
[41]Mark DeWolfe Howe, *Justice Oliver Wendell Holmes: The Proving Years, 1870–1882* (1963), pp. 10–17.
[42]Charles Warren, *A History of the American Bar* (1912) pp. 551–62.

of law: railroads, business corporations, and torts. John Forrest Dillon's *Law of Municipal Corporations*, first published in 1872, was a pioneering book, written over a period of nine years, in moments snatched in the "interstices" of this judge's busy life. The book was needed; it was an immediate success. Victor Morawetz threw himself into the work of writing a treatise on corporations. It appeared in 1882, and made his reputation; later he earned a fortune at the bar. John Chipman Gray (1839–1915), on the other hand, a distinguished Boston lawyer, one of the founders of the firm of Ropes and Gray, professor of law at Harvard, dipped into the older cellars of the common law and exhausted the subject of *The Rule Against Perpetuities* (1886) in a dark and dreary book which (according to tradition) no one has ever really read, though countless lawyers and students have skimmed through its pages in search of light. Gray also wrote a little treatise on *Restraints on the Alienation of Property* (1883).

Not surprisingly, law professors were among the most prolific and successful writers of treatises. Emory Washburn of Harvard wrote a treatise on *Real Property* (two volumes, 1860–1862); it was a great success. Theophilus Parsons's *Contracts* was, as we noted, a huge best seller; and Parsons wrote seven other treatises. One of them reportedly brought him $40,000, an enormous fortune for the day. Christopher Tiedeman, professor at the University of Missouri, wrote another popular treatise on real property (1884). Langdell's daring practice of hiring young full-time teachers and scholars, rather than elderly judges and lawyers, created a new occupation, the legal academic; at least in theory, these men could devote most of their lives to the literature of law. Some of their creative energy, of course, went into casebooks rather than textbooks or treatises. Langdell himself wrote very little besides his casebooks. But on the whole the academics did produce a substantial body of literature.

The most famous treatises were those which treated large, basic blocks of law, such as torts or property. But there were many highly specialized books, for example, Edward Keasbey's *Law of Electric Wires in Streets and Highways,* published in 1892. It is dangerous to generalize, but the treatises after 1870 seemed somewhat drier and less imaginative than the best work of the prior generation. Late 19th-century treatises tended to be humorless, impersonal, less concerned with praise and blame than with bare exposition of law. James Schouler, himself a treatise-writer (Volume I of his *Personal Property* appeared in 1873), pleaded for more skill in synthesizing cases and other legal materials; in his view, even this talent was frequently lacking. The standard editions of texts were becoming so "honeycombed with this insect annotation that the text seems to belong to the foot-notes, not the foot-notes to the text."[43] In this kind of book, there was no place for critique or for culture.

Not much, of course, could be expected from books written strictly for the lawyer's market. But in truth not much could be expected from legal literature in general. Common-law thought, in and out of universities, was isolated and inbred. The dominant culture of legal scholarship was infected by Langdell's ideas of legal science, or converged on the same state, for similar reasons. Few text-writers indulged in social commentary, or any commentary at all. John Forrest Dillon, a man of high intelligence, explained, in the preface to the fourth edition of his treatise on local government: "No writer on our jurisprudence is authorized to speak oracularly, to excogitate a system, or to give to his views any authoritative sanction. To this rule the most eminent are no exception." Dillon saw a role for the author's "reflections, criticisms, and conclusions"; but it was a limited role, and most of his colleagues did without these "reflections, criticisms, and conclusions."[44] After 1870, the tone of John Chipman Gray was more representative of the better treatises—logical, pseudoscientific, frankly jejune. Authors tended to confine personal opinions about social worth and social impact to the preface, if anywhere. There were exceptions. Joel Bishop made mordant comments throughout his treatises. Even he was proud to assert that "nothing merely theoretical" was "admitted" into his pages. And he was convinced that the "student, the practitioner, and the judge" all needed "the same learning," and therefore the same kind of book.[45] Thomas Cogley wrote a cranky, obstreperous book on the *Law of Strikes, Lock-outs and Labor Organizations* (1894), more a tract than a treatise. But there was nothing before 1900 to match the magnificent treatise on evidence (1904–05) by John H. Wigmore, scholarly, yet critical, the product of a glowing intelligence. Gray's style led directly to Samuel Williston, whose treatise on contracts in the 1920s was, from the standpoint of legal or social thought, volume after volume of a heavy void.

---

[43]James Schouler, "Text and Citations," 22 Am. L. Rev. 66, 73 (1888).
[44]John F. Dillon, *Commentaries on the Law of Municipal Corporations* (4th ed., 1890), preface, pp. vii–viii.
[45]Joel P. Bishop, *Commentaries on the Criminal Law* (7th ed., 1882), p. xiv.

Basically, legal literature was pragmatic; the differences between the famous treatises and strictly local manuals—and even such subliminal stuff as layman's guides and the many versions of *Every Man His Own Lawyer*—was a difference not of kind but of degree. Legal literature, with some exceptions, was empty of philosophy or social science. European jurisprudence was occasionally studied; the German historical school influenced the writing of James Carter, Field's great antagonist. John Chipman Gray's early 20th-century book *The Nature and Sources of the Law* (1909), well written and well balanced, is still worth reading. A school of legal history did develop in the latter part of the 19th century. It was concerned not with the history of the legal system so much as with the history of common-law doctrine, rather narrowly defined. Hence it was mostly English legal history, and fairly ancient history at that. The essays of James Barr Ames were among the best of these works.

Oliver Wendell Holmes's exploration of origins, *The Common Law* (1881), an authentic classic, was easily the most distinguished book on law, by an American, published between 1850 and 1900.[46] "The life of the law," wrote Holmes at the beginning of this book, "has not been logic; it has been experience." This famous line, endlessly quoted, served almost as a slogan or motto for the legal realists of the 1920s and '30s. It has been an important, even revolutionary, maxim for jurisprudence and legal research. To Langdell, and his disciple Ames, conceptual clarity and logic were at the very heart of law, or at any rate at the heart of legal science. Holmes understood that aspect of their thought; he called Langdell "the greatest living legal theologian." But Holmes saw logic as an "evening dress which the newcomer puts on to make itself presentable"; the "important phenomenon is the man underneath it, not the coat."[47] Despite their difference in viewpoint, Holmes was not so distant in historical technique from Langdell's disciple Ames. The "experience" which most fascinated Holmes was a common-law experience. He was as eager as Ames to look into the Year Books; and he searched for an understanding of common-law roots among Norman and Germanic materials. At times he seemed to care more for these origins than for fulfillments of law in his own generation.

---

[46]On the genesis of this book, see Mark DeWolfe Howe, *Justice Oliver Wendell Holmes: The Proving Years, 1870–1882* (1963), pp. 135–59.

[47]Quoted in Howe, *op. cit.*, pp. 155–57.

Outside the academy, there was hardly any historical literature of law that was worthy of the name. Most "Histories of Bench and Bar"—there were scores of these—were trivial, bombastic, maddeningly repetitious. One of the best of a bad lot was John Belton O'Neall's *Biographical Sketches of the Bench and Bar of South Carolina,* a two-volume work published in 1859. The prose was execrable:

> William Henry Drayton is a name not to be forgotten while liberty is appreciated. I turn to it with the delight with which the awakened sleeper witnesses the Aurora of a bright day.[48]

Many later histories were a hodgepodge, put together from the reminiscences of aging lawyers. When the upstarts of the "flush times" grew gray and respectable, they delighted in telling tall tales of their youth. Their memory, of course, was not to be trusted. Occasionally, though, these books preserved traditions and sources that had some historical value. Court histories were only a little better; they tended to be nothing but strings of anecdotes, punctuated with cameo descriptions of judges. In this wilderness, any careful and balanced study stood out dramatically. Such a book was Judge Charles P. Daly's *History of the Court of Common Pleas* (New York), a slim but valuable work that appeared in 1855.

More lasting and important work was written by constitutional theorists. If Holmes's *Common Law* was the most important 19th-century book, from the 20th-century standpoint, Thomas M. Cooley's *Constitutional Limitations,* written in 1868, was the most important book in its own time. Its full title was: *A Treatise on the Constitutional Limitations Which Rest Upon the Legislative Power of the States of the American Union.* Benjamin Twiss has claimed that Cooley's book supplied "capitalism . . . with a legal ideology . . . almost a direct counter to the appearance a year earlier of Karl Marx's *Das Kapital.*"[49] This was certainly an exaggeration. But the sentiment is understandable. The book appeared ahead of its time, before the full flowering of the due-process clause. It anticipated these developments. Ultimately, Cooley's book ran through several editions, and some prophecies of the first edition were fulfilled by the courts in time to appear as settled law in the later ones. Cooley's

[48]Vol. I. p. 13.
[49]Benjamin R. Twiss, *Lawyers and the Constitution* (1942), p. 18.

treatise was useful; it provided a beautiful constitutional theory for those who wanted limited government, who were frightened of impulsive and radical lawmaking, who wanted no more hostile regulation of business, no laws on the side of organized labor and the mob. This, the *laissez-faire* or social Darwinist point of view, found its champion in some passages in Cooley's text. (Cooley himself was much less of a cardboard reactionary than he has been pictured.)[50] The book was solidly written, well thought out, and was the product of an inventive mind. Its actual influence is a matter of some dispute. As we have seen, conservatism won some important victories in the courts toward the end of the century. The judges in these cases often cited Cooley; he has therefore been accused of inventing a lot of (bad) constitutional law. He did supply authority and text for those who needed and wanted these. But the Supreme Court was not hypnotized by Cooley. Rather, both Cooley and the judges were hypnotized by similar ideas. One wrote a book, the others decided cases, from similar impulses. Cooley was architect, prophet, and publicist, of a stern but satisfying order, in a period when the specter of "socialism" sent waves of panic through the upper stories of society. For the solid citizen, who watched gangs of immigrants pour into the country, and who worried about the staying power of American values, the Supreme Court was a mighty shield, preventing collapse. In the next generation, Christopher Tiedeman's book, *A Treatise on the Limitations of Police Power in the United States* (1889), took a position further to the right than Cooley. Tiedeman's idea of limited government gave the courts another text to refer to; once again, then, the theorists could cite, in their next edition, the courts who cited them.[51]

[50]See Alan Jones, "Thomas M. Cooley and the Michigan Supreme Court: 1865–1885," 10 Am. J. Legal Hist. 97 (1966).

[51]John Forrest Dillon, in his treatise on local government (1872), was also responsible for a few notions which became important in conservative decision-making. See Clyde Jacobs, *Law Writers and the Courts* (1954), for a good assessment of the work and importance of Cooley, Tiedeman, and Dillon.

LEGAL PERIODICALS AND CASEBOOKS

When West began to publish the *National Reporter System*, it undercut the reason for being of many law magazines. These periodicals contained little essays and comments about the law; they also brought the profession news about recent, interesting cases. The *Albany Law Journal*, the *Central Law Journal* and the *American Law Review* of St. Louis, the *American Law Register* of Philadelphia, and the *Virginia Law Journal* of Richmond still appeared in the 1880s.[52] But their day was almost done. A few journals specialized in insurance, or patents, or corporation law. Thomas B. Paton launched a *Banking Law Journal* in New York in 1889. *Green Bag*, begun in 1889, was an uninhibited potpourri of interesting articles and comments on the law.

A more significant event was the birth of the university law review. The first issue of the *Harvard Law Review* appeared in April 15, 1887. It was (and is) edited by students at the law school; every issue contained some of their work, along with the work of professors, lawyers, and judges. The first issues included law-school news, and notes "taken by students from lectures delivered as part of the regular course of instruction in the school."[53] The *Review* proposed to appear monthly "during the academic year," at a subscription price of $2.50 a year, or $.35 per number. The *Review* did not intend "to enter into competition with established law journals," but rather to "give...some idea of what is done under the Harvard system of instruction." Yet the staff did hope that its work might "be serviceable to the profession at large."[54] Most articles discussed points of laws, doctrinally, and more or less in the Langdell mode of thought. But there were other kinds of articles as well. William H. Dunbar, in the first volume, contributed an essay on "The Anarchists' Case before the Supreme Court of the United States"; and Samuel B. Clarke produced

---

[52]For a list of periodicals, see 21 Am. L. Rev. 150 (1887). Some of the reviews did not print cases, and were more strictly scholarly, like the later university reviews. One of these was the Southern Law Review, New Series, which Seymour D. Thompson began to edit at St. Louis in 1875. Thompson discontinued case digests, and promised to present instead "the *best legal thought* in America and Europe."

[53]See, for example, 1 Harv. L. Rev. 103 (1887).

[54]1 Harv. L. Rev. 35 (1887).

"Criticisms upon Henry George, Reviewed from the Stand-point of Justice."[55]

The *Yale Law Journal* was launched four years later, in October 1891; its first article was on "Voting-Trusts," by Simeon Baldwin. Other law reviews followed—Columbia in 1900, for example. The university law review proved an apt vehicle for speculative writing on law. It was the perfect outlet for shorter works by the new class of teaching scholars. The law review could justify itself as a training device for students, and as a scholarly journal; it did not have to meet the immediate demands of the marketplace. The writing in the early reviews was not uniformly good; but some distinguished articles were published. In a few notable instances, the reviews even seemed to affect the growth and development of law. A striking example was the article by Samuel D. Warren and Louis D. Brandeis in 1890, in the *Harvard Law Review*, on "The Right to Privacy."[56] Out of a few scraps of precedent, the article invented a brand-new tort, invasion of privacy. With the curious modesty of the common lawyer, the authors disclaimed this tort as their own child. They preferred to pass it off as a foundling. It was already born, they said, citing existing principles and cases; but the courts and the public had simply not been aware of the concepts that underlay a handful of these cases. The question was "whether the existing law affords a principle which can properly be invoked to protect the privacy of the individual?" Their answer was yes. The response of courts to this suggestion was not overwhelming; but when a time rolled around which was more sympathetic to privacy issues, Warren and Brandeis's child, like Cooley's theories in *their* realm, was available for adoption and support.

One final form of legal literature should also be mentioned: the casebook. This was, of course, a by-product of Langdell's reforms; and Langdell himself published the first teaching casebook, on contracts, in 1871. His disciples and converts followed with casebooks of their own.[57] James Barr Ames edited cases on

[55] 1 Harv. L. Rev. 265, 307 (1888).

[56] 4 Harv. L. Rev. 193 (1890).

[57] Collections of cases, of course, were not entirely new. For example, Edmund Bennet and Franklin Heard published *A Selection of Leading Cases in Criminal Law* in two volumes, in 1856. In the preface they noted that the "selection of important Cases on different branches of the Law, and the elucidation and development of the principles involved in them, in the form of Notes," had become an "acceptable mode of presenting legal subjects to the Profession." Langdell's was the first collection, however, arranged systematically, in accordance with his theory of legal education.

Bills and Notes in 1881. John Chipman Gray brought out a six-volume casebook on *Property* (1888–92).[58] The early casebooks were pure and austere; there was nothing in them but cases. They were totally devoid of any commentary. Finding, pasting, and stitching cases together was not so simple as it might appear. The best casebooks required a great deal of creative imagination. But these bare, spare books carried to its extreme a most striking characteristic of the style of teaching they reflected. This was the Socratic masquerade: the art of saying everything while appearing to say nothing at all.

[58]Interestingly, Gray arranged his materials to follow the organization of Emory Washburn's textbook on property, which had been published in 1860. See Sutherland, *op. cit.*, p. 152.

CHAPTER XII

THE LEGAL PROFESSION: AT WORK

THE NIMBLE PROFESSION

In 1850 there were, according to one estimate, 21,979 lawyers in the country.[1] As we have seen, the number of lawyers grew very rapidly after the Revolution. In the last half of the century, there was even greater increase. The transformation of the American economy after the Civil War profoundly affected the demand for lawyers, and hence the supply. By 1880, there were perhaps 60,000 lawyers; by 1900, about 114,000.

The functions of the profession changed along with its numbers. The New York Code of Civil Procedure, of 1848, symbolized one kind of change. The code did not end the lawyer's monopoly of courtroom work. It did not abolish the bag of jargon and artifice that was as much a part of his equipment as the doctor's black bag with stethoscope and tools. But the code symbolized, in a way, the end of the hegemony of the courtroom. One reason why procedural codes had become necessary in the first place was because lawyers were less talented in the art of pleading, less oriented toward procedure and litigation. The codes in turn dethroned the ancient pleading arts. The slow estrangement of the lawyer from his old and natural haunt, the court, was an outstanding fact of the practice in the second half of the century. Most lawyers still went to court; but the Wall Street lawyer, who perhaps never spoke to a judge except socially, made more money and had more prestige than any courtroom lawyer could.

The change of function reflected changes in the law itself. Life and the economy were more complicated; there was more, then, to be done, in the business world especially; and the lawyers proved able to do it. There was nothing inevitable in the process. It did not happen, for example, in Japan. The legal profession might

---

[1] [John] *Livingston's Law Register* (1851), preface, p. iv.

have become smaller and narrower, restricted like the English barrister, or the brain surgeon, to a few rare, complex, and lucrative tasks. Automation and technological change posed dangers to lawyers, just as they posed dangers to other occupations. Social invention constantly threatened to displace them. It was adapt or die. For example, lawyers in the first half of the century had a good thing going in title searches and related work. After the Civil War, title companies and trust companies proved to be efficient competitors. By 1900, well-organized, efficient companies nibbled away at other staples of the practice, too: debt collection and estate work, for example.

Nevertheless the lawyers prospered. The truth was that the profession was exceedingly nimble at finding new kinds of work and new ways to do it. Its nimbleness was no doubt due to the character of the bar: open-ended, unrestricted, uninhibited, attractive to sharp, ambitious men. In so amorphous a profession, lawyers drifted in and out; many went into business or politics because they could not earn a living at their trade. Others reached out for new sorts of practice. At any rate, the profession did not shrink to (or rise to) the status of a small, exclusive elite. Even in 1860, the profession was bigger, wider, more diverse than it had been in years gone by. In 1800, lawyers in Philadelphia came "predominantly from families of wealth, status, and importance." In 1860, a much higher percentage came from the middle class— sons of shopkeepers, clerks, small businessmen.[2] In Massachusetts, too, in the period 1870–1900, there was an increase in the percentage of lawyers who were recruited from business and white-collar backgrounds, rather than professional or elite backgrounds, compared to the prewar period.[3]

The external relations of the bar were always vitally important. After 1870, there was another line of defense against competition: the lawyers' unions (never called by that name), which fought vigorously to protect the boundaries of the calling. The organized profession raised (or tried to raise) its "standards"; tried to limit entry into the field, and (above all) tried to resist conversion of the profession into a "mere" business or trade. In fact, lawyers did not incorporate and did not become fully bureaucratized. The

[2]Gary B. Nash, "The Philadelphia Bench and Bar, 1800–1861," in *Comparative Studies in Society and History*, vol. VII, no. 2 (1965), p. 203.

[3]Gerard W. Gawalt, "The Impact of Industrialization on the Legal Profession in Massachusetts, 1870–1900," in Gerard W. Gawalt, ed., *The New High Priests: Lawyers in Post-Civil War America* (1984), pp. 97, 102.

bar was able to prevent the corporate practice of law. Large private law firms were able to compete with captive legal departments and house counsel staffs of large corporations. For the time being, at least, the private lawyer kept his independent status as a middle-class craftsman and entrepreneur. The lawyer's role in American life had never been too clearly defined. The practice of law was what lawyers did. This was a truth as well as a tautology. The upper echelons of the profession never quite succeeded in closing the doors against newcomers and outsiders. They dreamt of a close-knit, guildlike bar. They longed for the honor and security of the barrister. But because it was easy to pass in and out of the profession, their dream could never be fulfilled.

The corporation lawyer, on Wall Street and its sister streets in other cities, was a dramatic new figure at the bar. But he did not chase the other kinds of lawyer out of business. He merely supplemented them; he superimposed another layer on the profession, which was already made up of many layers and strata. Before the Civil War, the most prominent, famous lawyers were lawyer-statesmen, who argued great cases before great courts, who went into politics, and, above all, were skilled in the arts of advocacy. Daniel Webster was the prototype. There was no Daniel Webster in the Gilded Age. But the orator-statesman was not quite extinct. Jeremiah Sullivan Black, one of the most colorful 19th-century lawyers, was a well-known survival.[4]

Black was born in 1810. He read law in the office of Chauncey Forward and formed his distinctive style of speech and writing from close study of Shakespeare, Milton, and the Bible. He served on the Pennsylvania supreme court in the 1850s, where his pungent prose spices the otherwise dry, brittle pages of these law reports. Later, Black served in Buchanan's cabinet, as attorney general (1857). Still later, Black got rich off the fat of California land cases, which he argued before the Supreme Court. He fought the good fight in two great cases after the Civil War, *Ex parte Milligan* and *Ex parte McCardle*.[5] He figured on the Democratic side of the Tilden-Hayes controversy, and died in 1883. Black was a fiery lawyer, and a superb orator. He could emit a flawless oral argument, for hours on end, without referring to his notes, and without misciting a single case. He was a lone wolf who never

---

[4]His biography has been written by William N. Brigance, *Jeremiah Sullivan Black* (1934).

[5]71 U.S. 2 (1866); 74 U.S. 506 (1869).

really maintained an office, never had a partner for any length of time. Nor did Black have any permanent clients; he was always hired for the one particular case. His income was said to have been enormous; the exact amounts are not known. He kept no records, and, indeed, rarely fixed a fee. Yet for one case alone, in 1879, he was paid the princely sum of $28,000.

Lawyers like Black were rare. One direct descendant was Clarence Darrow, also a loner, also a dramatic courtroom warrior, whose amazing career began toward the end of the century.[6] Other modern examples are the great civil rights lawyers, on the one hand, and, on the other, the famous tort and criminal lawyers whose clients keep changing and whose livelihood depends on publicity and word of mouth. Howe and Hummel were not entirely aberrations. It is possible to be shy and bookish and make a fortune as a tax lawyer; to be a king of torts, or a Perry Mason, one must be made of more sensational stuff. Such lawyers are not necessarily ignoble. There were great careers made on the prosecutor's side, too—one example was the New York career of William Travers Jerome (1859–1934), the enemy of Tammany Hall; and there were chances, too, for political fortune, as the career of Thomas E. Dewey would later testify. But the big money was mainly elsewhere—on Wall Street. The Wall Street lawyer has always been in one sense self-effacing. He has no hunger, or need, for publicity. What he wants is a steady and permanent group of well-paying clients.

There is no question that the rise of the Wall Street lawyer was the most important event in the life of the profession during this period. Considering its importance, this event has been surprisingly little studied. First-hand accounts are rare. We are indebted to Robert T. Swaine, the historian of the Cravath firm of New York, for a detailed account of the rise of one Wall Street office.[7] For most of the 19th century, the firm was extremely small, a two-man partnership. Members of the Seward and Blatchford families were dominant figures in the early history of the firm. The firm was originally based in Auburn, New York. When William H. Seward became a United States senator in 1849, he loosened his ties to the office. But he never gave up the business of law, even though his career led him into Lincoln's cabinet, as secretary of state. In the 1850s, the firm did a great deal of debt collection,

---

[6]Darrow's career is described in Kevin Tierney, *Darrow: A Biography* (1979).
[7]*The Cravath Firm and Its Predecessors*, vol. I (1946).

real estate, and title business; wills and trusts were drafted. Cyrus McCormick retained the firm for a patent matter in 1850. In 1854, the firm moved to New York City. It was by then already active in patent litigation. The Bank of North America and the Girard Trust Company were among its clients.

After the Civil War, the booming express companies took over as the firm's biggest clients. Corporate business expanded; patent litigation gradually slackened off. The firm added new members. In 1869, Charles M. Da Costa joined the firm. He was an expert on admiralty matters, but he soon gravitated toward work on corporate reorganization. In 1880, the firm became involved with Kuhn, Loeb & Co., and hence with corporate securities and finance. William D. Guthrie became a partner in 1883; Victor Morawetz, the author of a treatise on corporations, joined in 1887. Between 1880 and 1900, the career of the firm was intimately bound up with Wall Street finance; it drew up papers merging businesses, it advised railroads on their legal affairs, handled stockholders' suits, floated bond issues. In 1896 Morawetz withdrew, to become general counsel for the Santa Fe; Charles Steele, a partner in the '90s, went over to the house of Morgan. The junior partners and clerks still handled small litigation for big clients; and the firm still argued cases before the Supreme Court (Guthrie's role in the income-tax case has been mentioned) but the partnership had become the very model of a Wall Street firm. It was a servant and advisor to big business, an architect of financial structures; it did not feed on lawsuits, rather it avoided them.

The Cravath story, of course, is one of continuous success. It is also, of course, a survivor. Nobody chronicles extinct firms. Many firms formed, reformed, split up, and disappeared from history.[8] Yet there were others, established in this period, that have had histories as long as the Cravath firm. Where these histories have been retold, they run quite parallel to that of Cravath—for example, the story of the firm of Thomas G. Shearman and John W. Sterling, which handled many of Jay Gould's tangled affairs, and later those of William Rockefeller.[9]

There were little Wall Streets in other cities, too. Each major

---

[8]Wayne K. Hobson, "Symbol of the New Profession: Emergence of the Large Law Firm, 1870–1915," in Gawalt, ed., *The New High Priests*, pp. 3, 5.

[9]The firm has been chronicled by Walter K. Earle, *Mr. Shearman and Mr. Sterling and How They Grew* (1963).

city had a corporate bar, though none so grand as New York. Outside New York, the literature on these firms is rather slim. Emily Dodge has studied the history of a Milwaukee law firm, dating back to 1842. Before the Civil War, real-estate matters dominated the firm's business. After the war, contract and business affairs took the lead. The firm grew and slowly took on staff. The growth of this firm ran roughly parallel to the growth of the great Wall Street houses.[10] The house chronicle of O'Melveny and Meyers, a great Los Angeles firm, shows how the founding father of the firm shifted his talents to municipal bonds when the title business threatened to dry up.[11]

By and large, the leading lawyers of the big Wall Street firms were solid Republican, conservative in outlook, standard Protestant in faith, old English in heritage. But the firms were never wholly monolithic. Morawetz was a southern Democrat. Guthrie, Seward's most militant and reactionary partner, was Roman Catholic; he began his career as an office boy. Da Costa, another partner, was descended from West Indian Jews. Charles O'Conor (1804–84), a dominant figure in the New York trial bar, was born in New York, of Irish parents. There were many others at the bar of Irish descent, like Charles P. Daly (1816–99), author, lawyer, and chief judge of the New York court of common pleas.[12] Good background and cultural compatibility were, however, helpful to the rising young lawyer. Old-line lawyers were never too happy about the influx of "Celts," Jews, and other undesirables. George T. Strong, writing in his diary in 1874, hailed the idea of a test for admission at the Columbia Law School: "either a college diploma, or an *examination including Latin.* This will keep out the little scrubs (German Jew boys mostly) whom the School now promotes from the grocery-counters . . . to be 'gentlemen of the Bar.'"[13] Meritorious outsiders sometimes reached the celestial heights of Wall Street or the equivalent—Louis Dembitz Brandeis, from a Jewish family of Louisville, Kentucky, was an extremely

---

[10]Emily P. Dodge, "Evolution of a City Law Office, Part II," 1956 Wis. L. Rev. 35, 41.

[11]William W. Clary, *History of the Law Firm of O'Melveny and Myers, 1885–1965,* Vol. 1 (1966), p. 102.

[12]Harold E. Hammond, *A Commoner's Judge: The Life and Times of Charles Patrick Daly* (1954).

[13]Quoted in Henry W. Taft, *A Century and a Half at the New York Bar* (1938), p. 146.

prominent Boston lawyer in the 1890s. But such people generally succeeded by adopting, to a greater or lesser extent, the protective coloration of the dominant culture.

Women and blacks were truly outsiders. No woman practiced law before the 1870s. Mrs. Myra Bradwell, born in 1831, married a lawyer in 1852, studied law, and passed her examination. She tried to get admitted to the Illinois bar in 1869; but she was turned down. She appealed, and lost her case. The legislature relented a few years later. Mrs. Arabella Mansfield was admitted to the Iowa Bar about the time of Mrs. Bradwell's failure.[14] Clara Foltz was the first woman lawyer in California. A California statute restricted the practice of law to "any white male citizen;" Mrs. Foltz had to struggle to get the law changed, in addition to all the other obstacles in her way.[15] It is hard to understand, in this day and age, the horror and disgust evoked by these few brave, stubborn women. Naturally, women who could fight the system were rare. At the turn of the century about fifty women practiced in Massachusetts.[16] Black lawyers, too, were unknown on Wall Street, and rare everywhere. The 1870 census listed only three in Massachusetts; there were fourteen listed for North Carolina in 1890, and something slightly above two dozen in Texas in 1900.[17]

Two charges have been leveled against the Wall Street firm: that it served its rich, evil clients rather than the public; and that it perverted the legal profession, turning free, independent craftsmen into workers in factories of law. Both charges were already heard in the late 19th century and have never completely subsided. The first charge is hard to evaluate. Most lawyers always served, mainly themselves, next their clients, last of all their conception of that diffuse, nebulous thing, the public interest. No

[14]On Myra Bradwell, see 49 Albany L.J. 136 (1894); on Arabella Mansfield, 4 Am. L. Rev. 397 (1870). The resistance to women lawyers only gradually diminished and is far from extinct in the 1980s.

[15]See Mortimer D. Schwartz, Susan L. Brandt and Patience Milrod, "Clara Shortridge Foltz: Pioneer in the Law," in D. Kelly Weisberg, ed., *Women and the Law*, vol. II (1982), p. 259.

[16]Gerard W. Gawalt, "The Impact of Industrialization on the Legal Profession in Massachusetts, 1870–1900," in Gawalt, ed., *The New High Priests*, pp. 97, 104–105.

[17]Gawalt, *op. cit.*, p. 104; Frenise A. Logan, *The Negro in North Carolina, 1876–1894* (1964), p. 108; Maxwell Bloomfield, "From Deference to Confrontation: The Early Black Lawyers of Galveston, Texas, 1895–1920," in Gawalt, *op. cit.*, pp. 151, 152–53.

doubt the Wall Street lawyer sincerely felt he served God by serving Mammon and Morgan.[18] Lawyers have to make a living. They go where the money and the practice are. As for the second charge, the rise of corporation law and big law firms was bound to change the myths and the outlook of the legal profession. A lawyer in a law firm, who rarely set foot in court, who did preventive-law work with big business clients, naturally organized his work life differently from the way a courtroom virtuoso, who worked alone, organized his. To help float a bond issue worth millions, or to reorganize a railroad, lawyers needed staff, and specialists, and a certain amount of investment in legal plant.

Indeed, the growth of the large law firm—large by standards of the day, though small by our standards—was one of the most striking developments of the late 19th century. Firms of more than three partners were rare before the Civil War. By 1900, they were much more common on Wall Street and in some of the other large cities. The largest firm in 1872 had six members, and there was only one this large. The largest firm at the turn of the century had about ten members; there were about seventy firms with five or more lawyers. More than half the big firms were in New York; Chicago was a distant second. Altogether, firms of this size made up a tiny percentage of the total practice; but they had a significance and influence beyond their mere numbers.[19]

The big firms were also more highly organized than individual practice could be. Firms hired growing numbers of clerks and associates. In the 1870s, three or four law students, on the average, took up space in the firm headed by Clarence A. Seward. Besides clerks and stenographers, the firm harbored about six associates. Student lawyers came, clerked, learned, and did service, partly on their own, partly for the firm's benefit. But as late as 1879, Seward wrote that it was "not the custom of my office, nor of any other with which I am acquainted, to give any compensation to students." At the end of the century, under the new "Cravath system," all lawyers who worked in the office were paid. Beginners

---

[18]Though not without a great deal of role strain, and even self-doubt. On the way in which lawyers in the period tried to reconcile their activities with their idealized conception of the legal order, see Robert W. Gordon, "'The Ideal and the Actual in the Law': Fantasies and Practices of New York City Lawyers, 1870–1910," in Gawalt, op. cit., p. 51.

[19]The figures in this paragraph are from Wayne K. Hobson, "Symbol of the New Profession: Emergence of the Large Law Firm, 1870–1915," in Gawalt, op. cit., p. 3.

received thirty dollars a month.[20] Law offices took up use of the telephone and the typewriter. The firms began to hire more office workers skilled in the use of business machines. In 1899, Cravath's firm started a filing system and took on a file clerk. In 1885, young Editha Phelps, daughter of a clergyman, applied to the Chicago firm of Williams and Thompson. She was, she said, "a first class stenographer and typewriter of two years experience ... Salary about $50 per month." She was hired, and stayed ten years.[21] Like Editha Phelps, the first women to appear in law offices did not come to practice law; they came to type and take shorthand.

The salaried lawyer became more common in the late 19th century. The big firms hired lawyers who were not immediately made partners; some never reached this rank at all. House counsel—lawyers on the full-time payroll of a company—were unheard of in 1800, exceedingly rare in 1850; by 1900 this was a well-worn groove of practice. The corporate giants hired their own law firms and had lawyers on their staffs as captives or collaborators. Other big corporations needed whole armies of lawyers to do their legal chores, big and small. In 1885, the Prudential Insurance Company "began to require the exclusive attention of its attorneys; the Mutual and the New York Life established their first full-time solicitors in 1893; the Metropolitan had a claim and law division by 1897."[22] To be general counsel of a major railroad, after the Civil War, was to occupy a position of great prestige and enormous salary. William Joseph Robertson left the Virginia supreme court to become general counsel for two railroads; Judge G. W. McCrary left the federal bench in the 1880s to take such a post on the Santa Fe; the chief justice of Kansas, Albert H. Horton, resigned and became attorney for the Missouri Pacific, in 1895.[23] Then as now, business attorneys sometimes moved up to top management. Thomas C. Cochran studied railroad leaders between

[20]Swaine, *op. cit.*, pp. 364, 658.

[21]Herman Kogan, *Traditions and Challenges: The Story of Sidley & Austin* (1983), p. 48. Williams and Thompson was a predecessor firm to Sidley & Austin. Theron Strong, looking back over a long career, praised the work of the women office workers; he felt that "the presence of a right-thinking and dignified young woman in an office tends to elevate its tone"; such women had a "restraining influence ...upon the clerks and students, preventing the use of language which might otherwise escape, and actions which might be open to criticism." Theron G. Strong, *Landmarks of a Lawyer's Lifetime* (1914), pp. 395–96.

[22]Morton Keller, *The Life Insurance Enterprise, 1885–1910* (1963), p. 187.

[23]J. Willard Hurst, *The Growth of American Law* (1950), pp. 297–98.

1845 and 1890; he found that many railroad presidents had begun as lawyers—for example, Frederick Billings (1823–90) of the Northern Pacific. Chauncey Depew (1834–1928) began his career as a lawyer, acted as a railroad attorney, then executive of the New York Central, then became a United States senator in 1899.[24]

Small-town and small-city practice were more timeless and unchanging than big-city practice; patterns of life remained much the same; hence the gap between Wall Street and Main Street practice was very wide. There were 143 items of business on the office docket, for 1874, of a "leading law firm" in a small Illinois city. They included three partition proceedings, one divorce, one petition for a writ of mandamus, three cases for specific performance, three attachments, one arbitration award, and a petition to sell real estate to pay debts. All the rest were collection matters, requiring either negotiation, or legal action before a justice of the peace or in county or circuit courts; twenty-two of these were foreclosures of mortgages on land. During the entire year, the firm appeared frequently in court, but in only the three lower courts just mentioned.[25] An Indiana lawyer later recalled life in the 1850s, in the fifth judicial circuit of Indiana. The firm of Fletcher, Butler, and Yandes had the most extensive practice in the circuit. But its work consisted largely of "the making of collections for eastern merchants."[26]

One instructive career was that of James Carr. He came to Missouri about 1850 from Pennsylvania. First he taught for some years at a country school in Monroe County, where he assumed a Virginia accent (the locals were not friendly to Yankees). Carr read law, and set up shop in Paris, Missouri, in a "small 14 × 14 office room." Since he could not afford a table, "he put a board on the arm of a 'split bottom' rocking chair, and on that he for some time did his studying and writing." Carr was, in the estimation of his peers, fairly learned, but nothing to write home about as a courtroom lawyer. He was not "a good judge of human nature," and "found it a difficult task to compete with the average country lawyer." So far, Carr's story was not much different from those of many other country lawyers, who eked out a bare living

[24]Thomas C. Cochran, *Railroad Leaders, 1845–1890* (1953), pp. 249, 309.
[25]R. Allan Stephens, "The 'Experienced Lawyer Service' in Illinois," 20 Amer. Bar Ass'n. J. 716 (1934).
[26]W. W. Woollen, "Reminiscences of the Early Marion County Bar," *Publications, Indiana Hist. Soc.*, Vol. VII (1923), pp. 185, 192.

at the law. But Carr "continued to fill his head with what the books said," especially books about the law of corporations. In 1865, he got work as attorney for the Hannibal & St. Joe Railroad, and moved to Hannibal, Missouri. Later, he transferred to St. Louis, where he practiced corporation law. When he died, late in the century, he "left a good estate for his family."[27] There were other small-town lawyers as successful as Carr, and some even more so. Sometimes they made their fortune without moving to the big city. They became rich country lawyers, like rich country doctors, and typically owed only part of their success to the practice of law. Law was a lever or an opening wedge: real estate, or local business, or political achievement were the spokes on their wheel of success.

By 1900, circuit riding was only a memory, part of the golden past. Even Abraham Lincoln, before he entered the White House, could have used the railroad to do all the traveling he needed, from county seat to county seat. Some of the romance of the practice was still alive, however, in the more remote parts of the country: the plains states, the Far West, the mountain and desert country. There were differences, of course, between the buckskin lawyer of the 1800s, in the Northwest Territory, and the lawyers of the Far West, in the cattle towns and mining camps. But there were also striking similarities—commonalities of frontier legal culture, whatever the period and place. These far-off spots still attracted adventurous young men: ambitious, variously educated, looking for a fortune in law, business, or politics, or simply interested in raising hell. David Dudley Field, in the East, fought for his codes, and made money as lawyer for the robber barons; his younger brother Stephen went to California during the gold-rush days. He became alcalde of Marysville, California; here he built a frame house and "dispensed justice for the community, holding court behind a dry goods box, with tallow candles for lights." He also made money in land speculation, fought or almost fought duels, rose to become justice of the California supreme court and from there was appointed to the United States Supreme Court.[28]

Field practiced in a rough community, during rough times. There was a certain element of toughness, among these Western lawyers. If we can believe what a Kansas lawyer (trained in New

[27]W. O. L. Jewett, "Early Bar of Northeast Missouri," in A. J. D. Stewart, ed., *History of the Bench and Bar of Missouri* (1898), pp. 54, 59.

[28]Carl Swisher, *Stephen J. Field, Craftsman of the Law* (1930), is the standard biography.

England) said, his colleagues at the bar were an "ignorant, detestable set of addle-headed numbskulls."[29] But the man who said these words was not himself of this sort. Stephen Field, too, was a person of education, culture, and great legal acumen. He was not the only one of this stamp in California. Joseph G. Baldwin, fresh from the "flush times" of the old Southwest, arrived in California in 1854: he, too, served on the state supreme court. Many territorial lawyers had been educated back East. Luther Dixon was born in Vermont, studied law under a Virginia judge, practiced for a while in Wisconsin, then settled in Colorado. Another Colorado attorney, Joseph N. Baxter, advertised himself in 1892 as "formerly of the Boston Bar." A Texas lawyer in the same year proudly proclaimed himself a "Graduate of Columbia College Law School, New York City, Class of 1884."[30]

The practice of the frontier lawyer was like frontier practice in earlier places and times. James M. Mathers, who practiced in Indian Territory, stated that "our practice...was by necessity a criminal practice...and the great bulk of cases were murder cases."[31] This was perhaps exceptional. Land law, claim law, real-estate brokerage and speculation, money brokerage, collection work, mortgage work—these were staples of practice in the more lightly settled territories. The letterhead of E. P. Caldwell, an attorney in Huron, Dakota Territory, in the 1860s, stated his business as follows: "Money Loaned for Eastern Capitalists. Taxes Paid for Nonresidents. Investments Carefully Made for Eastern Capitalists. General Law, Land and Collection Business Transacted. Buy and Sell Real Estate. U.S. Land Business promptly Attended to. Contests a Specialty."[32] An attorney in Waco, Texas, advertised in 1892: "Have splendid facilities for lending money on first-class real estate security." In Utah, in the same year (1892), the American Collecting Agency, an association of attorneys, reported that:

> A prosperous business year has enabled us to enlarge our offices and put in them an immense fireproof safe to protect our clientage. We have added to our home force, secured detectives in all parts of Utah, and engaged first-class cor-

[29]Quoted in Everett Dick, *The Sod House Frontier, 1854–1890* (1954), p. 450.
[30]*Hubbell's Legal Directory* (1892), Appendix, pp. 14, 197.
[31]Quoted in Marshall Houts, *From Gun to Gavel* (1954), p. 33.
[32]Howard R. Lamar, *Dakota Territory, 1861–1889: A Study of Frontier Politics* (1956), p. 127.

respondents.... We make no charge unless we collect. Our
charges are reasonable. We remit promptly. We are a godsend
to honest creditors—a holy terror to delinquents.[33]

Not every lawyer, of course, was a glorified collection agent.
But no Wall Street or Wall Street practice was possible in these
dry and far-off places. One novelty was railroad work. As the
railroads pushed west, they constantly needed local attorneys, to
handle affairs along the route. In Dakota Territory, in 1889, the
"assistant solicitor" of the Milwaukee Road heard young Thomas
J. Walsh argue a case before the supreme court of the Territory.
The man was impressed, and the future Montana senator was
appointed "local attorney" for the railroad in Redfield, Dakota
Territory. This entitled him to a free pass on the railroad, as a
"retainer."[34] Mining companies needed skilled lawyers, too; and
so did the big landowners, merchants, and ranchers.

Some Western lawyers were almost as peripatetic as prospec-
tors, who wandered from mining camp to mining camp, looking
for gold. Homebodies stayed home in the East; and most lawyers,
it seems, were homebodies.[35] The West was the place for rolling
stones. James Clagett, born in Maryland, migrated with his parents
to Iowa in 1850. He was admitted to the Iowa bar in 1858. In
1861, he moved to Carson City, Nevada, and in 1862 served as a
member of the territorial house. The discovery of gold drew him
to Montana in 1867; here he became territorial delegate to Congress. In 1873, he turned up in Denver, Colorado. Later, he shifted
his base of operations to Deadwood, Dakota Territory, where he
"thrived on the intrigues and law suits brought by the large mining
companies against one another." In 1882, he moved to Butte,
Montana, to engage in the mining business. Next, Clagett was
president of the Idaho constitutional convention, in 1889. Un-
successful in Idaho politics, he moved to Spokane, Washington,

[33]Hubbell, *op. cit.*, Appendix, pp. 206, 208.
[34]Walsh to Elinor C. McClements, Feb. 13, 1889, in J. Leonard Bates, ed., *Tom Walsh in Dakota Territory* (1966), p. 218.
[35]On this point, Gawalt's figures for Massachusetts are enlightening. Nearly 90 percent of the lawyers admitted to the bar in the state between 1870 and 1890 practiced in one town or city for their entire career; less than 5 percent moved out of state. Lawyers admitted before 1840 were much more mobile, geograph-ically; only 70 percent practiced in a single town; nearly 18 percent left the state. Gawalt, "The Impact of Industrialization on the Legal Profession in Massachusetts, 1870–1900," in Gawalt, ed., *The New High Priests*, pp. 97, 102.

where he died in 1901. Clagett was "an excellent example of the mobility which was a primary feature of political life in the West. . . . It was the Clagetts . . . who wrote the codes, and who were elected to such offices as register of deeds, county commissioner, or territorial delegate. They were the men who organized political parties in the wild lawless towns situated in some narrow gulch where a shallow creek ran, with a fortune hidden in its wet sands."[36]

In the far western states, legal systems had to be borrowed or invented in a hurry; lawyers were the only ones who could do this job. J. Warner Mills of Colorado lent his name to the annotated Colorado Statutes. Matthew Deady (1824–93) did the same service in Oregon. But he was also a maker of laws. He drew up many of the Oregon codes, played a crucial role in revising Oregon's statutes between 1859 and 1872 and drafted much legislation himself.[37] Many Western lawyers rose to eminent positions, and not only in the West. Few of them, of course, were born in the West. James Mills Woolworth, born in New York, settled in Omaha in 1856, two years after the area had been wrested from the native tribes. In 1896 he was elected president of the American Bar Association. Charles F. Manderson, president of the Association in 1899, was born in Pennsylvania, practiced in Ohio, rose to the rank of brigadier general during the Civil War, moved to Omaha, Nebraska, in 1869, served as United States senator, and became general solicitor for the western portion of the trackage of the Burlington Railroad in 1895.[38] These careers were not typical; but neither were they unique. Lawyers came early to the frontier boom towns, eager to turn a quick dollar. Lawyers who placed money and collected on notes often turned to banking and merchandising to earn a better living. For others, politics was the best way to scramble up the greasy pole. In these small communities, one of the biggest businesses was government. Politics was bread-and-butter work. For lawyers, county, state, territorial and federal jobs were sources of income and, in addition, advertisements for themselves. Politics, lawmaking, law administration, were as much a part of the practice as collection work and lawsuits over land. The frontier attorney "was always a politician. Law and politics

[36]Howard R. Lamar, *Dakota Territory, 1861–1889: A Study of Frontier Politics* (1956), pp. 168–69.

[37]Harrison Gray Platt, "Matthew P. Deady," in *Great American Lawyers*, vol. VII (1909), p. 357.

[38]James G. Rogers, *American Bar Leaders* (1932), pp. 90, 104.

went hand in hand.... The lawyer filled all the 'respectable government offices.'"[39]

The lawyer-politician was, of course, not only a Western phenomenon. Lawyers were in the midst of politics everywhere. They were always an influential bloc in state legislatures, sometimes an absolute majority. Many Presidents after 1850 were lawyers: Buchanan, Lincoln, Chester A. Arthur, Garfield, Cleveland. From 1790 to 1930, two thirds of the senators and about half of the members of the House of Representatives were lawyers; the percentage seems to have stayed fairly stable. Between one half and two thirds of the state governors were also lawyers. Lawyers were especially numerous in Southern legislatures. Lawyers in the North tended to represent metropolitan areas in the legislatures of their states.[40] Lawyers were prominent at constitutional conventions, too. Of 133 delegates to the 1872 Pennsylvania constitutional convention, 103 were lawyers.[41] This was, perhaps, an unusual percentage; but lawyers swarmed in thick numbers at other conventions, too. In Ohio, 43 out of 108 delegates at the constitutional convention of 1850–51 were lawyers; in the 1872–74 convention, 62 out of 105.[42]

It was not so much the case that public office required legal skill as that lawyers were skillful at getting and holding these offices. They were by instinct political; political animals gravitated toward the practice of law. A public career was helpful to private practice, which cannot be easily said for doctors, bankers, or farmers. After 1850, too, the civil-servant lawyer became more common. Lawyers had always worked in Washington, at state capitals, in city hall, and in the county seats. As government grew, so did the number of government lawyers. In 1853, the attorney general of the United States, Caleb Cushing, performed all his duties with the help of two clerks and a messenger. In 1897, Attorney General Joseph McKenna was the head of a respectable staff, including a solicitor general, four assistant attorneys general, seven "assistant attorneys," and one "attorney in charge of pardons," not to mention three law clerks, forty-four general clerks, and miscellaneous other employees, among them eight charwomen. The "Office of

[39]Raymond T. Zillmer, "The Lawyer on the Frontier," 50 Am. L. Rev. 27, 35 (1916).
[40]J. Willard Hurst, The Growth of American Law (1950), p. 352.
[41]Rosalind L. Branning, Pennsylvania Constitutional Development (1960), p. 61.
[42]See Isaac F. Patterson, The Constitutions of Ohio (1912), pp. 109, 176.

Solicitor of the Treasury" had sixteen employees.[43] Lawyers were scattered about other government departments as well. The same growth occurred at the state and city level. In the last third of the century, the job of corporation counsel for big cities took on greater and greater importance. By 1895, the Law Department of New York City "was the largest law office in the country;" twenty-eight lawyers worked there, with 64 clerical assistants.[44]

ORGANIZATION OF THE BAR

For most of the 19th century, no organization even pretended to speak for the bar as a whole, or any substantial part, or to govern the conduct of lawyers. Lawyers formed associations, mainly social, from time to time; but there was no general bar group until the last third of the century. On February 15, 1870, a group of lawyers, responding to a call that had gone out in December, 1869, with eighty-five signatures, met, formed the Association of the Bar of the City of New York, and acquired a house at 20 W. 27th Street as headquarters. In the first year, about 450 lawyers joined the organization, representing the "decent part" of the profession, that is, primarily well-to-do business lawyers, predominantly of old-American stock.[45]

In the immediate background was the odor of corruption, emanating from the courtrooms of New York City. Justice, in Tweed's New York, seemed to be blatantly for sale. The robber barons fought each other with injunctions and writs; some of the judges— Barnard and Cardozo, for example—were visibly corrupt. On February 13, 1870, Dorman B. Eaton, a lawyer who had taken

[43]*Official Register of the United States*, 1853, p. 254; 1897, vol. I, pp. 827–29.

[44]On these city lawyers, see Jon C. Teaford, *The Unheralded Triumph: City Government in America, 1870–1900* (1984), pp. 61–64. Corporation counsel jobs were good stepping stones to success; talented young men held positions in these offices—men like Francis L. Stetson, in New York, who later became J. P. Morgan's attorney; Clarence Darrow was acting corporation counsel in Chicago in the early 1890s.

[45]On the formation of the Association, see George Martin, *Causes and Conflicts: The Centennial History of the Association of the Bar of the City of New York, 1870–1970* (1970); see also John A. Matzko, "'The Best Men of the Bar': The Founding of the American Bar Association," in Gawalt, *op. cit.*, p. 75; see also the remarks of George T. Strong, quoted in Henry W. Taft, *A Century and a Half at the New York Bar* (1938), p. 148; other details are in Theron G. Strong, *Landmarks of a Lawyer's Lifetime* (1914), ch. 6.

part in some of the Erie litigation, was savagely beaten. This incident alarmed the "decent part" of the bar and quickened their interest in action. The new Association, like any club, aimed to "cultivate social relations among its members." But it also promised to promote "the due administration of justice"; and the articles of incorporation stated as one of the Association's purposes "maintaining the honour and dignity of the profession of the law."

The crisis in the profession was more than a crisis in decency. There was also a dim but real sense of business crisis. The bar felt the hot breath of competition; and, in the late 19th century, the characteristic response of any trade group to a business threat was to organize and fight back. At the meeting of the New York bar, "for the purpose of forming an Association," James Emott complained that the profession had lost its independence. "We have become simply a multitude of individuals, engaged in the same business. And the objects and the methods of those engaged in that business are very much dictated by those who employ them. [Lawyers]...are and do simply what their employers desire."[46] In union, it was hoped, there would be strength against the outside world. The bar-association movement began and spread at a time when farmers and workers were also organizing, and shortly before the great outburst of occupational licensing laws.

The movement soon expanded outside of New York. The bar of Iowa organized on a statewide basis in 1874. During its brief span of life, the Iowa State Bar Association discussed ways to raise standards for admission to the bar, and the need for laws to punish and disbar attorneys "guilty of shystering and unprofessional conduct." The bar also discussed problems of judicial organization and whether it was desirable or not to enact a statutory "fee-bill, or system of costs." The association was also a club and a social organization. The Hon. Edward H. Stiles, of Ottumwa, in 1876, regaled the membership with a talk on "the relation which law and its administration sustain to general literature," and Judge James M. Love, before a "very fine audience assembled in the Opera House," gave out "one of the most scholarly efforts ever delivered in Des Moines, rich in historic lore, beautiful in diction, and philosophical in style." A "bountifully laden table" in 1881 inspired a toast to "Good Digestion: its compatibility with a law-

---

[46]Quoted in 1 Albany L.J. 219 (1870). Somewhat naïvely, Emott blamed the degeneracy of the profession on the New York constitution of 1846, which brought in an elective judiciary and "broke down the bar."

yer's conscience."[47] Chicago lawyers, too, formed a bar association, in 1874, prodded into life by the "activities of a notorious fringe of unlicensed practitioners." Between 1870 and 1878, eight city and eight state bar associations were founded in twelve different states. Most of them, like the groups in Chicago and New York, had a reform ideology, and wanted to improve the image and performance of the bar.[48] But their successes were probably mostly social. The New York City group moved very slowly and cautiously against Tweed and other malefactors; it moved smartly on other fronts, buying a nice brownstone in which the association installed a librarian, old books, busts of lawyers, and a punch bowl filled with a drink made "according to a special recipe furnished by the nearby Century club."[49]

With few exceptions, state and city bar associations were not open to everybody; they did not invite the bar as a whole, but sent out feelers to a select group, the "decent part" of the bar. There was the same genteel choosiness at work when the American Bar Association was formed in 1878. "Seventy-five gentlemen from twenty-one jurisdictions" (out of the country's 60,000 lawyers) got together in Saratoga, New York.[50] Simeon E. Baldwin, of Connecticut, was prime mover. The purpose of the Association was to "advance the science of jurisprudence, promote the administration of justice and uniformity of legislation ... uphold the honor of the profession ... and encourage cordial intercourse among the members of the American Bar." During the Saratoga years, the American Bar Association paid a great deal of attention to the "cordial intercourse" part of its mandate; but Simeon Baldwin was a good organizer, and a man of conviction; he put his stamp on the ABA in these early years. The ABA grew only slowly in size. In 1902 there were 1,718 members. But as a reform group, it was far from inert.[51]

From the outset, the Association did much of its work through

[47]A. J. Small, comp., *Proceedings of the Early Iowa State Bar Association, 1874–1881* (1912), pp. 36, 37, 42, 83, 84, 141.

[48]J. Willard Hurst, *The Growth of American Law,* p. 286.

[49]John A. Matzko, "'The Best Men of the Bar': The Founding of the American Bar Association," in Gawalt, *op. cit.,* pp. 75, 79.

[50]Alfred Z. Reed, *Training for the Public Profession of the Law* (1921), p. 208. Material on the early history of the ABA comes from Reed, Matzko, *op. cit., supra,* n. 45, and from Edson R. Sunderland, *History of the American Bar Association and Its Work* (1953).

[51]On Baldwin's work, and the early history of the ABA, see Matzko, *op. cit. supra,* n. 45.

committees. Early on, a number of standing committees were appointed—on jurisprudence and law reform, judicial administration and remedial procedure, legal education and admission to the bar, commercial law and international law; the committee on obituaries, established in 1881, reported names and achievements of dead members, to be duly published in the annual reports. A flock of special committees, however, worked on law-reform issues (for example, on the problem of the low salaries of federal judges, 1888), or issues of interest to the working profession (on trademarks, 1898). The ABA never really clarified its relationship to local bar associations during the Saratoga period. In 1887, a group of lawyers formed a rival organization, the National Bar Association, expressly to serve as the apex of the pyramid of local and state associations. It proved ephemeral. The ABA encouraged state and local bar groups to send delegates to its Saratoga meetings. At first, few came—two lonely delegates from South Carolina were the only ones at the third annual meeting, in 1880. By the end of the century, there was a more respectable turnout; eighty delegates, from twenty-nine states, were accredited to the annual meeting in 1902; and forty-one actually attended.

Still, the ABA before 1900, despite its efforts, never proved to be much more than a gathering of dignified, well-to-do lawyers enjoying the comfort and elegance of Saratoga. Its prime significance, perhaps, was the way in which it expressed, in concrete form, the ambitions of the "best men" of the bar for status and organization. Speeches and reports to the meetings voiced conventional sentiments about law reform—ways and means to keep the profession decent, well-liked, and well paid. The lowlifes of the bar—the ambulance chasers, the sleazy lawyers who hung around the rear of criminal courtrooms, the small-time debt collectors—were definitely not represented; and the speeches also voiced fear that too warm an embrace from big business might threaten the independence of the bar. The ABA aspired to a moderate, middling role, a role of mild, beneficial reform.

Uniformity in the law was frequently discussed; the systems of the various states could strangle interstate business, or corrode wholesome laws with out-of-state laxity; all this was deplored. In 1889, the Association, by resolution, directed its president to appoint a committee, consisting of one member from each state, to "compare and consider" the laws on marriage and divorce, inheritance, and "acknowledgment of deeds" and to report measures that would promote the uniformity of law. Shortly thereafter, New York State created a board of three "Commissioners for the Promotion of Uniformity of Legislation in the United States." The ABA seized on this law, touted it to its members, and recommended it for other states as well. A National Conference of Commissioners on Uniform State Laws was organized in 1892, in Saratoga, and began to hold annual meetings in close connection with those of the ABA. Out of the work of the conference ultimately came a series of recommendations for uniform laws, endorsed by the ABA as well, and proposed to the states.

ADMISSION TO THE BAR

Nothing so dissatisfied the "decent part" of the bar as the fact that it was so easy to set up as a lawyer. The country was flooded with lawyers who were mediocre or worse. Few states controlled admission to the bar through a single agency or court. In 1860, ten out of thirty-nine jurisdictions did so; in 1890, sixteen out of forty-nine. Even in these jurisdictions, the control was often slight, the standards of admission vacuous. Where local courts each passed on admission to their bar, the exams were usually oral, and so cursory as to be almost a joke. Recommendations from well-known lawyers weighed more heavily than actual answers to questions. Before 1890, only four states had boards of bar examiners; only a few required a written examination. Nothing in the way Oliver Wendell Holmes, Jr., was admitted to the Massachusetts bar would inspire confidence that the state could select a Holmes and reject the unqualified. Judge Otis P. Lord of the superior court appointed two examiners; they separately asked Holmes a few questions; Holmes answered the questions, paid his five dollars, and was admitted to the bar.[52] Charles Francis Adams, after "about twenty months of desultory reading" in a law office, went to his friend and neighbor, Justice George T. Bigelow of Massachusetts, and asked for an examination. Bigelow invited him "into the Supreme Court room, where he was then holding court." A clerk handed him "a list of questions, covering perhaps, one sheet of letter paper." Adams "wrote out answers to such of them as I could....On several...subjects...I knew absolutely nothing. A

[52]Mark deWolfe Howe, *Justice Oliver Wendell Holmes: The Shaping Years, 1841–1870* (1957), pp. 263–64.

few days later I met the Judge on the platform of the Quincy station, and he told me I might come up to the court room and be sworn in.... I was no more fit to be admitted than a child."[53] This was in the late 1850s.

In other parts of the country, admission to the bar was even more perfunctory. L. E. Chittenden, in Vermont in the 1850s, was chairman of the committee to examine candidates for admission. Two young men came before him: "Of any branch of the law, they were as ignorant as so many Hottentots.... I frankly told them that for them to attempt to practice law would be wicked, dangerous, and would subject them to suits for malpractice. They begged, they prayed, they cried." Anyway, they wanted to go west: "I, with much self-reproach, consented to sign their certificates, on condition that each would buy a copy of Blackstone, Kent's Commentaries, and Chitty's Pleadings, and immediately emigrate to some Western town."[54] James Mathers, born in 1877, took a two-year course at Cumberland; this made him automatically a member of the Tennessee bar. Immediately, he moved to Indian country, in what is now Oklahoma, around the turn of the century.

> We went over to the courthouse and I shook hands with Judge Kilgore.... He examined my diploma from Cumberland, which was about a yard square and had to be rolled up for easy carrying, and then he looked at my license from Tennessee. That was all I needed to get his permission to practice in his court.

Kilgore asked Mathers the next day to become a law examiner, with two others, and screen applicants to the bar in Indian Territory. Mathers used no written examination or set questions. In his view, two or three hours at a dinner table or relaxing over coffee or a drink was enough; this told him all he needed to know. He did not expect applicants to have "a great knowledge of case law since none of us did; but... good, reasonable common sense."[55]

At one time, educational requirements for admission to the bar had been rather stringent, at least on paper. Before the Civil War, these requirements had considerably eroded. Four states actually abolished educational or training requirements altogether: Maine

---

[53]*Charles Francis Adams (1835–1915), An Autobiography* (1916), pp. 41–42; for a similar account, from 1861, see George A. Torrey, *A Lawyer's Recollections* (1910), p. 81.

[54]L. E. Chittenden, "Legal Reminiscenses," 5 Green Bag 307, 309 (1893).

[55]Marshall Houts, *From Gun to Gavel* (1954), pp. 28, 31.

(1843–59), New Hampshire (1842–72), Wisconsin (1849–59), and Indiana (from 1851).[56] After the Civil War, the trend toward laxity was reversed, particularly in the East. In 1860, only nine out of thirty-nine states and territories prescribed some minimum preparation for the practice. In 1890, twenty-three jurisdictions asked for some formal period of study, or apprenticeship. In 1878, New Hampshire set up a permanent committee to examine potential lawyers. A written bar exam became increasingly the norm.[57] In much of this development, the bar as an interest group supplied the lobbying muscle. The motives were, as usual, mixed. Many lawyers had a genuine desire to upgrade the profession; this was, of course, mingled with a selfish desire to control the supply of lawyers, and keep out price cutters and undesirables. Control was, arguably, in the public interest. To keep out bad lawyers was as beneficial as to outlaw quacks, or to police the training of midwives; as defensible too as license laws for barbers, plumbers, and embalmers of the dead.

[56]Reed, *op. cit.*, pp. 87–88.
[57]Robert Stevens, *Law School* (1983), p. 2.

AMERICAN LAW IN THE 20TH CENTURY

CENTER AND PERIPHERY:
FEDERALISM IN THE 20TH CENTURY

It would be more than presumptuous to deal with 20th-century law in a few short pages. The 20th century is, in the first place, over eighty years of history, at this writing. In the second place, the 20th century has been by common consent a period of fantastic social change—and therefore a period of tremendous legal change as well. In the third place, it is notoriously hard for a person to stand back and deal with his own times. When enough years go by, historians develop a certain perspective, a certain consensus, which makes it easier for them to get a handle on a "period," even though they may be really relying on half-truths, distorted mirrors, hindsight, and faulty memory.

For these three reasons, or excuses, I will not try to give a narrative account of American law in the 20th century, not even in the limited sense in which the older law was covered. Instead, this epilogue will sketch, very broadly, some of the lines along which law in the 20th century seemed to evolve, and will briefly discuss the meaning of this process: is American law in our times only a continuation of what has gone before, or a fulfillment; or is there some sort of sharp and precipitous break with the past?

The main political and social events of the century are familiar enough. In the 20th century the United States emerged, without question, as a major world power. It began the century with a small empire overseas. It played a decisive role in two world wars; after the second, the United States was without doubt the richest, strongest country in the world. It was also, for a time, the only country with an atom bomb. It is as of now (1985) still the only country that has, with technology, sent men to the surface of the moon. The United States is not the only superpower; it has taken its lumps, in Vietnam for example; but it is still *the* powerhouse of the Western world.

Internally, this has been an age of central, national power. The relative strength of the states has been slipping away; the federal government has grown to giant size. The federal Caesar fed on the meat of social upheaval, the two great wars and the cold war, a vast depression, and a technological revolution. The word Caesar is not much out of place. The main beneficiary of power at the center was not the national Congress, not the Supreme Court, but the national President, and the executive branch in general. The man who holds the office of President has become, as Presidents like to think, the most important, the most powerful person in the world. Theodore Roosevelt and Woodrow Wilson already sensed this role; Franklin Roosevelt glorified in it; Harding and Coolidge, small men with small conceptions of their job, were only detours on the way. Weak Presidents are still possible, but a weak Presidency is not.

Every major event of the century has seemed to conspire to make the central government stronger. Even Prohibition, the "noble experiment" (1919 to 1933)—the national ban on liquor—which in some ways was the last stand of a dying order, only fed the federal colossus. Prohibition had no chance to succeed except on a federal basis. The individual states were powerless to stamp out the curse of liquor, or even to try—just as they had been powerless to control the railroads; to pass a satisfactory law against the trusts; to uplift the quality of food products; to raise an army. Prohibition did not stop people from getting drunk, if they really wanted to. On the whole, Prohibition proved to be a costly failure. But it led to mammoth changes in the system of criminal justice. Prohibition filled the federal jails; it jammed the federal courts. In the 19th century, criminal justice was as local as local could be. It was a matter primarily for the cities and towns, secondarily for the states, for the federal government, hardly at all. Until the 1890s, the federal government did not own or run any prisons. The few federal prisoners were lodged in state prisons; the national government paid their room and board. After Prohibition, the idea of a national police force became no longer unthinkable.

Criminal justice is still local; but it is not *exclusively* local. There is a strong federal presence. The federal government still plays only a bit part in the drama of finding, catching, and trying thieves, murderers, and rapists. But it gets involved: in interstate crimes, in tax fraud, in kidnappings where state lines are crossed, and, perhaps most significantly, in helping to pay for state and local programs. And what has happened in criminal justice has happened in other purely "local" fields of government and law: education, land use, family affairs. The federal government is a partner—big or little—in every aspect of social control.

It is probably wrong to explain the growth of the national government in terms of wars, depressions, and other aberrations; even had none of these happened, it is fair to say that the great growth of the central government would have occurred nonetheless. How could it be otherwise? It was already plain in the late 19th century that the separate legal sovereignties could not manage the economic forces that industrialism seemed to let loose. The primitive conception of a country of yeoman, a federalism of smallholders, no longer suited reality. The trend was already marked in the 19th century, and it continued; the population grew and grew; big business got bigger; a smaller and smaller proportion of the population lived on the land; a larger and larger proportion lived in cities. More and more, people were interdependent, but in a new way: not the interdependence of small, face-to-face groups, but the interdependence of strangers—buyers who never saw their sellers; patients without close ties to their doctors; workers who did not know the boss's name. They were laced together, too, into a single huge nation. Technology created common ties of communication and transport; the market was national; radio and television nets became national; in the 1980s, New York and Los Angeles were a yawn, a drink, and a movie apart, as the jets flew.

Crucial too was the rising level of demands upon government. When we write history, we find it easy to fall into slipshod use of impersonal phrases and the passive voice. It is easy to write that government got bigger, that federal power was extended over more and more areas, as if we were talking about natural processes, like chemical reactions, or an evolution almost biologically programmed, like the transformation of an egg into a chicken. Politicians love to talk, too, about bloated government, as if the regime were some sort of fat man with an uncontrollable appetite. There is a grain of truth in this, but only a grain. Parkinson's law, and the greed of bureaucrats, explain some but not most of the growth. Organizations do want to get bigger and stronger and better; the people who run them are ambitious and expansionistic. But the gargantuan scope of modern government is not built entirely, or even mostly, on this base of red tape. It is built on a foundation of concrete demands, made by concrete groups, who clamor for public, that is, governmental, response.

The New Deal probably is the best and sharpest illustration of the way government grew in response to consumer demand. In 1932, the country was hungry for leadership. The economy was in a shambles. Local government was bankrupt and distraught. People looked to the Presidency for jobs, relief, economic reform. The New Deal program was immensely popular in its day; and what began in the 1930s has become so deeply ingrained in American life that nobody dares touch the essential New Deal, not even a Republican President as conservative as Ronald Reagan. Social Security, the SEC, some sort of federal housing effort, and national labor legislation are as permanently ensconced in the legal system as anything can be in a changing world. They are certainly politically untouchable, in the short run. The mere suggestion, by Barry Goldwater, that he might alter the Social Security system (1964) was greeted with outrage, as if he had befouled the Holy of Holies.

Big government also has a kind of snowball effect. The more government does, the more money it needs, and the more men to run its show. Big government develops, then, an enormous taxing apparatus, and it becomes a major employer, which gives it yet another lever of control over the economy. In this process, wars, hot and cold, have been a major, even if not indispensable, conditioning factor. Before Franklin D. Roosevelt, a federal budget of eighty billion dollars a year was inconceivable, astronomical, science-fiction. Now the federal government spends, each year, an amount that Roosevelt—or Kennedy, or even Nixon—would find absolutely staggering, on war and national defense alone. The defense budget in the mid-1980s is on the order of 300 billion dollars.

But the growth of big government does not repeal the law of demand and response. Perhaps the main effect of big government is on the mentality of citizens—on legal culture. In 1900, nobody expected much out of a national government. It ran the Army, the post office, supervised railroads—all this was important, of course, but the bulk of the governing process was lodged in the states. Every event of the 20th century seems to conspire to aggrandize the center. Then the attention of the public is focused on Washington, and away from state capitals. Thus people who are troubled by a problem—crime, or the fact that their children don't read—want action from Washington, above all. In the end, this means partial federalization of the whole legal system, from top to bottom, side to side.

The decline of state and local government has been relative, not absolute. By any measure, these second and third levels of government are themselves of colossal size. State and local governments still carry heavy responsibility in all sorts of vital areas. They build roads, run schools, operate the welfare system, hire policemen and firemen, issue marriage licenses and grant divorces. Every one of these has been a growth industry in the 20th century. Again, the New Deal was a great watershed. The local monopoly of poor relief disappeared. The federal government moved in with money and muscle. Later, it extended its hand into education, research, hospital-building, and interstate highways. But the everyday administration of these affairs remains mostly subfederal. The country is still, compared to France or the Soviet Union, extremely decentralized, and power is extremely dispersed.

This is, in part, because decentralization continues to be part of the legal culture. Fragmentation is useful, too, in many politically appealing ways. When people or groups demand central control, they do not want big government as such. Few people care (and why should they?) whether government is big or not at any level. They care about results. Arguments about centralism and decentralism have little political appeal, in themselves. They are surrogates for something else. Southerners who used to preach states' rights were not really professing a political theory. They had a shopping list of interests and demands, and they knew which stores carried the goods. Often, too, when local people and local government ask for federal intervention, they do not want central control; they want money, which the central government raises more easily than they do. Many so-called federal programs are hardly centralized at all; they are simply statutory pots of gold to be distributed among local interests and power groups. Urban redevelopment was a classic example. This program began in 1949; though it developed the usual thick texture of federal regulation, it was essentially, into the late 1960s, a device for siphoning funds. Efficient federal machines collect taxes and dispense the money once again to cities and local authorities, who do with it more or less as they please, subject to very loose, very general limits and controls.

So, despite all the events of the last eighty years or so, despite the hundreds of billions of dollars taxed and spent through Washington, despite the (literally) thousands of federal agencies and problems, the idea—or disease—of checks and balances has by no means run its course. The legal system is still in many ways a patchwork of power, a rug made of rags. On the one hand, federal law is infinitely more important than a century ago—in taxation, regulation of business, civil rights, protection of the environment. It is now massive, dominant, overbearing. The President is almost a czar over foreign affairs. Despite attempts by Congress to cut him down to size, after the disillusionment of the Vietnamese war, the President still has the power to move his troops—into and out of Lebanon, for example, as Ronald Reagan did in the early '80s.

But in other areas, the power of the President is still checked and limited, formally or informally, by other power-holders within the government. "Federal law" is a crazy quilt; federal programs are a diverse lot. Consider, for example, the differences between the way the post office is run and the way "little groups of neighbors" ran the system that drafted soldiers during the war in Vietnam; think of the position of the Federal Reserve Board, or the Supreme Court, or the Social Security Administration, or the National Science Foundation, or the FBI.

State law remains vigorous. The states continue to have the last word in much of that kingdom which Continental scholars call private law: the law of ordinary commerce, tort law, property law; the law of marriage and divorce. States and cities make up and enforce thousands of simple, ordinary rules that affect the daily life of the average person. They draft building codes, plumbing codes, and electrical codes for cities and towns.[1] They devise speed limits and set out parking zones. They regulate dry cleaners, license plumbers, and dictate the open season on pheasants and deer. They control the right to marry, to own a dog, to sell vegetables, to open a saloon. As we noted, they share with the federal government responsibility and rule-making power over schools, but the main share of the work is local, not national. They also do the dirty work of running the welfare system.

The warlord system in American politics and law is very much alive. The system continues to reject any hint of absolute power. State government has always been a force to reckon with. The counties have some (limited) powers. The cities, with or without

[1]Signs of federal encroachment here, however, are plainly visible as of the 1980s.

home rule, contradict and overlap the larger jurisdictions; since the Second World War, they have in some instances dealt directly with the federal government, as its special client. This tendency, under rather fancy names, seems bound to grow. Besides all these, there are little zones of power without number: sewer districts, school districts, air-pollution districts; and such mighty vassals as the New York Port Authority. Some of these districts and authorities are accountable, it seems, to no one in particular; some have gigantic mouths to feed on the plankton of nickels, dimes, and quarters thrown into the maw by motorists; with this food, they expand to monstrous size.

Since 1900, too, local government has become steadily *less* rational in at least one important sense. In the 19th century, as a rule, a city grew in physical size as it grew in population. This process ground to a halt about 1900; and since 1930, most big cities (except in parts of the West and South) have actually lost population, some of them quite dramatically. As everyone knows, this does not mean that people are returning to their farms. Quite the opposite: the countryside continued to shrink. Its people fled to the city as if a pack of wild dogs was after them. But the city's boundaries are fixed. The metropolitan areas, now truly gigantic, are made up of central cities, old suburbs, new suburbs, and little fragment settlements, some of them nothing more than incorporated neighborhoods, but as autonomous (in theory) as New York City or Chicago. These little fragments stoutly resist the large agglomerations that might want to swallow them up. They expect to rule their own roost. They want, in particular, to resist the influx of blacks and low-income people; they want to be warlords on their own. For this purpose, land-use control is essential; and the kind of control they want is most practical in small areas. There are hundreds of "villages" that are little more than restrictive covenants, or zoning ordinances, which have incorporated, giving themselves a lofty name and a show of undeserved power.

These brief remarks show that one persistent theme of American legal development, the struggle between uniformity and diversity, between centralism and localism, goes on without let and without end. And perhaps it should. The struggle is in no sense a "problem," to be resolved once and for all. It is not a problem, but a fact; and it cannot have a solution. The sophistry of some forms of conceptual jurisprudence, and some movements for "law reform," lies precisely in this: to imagine that uniformity or lack of uniformity is a problem in itself; or that diversity of power or of legal culture is a problem in itself, or that centralization or decentralization is a problem in itself. They are problems only from the standpoint of legal dogmatics. In real life, problems are specific: poverty, or air pollution, or crime, or low economic growth, or whatever society defines as a situation gone wrong. Structural features are tools or effects.

Yet tools or effects are not unimportant. The basic issue is power: where it is placed, and who should exercise it. The structural features of the legal system reflect the distribution of power, and, at the same time, influence or perpetuate power. A good distribution for one purpose is not a good one for another. Juries are good; but white juries in a prejudiced South may be bad. Politically sensitive and influential Americans have a flair for sensing these practical problems; the classic response is to build up more and more layers of countervailing power. The result is a delicately balanced system, incredibly complicated, with tremendous tensile strength. Its flaws are also massive; it is tremendously hard to unravel or reform; and it may, at some point, finally rip apart.

MODERN AMERICAN LEGAL CULTURE: PLURALISM AND INSTRUMENTALISM

In short, decentralization does not vanish, even in the teeth of the master trend of American legal history: the trend to create one legal culture out of many; to reduce legal pluralism; to broaden the base of the formal, official system of law; to increase the proportion of persons, relative to the whole population, who are consumers or objects of that law. This master trend continues, and accelerates, in the 20th century. In medieval England, only a tiny circle of people were really subjects or objects of common law. Since then, the ambit, scope, focus, and pretensions of the official law have grown; it now includes practically everybody in the commonwealth.

This last statement should be taken with a certain grain of salt. In the first place, the "common law" in England meant, primarily, the great royal courts, and the doctrines they wove. The peasant on the English manor had nothing much to do with this "common law"; but there was plenty of "law" on the manor, in the form of local "customs." In the colonies, astounding proportions of the adult population appeared somewhere in the court records in any given year. This was perhaps less so in cities and settled farm-

communities in the 19th century. The law today affects everyone—from giant corporations down to the homeless, sleeping on hot-air grates in the big cities. It touches some aspect of everybody's life. But this does not mean that the citizen of 1985, on the whole, is less free, than the citizen of 1785 or 1885. That is a different and a difficult issue.

In the second place, official law and living law are not, and never have been, the same in this country, or even close to it. Of all the mysteries of legal history, perhaps the most impenetrable is the history of law in action, law as living, breathing reality, not as myth or official norm. But informal law (and corruption) do not leave behind the neat and orderly records that official law does; statutes, cases, reports, rules, and pronouncements of authorities, survive; the rest either vanishes or was never there to read. In the contemporary world, sociologists of law take it as their task to explore what police, judges, and legislators actually do, rather than what they are supposed to do, or what they say they do—an idea blindingly simple as a matter of theory, not so easy as a matter of fact. The letter of the law no doubt did not carry itself out in the past any more than in the present. What evidence there is confirms this impression.

Nonetheless, there is undoubtedly a trend toward a single legal culture—a trend that is persistent, genuine, and significant. The country is a single economic unit for most purposes, and in many ways a single social unit. Mass media and mass transport are great levelers. Americans have always been ferocious travelers—a restless, shifting breed of men and women. The forces that level off regional variation are terribly strong. This was—compared to old-world countries—never a country with great variation in dialect and custom. In fact, *legal* dialect (the fifty state versions of a single legal language) was in some ways one of the most striking and persistent forms of localism. But in the 1980s, there is less and less scope for regionalism, including the regionalism of law.

This is partly the case on sheer efficiency grounds. Regionalism is not tolerable in a mass-market age. A company that sells in fifty states would prefer to talk one language, use one sales form, confront one body of laws. There is also, in the 20th-century mind, a great straining toward rationality. This trait, which seems fairly general in the western world, has a particularly virulent American form. Americans, at least at one level of their consciousness, have no patience for irregularities. Customs and traditions that are cherished in England have been rudely chased out of the United

States; Americans would consider them stupid or infantile. Modern law, for example, does not tolerate the classical common-law legal fiction, even where the device might be useful. Blatant, surface irrationality is not in fashion any more.

This state of mind is part of the general debris of a world-wide movement of recent centuries that can be called, for want of a better name, rationalism. Rationalism has been central to Western thought, at least since the Industrial Revolution, if not before. Its progress has been noted and chronicled, in law and out, by a number of scholars and historians; and the growth of "rationality" was one of the master themes of Max Weber's powerful work on law and society.[2] The essence of the story is the breakdown of older, traditional forms of legitimacy.

"Rational" is a tricky word. But contemporary men and women are "rational" in one important sense: they tend on the whole not to accept ideas and institutions simply because they are traditional; or for religious or supernatural reasons. (The words "tend" and "on the whole" are of course used deliberately here; tradition and religion are neither dying nor dead. Americans are, on the whole, a religious people, and in the 1980s the political and social force of organized religion seems stronger than it had been for some generations.) Actions and proposals have to pass a more-or-less utilitarian test. The legal system is taken as a tool, an instrument. For any proposed law or legal act, individuals ask, what is in it for me, or my family or my group? (These calculations, of course, are not necessarily crudely economic.) Governments and whole societies ask a similar question. Very little is given or fixed.

The consequences of instrumentalism are colossal; they have not yet played themselves out on the stage of time. Political democracy has been one consequence. Another has been the rise of the welfare state. Still a third is modern science. A fourth is the idea of equality before the law. A fifth is the—more recent—demand for equality of opportunity, which follows when formal equality fails in its purposes (from the standpoint of an oppressed or subordinate group). Instrumentalism, therefore, is in the long run an enemy of legal pluralism, not in the regional sense, but in the vertical sense: a pluralism of classes or degrees, each with its fixed position in the order, some near the bottom, some near the top, the bottom placid, deferential, and accepting.

[2]See, in general, Max Rheinstein, ed., *Max Weber on Law in Economy and Society* (1954).

Vertical pluralism of course does not give up easily. For reasons of rational self-interest, people on top bitterly resist threats both to their power and to their moral and ethical domination. There was a time, mostly in the 19th century, when a bite or two of formal equality *apparently* satisfied the many groups that never got a slice of the big pie, the main pie, the rich and filling pie. There was mobility for the few and dreams for the many. In England, perhaps, the sheer strength of traditional behavior acted to cushion the transfer of power from an elite to a broader group. The mass of the population was willing to let elites, so it seems, act as executioners of their own class system. In the United States, there were somewhat different cushions; the frontier, real opportunities, and the cult of free enterprise. At any rate, some combination of factors acted as a brake on demands for redistribution of the social product. The frontier was not the only "safety valve"; there was also the hope of success, the culture and cult of opportunity. Life was a lottery, but tickets were hawked for a few cents on every corner, and in every town.

THE STRUGGLE FOR RIGHTS

At any rate, there *was* a breathing space, and no revolution. But only for a while, it seemed. In the United States, volcanic eruptions of labor unrest terrorized the cities in the late 19th century. In the 20th century, after many zigs and zags, organized labor won a series of smashing legal victories. How much was due to political struggle, how much was made possible by plain economic growth and the gifts of modern technology, is beside the point here. The most significant legal triumphs took place during the New Deal period (the 1930s). The government in power was willing and able to press for laws that expressed the package of trade-union goals. Many New Dealers were antibusiness in their outlook. The New Deal upset the balance of honor and prestige between labor and capital. It enacted a tremendous number of regulatory laws, many of which created administrative agencies. The National Labor Relations Act (1935)[3] guaranteed the right to unionize, declared that it was an "unfair labor practice" to interfere with this right, and set up a board to enforce the act.[4] The New Deal also

---

[3] 49 Stats. 449 (act of July 5, 1935).
[4] The Norris-LaGuardia Act, passed in 1932, while Hoover was still President, did away with the labor injunction. 47 Stats. 70 (act of March 23, 1932).

launched the first meaningful programs of unemployment insurance, old-age pensions, and public housing.

Business was stunned, and shattered in morale, by the great crash of 1929 and the ensuing depression. Politically, business had never been feebler than in the early '30s. While the army of enterprise was in flight, the working class swarmed into the burned and deserted palaces. But prosperity, which the Second World War brought back, probably meant more to the working class in the long run than most New Deal reforms. Prosperity revived the strength and power of business as well. Much—not all—of its influence also returned. There was no more of the crude, overt hatred of the 1930s; very few people in the '60s, or the '70s, or the '80s, talked about "economic royalists" any more. The economy surged ahead so rapidly after the war that labor and business both shared in the product. Good times made for good feelings. The interests of master and servant seemed much more congruent. For example, the government set out, even before 1945, to help the veteran on a scale never before attempted. The government sent millions of soldiers and sailors to college. Among other things, this kept veterans from glutting the labor market. The government gave loans to those who wanted to start a small business. It made money available to fulfill the dream of the average family, to own a house in the suburbs, with a yard, a garage, a new kitchen. The program also made jobs for bricklayers and plumbers; it put money in the pockets of contractors and mortgage bankers, and manufacturers of plaster, glass, pipe, and toilet bowls.

CIVIL RIGHTS AND BEYOND

By the 1950s, the economy had moved so far so fast that some had conveniently put out of mind that there were underclasses in America. Scholars wrote books about the affluent society; they worried about an excess of leisure; the kind of enforced leisure called unemployment seemed almost forgotten. Into this Panglossian dream world, the black revolt, followed by brown, yellow, red, and women's revolts, burst like a bombshell. Lyndon Johnson's war against poverty (1964–65) had been conceived of as a mopping-up exercise. It turned into more of a war than its proponents bargained for. To many people, it seemed as if somebody had opened Pandora's box: out of it came hate, class struggle, backlash, and despondency, to poison the national air. The war in Vietnam made everything worse: socially and economically too. These were the years of the 1960s: restlessness of almost earthquake proportions; riots in the streets; fires burning on campus; the sense of oncoming ecological catastrophe; a government paranoid with fear of its subjects; an almost physical fear of crime, which stalked the streets like the Black Death. Every group or class that had been dependent, that had been put down, or put away, or taken for granted, now showed its fangs: blacks, prisoners, poor people, students, homosexuals, nuns. There seemed to be no respect for the slots in which society had placed its subordinate groups. There was little respect for society itself. Or so it appeared to millions of alarmed and threatened people.

Then, almost as suddenly as it came, the ferment seemed to end; a strange calm settled over the country. Not even the travails of Watergate, in which the very government tottered, and a President (Richard Nixon) resigned in disgrace; not even the unpopularity of the Carter administration, and the shame of the hostage crisis in Iran; not even the deep, destructive recession of the early Reagan years seemed able to raise the temperature of public life to the boiling point.

This, of course, is not history; it is the world outside the door, right now. The strands that have gone to make the 1970s what they were, and which make the 1980s what they are, are far too complex for general treatment. Certainly, the rebellion in the air—and the counterrebellion—had been fed by many springs; people spoke loosely about the war in Vietnam, permissive toilet training, Dr. Spock and his theories of child care, the decline of religion, or all or none of these things. Similarly, after 1980, they spoke of a backlash against the civil rights revolution, or the Warren court, or the cynicism of the post-Vietnam generation, the rebirth of religion and traditional morals, the rise of the radical right, and various other factors.

It may be, in the long course of history (which may be inaccurate too), that people tended to exaggerate both the rebelliousness of the 1960s and the reaction of the 1970s and beyond. These were blips or bumps in a single greater, larger master trend. In one sense, the "rebellion" was the unpeeling of one more layer of the onion of rationalism, one further consequence of the sunburst of modern secular thought. In our parochial legal terms, we can describe it as part of the process of making the legal culture one— the process of evening out some of the vertical pluralism of past generations. Nobody, of whatever color or condition, seemed willing to accept a lower or despicable status, in law or in fact; to accept the detrimental definitions that an outside majority (or minority) had fastened on its head. This recent and important revolution is of course not completely a bolt from the blue. As we have seen, it was merely the next step in a long series; and some parts of this book have been devoted to describing the earlier steps. In this latest phase, law played a direct, if narrow, part. The civil-rights revolution of the 1950s and the 1960s, in the historical clothing it wore, would be unthinkable without the federal courts. This is not to say that the revolution itself would be unthinkable without courts. But it would have worn a different aspect. It would have taken a different—perhaps more brutal—form.

Black people fought for their rights on many battlefields. Probably the most important one was in the streets—or in the buses, where black passengers refused to stay in their place, in lunch-counters, where they stubbornly insisted on service, in schools where they demanded the right to get in. On the legal side, they appealed to the words of an 18th-century document, the Bill of Rights, and the 14th Amendment to the Constitution, which itself was a century old (1868). The strength of this amendment lay in its potential effect on the way function and power were divided between federal and state governments, between federal judges and state judges, between judges, legislators, local officials, and whatever passed for public opinion. The law that grew up about these constitutional scraps of phrases was essentially modern. Even before 1868—often before 1800—the states had their own bills of rights, full of lofty, well-phrased statements of fundamental principle. Yet the case law on civil rights and civil liberties—on freedom of speech and religion, for example—is practically speaking a product of the 20th century. In the 19th century, there was not much litigation; this branch of constitutional law was on the whole rather tepid and torpid. This does not mean of course that the Bill of Rights was a bill of dead letters. But there is an aggressive, expansive tone to modern case law that was wholly lacking before.

Nothing shows better than the history of civil liberties and civil rights how foolish it is to imagine that legal words, concepts, phrases have an important life of their own. Take the vexed question of the line between free speech, which is sacred, and "obscenity," which presumably is not, and which can be squashed or suppressed by law. The basic legal concepts and texts—the very words—were around in 1790 as well as in 1980. There were also,

one might add, dirty books as well; they passed from clammy
hand to clammy hand, under the table. In fact, one of the ironies
of recent case law is that some key decisions passed judgment on
a famous old book, *Memoirs of a Woman of Pleasure,* usually called
Fanny Hill. Fanny has been around since the late 18th century,
just like the First Amendment. The idea of matching this odd
couple basically did not occur to 19th-century publishers and read-
ers. Why that was so is a complex question. In any event, a sharp
decline in conventional morality, together with the greed of publishers, burst the dam, and a pent-up flood of litigation spilled
over its ancient barriers. In short, things that were unthinkable
(but had been thought) and unprintable (but had been printed)
showed their brazen faces in public. And nobody boycotted these
authors and publishers or stopped having them over for dinner.
The books sold by the millions; and the courts, on the whole,
acquiesced.

Why, however, did courts have to say yes? There was, first of
all, a constitutional tradition and an activist bench. The country
was used to the idea that disputes of all sorts, social, economic,
and political, were not out of place dressed in robes and brought
to court. Nobody had the slightest idea, at the outset, in 1800,
say, or even 1900, that courts would be kind to *Fanny Hill,* or to
radical pamphlets, or to Jehovah's Witnesses. The courts became
the forum of civil liberties by a process of trial and error. When
legislative help was not politically possible—as was true for blacks,
for unpopular minorities, and for the publisher of *Fanny Hill*—
blocked interest groups, at least those with strong purposes, tried
other paths, like mice running through a maze, until they found
the one with the cheese. The first time is the hardest; then the
route becomes easier to follow; a receptive court invites further
litigation. If unpopular minorities—Jehovah's Witnesses in the
'40s; criminal defendants and radicals in the '50s and '60s—found
a court or two receptive, they tended to pursue judicial remedies
that much more avidly. The increase in this form of litigation,
then, adds to the pressure on courts to extend prior holdings just
a little bit further. Especially was this so of strong claims, claims
that, denied, did not simply vanish or die, claims that *demanded* a
response, claims (in short) with political and moral strength behind them: claims backed by a movement, a force.

A serious body of law on the subject of free speech did not
come together until around the time of the First World War. The
war set a whole caldron of chauvinism boiling. Espionage and

sedition acts were passed. A great witch hunt and red scare began, which lasted into the 1920s.[5] The courts were not as heroic as modern tastes would prefer. Oliver Wendell Holmes's clear and present danger test came out of this period—Congress could suppress words "used in such circumstances and . . . of such a nature as to create a clear and present danger that they will bring about the substantive evils that Congress has a right to prevent."[6]

Later cases dealt with other sensitive issues—for example, the scope of congressional investigations, which was much debated during the feverish days of the McCarthy period (1950s); the case law on censorship of movies and books also began in earnest in the 1950s. In the 1940s and beyond, some noted decisions concerned Jehovah's Witnesses, a troublesome and unpopular sect; these were followed by other dramatic cases which seemed to some people to build the wall of separation between church and state too high and too thick. The most notorious of these were cases, in the 1960s, which outlawed prayers and Bible-reading in the public schools. Every poll shows that these decisions are quite unpopular; and attempts have been made over the last 20 years to undo them—but as of now (1985) the court and the cases still hold.

The Supreme Court, particularly when Earl Warren was Chief Justice (1953–69), also took a stand far in advance of public opinion, in protecting unpopular minorities and furthering their interests. The cases on criminal procedure were particularly striking. In case after case, the Supreme Court took the side of the prisoner, requiring strict adherence to principles of fair search, arrest, and trial—principles which, it sometimes seemed, the judges created themselves. These were dramatic cases. On the one side, the state; on the other, some broken figure of a man, shuffling into court, a drunk, a gambler, a dope addict, a four-time loser, a petty thief, a creature at the bottom of the ladder. The Warren court sided with this underdog (and his lawyers) often enough, and forcefully enough, to draw cries of pain from the temples of order and law. Earl Warren was replaced by Warren Burger (1969–); the court stopped the thrust and momentum of these cases, retreated a bit here and there, threw a sop or two to the law-and-order crowd;

[5]See Harry N. Scheiber, *The Wilson Administration and Civil Liberties, 1917–1921* (1960); Stanley Coben, *A. Mitchell Palmer: Politician* (1963).
[6]*Schenck* v. *United States,* 249 U.S. 47, 52 (1919).

but despite a reputation for conservatism, the Burger court has kept most of the law it inherited, thus far.

Even more dramatic were the Court's incursions into the thickets of morality; here too there was basically no retreat. The court discovered a constitutional right of privacy, threw out the archaic law of Connecticut which tried to restrict the sale of contraceptives and, most sensationally of all, in *Roe* v. *Wade* (1972), struck down every single law in the country that dealt restrictively with abortion. It replaced these laws with a complex formula which, essentially, gave women total freedom to abort the unborn, without state interference, during the early stages of pregnancy. No decision since *Dred Scott,* perhaps, has created quite such a storm; but here too more than a decade has gone by, all turbulent years, and so far the court has not turned decisively back; attempts to undo *Roe* v. *Wade* by constitutional amendment have also failed.

Blacks were by far the most important minority group looking to the courts for firm support. Litigation on questions of race had never been absent from the courts. Black leaders never really accepted *Plessy* v. *Ferguson* (1896),[7] the case that put a mask of legitimacy on segregation. The National Association for the Advancement of Colored People was founded in 1909. Almost from the start, the NAACP used litigation as a strategy, and put pressure on the courts for racial equality. As early as 1915 the NAACP achieved an important, concrete result; the Supreme Court, in *Guinn* v. *U.S.*[8] held the "grandfather clause" of the Oklahoma constitution void. (The Oklahoma constitution of 1908, art. 3, sec. 4A, required voters to be "able to read and write any section of the Constitution of the State of Oklahoma"; but excused anyone who was "entitled to vote under any form of government" on January 1, 1866, or who "at that time, resided in some foreign nation," and any "lineal descendant" of any such persons. This meant that almost everybody was excused—except blacks, who of course could not vote before 1866.)

After 1940, the changing attitude of the Supreme Court toward black litigants became very marked. At first, the constitutional war on racism achieved only incremental results. In a series of cases, the Supreme Court declared this or that situation or practice (segregated law schools, for example) unconstitutional; but it did

[7]163 U.S. 537 (1896).
[8]238 U.S. 347 (1915).

not want to reach the ultimate issue: whether segregation, under the fig leaf of the "separate but equal" doctrine, had any warrant in law at all. The NAACP pushed and pulled; the Court was a reluctant bridegroom. Its decisions were clearly compromises; the blacks won, most of the time, in each particular case; on the other hand, the larger issue was avoided. During the Second World War, in a notable lapse, the Supreme Court refused to strike down the wartime internment of American citizens of Japanese ancestry; these decisions, shot through with racism and hysteria, are a blot on the court's reputation.[9]

The Court came closer to the heart of segregation in *Shelley* v. *Kraemer* (1948).[10] This struck down, as unenforceable, land covenants that forbade sale or rental of property to blacks. But the climax of the long struggle for equality was "black Monday," in 1954, when the Court handed down its decision in *Brown* v. *Board of Education*.[11] This was surely one of the most momentous of all Supreme Court decisions; to find a basis for comparison, one has to reach back as far as the *Income Tax* case, or even *Dred Scott,* or perhaps forward to *Roe* v. *Wade*. The *Brown* case ordered an end to segregated schools. To be sure, even today most blacks, North and South, go to schools which are totally black, or almost so. Nonetheless, *Brown* had an enormous impact, not least of all on the schools. It sounded the death knell of *Plessy* v. *Ferguson,* though at first only by indirection. Later cases made the Supreme Court's meaning abundantly clear. No form of segregation was permissible. The case also—like *Dred Scott*—involved the Court in a storm of controversy. Vilification and "massive resistance" in the South did not move the Court; it seemed if anything to make Earl Warren and the justices surer of their moral premises. Since 1954, the Court, on this point, has never budged.

The segregation cases affected, and joined forces with, the general black revolt. The case was just one thread in a carpet. Its influence cannot be measured and must not be overrated. The movement has not, at this writing, lost all its momentum. Much of the history of the United States, since the 1950s, domestically

[9]For an exhaustive—and depressing—treatment of these cases, see Peter Irons, *Justice at War: The Story of the Japanese-American Internment Cases* (1983).

[10]334 U.S. 1 (1948). On this case, and the role of the NAACP in general in the Civil Rights movement up to that point, see Clement E. Vose, *Caucasians Only: The Supreme Court, the NAACP, and the Restrictive Covenant Cases* (1959).

[11]347 U.S. 483 (1954).

speaking, has been a gloss on black-white relations. Every major domestic issue—the war on poverty, white backlash, urban renewal, unrest in the schools, crime in the streets—is bound up with, caused by, complicated by, disturbed by, the sickness and rot which affects race relations. White reaction has been as complicated as the great leap forward of the blacks. Different levels and groups of the population have reacted quite differently. A new series of civil-rights laws (1964, 1965), more sweeping than any since the false dawn of radical reconstruction, are one legal symptom of this reaction. Segregation is completely dead in hotels, restaurants, public facilities. It is still alive, but less virulent, in housing and employment. Blacks now vote in the South, as in the North, in vast numbers; the mayors of Atlanta, Chicago, Philadelphia, and Los Angeles are black (1985).

There is also white backlash, and it is not to be underestimated. It feeds on the fact that there remains an enormous black underclass. *Brown* and its successors, and the whole civil rights movement, freed the black middle class; blacks sing with the Metropolitan Opera, play baseball, and run for Congress; a few blacks become executives or partners in law firms; blacks appear on TV ads and in the movies. All this is important; but the black masses are still poor, still behind the white majority in every regard. Legally speaking, there are the problems posed by "affirmative action" and "reverse discrimination"; one climax was the famous *Bakke* case, in which a white, Alan Bakke, successfully fought exclusion from the University of California medical school, at Davis, on the grounds that he was (as a white) disfavored. What *Bakke* actually decided is, to say the least, unclear (*Regents of the University of California* v. *Bakke*, 438 U.S. 265, 1978). What is certain is that some (most?) whites are disturbed by the civil rights revolution. Progress is real, but so is rage and reaction; there is a connection between this reaction and the law-and-order movement (though the problem of crime is also very real). The flight to the suburbs is a reaction as well; and the ever-growing unpopularity of welfare programs, whose clients are disproportionately black. All this is as fundamental to the white reaction as Brotherhood Week, if not more so.

LAW REFORM AND UNIFICATION:
THE IVORY TOWER

Compared to the mighty events of the civil rights revolution and the massive changes in the structure and substance of law, the "law reform movement," strictly speaking, is small potatoes indeed. It too represents the working out of rationalism and the flight from legal pluralism, but in a pale and indistinct way. Law reform deserves comment only because of its parochial importance to lawyers. The organized bar and the academic side of the profession continued their own little battle in the 20th century for uniformity, codification of law, consistency and order on the statute books, and similar toys of the trade.

Indeed, the law-reform movement, on the surface, has been successful beyond the wildest dreams of the 19th century. This should not come as a surprise. "Law reform," in the sense the organized bar uses this term, is really a measure for professional defense. It responds mostly to the sense of beleaguered comradeship, which characterizes the elite of the profession. In the 20th century, the profession grew enormously—there were approximately 600,000 practicing lawyers in the early 1980s—and the profession was, as always, controversial. The leaders of the profession—the great Wall Street and Washington lawyers in particular—looked back in sentimental nostalgia to what they imagined was the golden age of the bar, before the flood of foreign-born lowlifes, ambulance chasers, divorce lawyers, and similar marginal people, who sullied the reputation of their noble calling.

Law reform was one way of showing the world that lawyers too served the public interest; and law reform has been historically linked, since the 1870s, with the official organization of the bar. Bar associations were just getting underway in 1870; they increased in importance throughout the 20th century, though they never approached the sheer power of the American Medical Association. The national Conference of Commissioners on Uniform State Laws and the Association of American Law Schools, founded around the turn of the century, were also concerned with law reform, and, incidentally, with the interests and good name of the profession. The American Law Institute, encouraged by the organized bar, had begun drafting uniform laws in the late 19th century. Many, many others followed in the 20th century. The

EPILOGUE 675

Uniform Sales Act (1906) was one of the most important, but no subject was too small; the Uniform Flag Act (1917) (forbidding anyone from defacing, defiling, defying, or trampling on the American flag), and a Uniform Simultaneous Death Act (1940), were other contributions of the Conference to the common good. After the Second World War, the Uniform Commercial Code, completed around 1950, was the most massive contribution to uniformity. Professor Karl Llewellyn was the Code's chief intellectual parent. The Code summed up all of the statute law of commerce, improved it (in theory), and replaced the old laws on sales, bills and notes, bulk sales, warehouse receipts, bills of lading, and secured transactions. (Many of these were themselves the subjects of "uniform" laws.)

The Code occupied the attention of leading academic specialists in commercial law for about a generation. First, they drafted it; then they lobbied for it; then they started to write about the way it was working. It took a heavy effort to sell it to the legislators, who had no idea they needed a code. Pennsylvania (1953) and Massachusetts (1957) were the pioneers; after years of agitation, the rest of the states gave in. In size and scale, the Code was a clear break with the past. American commercial legislation had usually been nothing but pieces and patches. In other respects, the Code was far less revolutionary. It was, in a way, curiously old-fashioned. The problems that it attacked were strictly "legal"; that is, they were problems of disorder in doctrine, clashing case law, and what seemed to be unlovely and unsympathetic arrangements of statutes. The draftsmen also believed that courts, and legislatures, did not understand what businessmen really needed, and how businessmen thought. This last point must be stressed, because it means that the Code was a mixture of two ideologies. One was the ideology of codes themselves, stressing system, order, logic, uniformity. The other was the ideology of the law merchant. This one flew the banner of service to the business community. But it was on the whole the first ideology that dominated. Devotion to business practice was deeply felt; nonetheless, it was window dressing at bottom. The draftsmen of the Code did not commission empirical studies of what business wanted, or even how business behaved; nor was there a coherent economic theory of what business needed at the base of the project. Some Wall Street lawyers and businessmen were asked their opinions; but there were no real explorations of what was wrong (if anything) with the way commercial law served the business world—or society. The Code was, however, ruthless in its attitude toward regionalism. The notion that any state in the Union might conceivably have an economic or social interest which called for an exception to the Code was considered heresy, and was in fact not tolerated. Nor was much attention paid to the interests of people outside the business community—labor or the consumer. It is unfair to make too much of a point of this. Academic interest in poor people, and in consumer problems, was not really in fashion among legal scholars, until the 1960s. The Code was a product of a time that now seems as quaint and old-fashioned as the era of high-button shoes. It was the work of a love feast among legal scholars, law schools, and Wall Street lawyers; and the only dissenting voices were old fogies at the bar who resisted any change.

At any rate, the Code was modernity itself compared to the restatements of the law, perhaps the high-water mark of conceptual jurisprudence. Work began in the late 1920s, under the sponsorship of the American Law Institute (founded in 1923). The proponents were hostile to the very thought of codification. They wanted to head it off, and save the common law, by reducing its principles to a simpler but more systematic form. The result would be a restatement, not a statute. Judges and professors would do the work, hacking away at the major common-law fields: contracts, trusts, property, torts, agency, business corporations, conflict of laws. They took fields of living law, scalded their flesh, drained off their blood, and reduced them to bones. The bones were arrangements of principles and rules (the black-letter law), followed by a somewhat barren commentary. The first restatement, on contracts, was finished in 1932. The restatements were, basically, virginally clean of any notion that rules had social or economic consequences. The arrangements of subject matter were, on the whole, strictly logical; the aim was to show order and unmask disorder. (Courts that were out of line could cite the restatement and return to the mainstream of common-law growth.) The chief draftsmen, men like Samuel Williston and Austin W. Scott of Harvard (contracts, trusts), were authors of massive treatises in the strict, conceptual, Langdell mold. They expended their enormous talents on an enterprise which, today, seems singularly fruitless, at least to those legal scholars who adhere to later streams of legal thought. Incredibly, the work of restating (and rerestating) is still going on.

All this law-reform activity in the 20th century had small social returns. Indeed, this was almost the name of the game. The subjects "reformed" were those that were quintessentially legal. In theory, public interest was king, and was the very soul and reason for reform; in practice the problems for reform came out of scanty appellate cases, and were problems of logic and consistency. Sometimes there was no doubt some incidental public benefit. And when judicial *structures* were reformed (as in New Jersey, under the leadership of Arthur Vanderbilt), the work probably paid a real social dividend. Model codes, a phenomenon later than the restatements, tended also to be more sophisticated. The draftsmen of the Model Penal Code were at least aware that their subject meant a lot to the outside world, and were attentive to clamorous voices from outside their doors. But basically, modern and uniform codes were mealymouthed or at best meliorative. The Uniform Probate Code, adopted (as of this writing) mostly by sparsely settled Western states, pruned away some of the expensive trimmings that gave the probate process a bad name; but it did not touch the heart of the probate system, which many scholars (and parts of the public) considered an expensive and archaic anomaly.

The ferment of the 1960s touched off what was, in many ways, a new style of law reform. Civil rights, Vietnam, the war against poverty, concern over pollution and population, and a general unrest in the universities—all these got the adrenalin going in the law schools and in the fringes of the profession. There had always been lawyers on the left: a persistent minority, socially conscious and sometimes even radical. What was different now was, first, the zeal, and second, the finances: the war on poverty of the Lyndon Johnson administration enlisted a corps of legal warriors, paid for by the government, charged with helping poor clients against their enemies (often enough this was the government itself). Poverty lawyers stepped up pressure on the system for far-reaching change.

In one sense, this was the second such wave. During the New Deal of the 1930s, too, lawyers came pouring out of law schools with a vision; they were determined to lead society onward and upward. They flocked to Washington to build the Roosevelt society. Their interests were mostly substantive, however—not the administration of justice, but administration of the economy. The radicals of the 1960s were interested in substance, too, of course. But they had a particular eye for justice: the courts, procedures, access to power. Here the push for law reform, *inside* the profession, joined with a genuine social movement coming from outside. Both demanded something more than formal equality before the law; both were in open revolt against vertical pluralism in American law and life; both were, moreover, vitally concerned with ways and procedures of justice.

Not all activist lawyers worked for the government, by any means. Some were members of so-called public interest law firms. The money came from the Sierra Club, or from contributors to the NAACP, or the like. The numbers involved were miniscule: hundreds, not thousands, in a profession that had reached and passed the half-million mark. But this small band accomplished a great deal—too much, some people thought. The largest number of this band were the legal services lawyers on the public payroll. These lawyers were at particular risk. The funds could be turned off in a second. The work of these lawyers offended powerful interests. They particularly irked a governor of California named Ronald Reagan; and when Reagan became President, he tried to eliminate the program. Congress refused; but funds were drastically cut. Whether the program will survive in the long run is still an open question.

THE GROWTH OF THE LAW

In the law itself, there was rapid, ceaseless change in the 20th century. Some of the main headings have been mentioned—for example, the rise of administrative law. Others, too numerous for adequate treatment, demand at least some passing recognition.

In land law, it was a century of land-use controls. The restrictive covenant and common-law nuisance doctrine were together not strong enough to hold the forces of change at bay in big cities. The 20th century tried zoning. New York City had the first comprehensive zoning ordinance (1916).[12] From this beginning, zoning became an almost universal feature of the land-use law of the cities. Planning and controls were used to monitor the growth of the city, to preserve the character of neighborhoods, to stop any downward slide of land values, to counterbalance the iron laws of the market. These were popular goals, and zoning was a popular tool; it served the interests of the middle-class homeowner, and (to some extent) the businessman too.

In general, land-use controls were popular because of the

[12]See Roy Lubove, *The Progressives and the Slums* (1962), pp. 229–45.

American custom of income segregation. Rich and poor were sorted out into their own little areas. This was standard enough; problems arose at the borders and in enclaves. From the period of the First World War and on, the black rural mass began to move north in search of jobs. This movement became a flood after the Second World War. White fear then became another dominant support for enforcement of land-use controls. Federal programs—urban renewal and redevelopment from 1949, Model Cities in the late 1960s—hardly made a dent in urban segregation. These programs took the form, by and large, of grants made to local warlords, and with their approval. Cities and neighborhoods made policy; the white majority never favored any plan that smacked of large-scale integration. *Shelley* v. *Kraemer* outlawed the restrictive covenant in 1948; in 1949, Urban Redevelopment popped out of its box. Not that the two events were directly connected. But the energy released by one act flowed into the other. If blacks and poor people could not be kept out of a neighborhood directly, then the job was best done indirectly, through some sort of fight-blight campaign.

Two important reformist goals acted as at least rhetorical pillars of Redevelopment and its later recensions. One was low-income housing; the other was the dream of the city beautiful. The actual impact of the programs was different, and far less salutary; neighborhoods were disrupted, and the slums were simply shifted about the city. Predictably, a backlash developed against urban renewal. The troops consisted of blacks, radicals, and (sometimes) white smallholders; those who saw the bulldozer approaching their own backyard. There had been, of course, protests against particular projects since the very beginning of redevelopment. In the good old American way, some of these went to court. In the 1950s, the courts uniformly brushed all objections aside. Stripped of jargon, the cases said, first, that papa knew best; second, that judges could not interfere with orderly decisions by respectable authorities.

In the 1960s, there were more cases; a few judges had second thoughts; a few housewives chained themselves to trees for publicity; and there was much hand-wringing and pamphlet-writing from Washington. The general decline in compliance and complacency had overtaken urban renewal. The economic forces that benefited from renewal were still strong; but so was the enemy. Planners had to contend now with a growing conservation movement; and urban decay lost some of its luster as a social problem.

It now had to reckon with the newest social problem to demand the center of the stage, the problem of mankind and the physical environment.

Air and water pollution, urban squeeze, and other symptoms of distress were old enough; there had always been voices crying in and for the wilderness. But the voices became more strident from the 1960s on. A real sense of doom began to hang over this small and limited world. Many sources fed the ecological movement. First, economic growth (in a society which, after all, had had a great deal of this otherwise scarce commodity) no longer satisfied everyone, particularly those with money to spare, and still no inner peace. Second, the crisis was real. Resources were *not* infinite. Big business was poisoning the rivers and darkening the air; lumber companies were chopping down irreplaceable trees; cities were pouring tons of muck into lakes and oceans; highway engineers were driving concrete paths through pieces of the American heart and heritage. This debauchery could be justified only by blind faith in the invisible hand of the market, and in "progress," and in the virtue and sense of public institutions. Faith of this sort was itself becoming a scarce commodity. Third, this was a society with many rich and leisured people; with enormous government and governments, peopled by professionals and bureaucrats; and with a growing number of academics and intellectuals looking for a place in the sun. All of these interest groups (it is fair to call them that) had consciences and needed causes. The government needed causes because its size was only excusable if it pursued the national interest; every part of every government had to have some sort of socially useful program. Academics and the leisure class had their own self-interest, as consumers, at stake; they also needed and wanted some way to spend their surplus time and money. Many expended energy collecting stamps, writing histories of China, going to antique shops, getting drunk, and otherwise, but a certain number hit on the environmental crisis, which was genuine, and for which the time was somehow ripe. Hence, an interest group with some power—particularly, power to mobilize the neutrals—joined forces on an issue which suited the '60s. By the late '60s, many prior issues had become inhospitable. (The blacks, for example, had rudely taken over, with hardly a thank-you, the job of their own liberation.)

The ecological movement also implied the rise to prominence of consumer interests. It was still a society whose law was forged in the struggles and compromises of interest groups. For the first time, however, the consumer formed an organized interest group. This made itself felt in many areas of public and private law. One notable instance was the growth of products liability. In one sense, products liability merely continued the long flight from *caveat emptor*. In the 20th century, this flight quite naturally claimed a higher governmental input than in prior times. Private lawsuits were, as before, mostly costly and impractical. Manufacturers and processors were made accountable therefore by statute. A federal food and drug law was passed in 1906. A bizarre episode of struggle preceded it. A pure-food movement had been going for a generation. Upton Sinclair's book *The Jungle* helped the final push immeasurably. The reading public nearly retched at the thought that their meat products were moldy, that pieces of rat were in their sausage, that acid and spices hid putrefaction in canned goods, and, worst of all, that their lard might make cannibals of them all. Sinclair wrote the book to expose the plight of "the wage-slaves of the beef trust,"[13] in Chicago's packing town. "I aimed at the public's heart," he said, in a celebrated sentence, "and I hit ...the stomach." Indeed, he had. Scandal cut the sale of meat products almost in half. This made a point the food industry understood better than sentiment or socialism. If pure-food legislation would restore public confidence in processed meat and food products, it was well worth the price of regulation, at least for the reputable firms.

Scandal continued to play a role, too, in the complex history of food and drug law after 1906. Over 100 people, mostly small children, died after taking "Elixir Sulfanilimide," in 1937; a drug company had had the happy thought of marketing the new wonder drug in liquid form; the solvent, alas, was a deadly poison. Legislation in 1938 then beefed up the FDA and outlawed the marketing of drugs before they were adequately tested.[14]

Deadly episodes helped spark state and federal laws on clean air and water as well. Environmental protection seemed to be, and remain, genuinely popular. But here too a certain backlash set in, in the late 1970s and the early 1980s. Had the pendulum swung too far? Was the economy going to rack and ruin, for the sake of a few little fish, teetering on the brink of extinction, or a lousewort (whatever that was), or some endangered worm? The

---

[13]Upton Sinclair, *American Outpost, a Book of Reminiscences* (1932), p. 154.

[14]James Harvey Young, "Three Southern Food and Drug Cases," 49 J. Southern Hist. 3 (1983).

EPA and its works stood at the center of controversy, and have continued to be; but there was every indication of vast popular support for the main pillars of its program.

FDA, EPA, and their fellows, share a common theme: control of what economists call externalities, that is, the effects of private actions that impose costs and burdens beyond the little circle of immediate actors. Of course, no person is an island; all behavior has ripple effects; the question is where to draw the line. New York (1984) has decided to force drivers to wear seat belts. Some people yelped about big brother, or about dictatorship; but a smashup on the highway inevitably affects a circle of people beyond the driver, and if seat belts reduce the effects, there is a case for requiring them. In any event, accident law has been amazingly socialized in the 20th century.

First, as to work accidents. By 1900, as we saw, the fellow-servant rule no longer worked very well. It was still cruel, but it no longer had the virtue of simplicity. It did not allocate the costs of industrial accidents with any efficiency. Congress swept the rule away for railroad workers, in 1906, when the Federal Employers' Liability Act was enacted.[15] Many states also abolished the rule; and between 1900 and 1910, there was vigorous debate and agitation over compensation plans. In the United States, industry resisted, but resistance gradually tapered off. Litigation and accident insurance cost industry a great deal of money. Was it possible that compensation would not really add much to the burdens? That more money would go directly to workers, less to parasites, lawyers, and middlemen? Perhaps such a plan would buy industrial peace as well. European countries, notably England and Germany, had adopted workmen's compensation, and the sky had not fallen in. New York passed a compensation statute in 1910; it was declared unconstitutional.[16] Next came Wisconsin (1911), this time successfully. Other states followed, avoiding the pitfalls that made New York's law offensive to the judges. The Supreme Court later held the most common types of plan constitutional. Mississippi, in 1948, was the last of the states to pass a compensation law.

Workmen's compensation was a compromise system. Each side

[15]34 Stats. 232 (act of June 11, 1906). The statute had constitutional problems; supposedly it covered more employees than federal power could lawfully extend to. This was so held in the Employers' Liability cases, 207 U.S. 463 (1908) (a 5–4 decision). A new act, passed in 1908, 35 Stats. 65 (act of April 22, 1908) side-stepped the problem.

[16]*Ives v. South Buffalo Railway Co.*, 201 N.Y. 271, 94 N.E. 431 (1911).

gave a little, got a little. The worker got compensation. If she was injured on the job, she collected for it, whether the employer was negligent or not.[17] The fellow-servant rule was abolished. So was the doctrine of assumption of risk. Nor did it matter whether the worker himself had been careless: unless his behavior was really gross, or he was drunk, most states still allowed compensation. On the other hand, what the employer had to pay to the workman was fixed by statute, and strictly limited. The worker would recover medical expenses and a fixed percent of wages actually lost, but with a definite ceiling. In Wisconsin in 1911, for example, a worker totally disabled could collect, as long as her disability lasted, 65 percent of average weekly wages, up to four times her average annual earnings; this was as high as she could go.[18] Statutes also commonly set a definite price for "permanent partial disability"— so many weeks' compensation for a finger, a toe, an eye, a foot, an arm. The employee could get no less; but he could also get no more; no more jury trials; no more chance at an inflated recovery. For this, the employers were grateful.

Workmen's compensation was supposed to do away with the plague of accident case law. In the main, it was successful. Almost all work accident cases are handled smoothly, and without litigation, by commissions and boards. But the new statutes did generate enough case law to surprise, and disappoint, some champions of the system. The case law has tended to extend liability in directions that early proponents hardly dreamt of. Now, in some states, workers recover for heart attacks suffered on the job; a secretary who strains her neck at the office, turning to talk to her girl friend, collects lost wages; dozens of cases deal with accidents at company parties or picnics. Partly, these extensions of liability were only to be expected. The plight of the individual, in "hard" cases, tends to tug at the heartstrings of judges and administrators. Besides, white-collar and service workers now outnumber blue-collar workers in the labor force. It is now *their* law, their piece of the welfare state. Since the nation has yet to adopt a general security law, cradle to grave, piecemeal bits accrue to existing institutions or are captured by "special-interest groups." Liability under compensation laws can be looked at in this light.

So much for the worker's injuries. For all its failings, workmen's

---

[17]The concept of contributory negligence was abolished, but certain kinds of gross misconduct on the job cost the workman his right to collect compensation.
[18]Laws Wis. 1911, ch. 50, pp. 46–47.

compensation has achieved its basic aims. Tort law, meanwhile, has been thoroughly revolutionized. Since the 1920s, the automobile has played a larger and larger role in everyday tort law. Practically speaking, most personal-injury lawyers work on auto-accident cases; and such cases dominated the tort docket of trial courts. In addition, in some states in the 1950s, wrecks on the highway accounted for up to forty percent of the cases decided by appellate courts. Mostly the insurance companies pay. The personal-injury bar makes use of the contingent fee system, and there are some very large recoveries; but trials cost money, and the vast majority of incidents get settled out of court. Legal scholars and others have suggested some sort of compensation scheme. So far, not much has happened. Workmen's compensation came out of a clear bilateral system, with organized workers on one side, organized employers on the other. The whole public rides in automobiles; and insurance makes the current system at least vaguely tolerable, for most people. As the costs of insurance skyrocket, the chance of change improves. A "no-fault" system was first enacted in Massachusetts. "No-fault" makes steady progress, though over the dead bodies (so to speak) of personal injury lawyers.

The automobile accident is the bread and butter of tort law; but the most dramatic changes have occurred in fields that hardly existed before 1900: products liability and medical malpractice. In 1916, in a decision clearly written for posterity, Judge Benjamin Cardozo of New York seized an opportunity, and helped change the course of liability law. The case was *MacPherson* v. *Buick Motor Co.*;[19] the occasion, a wheel "made of defective wood," whose spokes "crumbled into fragments" and led to serious injury for Mac-Pherson. Cardozo held that the buyer of the car, which was defective, could bring a lawsuit directly against the manufacturer for his injuries. There had been a technical barrier. No "privity," no direct relationship, connected plaintiff and defendant. MacPherson did not buy his car from Buick; he bought it from a dealer. According to the older case law, he could only sue the dealer. Despite this, Cardozo's court gave MacPherson a cause of action against the far-off manufacturer. When a manufactured item is or can be dangerous, and the maker knows that the product will be used by third-person consumers, he must make his product "carefully," or suffer the consequences.

Cardozo's language was eloquent, his reasoning clever. The case

---

[19]217 N.Y. 382, 111 N.E. 1050 (1916).

created a stir in legal circles; it encouraged more cases to be brought. Some of these were successful. After a generation or so, most state courts accepted the innovation. But it would be wrong to say that the other courts had *followed* Cardozo. Certainly, they cited him. Whether his opinion persuaded, in itself, is another question. If it did, it was less because of its own eloquence than because it eloquently summed up a state of mind which would have made its way on any account. The 20th century was bound to accept the basic idea of products liability, that is, that manufacturers ought to be responsible to ultimate consumers. In recent years, courts have carried products liability further than Cardozo would have dreamed. In place of a negligence standard, there is strict or absolute liability: if a defective product injures someone, the company must pay. In a few, dramatic cases, recoveries have soared into the millions.

There has been a similar explosion in malpractice cases. These are mostly brought against doctors, though dentists, nurses, and hospitals also take their lumps; and recently, too, lawyers, accountants, even teachers and preachers. In the 19th century, and well into the 20th century, cases of this kind were very rare. By the 1970s, partly because of a small but important group of cases that produced huge recoveries, insurance premiums soared, and the doctors screamed in wounded rage. Some states even put a cap on recovery. Statistically speaking, these were not common cases; but they created a sense that lawsuits had become a serious threat to everyone in professional life.

It is a striking fact that the tort law revolution was mostly made by judges. This tempts jurists to imagine that courts have played an enormous role in reworking the law in the twentieth century. They have undoubtedly played a role; but of what size? What they accomplished must not be exaggerated. Courts were, of course, exceedingly busy and active in the 20th century. In a number of dramatic instances—*Brown* v. *Board of Education* was one—they left their mark on national affairs. They altered old rules and developed new ones. But there were limits to their power. The courts began the century with huge pretensions, often exercised in a conservative direction. In the 1930s, the Supreme Court's veto power wrecked some of the New Deal's most precious legal engines. Franklin Roosevelt, at this point, threatened to pack the Court—to increase its size with new appointments, presumably loyal New Dealers. Despite Roosevelt's great popularity, this plan notoriously backfired. The court-packing plan was killed.

Roosevelt had the last laugh. He was elected four times, and he simply outlasted the "nine old men." New appointments, and some second thoughts, brought the Court into a more reasonable mood. It was no longer (at least through 1985) offensive to liberal thought in the country. Indeed, under Earl Warren, in the 1950s and 1960s, the tables were turned. It was the conservatives' moment to scream.

After the Supreme Court abdicated, as it were, in the late 1930s, no *judicial* barrier stood in the way of the enormous increase in the power of the central government, and the incredible expansion of the welfare and regulatory business of government. The main economic power was firmly in the hands of legislature and executive. The courts were (in Alexander Bickel's phrase) the "least dangerous branch"; were they also the least important? Even private law, so-called, was turning statutory. The lion's share of the norms and rules that actually governed the country came out of Congress and the legislatures, usually drafted in the office of the President or governor, or by their delegates and agents within the bureaucracy. The rules of the countless administrative agencies were themselves an important, even crucial, source of law. Tax law can serve as an illustration. In 1913, after the 16th amendment undid the damage of the *Pollock* case, Congress passed a new income-tax law. Over the years, Congress repeatedly raised the rates, and added to the law's provision. By 1950 or so, the Internal Revenue Code (dominated by federal income-tax law) was the longest, most complicated, most densely packed enactment in the country; and the one which probably affected more persons and businesses (and gave work to more lawyers and accountants) than any other piece of legislation or for that matter any other single law. Tax laws raised, and had to raise, billions of dollars each year. This was the fuel that big government had to have; hence all this attention was not surprising. A stupendous body of regulations, rulings, and occasional orders of the Treasury clarified and supplemented the statutes. Court cases ranked a poor third as a source of policy in tax law.

Virtually the whole population was affected, too, by the welfare laws of the 20th century. The biggest changes and the biggest breakthroughs came during the presidency of Franklin D. Roosevelt. Unemployment compensation, categorical grants in aid, public housing, old-age insurance, aid to families of dependent children—all these either began in the 1930s, or were substantially revised and revamped. The depression had cast millions down into poverty. These were the millions who lost faith in business hegemony, and who demanded government action to relieve them from a misery they were not used to and felt they did not deserve. The people in distress were no tiny underclass to be safely ignored; they were an enormous mass, and many of them had recently dropped from the middle class. The resurgent Democratic party built a political fortress out of these stones. Every new administration after the 1930s felt compelled to keep intact the core of the New Deal's essays in social insurance. It became a regular ritual to raise social-security payments. In the 1960s Medicare, Medicaid, expanded federal funds for education, and the Economic Opportunity Act, joined the great family of welfare.

All was not rosy, however, in the world of social legislation and welfare administration. The success of the middle class, after 1939, had a poisonous effect on some of these programs, notably AFDC and public housing, which were inherited by poorer and poorer customers. At one time these were programs for the submerged middle class. The blacks and the dispossessed moved in as the fattened middle class moved out. But this meant the loss of that all-important factor, political popularity. The long shadow of the old pauper laws began to fall once more on these programs. They became stingy, harried by onerous conditions, and easy prey for political snipers. This in turn increased disaffection within the ranks of beneficiaries. The programs were ripe, then, for the revolts and the counterrevolts of the 1960s. And in the late '70s and early '80s, financial doubts and worries began to plague the *middle-class* core of the welfare state: the old-age pensions under social security, medicare. A crisis loomed ahead, most critics believed. How it would be resolved was not yet clear. There was a tendency to muddle on, from election to election, dodging the hardest issues and choices.

BENCH AND BAR

Despite the retreat of the 1930s, the United States Supreme Court never stood higher in prestige or in power than in the middle 20th century. It replaced its powerful voice on economic issues with an even more powerful voice on "social" issues: race segregation, the death penalty, criminal defense, contraception and abortion. Its decisions were front-page news. A book that promised to tell its secrets, to rip aside its curtain of secrecy, climbed to the top of the best-seller lists in 1979.[20]

This was of course an exceptional court. There was, indeed, a growing role and a growing activism in the federal court system; state courts and judges on the other hand, though they may have kept (or even gained) power in absolute terms, surely lost power, relatively speaking, to the central branches of government in the 20th century. Certainly, few state-court judges ever achieved much fame. Benjamin Cardozo (1870–1938) of New York was a rare exception. (Cardozo also served on the United States Supreme Court, from 1932 on.) In the 1950s and 1960s, Roger Traynor of California had perhaps the largest reputation of any state-court judge. Probably few nonlawyers had ever heard of him. A few later judges were famous or notorious for one reason or another—for example, Rose Bird, the controversial chief justice of California. But almost all state court judges remained obscure and unsung.

The differences between Cardozo and Traynor were, in one respect, highly revealing. The two men lived a generation apart. Both were best known as innovating judges. Cardozo, however, preferred to dress change in common-law clothes; he liked to show continuity in the midst of change, to argue that the genius or spirit of the common law required him to move as he did. He was, or posed as, a craftsman molding traditional clay. Traynor was more likely to cut and break with the past; he spoke a different, franker language.

One philosophy affected both these judges, as it affected legal education, and the intellectual life of the law. This was the set of ideas called *legal realism,* ultimately associated with a group of writers in the 1930s, notably Jerome Frank and Karl Llewellyn. Realism was, in fact, less a philosophy than an attitude. It rejected the mind-set of judges and scholars of the late nineteenth century, who had emphasized legal logic and purity of concepts; it rejected, in other words, the philosophy of Langdell. The realists had no great reverence for legal tradition as such. Realist judges and writers were openly instrumental; they asked: what use is this doctrine or rule? A string of citations was definitely not a sufficient answer; it was no answer to invoke noble judges from the past,

[20]Bob Woodward and Scott Armstrong, *The Brethren: Inside the Supreme Court* (1979).

or to appeal to so-and-so's treatise, or to deduce a result logically from principles expressed in prior cases. There was less and less tolerance of artifice, fictions, real and apparent irrationalities. Law had to be a working social tool; and it had to be *seen* in that light.

These attitudes were not entirely new; and they never captured the minds of all judges and lawyers. But they did affect an important elite. Realism made a difference in the way a small but important group of judges wrote, and perhaps (though here we are on thinner ice) in the way they behaved and decided. On the surface, their cases contained more (and more explicit) appeals to "public policy." Over the last century or so, judges have become more willing to overrule cases directly. Overruling had always been possible in America; but the power was rarely used. In Earl Warren's court, overruling became positively epidemic. Modern high court judges also dissent more than their predecessors, and they write more concurring but separate opinions. In Michigan, in the 1870s, about 95 percent of all high court cases were unanimous; in the 1960s, there were dissents or concurrences in 44 percent of the published opinions.[21]

The trend is most marked in the United States Supreme Court. Oliver Wendell Holmes and Louis Brandeis were "great dissenters" in the first third of the century; but in their day dissent was still not as normal as it later became. By the late 1950s, a unanimous decision was unusual, at least in cases of first importance. The school-segregation case was, in fact, unanimous; this in itself suggested ardent diplomacy by Warren behind the scenes. Frequently, the Supreme Court splits down the middle, 5 to 4; in some cases, the justices write three, four, five, or even more separate opinions; it became a nice preoccupation of political scientists to analyze blocs on the Court, and the games that justices played.

In the 20th century, the bench and bar continued their progress (if that is the word) toward full professional status. In most states, lay judges—even lay justices of the peace—went the way of the heath hen and the Carolina parakeet. To be sure, judges were

[21]Lawrence M. Friedman et al., "State Supreme Courts: A Century of Style and Citation," 33 Stan. L. Rev. 773, 790 (1981). Michigan was one of 16 state supreme courts studied; there was tremendous variation among states (dissent rates actually *fell* in West Virginia between 1870 and 1970; in the decade of the '60s, more than 98 percent of the West Virginia high court cases were unanimous); but the number of nonunanimous decisions, in general, doubled over the course of the century.

still elected; they were, in this sense, politicians rather than part of the civil service. But the election of judges tended to be a routine affair, an electoral rubber stamp. Most often, a judge got his seat on the bench through appointment, when an old judge died or resigned. After a long term of office, the new judge would run for re-election, but without any real opposition. Few high court judges were ever defeated, or even threatened with defeat.

The Missouri plan (1940) proposed ending the electoral charade. This plan shifted responsibility for selecting judges to a panel made up of lawyers chosen by the local bar, a sitting judge, and laymen appointed by the governor. The panel would suggest three names; the governor would choose one of the three. This judge then served one year on the bench; at that point he or she would run for re-election, but unopposed. Since it is hard to defeat a somebody with nobody, the unopposed judge would certainly win (Rose Bird, the controversial Chief Justice of California, appointed in the late 1970s, narrowly survived one such attempt to unseat her). In the 1960s, a number of states followed Missouri's example. As early as the 1940s, also, the ABA lobbied, with some success, for a greater say in the selection of federal judges. It is now routine to ask the opinion of an ABA committee, on whether some proposed judge is qualified or not. This is not binding on anybody, but has an impact on selection and confirmation.

In 1908, the American Bar Association adopted a canon of professional ethics. Most states accepted this or a similar code as the official rules for the conduct of lawyers. The bar became "integrated" in many states from about the middle of the century. This meant that all lawyers in the state had to belong to a single (state) bar association, which collected dues and had power, at least in theory, to discipline its members. By 1960, more than half of the states had integrated bars. There is still a trend in this direction—Illinois, for example, integrated its bar in the 1970s. Still, compared to the hold of the American Medical Association over doctors (largely through control of hospitals), the legal profession has been loose and liberal indeed. At no point did more than half the lawyers even bother to join their national association. And although the bar tried to speak with one voice, it never quite persuaded the outside world to listen.

Some would say this is all to the good. The performance of the organized bar, compared to its ballyhoo, has been retrograde and weak. In times when justice or civil liberty were in crisis, the organized bar was not on the side of the angels. It was racist in the early part of the century (no blacks were allowed in the ABA); during the McCarthy period, the ABA was eager for loyalty oaths and purges.[22] Its "ethics" meant, for the most part, squelching advertising and protecting lawyers against competition. In the last generation or so, the bar has somewhat mended its ways. In any event, it has moved toward the political center. The Supreme Court gave it a push when it struck down the ban on advertising. One can now hear lawyers on TV, hustling for the business of drunk drivers; legal "clinics" are spreading like shops that sell fried chicken. The old lawyers of Wall Street would turn over in their graves.

But Wall Street itself has changed dramatically. At one time a big firm had 20 lawyers; only a generation ago, 100 lawyers meant a giant firm. In the 1980s, Baker and McKenzie had over 500 lawyers. Not only were the megafirms growing like weeds, they had discovered the virtues of branching. This was, before the Second World War, distinctly a rarity. Until recently, only a few law firms had branches—perhaps in Washington, D.C.; one or two firms maintained a tiny overseas office. Branching is now much more common; there are firms with five or six branches— as far away as Riyadh, Saudi Arabia, or as close as the flashier suburbs.

By now, the law schools have a virtual monopoly on access to the bar.[23] There were more of them than medical schools—something on the order of 200, by 1980. Almost every state had at least one—a few holdouts, like Hawaii and Vermont, succumbed after the Second World War. Law schools were not so expensive to run or so carefully controlled as medical schools—not that they were as diverse as they might or ought to have been. The Langdell method and conceptual jurisprudence dominated legal education in the first half of the century. All over the country in, say, 1930 or 1950, small, poorly financed schools, some with night divisions, pathetically tried to imitate Harvard, using her methods and her casebooks, rather than searching for their own mission and soul. In the '60s and '70s, an incredible flood of applicants meant that almost all schools were able to become more selective; the top

[22]Jerold S. Auerbach, *Unequal Justice: Lawyers and Social Change in Modern America* (1976).

[23]See, in general, Robert B. Stevens, *Law School: Legal Education in America from the 1850s to the 1980s* (1983).

schools in prestige skimmed off the cream of the crop. Many schools also made an attempt to reach out for minority students. There was an incredible increase in the number of women who studied for the bar. From about one percent or so in some schools, as late as the 1960s, they rose to a quarter, a third, or even half by 1980.

During most of the period, Langdell and conceptualism had the upper hand in literature as well. This was the age of great treatises. Samuel Williston built a monumental fortress (1920–22) out of the law of *Contracts,* volume after volume, solid, closely knit, fully armored against the intrusion of any ethical, economic, or social notions whatsoever.[24] After 1920, the legal realist movement threw down the gauntlet and became a serious rival of the dominant school. Karl Llewellyn and Jerome Frank, among others, did battle against the jurisprudence of concepts; there were even realist treatises, like Arthur Corbin's *Contracts,* a counterpoise out of Yale to the old man of Harvard. The realist idea also had an effect on the curriculum. Administrative law and taxation entered the ranks of the courses; and there was some attempt to change content in older courses, in line with the new temper of the times. On the whole, though, law school curricula have remained amazingly resistant to radical transformation, despite generations of manifestoes. Some schools have added "enrichment" courses; some have tinkered with clinical training. The center seems to hold, for better or for worse. The core curriculum has proved incredibly tough and impermeable.

There has been, from time to time, a movement to bring law back into the intellectual world. There were experiments in integrating law and social science in the 1920s and 1930s at Columbia, Johns Hopkins, and Yale, and a fling or two at curricular reform. These essays failed. After the Second World War, there were more serious efforts. Now, at last, government and foundation money began to trickle into the law schools. In the 1950s, an empirical study of the jury, at the University of Chicago, showed that collaboration between legal scholars and their social science colleagues was at least possible. Mostly, law and social science was still only a promise; but the promise seemed a little less hollow and dreamlike. In a few schools—notably Wisconsin and Berkeley—there was something more than lip service to the idea. In the 1960s, law study broadened to include more social issues—

[24]Williston was born in 1861 and died in 1963 at the age of 101.

law and poverty, for example, and a richer, more varied dose of foreign law. The social sciences, basically, made hardly a dent, except for economics. Here Chicago was a leader; and Richard Posner, later a federal judge, was a major contributor. The "law and economics" school was widely attacked as right-wing and excessively narrow; but it had gained, by the 1980s, a significant place in legal teaching, thought, and research.

Of the making of books, quality aside, there was truly no end. The few university law reviews of the 19th century had grown to an incredible number by the 1980s. There were probably on the order of one hundred and fifty. Virtually every law school, no matter how marginal, published a review as a matter of local pride. Somehow, all of these thousands of pages filled up with words. The more prestigious schools put out more issues per year than the weaker schools; then, when thick volumes became commonplace, they put out two journals, or more. By law school tradition, students ran the journals; law-review editors were the student elite of their schools. They had the best grades, the best, or only, rapport with the faculty, and went to the best firms when they got their degrees. (Some schools, in a burst of 1960s egalitarianism, opened law-review competition to all students who wished to try, regardless of grades.) It was a rare and daring event when Duke University, in the early 1930s, began to publish a journal called *Law and Contemporary Problems*. Each issue was a symposium on some topical subject; and there was no section set aside for the work of students. Later, specialized and scholarly journals, for example, the *American Journal of Legal History,* began to appear. The first issue of *The Law & Society Review* was published in 1966.

On the whole, despite the baleful influence of conceptualism, legal literature was never richer than in the 20th century. During his long life, Roscoe Pound (1870–1964), a product of Nebraska who switched from the study of fungus to law, poured his enormous creative energy into many subjects, sometimes erratically, but always provocatively. Between the two world wars, Charles Warren wrote a number of seminal studies of the American legal past. Legal history emerged once more from the shadows after the Second World War, and produced at least one major figure, Willard Hurst of Wisconsin. Hurst and his followers—the so-called Wisconsin school—focused a major part of their effort on the relationship between law and the economy. In the 1970s, a group of younger historians, somewhat more radical, began questioning the work of the Hurst school; but this too was a mark of its permanent influence. Scholars from other disciplines, too, began to look *at* law with a fresh and sometimes illuminating eye. Most of these—but not all—stood outside the law school world.

In the late 1960s, volcanic rumblings began to disturb the peace of the law schools. Students led the way: their banners flew slogans of civil rights and civil liberties; then those of the war against poverty; then general radicalism and revulsion with the established order. The richest and most famous schools were most affected; and within the schools, on the whole, it was the most intellectually active students who most strongly joined in with the currents of protest. The whole profession began to taste the consequences. When the Office of Economic Opportunity put money into neighborhood law offices, young lawyers eagerly turned out to work in the ghettos. Wall Street had to raise its price to keep its pools of talent from drying up. Things (it appeared) would never be the same. Classical legal education looked like a Humpty Dumpty, teetering on the wall. Would it bounce, or would it break?

The vast ocean of law, the bottomless pit of law, seemed caught up, along with the rest of society, in crisis. The pillars on which it rested seemed to be crumbling. Everybody agreed, for example, that criminal justice was rotten to the core. The left considered it oppressive and unjust; the right complained that it was too tenderhearted to do the job. In the late 1970s, the welfare state seemed to some to be dangerously overextended; and this included its legal component. Meanwhile, everybody, left, right, and center, was complaining about a litigation explosion (largely mythical, perhaps), and society seemed to be choking to death on its own secretions.

Yet, by 1970, the student movement had peaked. And in the 1980s, the riots stopped happening; the country seemed remarkably quiescent; there was a hunger for old-fashioned verities; the most conservative President in decades (Ronald Reagan) smiled soothingly from the White House and on TV screens. In many law schools, professors complained that students were boring, complacent, vocational. New radical movements sprang up among the professorate; but the student body (and the bar) hardly blinked. The public complained of too much law; but it was, in some ways, a monster of its own making—if it was indeed a monster at all.

Still, people asked: where was all this coming to? What was the future of this amazing system of law? Of course, it had a future— that much was clear. If law means an organized system of social control, any society of any size and complexity has such a system, and lots of it. As long as the country endures, so will its system of law, coextensive with society itself, reflecting its wishes and needs, in all their irrationality, ambiguity, and inconsistency. It will follow every twist and turn of development. It will reflect the yearnings for justice—and also the thirst for power, the deep inequality built into the structure of society. The law, after all, is a mirror held up against life. It is order: it is justice; it is also fear, insecurity, and emptiness; it is whatever results from the scheming, plotting, and striving of people and groups, with and against each other. None of this is going to change. A full history of American law would be nothing more or less than a full history of American life. The future of one is the future of the other. If American institutions can support a society that is prosperous, efficient, and satisfying, that society might also be lawful and just. The fate of the system is beyond the capacity of history to say.

BIBLIOGRAPHICAL ESSAY

In the Bibliography, I have listed those books and articles cited and made use of in the text, omitting chiefly such primary sources as cases, statutes, and so on. This list might serve the reader as a kind of guide to additional secondary studies in American legal history. In these few pages, however, I have singled out a short, selective group of books (and a few articles). These are exceptionally cogent, or comprehensive, or well-written, or in some other way worthy of special notice.

There is a profound shortage of *general* books on American legal history. The present text is basically the only one that covers the whole subject (or most of it). There are essentially no other concise (or for that matter, wordy) narrative accounts of the story of American law and American legal institutions, except for a coffee-table book or two. On the other hand, there is a literature on particular topics, and it is not without its glories. Since the first edition of this book (1973), this literature has grown very rapidly, and the future looks even brighter. Kermit Hall has produced a five-volume bibliography on American legal and constitutional history which was published in late 1984 under the title *A Comprehensive Bibliography of American Constitutional and Legal History, 1896–1979*. Also, Borzoi Books/Knopf has brought out a series of short paperbacks, which together cover the main periods of American legal history. Each of these books—there are five—contains an introductory essay (usually about 50 or 60 pages long), followed by some representative documents. The books are: Stephen Botein, *Early American Law and Society* (1983); George Dargo, *Law in the New Republic: Private Law and the Public Estate* (1983); Jamil Zainaldin, *Law in Antebellum Society: Legal Change and Economic Expansion* (1983); Jonathan Lurie, *Law and the Nation, 1865–1912* (1983); and Gerald L. Fetner, *Ordered Liberty: Legal Reform in the Twentieth Century* (1982).

No student of American legal history can ignore the work of J. Willard Hurst. Of his many books, *The Growth of American Law: The Law Makers* (1950), is the most general and accessible; it treats the work of certain "principal agencies of law" (the bar, the bench, the legislatures, the constitution makers), between 1790 and 1940, all with great clarity and insight. *Law and the Conditions of Freedom in the Nineteenth Century United*

States (1956) is a short but brilliant essay that digs below the surface of American legal culture in the 19th century. Perhaps the most ambitious of Hurst's books is *Law and Economic Growth: The Legal History of the Lumber Industry in Wisconsin, 1836–1915* (1964). This is a case study, tied to a concrete time, place, and industry, but it deserves close attention for its thoughtfulness, care, and detail. Among Hurst's more recent works are *Law and Social Order in the United States* (1977), and *Law and Markets in United States History: Different Modes of Bargaining among Interests* (1982).

There are not many books besides Hurst's that present a general theory or a broad, wide-ranging approach to our legal history, or even a substantial portion of it. Two books about the transition between the colonial period and the period of the Republic, or rather between a less and a more modern phase of legal history, have evoked considerable discussion. One is Morton J. Horwitz's *The Transformation of American Law, 1780–1860* (1977); the other is William Nelson's *Americanization of the Common Law: The Impact of Legal Change on Massachusetts Society, 1760–1830* (1975).

The reader interested in the *colonial period* will want to begin with George L. Haskins's *Law and Authority in Early Massachusetts* (1960), a seminal book. There is no general overview of the period, but there are a number of collections of essays, notable David H. Flaherty, ed., *Essays in the History of Early American Law* (1969); and see also Richard B. Morris, *Studies in the History of American Law, with Special Reference to the 17th and 18th Centuries* (2nd edition, 1959), which is still valuable, though it has been superseded on many points by more recent work. There are also collections of essays on the legal history of particular colonies, for example, Herbert A. Johnson, *Essays on New York Colonial Legal History* (1981).

There are some well-crafted recent monographs on particular places and subjects. There is, to begin with, William E. Nelson's study, *Dispute and Conflict Resolution in Plymouth County, Massachusetts, 1725–1825* (1981), which, as the name suggests, laps over into the Republican period. David L. Konig, *Law and Society in Puritan Massachusetts, Essex County, 1629–1692* (1979), is one of the most insightful attempts to make sense of the colonial tapestry. The transition from English to American ways is dealt with in David G. Allen's book, *In English Ways* (1981). For a rich treatment of the work of the county courts, there is Hendrik Hartog's "The Public Law of a County Court: Judicial Government in Eighteenth-Century Massachusetts," 20 Am. J. Legal Hist. 282 (1976). Now if only more of the talent at work on the colonial period would spill over into studies of colonies other than Massachusetts (and a bit of Virginia and New York)!

The reader interested in the colonial period has another advantage: there are quite a few good modern editions of colonial court records. Joseph H. Smith's *Colonial Justice in Western Massachusetts (1639–1702), The Pynchon Court Record* (1961) is particularly outstanding, because of its long and informative introduction. Studies of particular aspects of colonial law are not, to say the least, overabundant; but Richard B. Morris, *Government and Labor in Early America* (1946) covers this important subject in fine detail. On criminal law, see Julius Goebel, Jr., and T. Raymond Naughton, *Law Enforcement in Colonial New York: A Study in Criminal Procedure* (1944); and Douglas Greenberg, *Crime and Law Enforcement in the Colony of New York, 1691–1776* (1974). Joseph H. Smith's *Appeals to the Privy Council from the American Plantations* (1950) is the definitive study of its subject.

The Revolution itself, and the period immediately following, have been somewhat neglected in legal history. Hendrik Hartog has edited a collection of review essays, *Law in the American Revolution and the Revolution in the Law* (1981). John Phillip Reid has written extensively on the legal events leading up to the Revolution; see, for example, *In Defiance of the Law: The Standing-Army Controversy, the Two Constitutions, and the Coming of the American Revolution* (1981).

From the time of the Constitution on, there is much more of a literature, particularly on institutional history. Legal historians, to no one's surprise, are particularly interested in courts. Unlike the colonial period, certain of the 19th century sources are to a degree readily available; reported appellate cases, and the state and federal statutes, can be found in any decent law library. The trial courts, alas, are if anything more obscure than in the colonial period.

Many scholars have worked on aspects of the history of courts. The United States Supreme Court, naturally, has garnered the lion's share of attention. Charles Warren's *The Supreme Court in United States History* (3 vols., 1922) is a genuine classic—engrossing, richly detailed, superbly easy to read. Warren had a point of view—or bias, if you will—and did not hide it; but nothing before or after provides so generous a look at the Court at work, or is so studiously attentive to the political context in which the Court does its labors. A new history of the Court, in many volumes, has been in process for what seems like forever. A few parts have actually appeared: Volume I, *Antecedents and Beginnings to 1801,* by Julius Goebel, Jr. (1971); Volume II, *Foundations of Power: John Marshall, 1801–15* (1981), by George L. Haskins and Herbert A. Johnson; Volume V, *The Taney Period, 1836–1864* (1974), by Carl B. Swisher; Volume VI, Part One, *Reconstruction and Reunion, 1864–1888,* by Charles Fairman (1971). These are all big books, in the physical sense, and extremely detailed. For specific periods, the reader can choose among a number of other books: Stanley I. Kutler, *Judicial Power and Reconstruction Politics* (1968); Harold M. Hyman and William M. Wiecek, *Equal Justice under Law: Constitutional Development, 1835–1875* (1982); William F. Swindler, *Court and Constitution in the Twentieth Century: The Old Legality, 1889–1932* (1969); Arnold M. Paul, *Conservative Crisis and the Rule of Law: Attitudes of Bar and Bench, 1887–1895* (1960).

There are also some interesting studies of particular decisions—for example, C. Peter Magrath, *Yazoo, Law and Politics in the New Republic:*

The Case of Fletcher v. Peck (1966); Stanley I. Kutler, *Privilege and Creative Destruction: The Charles River Bridge Case* (1971). Don E. Fehrenbacher's *The Dred Scott Case: Its Significance in American Law and Politics* (1978) is a massive and definitive study, not only of the case itself, but of many salient features in the legal and constitutional background. A shorter version, *Slavery, Law, and Politics: The Dred Scott Case in Historical Perspective,* appeared in 1981. Tony Freyer's book, *Harmony and Dissonance: The Swift and Erie Cases in American Federalism* (1981), follows the career of one important case through time. On the technical growth of the jurisdiction of the Supreme Court, Felix Frankfurter and James M. Landis, *The Business of the Supreme Court: A Study in the Federal Judicial System* (1928), still has value.

Some of the best work on the Supreme Court lurks in judicial biographies. Three older but excellent examples are Charles Fairman, *Mr. Justice Miller and the Supreme Court, 1862–1890* (1939), and two studies by Carl B. Swisher, *Stephen J. Field: Craftsman of the Law* (1930) and *Roger B. Taney* (1935). The old biography of John Marshall, by Albert Beveridge, is long-winded and biased, but the writing is sprightly. Gerald T. Dunne has published a biography of Joseph Story, *Joseph Story and the Rise of the Supreme Court* (1970). For the same period, there is Donald G. Morgan's *Justice William Johnson: The First Dissenter* (1945). Mark DeWolfe Howe's study of the life of Oliver Wendell Holmes, Jr., was cut short by Howe's death. Two volumes had appeared: *Justice Oliver Wendell Holmes: The Shaping Years, 1841–1870* (1957); and *Justice Oliver Wendell Holmes: The Proving Years, 1870–1882* (1963). The work stops just at the point of Holmes's appointment to the Massachusetts bench. Finally, Leon Friedman and Fred L. Israel have edited *The Justices of the United States Supreme Court, 1789–1969* (1969), in four volumes.

The lower federal courts, and the state courts, have done much more poorly in legal scholarship. Richard E. Ellis, *The Jeffersonian Crisis: Courts and Politics in the Young Republic* (1971), is exceptional, in that it looks at courts in selected states, as well as on the federal level. A rare study of a lower federal court is Mary K. Bonsteel Tachau, *Federal Courts in the Early Republic: Kentucky, 1789–1816* (1978). On the federal judiciary, see Kermit L. Hall, *The Politics of Justice: Lower Federal Judicial Selection and the Second Party System, 1829–61* (1979). Studies of state courts—one older example is Carroll T. Bond, *The Court of Appeals of Maryland: A History* (1928)—are rare, and leave a lot to be desired. There are also a few biographies of state judges which have merit, for example, John Philip Reid, *Chief Justice, the Judicial World of Charles Doe* (1967), and Leonard Levy, *The Law of the Commonwealth and Chief Justice Shaw* (1957).

Historical studies of the actual work of American courts—the flow of business through them; the kinds of disputes they handle—are also not common. For a long time, the only book that could be cited here was Francis W. Laurent's *The Business of a Trial Court: 100 Years of Cases* (1959), an intriguing but somewhat unsatisfying study of the work of the trial courts of general jurisdiction in Chippewa County, Wisconsin. Recently, the literature has grown; it now includes Lawrence M. Friedman and Robert V. Percival, "A Tale of Two Courts: Litigation in Alameda and San Benito Counties," 10 Law & Society Review 267 (1976), and Robert Silverman, *Law and Urban Growth: Civil Litigation in the Boston Trial Courts, 1880–1900* (1981). The very lowest courts never get much of a break in research, but justice courts were the subject of John R. Wunder, *Inferior Courts, Superior Justice: A History of the Justices of the Peace on the Northwest Frontier, 1853–1889* (1979).

For those interested in the history of the legal profession, Anton-Hermann Chroust's *The Rise of the Legal Profession in America*, in two volumes (Volume 1, *The Colonial Experience*, Volume 2, *The Revolution and the Post-Revolutionary Era*, 1965), at least provides a good deal of information, though this is a fairly uncritical work. More solid scholarship is in Gerard W. Gawalt's book, *The Promise of Power: The Emergence of the Legal Profession in Massachusetts, 1760–1840* (1979); Maxwell Bloomfield's essays on the profession are collected in *American Lawyers in a Changing Society* (1976); and Gerard W. Gawalt has edited an (uneven) group of essays in *The New High Priests: Lawyers in Post-Civil War America* (1984). William F. English, *The Pioneer Lawyer and Jurist in Missouri* (1947), makes lively reading.

Another good read is William F. Keller, *The Nation's Advocate, Henry Marie Brackenridge and Young America* (1956). This book also represents a large and very mixed literature: biographies of lawyers. If the "lawyer" has made his mark in another field, too, the material tends to balloon— for example, Abraham Lincoln, treated in John P. Frank, *Lincoln as a Lawyer* (1961); and John J. Duff, *A. Lincoln, Prairie Lawyer* (1960). Thus there are many biographies of Daniel Webster, including one by Irving H. Bartlett, *Daniel Webster* (1978). But rare indeed are books which open the door to the lawyer's office, so to speak.

The monumental edition of *The Law Practice of Alexander Hamilton: Documents and Commentary*, in five volumes (Vol I, 1964, and Vol. II, 1969, edited by Julius Goebel Jr.; Vol. III, 1980, Vol. IV, 1980, and Vol. V, 1981, edited by Goebel and Joseph Smith), does nobly for the period around 1800; Webster's legal papers, too, are in the process of getting themselves edited; two volumes, edited by Alfred S. Konefsky and Andrew J. King, have so far appeared. One wishes a similar job could be done for the Wall Street lawyer of the late nineteenth century; but there is at least some raw material in the law-office histories that have appeared, notably, Robert T. Swaine, *The Cravath Firm and Its Predecessors, 1819–1947*, Vol I, *The Predecessor Firms, 1819-1906* (1946). Henry W. Taft's book, *A Century and a Half at the New York Bar* (1938), is entertaining reading.

On legal education, Alfred Z. Reed, *Training for the Public Profession of the Law* (1921), is old but useful. Robert B. Stevens, *Law School: Legal Education in America from the 1850s to the 1980s* (1983), is the most comprehensive treatment of the subject. In addition, a number of law schools, most notably Harvard, have had their chroniclers; Arthur E. Sutherland's *The Law at Harvard: A History of Ideas and Men, 1817–1967* (1967) is quite readable. Frank L. Ellsworth, *Law on the Midway: The Founding of the University of Chicago Law School* (1977), is particularly interesting for the light it sheds on the spread of the influence of Harvard. Elizabeth G. Brown, *Legal Education in Michigan, 1859–1959* (1959), covers the first century of this important school.

The literature on legal literature, and on legal thought, is not very full or very satisfactory. Perry Miller collected some snippets and edited them under the title *The Legal Mind in America: From Independence to the Civil War* (1962). Miller's own treatment of the subject, in *The Life of the Mind in America: From the Revolution to the Civil War* (1965), is, to me at least, not very enlightening. There is also Charles M. Cook, *The American Codification Movement: A Study of Antebellum Legal Reform* (1981). For the end of the century, one can cite Clyde Jacobs, *Law Writers and the Courts: The Influence of Thomas M. Cooley, Christopher G. Tiedeman, and John F. Dillon upon American Constitutional Law* (1954). On civil procedure, there is a rather ponderous but carefully executed book by Robert W. Millar, *Civil Procedure of the Trial Court in Historical Perspective* (1952).

A number of monographs have appeared on the subject of state constitution-making; of special interest are Willi P. Adams, *The First American Constitutions: Republican Ideology and the Making of the State Constitutions in the Revolutionary Era* (1980); Fletcher M. Green, *Constitutional Development in the South Atlantic States, 1776–1860* (1966); and Carl B. Swisher, *Motivation and Political Technique in the California Constitutional Convention, 1878–9* (1930). One interesting side show in American legal history is treated in William M. Robinson, Jr., *Justice in Grey: A History of the Judicial System of the Confederate States of America* (1941); another is considered in Carol Weisbrod, *The Boundaries of Utopia* (1980), which deals with the internal affairs of "self-contained communities" in the United States (the Oneida community, for example). Frontier law has generated far more heat and romance than light. A careful glimpse of an early period is in William Baskerville Hamilton, *Anglo-American Law on the Frontier: Thomas Rodney and His Territorial Cases* (1953); for later periods, it is hard to resist a book as lively as Glenn Shirley's *Law West of Fort Smith: A History of Frontier Justice in the Indian Territory, 1834–1896* (1957). An important study of legal culture in the West is John Phillip Reid's book, *Law for the Elephant: Property and Social Behavior on the Overland Trail* (1980), which deals with the living law of the pioneers who followed the trails to Oregon and California in the middle of the 19th century.

The *substantive* law is a mixed bag. Many areas have never gotten their due. No one seriously interested in American legal history should ignore the series of books that emerged from the workshops of the University of Wisconsin law school, under the direct or indirect influence of J. Willard Hurst, all dealing with one or another aspect of law in Wisconsin, chiefly in the 19th century. Taken as a whole, these books provide the fullest available picture of the law in action in a single state. Some are better or more readable than others, of course. Robert S. Hunt's *Law and Locomotives: The Impact of the Railroad on Wisconsin Law in the Nineteenth Century* (1958) is particularly fascinating. Others in the series include Lawrence M. Friedman, *Contract Law in America: A Social and Economic Case Study* (1965); Spencer Kimball, *Insurance and Public Policy: A Study in the Legal Implementation of Social and Economic Public Policy* (1960); and George J. Kuehnl, *The Wisconsin Business Corporation* (1959).

The Wisconsin school of legal history has had a special interest in the relationship between law and the economic system, and between law and business. This aspect of law has been treated rather better than certain other aspects of law in the 19th century, though no one would say that anywhere near enough work had been done. The area, too, is much illuminated by the literature on government's role in the economy—works such as Oscar and Mary Handlin, *Commonwealth: A Study of the Role of Government in the American Economy: Massachusetts, 1774–1861* (rev. ed., 1969); and Louis Hartz, *Economic Policy and Democratic Thought: Pennsylvania, 1776–1860* (1948); Harry N. Scheiber, *Ohio Canal Era: A Case Study of Government and the Economy, 1820–1861* (1969). Bray Hammond has written the major book on banking and the law: *Banks and Politics in America from the Revolution to the Civil War* (1957); he also published *Sovereignty and an Empty Purse, Banks and Politics in the Civil War* (1970). On railroad regulation, there is the Hunt study, mentioned above, for Wisconsin; Edward C. Kirkland, *Men, Cities and Transportation: A Study in New England History, 1820–1900* (2 vols., 1948); George H. Miller, *Railroads and the Granger Laws* (1971); and the iconoclastic study by Gabriel Kolko, *Railroads and Regulation, 1877–1916* (1965). On the ICC act, and administrative development in general, see Stephen Skowronek, *Building a New American State: The Expansion of National Administrative Capacities, 1877–1920* (1982). For the background and early history of the antitrust laws, see William R. Letwin, *Law and Economic Policy in America: The Evolution of the Sherman Antitrust Act* (1965). Charles Warren's *Bankruptcy in United States History* (1935) is still useful, though it should now be supplemented by Peter Coleman's study, *Debtors and Creditors in America: Insolvency, Imprisonment for Debt, and Bankruptcy, 1607–1900* (1974). On corporation law, there is John William Cadman, *The Corporation in New Jersey: Business and Politics* (1949); and Ronald E. Seavoy, *The Origins of the American Business Corporation, 1784–1855* (1982). On taxation, there is Randolph E. Paul, *Taxation in the United States* (1954); on the development of the law of municipal corporations, Hendrik Hartog, *Public Property and Private Power: The Corporation of the City of New York in American Law, 1730–1870* (1983), and Jon C. Teaford, *The Unheralded Triumph: City Government in America, 1870–1900* (1984).

In general, the law of property is still waiting for its prince to come and rouse it from the long sleep of obscurity. Public land law has done a bit better than the rest of this field. A comprehensive, older account is Benjamin H. Hibbard, A History of the Public Land Policies (1924); a more recent treatment is Paul Gates, History of Public Land Law Development (1968). Vernon Carstensen collected important essays and edited them under the title of The Public Lands: Studies in the History of the Public Domain (1963). A key essay on eminent domain law is Harry N. Scheiber's "The Road to Munn: Eminent Domain and the Concept of Public Purpose in the State Courts," in Donald Fleming and Bernard Bailyn, eds., Law in American History (1971), p. 329.

For a long time, there was surprisingly little good work on the history of criminal law and criminal justice. But the situation has much improved, and the volume is steadily increasing. On the criminal justice system, see Jack K. Williams, Vogues in Villainy: Crime and Retribution in Ante-Bellum South Carolina (1959); Michael S. Hindus, Prison and Plantation: Crime, Justice, and Authority in Massachusetts and South Carolina, 1767–1878 (1980); Lawrence M. Friedman and Robert V. Percival, The Roots of Justice: Crime and Punishment in Alameda County, California, 1870–1910 (1981); Edward L. Ayers, Vengeance and Justice, Crime and Punishment in the 19th-Century American South (1984). Samuel Walker, Popular Justice: A History of American Criminal Justice (1980) is a readable general survey. On the police, see Roger Lane, Policing the City: Boston, 1822–1885 (1967); and Wilbur R. Miller, Cops and Bobbies: Police Authority in New York and London, 1830– 1870 (1977). There are useful essays in Violence in America: Historical and Comparative Perspectives, edited by Hugh D. Graham and Ted R. Gurr (1969), a report submitted to the National Commission on the Causes and Prevention of Violence. Other relevant studies include Richard Maxwell Brown, Strain of Violence: Historical Studies of American Violence and Vigilantism (1975); and Roger Lane, Violent Death in the City: Suicide, Accident and Murder in 19th Century Philadelphia (1979).

David J. Rothman's provocative book, The Discovery of the Asylum, Social Order and Disorder in the New Republic (1971), illuminates many areas of legal and social history. The theme of the book is the shift to institutional treatment of deviants in the 19th century—the rise to prominence of the penitentiary, poorhouse, insane asylum, and the juvenile house of refuge. Rothman continued the story in Conscience and Convenience: The Asylum and Its Alternatives in Progressive America (1980). His work thus straddles welfare history and the history of criminal justice; this double treatment is found also in Eric H. Monkkonen's book, The Dangerous Class: Crime and Poverty in Columbus, Ohio, 1860–1885 (1975). This is perhaps also the best place to mention Joseph Gusfield's stimulating study of the liquor laws, Symbolic Crusade: Status Politics and the American Temperance Movement (1963).

Welfare law itself does not have an adequate literature. In the 1930s, a series of studies of the poor laws came out of the University of Chicago, under the sponsorship of the School of Social Service Administration. A typical example was Alice Shaffer, Mary W. Keefer, and Sophonisba P.

Breckinridge, *The Indiana Poor Law* (1936). But the overall quality was low. Henry Farnam, *Chapters in the History of Social Legislation in the United States to 1860* (1938), is still of value; another monograph is James Leiby, *Charity and Correction in New Jersey* (1967). Joel Handler has edited *Family Law and the Poor: Essays by Jacobus ten Broek* (1971). On the early history of housing law, see Lawrence M. Friedman, *Government and Slum Housing: A Century of Frustration* (1968); on environmental law, Earl F. Murphy, *Water Purity: A Study in Legal Control of Natural Resources* (1961).

Family law, too, is relatively neglected, but there are signs of progress here. Nelson M. Blake, *The Road to Reno: A History of Divorce in the United States* (1962), is good reading; and William L. O'Neill's book, *Divorce in the Progressive Era* (1967), is provocative; the bulk of it, however, deals with the early 20th century. Another study of the same period is Elaine Tyler May, *Great Expectations: Marriage and Divorce in Post-Victorian America* (1980). A literature on married women's property laws has begun to grow; the best book on the subject so far is Norma Basch, *In the Eyes of the Law: Women, Marriage, and Property in Nineteenth-Century New York* (1982). D. Kelly Weisberg has edited two volumes on *Women and the Law: The Social Historical Perspective* (1982); the essays collected here vary in quality and theme, but they give a good overview of the present state of women's legal history. The law of slavery and race relations is often treated in general books on these subjects, for example, Kenneth Stampp's *The Peculiar Institution: Slavery in the Ante-Bellum South* (1956); or C. Vann Woodward's *The Strange Career of Jim Crow* (revised edition, 1966). There is also a developing literature on the subject which stresses the legal side— criminal justice is treated in Hindus's and Ayers's books, cited above; and there is also Robert M. Cover, *Justice Accused: Antislavery and the Judicial Process* (1975); Paul Finkelman, *An Imperfect Union: Slavery, Federalism, and Comity* (1981); and A. E. Keir Nash's long essay, "Reason of Slavery: Understanding the Judicial Role in the Peculiar Institution," in 32 Vanderbilt Law Review 7 (1979). No doubt more will be heard on this subject.

BIBLIOGRAPHY

Abbott, Martin, *The Freedmen's Bureau in South Carolina, 1865–1872* (1967).

Abel-Smith, Brian, and Stevens, Robert, *Lawyers and the Courts: A Sociological Study of the English Legal System, 1750–1965* (1967).

Adams, Charles Francis, (1835–1915), *An Autobiography* (1916).

Adams, Willi Paul, *The First American Constitutions: Republican Ideology and the Making of the State Constitutions in the Revolutionary Era* (1980).

Addison, Alexander, *Charges to Grand Juries of the Counties of the Fifth Circuit in the State of Pennsylvania* (1800).

Addison, Charles G., *Wrongs and Their Remedies* (1860).

Allen, David Grayson, *In English Ways: The Movement of Societies and the Transferal of English Local Law and Custom to Massachusetts Bay in the Seventeenth Century* (1981).

Allen, Neal W., Jr., ed., Province and Court Records of Maine, Vol. IV, *The Court Records of York County, Maine* (1958).

American Law Institute, *A Study of the Business of the Federal Courts;* Part I, *Criminal Cases,* Part II, *Civil Cases* (1934).

Ames, James B., "The Failure of the 'Tilden Trust,'" 5 Harv. L. Rev. 389 (1892).

Anderson, Oscar E., *The Health of a Nation: Harvey W. Wiley and the Fight for Pure Food* (1958).

Angell, Joseph K., and Ames, Samuel, *A Treatise on the Law of Private Corporations Aggregate* (2nd ed., 1843).

Aronson, Sidney H., *Status and Kinship in the Higher Civil Service* (1964).

Asbury, Herbert, *The Gangs of New York: An Informal History of the Underworld* (1928).

Atiyah, Patrick S., *The Rise and Fall of Freedom of Contract* (1979).

Atkinson, Thomas E., "The Development of the Massachusetts Probate System," 42 Mich. L. Rev. 425 (1943).

Auerbach, Jerold S., *Justice without Law? Non-legal Dispute Settlement in American History* (1983).

———, *Unequal Justice: Lawyers and Social Change in Modern America* (1976).

Aumann, Francis R., *The Changing American Legal System: Some Selected Phases* (1940).

Ayers, Edward L., *Vengeance and Justice: Crime and Punishment in the Nineteenth-Century American South* (1984).

Baade, Hans W., "Marriage Contracts in French and Spanish Louisiana: A Study in 'Notarial' Jurisprudence," 53 Tulane L. Rev. 3 (1978).

Babb, James E., "The Supreme Court of Illinois," 3 Green Bag 217 (1891).

Bacote, Clarence A., "Negro Proscriptions, Protests, and Proposed Solutions in Georgia, 1880–1908," 25 J. Southern Hist. 471 (1959).

Bailey, Thomas A., "Congressional Opposition to Pure Food Legislation, 1879–1906," 36 Am. J. Sociol. 52 (1930).

"Bailments and Conditional Sales," 44 Am. Law Rev. 335 (1896).

Baker, Elizabeth F., *Henry Wheaton, 1785–1848* (1937).

Bakken, Gordon M., *The Development of Law on the Rocky Mountain Frontier: Civil Law and Society, 1850–1912* (1983).

———, "The Impact of the Colorado State Constitution on Rocky Mountain Constitution Making," 47 Colo. Magazine, No. 2, 152 (1970).

Baldwin, Joseph G., *The Flush Times of Alabama and Mississippi, A Series of Sketches* (1957).

Bancroft, Hubert, *Popular Tribunals* (2 volumes, 1887).

Barnes, I. R., *Public Utility Control in Massachusetts* (1930).

Bartlett, Irving H., *Daniel Webster* (1978).

Basch, Norma, *In the Eyes of the Law: Women, Marriage, and Property in Nineteenth-Century New York* (1982).

Bassett, John Spencer, *Slavery and Servitude in the Colony of North Carolina* (1896).

Bates, J. Leonard, ed., *Tom Walsh in Dakota Territory* (1966).

Baumgartner, M. P., "Law and Social Status in Colonial New Haven, 1639–1665," *Research in Law and Sociology*, Vol. 1 (1978).

Bay, W. V. N., *Reminiscences of the Bench and Bar of Missouri* (1878).

Beach, Charles F., *Commentaries on the Law of Public Corporations* (2 volumes, 1893).

Beard, Earl S., "The Background of State Railroad Regulation in Iowa," 51 Iowa J. of Hist. 1 (1953).

Beitzinger, Alfons J., *Edward G. Ryan, Lion of the Law* (1960).

Benjamin, Judah P., *A Treatise on the Law of Sale of Personal Property* (3rd American edition, Edmund Bennett, ed., 1881).

Bennett, Edmund, and Heard, Franklin, *A Selection of Leading Cases in Criminal Law* (2 volumes, 1856–57).

Benson, George C. S., et al., *The American Property Tax: Its History, Administration and Economic Impact* (1965).

Benson, Lee, *Merchants, Farmers, and Railroads: Railroad Regulation and New York Politics, 1850–1887* (1955).

Bentham, Jeremy, *Defence of Usury* (3rd ed., 1816).

———, *Rationale of Judicial Evidence*, Vol. IV (1827).

Benton, Josiah H., *Warning Out in New England* (1911).

Berger, Raoul, "Impeachment of Judges and 'Good Behavior' Tenure," 79 Yale L. J. 1475 (1970).

Beutel, Frederick K., "Colonial Sources of the Negotiable Instruments Law of the United States," 34 Ill. L. Rev. 137 (1939).

———, "The Development of State Statutes on Negotiable Paper Prior to the Negotiable Instruments Law," 40 Columbia L. Rev. 836 (1940).

Beveridge, Albert J., *The Life of John Marshall* (4 volumes, 1916–19).

Billings, Warren M., "Pleading, Procedure, and Practice: The Meaning of Due Process of Law in Seventeenth-Century Virginia," 47 J. Southern Hist. 569 (1981).

Binney, Horace, *The Leaders of the Old Bar of Philadelphia* (1866).

Bishop, Joel P., *Commentaries on the Criminal Law* (7th ed., 1882).

———, *Commentaries on the Law of Marriage and Divorce* (4th ed., 1864).

Blackstone, Sir William, *Commentaries on the Laws of England* (4 volumes, 1765–69).

Blake, Nelson M., *The Road to Reno: A History of Divorce in the United States* (1962).

Blandi, Joseph G., *Maryland Business Corporations, 1783–1852* (1934).

Bloomfield, Maxwell, *American Lawyers in a Changing Society, 1776–1876* (1976).

———, "From Deference to Confrontation: The Early Black Lawyers of Galveston, Texas, 1895–1920," in Gerard W. Gawalt, *The New High Priests: Lawyers in Post-Civil War America* (1984).

———, "Law vs. Politics: The Self-Image of the American Bar (1830–1860)," 12 Am. J. Legal Hist. 306 (1968).

———, "William Sampson and the Codifiers: The Roots of American Legal Reform, 1820–1830," 11 Am. J. Legal Hist. 234 (1967).

Blume, William W., "Civil Procedure on the American Frontier," 56 Mich. L. Rev. 161 (1957).

———, "Legislation on the American Frontier," 60 Mich. L. Rev. 317 (1962).

———, "Probate and Administration on the American Frontier," 58 Mich. L. Rev. 209 (1959).

———, ed., *Transactions of the Supreme Court of the Territory of Michigan,* Vol. I (1935).

Blume, William W., and Brown, Elizabeth G., "Territorial Courts and Law: Unifying Factors in the Development of American Legal Institutions," 61 Mich. L. Rev. 39, 467 (1962–63).

Boan, Fern, *A History of Poor Relief Legislation and Administration in Missouri* (1941).

Bodenhamer, David J., "The Democratic Impulse and Legal Change in the Age of Jackson: The Example of Criminal Juries in Antebellum Indiana," 45 The Historian 206 (1982).

———, "Law and Disorder on the Early Frontier: Marion County, Indiana, 1823–1850," 10 Western Hist. Q. 323 (1979).

Bodenhamer, David J., and Ely, James W., Jr., eds., *Ambivalent Legacy: A Legal History of the South* (1984).

Bogue, Allan G., "The Iowa Claim Clubs: Symbol and Substance," 45 Miss. Valley Hist. Rev. 231 (1958).

Bohlen, Francis H., "The Rule in *Rylands* v. *Fletcher*," 59 U. Pa. L. Rev. 298, 373, 423 (1911).

Bond, Beverley W., Jr., *The Quit-Rent System in the American Colonies* (1919).

Bond, Carroll T., *The Court of Appeals of Maryland, a History* (1928).

———, *Proceedings of the Maryland Court of Appeals, 1695–1729* (1933).

Boorstin, Daniel J., *The Americans: The Colonial Experience* (1958).

———, *Delaware Cases, 1792–1830* (3 volumes, 1943).

Borkin, Joseph, *The Corrupt Judge* (1962).

Botein, Stephen, *Early American Law and Society* (1983).

———, "The Legal Profession in Colonial North America," in Wilfrid Prest, ed., *Lawyers in Early Modern Europe and America* (1981).

Bourguignon, Henry J., *The First Federal Court: The Federal Appellate Prize Court of the American Revolution, 1775–1787* (1977).

Bowker, Richard Rogers, *Copyright, Its History and Its Law* (1912).

Boyer, Paul, and Nissenbaum, Stephen, *Salem Possessed: The Social Origins of Witchcraft* (1974).

Branning, Rosalind L., *Pennsylvania Constitutional Development* (1960).

Branscombe, Martha, *The Courts and the Poor Laws in New York State, 1784–1929* (1943).

Breckinridge, Sophonisba P., *The Illinois Poor Law and Its Administration* (1939).

———, *Public Welfare Administration in the United States* (2nd ed., 1938).

Bridenbaugh, Carl, *Cities in the Wilderness* (1938).

Brigance, William N., *Jeremiah Sullivan Black* (1934).

Bringhurst, Bruce, *Antitrust and the Oil Monopoly: The Standard Oil Cases, 1890–1911* (1979).

Bronner, Edwin B., *William Penn's "Holy Experiment"* (1962).

Brown, Elizabeth G., "The Bar on a Frontier: Wayne County, 1796–1836," 14 Am. J. Legal Hist. 136 (1970).

———, *British Statutes in American Law, 1776–1836* (1964).

———, "Husband and Wife—Memorandum on the Mississippi Women's Law of 1839," 42 Mich. L. Rev. 1110 (1944).

———, "The Law School of the University of Michigan, 1859–1959," 38 Mich. St. Bar J. 16 (August, 1959).

———, *Legal Education at Michigan, 1859–1959* (1959).

———, "Legal Systems in Conflict: Orleans Territory, 1804–1812," 1 Am. J. Legal Hist. 35 (1957).

———, "Poor Relief in a Wisconsin County, 1846–1866: Administration and Recipients," 20 Am. J. Legal Hist. 79 (1976).

Brown, Richard Maxwell, "The American Vigilante Tradition," in Hugh D. Graham and Ted R. Gurr, eds., *Violence in America: Historical and Comparative Perspectives* (1969).

————, "Historical Patterns of Violence in America," in Hugh D. Graham and Ted R. Gurr, eds., *Violence in America: Historical and Comparative Perspectives* (1969).

————, *Strain of Violence: Historical Studies of American Violence and Vigilantism* (1975).

Browne, William H., ed., Archives of Maryland, Vol. IV, *Judicial and Testamentary Business of the Provincial Court, 1637–1650* (1887).

Browning, Grace A., *The Development of Poor Relief Legislation in Kansas* (1935).

Bruce, Isabel C., and Eickhoff, Edith, *The Michigan Poor Law* (1936).

Bryson, W. Hamilton, *Legal Education in Virginia, 1779–1979: A Biographical Approach* (1982).

Buchanan, A. Russell, *David S. Terry of California, Dueling Judge* (1956).

Bugbee, Bruce W., *Genesis of American Patent and Copyright Law* (1967).

Cadman, John W., *The Corporation in New Jersey: Business and Politics, 1791–1875* (1949).

Cahill, Marion C., *Shorter Hours* (1932).

Cahn, Frances, and Bary, Valeska, *Welfare Activities of Federal, State, and Local Governments in California, 1850–1934* (1936).

Calhoun, Daniel H., *Professional Lives in America: Structure and Aspiration, 1750–1850* (1965).

Callow, Alexander B., Jr., *The Tweed Ring* (1966).

Canady, Hoyt P., "Legal Education in Colonial South Carolina," in Herbert Johnson, ed., *South Carolina Legal History* (1980).

Capen, Edward W., *The Historical Development of the Poor Law of Connecticut* (1905).

Carr, Lois Green, "The Development of the Maryland Orphans' Court," in Aubrey C. Land, Lois Green Carr, and Edward C. Papenfuse, eds., *Law, Society, and Politics in Early Maryland* (1977).

Carter, James C., *The Proposed Codification of Our Common Law* (1884).

————, *The Provinces of the Written and the Unwritten Law* (1889).

Casner, Andrew J., ed., *American Law of Property: A Treatise on the Law of Property in the United States* (7 volumes, 1952).

Caton, John D., *Early Bench and Bar of Illinois* (1893).

Caughey, John W., *Their Majesties, the Mob* (1960).

Centennial History of the Harvard Law School: 1817–1917 (1918).

Chandler, Alfred D., Jr., *The Visible Hand: The Managerial Revolution in American Business* (1977).

"The Changing Role of the Jury in the Nineteenth Century," 74 Yale L. J. 170 (1964).

Chapin, Bradley, *The American Law of Treason: Revolutionary and Early National Origins* (1964).

————, *Criminal Justice in Colonial America, 1606–1660* (1983).

Chase, Frederic Hathaway, *Lemuel Shaw, Chief Justice of the Supreme Judicial Court of Massachusetts* (1918).

Chase, William C., *The American Law School and the Rise of Administrative Government* (1982).

Child, Robert, *New Englands Jonas Cast up at London,* ed. W. T. R. Marvin (1869).

Chipman, Daniel, *The Life of the Hon. Nathaniel Chipman, Ll.D.* (1846).

Chittenden, L. E., "Legal Reminiscences," 5 Green Bag 307 (1893).

Chitty, Joseph, *Treatise on Pleading* (8th ed., 1840).

Christman, Henry, *Tin Horns and Calico* (1945).

Chroust, Anton-Hermann, *The Rise of the Legal Profession in America* (2 volumes, 1965).

Chused, Richard H., "Married Women's Property Law: 1800–1850," 71 Georgetown L.J. 1359 (1983).

Clark, Charles E., "The Union of Law and Equity," 25 Columbia L. Rev. 1 (1925).

Clark, Cornelia Anne, "Justice on the Tennessee Frontier: The Williamson County Circuit Court, 1810–1820," 32 Vanderbilt L. Rev. 413 (1979).

Clark, William L., *Handbook of the Law of Private Corporations* (1897).

Clarke, Samuel B., "Criticisms upon Henry George, Reviewed from the Stand-Point of Justice," 1 Harv. L. Rev. 265 (1888).

Clary, William W., *History of the Law Firm of O'Melveny and Myers, 1885–1965,* Vol. I (1966).

Coan, Titus M., ed., *Speeches, Arguments, and Miscellaneous Papers of David Dudley Field,* Vol. III (1890).

Coates, Albert, "The Story of the Law School at the University of North Carolina," N. Car. L. Rev., Special Issue (Oct. 1968).

Coben, Stanley, *A. Mitchell Palmer: Politician* (1963).

Cochran, Thomas C., *Railroad Leaders, 1845–1890* (1953).

Coe, Mildred V., and Morse, Lewis W., "Chronology of the Development of the David Dudley Field Code," 27 Cornell L. Q. 238 (1942).

Cohen, William, "Negro Involuntary Servitude in the South, 1865–1940: A Preliminary Analysis," 42 J. Southern Hist. 31 (1976).

Colden Letter Books, 1765–1775, Vol. II (Collections of the New York Historical Society, 1877).

Coleman, Peter J., *Debtors and Creditors in America: Insolvency, Imprisonment for Debt, and Bankruptcy, 1607–1900* (1974).

———, *The Transformation of Rhode Island, 1790–1860* (1963).

Commons, John R., *Races and Immigrants in America* (1907).

Commons, John R., and Andrews, John B., *Principles of Labor Legislation* (Rev. ed., 1927).

Compton, William R., "Early History of Stock Ownership by Corporations," 9 Geo. Wash. L. Rev. 125 (1940).

Conmy, Peter T., *The Historic Spanish Origin of California's Community Property Law and Its Development and Adaptation to Meet the Needs of an American State* (1957).

Connelly, Mark T., *The Response to Prostitution in the Progressive Era* (1980).

Conover, Milton, "The Abandonment of the 'Tidewater' Concept of Admiralty Jurisdiction in the United States," 38 Oregon L. Rev. 34 (1958).

"The Contingent Fee Business," 24 Albany L. J. 24 (1881).

Cook, Charles M., *The American Codification Movement: A Study of Antebellum Legal Reform* (1981).

Cook, William W., *A Treatise on Stock and Stockholders, Bonds, Mortgages, and General Corporation Law* (2 volumes, 3rd ed., 1894) (3 volumes, 5th ed., 1903).

Cooley, Thomas M., *A Treatise on Constitutional Limitations* (5th ed., 1883).

———, *A Treatise on the Law of Torts, or the Wrongs Which Arise Independent of Contract* (1879).

Corwin, Edward S., *Court over Constitution: A History of Our Constitutional Theory* (1938).

———, *The Twilight of the Supreme Court* (1934).

Cover, Robert, *Justice Accused: Antislavery and the Judicial Process* (1975).

Cowan, Thomas A., "Legislative Equity in Pennsylvania," 4 U. Pitt. L. Rev. 1 (1937).

Craven, Wesley Frank, *The Southern Colonies in the Seventeenth Century, 1607–1689* (1949).

Crawford, John J., *Negotiable Instruments Law* (1897).

"The Creation of a Common Law Rule: The Fellow-Servant Rule, 1837–1860," 132 U. Pa. L. Rev. 579 (1984).

Creech, Margaret, *Three Centuries of Poor Law Administration: A Study of Legislation in Rhode Island* (1936).

Crèvecoeur, St. John, *Letters from an American Farmer* (1782).

Cullen, Charles T., "New Light on John Marshall's Legal Education and Admission to the Bar," 16 Am. J. Legal Hist. 345 (1972).

Curti, Merle, *The Making of an American Community* (1959).

Curtis, George B., "The Colonial County Court: Social Forum and Legislative Precedent, Accomack County, Virginia, 1633–1639," 85 Va. Mag. Hist. & Biog. 274 (1977).

Curtis, George T., *Life of Daniel Webster* (2 volumes, 1872).

D'Agostino, Lorenzo, *History of Public Welfare in Vermont* (1948).

Dalzell, George W., *Benefit of Clergy in America and Related Matters* (1955).

Dane, Nathan, *A General Abridgment and Digest of American Law* (9 volumes, 1823–29).

Daniel, John W., *A Treatise on the Law of Negotiable Instruments* (2 volumes, 5th ed., 1903).

Danzig, Richard, "*Hadley* v. *Baxendale*: A Study in the Industrialization of the Law," 4 J. Legal Studies 249 (1975).

Dargo, George, *Jefferson's Louisiana: Politics and the Clash of Legal Traditions* (1975).

———, *Law in the New Republic: Private Law and the Public Estate* (1983).

Davies, Pearl J., *Real Estate in American History* (1958).

Davis, David B., "The Movement to Abolish Capital Punishment in America, 1787–1861," 63 Am. Hist. Rev. 23 (1957).

Davis, Joseph S., *Essays in the Earlier History of American Corporations* (2 volumes, 1917).

Davis, Ray Jay, "The Polygamous Prelude," 6 Am. J. Legal Hist. 1 (1962).

Davis, Thomas J., introduction to Daniel Horsmanden, *The New York Conspiracy* (1971).

Day, Alan F., "Lawyers in Colonial Maryland, 1660–1715," 17 Am. J. Legal Hist. 145 (1973).

Dearing, Mary R., *Veterans in Politics: The Story of the G.A.R.* (1952).

Deen, James W., "Patterns of Testation: Four Tidewater Counties in Colonial Virginia," 16 Am. J. Legal Hist. 154 (1972).

de Ford, Miriam Allen, *Stone Walls: Prisons from Fetters to Furloughs* (1962).

Degler, Carl N., *Out of Our Past: The Forces that Shaped Modern America* (1959).

de Beaumont, Gustave, and de Tocqueville, Alexis, *On the Penitentiary System in the United States and Its Application to France* (1833).

de Tocqueville, Alexis, *Democracy in America* (J. P. Mayer and M. Lerner, eds., 1966).

de Valinger, Leon, Jr., ed., *Court Records of Kent County, Delaware, 1680–1705* (1959).

Dick, Everett N., *The Lure of the Land* (1970).

——, *The Sod House Frontier* (1954).

Dickens, Charles, *American Notes* (1842).

Dillon, John F., *Commentaries on the Law of Municipal Corporations* (2 volumes, 4th ed., 1890).

Dimsdale, Thomas J., *The Vigilantes of Montana, or Popular Justice in the Rocky Mountains* (new edition, 1953).

Dobkins, Betty E., *The Spanish Element in Texas Water Law* (1959).

Dodd, E. Merrick, "Statutory Developments in Business Corporation Law, 1886–1936," 50 Harv. L. Rev. 27 (1936).

Dodd, Walter F., *Administration of Workmen's Compensation* (1936).

Dodge, Emily P., "Evolution of a City Law Office, Part II," 1956 Wis. L. Rev. 35.

Dorfman, Joseph, "Chancellor Kent and the Developing American Economy," 61 Columbia L. Rev. 1290 (1961).

Doris, Lillian, ed., *The American Way in Taxation: Internal Revenue, 1862–1963* (1963).

Dressler, David, *Practice and Theory of Probation and Parole* (1959).

Dulles, Foster R., *Labor in America* (2nd rev. ed., 1960).

Dunbar, William H., "The Anarchists' Case before the Supreme Court," 1 Harv. L. Rev. 307 (1888).

Dunne, Gerald T., "Joseph Story: The Germinal Years," 75 Harv. L. Rev. 707 (1962).

——, *Justice Joseph Story and the Rise of the Supreme Court* (1970).

DuRelle, George, "John Boyle," in William D. Lewis, ed., *Great American Lawyers*, Vol. II (1907).

Earle, Walter K., *Mr. Shearman and Mr. Sterling and How They Grew* (1963).

Eaton, Amasa, "Proposed Reforms in Marriage and Divorce Laws," 4 Columbia L. Rev. 243 (1904).

Eblen, Jack E., *The First and Second United States Empires: Governors and Territorial Government, 1784–1912* (1968).

Edsall, Preston W., ed., *Journal of the Courts of Common Right and Chancery of East New Jersey, 1683–1702* (1937).

Eggert, Gerald G., *Railroad Labor Disputes: The Beginnings of Federal Strike Policy* (1967).

Elkins, Stanley M., *Slavery, A Problem in American Institutional and Intellectual Life* (1959).

Ellis, Richard E., *The Jeffersonian Crisis: Courts and Politics in the Young Republic* (1971).

Ellsworth, Frank L., *Law on the Midway: The Founding of the University of Chicago Law School* (1977).

Ely, James W., Jr., "Patterns of Statutory Enactment in South Carolina, 1720–1770," in Herbert A. Johnson, ed., *South Carolina Legal History* (1980).

Emery, J. Gladston, *Court of the Damned* (1959).

English, William F., *The Pioneer Lawyer and Jurist in Missouri* (1947).

Erickson, Nancy S., "Historical Background of 'Protective' Labor Legislation: *Muller v. Oregon*," in D. Kelly Weisberg, ed., *Women and the Law*, Vol. II (1982).

Erikson, Kai T., *Wayward Puritans* (1966).

Ewing, Cortez A. M., *The Judges of the Supreme Court, 1789–1937* (1938).

Ezell, John S., *Fortune's Merry Wheel: The Lottery in America* (1960).

Faber, Eli, "Puritan Criminals: The Economic, Social, and Intellectual Background to Crime in Seventeenth-Century Massachusetts," 11 Perspectives in Am. Hist. 81 (1977–78).

Fairman, Charles, *History of the Supreme Court of the United States*, Vol. VI, Part One, *Reconstruction and Reunion, 1864–1888* (1971).

———, "Mr. Justice Bradley," in Allison Dunham and Philip Kurland, eds., *Mr. Justice* (1956).

———, *Mr. Justice Miller and the Supreme Court, 1862–1890* (1939).

Farnam, Henry, *Chapters in the History of Social Legislation in the United States to 1860* (1938).

Farrell, John T., ed., *The Superior Court Diary of William Samuel Johnson, 1772–1773* (1942).

Faulkner, Harold U., *Politics, Reform and Expansion, 1890–1900* (1959).

Faust, Drew Gilpin, *James Henry Hammond and the Old South: A Design for Mastery* (1982).

Feder, Leah H., *Unemployment Relief in Periods of Depression, 1857–1922* (1936).

Fehrenbacher, Don E., *The Dred Scott Case: Its Significance in American Law and Politics* (1978).

———, *Slavery, Law, and Politics: The Dred Scott Case in Historical Perspective* (1981).

Fetner, Gerald L., *Ordered Liberty: Legal Reform in the Twentieth Century* (1983).

Field, Arthur S., *The Child Labor Policy of New Jersey* (1910).

Field, Henry M., *The Life of David Dudley Field* (1898).

Field, Oliver P., "Unconstitutional Legislation in Indiana," 17 Ind. L. J. 101 (1941).

———, "Unconstitutional Legislation in Minnesota," 35 Am. Pol. Science Rev. 898 (1941).

Field, Richard S., *The Provincial Courts of New Jersey* (1849).

Finkelman, Paul, *An Imperfect Union: Slavery, Federalism, and Comity* (1981).

Fischer, Roger A., "Racial Segregation in Ante Bellum New Orleans," 74 Am. Hist. Rev. 926 (1969).

Flaherty, David H., ed., *Essays in the History of Early American Law* (1969).

Flexner, Eleanor, *Century of Struggle: The Woman's Rights Movement in the United States* (1972).

Foner, Philip S., ed., *Complete Writings of Thomas Paine*, Vol. II (1945).

Ford, Thomas, *A History of Illinois from Its Commencement as a State in 1818 to 1847* (1854).

Fox, Dixon R., ed., *Minutes of the Court of Session, Westchester County, 1657–1696* (1924).

Frank, John P., *Justice Daniel Dissenting* (1964).

Frankfurter, Felix, and Greene, Nathan, *The Labor Injunction* (1930).

Frankfurter, Felix, and Landis, James M., *The Business of the Supreme Court: A Study in the Federal Judicial System* (1928).

Franklin, John Hope, *From Slavery to Freedom* (2nd ed., 1956).

Frantz, Joe B., "The Frontier Tradition: An Invitation to Violence," in Hugh D. Graham and Ted R. Gurr, eds., *Violence in America: Historical and Comparative Perspectives* (1969).

Frazier, Edward Franklin, *The Negro in the United States* (rev. ed., 1957).

Freedman, Estelle B., *Their Sisters' Keepers: Women's Prison Reform in America, 1830–1930* (1981).

Freund, Ernst, *Standards of American Legislation* (1917).

Freyer, Tony A., "The Federal Courts, Localism, and the National Economy, 1865–1900," 53 Bus. Hist. Rev. 343 (1979).

———, *Forums of Order: The Federal Courts and Business in American History* (1979).

———, *Harmony and Dissonance: The Swift & Erie Cases in American Federalism* (1981).

Friedman, Lawrence M., *Contract Law in America: A Social and Economic Case Study* (1965).

———, "The Devil Is Not Dead: Exploring the History of Criminal Justice," 11 Ga. L. Rev. 257 (1977).

———, "The Dynastic Trust," 73 Yale L. J. 547 (1964).

———, "Freedom of Contract and Occupational Licensing, 1890–1910: A Legal and Social Study," 53 Cal. L. Rev. 487 (1965).

———, *Government and Slum Housing: A Century of Frustration* (1968).

———, "History, Social Policy, and Criminal Justice," in David J. Rothman and Stanton Wheeler, eds., *Social History and Social Policy* (1981).

———, "Law and Small Business in the United States: One Hundred Years of Struggle and Accommodation," in Stuart W. Bruchey, ed., *Small Business in American Life* (1980).

———, "Law Reform in Historical Perspective," 13 St. Louis U. L. J. 351 (1969).

———, "Notes Toward a History of American Justice," 24 Buffalo L. Rev. 111 (1974).

———, "Patterns of Testation in the 19th Century: A Study of Essex County (New Jersey) Wills," 8 Am. J. Legal Hist. 34 (1964).

———, "Plea Bargaining in Historical Perspective," 13 Law & Society Rev. 247 (1979).

———, "San Benito 1890: Legal Snapshot of a County," 27 Stan. L. Rev. 687 (1975).

———, "The Usury Laws of Wisconsin: A Study in Legal and Social History," 1963 Wis. L. Rev. 515.

Friedman, Lawrence M., and Ladinsky, Jack, "Social Change and the Law of Industrial Accidents," 67 Columbia L. Rev. 50 (1967).

Friedman, Lawrence M., and Percival, Robert V., *The Roots of Justice: Crime and Punishment in Alameda County, California, 1870–1910* (1981).

———, "A Tale of Two Courts: Litigation in Alameda and San Benito Counties," 10 Law & Society Rev. 267 (1976).

———, "Who Sues for Divorce? From Fault through Fiction to Freedom," 5 J. Legal Studies 61 (1976).

Friedman, Lawrence M.; Kagan, Robert; Cartwright, Bliss; and Wheeler, Stanton, "State Supreme Courts: A Century of Style and Citation," 33 Stan. L. Rev. 773 (1981).

"From Judicial Grant to Legislative Power: The Admiralty Clause in the Nineteenth Century," 67 Harv. L. Rev. 1214 (1954).

Garfinkel, Harold, "Conditions of Successful Degradation Ceremonies," 61 Am. J. Sociol. 420 (1956).

Garlock, Peter D., "'Wayward' Children and the Law, 1820–1900: The Genesis of the Status Offense Jurisdiction of the Juvenile Court," 13 Ga. L. Rev. 341 (1979).

Gaskins, Richard, "Changes in the Criminal Law in Eighteenth-Century Connecticut," 25 Am. J. Legal Hist. 309 (1981).

Gates, Paul W., *Frontier Landlords and Pioneer Tenants* (1945).

———, *History of Public Land Law Development* (1968).

———, "The Homestead Law in an Incongruous Land System," in Vernon Carstensen, ed., *The Public Lands* (1963).

———, "An Overview of American Land Policy," 50 Agricultural History 213 (1976).

Gawalt, Gerard W., "The Impact of Industrialization on the Legal Profession in Massachusetts, 1870–1900," in Gerard W. Gawalt, ed., *The New High Priests: Lawyers in Post-Civil War America* (1984).

———, ed., *The New High Priests: Lawyers in Post-Civil War America* (1984).

———, *The Promise of Power: The Emergence of the Legal Profession in Massachusetts, 1760–1840* (1979).

Gische, David M., "The New York City Banks and the Development of the National Banking System, 1860–1870," 23 Am. J. Legal Hist. 21 (1979).

Goebel, Julius, Jr., ed., *A History of the School of Law, Columbia University* (1955).

———, *History of the Supreme Court of the United States*, Vol. I, *Antecedents and Beginnings to 1801* (1971).

———, "King's Law and Local Custom in Seventeenth-Century New England," 31 Columbia L. Rev. 416 (1931).

———, *The Law Practice of Alexander Hamilton: Documents and Commentary, 1757–1804* (Vol. I, 1964, Vol. II, 1969).

Goebel, Julius, Jr., and Smith, Joseph H., *The Law Practice of Alexander Hamilton* (Vol. III, 1980, Vol. IV, 1980, Vol. V, 1981).

Goff, John S., "Old Age and the Supreme Court," 4 Am. J. Legal Hist. 95 (1960).

Gold, David M., "Redfield, Railroads, and the Roots of 'Laissez Faire Constitutionalism,'" 27 Am. J. Legal Hist. 254 (1983).

Goodell, William, *The American Slave Code in Theory and Practice* (1853).

Goodrich, Carter, *Government Promotion of American Canals and Railroads, 1800–1890* (1960).

Goodrich, Carter, *et al.*, *Canals and American Economic Development* (1961).

Gordon, Robert W., "'The Ideal and the Actual in the Law': Fantasies and Practices of New York City Lawyers, 1870–1910," in Gerard W. Gawalt, ed., *The New High Priests: Lawyers in Post-Civil War America* (1984).

Grabosky, Peter N., *Rogues, Rebels, and Reformers: A Political History of Urban Crime and Conflict* (1976).

Graves, John William, "The Arkansas Separate Coach Law of 1891," 7 Journal of the West 531 (1968).

Green, Fletcher M., *Constitutional Development in the South Atlantic States, 1776–1860* (1930).

Greenberg, Douglas, "Crime, Law Enforcement, and Social Control in Colonial America," 26 Am. J. Legal Hist. 293 (1982).

———, *Crime and Law Enforcement in the Colony of New York, 1691–1776* (1976).

Greenberg, Irwin F., "Justice William Johnson: South Carolina Unionist, 1823–1830," 36 Pa. Hist. 307 (1969).

Greene, Lorenzo J., *The Negro in Colonial New England, 1620–1776* (1942).

Gregorie, Anne K., ed., *Records of the Court of Chancery of South Carolina, 1661–1779* (1950).

Gregory, Charles O., "Trespass to Negligence to Absolute Liability," 37 Va. L. Rev. 359 (1951).

Grey, Thomas C., "Langdell's Orthodoxy," 45 U. Pitt. L. Rev. 1 (1983).

Griswold, Robert L., *Family and Divorce in California, 1850–1890: Victorian Illusions and Everyday Realities* (1980).

Grob, Gerald N., *The State and the Mentally Ill* (1966).

Grossberg, Michael, "Guarding the Altar: Physiological Restrictions and the Rise of State Intervention in Matrimony," 26 Am. J. Legal Hist. 197 (1982).

Guice, John D. W., *The Rocky Mountain Bench: The Territorial Supreme Courts of Colorado, Montana, and Wyoming, 1861–1890* (1972).

Gunderson, Joan R. and Gampel, Gwen V., "Married Women's Legal Status in Eighteenth-Century New York and Virginia," 39 William and Mary Q. (3rd ser.) 114 (1982).

Gurr, Ted R., and Gossett, Thomas F., *Race: The History of an Idea in America* (1963).

Gusfield, Joseph, *Symbolic Crusade: Status Politics and the American Temperance Movement* (1963).

Gutman, Herbert G., *The Black Family in Slavery and Freedom, 1750–1925* (1976).

Habenstein, Robert W., and Lamers, William M., *History of American Funeral Directing* (1955).

Haines, Charles Grove, *The Role of the Supreme Court in American Government and Politics, 1789–1835* (1944).

Hall, Jerome, *Theft, Law, and Society* (2nd ed., 1952).

Hall, Kermit L., "The Judiciary on Trial: State Constitutional Reform and the Rise of an Elected Judiciary, 1846–1860," 45 The Historian 337 (1983).

———, *The Politics of Justice: Lower Federal Judicial Selection and the Second Party System, 1829–1861* (1979).

Hall, Livingston, "The Substantive Law of Crimes, 1887–1936," 50 Harv. L. Rev. 616 (1937).

Haller, Mark H., *Eugenics: Hereditarian Attitudes in American Thought* (1963).

Hamilton, Walton, "The Ancient Maxim Caveat Emptor," 40 Yale L. J. 1133 (1931).

Hamilton, William B., *Anglo-American Law of the Frontier: Thomas Rodney and his Territorial Cases* (1953).

Hamlin, Paul M., *Legal Education in Colonial New York* (1939).

Hamlin, Paul M., and Baker, Charles E., *Supreme Court of Judicature of the Province of New York, 1691–1704* (3 volumes, 1959).

Hammond, Bray, *Banks and Politics in America, From the Revolution to the Civil War* (1957).

——, *Sovereignty and an Empty Purse: Banks and Politics in the Civil War* (1970).

Hammond, Harold E., *A Commoner's Judge: The Life and Times of Charles Patrick Daly* (1954).

Handler, Joel F., ed., *Family Law and the Poor: Essays by Jacobus ten Broek* (1971).

Handlin, Oscar, and Handlin, Mary, *Commonwealth: A Study of the Role of Government in the American Economy: Massachusetts, 1744–1861* (rev. ed., 1969).

Harno, A. J., *Legal Education in the United States* (1953).

Harring, Sidney L., *Policing a Class Society: The Experience of American Cities, 1865–1915* (1983).

Harris, Virgil M., *Ancient, Curious, and Famous Wills* (1911).

Hartog, Hendrik, "Distancing Oneself from the Eighteenth Century: A Commentary on Changing Pictures of American Legal History," in Hendrik Hartog, ed., *Law in the American Revolution and the Revolution in the Law* (1981).

——, ed., *Law in the American Revolution and the Revolution in the Law* (1981).

——, "The Public Law of a County Court: Judicial Government in Eighteenth-Century Massachusetts," 20 Am. J. Legal Hist. 282 (1976).

——, *Public Property and Private Power: The Corporation of the City of New York in American Law, 1730–1870* (1983).

Hartz, Louis, *Economic Policy and Democratic Thought: Pennsylvania, 1776–1860* (1948).

Haskins, George L., "The Beginnings of the Recording System in Massachusetts," 21 Boston U. L. Rev. 281 (1941).

——, "Codification of the Law in Colonial Massachusetts: A Study in Comparative Law," 30 Ind. L. J. 1 (1954).

——, "The First American Reform of Civil Procedure," in Roscoe Pound, ed., *Perspectives of Law; Essays for Austin Wakeman Scott* (1964).

——, "Influences of New England Law on the Middle Colonies," 1 Law and Hist. Rev. 238 (1983).

——, *Law and Authority in Early Massachusetts* (1960).

Haskins, George L., and Ewing, Samuel E., "The Spread of Massachusetts Law in the Seventeenth Century," 106 U. Pa. L. Rev. 413 (1958).

Haskins, George L., and Johnson, Herbert A., *History of the Supreme Court of the United States*, Vol. II, *Foundations of Power: John Marshall, 1801–15* (1981).

Hassam, John T., "Land Transfer Reform," 4 Harv. L. Rev. 271 (1891).

Hatcher, William B., *Edward Livingston* (1940).

Hay, Douglas, "Property, Authority and the Criminal Law," in Douglas Hay et al., eds., *Albion's Fatal Tree: Crime and Society in Eighteenth-Century England* (1975).

Haynes, Evan, *The Selection and Tenure of Judges* (1944).

Heath, Milton S., *Constructive Liberalism: The Role of the State in Economic*

Development in Georgia to 1860 (1954).

Heiberg, Robert A., "Social Backgrounds of the Minnesota Supreme Court Justices: 1858–1968," 53 Minn. L. Rev. 901 (1969).

Heizer, Robert F., and Almquist, Alan J., *The Other Californians* (1971).

Henry, Robert S., "The Railroad Land Grant Legend in American History Texts," 32 Miss. Valley Hist. Rev. 171 (1945).

Hepburn, Charles M., *The Historical Development of Code Pleading in America and England* (1897).

Heumann, Milton, "A Note on Plea Bargaining and Case Pressure," 9 Law & Society Rev. 515 (1975).

Hibbard, Benjamin H., *A History of the Public Land Policies* (1924).

Hickman, Martin B., "Judicial Review of Legislation in Utah," 4 Utah L. Rev. 50 (1954).

Hicks, Frederick C., ed., *High Finance in the Sixties* (1929).

Higginbotham, S. W., *The Keystone in the Democratic Arch: Pennsylvania Politics, 1800–1816* (1952).

High, J. L., "What Shall Be Done with the Reports?" 16 Am. L. Rev. 429 (1882).

Hilliard, Francis, *The Law of Torts, or Private Wrongs* (1859).

Hindus, Michael S., *Prison and Plantation: Crime, Justice and Authority in Massachusetts and South Carolina, 1767–1878* (1980).

Hindus, Michael S., and Withey, Lynne E., "The Law of Husband and Wife in Nineteenth-Century America: Changing Views of Divorce," in D. Kelly Weisberg, ed., *Women and the Law,* Vol. II (1982).

Hirsch, Adam J., "From Pillory to Penitentiary: The Rise of Penal Incarceration in Early Massachusetts," 80 Mich. L. Rev. 1179 (1982).

Hobson, Wayne K., "Symbol of the New Profession: Emergence of the Large Law Firm, 1870–1915," in Gerard W. Gawalt, ed., *The New High Priests: Lawyers in Post-Civil War America* (1984).

Hollister, Ovando J., *The Mines of Colorado* (1867).

[Holmes, Oliver Wendell, Jr.] "The Theory of Torts," 7 Am. L. Rev. 652 (1873).

Homer, Michael W., "The Territorial Judiciary: An Overview of the Nebraska Experience, 1854–1867," 63 Nebraska History 349 (1982).

Hopkins, James F., ed., *The Papers of Henry Clay,* Vol. I, *The Rising Statesman, 1797–1814* (1959).

Horton, John T., *James Kent: A Study in Conservatism, 1763–1847* (1939).

Horwitz, Morton J., "The Rise of Legal Formalism," 19 Am. J. Legal Hist. 251 (1975).

———, *The Transformation of American Law, 1780–1860* (1977).

Houts, Marshall, *From Gun to Gavel* (1954).

Hovenkamp, Herbert, "Pragmatic Realism and Proximate Cause in America," 3 J. Legal Hist. 3 (1982).

Howard, Warren S., *American Slavers and the Federal Law, 1837–1862* (1963).

Howe, Mark DeWolfe, *Justice Oliver Wendell Holmes: The Proving Years, 1870–1882* (1963).

——, *Justice Oliver Wendell Holmes: The Shaping Years, 1841–1870* (1957).

Hubbell's Legal Directory (1892).

Huffcut, Ernest W., "A Decade of Progress in Legal Education" *Report, 25th Ann. Meeting ABA* (1902).

Hughes, Robert M., *Handbook of Admiralty Law* (1901).

Hunt, Aurora, *Kirby Benedict, Frontier Federal Judge* (1961).

Hunt, Robert S., *Law and Locomotives: The Impact of the Railroad on Wisconsin Law in the Nineteenth Century* (1958).

Hurst, J. Willard, *The Growth of American Law: The Law Makers* (1950).

——, *Law and the Conditions of Freedom in the Nineteenth Century United States* (1956).

——, *Law and Economic Growth: The Legal History of the Lumber Industry in Wisconsin, 1836–1915* (1964).

——, *Law and Markets in United States History: Different Modes of Bargaining among Interests* (1982).

——, *Law and Social Order in the United States* (1977).

——, *A Legal History of Money in the United States, 1774–1970* (1973).

——, "Treason in the United States," 58 Harv. L. Rev. 226 (1944).

——, "The Uses of Law in Four 'Colonial' States of the American Union," 1945 Wisconsin L. Rev. 577.

Hurwitz, Howard L., *Theodore Roosevelt and Labor in New York State, 1880–1900* (1943).

Hyman, Harold M., and Wiecek, William M., *Equal Justice under Law: Constitutional Development, 1835–1875* (1982).

Ingersoll, Henry H., "Some Anomalies of Practice," 1 Yale L. J. 89 (1891).

Ireland, Robert M., *The County Courts in Antebellum Kentucky* (1972).

Irons, Peter, *Justice at War: The Story of the Japanese-American Internment Cases* (1983).

Jacobs, Clyde, *Law Writers and the Courts* (1954).

James, Henry, *Richard Olney and His Public Service* (1923).

Jenks, W. L., "History of Michigan Constitutional Provision Prohibiting a General Revision of the Laws," 19 Mich. L. Rev. 615 (1921).

Jensen, Merrill, *The New Nation: A History of the United States During the Confederation, 1781–1789* (1950).

Jewett, W. O. L., "Early Bar of Northeast Missouri," in A. J. D. Stewart, ed., *History of the Bench and Bar of Missouri* (1898).

Johnson, Edward, *Johnson's Wonder-Working Providence, 1628–1651,* Jameson, J. Franklin, ed. (1910).

Johnson, Emory R., *American Railway Transportation* (rev. ed., 1907).

Johnson, Herbert A., "Civil Procedure in John Jay's New York," 11 Am. J. Legal Hist. 69 (1967).

——, *Essays on New York Colonial Legal History* (1981).

——, *Imported Eighteenth-Century Law Treatises in American Libraries, 1700–1799* (1978).

————, "The Prerogative Court of New York, 1686–1776," 18 Am. J. Legal Hist. 95 (1973).

————, ed., *South Carolina Legal History* (1980).

Johnson, William R., *Schooled Lawyers: A Study in the Clash of Professional Cultures* (1978).

Jones, Alan, "Thomas M. Cooley and the Interstate Commerce Commission: Continuity and Change in the Doctrine of Equal Rights," 81 Polit. Sci. Q. 602 (1966).

————, "Thomas M. Cooley and the Michigan Supreme Court: 1865–1885," 10 Am. J. Legal Hist. 97 (1966).

Jones, Douglas L., "The Strolling Poor: Transiency in Eighteenth Century Massachusetts," 8 J. Social Hist. 28 (1975).

Jones, Maldwyn A., *American Immigration* (1960).

Jordan, Wilbur K., *Philanthropy in England, 1480–1660* (1959).

Jordan, Winthrop D., *White Over Black: American Attitudes Toward the Negro, 1550–1812* (1968).

Kagan, Robert A.; Cartwright, Bliss; Friedman, Lawrence M.; and Wheeler, Stanton, "The Business of State Supreme Courts, 1870–1970," 30 Stan. L. Rev. 121 (1977).

————, "The Evolution of State Supreme Courts," 76 Mich. L. Rev. 961 (1978).

Keasbey, Edward Q., "New Jersey and the Great Corporations," 13 Harv. L. Rev. 198 (1899).

Keedy, Edwin R., "History of the Pennsylvania Statute Creating Degrees of Murder," 97 U. Pa. L. Rev. 759 (1949).

Keller, Morton, *Affairs of State: Public Life in Late 19th-Century America* (1977).

————, *The Life Insurance Enterprise, 1885–1910* (1963).

Keller, William F., *The Nation's Advocate: Henry Marie Brackenridge and Young America* (1956).

Kennedy, Duncan, "Form and Substance in Private Law Adjudication," 89 Harv. L. Rev. 1685 (1976).

Kent, James, *Commentaries on American Law* (1st ed., 4 vols., 1826–1830).

————, *An Introductory Lecture to a Course of Law Lectures, Delivered November 17, 1794* (1794).

Kent, William, *Memoirs and Letters of James Kent, Ll. D.* (1898).

Kettner, James H., *The Development of American Citizenship, 1608–1870* (1978).

Kim, Sung Bok, *Landlord and Tenant in Colonial New York: Manorial Society, 1664–1775* (1978).

Kimball, Edward L., "Criminal Cases in a State Appellate Court: Wisconsin, 1839–1959," 9 Am. J. Legal Hist. 95 (1965).

Kimball, Spencer L., *Insurance and Public Policy: A Study in the Legal Implementation of Social and Economic Public Policy, Based on Wisconsin Records 1835–1959* (1960).

Kirkland, Edward C., *Men, Cities and Transportation: A Study in New England History, 1820–1900* (2 vols., 1948).

Klein, Herbert S., *Slavery in the Americas: A Comparative Study of Virginia and Cuba* (1967).

Klein, Milton M., ed., *The Independent Reflector; or, Weekly Essays on Sundry Important Subjects* (1963).

Kogan, Herman, *Traditions and Challenges: The Story of Sidley & Austin* (1983).

Kolko, Gabriel, *Railroads and Regulation, 1877–1916* (1965).

Konefsky, Alfred S., and King, Andrew J., eds., *The Papers of Daniel Webster: Legal Papers*, Vol. 2: *The Boston Practice* (1983).

Konig, David T., "'Dale's Laws' and the Non-Common Law Origins of Criminal Justice in Virginia," 26 Am. J. Legal Hist. 354 (1982).

——, *Law and Society in Puritan Massachusetts: Essex County, 1629–1692* (1979).

Kuehnl, George J., *The Wisconsin Business Corporation* (1959).

Kurtz, Paul M., "Nineteenth Century Anti-Entrepreneurial Nuisance Injunctions—Avoiding the Chancellor," 17 William & Mary L. Rev. 621 (1976).

Kutler, Stanley I., ed., *The Dred Scott Decision: Law or Politics?* (1967).

——, *Judicial Power and Reconstruction Politics* (1968).

——, *Privilege and Creative Destruction: The Charles River Bridge Case* (1971).

Lamar, Howard R., *Dakota Territory, 1861–1869: A Study of Frontier Politics* (1956).

Lane, Roger, *Policing the City: Boston, 1822–1885* (1967).

——, "Urbanization and Criminal Violence in the 19th Century: Massachusetts as a Test Case," in Hugh D. Graham and Ted R. Gurr, eds., *Violence in America: Historical and Comparative Perspectives* (1969).

——, *Violent Death in the City: Suicide, Accident and Murder in 19th Century Philadelphia* (1979).

Langsam, Miriam Z., *Children West: A History of the Placing-Out System of the New York Children's Aid Society, 1853–1890* (1964).

Langum, David J., "Pioneer Justice on the Overland Trails," 5 Western Hist. Q. 420 (1974).

Laurent, Francis W., *The Business of a Trial Court: One Hundred Years of Cases* (1959).

The Laws and Liberties of Massachusetts, Reprinted from the Copy of the 1648 Edition in the Henry G. Huntington Library (1929).

Lechford, Thomas, *Plaine Dealing, or Newes from New England* (1867 ed.).

Lee, Charles R., Jr., *The Confederate Constitutions* (1963).

Lefler, H. T., ed., *North Carolina History as Told by Contemporaries* (1956).

Leiby, James, *Charity and Correction in New Jersey* (1967).

Lermack, Paul, "Peace Bonds and Criminal Justice in Colonial Philadelphia," 100 Pa. Mag. Hist. & Biog. 173 (1976).

Letwin, William, "Congress and the Sherman Antitrust Law, 1887–1890," 23 U. Chi. L. Rev. 221 (1956).

———, *Law and Economic Policy in America: The Evolution of the Sherman Antitrust Act* (1965).

Levy, Leonard W., *The Law of the Commonwealth and Chief Justice Shaw* (1957).

Lewis, Orlando F., *The Development of American Prisons and Prison Customs, 1776–1845* (1922).

Lewis, W. David, *From Newgate to Dannemora: The Rise of the Penitentiary in New York, 1796–1848* (1965).

Lewis, William Draper, ed., *Great American Lawyers* (8 volumes, 1907–09).

Licht, Walter, *Working for the Railroad: The Organization of Work in the Nineteenth Century* (1983).

Lillich, Richard B., "The Chase Impeachment," 4 Am. J. Legal Hist. 49 (1960).

Litwack, Leon F., *North of Slavery: The Negro in the Free States, 1790–1860* (1961).

Liverant, Spencer R., and Hitchler, Walter H., "A History of Equity in Pennsylvania," 37 Dickinson L. Rev. 156 (1933).

Livermore, Shaw, *Early American Land Companies: Their Influence on Corporate Development* (1939).

Livingston's [John] *Law Register* (1851).

Llewellyn, Karl N., *The Common Law Tradition: Deciding Appeals* (1960).

———, "Remarks on the Theory of Appellate Decision and the Rules or Canons about How Statutes Are To Be Construed," 3 Vanderbilt L. Rev. 395 (1950).

Llewellyn, Karl N., and Hoebel, E. A., *The Cheyenne Way* (1941).

Lockwood, James H., "Early Times and Events in Wisconsin," *Second Annual Report and Collections of the State Historical Society of Wisconsin,* Vol. II (1856).

Logan, Frenise A., *The Negro in North Carolina, 1876–1894* (1964).

Lou, Herbert H., *Juvenile Courts in the United States* (1927).

Lubove, Roy, *The Progressives and the Slums: Tenement House Reform in New York City, 1890–1917* (1962).

Luepke, Henry F., Jr., "Comments on the Evidence in Missouri," 5 St. Louis U. L. J. 424 (1959).

Lurie, Jonathan, "Commodities Exchanges as Self-Regulating Organizations in the Late 19th Century: Some Parameters in the History of American Administrative Law," 28 Rutgers L. Rev. 1107 (1975).

———, *Law and the Nation, 1865–1912* (1983).

Lutz, Harley L., *The State Tax Commission* (1918).

McAdam, David, ed., *History of the Bench and Bar of New York* (2 volumes, 1897–99).

McCain, Paul M., *The County Court in North Carolina before 1750* (1954).

McCurdy, Charles W., "American Law and the Marketing Structure of the Large Corporation, 1875–1890," 38 J. Econ. Hist. 631 (1978).

———, "Justice Field and the Jurisprudence of Government-Business Relations: Some Parameters of Laissez Faire Constitutionalism, 1863–1897," 61 J. Am. Hist. 970 (1975).

———, "The *Knight* Sugar Decision of 1895 and the Modernization of American Corporation Law, 1869–1903," 53 Bus. Hist. Rev. 304 (1979).

McDade, Thomas M., *The Annals of Murder: A Bibliography of Books and Pamphlets on American Murders from Colonial Times to 1900* (1961).

McIntosh, Wayne V., "150 Years of Litigation and Dispute Settlement: A Court Tale," 15 Law and Society Rev. 823 (1981).

McKirdy, Charles R., "The Lawyer as Apprentice: Legal Education in Eighteenth-Century Massachusetts," 28 J. Legal Educ. 124 (1976).

McKnight, Joseph W., "The Spanish Legacy to Texas Law," 3 Am. J. Legal Hist. 222, 299 (1959).

McNulty, John W., "Sidney Breese, The Illinois Circuit Judge, 1835–1841," 62 J. Ill. State Hist. Soc. 170 (1969).

Maestro, Marcello T., *Voltaire and Beccaria as Reformers of Criminal Law* (1942).

Magrath, C. Peter, *Yazoo, Law and Politics in the New Republic: The Case of Fletcher v. Peck* (1966).

Maier, Pauline, "Popular Uprisings and Civil Authority in Eighteenth-Century America," 27 William and Mary Q., 3rd ser., 3 (1970).

Maine, Sir Henry, *Ancient Law* (1861).

Malone, Wex S., "The Formative Era of Contributory Negligence," 41 Ill. L. Rev. 151 (1946).

———, "The Genesis of Wrongful Death," 17 Stan. L. Rev. 1043 (1965).

Mann, Bruce H., "The Formalization of Informal Law: Arbitration before the American Revolution," 59 N.Y.U. L. Rev. 443 (1984).

———, "Rationality, Legal Change, and Community in Connecticut, 1690–1760," 14 Law & Society Rev. 187 (1980).

Markham, Edward L., Jr., "The Reception of the Common Law of England in Texas and the Judicial Attitude Toward That Reception, 1840–1859," 29 Texas L. Rev. 904 (1951).

Martin, George, *Causes and Conflicts: The Centennial History of the Association of the Bar of the City of New York, 1870–1970* (1970).

Matzko, John A., "'The Best Men of the Bar': The Founding of the American Bar Association," in Gerard W. Gawalt, ed., *The New High Priests: Lawyers in Post-Civil War America* (1984).

May, Elaine T., *Great Expectations: Marriage and Divorce in Post-Victorian America* (1980).

Mennel, Robert M., *Thorns and Thistles: Juvenile Delinquents in the United States, 1825–1940* (1973).

Merk, Frederic, *Economic History of Wisconsin During the Civil War Decade* (1916).

Metcalf, Theron, *Principles of the Law of Contracts* (1874).

Millar, Robert W., *Civil Procedure of the Trial Court in Historical Perspective* (1952).

Miller, George A., "James Coolidge Carter, 1827–1905," in William D. Lewis, ed., *Great American Lawyers*, Vol. VIII (1909).

Miller, George H., *Railroads and the Granger Laws* (1971).

Miller, Howard S., *The Legal Foundations of American Philanthropy, 1776–1844* (1961).

Miller, Perry, *The Legal Mind in America: From Independence to the Civil War* (1962).

Miller, Wilbur R., *Cops and Bobbies: Police Authority in New York and London, 1830–1870* (1977).

Moffet, S. E., "The Railroad Commission of California: A Study in Irresponsible Government," 6 Annals 469 (1895).

Mohr, James C., *Abortion in America: The Origins and Evolution of National Policy, 1800–1900* (1978).

Moley, Raymond, *Politics and Criminal Prosecution* (1929).

Monkkonen, Eric, "Can Nebraska or Any State Regulate Railroads? *Smyth v. Ames*, 1898," 54 Nebraska History 365 (1973).

———, *The Dangerous Class: Crime and Poverty in Columbus, Ohio, 1860–1885* (1975).

———, "A Disorderly People? Urban Order in the Nineteenth and Twentieth Centuries," 68 J. Am. Hist. 539 (1981).

———, *Police in Urban America, 1860–1920* (1981).

Morawetz, Victor, *The Law of Private Corporations* (2 volumes, 2nd ed., 1886).

Morgan, Donald G., *Justice William Johnson: The First Dissenter* (1954).

Morgan, Edmund S., and Morgan, Helen M., *The Stamp Act Crisis* (1953).

Morris, Richard B., *Government and Labor in Early America* (1946).

———, *Studies in the History of American Law, with Special Reference to the 17th and 18th Centuries* (2nd ed., 1959).

———, ed., *Select Cases of the Mayor's Court of New York City, 1674–1784* (1935).

Morris, Thomas D., "'Society is Not Marked by Punctuality in the Payment of Debts': The Chattel Mortgages of Slaves," in David J. Bodenhamer and James W. Ely, Jr., eds., *Ambivalent Legacy: A Legal History of the South* (1984).

Mueller, Gerhard O. W., "Inquiry into the State of a Divorceless Society: Domestic Relations Law and Morals in England from 1660 to 1857," 18 U. Pitt. L. Rev. 545 (1957).

Murphy, Earl F., *Water Purity: A Study in Legal Control of Natural Resources* (1961).

Murrin, John M., *Anglicizing an American Colony: The Transformation of Provincial Massachusetts* (unpublished Ph.D. thesis, Yale University, 1966).

——, "The Legal Transformation: The Bench and Bar of Eighteenth-Century Massachusetts," in Stanley N. Katz, ed., *Colonial America: Essays in Politics and Social Development* (1971).

Narrett, David E., "Preparation for Death and Provision for the Living: Notes on New York Wills (1665–1760)," 57 N.Y. Hist. 417 (1976).

Nash, A. E. Keir, "A More Equitable Past? Southern Supreme Courts and the Protection of the Antebellum Negro," 48 N. Car. L. Rev. 197 (1970).

——, "Reason of Slavery: Understanding the Judicial Role in the Peculiar Institution," 32 Vanderbilt L. Rev. 7 (1979).

Nash, Gary B., "The Philadelphia Bench and Bar, 1800–1861," *Comparative Studies in Society and History*, Vol. VII, No. 2 (1965).

Nash, Gerald D., *State Government and Economic Development: A History of Administrative Policies in California, 1849–1933* (1964).

Nelson, Margaret V., *A Study of Judicial Review in Virginia, 1789–1928* (1947).

Nelson, William E., *Americanization of the Common Law: The Impact of Legal Change on Massachusetts Society, 1760–1830* (1975).

——, *Dispute and Conflict Resolution in Plymouth County, Massachusetts, 1725–1825* (1981).

——, "Emerging Notions of Modern Criminal Law in the Revolutionary Era: An Historical Perspective," 42 N.Y.U. L. Rev. 450 (1967).

Nevins, Allan, and Thomas, Milton H., eds., *The Diary of George Templeton Strong* (4 volumes, 1952).

Nortrup, Jack, "The Education of a Western Lawyer," 12 Am. J. Legal Hist. 294 (1968).

Norvell, James R., "The Reconstruction Courts of Texas, 1867–1873," 62 Southwestern Hist. Q. 141 (1958).

Novak, Daniel A., *The Wheel of Servitude: Black Forced Labor after Slavery* (1978).

Nye, Russel B., *Fettered Freedom: Civil Liberties and the Slavery Controversy, 1830–1860* (1963).

"Observations on the Pernicious Practice of the Law," 13 Am. J. Legal Hist. 244 (1969).

O'Connor, John E., "Legal Reform in the Early Republic: The New Jersey Experience," 22 Am. J. Legal Hist. 95 (1978).

O'Dea, Thomas F., *The Mormons* (1957).

Olsen, Otto H., *Carpetbagger's Crusade: The Life of Albion Winegar Tourgée* (1965).

O'Neall, John Belton, *Biographical Sketches of the Bench and Bar of South Carolina* (2 volumes, 1859).

O'Neill, William L., *Divorce in the Progressive Era* (1967).

Osborn, William C., "Liquor Statutes in the United States," 2 Harv. L. Rev. 125 (1888).

"Overruled Their Judicial Superiors," 21 Am. L. Rev. 610 (1887).

Page, Elwin L., *Judicial Beginnings in New Hampshire, 1640–1700* (1959).

Parsons, Theophilus, *The Law of Contracts* (2 volumes, 3rd ed., 1857).

Patterson, Isaac F., *The Constitutions of Ohio* (1912).

Patterson, Lyman R., *Copyright in Historical Perspective* (1968).

Patteson, S. S. P., "The Supreme Court of Appeals of Virginia," 5 Green Bag 310 (1893).

Paul, Arnold M., *Conservative Crisis and the Rule of Law: Attitudes of Bar and Bench, 1887–1895* (1960).

Paul, Randolph E., *Taxation in the United States* (1954).

Peterson, Merrill D., ed., *Democracy, Liberty and Property: The State Constitutional Conventions of the 1820's* (1966).

Philbrick, Francis S., ed., *The Laws of Indiana Territory, 1801–1809* (1930).

——, *Pope's Digest, 1815* (2 volumes, 1938–1940).

Pierce, Harry H., *Railroads of New York: A Study of Government Aid* (1953).

Pivar, David J., *Purity Crusade: Sexual Morality and Social Control, 1868–1900* (1973).

Platt, Anthony, *The Child Savers: The Invention of Delinquency* (1969).

Platt, Harrison Gray, "Matthew P. Deady," in William D. Lewis, ed., *Great American Lawyers*, Vol. VII (1909).

Pleasants, J. Hall, ed., *Archives of Maryland*, Vol. XLIX, *Proceedings of the Provincial Court of Maryland, 1663–1666* (1932).

——, *Archives of Maryland*, Vol. LIII, *Proceedings of the County Court of Charles County, 1658–1666, and Manor Court of St. Clement's Manor, 1659–1672* (1936).

Plucknett, Theodore F. T., *A Concise History of the Common Law* (5th ed., 1956).

Poldervaart, Arie W., *Black-Robed Justice: A History of the Administration of Justice in New Mexico from the American Occupation in 1846 until Statehood in 1912* (1948).

Pomeroy, Earl S., *The Territories and the United States, 1861–1890* (1947).

Posner, Richard A., "A Theory of Negligence," 1 J. Legal Studies 29 (1972).

Potter, David M., *People of Plenty* (1954).

Pound, Roscoe, *Appellate Procedure in Civil Cases* (1941).

——, *Criminal Justice in America* (1930).

——, *Organization of Courts* (1940).

——, "The Place of Judge Story in the Making of American Law," 48 Am. L. Rev. 676 (1914).

Powell, Elwin H., "Crime as a Function of Anomie: Buffalo, 1854–1956," 57 J. Crim. Law, Criminology, & Police Sci. 161 (1966).

Powell, Richard R., *Registration of the Title to Land in the State of New York* (1938).

Powell, Sumner C., *Puritan Village: The Formation of a New England Town* (1965).

Powers, Edwin, *Crime and Punishment in Early Massachusetts, 1620–1692: A Documentary History* (1966).

Pratt, Walter F., "Rhetorical Styles on the Fuller Court," 24 Am. J. Legal Hist. 189 (1980).

Preyer, Kathryn, "Crime, the Criminal Law and Reform in Post-Revolutionary Virginia," 1 Law and Hist. Rev. 53 (1983).

———, "Penal Measures in the American Colonies: An Overview," 26 Am. J. Legal Hist. 326 (1982).

Priest, George L., "Law and Economic Distress: Sangamon County, Illinois, 1837–1844," 2 J. Legal Studies 469 (1973).

Prince, W. F., "The First Criminal Code of Virginia," *Ann. Rpt. Am. Hist. Ass'n.*, Vol. 1 (1899).

Prosser, William, *Handbook of the Law of Torts* (3rd ed., 1964).

Pumphrey, Ralph E. and Muriel W., eds., *The Heritage of American Social Work* (1961).

Rabalais, Raphael J., "The Influence of Spanish Laws and Treatises on the Jurisprudence of Louisiana: 1762–1828," 42 La. L. Rev. 1485 (1982).

Rabin, Robert L., "The Historical Development of the Fault Principle: A Reinterpretation," 15 Ga. L. Rev. 925 (1981).

Rabinowitz, Howard N., "From Exclusion to Segregation: Southern Race Relations, 1865–1890," 63 J. Am. Hist. 325 (1976).

Rabkin, Peggy, *Fathers to Daughters: The Legal Foundations of Female Emancipation* (1980).

Rahl, James A., and Schwerin, Kurt, "Northwestern University School of Law, A Short History," 55 Northwestern U. Law Rev. 131 (1960).

Rankin, Hugh F., *Criminal Trial Proceedings in the General Court of Colonial Virginia* (1965).

Ransom, Roger L., and Sutch, Richard, *One Kind of Freedom: The Economic Consequences of Emancipation* (1977).

Records of the Court of Assistants of the Colony of the Massachusetts Bay, 1630–1692, Vol. II (1904).

Redlich, Josef, *The Common Law and the Case Method in American University Law Schools* (1914).

Reed, Alfred Z., *Training for the Public Profession of the Law* (1921).

Reed, H. Clay, and Miller, George J., eds., *The Burlington Court Book: A Record of Quaker Jurisprudence in West New Jersey, 1680–1709* (1944).

Reid, John P., *Chief Justice: The Judicial World of Charles Doe* (1967).

———, *In Defiance of the Law: The Standing-Army Controversy, the Two Constitutions, and the Coming of the American Revolution* (1981).

———, *A Law of Blood: The Primitive Law of the Cherokee Nation* (1970).

———, *Law for the Elephant: Property and Social Behavior on the Overland Trail* (1980).

"Report of the Committee on Uniform State Laws," in *Report, 14th Annual Meeting, American Bar Ass'n.*, p. 365 (1891).

Report of the Trial of the Hon. Samuel Chase (1805).

Rennie, Ysabel, *The Search for Criminal Man: A Conceptual History of the Dangerous Offender* (1978).

Reppy, Alison, "The Field Codification Concept," in Alison Reppy, ed., *David Dudley Field Centenary Essays* (1949).

Rheinstein, Max, ed., *Max Weber on Law in Economy and Society* (1954).

Riesenfeld, Stefan A., "Law-making and Legislative Precedent in American Legal History," 33 Minn. L. Rev. 103 (1949).

Robinson, William M., Jr., *Justice in Grey: A History of the Judicial System of the Confederate States of America* (1941).

Robinson, W. W., *Land in California* (1948).

Roeber, A. G., *Faithful Magistrates and Republican Lawyers: Creators of Virginia Legal Culture, 1680–1810* (1981).

Rogers, James G., *American Bar Leaders* (1932).

Rogers, W. McDowell, "Free Negro Legislation in Georgia Before 1865," 16 Ga. Hist. Q. 27 (1932).

Rohrbough, Malcolm J., *The Land Office Business: The Settlement and Administration of American Public Lands, 1789–1837* (1968).

Rosenberg, Charles, *Trial of the Assassin Guiteau* (1968).

Rothbard, Murray N., *The Panic of 1819: Reactions and Policies* (1962).

Rothman, David J., *Conscience and Convenience: The Asylum and Its Alternatives in Progressive America* (1980).

———, *The Discovery of the Asylum: Social Order and Disorder in the New Republic* (1971).

Rovere, Richard, *The Magnificent Shysters* (1947).

Rowland, Dunbar, *Courts, Judges and Lawyers of Mississippi, 1798–1935* (1935).

Russell, John H., *The Free Negro in Virginia, 1619–1865* (1913).

Rutland, Robert Allen, *The Birth of the Bill of Rights, 1776–1791* (1962).

Salmon, Marylynn, "The Legal Status of Women in Early America: A Reappraisal," 1 Law and Hist. Rev. 129 (1983).

———, "Women and Property in South Carolina: The Evidence from Marriage Settlements, 1730 to 1830," 39 William and Mary Q., 3rd ser., 655 (1982).

Scafidel, Beverly, "The Bibliography and Significance of Trott's Laws," in Herbert Johnson, ed., *South Carolina Legal History* (1980).

Schafer, Joseph, "Wisconsin's Farm Loan Law, 1849–1863," in *Proceedings, State Historical Society of Wisconsin, 68th Ann. Meeting* (1920).

Scheiber, Harry N., "Instrumentalism and Property Rights: A Reconsideration of American 'Styles of Judicial Reasoning' in the 19th Century," 1975 Wis. L. Rev. 1.

———, *Ohio Canal Era: A Case Study of Government and the Economy, 1820–1861* (1969).

———, "The Road to *Munn*: Eminent Domain and the Concept of Public Purpose in the State Courts," in Donald Fleming and Bernard Bailyn, eds., *Law in American History* (1971).

———, "The Transportation Revolution and American Law: Constitutionalism and Public Policy," in *Transportation and the Early Nation* (1982), p. 1.

———, *The Wilson Administration and Civil Liberties, 1917–1921* (1960).

Schlesinger, Arthur, "Biography of a Nation of Joiners," 50 Am. Hist. Rev. 1 (1944).

Schneider, David M., *The History of Public Welfare in New York State, 1609–1866* (1938).

Schneider, John C., *Detroit and the Problem of Order, 1830–1880* (1980).

Schouler, James, "Text and Citations," 22 Am. L. Rev. 66 (1888).

———, *A Treatise on the Law of Wills* (2nd ed., 1892).

Schuckers, J. W., *The Life and Public Services of Salmon Portland Chase* (1874).

Schwartz, Gary, "Tort Law and the Economy in Nineteenth-Century America: A Reinterpretation," 90 Yale L.J. 1717 (1981).

Schwartz, Mortimer D., and Hogan, John C., eds., *Joseph Story* (1959).

Schwartz, Mortimer D., Brandt, Susan L., and Milrod, Patience, "Clara Shortridge Foltz: Pioneer in the Law," in D. Kelly Weisberg, ed., *Women and the Law: The Social Historical Perspective*, Vol. II (1982).

Schwartz, Philip J., "Forging the Shackles: The Development of Virginia's Criminal Code for Slaves," in David J. Bodenhamer and James W. Ely, Jr., eds., *Ambivalent Legacy: A Legal History of the South* (1984).

Scott, Arthur P., *Criminal Law in Colonial Virginia* (1930).

Scribner, Charles H., *Treatise on the Law of Dower* (2 volumes, 2nd ed., 1883).

Seavoy, Ronald E., *The Origins of the American Business Corporation, 1784–1855* (1982).

Sedgwick, Theodore, *A Treatise on the Measure of Damages* (2nd ed., 1852).

Segal, Ronald, *The Race War* (1966).

Seligman, Edwin R., *Essays in Taxation* (6th ed., 1909).

Selsam, J. Paul, *The Pennsylvania Constitution of 1776* (1936).

Shalloo, J. P., *Private Police, with Special Reference to Pennsylvania* (1933).

Shambaugh, Benjamin F., *History of the Constitutions of Iowa* (1902).

Sharfman, I. L., *The Interstate Commerce Commission*, Vol. I (1931).

Sheldon, Theodore, *Land Registration in Illinois* (1901).

Shepard, E. Lee, "Breaking Into the Profession: Establishing a Law Practice in Antebellum Virginia," 48 J. Southern Hist. 393 (1982).

———, "Lawyers Look at Themselves: Professional Consciousness and the Virginia Bar," 25 Am. J. Legal Hist. 1 (1981).

Sheppard, William, *The Faithful Councellor, or the Marrow of the Law in English* (2nd ed. 1653).

Shirley, Glenn, *Law West of Fort Smith: A History of Frontier Justice in the Indian Territory, 1834–1895* (1957).

Shryock, Richard H., *Medical Licensing in America, 1650–1965* (1967).

Siegel, Stephen A., "Understanding the *Lochner* Era: Lessons from the Controversy over Railroad and Utility Rate Regulation," 70 Va. L. Rev. 187 (1984).

Silverman, Robert A., *Law and Urban Growth: Civil Litigation in the Boston Trial Courts, 1880–1900* (1981).

Sims, Henry U., *A Treatise on Covenants Which Run with Land* (1901).

Sinclair, Upton, *American Outpost: A Book of Reminiscences* (1932).

Sirmans, M. Eugene, "The Legal Status of the Slave in South Carolina, 1670–1740," in Stanley N. Katz, ed., *Colonial America: Essays in Politics and Social Development* (1971).

Skilton, Robert H., "Developments in Mortgage Law and Practice," 17 Temple L. Q. 315 (1943).

Skowronek, Stephen, *Building a New American State: The Expansion of National Administrative Capacities, 1877–1920* (1982).

Small, A. J., comp., *Proceedings of the Early Iowa State Bar Association, 1874–1881* (1912).

Smith, Abbot E., *Colonists in Bondage: White Servitude and Convict Labor in America, 1607–1776* (1947).

Smith, Charles P., *James Wilson, Founding Father, 1742–1798* (1956).

Smith, Chauncey, "A Century of Patent Law," 5 Quarterly J. of Economics 44 (1890).

Smith, James G., *The Development of Trust Companies in the United States* (1928).

Smith, James Morton, *Freedom's Fetters: The Alien and Sedition Laws and American Civil Liberties* (1956).

Smith, Joseph H., *Appeals to the Privy Council from the American Plantations* (1950).

Smith, Joseph H., ed., *Colonial Justice in Western Massachusetts (1639–1702), The Pynchon Court Record* (1961).

Smith, Joseph H., and Crowl, Philip A., eds., *Court Records of Prince Georges County, Maryland, 1696–1699* (1964).

Smith, Matthew Hale, *Sunshine and Shadow in New York* (1880).

Smith, Warren B., *White Servitude in Colonial South Carolina* (1961).

Spector, Robert, "Emory Washburn: Conservator of the New England Legal Heritage," 22 Am. J. Legal Hist. 118 (1978).

Speth, Linda E., "The Married Women's Property Acts, 1839–1856: Reform, Reaction, or Revolution?," in D. Kelly Weisberg, ed., *Women and the Law: The Social Historical Perspective*, Vol. II (1982).

Spindel, Donna J., "The Administration of Criminal Justice in North Carolina, 1720–1740," 25 Am. J. Legal Hist. 141 (1981).

Stampp, Kenneth M., *The Peculiar Institution: Slavery in the Ante-Bellum South* (1956).

"State Interference with Patent Rights," 16 Albany L. J. 360 (1877).

Steinberg, Allen R., "The Criminal Courts and the Transformation of Criminal Justice in Philadelphia, 1815–1874," (Ph.D thesis, Columbia University, 1983).

Stephens, R. Allan, "The 'Experienced Lawyer Service' in Illinois," 20 Amer. Bar Ass'n. J. 716 (1934).

Stevens, Robert, *Law School: Legal Education in America from the 1850s to the 1980s* (1984).

Stimson, Frederic J., *Handbook to the Labor Law of the United States* (1896).

————, *Popular Law-Making* (1910).

Story, Joseph, "An Address Delivered Before the Members of the Suffolk Bar, Sept. 4, 1821," 1 Am. Jurist 1 (1829).

————, *Commentaries on Equity Jurisprudence* (1836).

————, *Commentaries on the Law of Promissory Notes* (1845).

Strong, Theron G., *Landmarks of a Lawyer's Lifetime* (1914).

Sullivan, James, *The History of Land Titles in Massachusetts* (1801).

Sunderland, Edson R., *History of the American Bar Association and Its Work* (1953).

Surrency, Erwin C., "The Judiciary Act of 1801," 2 Am. J. Legal Hist. 53 (1958).

Sutherland, Arthur E., *The Law at Harvard, A History of Ideas and Men, 1817–1967* (1967).

Swaine, Robert T., *The Cravath Firm and Its Predecessors, 1819–1947*, Vol. I, *The Predecessor Firms, 1819–1906* (1946).

Swift, Zephaniah, *Digest of the Law of Evidence in Civil and Criminal Cases* (1810).

————, *A System of the Laws of the State of Connecticut* (1795).

Swindler, William F., *Court and Constitution in the 20th Century: The Old Legality, 1889–1932* (1969).

Swisher, Carl B., *History of the Supreme Court of the United States*, Vol. V, *The Taney Period, 1836–1864* (1974).

————, *Motivation and Political Technique in the California Constitutional Convention, 1878–9* (1930).

————, *Stephen J. Field, Craftsman of the Law* (1930).

Tachau, Mary K. Bonsteel, *Federal Courts in the Early Republic: Kentucky, 1789–1816* (1978).

Taft, Henry W., *A Century and a Half at the New York Bar* (1938).

Taft, Philip, and Ross, Philip, "American Labor Violence: Its Causes, Character, and Outcome," in Hugh D. Graham and Ted R. Gurr, eds., *Violence in America: Historical and Comparative Perspectives* (1969).

Teaford, Jon C., "Special Legislation and the Cities, 1865–1900," 23 Am. J. Legal Hist. 189 (1979).

————, *The Unheralded Triumph: City Government in America, 1870–1900* (1984).

Teeters, Negley K., and Shearer, John D., *The Prison at Philadelphia: Cherry Hill* (1957).

ten Broek, Jacobus, "California's Dual System of Family Law: Its Origin, Development and Present Status," Part II, 16 Stan. L. Rev. 900 (1964).

Thayer, James B., *A Preliminary Treatise on Evidence at the Common Law* (1898).

Thornbrough, Emma Lou, *The Negro in Indiana* (1957).

Thurman, Kay Ellen, *The Married Women's Property Acts* (unpublished LL.M. thesis, University of Wisconsin Law School, 1966).

Tiedeman, Christopher G., *An Elementary Treatise on the American Law of Real Property* (1885).

———, *A Treatise on the Limitations of Police Power in the United States* (1886).

Tierney, Kevin, *Darrow: A Biography* (1979).

Tighe, Janet A., "Francis Wharton and the Nineteenth-Century Insanity Defense: The Origins of a Reform Tradition," 27 Am. J. Legal Hist. 223 (1983).

Tindall, George B., *South Carolina Negroes, 1877–1900* (1952).

Torrey, George A., *A Lawyer's Recollections* (1910).

Trattner, Walter I., *From Poor Law to Welfare State: A History of Social Welfare in America* (1974).

Tunnard, Christopher, and Reed, Henry H., *American Skyline* (1956).

Turner, Lynn W., "The Impeachment of John Pickering," 54 Am. Hist. Rev. 485 (1949).

Twiss, Benjamin R., *Lawyers and the Constitution: How Laissez Faire Came to the Supreme Court* (1942).

Two Centuries' Growth of American Law, 1701–1901 (1901).

Ubbelohde, Carl, *The Vice Admiralty Courts and the American Revolution* (1960).

Updike, Wilkins, *Memoirs of the Rhode Island Bar* (Boston, 1842).

Urofsky, Melvin I., "Proposed Federal Incorporation in the Progressive Era," 26 Am. J. Legal Hist. 160 (1982).

Valentine, Alan, *Vigilante Justice* (1956).

Van Alstyne, Arvo, *The California Civil Code* (1954).

Vander Velde, Lewis G., "Thomas McIntyre Cooley," in Earl D. Babst and Lewis G. Vander Velde, eds., *Michigan and the Cleveland Era* (1948).

Vaughan, Floyd L., *The United States Patent System: Legal and Economic Conflicts in American Patent History* (1956).

Verlie, Emil J., ed., *Illinois Constitutions* (1919).

Vose, Clement E., *Caucasians Only: The Supreme Court, the NAACP, and the Restrictive Covenant Cases* (1959).

Wagner, Samuel, "The Advantages of a National Bankrupt Law," *Report, 4th Ann. Meeting ABA* (1881).

Walker, Albert H., "George Harding," in William D. Lewis, ed., *Great American Lawyers*, Vol. VIII (1909).

Walker, Samuel, *Popular Justice: A History of American Criminal Justice* (1980).

Walsh, Lorena S., "Servitude and Opportunity in Charles County, Maryland, 1658–1705," in Aubrey C. Land, Lois Green Carr, and Edward C. Papenfuse, *Law, Society, and Politics in Early Maryland* (1977).

Warden, G. B., "Law Reform in England and New England, 1620–1660," 35 William and Mary Q., 3rd ser., 668 (1978).

Warner, Amos G., *et al. American Charities and Social Work* (3rd ed., 1919; 4th ed., 1930).

Warren, Charles, *Bankruptcy in United States History* (1935).

———, *A History of the American Bar* (1911).

———, *History of the Harvard Law School and of Early Legal Conditions in America* (3 volumes, 1908).

———, *The Supreme Court in United States History* (3 volumes, rev. ed., 1935).

Warren, Edward H., *Corporate Advantages Without Incorporation* (1929).

Warren, Samuel D., and Brandeis, Louis D., "The Right to Privacy," 4 Harv. L. Rev. 193 (1890).

Washburn, Emory, *Sketches of the Judicial History of Massachusetts, 1630– 1775* (1840).

Washburn, Wilcomb E., *The Assault on Indian Tribalism: The General Allotment Law (Dawes Act) of 1887* (1975).

Webb, Walter P., *The Great Plains* (1931).

Weisberg, D. Kelly, ed., *Women and the Law: The Social Historical Perspective* (2 vols., 1982).

Weisbrod, Carol, *The Boundaries of Utopia* (1980).

Wettach, Robert H., ed., *A Century of Legal Education* (1947).

Wharton, Francis, *A Treatise on the Criminal Law of the United States* (4th ed., 1857).

White, G. Edward, *Tort Law in America: An Intellectual History* (1980).

White, Leonard D., *The Republican Era: 1869–1901* (1958).

Whitehead, John, "The Supreme Court of New Jersey," 3 Green Bag 493 (1891).

Whitin, E. S., *Factory Legislation in Maine* (1908).

Wiecek, William M., "The Statutory Law of Slavery and Race in the Thirteen Mainland Colonies of British America," 34 William and Mary Q., 3rd ser., 258 (1977).

Wigmore, John H., *A Treatise on the System of Evidence in Trials at Common Law* (4 volumes, 2nd ed., 1923).

Williams, Jack K., "Crime and Punishment in Alabama, 1819–1840," 6 Ala. R. 1427 (1953).

———, *Vogues in Villainy: Crime and Retribution in Ante-Bellum South Carolina* (1959).

Williamson, Joel, *After Slavery: The Negro in South Carolina during Reconstruction, 1861–1877* (1965).

Willis, William, *A History of the Law, the Courts, and the Lawyers of Maine* (1863).

Wines, Frederick H., *Punishment and Reformation: A Study of the Penitentiary System* (2nd edition, 1910).

Winthrop, John, *The History of New England from 1630–1649* (2 volumes, 1853).

Woodford, Frank B., *Mr. Jefferson's Disciple: A Life of Justice Woodward* (1953).

Woodward, Bob, and Armstrong, Scott, *The Brethren: Inside the Supreme Court* (1979).

Woodward, C. Vann, *Origins of the New South, 1877–1913* (1951).
———, *The Strange Career of Jim Crow* (2nd rev. ed., 1966).
Woollen, W. W., "Reminiscences of the Early Marion County Bar," *Publications, Indiana Hist. Soc.*, Vol. VII (1923).
Woolsey, Theodore D., *Divorce and Divorce Legislation* (2nd ed., 1882).
Woytinsky, W. S., *et al.*, *Employment and Wages in the United States* (1953).
Wright, James M., *The Free Negro in Maryland, 1634–1860* (1921).
Wright, Louis B., *The Cultural Life of the American Colonies, 1607–1763* (1957).
Wroth, L. Kinvin, "The Massachusetts Vice Admiralty Court and the Federal Admiralty Jurisdiction," 6 Am. J. Legal Hist. 250, 347 (1962).
Wroth, L. Kinvin, and Zobel, Hiller B., *Legal Papers of John Adams,* Vol. I (1965).
Wunder, John R., "The Chinese and the Courts in the Pacific Northwest: Justice Denied?" 52 Pac. Hist. Rev. 191 (1983).
———, *Inferior Courts, Superior Justice: A History of the Justices of the Peace on the Northwest Frontier, 1853–1889* (1979).
Wyckoff, Vertrees J., *Tobacco Regulation in Colonial Maryland* (1936).
Young, James Harvey, "Three Southern Food and Drug Cases," 49 J. Southern Hist. 3 (1983).
Young, William T., *Sketch of Life and Public Services of General Lewis Cass* (1853).
Younger, Richard D., *The People's Panel: The Grand Jury in the United States, 1634–1941* (1963).
Zainaldin, Jamil, "The Emergence of a Modern American Family Law: Child Custody, Adoption and the Courts, 1796–1851," 73 Northwestern U. L. Rev. 1038 (1979).
———, *Law in Antebellum Society: Legal Change and Economic Expansion* (1983).
Zelizer, Viviana A. Rotman, *The Development of Life Insurance in the United States* (1979).
Zillmer, Raymond T., "The Lawyer on the Frontier," 50 Am. L. Rev. 27 (1916).
Zilversmit, Arthur, *The First Emancipation: The Abolition of Slavery in the North* (1967).
ZoBell, Karl, "Division of Opinion in the Supreme Court: A History of Judicial Disintegration," 44 Cornell L. Q. 186 (1959).

Index

ABOUT THE AUTHOR

LAWRENCE M. FRIEDMAN was born in 1930, educated at the University of Chicago where he earned his law degree, and admitted to the Illinois bar in 1951. He received a graduate degree from the University of Chicago Law School in English legal history. After serving in the United States Army, he practiced with a law firm in Chicago and subsequently entered the teaching profession. He has taught at St. Louis University, the University of Wisconsin, and, since 1968, at Stanford University, where he is now Marion Rice Kirkwood Professor of Law. He is the author of *Contract Law in America: A Social and Economic Case Study* (1965); *Government and Slum Housing: A Century of Frustration* (1968); *Law and the Behavioral Sciences* (coeditor; 1969, 2nd edition, 1977); *The Legal System: A Social Science Perspective* (1975); *Law and Society: An Introduction* (1977); *American Law and the Constitutional Order: Historical Perspectives* (coeditor, 1978); *Law and Social Change in Mediterranean Europe and Latin America* (coeditor, 1979); *The Roots of Justice: Crime and Punishment in Alameda County, California, 1870–1910* (coauthor, 1981); *American Law* (1984); *Your Time Will Come* (1985); and *Total Justice* (1985). He has contributed more than eighty articles to legal and associated journals. Professor Friedman is the past president of the Law and Society Association, and a past Fellow of the Center for Advanced Study in the Behavioral Sciences and of the Institute for Advanced Study in Berlin. He is a Fellow of the American Academy of Arts and Sciences, and the recipient of a number of awards for writing and teaching. He is married and has two daughters.